S0-BTD-193

**Model
Activities**

Intermediate-Level Lesson on Context Clues

Write one of the sentences mentioned previously on the board or display it using a transparency. Say: "Rather than encountering hostile natives, as they had ex- natives to be amicable. I wonder what *amicable* means? Let's see; the sentence says *'Rather than encountering hostile natives.'* That means the natives weren't hostile. *Hostile* means *unfriendly*; so maybe *amicable* means *friendly.*"

**Model
Student Activities
for All Levels**

**Model
Activities**

Inferring Unstated Main Ideas

Model the generation of a main idea for a paragraph from one of the students' textbooks that has an unstated main idea. Be sure to show how each sentence in the paragraph supports the main idea you generated. Then display a copy of the following paragraph (or a similar one textbooks) and main idea choices o or a transparency.

The mayor of this town has alwa political campaigns as name-call once has he approached the basi paign. Nevertheless, he builds hir statesman, ignoring the irregu been discovered during his term: want a person like this to be reele

The main idea of this selection is:

1. The current mayor is not a good person to re-elect to office.

2. The mayor doesn't say nice things about his op-ponents.

3. The mayor is a crook.

**Model
Activities**

Listening for Information

Set up a science center with books and displays about plants. Say to the children: "Today we are going to talk about plants. First, I am going to read you a book about plants. Listen to see if you can find out how plants grow. Then we will plant something for our room." Read the book and ask questions like the following:

Questions

Where do seeds come from?

What do plants need to make them grow?

How are seeds planted?

If we want to plant something, what will we need?

For Your Journal...and Your Portfolio

For your journal...

1. Write a description of how you would teach sight recognition of function words that do not represent concrete images, words such as *for* and *which*.

2. React to the following statement: "Going back to teaching basic phonics skills will cure all of our count

3. After observing a teacher teac teacher teaching an analytic p two approaches, based upon y methods, not the instructors.

4. React to the following stateme to use context clues. It just pro

...And your portfolio

1. Plan a lesson to teach one or n popular picture book that con structural analysis elements.

2. Develop a collection of rhyme auditory discrimination skills.

Classroom Scenarios

Classroom
Scenario

Metacognition

As Ina Maxwell works at her desk one January morning, a student comes by to share a discovery about her reading. The girl is currently reading *Dark Hour of Noon*.

"*Dark Hour of Noon* reminds me of *Number the Stars*, that book we read last fall," she says. "In *Number the Stars,* the Nazis came and told the Jews to move to camps. They took butter and other foods. The Nazis were killing Jews. Adolf Hitler was in charge of the Germans."

Analysis of Scenario

Ms. Maxwell encourages her students to make connections with life experiences and previous reading material as they read. Her encouragement and openness to students' comments lead students to share these connections with her, even when they are unsolicited.

Teaching Reading in Today's Elementary Schools

Teaching Reading in Today's Elementary Schools

Seventh Edition

Paul C. Burns
Late of University of Tennessee at Knoxville

Betty D. Roe
Tennessee Technological University

Elinor P. Ross
Tennessee Technological University

Houghton Mifflin Company
Boston   New York

Dedicated to Michael H. Roe
and James R. Ross

Senior Sponsoring Editor: Loretta Wolozin
Associate Editor: Lisa Mafrici
Project Editor: Kellie Cardone
Senior Production/Design Coordinator: Carol Merrigan
Senior Manufacturing Coordinator: Marie Barnes

Cover Designer: Rebecca Fagan
Cover Image: © Joanne Dugan/Graphic Stock

Printed in the U.S.A.

Library of Congress Catalog Card Number: 98-72006

ISBN: 0-395-90347-5

123456789-QF-02 01 00 99 98

40483640

Contents

Reading/Study Techniques   365

9

Reading in the Content Areas   405

10

Reading instruction in most schools currently includes much use of authentic literature, more integration of instruction in the language arts and across the curriculum, more holistic instruction, more active involvement of students in learning activities, and more use of alternative assessment measures than was generally true in the past. There is also increased use of technology in reading instruction today within a rapidly evolving information age. This seventh edition of *Teaching Reading in Today's Elementary Schools* addresses all of these movements, including new information on theory, research, and techniques while retaining solid, time-tested ideas and procedures—all within the familiar and practical framework of previous editions. We have included new concepts, materials, techniques, and positions and integrated them with valid traditional ideas in the balanced, even-handed way that has characterized our book from the start.

We hope to empower teachers to become decision makers, rather than merely followers of plans provided by others. Thus, we have offered information about many methods and materials for reading instruction, along with principles to help teachers choose among these options for their specific students and situations.

Audience and Purpose

Teaching Reading in Today's Elementary Schools is intended for use in introductory reading education courses for both preservice and inservice elementary school classroom teachers. It will also be beneficial in introductory courses for teachers preparing to become reading specialists, and it contains much information that will help administrators direct their schools' reading programs.

This book is designed to familiarize teachers with all the important aspects of elementary reading instruction. It presents much practical information about the process of teaching reading. Theoretical background and the research base behind suggestions have also been included to give the teacher or prospective teacher a balanced perspective.

The primary aim of the book is to prepare teachers to develop their students' abilities to read fluently and to foster their students' enjoyment of reading. The large amount of the school day spent on reading instruction in the primary grades makes this content especially important to the primary grade teacher. In the intermediate grades students must handle reading assignments in the content areas as well as in reading periods. Our book—particularly the chapters on content area reading and reading/study techniques—contains information that will help teachers implement reading instruction across the curriculum.

Revisions in This Edition

This edition represents a substantial revision. As always, the research base for understandings about reading instruction has been fully updated. A number of topics of recent concern, such as theoretical issues about developmentally appropriate practice and Vygotsky's theories about the zone of proximal development, Rosenblatt's reader-response theories, thematic teaching, technology uses in reading instruction, alternative assessment, family literacy, and a balanced approach to reading instruction, are given special attention in this edition.

Each chapter has undergone thorough revision. Chapter 1 has new information about motivation and emphasizes a balanced approach to reading instruction. Chapter 2 has information on developmentally appropriate practice and Vygotsky's theories. Chapter 3 now includes more information about phonemic awareness and onsets and rimes. Chapter 4 has additional information about analogies. Chapter 5 has new information on multiple intelligences, visual representations as postreading strategies, understanding characterization and themes in stories, Concept-Oriented Reading Instruction, and educational television. In Chapter 6 there is new information about the effectiveness of seven types of open-ended reading response formats, some new suggestions for critical reading instruction, and some new information on student-generated questions. Chapter 7 has added information about literature-based approaches and eclectic approaches, and there has been some reorganization of information, due primarily to the addition of Chapter 11, which covers many technology issues that were previously covered in this chapter in a condensed form. Chapter 8 has new material on double-entry journals and Rosenblatt's reader-response theory. In Chapter 9 the connection between libraries and research skills, including multimedia production, is made. Chapter 10 has been updated and tightened. Chapter 11 is a new chapter on the use of technology for literacy learning. It addresses the role of the teacher in the use of technology, technology as an instructional tool, and adjusting instruction through technology. Areas of technology covered include instructional transparencies, television programs, audiotapes, videotapes, CD-ROMs and videodiscs, computer applications, and multimedia applications. Chapter 12 reflects current thinking on assessment by presenting new material on alternative assessment and rubrics. Chapter 13 now has more on themes and the social-emotional environment. Chapter 14 addresses family literacy and direct instruction.

Facsimiles of elementary school reading materials, focused examples, model activities, classroom scenarios, and vignettes that focus on strategies continue to be plentiful.

New to this edition are *Time for Reflection* features occurring several times in each chapter. These features encourage students to reflect on what they believe about current issues and debates in the reading field. New chapter end matter offers suggestions for use with *journals* and *portfolios*—keys to ongoing professional development.

Coverage

The first chapter discusses components of the reading act, theories related to reading, and principles of teaching reading. Chapter 2 presents information on emergent literacy. The next two chapters are devoted to techniques of teaching word recognition and meaning vocabulary. Comprehension strategies and skills are covered in the two comprehension chapters, 5 and 6. Major approaches and materials for reading instruction are described in Chapter 7. Chapter 8 deals with language and literature; Chapter 9 discusses methods of teaching reading/study techniques; and Chapter 10 tells how to present the reading skills necessary for reading in individual content areas. Chapter 11 addresses use of technology for literacy instruction and learning. Assessment of student progress is discussed in Chapter 12, and classroom management and organization are treated in Chapter 13. Chapter 14 covers the teaching of reading to students with special needs. The Appendix contains answers to Test Yourself quizzes.

Features of the Text

This text provides an abundance of practical activities and strategies for improving students' reading performance. *Illustrative lesson plans, classroom scenarios, focus on strategies vignettes, learning-center ideas, model activities,* and *instructional games* are all presented. Thus, this text should continue to be a valuable reference for inservice teachers.

In order to make this text easy to study, we have included the following features:

Setting Objectives, part of the opening material in each chapter, provides objectives to be met as the chapter is read.

Key Vocabulary, a list of important terms which readers should know, is included to help students focus on key chapter concepts.

Introductions to each chapter help readers develop a mental set for reading the chapter and give them a framework into which they can fit the ideas they will read about.

Examples, Model Activities, Classroom Scenarios, and Focus on Strategies sections clarify the material in the text and put it into perspective.

Time for Reflection is a new feature located at strategic points throughout each chapter to encourage readers to think about the subject matter that has been presented and decide where they stand on debated issues.

Test Yourself, a section at the end of each chapter, includes questions that check retention of the chapter's material as a whole; these questions may also serve as a basis for discussion.

For your journal . . . presents topics the readers can write about in order to further their understanding of the ideas and methods presented in the chapter.

. . . **And your portfolio** presents ideas to include in a portfolio for assessment purposes.

A **Glossary** contains meanings of specialized terms used in this book.

Instructional Components That Accompany the Text

Instructor's Resource Manual with Test Items   This teaching aid provides supplementary material including model syllabi, chapter outlines, key vocabulary terms and definitions, instructional media selections, suggested teaching strategies, and suggested readings. It also includes listings of resources for independent reading activities, multimedia materials, and computer software. In addition, essay and objective questions are provided for each chapter, as well as ideas for implementing authentic assessment.

Computerized Test Bank   Questions from the Instructor's Resource Manual are available in computerized format as well.

Transparencies   A set of 80 overhead transparencies reproduce important text figures, lists, strategies, and activities, and also present new graphics designed for the transparency package. The transparency package is available upon adoption of the text.

Teacher Education Station Web Site (http://www.hmco.com/college/, click on "**Education**")   This web site provides additional pedagogic support and resources for beginning and experienced professionals in education.

Acknowledgments

We are indebted to many people for their assistance in the preparation of this text. In particular, we would like to recognize the contribution that Paul C. Burns made to the first and second editions of this book. His death in the summer of 1983 was a loss to us as his colleagues and friends and a loss to the field of reading as well. As a prolific writer and an outstanding teacher, his contributions to reading education were exceptional.

Although we would like to acknowledge the many teachers and students whose inspiration was instrumental in the development of this book, we cannot name all of them. We offer grateful recognition to the following reviewers, whose constructive advice and criticism helped greatly in the writing and revision of the manuscript:

Thyria G. Ansley, *Florida A & M University*

June E. Barnhart, *Northern Illinois University*

Ashley Bishop, *California State University, Fullerton*

James F. Buff, *Mercer University*

Rosemary Cameron, *College of St. Rose*

Susan K. Leone, *Clarion University of Pennsylvania*

Patricia Ruggiano Schmidt, *Le Moyne College*

Kathleen M. Scott, *College of St. Rose*

Kenneth J. Weiss, *Nazareth College*

In addition, we express appreciation to those who have granted permission to use sample materials or citations from their respective works. Credit for these contributions has been given in the source lines.

The invaluable assistance provided by Michael Roe in proofreading and obtaining permissions is greatly appreciated. Grateful acknowledgment is also given to our editors—Merryl Maleska Wilbur, Kellie Cardone, Lisa Mafrici, and Loretta Wolozin—for their assistance throughout the development and production of the book.

Betty D. Roe

Elinor P. Ross

The Reading Act

Key Vocabulary

Pay close attention to these terms when they appear in the chapter.

affective
auditory acuity
auditory discrimination
automaticity
bottom-up models
grapheme
interactive theories
kinesthetic
metacognitive strategies
modality
motivation
perception
phoneme
regressions
reinforcement
schemata
self-concept
semantic clues
subskill theories
syntactic clues
tactile
top-down models
transactive theories
vicarious experience
visual acuity
visual discrimination
whole language
  philosophy

SETTING OBJECTIVES

When you finish reading this chapter, you should be able to

▶ Discuss the reading product.

▶ Describe the reading process.

▶ Explain three types of theories of the reading process: subskill, interactive, and transactive.

▶ Identify some attributes of the whole language philosophy.

▶ Name some principles on which effective reading instruction is based.

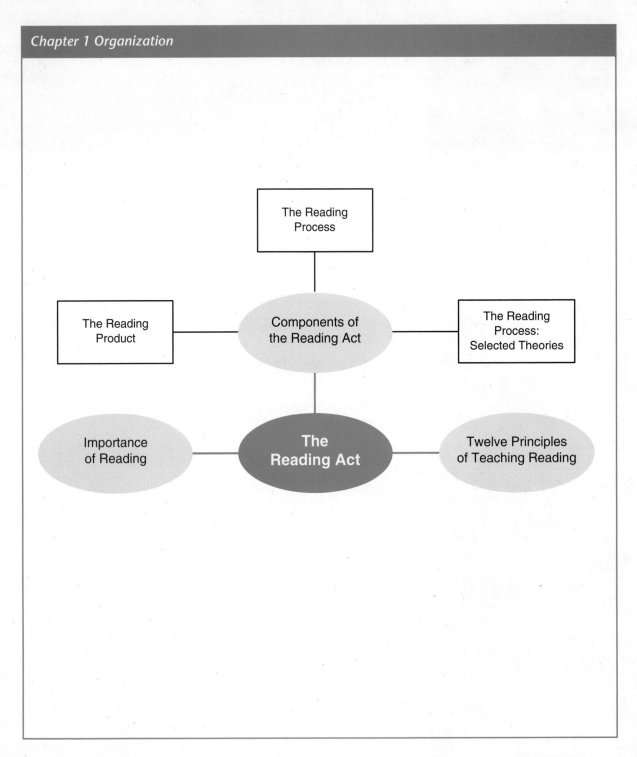

Few adults would question the importance of reading to effective functioning in our complex technological world. Educators have long made reading instruction a priority in the school curriculum, and many children come to school with a sense of the importance of reading in their lives. Unfortunately, however, not all students have this vision. One of the tasks teachers face is to help students see the importance of acquiring reading ability for performing everyday tasks effectively and the value of reading as a source of information, enjoyment, and recreation. To accomplish this task effectively, teachers need to know something about the reading act, know some useful principles of reading instruction, and understand some of the theories on which instructional practices in reading are based. They will also benefit from exposure to current philosophical positions related to reading instruction, such as the whole language philosophy and the belief in a balanced approach to reading instruction.

Reading is a highly complex act. It includes two major components—a process and a product—each of which is also complicated. Teachers need to be aware of these components and their different aspects in order to respond effectively to their students' reading needs.

This chapter analyzes the reading product and process. It describes three theories of the reading process and presents some sound principles for reading instruction, with explanatory comments.

The Importance of Reading

The ability to read is vital to functioning effectively in a literate society such as ours. However, children who do not understand the importance of learning to read will not be motivated to learn. Learning to read takes effort, and children who see the value of reading in their personal activities will be more likely to work hard than those who fail to see the benefits.

Teachers should have little trouble demonstrating to children that reading is important. Every aspect of life involves reading. Road signs direct travelers to particular destinations, inform drivers of hazards, and remind people about traffic regulations. There are menus in restaurants, labels on cans, printed advertisements, newspapers, magazines, insurance forms, income tax forms, and campaign and travel brochures. These reading situations are inescapable. Even very young children can be helped to see the need to read the signs on restrooms, the labels on individual desks in their classrooms, and the labeled areas for supplies. In fact, these young children are often eager to learn to read and are ready to attack the task enthusiastically. However, children do not automatically realize the "profusion of literacy activities in the nonschool world" (Kotrla, 1997, p. 702).

Reading tasks become increasingly complex as students advance through the grades and require continuing improvement. Anderson (1988) suggests sparking the interest of middle grade students through career education activities, helping them in this way to see that reading is a life skill that is relevant to their future success. The children can choose occupations that interest them and list the reading skills each occupation requires. They can take one or more field trips to

Students may read for relaxation, vicarious adventure, or aesthetic pleasure, as well as to gain information. (© *Laimute E. Druskis/Stock Boston*)

businesses to see workers using reading to carry out their jobs, and they can hear resource people speak to their classes about how they personally need reading in their jobs. These resource people may bring to class examples of the reading materials they must use to perform their daily tasks. The students may also interview parents and others to learn about reading demands in a wide variety of careers. In many cases, the reading activities involve such applications as use of computer databases and electronic mail.

As important as functional reading is to everyday living, another important goal of reading is enjoyment. Teachers must attempt to show students that reading can be interesting to them for reasons other than strictly utilitarian ones. Students may read for relaxation, vicarious adventure, or aesthetic pleasure as they immerse themselves in tales of other times and places or those of the here and now. They may also read to obtain information about areas of interest or hobbies to fill their leisure time. To help children see reading as a pleasurable activity, teachers should read to them each day on a variety of themes and topics, from a variety of genres, and from the works of many authors. They should also make many books available for children to look at and read for themselves, and they should set aside time for children to read from self-selected materials. Students should be given opportunities to share information from and reactions to their reading in both oral and written forms. They should be encouraged to think about the things they are reading and to relate them to their own experiences.

Components of the Reading Act

The reading act is composed of two parts: the *reading process* and the *reading product*. Nine aspects of the reading process—sensory, perceptual, sequential, experiential, thinking, learning, association, affective, constructive—combine to produce the reading product. When these aspects blend and interact harmoniously, good communication between the writer and reader results. But the sequences involved in the reading process are not always exactly the same, and they are not always performed in the same way by different readers.

The product of reading is the communication of thoughts and emotions by the writer to the reader. Communication results from the reader's construction of meaning through integrating his or her prior knowledge with the information presented in the text. Because the goal of communication is central to reading instruction, we will discuss the reading product first.

The Reading Product

As we have pointed out, the product of the reading act is communication, the reader's own understanding of ideas that the writer has put into print. Today's readers have a wealth of knowledge available to them because they are able to read material that others wrote in the past. Americans can read of events and accomplishments that occur in other parts of the globe. Knowledge of great discoveries need not be laboriously passed from person to person by word of mouth; such knowledge is available to all who can read.

In addition to being a means of communicating generally, reading is a means of communicating specifically with friends and acquaintances. A note may tell a child that Mother has gone to the store or inform a baby-sitter about where to call in case of an emergency. A memo from a person's employer can identify the work to be done. Reading can be a way to share another person's insights, joys, sorrows, or creative endeavors. Reading can also enable a person to find places he or she has never visited before (through maps and directional signs), to take advantage of bargains (through advertisements), or to avert disaster (through warning signs). It is difficult to imagine what life would be like without this vital means of communication.

Communication depends on comprehension, which is affected by all aspects of the reading process. Word recognition strategies, a part of the associational aspect of the reading process, are essential, but comprehension involves much more than decoding symbols into sounds; the reader must construct meaning while interacting with the printed page. Some people mistakenly view reading as a single skill, that of pronouncing words, rather than a combination of many skills that lead to the derivation of meaning. Thinking of reading in this way may have fostered the misguided practice of using a reading period for extended drill on word calling, in which the teacher asks each child to "read" aloud while classmates follow in their books. When a child cannot pronounce a word, the teacher may supply the pronunciation or ask another child to do so. When a child miscalls, or mispronounces, a word, the teacher usually corrects the mistake. Some students may be good pronouncers in such a situation, but are they readers? They may pronounce words perfectly, but fail to understand anything they have read. Although pronunciation is important, reading involves much more.

Teachers who realize that all aspects of the reading process affect comprehension of written material will be better able to identify children's reading difficulties and, as a result, offer effective instructional programs based on children's needs. Faulty performance related to any aspect of the reading process may result in an inferior product or in no product at all.

Time for Reflection	Some people believe that just teaching children to pronounce words allows them to achieve communication with the authors of written materials. Others view pronunciation as a step toward the goal of communication, but not a final goal. What do *you* think?

The Reading Process

Reading is an extremely complex process. When they read, children must be able to perceive the symbols set before them (*sensory* aspect); interpret what they see (*perceptual* aspect); follow the linear, logical, and grammatical patterns of the written words (*sequential* aspect); relate words back to direct experiences to give the words meaning (*experiential* aspect); make inferences from and evaluate the material (*thinking* aspect); remember what they learned in the past and incorporate new ideas and facts (*learning* aspect); recognize the connections between symbols and sounds, between words and what they represent (*associational* aspect); deal with personal interests and attitudes that affect the task of reading (*affective* aspect); and put everything together to make sense of the material (*constructive* aspect).

Reading seems to fit into the category of behavior called a *skill*, which Frederick McDonald has defined as an act that "demands complex sets of responses—some of them cognitive, some attitudinal, and some manipulative" (Downing, 1982, p. 535). Understanding, rather than simple motor behavior, is essential. The key element in skill development is *integration* of the processes involved, which "is learned through practice. Practice in integration is supplied only by performing the whole skill or as much as is a part of the learner's 'preliminary fix.' . . . one learns to read by reading" (Downing, 1982, p. 537). Whereas reading can be broken down into subskills, reading takes place only when these subskills are put together into an *integrated* whole. Performing subskills individually is not reading (Anderson et al., 1985).

Not only is the reading process complex, but each aspect of the process is complex as well. As Example 1.1 shows, the whole process can be likened to a series of books, with each aspect represented by a hefty volume. A student would have to understand the information in every volume to have a complete grasp of the subject. Therefore, the student would have to integrate information from *all* of the volumes in order to perform effectively in the area of study. The *series* would be more important than any individual volume.

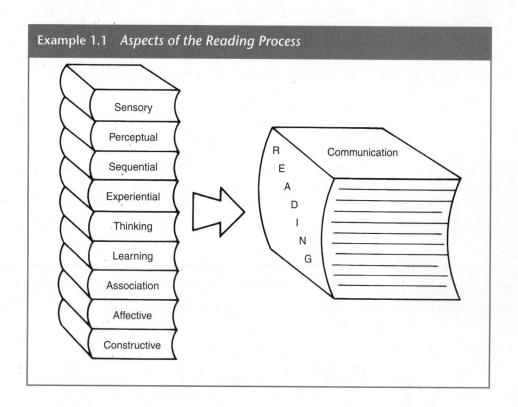

Example 1.1   *Aspects of the Reading Process*

Sensory
Perceptual
Sequential
Experiential
Thinking
Learning
Association
Affective
Constructive

R E A D I N G   Communication

Sensory Aspects of Reading

The reading process begins with a sensory impression, either visual or tactile. A normal reader perceives the printed symbol visually; a blind reader uses the tactile sense. (Discussion of the blind reader is beyond the scope of this text.) The auditory sense is also very important, since a beginning stage in reading is the association of printed symbols with spoken language. A person with poor auditory discrimination may find some reading skills, especially those involved with phonics, difficult to master.

Vision.   The reading act imposes many visual demands on children. They must be able to focus their eyes on a page of print that is generally fourteen to twenty inches away, as well as on various signs and visual displays that may be twenty or more feet away. Besides possessing *visual acuity* (or sharpness of vision), children must learn to discriminate visually among the graphic symbols (letters or words) that are used to represent spoken language. Reading is impossible for a person who cannot differentiate between two unlike graphic symbols. Because of these demands, teachers should be aware of the way in which a child's sight develops and of the physical problems that can handicap reading.

Many first graders have not yet attained 20/20 vision. Far-sighted first graders may learn reading skills more easily by working on charts and chalkboards than by using workbooks and textbooks. Teachers should avoid requiring far-sighted children to do a great deal of uninterrupted reading, and they should also use large print for class handouts (Biehler and Snowman, 1986). Although near-sighted children may do well when working with books, they are often unable to see well enough to respond to directions or exercises written on charts or chalk-boards.

Some children may have an eye disorder called *astigmatism,* which results in blurred vision. This problem, as well as nearsightedness and farsightedness, can generally be corrected by glasses.

If a child's eyes do not work well together, he or she may see two images in-stead of one. Sometimes when this occurs, the child manages to suppress the im-age from one eye. If suppression continues over a period of time, he or she may lose sight in that eye entirely. If suppression occurs for only short periods, the child may lose the appropriate place on the page when reading and become con-fused and frustrated.

Eye movements back to a previously read word or phrase in order to reread are called *regressions.* Although regressions can become an undesirable habit, they are useful if the reader performs them to correct false first impressions.

It takes time for children to learn to move their eyes across a page in a left-to-right progression and to execute a return sweep from the end of one line to the beginning of the next line. This is a difficult maneuver. Children who have not yet mastered the process will find themselves rereading and skipping lines, both of which hamper comprehension. Although teachers often attempt to cor-rect faulty eye movements, such movements may be *symptoms* of other problems (for example, poor muscle coordination or poor vocabulary) rather than *causes* of problems. When the other problems are removed, these symptoms usually disappear.

Hearing. A child who cannot discriminate among the different sounds (*phonemes*) represented by graphic symbols will be unable to make the sound-symbol associa-tions necessary for decoding unfamiliar words. Of course, before a child can dis-criminate among sounds, he or she must be able to hear them; that is, *auditory acuity* must be adequate. Thus, deaf and hearing-impaired children are deprived of some methods of word identification.

Perceptual Aspects of Reading

Perception involves interpretation of the sensory impressions that reach the brain. Each person processes and reorganizes sensory data according to his or her back-ground of experiences. When a person is reading, the brain receives a visual sen-sation of words and phrases from the printed page. It recognizes and gives meaning to these words and phrases as it associates them with the reader's previous experience with the objects, ideas, or emotions represented.

Because readers' experiences vary, different readers may interpret a single text differently (Anderson et al., 1985). For example, the printed words *apple pie* have no meaning for a person until that person associates them with the object they represent. Perception of the term *apple pie* can result not only in a visual image of a pie but also in a recollection of its smell and taste. Of course, the person must have prior experience with the thing named by the word(s) in order to make these associations.

Since different people have had different experiences with apple pies, and apple pies can vary in smell, taste, and appearance, people will attach different meanings to *apple pie.* Therefore, individuals will have slightly different perceptions when they encounter these or any other words. The clusters of information that people develop about things (such as apple pies), places (such as restaurants or airports), or ideas (such as justice or democracy) are sometimes referred to as *schemata.* Every person has many schemata. Reading comprehension has been described as the act of relating textual information to existing schemata (Pearson et al., 1979). Chapter 5 presents more information about this relationship.

Visual Perception. Visual perception involves identification and interpretation of size, shape, and relative position of letters and words. *Visual discrimination,* the ability to see likenesses and differences in visual forms (for example, between the printed words *big* and *dig*), is an important part of visual perception because many letters and words are very similar in form but very different in pronunciation and meaning. Accurate identification and interpretation of words results from detecting the small variations in form. A child may have good visual acuity (see images clearly) but be unable to discriminate well visually. Teachers can help children develop this skill through carefully planned activities (discussed in Chapter 3). The final step in visual perception, of course, is attaching meaning to the words by using past experiences, as described earlier.

Auditory Perception. Auditory perception involves *auditory discrimination,* detecting likenesses and differences in speech sounds (for example, recognizing the difference in the spoken words *big* and *dig*) and interpreting the result. Children must be able consciously to separate a phoneme (sound) from one spoken word and compare it with another phoneme separated from another word. As is true of visual discrimination, a child can have good auditory acuity (hear sounds clearly), but be unable to discriminate well auditorily. The skill can be taught, however. (Instructional activities for enhancing auditory discrimination are discussed in Chapter 3.) The final step in auditory perception is to attach meaning to the words heard by using past experiences.

Sequential Aspects of Reading

English-language printed material generally appears on a page in a left-to-right, top-to-bottom sequence. A person's eyes must follow this sequence in order to read. We pointed out earlier that readers occasionally regress, or look back to earlier words and phrases, as they read. Although these regressions momentarily interrupt the reading process as the reader checks the accuracy of initial impressions, the reader eventually returns to the left-to-right, top-to-bottom sequence.

Another reason reading is a sequential process is that oral language is strung together in a sequential pattern of grammar and logic. Since written language is a way of representing speech, it is expressed in the same manner. The reader must be able to follow the grammatical and logical patterns of spoken language in order to understand written language.

Experiential Background and Reading

As indicated in the section on perceptual aspects, meaning derived from reading is based on the reader's experiential background. Children with rich background experiences have had more chances to develop understanding of the vocabulary and concepts they encounter in reading than have children with limited experiences. For example, a child who has actually been in an airport is more likely to be able to attach appropriate meaning to the word *airport* when he or she encounters it in a reading selection than a child who has not been to an airport. Direct experiences with places, things, and processes described in reading materials make understanding of the materials much more likely.

Vicarious (indirect) *experiences* also enhance conceptual development, although they are probably less effective than concrete experiences. Hearing other people tell of or read about a subject; seeing photos or a movie of a place, event, or activity; and reading about a topic are examples of vicarious experiences that can build concept development. Since vicarious experiences involve fewer senses than do direct, concrete experiences, the concepts gained from them may be developed less fully.

Some parents converse freely with their children, read to them, tell them stories, show them pictures, and take them to movies and on trips. These parents are providing rich experiences. Other parents do not offer these experiences to their children. Teachers can help broaden children's concrete experiences through field trips, displays of objects, and class demonstrations. They can also help by providing rich vicarious experiences, such as photographs, filmstrips, movies, records and tape recordings, classroom discussions, and storytelling and story-reading sessions.

If reading materials contain vocabulary, concepts, and sentence structures that are unfamiliar to children, teachers must help them develop the background they need to understand the materials. Because children's experiential backgrounds differ, some need more preparation for a particular selection than others do.

Teachers can help children learn the Standard English found in most books by telling and reading stories, encouraging show-and-tell activities, leading or encouraging class discussions, using language experience stories (accounts developed cooperatively by teacher and class members about actual events), and encouraging dramatic play (enactment of roles or imitation of people or things). The new words encountered during field trips and demonstrations will also be valuable.

Good readers can skillfully integrate information in the text with prior knowledge about the topic, but poor readers may either overemphasize the symbols in the text or rely too heavily on their prior knowledge of the topic. Poor readers who focus primarily on the text may produce nonsense words that are graphically similar to the ones in the text. This occurs because such readers are not attempting to connect what they read to their experiences or to demand sense from reading. Poor readers who depend too much on prior knowledge may fail to make sufficient use of clues in the text to come close to the intended message (Anderson et al., 1985).

The Relationship Between Reading and Thinking

Reading is a thinking process. The act of recognizing words requires interpretation of graphic symbols. To comprehend a reading selection thoroughly, a person must be able to use the information to make inferences and read critically and creatively—to understand the figurative language, determine the author's purpose, evaluate the ideas presented, and apply the ideas to actual situations. All of these skills involve thinking processes.

Teachers can guide students' thinking by asking appropriate questions. Students will be more likely to evaluate the material they are reading if they have been directed to do so. *How* and *why* questions are particularly good. Appropriate questions can help involve a reader in the material and help the reader make personal connections with it. Questions can also limit thinking, however; if children are asked only to locate isolated facts, they will probably not be very concerned about main ideas in a passage or about the author's purpose. Test questions also affect the way students read assignments: if the usual test questions ask for evaluation or application of ideas, children will be apt to read the material more thoughtfully than they will if they are asked to recall isolated facts.

The Relationship of Reading to Learning

Reading is a complex act that must be learned. It is also a means by which further learning takes place. In other words, a person learns to read and reads to learn.

Learning to read depends on motivation, practice, and reinforcement. Teachers must show children that being able to read is rewarding in many ways: it increases success in school, helps in coping with everyday situations outside of school, bestows status, and provides recreation. Children are motivated by the expectation that they will receive these rewards, which then provide reinforcement to continue reading. Reinforcement encourages them to continue to make associations between printed words and the things to which they refer and to practice the skills they need for reading.

After children have developed some facility in reading, it becomes a means through which they learn other things. They read to learn about science, mathematics, social studies, literature, and all other subjects, a topic treated in depth in Chapter 10.

We should clarify one additional idea at this time. Teachers sometimes assume the existence of a dichotomy: that children "learn to read" in the primary grades and "read to learn" in the intermediate and upper grades. Although it may be true that teachers devote less attention to the actual process of learning to read at the intermediate level, there is still a need there for attention to primary, as well as higher-level, strategies. On the other hand, primary students can and do read for information.

Reading as an Associational Process

Learning to read depends on a number of types of associations. First, children learn to associate objects and ideas with spoken words. Next, they are asked to build up associations between spoken words and written words. In some cases— for instance, when a child encounters an unfamiliar written word paired with a picture of a familiar object—the child makes a direct association between the object or event and the written word without an intermediate connection with the spoken word. In teaching phonics, teachers set up associations between graphic symbols (*graphemes*) and sounds (*phonemes*).

When children practice the associations through classroom activities, immediate reinforcement of correct answers and correction of wrong ones can help to establish the associations. The sooner the teacher provides the reinforcement after the child makes the response, the more effective the reinforcement is likely to be. For example, the teacher might show a child the word *time* and say that this printed word is *time*. Then the teacher would show the word again and ask the child to respond with the word *time*. The teacher may offer the child opportunities for repetition of this response in a variety of situations, and the child can respond appropriately, using the association each time he or she sees that word.

Practice in and of itself, however, is not always enough to set up lasting associations. The more meaningful an association is to a child, the more rapidly he or she will learn it. Children can learn words after only a single exposure if the words have vital meaning for them (Ashton-Warner, 1963).

Affective Aspects of the Reading Process

Interests, attitudes, and self-concepts are three affective aspects of the reading process. These aspects influence how hard children will work at the reading task. For example, children who are interested in the materials presented to them will put forth much more effort in the reading process than will children who have no interest in the available reading materials.

In the same manner, children with positive attitudes toward reading will expend more effort on the reading process than will children with negative attitudes. Positive attitudes are nurtured in homes where the parents read for themselves and to their children and where reading materials are provided for children's use. In the classroom, teachers who enjoy reading, who seize every opportunity to provide pleasurable reading experiences for their students, and who allow time for recreational reading during school hours are encouraging positive attitudes. Reading aloud to the children regularly can also help accomplish this objective, and this activity should continue beyond the primary grades (Daisey, 1993; Duchein and Mealey, 1993; Schumm and Saumell, 1994). Also, if a child's peers view reading as a positive activity, that child is likely to view reading in the same way.

Ruddell (1992) believes internal motivation and identification with a piece of literature can take several forms: seeing oneself as a successful problem solver, viewing oneself as a person of significance, evoking an aesthetic sense, finding escape from daily life, piquing intellectual curiosity, and understanding oneself. These types all invite the reader to "step into the story" and be a part of it. External motivations for reading may include peer pressure, teacher expectations, or means to meet responsibilities.

Negative attitudes toward reading may develop in a home environment where parents, for a variety of reasons, do not read. Children from some homes may be given the impression that reading is a female activity. They may bring this idea to the classroom and spread it among children who have not previously been exposed to it. This attitude affects everyone in the classroom negatively, regardless of gender.

**Focus on
Strategies**

Attitude Toward Reading

James, a sixth grader, grumbled about being asked to participate in any reading activities. One day he told Mr. Hyde, his teacher, "I don't need to be able to read. My dad is a construction worker who drives heavy equipment, and that's what I'm going to be. I won't need to read to do that."

Mr. Hyde responded, "What will you do if you are given written instructions to get to the construction site? Won't you need to read then?"

"I'll ask somebody," James replied.

"What if nobody else is there?" Mr. Hyde persisted.

"I don't think that will happen," James countered.

"Well, what if you can't read the road signs to find the place that you are going? You might even need to read a map to find the place. Or what will you do if you get letters from people? You may not want to ask someone else to read them to you. They could be private. Can't you see some advantages to being able to read, even if you don't have to read a lot at work?"

"I guess so," James mumbled reluctantly.

Mr. Hyde had some arguments that were difficult to refute, but probably did not change James's attitude with this one conversation. He needed to be shown repeatedly the benefits that could accrue from reading ability. He also needed to be helped to see that reading can be fun. Mr. Hyde found an informational book containing

(continued)

lots of pictures of heavy equipment and gave James the book to look through when-ever he had some time. He did not choose to look at it immediately, but a couple of days later, when the children were having a supervised study time, he took out the book in preference to doing mathematics homework. At first he just thumbed through the pages, but eventually he began to pay closer attention to specific parts of the book. After a day or two, he returned the book and remarked that it was "okay." Mr. Hyde saw a possible avenue to helping James become a reader and pur-sued it for the rest of the year.

Maudeville (1994) believes that if readers make decisions about what inter-ested them or what information was important to them in a selection they have just read, they will understand and retain that information better. Reflecting on changes in attitude about the topic may also help. Discussion of these personal responses is also important. Giving students opportunities for self-expression is a key to intrinsic motivation (Oldfather, 1995). Open-ended tasks promote student motivation because they allow personal choices, challenges, and control. Social interaction during literacy tasks, book-rich environments, and teachers who model reading also enhance motivation (Turner and Paris, 1995; Gambrell, 1996).

Children with poor opinions of themselves may be afraid to attempt a read-ing task because they are sure they will fail. They find it easier to avoid the task altogether and to develop "don't care" attitudes than to risk looking "dumb." Children with positive self-concepts, on the other hand, are generally not afraid to attack a reading task, since they believe they are going to succeed.

There are several ways to help children build positive self-concepts. First, in every possible way, the teacher should help the children feel accepted. A definite relationship exists between a teacher's attitude toward a child, as the child per-ceives it, and the child's self-concept. One of the best ways to make children feel accepted is for the teacher to share their interests, utilizing those interests in plan-ning for reading instruction. Second, the teacher can help children feel successful by providing activities that are simple enough to guarantee satisfactory comple-tion. Third, the teacher should avoid comparing a child with other children. In-stead, reading progress should be compared with the child's own previous work. Fourth, if the teacher uses reading groups, he or she should minimize the focus on the differences among these groups to avoid giving children the idea that, un-less they are members of the top group, they are not worthy people. Comparisons and competition among groups should be avoided, and the bases on which groups are formed should be varied.

Constructive Aspect of the Reading Process

The reader puts together input from sensory and perceptual channels with expe-riential background and affective responses and constructs a personal meaning for the text. This meaning is based on the printed word, but does not reside completely in it; it is transformed by the information the reader brings to the text, the reader's feelings about the material, the purposes for the reading, and the context in which the reading takes place. Readers with different backgrounds of experience and different affective reactions will derive different meanings from the same text, as may those with divergent purposes and those reading under varying conditions. A person from the Middle East will understand an article about dissension among Middle Eastern countries differently than will one from the United States. A person reading to find a single fact or a few isolated facts will derive a different meaning from an article from someone reading to get an overall picture of the topic. A person reading a horror story alone in the house at night may well construct a different understanding of the text from one reading the same story in broad daylight in a room full of family members.

The Reading Process: Selected Theories

A theory is a set of assumptions or principles designed to explain phenomena. Theories that are based on good research and practical observations can be helpful when planning reading instruction, but teachers should not lose sight of the fact that current theories do not account for all aspects of this complex process. In addition, theories grow out of hypotheses—educated guesses. New information may be discovered that proves part or all of a theory invalid.

It would not be practical to present all the theories related to reading in the introductory chapter of a survey textbook. Therefore, we have chosen to discuss three theoretical approaches—subskill, interactive, and transactive theories—to give you a feeling for the complexities inherent in choosing a theoretical stance. The choices that teachers make about types of instruction and emphases in instructional programs are affected by their theoretical positions concerning the reading process.

Subskill Theories

Some educators see reading as a set of *subskills* that children must master and integrate. They believe that, although good readers have learned and integrated these subskills so well that they use them automatically, beginning readers have not learned them all and may not integrate well those that they have learned. Beginning readers, therefore, may exhibit slow, choppy reading and perhaps have reduced comprehension, because the separate skills of word recognition take so much concentration. Teaching these skills until they become automatic and smoothly integrated is thus the approach these educators take to reading instruction (Weaver and Shonhoff, 1984). *Automaticity* is "the ability to perform a task with little attention" (Samuels, 1994, p. 819). It is evident when a high level of accuracy is combined with speed, and readers who read orally with good expression are exhibiting automaticity in word recognition.

R. J. Smith and colleagues (1978) assert that teachers need to teach specific skills in order to focus instruction. Otherwise, instruction in reading would be reduced to assisted practice—a long, laborious trial-and-error approach. Weaver and

Shonhoff (1984) state that "although some research suggests that *skilled* reading is a single, holistic process, there is no research to suggest that children can learn to read and develop reading skill if they are taught using a method that treats reading as if it were a single process. Therefore, for instructional purposes, it is probably best to think of reading as a set of interrelated subskills" (p. 36).

Similarly, LaBerge and Samuels (1985) point out that a child who is slow in learning to read "often must be given extensive training on each of a variety of tasks, such as letter discrimination, letter-sound training, blending, etc. In this manner a teacher becomes aware of the fact that letter recognition can be considered a skill itself" (p. 713). LaBerge and Samuels's hierarchical model of perceptual learning suggests that students master smaller units before larger ones and integrate them into larger units after mastery (Samuels and Schachter, 1984).

Since fluent readers have mastered each of the subskills to the point where they use and integrate the subskills automatically, they do not clearly see the dividing lines among these skills during their daily reading. "One of the hallmarks of the reader who learned the subskills rapidly is that he was least aware of them at the time, and therefore now has little memory of them as separate subskills" (LaBerge and Samuels, 1985, p. 714). Guthrie (1973) found that reading subskills correlated highly with one another for students who were good readers. The correlations among reading subskills for poor readers were low. These students seemed to be operating at a level of separate rather than integrated skills. Guthrie's findings led to the conclusion that "lack of subskill mastery and lack of integration of these skills into higher order units" were sources of disability among poor readers (Samuels and Schachter, 1984, p. 39).

Samuels and Schachter (1984) report a study showing that "roughly 50 percent of the variability in oral reading of connected words is associated with how well one can read these words in isolation" (p. 40). Recognition of words in isolation (sight words) is one decoding subskill, so this study tends to support subskill theory.

Those who teach a set of subskills as a means of instructing children in reading generally recognize the importance of practicing the subskills in the context of actual reading in order to ensure integration. But some teachers overlook this vital phase and erroneously focus only on the subskills, overlooking the fact that they are the means to an end and not an end in themselves. Samuels (1994) points out that students can build automaticity only by spending much time reading. Although he acknowledges the need for practice with important subskills, he cautions that practice time must also be "spent on reading easy, interesting, meaningful material" (p. 834).

Adams (1994) feels much the same way. She says, "Deep and ready working knowledge of letters, spelling patterns, and words, and of the phonological translations of all three, are of inescapable importance to both skillful reading and its acquisition—not because they are the be all or the end all of the reading process, but because they enable it" (p. 859). She points out that frequent broad reading is important in developing reading proficiency.

Whereas beginning readers first focus on decoding and then switch their attention to comprehension, fluent readers decode automatically, and thus can focus attention on comprehension. Samuels (1994) points out that although the meanings of familiar words may be automatic for skilled readers, "the ability to get the meaning of each word in a sentence, however, is not the same as the ability to comprehend a sentence. In comprehending a sentence one must be able to interrelate and combine the separate meanings of each of its words. From this point of view, comprehension is a constructive process of synthesis and putting word meanings together in special ways, much as individual bricks are combined in the construction of a house" (p. 820).

Interactive Theories

An *interactive* theoretical model of the reading process depicts reading as a combination of two types of processing—top-down (reader-based) and bottom-up (text-based)—in continuous interaction. In *top-down* processing, the act of reading begins with the reader generating hypotheses or predictions about the material, using visual cues in the material to test these hypotheses as necessary (Walberg, Hare, and Pulliam, 1981). For instance, the reader of a folktale that begins with the words "Once upon a time there was a man who had three sons . . . " forms hypotheses about what will happen next, predicting that there will be a task to perform or a beautiful princess to win over and that the oldest two sons will fail but the youngest will attain his goal. Because of these expectations, the reader may read the material fairly quickly, giving attention primarily to words that confirm the expectations. Close reading occurs only if the hypothesis formed is not confirmed and an atypical plot unfolds. Otherwise, the reader can skip many words while skimming for key words that move the story along. Processing of print obviously cannot be a totally top-down experience, because a reader must begin by focusing on the print (Gove, 1983).

In *bottom-up* processing, reading is initiated by examining the printed symbols and requires little input from the reader (Walberg, Hare, and Pulliam, 1981). Gove (1983) says, "Bottom-up models assume that the translation process begins with print, i.e., letter or word identification, and proceeds to progressively larger linguistic units, phrases, sentences, etc., ending in meaning" (p. 262). A reader using bottom-up processing might first sound out a word letter by letter and then pronounce it, consider its meaning in relation to the phrase in which it is found, and so on.

An interactive model assumes parallel processing of information from print and information from background knowledge. Recognition and comprehension of printed words and ideas are the result of using both types of information (Gove, 1983). Rumelhart's early model indicated that "at least for skilled readers, top-down and bottom-up processing occur simultaneously. . . . Because comprehension depends on both graphic information and the information in the reader's mind, it may be obstructed when a critical skill or a piece of information is missing" (Harris and Sipay, 1985, p. 10). For example, a reader who is unable to use context clues may fail to grasp the meaning of an unfamiliar word that is central to understanding the passage. Similarly, a reader who has no background knowledge about the topic may be unable to reconstruct the ideas the author is trying to convey.

Ruddell and Unrau (1994) bring social context into the picture, along with the reader and the text. They assert that "meaning results from the reader's meaning-construction process. That meaning is not entirely in either the text or the reader but is created as a result of the interactions among reader, text, teacher, and classroom community" (p. 1032).

Transactive Theories

Rosenblatt (1994) believes that "every reading act is an event, or a transaction involving a particular reader and . . . a text, and occurring at a particular time in a particular context. . . . The meaning does not reside ready-made 'in' the text or 'in' the reader but happens or comes into being during the transaction between reader and text" (p. 1061). Meaning results during the transaction. McGee (1992) points out that readers employ knowledge gained through past experiences to help them select interpretations, visualize the message, make connections between the new information and what they know, and relate affectively to the material. The transaction between reader and text is dynamic. The reader is highly important to this view of reading, and the stance the reader chooses must be considered. The reader may focus on obtaining information from the text (an efferent stance) but may also focus on the experience lived through during the reading, the feelings and images evoked and the memories aroused by the text (an aesthetic stance). Both stances are appropriate at times, and it is up to the reader to choose the approach to the reading. Even when reading a single work, readers may shift their stances from more efferent to more aesthetic, or vice versa, but fiction and poetry should involve a more aesthetic stance (Probst, 1988; Rosenblatt, 1978, 1991; McGee, 1992). Beach and Hynds (1991) believe that reading must be viewed as constructing an evolving experience, instead of a static meaning. The readers' stances, beliefs, and attitudes affect their responses, as does the context.

Rosenblatt's idea of an efferent–aesthetic continuum helps teachers see that there are both cognitive and affective aspects of all reading activities for both fiction and nonfiction and that the relative importance of each aspect will vary with the text and the reading situation. Frager (1993) suggests encouraging a wider range of aesthetic responses to content area reading by asking readers what feelings the text aroused in them. Students should both think about the concepts and experience the feelings evoked by the words.

Goodman (1973, p. 31) sees reading as a psycholinguistic guessing game in which readers "select the fewest, most productive cues necessary to produce guesses which are right the first time." Goodman believes that, although the ability to combine letters to form words is related to learning to read, it has little to do with the process of fluent reading. A person who is reading for meaning does not always need to identify individual words; a reader can comprehend a passage without having identified all the words in it. The more experience a reader has had with language and the concepts presented, the fewer clues from visual configurations (graphophonic clues) he or she will need to determine the meaning of the material. Fluent readers make frequent use of *semantic* (meaning) and *syntactic* (word-order) clues within the material as well (Cooper and Petrosky, 1976). Goodman points out the importance of the reader's ability to anticipate material that he or she has not yet seen. He also stresses that readers bring to their reading all their accumulated experience, language development, and thought in order to anticipate meanings in the printed material (p. 34).

Goodman acknowledges that Rosenblatt (1938/1983) has influenced his thinking (Aaron et al., 1990), and he has moved from a strictly psycholinguistic focus to embrace a *transactive* focus. "The reader . . . constructs a text during reading through transactions with the published text and the reader's schemata are also transformed in the process. . . . In the receptive processes (listening and reading), meaning is constructed through transactions with the text and indirectly through the text with the writer" (Goodman, 1985, p. 814). He now asserts that the text a writer constructs has a meaning potential, although the text itself does not have meaning. Readers will use this meaning potential to construct their own meaning (Goodman, 1994).

The transactive theory appeals to advocates of a *whole language philosophy* toward reading. These educators want students to be involved with authentic reading, writing, listening, and speaking activities; that is, activities that are not just contrived to teach particular skills but are designed to communicate. Further description of the whole language philosophy follows.

Time for Reflection	Some people believe that, for the reader, meaning resides in the text. Others believe that the reader brings meaning to the text. Still others believe that, for the reader to comprehend the meaning fully, reading must involve using both the information in the text and the information that the reader brings to the text in the context in which the reading takes place. **What do *you* think?**

Whole Language Philosophy

Whole language is a curricular philosophy, or belief system, in which the teacher is an initiator and mediator of learning experiences, a kidwatcher (observer of children), a liberator from constraints on learning, and a curriculum developer who links the curriculum to the learner. The social context for whole language instruction is a collaborative, mutually supportive, learner-centered classroom in which all learners are viewed positively and accepted as a part of the community of learners regardless of individual differences. Language is seen as central to learning; whole literature selections are used in reading programs; writing and reading are connected; functional language, reading comprehension, and written expression are emphasized; and teachers and students, rather than textbooks and tests, are in control of the curriculum. There is no packaged set of materials to rely on. The teacher, with student input, must be the decision maker. Students are involved in making choices, self-evaluating, and taking responsibility for their learning. In addition, learning is viewed as fulfilling and joyous (Goodman, 1992; Cullinan, 1992; Pahl and Monson, 1992; Oldfather, 1993; Walmsley and Adams, 1993; Moss and Noden, 1993/1994; Church, 1994; Watson, 1994). Students are motivated to learn when they are given opportunities to express themselves and have choices about their learning. They need to know that they will have a chance to share their ideas and products with others and that the teacher and other students will listen and respond to their spoken and written ideas (Oldfather, 1993).

Whole language classrooms are not devoid of skills instruction. Phonics *is* taught, but not separately from reading and writing. Spelling and grammar are viewed as means to an end (Newman and Church, 1990).

Church (1994) points out that "the shift to a whole language perspective involves fundamental changes in how teachers work. To implement a whole language philosophy, teachers need to know about language and literacy development, about language itself, about collaborative learning, about children's literature, about the reading and writing processes, and about language for learning across subject disciplines" (p. 368). There is no "one way" to be a whole language teacher (Newman and Church, 1990).

Whole language classrooms make much use of literature. Literature-based reading approaches are discussed in Chapters 7 and 8. Sustained silent reading, a technique in which everyone reads a self-selected book without interruption for a predetermined period of time, is a particularly appropriate technique for use in a school that embraces a whole language philosophy. (See more about this in Chapter 8.) The following Classroom Scenario describes a successful sustained silent reading period.

Classroom Scenario

Sustained Silent Reading

A group of educators visited a middle school in West Tennessee shortly after 8 o'clock one morning. When they entered the school, it was extremely quiet. They went directly to the office, where they found the secretary reading a paperback book. One member of the group explained that they had entered the building during the sustained silent reading period and would not be able to talk to anyone until it was over, because interruptions to the reading of students, teachers, and staff members were not allowed. The visitors walked quietly through the school, observing the reading that was going on in every classroom. In some classrooms, students were sitting in chairs in a variety of postures or were sprawled on the carpet on their backs or stomachs. All seemed to be completely absorbed in reading books, magazines, or newspapers. At the end of the period a bell rang and the students, many reluctantly, put aside their reading materials and readied themselves for classwork. Some whispered excitedly to their neighbors, perhaps about the materials they had been reading. The overall impression the visitors received was that children and adults alike were pleased with the opportunity to read self-chosen material without interruption.

Analysis of Scenario
The use of sustained silent reading in this school obviously gave students the opportunity to read entire stories independently. The students were also allowed to select their own reading material, making it more likely that the material would be meaningful to them. Motivation to read was high under these conditions.

Resolving the Teacher's Dilemma: Taking a Balanced Approach

The current educational situation in many areas poses a dilemma for teachers. Accountability is a big issue, and in most cases it is monitored by standardized tests. In general, the standardized tests of reading consist of performance of isolated skill activities rather than reading of whole pieces of text and responding to the text in a variety of ways. To prepare their students to score well on standardized tests, teachers may choose to follow a subskill approach to reading, even if they would more likely embrace an interactive or a transactive theory and set up classrooms filled with activities related to reading and writing whole pieces of literature, if left to their own decisions about what would be best for the students. Mosenthal (1989) suggests that researchers need to focus on the complementarity between the approaches (subskills and holistic) rather than on their incompatibility.

Today, many teachers are moving toward a balanced approach to reading instruction in which they combine elements of direct skills instruction and elements of holistic instruction in their teaching. They offer authentic literacy activities in the classroom, but teach skills directly to help students succeed in those activities. As Spiegel (1992, p. 44) states, "Systematic direct instruction and many aspects of whole language can be blended in ways that strengthen both approaches."

The need for balance is recognized by educators from many philosophical backgrounds. For example, constructivist theory emphasizes student autonomy, student construction of meaning, and student interest. It pictures an active, involved, creative learner, with the teacher coordinating and critiquing student construction. This position is typical of whole language instruction, but Airasian and Walsh (1997) point out that students can engage in construction of meaning as part of any teaching approach. Even memorization and rote learning may be useful to learning activities under some circumstances. "One's task is to find the right balance between the activities of constructing and receiving knowledge, given that not all aspects of a subject can or should be taught in the same way or be acquired solely through 'hands-on' or student-centered means" (Airasian and Walsh, 1997, p. 447). Airasian and Walsh (1997) also advocate a balance between teacher involvement and noninvolvement in constructions.

Instruction should also maintain a balance between focusing on word recognition and focusing on comprehension, with word recognition viewed as a means to enable comprehension, not as a final goal. Comprehension instruction should be emphasized from the very beginning. Children should not have to wait until they can sound out most words to have an emphasis on meaning.

Some people think that skills instruction is unnecessary if students are surrounded by print and immersed in a literacy-rich environment. Others think that systematic, direct skills instruction is necessary for a successful reading program. **What do *you* think?**

Twelve Principles of Teaching Reading

Principles of teaching reading are generalizations about reading instruction based on research in the field of reading and observation of reading practices. The principles listed here are not all-inclusive; many other useful generalizations about teaching reading have been made in the past and will continue to be made in the future. They are, however, the ones we believe are most useful in guiding teachers in planning reading instruction.

Principle 1 Reading is a complex act with many factors that must be considered.

The discussion earlier in this chapter of the nine aspects of the reading process makes this principle clear. The teacher must understand all parts of the reading process in order to plan reading instruction wisely.

Principle 2 Reading involves the construction of the meaning represented by the printed symbols.

A person who fails to derive meaning from a passage has not been reading, even if he or she has pronounced every word correctly. Chapters 4, 5, and 6 focus on constructing meaning from reading materials. "In addition to obtaining information from the letters and words in a text, reading involves selecting and using knowledge about people, places, and things, and knowledge about texts and their organization. A text is not so much a vessel containing meaning as it is a source of partial information that enables the reader to use already-possessed knowledge to determine the intended meaning" (Anderson et al., 1985, p. 8).

Readers construct the meanings of passages by using both the information conveyed by the text and their prior knowledge, which is based on their past experiences. Obviously, different readers construct meaning in somewhat different ways because of their varied experiential backgrounds. Some readers do not have enough background knowledge to understand a text; others fail to make good use of the knowledge they have (Anderson et al., 1985). For example, suppose a text mentions how mountains can isolate a group of people living in them. Students familiar with mountainous areas will picture steep grades and rough terrain, which make road building difficult, and will understand the source of the isolation, although the text never mentions it. Affective factors, such as the reader's attitudes toward the subject matter, also influence the construction of meaning, as does the context in which the reading takes place.

Principle 3   There is no one correct way to teach reading.

Some methods of teaching reading work better for some children than for others. Each child is an individual who learns in his or her own way. Some children are visual learners; some are auditory learners; some are kinesthetic learners. Some need to be instructed through a combination of modalities, or avenues of perception, in order to learn. The teacher should differentiate instruction to fit the diverse needs of the students. Of course, some methods also work better for some teachers than they do for others. Teachers need to be acquainted with a variety of methods, including ones that involve technology, so that they can help all of their students. Chapter 7 covers a number of approaches to reading instruction, and Chapter 11 discusses the use of technology in literacy instruction.

Principle 4   Learning to read is a continuing process.

Children learn to read over a long period of time, acquiring more advanced reading skills after they master prerequisite skills. Even after they have been introduced to all reading skills, the process of refinement continues. No matter how old they are or how long they have been out of school, readers continue to refine their reading skills. Reading skills require practice. If readers do not practice, the skills deteriorate; if they do practice, their skills continue to develop.

Principle 5   Students should be taught word recognition strategies that will allow them to unlock the pronunciations and meanings of unfamiliar words independently.

Children cannot memorize all the words they will meet in print. Therefore, they need to learn techniques for figuring out unfamiliar words so that they can read when the assistance of a teacher, parent, or friend is not available. Chapter 3 focuses on word recognition strategies that children need.

Principle 6   The teacher should assess each student's reading ability and use the assessment as a basis for planning instruction.

Teaching all children the same reading lessons and hoping to deal at one time or another with all the difficulties students encounter is a shotgun approach and should be avoided. Such an approach wastes the time of those children who have attained the skills currently being emphasized and may never meet some of the desperate needs of other children. Teachers can avoid this approach by using assessment instruments and techniques to pinpoint the strengths and weaknesses of each child in the classroom. Then they can either divide the children into needs groups for pertinent instruction or give each child individual instruction. Chapter 12 describes many useful tests and other assessment procedures.

Principle 7   Reading and the other language arts are closely interrelated.

Reading—the interaction between a reader and written language through which the reader tries to reconstruct the writer's message—is closely related to the other major language arts (listening, speaking, and writing). Learning to read should be treated as an extension of the process of learning spoken language, a process that generally takes place in the home with little difficulty if children are given normal language input and feedback on their efforts to use language.

A special relationship exists between listening and reading, which are *receptive* phases of language, as opposed to the *expressive* phases of speaking and writing. Mastering listening skills is important in learning to read, for direct association of sound, meaning, and word form must be established from the start. The ability to identify sounds heard at the beginning, middle, or end of a word and the ability to discriminate among sounds are essential to successful phonetic analysis of words. Listening skills also contribute to the interpretation of reading material.

Students' listening comprehension is generally superior to their reading comprehension in the elementary school years. Although reading and listening are not identical and each has its own advantages, they are alike in many ways. For example, both are constructive processes. In reading, the reader constructs the message from a printed source with the help of background knowledge; in listening, the listener constructs the message from a spoken source with the help of that same background knowledge.

People learn to speak before they learn to read and write. Children's reading vocabularies generally consist largely of words in their oral language (listening and speaking) vocabularies. These are words for which they have previously developed concepts and thus, can comprehend.

Speaking, like the other language arts, is a constructive process. The speaker puts together words in an attempt to convey ideas to one or more listeners. The reader works at constructing meaning from the words the writer has put on paper.

The connection between reading and writing is particularly strong. First, both reading and writing are basically constructive processes. Readers must construct or attempt to reconstruct the message behind a written text. Readers evaluate the accuracy of their message construction as they monitor their reading processes; they may revise the constructed meaning if the need is apparent.

Starting with purposes for writing that affect the choice of ideas and the way these ideas are expressed, writers work to create written messages for others to read. In completing the writing task, they draw on their past experiences and their knowledge of writing conventions. As they work, they tend to read and review their material in order to evaluate its effectiveness and to revise it, if necessary.

One means of relating early writing experiences to reading experiences—the language experience approach—is described in Chapter 7. Chapters 7 and 8 describe having children construct written responses to their reading of literature. Writing is also sometimes used as a follow-up or enrichment activity in basal reading lessons.

The strategies and skills needed for the language arts are interrelated. For example, the need to develop and expand concepts and vocabulary, which is essential to reading, is evident in the entire language arts curriculum. Concepts and vocabulary terms to express these concepts are basic to listening, speaking, and writing as well as to reading activities. Spoken and written messages are organized around main ideas and supporting details, and people listen and read to identify the main ideas and supporting details conveyed in the material. Chapter 6 contains many examples of reading skills that have parallel listening skills and related writing and speaking skills.

Principle 8   *Using complete literature selections in the reading program is important.*

Students need to experience the reading of whole stories and books to develop their reading skills. Reading isolated words, sentences, and paragraphs does not give them the opportunity to use their knowledge of language and story structure to the fullest, and reading overly simplified language both reduces the opportunities to use their language expertise *and* dampens interest in reading the material. Whole pieces of literature can include students' own writing and the writing of other children as well as the works of commercial authors.

Principle 9   *Reading is an integral part of all content area instruction within the educational program.*

Teachers must consider the relationship of reading to other subjects within the curriculum of the elementary school. Frequently other curricular areas provide applications for the skills taught in the reading period. Textbooks in the various content areas are often the main means of conveying content concepts to students. Supplementary reading of library materials, magazines, and newspapers is also frequently used. Inability to read these materials with comprehension can mean failure to master important ideas in science, mathematics, social studies, and other areas of the curriculum. Students who have poor reading skills may therefore face failure in other areas of study because of the large amount of reading these areas often require. In addition, the need to write reports in social studies, science, health, or other areas can involve many reading and study skills: locating information; organizing information; and using the library and multimedia reference sources, including the Internet. Chapter 11 addresses use of multimedia references and the Internet.

Teachers who give reading and writing instruction only within isolated periods and treat reading and writing as separate from the rest of the curriculum will probably experience frustration rather than achieve student change and growth. Although a definite period scheduled specifically for language instruction (listening, speaking, reading, and writing) may be recommended, this does not mean that teachers should ignore these areas when teaching content subjects. The ideal situation at any level is not "reading" and "writing" for separate time periods, followed by "study" of social science or science for the next period. Instead, although the emphasis shifts, language learning and studying should be integrated during all periods at all levels. Chapters 9, 10, and 13 elaborate on these points.

Principle 10   *The student needs to see that reading can be an enjoyable pursuit.*

It is possible for our schools to produce capable readers who do not read; in fact, today this is a common occurrence. Reading can be entertaining as well as

Reading can be an enjoyable pursuit.
(© *Laimute E. Druskis/ Stock Boston*)

informative. Teachers can help students realize this fact by reading stories and poems to them daily and setting aside a regular time for pleasure reading, during which many good books of appropriate levels and from many interest areas are readily available. Teachers can show children that reading is a good recreational pursuit by describing the pleasure they personally derive from reading in their spare time and by reading for pleasure in the children's presence. When the children read recreationally, the teacher should do this also, thereby modeling desired behavior. Pressures of tests and reports should not be a part of recreational reading times. Chapter 8 provides some guidance for teachers in this area. Students in literature-based reading instructional programs that include self-selection of reading materials and group discussion of chosen reading materials are likely to discover the enjoyable aspects of reading for themselves. Chapter 7 discusses such programs.

Principle 11 Reading should be taught in a way that allows each child to experience success.

The stage of the child's literacy development should be considered for all instructional activities throughout the grades. Not only when reading and writing instruction begins, but whenever instruction in any language strategy takes place, at all grade levels, teachers should consider each child's readiness for the instructional activity. If the child's literacy development is not adequate for the task, the teacher should adjust the instruction so that it is congruent with the student's literacy level. This may involve instruction to provide a child with readiness to incorporate the new learning into his or her store of concepts.

Asking children to try to learn to read from materials that are too difficult for them ensures that a large number will fail. Teachers should give children instruction at their own levels of achievement, regardless of grade placement. Success generates success. If children are given a reading task at which they can succeed, they gain the confidence to attack the other reading tasks they must perform in a positive way. This greatly increases the likelihood of their success at these later tasks. In addition, some studies have shown that if a teacher *expects* students to be successful readers, they will in fact *be* successful.

Teachers tend to place poor readers in materials that are too hard for them more frequently than they place good readers in such materials. Children who are given difficult material to read use active, comprehension-seeking behaviors less often than do children who are reading material they can understand with a teacher's assistance. Placing poor readers on levels that are too high tends to reinforce the inefficient reading strategies that emerge when material is too difficult, making it less likely that these readers will develop more efficient strategies. Although they do not have high expectations of success under any circumstances, their expectations of success decrease more after failure than do those of good readers (Bristow, 1985).

Teachers should place poor readers in material they can read without undue focus on word recognition. This approach allows poor readers to focus on comprehending the text. Poor readers must be convinced that they will gain greater understanding during reading if they apply strategies they have learned (Bristow, 1985).

Asking children to read from materials that do not relate to their backgrounds of experiences can also result in less successful experiences. In view of the wide cultural diversity found in schools today, teachers must be particularly sensitive to this problem and must provide relevant materials for children that offer them a chance for success.

Principle 12   Encouragement of self-direction and self-monitoring of reading is important.

Good readers direct their own reading, making decisions about how to approach particular passages, what reading speed is appropriate, and *why* they are reading the passages. They are able to decide when they are having difficulties with understanding and can take steps to remedy their misunderstandings (Anderson et al., 1985). When they do this, they are using metacognitive strategies. Chapters 5 and 9 present more information about the way good readers read flexibly and monitor their reading.

No matter what teaching approaches are used in a school or what patterns of organization predominate, these principles of teaching reading should apply. Each teacher should consider carefully his or her adherence or lack of adherence to such principles.

Time for Reflection

Some people think reading should be taught *only* during reading class. Others think reading instruction should take place, as needed, throughout the entire day. What do *you* think?

Summary

The reading act is composed of two major parts: the reading process and the reading product. The reading process has nine aspects—sensory, perceptual, sequential, experiential, thinking, learning, association, affective, and constructive—that combine to produce the reading product, communication.

Three of the many types of theories about the reading process are subskill theories, interactive theories, and transactive theories. Subskill theories depict reading as a series of subskills that children must master so that they become automatic and smoothly integrated. Interactive theories depict reading as the interaction of two types of processing: top-down and bottom-up. Both types of processing are used to recognize and comprehend words. According to the bottom-up view, reading is initiated by the printed symbols (letters and words) and proceeds to larger linguistic units until the reader discovers meaning. According to the top-down view, reading begins with the reader's generation of hypotheses or predictions about the material, with the reader using the visual cues in the material to test these hypotheses as necessary. Therefore, according to interactive theories, both the print and the reader's background are important in the reading process. Transactive theories depict every reading act as a transaction involving a reader and a text at a particular time in a specific context. Readers generate and test hypotheses about the reading material and get feedback from the material. Whole language activities fit well with the transactive theoretical stance, since the whole language philosophy embraces the idea of encouraging authentic transactions with text. Whole language philosophy also encourages collaborative, learner-centered classroom environments, much reading and writing of whole selections, and student choice.

Some principles related to reading instruction that may be helpful to teachers include the following:

1. Reading is a complex act with many factors that must be considered.
2. Reading involves the construction of the *meaning* represented by the printed symbols.
3. There is no one correct way to teach reading.
4. Learning to read is a continuing process.
5. Students should be taught word recognition skills that will allow them to unlock the pronunciations and meanings of unfamiliar words independently.
6. The teacher should assess each student's reading ability and use the assessment as a basis for planning instruction.
7. Reading and the other language arts are closely interrelated.

8. Using complete literature selections in the reading program is important.
9. Reading is an integral part of all content area instruction within the educational program.
10. The student needs to see that reading can be an enjoyable pursuit.
11. Reading should be taught in a way that allows each child to experience success.
12. Encouragement of self-direction and self-monitoring of reading is important.

Test Yourself

True or False

_F_____ 1. Over a period of time a single, clear-cut definition of reading has emerged.

_T_____ 2. Reading is a complex of many skills.

_T_____ 3. Faulty eye movements usually cause serious reading problems.

_F_____ 4. Regressions are always undesirable.

_T_____ 5. Perception involves interpretation of sensation.

_T_____ 6. Prereading questions can affect the way students think while reading.

_T_____ 7. The more meaningful learning is to a child, the more rapidly associative learning takes place.

_F_____ 8. Word calling and reading are synonymous.

_F_____ 9. Teachers go to school so that they can learn the one way to teach reading.

_T_____ 10. People can continue to refine their reading skills as long as they live.

_F_____ 11. Assessing the reading problems of every child in a class is a waste of a teacher's valuable time.

_T_____ 12. Assessment can help a teacher plan appropriate instruction for all children in a class.

_T_____ 13. Reading and the other language arts are closely interrelated.

_F_____ 14. Content area instruction should not have to be interrupted for teaching of reading strategies; reading instruction should remain strictly within a special reading period.

_F_____ 15. Understanding the importance of reading is unimportant to a child's reading progress.

_T_____ 16. Teachers should stress reading for enjoyment as well as for information.

_T_ 17. Reading seems to fit in the "skill" category of behavior.

_F_ 18. Current theories about reading account for all aspects of the reading process.

_F_ 19. No research supports the view that reading is a set of subskills that must be mastered and integrated.

_T_ 20. A bottom-up model of the reading process assumes that reading is initiated by the printed symbols, with little input required from the reader.

_F_ 21. According to an interactive model of reading, parallel processing of information from print and from background knowledge takes place.

_T_ 22. Reading involves constructing the meaning of a written passage.

_T_ 23. Reading and writing are both constructive processes.

_I_ 24. Teachers give good readers materials that are too hard for them more often than they give poor readers such materials.

_T_ 25. Metacognitive processes are self-monitoring processes.

_F_ 26. Whole language teachers personally make all of the decisions about classroom materials and activities.

_T_ 27. Transactive theories of the reading process take into account the reader, the text, and the context in which the reading takes place.

_F_ 28. A transactive theory would support the position that the meaning resides in the text.

For your journal...

1. Study the following definitions of reading, which have been suggested by well-known authorities. Indicate in your journal which aspect or combination of aspects of the reading process each definition emphasizes most.

   a. "Reading is a process in which information from the text and the knowledge possessed by the reader act together to produce meaning." (Richard C. Anderson et al., *Becoming a Nation of Readers*. Washington, D.C.: National Institute of Education, 1985, p. 8.)

   b. Reading is "a sampling, selecting, predicting, comparing and confirming activity in which the reader selects a sample of useful graphic cues based on what he sees and what he expects to see." (Kenneth Goodman, quoted in *The Literacy Dictionary: The Vocabulary of Reading and Writing*, edited by Theodore L. Harris and Richard E. Hodges. Newark, Del.: International Reading Association, 1995, p. 207.)

   c. "Reading means getting meaning from certain combinations of letters. Teach the child what each letter stands for and he can read."

(Rudolph Flesch, *Why Johnny Can't Read and What You Can Do about It.* New York: Harper & Row, 1955, pp. 2–3.)

d. "Reading is a process of looking at written language symbols, converting them into overt or covert speech symbols, and then manipulating them so that both the direct (overt) and implied (covert) ideas intended by the author may be understood." (Lawrence E. Hafner and Hayden B. Jolly, *Teaching Reading to Children,* 2d ed. New York: Macmillan, 1982, p. 4.)

e. "Reading is thinking . . . reconstructing the ideas of others." (Robert Karlin, *Teaching Elementary Reading: Principles and Strategies,* 3d ed. New York: Harcourt Brace Jovanovich, 1980, p. 7.)

f. "Reading involves the identification and recognition of printed or written symbols which serve as stimuli for the recall of meaning built up through past experience, and further the construction of new meanings through the reader's manipulation of relevant concepts already in his possession. The resulting meanings are organized into thought processes according to the purposes that are operating in the reader." (Miles A. Tinker and Constance M. McCullough, *Teaching Elementary Reading,* 4th ed. Englewood Cliffs, N.J.: Prentice-Hall, 1975, p. 9.)

g. "Reading involves nothing more than the correlation of a sound image with its corresponding visual image, that is, the spelling." (Leonard Bloomfield and Clarence L. Barnhart, *Let's Read: A Linguistic Approach.* Detroit: Wayne State University Press, 1961, dustjacket.)

h. "Reading typically is the bringing of meaning *to* rather than the gaining of meaning *from* the printed page." (Henry P. Smith and Emerald V. Dechant, *Psychology in Teaching Reading.* Englewood Cliffs, N.J.: Prentice-Hall, 1961, p. 22.)

2. Note the points of agreement in the various definitions given in item 1.

3. Find more recent definitions of reading in this text or in journal articles, and compare them to the definitions in item 1.

4. After studying the principles of reading instruction presented in this chapter, see if you can formulate other principles based on your reading in other sources.

. . . And your portfolio

Write a description of the theoretical stance on reading instruction that makes most sense to you. Give reasons for your position.

2

Emergent Literacy

SETTING OBJECTIVES

When you finish reading this chapter, you should be able to

▶ Discuss the relationship between cognitive development and language learning.

▶ Understand the concept of *emergent literacy*.

▶ List some features of a print-rich classroom environment.

▶ Explain the influence of the home on a child's early language growth.

▶ Discuss the roles of listening comprehension and oral expression in the development of literacy.

▶ Identify some ways children learn to read in an emergent literacy classroom.

▶ Explain how children's growth in writing occurs.

▶ Describe some appropriate assessment techniques for young readers and writers.

alphabetic principle

big book

cognitive development

creative dramatics

developmentally
  appropriate practice

dramatic play

emergent literacy

environmental print

experience chart

invented spelling

literacy club

phonemic awareness

predictable story

print conventions

scaffolding

shared-book experience

sight word

zone of proximal
  development

This chapter opens with a discussion of the close relationship between cognitive development and language learning. Jean Piaget's and Lev Vygotsky's theories are considered, and attention is given to developmentally appropriate practice.

The whole chapter is informed by a current view of beginning reading, a view supporting the position that during early childhood and beyond, youngsters go through a period of *emergent literacy,* or a developing awareness of the interrelatedness of oral and written language (Teale and Sulzby, 1986). The word *emergent* implies that development occurs from within the child, that it happens gradually over time, that some fundamental abilities for making sense of the world must already exist within the child, and that *literacy* (the ability to read and write) will emerge when conditions are right (Hall, 1987).

The emergent literacy classroom places the child at the center of the learning experiences and provides many opportunities for language development. A central emergent literacy concept is that most children know a great deal about literacy from early experiences in the home, and the teacher should build on this knowledge when planning classroom learning activities. The teacher should provide a print-rich environment to nurture growth in reading and writing and should offer children authentic purposes for learning language. As in the home, reading and writing should develop concurrently through the use of a wide variety of literacy experiences and materials.

The chapter presents a variety of ways teachers can facilitate language development in young children. It discusses ideas for enhancing listening comprehension and oral expression and gives special attention to informal drama as a means of stimulating such development. Then it examines the ways children learn to read and write by applying knowledge they have gained from their background experiences and their familiarity with print. Strategies for encouraging children to use invented spellings are considered for promoting both writing and reading. A discussion of assessment techniques concludes the chapter.

Development of Cognition and Language

In recent years, the study of language development in isolation has shifted to the study of language learning in relation to *cognitive development* (Finn, 1985). This means there is a connection between the way children learn to use language and the way they grow in the ability to know and understand concepts or ideas. Thought and language are closely related; language is a vehicle for understanding and communicating thoughts.

Cognitive Development

Jean Piaget, a Swiss psychologist highly respected for his theory of cognitive development, asserted that thought comes before language and that language is a way of representing thought. Piaget divided cognitive development into four periods:

Chapter 2 Organization

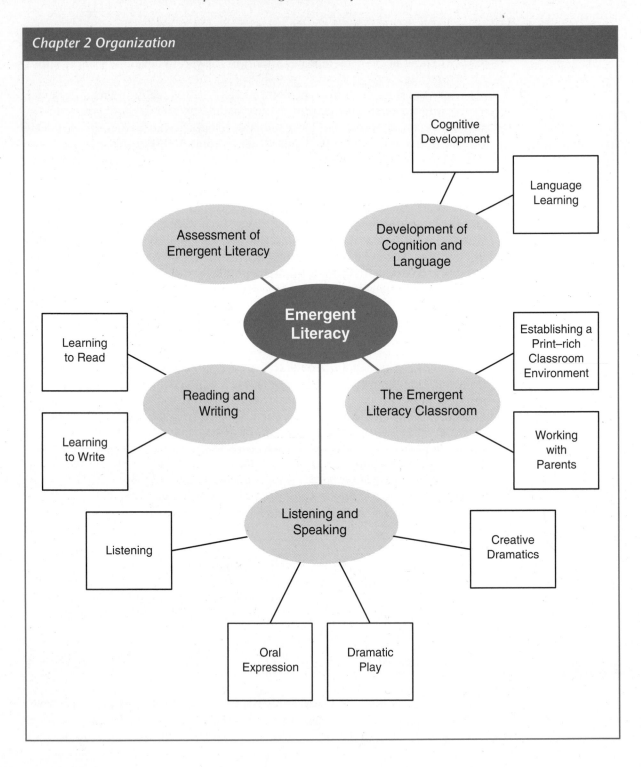

sensorimotor, preoperational, concrete-operational, and formal-operational. Because this chapter deals with the child's early school years, this discussion of Piaget's theory will focus on the *preoperational period.*

The preoperational period is divided into two stages, the *preconceptual stage* from age two to four and the *intuitive stage* from age four to six or seven (Burmeister, 1983). During the preconceptual stage, children begin to engage in symbolic thought by representing ideas and events with words and sentences, drawings, and dramatic play. As they begin to use symbols to stand for spoken words, they realize that writing represents meaning, a concept that is basic to reading comprehension (Waller, 1977).

At the intuitive stage, children are rapidly developing concepts but are limited in their ability to use adult logic. They are egocentric; that is, they consider things only from their own points of view. This characteristic prevents children from thinking clearly about the events in a story, except from their own limited perspectives. Although most children at this stage are unable to state the rules governing syntax, they do demonstrate syntactic or grammatical awareness in their speech; that is, they are able to use words in a logical order as they form sentences.

Children at the preoperational level lack many of the concepts needed to understand reading and writing processes, and they are often frustrated when teachers expect them to perform such beginning reading tasks as memorizing rules and deciding which words follow the rule, understanding that a single letter can represent multiple sounds, and changing letters to sounds and back to letters (Harp, 1987). Children at this level would probably be more successful in whole language or child-centered classrooms with a wide variety of language materials and experiences that would allow them to form their own concepts about print.

Not all children go through Piaget's stages at the same ages; in fact, children may be advanced in some areas but delayed in others (Sameroff and McDonough, 1996–1997). Such factors as the child's characteristics, the home environment, the type of support given, sensory-perceptual experiences, cultural context, and emotional involvement account for much of the variability in the ages at which children move from one stage to another (Fortson and Reiff, 1995; Sameroff and McDonough, 1996–1997).

Realizing that children in any classroom are at a variety of levels, the teacher should apply *developmentally appropriate practice,* a framework or an approach for working with young children in which the teacher considers each child's competencies and adjusts instruction accordingly (Gestwicki, 1995). This practice is based on Piaget's theory that a child's education depends on finding a match between the curriculum and the child's level of thinking (Elkind, 1989). Knowledge of developmental stages indicates which practices are appropriate for beginning readers and writers (e.g., dictating stories, illustrating a field trip, and enjoying picture books) and which practices (such as isolated skill development and worksheets) are inappropriate (Gestwicki, 1995).

Developmentally appropriate activities promote self-esteem because children feel good about themselves when they complete tasks successfully. Positive self-esteem affects how well a child performs in school, and it should be established early because it becomes more difficult to change as the child grows older (Sameroff and McDonough, 1996–1997). Negative influences on self-esteem include too-difficult learning tasks, teaching methods that ignore natural learning styles, and unreasonably high expectations (Gestwicki, 1995). Some teaching procedures cover a range of abilities so that each child can experience success within a whole-class setting. For example, during shared book reading, some children may simply be learning directionality by following the pointer from left to right; others may be acquiring letter-sound correspondences; and a few may be matching printed words to spoken words. Because each child participates at some level, each can feel successful.

Time for Reflection	Some educators support developmentally appropriate practice, but others believe all children should meet grade-level standards. What do *you* think?

Vygotsky stated that childhood experiences give rise to two different groups of concepts—*spontaneous* and *scientific* (Dixon-Krauss, 1996; Vygotsky, 1986). Vygotsky defines spontaneous concepts as those that children learn informally in the course of everyday concrete experiences at home and elsewhere. Verbal interactions with parents and others help children negotiate meaning from these experiences. Vygotsky defines scientific concepts as those that children learn during systematic classroom instruction when teachers present information. In other words, spontaneous concepts result from what children directly see or manipulate, and scientific concepts help children formalize their understandings as the teacher transmits knowledge verbally. Therefore, children need exposure to a wide variety of experiences combined with structured class activities in order to advance cognitive development.

Vygotsky's *zone of proximal development* is the span between a child's actual level and his or her potential level with assistance, or the difference between what a child can do alone and what the child can do with help (Vygotsky, 1986). The teacher can be most effective by serving as a mediating adult within this zone. As such, the teacher provides *scaffolding,* or support that is gradually withdrawn as learners become capable of doing for themselves. With beginning readers, one way that a teacher creates a scaffold is by taking the lead during interactive storybook reading, then gradually turning the responsibility for interaction over to the students (Dixon-Krauss, 1996).

Language Learning

Developmental learning occurs naturally, with minimal instruction, as a child grows up. It "is highly individual and noncompetitive; it is short on teaching and long on learning; it is self-regulated rather than adult-regulated; it goes hand in hand with the fulfillment of real life purposes; it emulates the behavior of people who model the skill in natural use" (Holdaway, 1979, p. 14). Speech develops in this way, and many educators argue that literacy should develop in a similar manner.

Language learning is a continuous, interactive, and purposeful process (Loughlin and Martin, 1987). Children learn to speak without instruction by imitating speech sounds and observing the interactions of language users. Language learning is more than imitation, however, because each individual constructs language according to personal needs and motivations. The child acquires speech through immersion in a language environment that provides speech models, motivation for speaking, and interactions with other speakers. The beginning speaker engages in trial and error and takes risks to establish communications with others.

A child's early attempts at language are intuitive; that is, the child uses language reasonably well but lacks *metalinguistic awareness,* the ability to think about language and manipulate it objectively. For example, a youngster may say, "I want some candy," but may be unable to tell how many words were spoken or recognize that this group of words is called a *sentence.* A discrepancy exists between the use of language and an awareness of the meanings of terms, such as *word, sentence, sound,* and *letter,* that refer to language (Hare, 1984). A teacher who wishes to develop children's skill in recognizing words as basic elements of speech might use the following Model Activity.

Model Activities

Recognition of the Concept of *Word*

Make two copies of a chart story based on an experience that children have shared. Run your fingers under the first sentence on one of the charts as you say to the children: "Read this sentence with me." Then use your hands to block off individual words as you say to them: "Look at the groups of letters between the spaces. We call each group of letters a *word.*" Ask them: "How many words are in this sentence?" Do the same thing with the other sentences on the chart. Then cut the sentences into strips and ask several children to cut the strips into words. Give each child a word. Say to the children: "Can you find your word on our other chart? If you can, put your word with the word on the chart."

It is important to realize that children develop an understanding of the concept of *word* gradually through many experiences. Also, because individual children are at various developmental levels for acquiring this concept, for some the lesson will verify what they were already beginning to realize and for others, who are less ready, the lesson will have little or no meaning.

Because many children fail to understand linguistic terminology, they cannot make sense of instruction based on these terms. If a child does not understand the meanings of language-related terms, he or she must experience considerable confusion when a teacher says, "Look at the *middle letter* of this *word*. The *vowel* has its *short sound* because it is followed by a *consonant.*"

Having children perform isolated drills and memorize rules without understanding their meanings is unlikely to help them learn to read. Beginning reading instruction should be based on language experiences and predictable or repetitive stories rather than on isolated phonics and structural analysis. It is the teacher's responsibility to provide a print-rich environment, ask questions about language and help children discover answers, read to and with the children, provide authentic reading and writing tasks, and encourage and guide children in their developing sense of language.

The Emergent Literacy Classroom

Emergent literacy is based on the assumption that language learning occurs naturally in the home and community as children see print and understand its function in their environment. They learn about literacy from adult models, particularly family members, and their knowledge of reading and writing develops concurrently. Before they understand letter-sound associations, they scribble messages or draw letterlike forms that have meaning for them and then "read" their messages to others. Children who have quite naturally acquired basic concepts about print are members of the *literacy club* (Smith, 1988), and researchers have found that many kindergarten children do indeed understand a great deal about how language works, as in the following examples (Mavrogenes, 1986; McLane and McNamee, 1990):

1. They make sense out of the writing in their environment by relating words (such as *McDonald's*) to corresponding places (a restaurant).

2. They expect print to be meaningful and to communicate ideas.

3. They understand some characteristics of written language, such as directionality, spacing, sequencing, and form.

4. They have some knowledge of letter names, auditory and visual discrimination, and correspondence between written and spoken words.

5. They know what books are and how to use them.

What the child learns about language at home should be the foundation for literacy learning in the classroom, and it makes sense for continued language growth to occur in much the same way that it did during the preschool years. In other words, language learning in the classroom should grow out of the child's natural curiosity about language, functional use of language in authentic situations, and experimentation with ways to use language for effective communication.

Early experiences with written language that may occur during the first year of life, such as playing with alphabet blocks and listening to stories read from books, lay the foundation for a lifelong process of learning to read and write (Teale and Sulzby, 1989). Children progress through developmental stages in oral language (from babbling to mature speech) and written language (from scribbling to legible writing), moving toward ever-higher levels of language proficiency. Thus, literacy evolves in a natural, connected way over an extended period of time as the learner discovers new insights about language and how it works.

In the emergent literacy classroom, children are the center of learning, many forms of print are available, and activities are purposeful. Reading and writing develop concurrently, with teacher guidance and encouragement. This does not mean skills are unimportant; indeed, children must learn them to become successful readers, writers, and speakers. The perspective has changed, however. The teacher's role is now one of setting conditions that enable children to explore language and make discoveries that will lead them to internalize reading and writing skills. The teacher is there sometimes to provide direct instruction, but more often to assist learners and intervene when they need help.

The teacher must build on children's existing knowledge about language by understanding each child and providing developmentally appropriate literacy experiences. It is important to remember that every child who enters school is an individual with a unique personality, a specific set of experiences, and special interests. Most children come to the classroom with reasonable control over oral language, but they are likely to have many misconceptions and incompletely formed concepts about written language. According to Kenneth Goodman (1986), teachers should accept children as natural and curious learners, recognize their special competencies and needs, find ways to serve them, and support them with patience and encouragement.

Children value their ability to make choices—what to do, with whom to work, where to work, which books to read, and how best to do chosen tasks (Rasinski, 1988). Freedom to choose enables children to make decisions and self-direct their learning. From a study involving six year olds, Fresch (1995) found that children select books and activities that meet special needs, such as facing a new challenge, talking with friends about reading and writing, and building confidence through familiar reading. Children can even help create curriculum if their teacher considers their interests, concerns, and inquiries when planning instruction (Fallon and Allen, 1994). The following Classroom Scenario illustrates the value of allowing children to make choices.

Classroom Scenario

Freedom to Choose

Following a unit on giants that included a section on whales, a prefirst grader chose to draw pictures of whales during language workshop. Sprawled on the floor in a corner of the room, Danny carefully sketched a different kind of whale in each of six frames of large segmented paper to be used for a roll movie. He marked the distinguishing features of each whale, then labeled each picture by copying the name of the type of whale. For Danny, such sustained attention was unusual, but whales fascinated him.

Analysis of Scenario
When children are free to choose their activities, their concentration and determination enable them to accomplish remarkable tasks.

Establishing a Print-Rich Classroom Environment

By establishing print-rich environments, teachers can encourage children to become aware of purposes for reading and writing. Charts on which teachers record dictations about students' experiences, as well as labels for identifying objects, remind students that print communicates meaning. Attractively displayed books invite children to read, and writing materials at play centers encourage them to write lists and memos (Booth, 1994).

Many children learn to read *environmental print*—words they frequently see around them—long before they enter school. By using advertisements and promotional materials for familiar products such as Crest or popular cereals, teachers link the home/community environment with that of the classroom (Neuman and Roskos, 1993; Sabey and Squier, 1993). Another advantage of using environmental print is that it is free and readily available. Often children bring examples to share, read them, and display them for others to read. Using the children's knowledge of environmental words, the teacher can begin teaching letter-sound relationships. See the following Model Activity.

Model Activities

Environmental Print

Since you have been encouraging the children to share examples of environmental print, they have responded enthusiastically. Today, as the children present their treasures, you notice a teaching opportunity. Say: "Tina and Jeff, will you please tell us what you brought?" (Tina has a label from a pizza box, and Jeff has an empty bag of potato chips.) Then say: "Who can tell me the name of the letter we see at the beginning of *pizza*? What letter do we see at the beginning of *potato chip*? Now let's say these words and listen to see if they sound alike at the beginning."

When the children have identified the letter and realized that the words begin with the same sound, say: "Can you find another word in the room that starts with the same letter?" When Carole finds the word *party* in a chart story about last week's Halloween party, ask: "Does *party* begin with the same sound we hear at the beginning of *pizza* and *potato chip*?" When the children reply affirmatively, put the letter *p* at the top of a chart and write *pizza, potato chip,* and *party* under the letter. Say: "Let's read these words again and listen for the sound that *p* makes. When we find other words that begin with the letter *p,* we can add them to our chart."

In a developmental classroom, the environment should provide opportunities for language growth that are similar to those provided in a natural home environment (Holdaway, 1979). Here are some guidelines based on this concept (Fisher, 1989; Wood and Nurss, 1988; Fortson and Reiff, 1995; Salinger, 1996).

1. Provide a wide variety of materials for purposeful writing and reading.

2. Place labels and key words around the room at the children's eye level.

3. Organize the room so that children can follow the classroom routine and take care of their belongings independently.

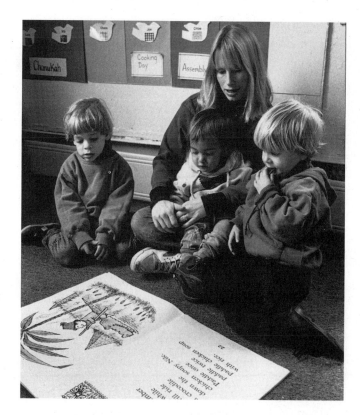

A teacher's daily reading aloud to children helps them develop an awareness of story structure, acquaints them with new words, and fosters their interest in reading. (© *Jean Claude Lejeune*)

4. Display children's work so that they can see it and discuss it with others. (In one room, the bulletin board is on the floor.)

5. Encourage children to compose stories from wordless picture books and to respond creatively to literature.

6. Provide opportunities for expressing ideas, thoughts, and feelings through talk.

7. Immerse children in literature and in early drawing, writing, and read-along experiences.

8. Use reading materials that relate to ongoing class activities, as shown in the following Model Activity.

Model Activities

Duty Chart

Say to the children: "In our classroom, we need many helpers. What kinds of helpers do we need?" The children suggest answers. Then say: "We will need different boys and girls to help us each week. I have made a duty chart to help us remember whose turn it is to help. Each week we will change the names beside the jobs. Let's read the chart together. We'll see who has a job this week."

In a print-rich, literate classroom environment, the following items might be found at learning centers (see Chapter 13 for a full description of centers), on walls, on shelves, on bulletin boards, or even suspended from the ceiling.

books of all types	stamp pads
typewriter and computer	variety of writing materials
captioned photographs	nature center with labels
individual chalkboards	displays of children's work
chart stories	calendars, weather reports
newspapers, magazines	unit displays and models
message boards	labels from familiar foods
child-made books	files of children's work
labels around classroom	pocket charts

Time for Reflection

Some teachers believe they should decorate the classroom with attractive displays so that children enter an intriguing, welcoming room on the first day of school. Other teachers prefer to leave the classroom nearly bare until the children create their own displays and charts; these teachers feel that children will develop a sense of ownership and pride if their contributions are recognized. **What do *you* think?**

Working with Parents

It is important that parents provide a positive environment for their youngsters' emerging literacy. Parents need to become aware that they are their children's first teachers and that the language experiences they provide will have a powerful effect on the children's growth in literacy. Teachers can help parents better understand and execute their critical role in promoting early literacy by encouraging them to respond enthusiastically to their children's curiosity about print. The continuity—or lack of continuity—between literacy experiences at home and in school strongly affects learning (McLane and McNamee, 1990).

Although teachers should not expect parents to provide direct instruction for their children, which may create anxieties and tensions (Clay, 1979), they can offer parents the following suggestions for guiding literacy development at home:

1. Read picture books, beginning at infancy.
2. Listen patiently and supportively when the child struggles to express an idea, and respond appropriately.
3. Share letters that come in the mail so that the child understands that writing can communicate messages.
4. Point out and read familiar signs, such as ones that say *Sears, Wendy's,* and *Stop.* Encourage the child to read them too.
5. Provide writing materials (including typewriters and computers, if possible) and encourage their use for writing messages, shopping lists, and letters.
6. Model good reading practices by reading books for your own pleasure. Explain why you are enjoying your book.
7. Carry on conversations with the child. Answer questions and explain "why" and "how."
8. Share newspapers and magazines. Encourage the child to find familiar words that appear in advertisements.
9. Sing songs, do finger plays, recite nursery rhymes, and play guessing games.
10. Take the child with you on visits and trips. Use specific terms when discussing the experience, such as *flight attendant, pilot, gate,* and *baggage area.*
11. Involve the child in activities around the home, such as cooking, gardening, and paying bills. Point out the usefulness of recipes, instructions on seed packets, and checkbooks.
12. Visit the children's section of the library; let the child get a library card and check out lots of books.
13. Read together cereal boxes, menus, place mats, street signs, coupons, and other forms of print.
14. Encourage the child to "talk like a book" when sharing a storybook with you.

Because of the importance of story reading with children, teachers might offer parents some specific pointers. Story reading can be a pleasurable experience for both the reader and the child, especially when accompanied by a lively verbal exchange about the story and the illustrations. Research on home storybook reading has supported the following interactive behaviors for their positive effects on literacy: questioning, praising, offering information, directing discussion, relating concepts to life experiences, modeling dialogue and responses, and sharing personal reactions (Strickland and Morrow, 1990). Here are examples of appropriate questions and comments based on *The Three Little Pigs.*

How is this little pig's house different from our house?

Uh-oh, that wolf is going to cause trouble! Can you read this part with me? (*I'll huff, and I'll puff, and I'll blow your house down.*)

What do you think will happen next?

That's a good idea! Let's read so that we can find out for sure.

I think this third little pig is pretty smart. What do you think?

By sharing books with their children, parents can make them aware of many print conventions. Behaviors such as pointing to words and letters, talking about words with similar sounds, and observing upper- and lower-case letters occur naturally during parent-child reading. Smolkin and Yaden (1992) found that children whose parents read with them were using correct linguistic terms (for example, *letter* and *word*) and becoming aware of directionality, letter forms, and sound-letter relationships. In addition, they were learning new word meanings and using prior knowledge to make sense of text.

Parents unaccustomed to emergent literacy classrooms may expect their children to bring home graded worksheets and may be dismayed by child-created stories using invented spelling. The teacher should communicate with parents, perhaps through weekly newsletters or regular parent workshops, to inform them about classroom practices (Enz, 1995).

Listening and Speaking

The language skills children have learned at home are the foundation for their further language development. Throughout the school day, children should have many opportunities to develop oral communication skills. In the accompanying Classroom Scenario, the children follow a procedure for sharing time that stresses courtesy in both speaking and listening behaviors.

Classroom Scenario

Sharing Time

At the beginning of school, Paula Franck modeled sharing time with her kindergartners, but now they are conducting it themselves. Paula and the children are sitting on the rug with Kelly, today's leader, on a chair in front of them. Kelly begins by saying: "Who has something to share today?" Jenny's hand goes up, and Kelly invites her to share. Jenny begins: "This is what my dad brought me from Washington." She shows a model of the Washington Monument and continues to talk about it. When Jenny finishes, she calls on the listeners to make comments and ask questions. Ted says: "I really like what you told us. What is it made of?" Jenny answers, then calls on Chris, who says: "That is very interesting. How big is the real one?"

Analysis of Scenario

Children who speak must be prepared to share and then be able to direct the discussion that follows. Basing their responses on careful listening, members of the audience must say something positive and then ask questions or make comments. Paula intervenes only when no one has a question or comment, which rarely occurs.

Listening

In teaching children to listen, the teacher should choose topics that interest them and make use of words and concepts they understand. To be members of an audience, children need to learn to concentrate and become good listeners.

Teachers can help children improve their listening comprehension by reading both story and informational books to them. When reading these books to the class, teachers should relate the children's experiences to the content of the books. They should read relevant books and make them available to children before and after visiting various places on field trips.

The following Model Activity shows how books could be used in a lesson on plants in a kindergarten room.

Model Activities

Listening for Information

Set up a science center with books and displays about plants. Say to the children: "Today we are going to talk about plants. First, I am going to read you a book about plants. Listen to see if you can find out how plants grow. Then we will plant something for our room." Read the book and ask questions like the following:

Questions

Where do seeds come from?

What do plants need to make them grow?

How are seeds planted?

If we want to plant something, what will we need?

Although the preceding Model Activity is an example of students' practicing listening skills in a subject-area learning center, centers can also be set up specifically *for* listening of all sorts. These dedicated listening areas should be equipped with tape recorders, headsets, story tapes, and multiple copies of read-along books. By recording themselves reading stories to the children, teachers can provide a wide variety of tapes easily and inexpensively (Ollila and Mayfield, 1992). Tapes of nonfiction books introduce children to expository text, and recorded commentaries on field trips help students recall special events with appropriate specialized vocabulary. Other ideas for listening center tapes include jump-rope rhymes, riddles and jokes, interviews, tongue twisters, and poems or jingles.

Oral Expression

Children learn about using language through informal conversations, which they may engage in while working together at centers or on class projects. Teachers' recognizing the value of talk reflects Vygotsky's theory that children develop intellectually as they interact socially with other children and with mediating adults (Fortson and Reiff, 1995). The classroom environment provides many subjects and opportunities for descriptive talk. Children can compare different building blocks and note their relationships (size, weight, color); they can observe several kinds of animals and consider differences in the animals' feet, skin covering, and size; and they can compare a variety of fabrics for texture, weight, and purpose.

Opportunities for oral expression occur frequently during the day. Teachers should encourage children to use these opportunities to develop their skills in oral communication. Here are some good ideas for class activities that develop oral expression:

    making the daily schedule

    choosing a current event to record on the chalkboard

    planning projects, activities, or experiences

    discussing a new bulletin board display

    interpreting pictures

    discussing what to include in an experience story

    brainstorming ideas from "What if . . ." situations (Example: "What if we had four arms instead of two arms?")

    acting out stories

    carrying on pretend telephone conversations with toy telephones

    reviewing the day's events

    engaging in dramatic play

Some teachers may wish to set up language centers to combine verbal communication with cognitive development (Hunter-Grundin, 1990). An adult (teacher, parent, or teaching assistant) leads a small group of children in a discussion that enables them to express opinions, justify points of view, challenge the opinions of others, or suggest possible alternatives. Appropriate topics include ideas for books children are coauthoring, solutions to problems, and subjects related to a theme. The discussion is not a question-answer session, but an open expression of thoughts and ideas. It should help students gain confidence in their ability to communicate, and it should stimulate them to think deeply about matters that concern them.

Dramatic Play

Dramatic play occurs when children simulate real experiences, such as cooking dinner or being a cashier. It requires both speaking and listening, but often incorporates reading and writing as well. It is spontaneous and unrehearsed, and children assume the roles of people they have observed from real-life experiences. They think, feel, move, react, and speak according to their interpretations of how these people perform their roles. Both Piaget and Vygotsky believe that children construct knowledge and develop intellectually through play (Wortham, 1996).

In the following Model Activity, children are able to practice language skills as they play the roles of customer, cashier, food preparer, and order taker. They learn to follow directions, fill out forms, and recognize the words for menu items. They also develop mathematical skills as they use play money to pay for their orders and make change.

Model Activities

Dramatic Play

After the children have discussed their experiences at various fast-food restaurants, say to them: "How could we make a pretend fast-food restaurant in our own classroom? Where could we put it? What are some things we would need? How could we get these things?" Have the children come up with answers and develop a plan. Ask some children to bring in cups, napkins, bags, and plastic containers from a fast-food restaurant, and have others paint a sign. One child can bring in a toy cash register.

Make an illustrated price list to place above an improvised counter, and provide copies of order forms for the children to use. Help the children learn to read the food words and the prices by asking: "What is the first item on the list? How much does it cost? Can you find it on the order form?" Keep the list simple at first, and add new items later. When the fast-food center is ready, different children can assume the roles of customers and workers (McNutt and Bukofzer, 1982).

Ideally, themes for dramatic play centers originate from the children's interests and ideas, with the teacher facilitating the development of the centers. A field trip to a grocery store or fire station may be the stimulus for a dramatic play center. Other typical centers are a kitchen, bakery, post office, bank, business office, hospital, beauty parlor, travel agency, aquarium, and restaurant (Dailey and Owen, 1994; Fields and Hillstead, 1990; Fisher, 1991). See Example 2.1 for an example of a library center.

The children can plan and prepare each center by bringing supplies, arranging the area, and painting cardboard walls or counters. The teacher should see

Example 2.1   *Dramatic Play Center: Library Theme*

Discussion:

To create interest in this center, have the children take a trip to the public library, or have the school librarian introduce the children to their library and its facilities. The children should understand that the library exists so that people may borrow books to read and that borrowers must take good care of the books.

Preparation:

The teacher writes an experience chart about the library visit from the children's dictation. Together, the children and teacher plan their own library, including the arrangement of the area and the supplies needed. With the teacher's help, the children plan ways to organize their space, put up signs, create shelves for books, decorate the walls, and get the books they'll use.

Center Props:

check-out table or desk	bookshelves
mats for sitting	book and author posters
books and magazines	telephone

Literacy Materials:

library cards (personal)	library book return cards
pencils, pens, markers	telephone directory
stamp pad	check-out/check-in paper
index cards	telephone pad
bookmarks	calendar

signs and labels (for library hours, book classifications, etc.)

that materials are available to stimulate the use of written language for communication, such as the following:

recipes	note paper
writing tools	envelopes
clipboards	briefcases
file folders	newspapers
coupons	menus

grocery lists   junk mail

bank checks   strips of tickets

Only a few materials should be available at first, and others may be added as needed. These items should be safe for children to handle, authentic in terms of their real-world environment, and useful for carrying out their roles (Neuman and Roskos, 1993; Roskos and Vukelich, 1991).

During dramatic play, the teacher acts primarily as an observer, but may also participate briefly to model appropriate behaviors and promote interaction. For instance, at a grocery store, the teacher might ask, "Do you have any specials today?" or "May I use my coupon to buy this soap?"

Dramatic play has many benefits. Because children need to carry on conversations, they must use good language skills. Frequently children use printed words in their play, which later become sight words. These words may be found on package labels, order forms, street signs, or ticket booths. Children discover the need to read when they have to recognize words to play the situation. Perceiving this need stimulates their interest in learning to read.

Creative Dramatics

Spontaneous story reenactments, or *creative dramatics,* heighten children's awareness of story structure and characterization, which in turn helps them to comprehend and recall stories (Martinez, 1993). Acting out stories spontaneously builds interest in reading because children love to hear stories and then perform them. As the teacher reads a story, the children need to pay close attention to the sequence of events, the personalities of the characters, the dialogue, and the mood. Before acting out the story, the class reviews what happened and identifies the characters. As they act, the children must use appropriate vocabulary, enunciate distinctly, speak audibly, and express themselves clearly. Children will want to dramatize some stories several times, switching roles each time. The rest of the class forms the audience and must listen carefully. There is little or no need for props, sets, or costumes. Here are some good stories to dramatize:

Polar Bear, Polar Bear, What Do You Hear? by Bill Martin, Jr. New York: Henry Holt, 1991.

One Fine Day by Nonny Hogrogian. New York: Macmillan, 1971.

Caps for Sale by Esphyr Slobodkina. New York: William R. Scott, 1947.

The Three Billy Goats Gruff by Peter Asbjornsen and Jorgan Moe. New York: Harcourt Brace Jovanovich, 1957.

The Ox-Cart Man by Barbara Cooney. New York: Viking, 1979.

Where the Wild Things Are by Maurice Sendak. New York: Harper & Row, 1963.

Seven Blind Mice by Ed Young. New York: Philomel, 1992.

Puppets are also useful in creative dramatics. Some shy children who are unwilling to speak as themselves are willing to talk through puppets. Children develop good language skills as they plan puppet shows and spontaneously speak their lines.

Reading and Writing

Several concepts are basic to understanding how growth in reading and writing occurs in an emergent literacy classroom (Strickland and Morrow, 1988):

1. Children construct their own knowledge of reading and writing through experimentation and discovery. By bringing the knowledge they already have to new situations, they make connections and look for patterns in printed words.

2. Growth in reading and writing occurs jointly and along with growth in oral language. Each language art supports the others in an interrelated way.

3. Children learn reading and writing by actively using them for real purposes. A major task for the teacher is to structure the environment so that children can explore language in meaningful ways.

4. Teachers need to consider individual differences in children's abilities, interests, and experiences when planning instruction.

5. When necessary, teachers intervene in language learning to help children make connections and move ahead.

6. Reading and writing activities take place throughout the school day, not in separate instructional periods.

In the Classroom Scenario "Kindergarten Literacy Activities," the teacher is using many of these concepts.

**Classroom
Scenario**

Kindergarten Literacy Activities

Before the school day officially begins in Linda Edwards's whole language kindergarten, the children are sitting at tables writing journal entries, gathering around the incubator watching newly hatched ducklings, or sharing books at the reading center. When Linda calls the children together, they discuss the date and the weather. They mark the calendar, and one child calculates the number of 1s and 10s in May 17. Linda then reads them a story from a big book, moving a pointer under the words as she reads. The children sing a song from the big book, with a parent using the pointer while the teacher plays the autoharp. When Linda questions the children about their favorite part, they respond enthusiastically. Then they read the story with her as she moves the pointer below the words again.

Analysis of Scenario
This scenario contains many opportunities for observing and discussing, writing purposefully, and reading independently, as well as learning math concepts, singing songs, and making decisions as a class. Reading and writing are not lessons to be taught during specific time periods but occur in various forms throughout the day.

It is important to keep in mind that reading and writing are complementary processes; children learn them interrelatedly. To give each process due consideration, however, we will examine them separately.

Learning to Read

Learning to read does not happen all at once when children enter school; it is a process that builds gradually from an early age as children acquire new understandings about reading and writing as communication. Let us consider some of the various factors that enter into a child's ability to read.

Experiential Background

A broad experiential background is essential for success in reading, because children must be familiar with the concepts and vocabulary they will see in written form to gain meaning from them. Through their individual experiences, children gain an understanding of concepts and learn words, or labels, for them. As children encounter a variety of experiences, they modify and refine their perceptions until they get a clear picture of each concept they have acquired. A child may need many experiences to attain a well-rounded impression of a single idea. *School,* for example, is a concept that children do not completely understand until they have experienced it in different ways.

Teachers should read aloud to children several times a day, because story sharing creates far-reaching benefits for the listener. Stories introduce children to new vocabulary, language patterns, concepts, cultures, and lifestyles. Children develop an awareness of story structure by listening to stories and discussing them. Hearing stories read aloud may bring about an interest in reading and a desire to learn to read. Well-chosen stories can be the basis for creative expression such as drama, music, and art.

Having a news period can be useful. The teacher can make a chart of classroom news, including items like "We had a fire drill today" or "We talked about the farm." Students can help compile the week's news, decide on headlines, and make illustrations for some items.

Experiences may be either direct or vicarious. Children generally remember direct experiences with actual physical involvement best, but it may not always be feasible to provide direct experiences. Good vicarious experiences, such as listening to stories and watching films, provide opportunities to expand concepts and vocabulary indirectly. Some appropriate experiences of both types are

field trips	films, filmstrips, slides, and tapes
resource people	selected television programs
story reading	photographs, pictures, posters
demonstrations	neighborhood walks
exhibits	class holiday celebrations

A class project like the following Model Activity can promote growth in vocabulary and concept development.

Model Activities

Direct Experience

Start by saying to the children: "Tomorrow we will make some vegetable soup. Try to remember to bring a vegetable to put in the soup. Now we will write a chart story about the ingredients we will need for our soup."

The next morning, say: "Tell us about your vegetable. What is it called? What color is it? How does it feel? How does it smell?" Give each child a chance to handle and talk about the vegetables. Then ask: "What do we need to do first to make the soup? What must we do to the vegetables before we put them in the pot? What else should we add?" (Answers include getting and heating the water, washing and cutting up the vegetables, and adding spices and alphabet noodles.)

When the soup is ready to eat, give each child a cupful. As the children eat, ask: "How does your soup taste? Are the colors of the vegetables the same as when we put them into the soup? How have the alphabet noodles changed? Can you name some of the letters that are in your soup?" After they have fin-

ished eating, let the children dictate another chart story about the sequence of making the soup and/or their reactions to eating it, or have the children write their own stories.

Some of the concepts you can help children acquire from this experience and related discussions are (1) soup can be made from firm, fresh, brightly colored vegetables; (2) after they are cooked, the vegetables change in texture and appearance; (3) the noodles get larger from absorbing the water; (4) it takes time to heat water and cook soup; (5) the water absorbs flavor and color from the vegetables and spices; (6) cold water becomes hot when it is placed on a heated surface; (7) certain foods are classified as vegetables.

As a result of the experience, children's vocabularies might now include *boil, simmer, dissolve, ingredients, squash, celery, turnips, slice, chop, shred, dice, liquid,* and *flavor.* A bonus comes from letting the children manipulate the alphabet letters—identifying them, matching them, and finding the first letters of their names.

Wordless picture books and pictures can provide vicarious experiences. By looking at the pictures in wordless picture books, children can use their own words to describe events and characters, thus building their experiences along with vocabulary and concepts. Pictures, particularly those that tell a story, are extremely fruitful sources of new ideas and experiences. To help children interpret pictures fully, teachers should ask them questions like those in the following Model Activity.

**Model
Activities**

Vicarious Experience

Show the children the picture and then ask the following questions:

1. Where is the little boy? How do you know?

2. What kinds of things usually happen at the veterinarian's office?

3. Why do you think he took his cat there?

4. Why are the other people there?

5. Who is at the door? How do you know?

6. Why is the boy there without his father or mother?

7. What is the boy doing?

8. What do you think will happen soon?

Story writing can be a logical extension of either direct or vicarious experiences. If a class writes a story after a field trip, the students should first discuss the trip. By asking carefully selected questions, the teacher can encourage them to form valid concepts and use appropriate vocabulary words. The students then dictate sentences for the teacher to write on an *experience chart* like that in Example 2.2. Dictated story experiences provide excellent opportunities to introduce the coordinated language experience approach, discussed in Chapter 7.

Stories about an experience may be dictated by a whole class, a group, or a single child. When individual children tell stories, parents, teaching assistants, older children, classroom volunteers, or the teacher can act as scribes. These stories should be about things that are important to the children, such as their families, pets, or favorite activities. The children may illustrate them and combine them into booklets that are then shared around the library table and eventually taken home by the authors. Following are some appropriate experiences for story writing:

Example 2.2 *Experience Chart Story*

Our Trip to the Zoo

We rode in the school bus.
Mr. Spring was the bus driver.
The bus took us to the zoo.
We saw many animals.
We ate popcorn and peanuts.
We thanked Mr. Spring.
Our trip was fun.

---

taking a field trip   observing an animal

watching an experiment   popping corn

visiting a science or book fair   experimenting with paints

tasting unusual foods   planting seeds or bulbs

entertaining a visitor   building a pretend space ship

Perhaps the most important reason for story writing is that children begin to realize that speech can be recorded and that print makes sense. This awareness occurs as the teacher reads the story back to the children in the words they have just dictated. After repeated readings by the teacher, the children may also be able to "read" the story. The teacher can make copies of the story for all the children to take home and share with their families. As a result of their involvement with the story, children may learn to recognize some high-interest words and words used more than once (such as *we, zoo,* and *bus* in the experience chart story).

Children learn many literacy concepts through story writing. They watch as the teacher forms letters that make up words. They notice that language consists of separate words that are combined into sentences. They see the teacher begin at the left side and move to the right and go from top to bottom. They become aware that dictated stories have titles in which the first letter of each important word is capitalized. They realize that sentences begin with capital letters and end with punctuation marks. Besides becoming familiar with mechanical writing skills, children develop their thinking skills. The teacher's questions help them develop skill in organizing and summarizing. As the children retell events in the order of occurrence, they begin to understand sequence. As they recall the important points, they begin to form a concept of *main idea.*

Some say children learn reading and writing naturally, just as they have learned to speak, and that a supportive environment and a wide variety of experiences are all they need to figure out the writing system on their own. Others, however, say that children need direct instruction in skills. **What do** *you* **think?**

Print Conventions

Many children, especially those who have been read to often, begin to "talk like a book" at a very young age (Clay, 1979; Dickinson, 1987; Hall, 1987). They pretend to read by imitating literary style and content instead of using conversational style. Illustrations and previous readings by adults help children construct the text they pretend to read, but of course these children are not yet able to read the actual words. Youngsters often practice "pretend reading" to a younger sibling or a grandparent. "Talking like a book" is an important step in learning to read because it helps children acquire basic literacy concepts, such as realizing that print can be turned into spoken words and that books use a special type of language. These and similar concepts are sometimes called *print conventions,* that is, generally accepted concepts about reading and writing. The reader expects the writer to use certain conventions, and the writer assumes the reader will follow them (Butler and Turbill, 1987).

Fisher (1991, 1995) focuses on four major types of print conventions as she helps her kindergartners increase their awareness of written language:

1. Book knowledge (awareness of title and author, knowing how to hold a book and turn pages)
2. Directionality (moving from top to bottom and left to right)
3. Visual connections (distinguishing between letter and word, understanding uses of punctuation, recognizing upper- and lower-case letters)
4. Auditory conventions (awareness of sound-letter relationships)

By demonstrating these conventions while reading, Fisher helps her children become more aware of them. She records the concepts she stresses during each lesson and evaluates the children's progress toward understanding and applying them in their reading and writing.

Sight Words

Children who enter school are rapidly acquiring *sight words,* words they recognize instantly without analyzing them. Teachers can encourage sight word recognition by exposing children to commonly used words, such as names, number and color words, and environmental words.

Sight vocabulary can be learned in a number of meaningful ways. Ashton-Warner (1963) described the use of *organic words,* words that are meaningful or emotionally charged, such as *ghost, kiss,* and *Mother.* Each child chooses a word that has special personal meaning, and the teacher writes that word on a card and gives it to the child. A word card is kept as long as the word is known; when a word is forgotten or is no longer meaningful to the child, the card is discarded.

Another child-centered strategy for teaching sight words is to create a "word wall" of words that children find interesting or important. Martha Dawson demonstrates how her children use their word wall in the following Classroom Scenario.

Classroom Scenario

Word Wall

Toward the end of the year, the word wall in her classroom contained a large number of words that Martha Dawson's kindergartners wanted to know. Martha had started the collection of words when the children asked how to spell words they needed to use. She encouraged them to suggest words for her to write on cards made from colored poster board strips. She attached the cards to the wall in alphabetical order, and the children read them daily—sometimes all of them in alphabetical order and sometimes just similar words classified by colors, such as blue words or yellow words.

Today Andy had a word to add to the wall. His word was *TV.* The children agreed this was an important word and should go with the group of words near the end of the list that began with *t.* There were already two *t* words, *thank* and *train,* so the children needed to decide where *TV* should go. With Martha's help, they checked the alphabet strip at the front of the room and decided that *TV* should go after *thank* and *train* because *V* comes after *h* and *r.* Martha then taped the word card in its proper place, and the class read all of the words on the wall, including the new one.

Analysis of Scenario
In Martha's classroom, children chose words they considered important, so they felt a sense of ownership with their word wall. It provided a quick reference for accurate spelling of frequently used words, and the children were learning to recognize these words by reading them often. They also found that alphabetical order was a convenient way to organize and locate words. By learning at this early stage to look at the first and second letters of a word for its alphabetical placement, they should find later dictionary study an easy task.

Letters and Sounds

To learn to read, children must acquire knowledge of letters and their corresponding sounds.

Letter Recognition. Teachers need to keep several points in mind while helping beginning readers learn letters and words. Children should learn letter names early so that the teacher and the class have a common referent—for example, understanding when the teacher talks about the letter *f* or the letter *n* (Farr and Roser, 1979). Knowledge of letter *names* is important for talking about similarities and differences among printed words, but knowledge of letter *sounds* is more useful in decoding words (Hafner and Jolly, 1982). Children who learn both the names and sounds of letters can read better than children who learn only letter names (Anderson et al., 1985).

Phonemic Awareness. *Phonemic awareness,* an understanding that speech consists of a series of small sound units, is a powerful predictor of success in reading (Adams, 1990; Pearson, 1993; Stanovich, 1993/1994; Yopp, 1992). It is both a prerequisite for learning to read and a consequence of an increased awareness of language that comes from learning to read (Yopp, 1992).

Teachers can help students develop phonemic awareness by encouraging them to use invented spellings so that they become conscious of the sounds that make up words (Pearson, 1993), exposing them to literature that plays with the sounds of language (Griffith and Olson, 1992), and involving them in songs and games that draw attention to the sounds of language (Yopp, 1992). When youngsters pay close attention to speech sounds and use their discoveries about letter-sound relationships to guide their writing and reading, they increase their functional and meaningful use of written language (Richgels et al., 1996).

Alphabetic Principle. It is critical that beginning readers understand the *alphabetic principle,* the concept that letters represent speech sounds (Pikulski, 1989). Some children learn this principle intuitively, but most need help. Holdaway (1979) suggests introducing two contrasting letter-sound combinations, such as *m* and *f,* and having children find these letters in familiar stories that the teacher has read with them. After they find many examples, which they can readily identify because of their familiarity with the stories, they work with other letter-sound relationships, including *b, g, s,* and *t.* Because of the insights they have gained, many children are now able to learn the remaining initial consonants and consonant blends on their own.

Reading Centers

A reading center is an area in which children gather to read and listen to stories. Books are arranged on shelves by categories, placed in storage crates by favorite authors, or enticingly displayed with their full covers showing. The classroom library should contain about five to eight books per child. These books should represent different levels of difficulty and should be rotated from time to time (Strickland and Morrow, 1988). Big books open to familiar stories rest on easels; smaller versions are nearby for independent reading. A carpeted area with a rocking chair and pillows completes the scene.

At reading centers, children may read independently or with partners from books, magazines, or newspapers. They may make and use such materials as roll movies, flannel boards, and puppets to expand on stories they have heard or read. If a library checkout system is operating, youngsters can write their names and dates on cards and file them. The children may find ways to make the center more attractive and meaningful for them, perhaps by decorating it with their own stories and illustrations. When children work independently on chosen tasks at developmentally appropriate levels, the teacher is free to work with small groups, hold individual reading conferences, and circulate to observe and offer support (Henderson, 1996).

Reading Materials

In a print-rich classroom environment, words are everywhere—on bulletin boards and walls, on children's work and book jackets, and as labels on objects around the room. There are charts dictated by the children and books on shelves and at centers.

Big books with enlarged pictures and print that the entire class can read together offer an excellent way for children to learn to read, even on the first day of school. (See the Classroom Scenario "First Day of School.") Many big books have *predictable* or patterned stories—stories that use repetition, rhythmic language patterns, and familiar concepts. (See Appendix A at the end of this chapter.) Even during a first reading by the teacher, children join in on the repetitive lines or familiar chants. For example, when the teacher reads, "And the little red hen said—," the children respond, "I'll do it myself!" This procedure enables a child to "confirm the predictability of written language" (Wiseman, 1984, p. 343). Stories such as Bill Martin, Jr.'s *Brown Bear, Brown Bear* and Audrey Wood's *The Napping House* contain familiar sequences of this sort. Children will soon read these books by themselves if the teacher has reread them and pointed out the corresponding words.

**Classroom
Scenario**

First Day of School

Early in the day, Oliver Jordan calls the children to the story rug and introduces the big book version of Bill Martin, Jr.'s *Brown Bear, Brown Bear, What Do You See?* Eagerly the children listen as he reads and watch as he turns the brightly colored pages. Soon they are chiming in on some of the words, helped along by the picture clues. When they beg him to read it again, he does so and invites all of them to read it with him. In additional readings throughout the day, children read pages by themselves and with partners. They listen with headphones as they follow along in small book versions, and by the end of the day they believe they are readers.

Across the hall, Mary Hill is also introducing her children to reading, but she does so by asking them to return to their seats and giving them new workbooks. She tells them to turn to the first page and explains the directions for marking the words that begin with the same letter. "Our letter today is the letter *m*," she says, "and I'd like you to take your pencil or crayon and mark each word that begins with this letter." The children finish the exercise, watch as Mary shows them how to print the letter *m*, and then make rows of *m*s.

Analysis of Scenario

Many children come to school eager to learn to read. In Oliver's class, the children were excited because they believed they were really reading. In Mary's class, the children were disappointed because they had not learned to read; they were unable to see any connection between their work and reading stories. According to Booth (1994), the way children encounter print at the beginning of school may determine their attitudes toward reading for the rest of their lives.

As children read and reread stories—by themselves and to one another—and engage in reading and writing activities related to the stories, they are participating in what Holdaway (1979) calls the *shared-book experience*. Teachers may use the following procedure for sharing big books with their children, which is an extension of the bedtime story shared between parent and child (Holdaway, 1979; Strickland, 1988):

1. Introduce the story by stimulating a discussion that relates students' experiences to the text, presenting the title and author (using these terms), guiding the children to make predictions about the story, and showing eager anticipation for reading the story.

2. Read the story with lively expression. Run a pointer slowly under the words as you read them so that the children can match the spoken words with the print and observe the directionality. While reading, think aloud about aspects of the story ("I wonder what will happen now!" or "Little Bear must feel very happy!"). Encourage children to make predictions and read familiar parts with you.

3. When the story is over, guide a discussion about major points; then find and reread corresponding parts of the text to confirm the points. Help the children reread the text together until they become fluent and confident.

A number of optional variations and follow-up activities are also useful. To focus on meaning, the teacher may use adhesive notes or flaps to cover meaningful, predictable words and then ask the children to identify the words underneath. The teacher may also select certain phonics or structural elements that are well represented in the story, call the children's attention to them, and lead the children to discover word recognition strategies for decoding words with these elements. The children may wish to illustrate parts of the text, write their own versions, find other books related to the same topic, or extend the text in some other way. Since many big books have accompanying audiotapes and sets of small books, the children may read a small version to a listener or listen to a tape of the big book while following along in the smaller one.

Believing that children gain confidence and skill in reading from free selection, Fisher (1991) explains her procedure for daily *choice time* reading. The children may choose whatever they wish to read: big books or small versions of them, trade books, magazines, books published by other children, poems, or songs written on charts around the room. They may follow along in a book as they listen to a tape of a familiar story, or they may read with her, with a friend, with a visitor, or alone. Sometimes they role-play a shared reading session, taking turns being the teacher and inviting a small group to respond.

The McCrackens (1987) use a *pocket chart* for teaching children to read. This consists of a large chart with rows of "pockets" that hold words, pictures that represent words, and sentence strips. The teacher has the children manipulate the words and sentences so that they can learn the story, become aware of print, match words, and build the story or sequence of events. See the following Classroom Scenario.

**Classroom
Scenario**

Reading from a Pocket Chart

As part of the morning activities, Tina DeStephen's prefirst graders read their daily schedule from a pocket chart.

Morning	Afternoon
Attendance/Tally	Lunch
Pledge/Song	Storytime
Calendar/Weather	Quiet self-selected reading
Language workshop	Buddy reading
Author's Chair	Reading conferences
Something Special	Self-selection
Recess	Clean-up
Math	Time to go home

Tina discusses the day's schedule with the children and talks about "something special," which may be a visitor, a trip, or an invitation to see another class perform a play. "Self-selection" refers to such options as playing with blocks, doing handwriting, reading to the bear, making a puppet show, playing instruments, painting at the easel, using math manipulatives, and playing in the housekeeping center. Before releasing the children to work independently, Tina makes sure that each child has decided what to do.

Analysis of Scenario

This daily ritual serves many purposes. Tina and the children anticipate the day's events together as they read and discuss the activities. The children are comfortable and secure in this familiar routine, and they consider their choices and make decisions about what they will do. They realize that reading is purposeful, they reread now familiar words, and they become aware of sequence.

Learning to Write

We have stressed that many youngsters know a great deal about written language before entering school. Children actually perceive themselves as writers long before they can write conventionally. They experiment with making scribbles, sometimes interspersing pictures and letterlike shapes, and believe that their "writing" conveys messages.

When teachers invite children to write in kindergarten, they should follow certain basic guidelines (based on Sulzby, Teale, and Kamberelis, 1989; Sulzby, 1994; Ollila and Mayfield, 1992):

1. Accept the form of writing the child can use; it does not have to be adult writing.

2. Allow children to share their writing and respond to what other children have written.

3. Let children "write" their own names on their work to give them a sense of ownership.

4. Encourage children to use writing to communicate with other people.

5. Provide a variety of writing materials that are readily available.

6. Be a model by letting children see you writing purposefully.

7. Provide ample time for children to write.

8. Help children realize the importance of writing in their lives.

Early Writing Strategies

For young children, writing is often a social event. Children confer with one another, sharing their skills and searching for resources and examples (Loughlin and

Martin, 1987). They may tentatively compose stories and tell them to their friends before writing them. When children actually get down to the serious business of writing, Donald Graves claims, they talk to themselves, audibly or subaudibly (Walshe, 1986). They verbalize as they physically form letters and words in the process of formulating their stories.

When children begin kindergarten and are given opportunities to write, some are in the prephonetic stage and place letters on paper without regard for the sounds they make, as in Example 2.3. They tell the teacher what they have written, and the teacher records what they dictate while helping them see relationships between spoken and written words (Coate and Castle, 1989). In kindergarten most children continue to scribble, draw, and use nonphonetic strings of letters (Sulzby, Teale, and Kamberelis, 1989).

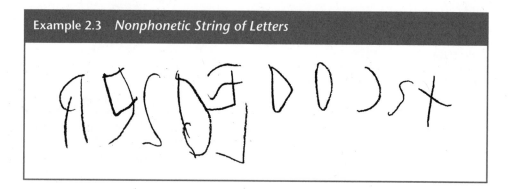

Example 2.3 *Nonphonetic String of Letters*

Once children have a sense of letter-sound relationships, they begin to use *invented,* or *temporary, spellings.* Richgels (1987, p. 523) defines invented spelling as "beginning writers' ability to write words by attending to their sound units and associating letters with them in a systematic, though unconventional, way." Writing with invented spellings enables children to apply their knowledge of letter-sound relationships for their own purposes. Example 2.4 shows how a kindergartner reacted to a dinosaur theme by drawing a picture and writing a story with invented spellings. Example 2.5 shows a first grader's use of invented spellings in a message to a friend.

Close observation of children's invented spellings provides insights into their awareness of letter-sound relationships. Because consonant sounds are more distinctive than vowel sounds, children often use them to represent the key sounds in the words they are trying to spell, either omitting or misrepresenting vowel sounds. Sometimes, in fact, beginning spellers use only the initial consonant of the word they wish to spell. In Example 2.4, Taylor shows considerable knowledge of phonics by systematically sounding through each word and representing each sound with the letter he hears, as in *dinaswrs.* Taylor also mixes

Example 2.4 *Kindergartner's Use of Invented Spellings*

This story reads as follows: The meat eater of the dinosaurs. Will Tyrannosaurus Rex survive?

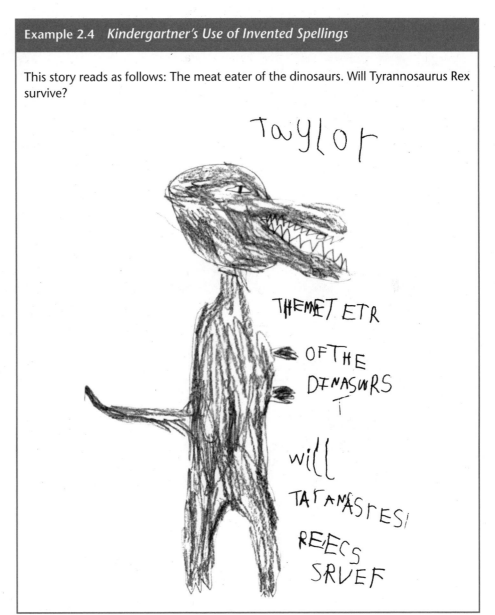

Source: Taylor Bennett, Sycamore Elementary School, Cookeville, Tennessee, 1987. Used with permission.

some conventional spelling (i.e., *of* and *the*) with his spelling inventions. Trudy (Example 2.5) also reveals excellent awareness of letter-sound relationships in the word *dadokaded.*

With each writing sample, the teacher can learn a great deal about a child's beginning reading and writing competencies. In Example 2.6, the teacher observes

---

Example 2.5 *First Grader's Use of Invented Spellings*

This story reads as follows: Roses are red. Violets are blue. These golden flowers remind me of you. Dedicated to Janet.

rosises   are   red   volits
are   blue   thes   goldn
fouers   reemid   me   of   you

dadokaded

to

Janet

by

Trudy

Source: Trudy Walker, Capshaw Elementary School, Cookeville, Tennessee, 1987. Used with permission.

that Sheila, a kindergartner, writes from left to right, leaves spaces between words, and writes in complete sentences. She has a good sense of sound-letter relationships, although she sometimes omits some sounds (*WH* for *went*). She spells the *ing* ending correctly. She is not clear about when to use upper- and lower-case letters, however, and she does not use punctuation.

Knowledge of which letters represent certain sounds within words is useful not only for writing, but also for decoding words in reading. Using invented spelling helps children develop phonemic awareness and understanding of the alphabetic principle (Adams, 1990). According to Cunningham and Cunningham (1992, p. 106), research indicates that "invented spelling and decoding are mirror-like processes that make use of the same store of phonological knowledge." Thus, as children learn to associate sounds with letters, they advance their knowledge of both reading and writing. The Model Activity on invented spelling and the Focus on Strategies demonstrate ways teachers can help children begin to write and read.

Example 2.6   *Beginning Writing*

The story reads as follows: I went to get a present for my mom. Everybody was shouting hoorah and singing happy birthday.

I WH to   GH A
PReSt   FoR my
mom   eVRX BuDY
WuS   ShoWINg
huRA AND
SEINg   hBe BRDA

Source: Sheila Vogel, Kingston Elementary School, Kingston, Tennessee, 1994. Used with permission.

Model Activities

Demonstrating Invented Spelling

Say to the children: "We've been talking about going camping, and today we set up a tent in our room. Some of you may want to write about tents in your journals. Can you help me spell *tent*?" The children eagerly agree. "Let's say *tent* slowly together and listen for the sounds. What letter makes the sound we hear at the beginning?" Most children suggest *t,* so write *t* on the board. Then ask: "Let's say *tent* again and stretch it out. Think about the sound we hear next. What letter makes that sound?" The children aren't quite sure; some say *t*; some say *n*; and a few offer other letters. For now,

write *n.* Then say "Is there another sound? Let's say *tent* once more, very slowly." After repeating the word, the children quickly say: "*t,* another *t* at the end." Complete the word for them by adding *t.*

To reinforce the sound-letter relationships, ask: "Can you find a word in our room that begins like *tent*?" The children turn to the charts and labels. Jamie finds *turtle,* and Allyson sees *ten.* She says excitedly: "*Tent* and *ten* sound almost alike! Can we put an *e* in *tent*?" Ask Allyson to come to the board and put the *e* where it should go; then ask the other children if they agree. After receiving an affirmative answer, ask the children to say the letters in *tent* and remind them to use these letters if they write about tents.

Getting Children Started in Writing

Ms. McLoughlin paused a moment as she moved from one kindergartner to another, offering encouragement as they worked in their journals. She thought back to the beginning of the year when only a few of them could even print their names. For the first few weeks, she had to write in their journals a sentence or two that they had dictated to her to help them grasp the concept that what they said could be written down.

When she had first asked the children to write, they told her they didn't know how. She supplied them with paper and a variety of writing tools, however, and encouraged them to first draw a picture and then write something about it. Some did this with scribbles, some with pictures only, and some with a few letters strewn haphazardly on the page. She accepted their work and asked them to read their stories to her, but she realized she needed to help them discover sound-letter relationships so that they could begin using the letters they needed to make words.

Ms. McLoughlin helped her children discover associations between sounds and letters by pointing them out during shared book reading and having the children pay attention to the letters and sounds in the environmental words at play centers. When the children had developed some knowledge of sound-letter relationships, she demonstrated how to spell words. Even though it took time, she shared individually with each of the children every day and noted in their journals if she helped them sound the words.

In a few weeks, some children were still scribble writing or drawing pictures, but a few had begun to string letters together, often using invented spelling to make words. Ms. McLoughlin remembered the day Tony asked her to spell *duck* and she had said, "What sounds do you hear? Stretch out the word so that you can hear all of its sounds." Slowly, Tony said the word, then wrote *dk*—a real breakthrough for him. As the children discovered sound-letter relationships, they eagerly attempted to spell any word they wanted to use in their stories.

Now, near the end of the school year, Ms. McLoughlin found that most of her children were writing longer and more readable journal entries. They were working on refining sentence structure, making sure there were spaces between words, and placing punctuation marks correctly. She looked at Hank's story and asked him to read it to her. He read:

> Once upon a time there was a tree that wanted to be yellow and he could not decide. So he waited for fall . . . And he turned yellow. The end. By Hank

Ms. McLoughlin complimented him on the way his story had a beginning, a middle, and an end—something she encouraged her children to consider as they wrote. They often discussed story structure as they read stories together.

Looking over at Judy's paper, Ms. McLoughlin could see that Judy still had not made the breakthrough to understanding the relationship between sounds and letters. She looked frustrated, so Ms. McLoughlin asked Hank to help Judy with the words she needed. Ms. McLoughlin smiled to herself as she heard Hank using her

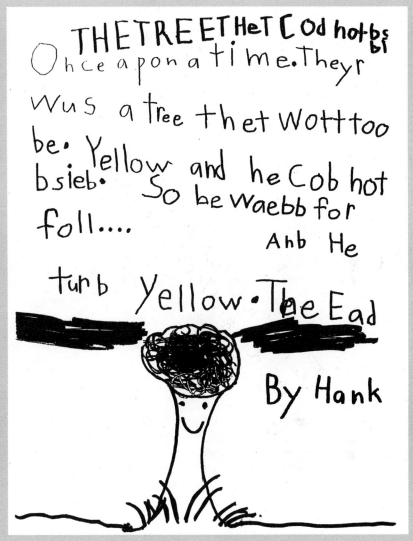

THE TREE ET HET COd hotb bi
Ohce apon a time. Theyr
Wus a tree thet Wotttoo
be. Yellow and he Cob hot
b.sieb. So he waebb for
foll....
Ahb He
turb Yellow. The Ead

By Hank

Source: Hank Replogle, Carthage Elementary School, Carthage, Tennessee, 1994. Used with permission.

exact words: "Think of the sounds in *dinner.* What letter makes the sound you hear at the beginning of the word?"

Moving on, Ms. McLoughlin overheard two children conferring. Al said, "You know. When we write *running,* all we have to do is think how to spell *run* and add *ing.* That's easy." When Chris asked Karen how to spell a word, Karen reminded him he could copy the word he needed from yesterday's chart. Ms. McLoughlin was

(continued)

pleased to hear that exchange, because she always encouraged the children to use the words displayed in the room to get the correct spelling. Tara wanted someone to listen to her story, and Joshua was asking Jeff to help him write his next word. The children learn so much from each other, Ms. McLoughlin thought as she watched them work.

When most of the children had finished, Ms. McLoughlin told them she was ready for them to read their journals to her. Martha came first with a two-page story about her big sister's birthday party. After letting Martha stamp the date on her story, Ms. McLoughlin asked her to select a book to read while the others came to her with their journals. Chuck came next with four pages filled with writing. He eagerly read her a long, involved story about dinosaurs, but she noted that his words were made of letters that had no relationship to the sounds in them. Chuck was a bright child and knew a great deal about dinosaurs, but he still could not use letter-sound relationships.

Even though Ms. McLoughlin sometimes asked the children to write about special topics related to holidays or themes, she often let them choose their own topics. Free choice worked well for Matt; his last entry was only three words, but today he produced a full-page story about his camping trip with his dad.

Glancing around, Ms. McLoughlin could see that nearly all the children had read their journals to her and were comfortably looking at books. Establishing this routine had taken considerable time and effort, but most of the children now understood the schedule and responded well. Even better, many of them were now able to write simple, well-constructed stories with invented spelling.

Time for Reflection

Many teachers encourage children to spell as best they can when they write stories, but others insist they spell words correctly. **What do *you* think?**

Purposes for Writing

When children write to communicate meaning, their writing is purposeful. Some classes support postal system/penpal programs with individual mailboxes for receiving letters and a central mailbox for sending letters. Many reasons for writing also occur at dramatic play centers, where children write telephone messages, take orders for food, make shopping lists, and so on. Other purposeful writing activities include sending messages to school personnel, making greeting cards, sending thank-you notes, writing stories, writing letters, and recording information.

Journal writing offers another purposeful writing activity and often gives the teacher insights into the child's understandings and misinterpretations (Fallon and Allen, 1994). The teacher gives each child a booklet, often made of folded unlined sheets of paper stapled together, to write in during a special time each day. Children may copy, scribble, print, or draw anything they wish in their journals, and sometimes the teacher records in conventional print what the children dictate (McGee and Richgels, 1990).

Writing Centers

A writing center should have a table with chairs around it, containers of writing tools, and newsprint or unlined paper in various sizes and colors. Children like to experiment with colored felt-tipped pens, crayons, pencils, and chalk for individual chalkboards. Resource materials to encourage children to write include greeting cards, note pads, books and magazines, envelopes, special words related to a unit or holiday, magnetic letters, and the alphabet in upper- and lower-case letters. Writing centers may also contain notice or message boards for the children and teacher to use for exchanging information. Computers should be available at writing centers to provide an option for communicating ideas. (See Chapter 11 for information about using computers.)

Invented spelling enables children to apply their knowledge of letter-sound relationships for their own purposes. (© *Elizabeth Crews*)

Assessment of Emergent Literacy

Assessment of each child's progress toward literacy is an essential component of the instructional program. Teachers sometimes administer formal tests at the end of kindergarten and/or the beginning of first grade to predict a child's likelihood

Example 2.7 *Writing Checklist*

Name _____

\multicolumn{6}{c}{*Six-Week Periods*}						*Criteria for Evaluation*
1	**2**	**3**	**4**	**5**	**6**	
						Shows interest in writing
						Writes name
						Draws recognizable picture and can tell story to go with it
						Writes letters or scribblings to represent words
						Reads back own writing
						Writes letter(s) for beginning sounds
						Writes letter(s) for ending sounds
						Writes some intermediate letters
						Copies words from various sources
						Writes from left to right and top to bottom
						Leaves spaces between words
						Uses punctuation appropriately
						Uses upper- and lower-case letters appropriately
						Writes complete sentences
						Writes complete stories

Key:

__+__ Shows normal progress.

__−__ Needs improvement.

__0__ Not expected at this time.

of success in reading, but few tests can reliably predict student performance (Lipson and Wixson, 1991). Instead, most teachers rely heavily on various forms of informal assessment. Chapter 12 presents additional information on assessment in the early grades.

Teachers can evaluate children's awareness of the function or purpose of writing by observing their responses to printed labels and messages. They can learn about children's comprehension strategies by noting their answers to questions about stories read to them. Children reveal a great deal about their emergent literacy when they pretend to read books, especially by the way they use pictures or print as a guide, by the formality of their language, and by their ability to construct stories. Their use of invented spellings when they write and their perceptions of the connections between reading and writing as they "read" their writings also indicate their literacy development. Other indications include the ability to dictate coherent stories, to retell stories they have heard, and to recognize environmental print (words on signs, for example).

Teachers can create their own informal checklists of literacy skills and behaviors. By filling out the forms periodically and dating each form, the teacher creates a written record of each child's progress. A checklist for writing appears in Example 2.7.

For a holistic or process-oriented assessment of a young child's literacy development, Marie Clay's *Concepts about Print Test: Sand* and *Concepts about Print Test: Stones* (both from Heinemann Educational Books, Portsmouth, New Hampshire, 1979) can provide insight into a child's knowledge of written language. The 20-page booklets used for administering the tests are similar to children's picture storybooks; in fact, the teacher may substitute children's books and follow the same procedure. This procedure enables the teacher to observe how a child responds to print as the teacher reads, discover what should be taught as the child interacts with the printed page, and find out which aspects of language the child is learning to control.

The teacher gives the test individually in about five or ten minutes using the following procedure (Clay, 1979). The teacher says to the child, "I'm going to read you this story, but I want you to help me." Teacher and child proceed through the test booklet, with the teacher questioning the child about significant concepts of written language. On the sample page given here (Example 2.8), the teacher tests for awareness of directionality and word-by-word pointing.

1. For directional rules.

   a. The teacher says: Show me where to start.
      Score: 1 for top left

   b. The teacher says: Which way do I go?
      Score: 1 for left to right

   c. The teacher says: Where do I go after that?
      Score: 1 for return sweep to left.

2. Word-by-word pointing.

   a. The teacher says: Point to it while I read it. (The teacher reads slowly, but fluently.)
      Score: 1 for exact matching.

Example 2.8 *Test Page from Sand Booklet*

> I dug a little hole
> and the waves
> splashed in.
>
> 4

Source: *SAND-Concepts About Print Test*. Marie M. Clay, Heinemann Publishers, Auckland, New Zealand, Heinemann Educational Books, Inc., Portsmouth, N.H., 1989.

Time for Reflection

Whereas some teachers believe in giving formal, commercially prepared tests at the end of kindergarten or beginning of first grade, others prefer to evaluate students through observation and informal checklists. **What do *you* think?**

Summary

Cognitive development and language learning occur together. Children learn language naturally by observing and imitating language users and then constructing language to meet their needs. *Emergent literacy,* a continuum of literacy growth beginning at birth, assumes that children already know a great deal about reading and writing before entering school. Teachers should build on and expand children's growing awareness of language as purposeful communication.

In the emergent literacy classroom, the teacher acts as a facilitator of learning by creating activities to meet the children's needs and interests. A print-rich classroom environment with books, charts, labels, environmental print, and centers provides a further stimulus for language development. Realizing the value of a literate home environment, the teacher may suggest strategies to parents for guiding their youngsters toward literacy.

Many children's listening and speaking skills are well developed when they enter school, and teachers provide opportunities for further growth in listening comprehension and oral expression. Through exposure to reading and writing materials and experiences, children gain knowledge of print conventions and sight words. Children's growth in reading and writing, based on what they already know, occurs concurrently and interrelatedly through experiences with big books, journal writing, listening to stories, and working on computers. Invented spelling helps children to connect letters with sounds. Although teachers may sometimes use formal assessment techniques, they are more likely to evaluate young children's progress through observation and checklists.

Test Yourself

True or False

_____ F 1. Language learning begins at birth and is continuous.

_____ T 2. The term *emergent literacy* refers to a child's language development after entering school.

_____ F 3. A child's phonemic awareness is a good predictor of future reading success.

_____ F 4. A close relationship exists between cognitive development and the growth of concepts about language.

_____ T 5. The preferred frequency for teachers to read aloud to children is once a week.

_____ T 6. Picture reading is an example of a direct experience through which a child can learn concepts and vocabulary.

_____ T 7. Jean Piaget developed a philosophy of whole language.

_____ E 8. According to Piaget, children at the preoperational level are more likely to be successful in child-centered classes than in classes where they are required to memorize rules.

_____ T 9. According to Piaget, language comes before thought.

_____ F 10. The literacy club consists of children who read and discuss stories with one another.

_____ F 11. The only way children can learn language is by imitation.

_____ T 12. Many children engage in unconventional forms of reading and writing before they enter school.

_____ T 13. Dramatic play centers should include materials for motivating written communication.

_____ F 14. Young children need direct instruction in how to speak when they first begin talking.

_____ F 15. Formal tests are the most appropriate form of assessment for young children.

_____ T 16. Home environment has little or no effect on language learning.

_____ T 17. In shared big book reading, children take turns reading from a large book.

_____ F 18. When children "talk like a book," they are most likely reading the exact words.

_____ T 19. Interactive story reading is a more worthwhile literacy experience than simply reading a story aloud without comments or questions.

_____ T 20. Parents should discourage a child who wants to read before entering school.

_____ T 21. Children must learn to read before they can learn to write.

_____ *T* 22. As presented in this chapter, a writing center is a place where children go to practice handwriting skills.

_____ *T* 23. Children use invented spellings to express the ways they perceive letter-sound associations.

_____ *F* 24. Isolated drills and memorization of rules are better than language experiences for helping children understand written communication.

_____ *T* 25. Early reading of environmental words helps children realize that print represents meaning.

_____ *F* 26. A teacher should intervene in language learning by providing help when students are having problems.

_____ *T* 27. Many big books have predictable language patterns.

_____ *F* 28. Piaget created the concept of zone of proximal development.

For your journal...

1. Respond to any practicum experiences with literacy in early childhood education.

2. Reflect on one or more of the following concepts: invented spelling, developmentally appropriate practice, shared book reading, zone of proximal development, and emergent literacy.

3. Observe one child carefully. How could you provide scaffolding that would move this child through the zone of proximal development?

...And your portfolio

1. Start an annotated bibliography of read-aloud, predictable, and repetitive books that you would like to use with your class.

2. Create a file of pictures that might stimulate children to tell or write their own stories.

3. On a continuing basis, observe a child's emergent literacy and suggest developmentally appropriate practices for providing instruction.

Chapter Appendix A

Predictable/Repetitive/Alliterative/Rhyming Books

Aardema, V. *Why Mosquitoes Buzz in People's Ears.* New York: Dial, 1978.
Aliki. *Go Tell Aunt Rhody.* New York: Macmillan, 1974.
Allen, R. V. *I Love Ladybugs.* Allen, Tex.: DLM, 1985.
Asch, F. *Just Like Daddy.* Englewood Cliffs, N.J.: Prentice-Hall, 1981.

Baer, G. *THUMP, THUMP, Rat-a-Tat-Tat*. Singapore: Harper & Row, 1989.

Barrett, J. *Animals Should Definitely Not Act Like People*. New York: Aladdin, 1987.

Carle, E. *Today Is Monday*. New York: Scholastic, 1993.

Carle, E. *The Very Busy Spider*. New York: Philomel, 1985.

Carle, E. *The Very Hungry Caterpillar*. Cleveland: Collins World, 1969.

Cowley, J. *Mrs. Wishy-Washy*. San Diego: The Wright Group, 1987.

Degen, B. *Jamberry*. New York: Scholastic, 1983.

Emberley, D. *Drummer Hoff*. Englewood Cliffs, N.J.: Prentice-Hall, 1967.

Fox, M. *Shoes from Grandpa*. Sydney, Australia: Ashton Scholastic, 1989.

Fox, M. *Time for Bed*. San Diego: Gulliver, 1993.

Galdone, P. *The Teeny, Tiny Woman*. New York: Clarion, 1984.

Grossman, B. *My Little Sister Ate One Hare*. New York: Crown, 1996.

Hutchins, P. *The Doorbell Rang*. New York: Greenwillow, 1986.

Hutchins, P. *Rosie's Walk*. New York: Macmillan, 1968.

Hutchins, P. *Titch*. New York: Penguin, 1985.

Johnson, T. *Yonder*. New York: Dial, 1988.

Kent, J. *The Fat Cat*. New York: Scholastic, 1987.

Langstaff, J. *Oh, A-Hunting We Will Go*. New York: Atheneum, 1974.

Langstaff, J. *Ol' Dan Tucker*. New York: Harcourt Brace & World, 1963.

Livingston, M. C. *Dilly Dilly Piccalilli*. New York: McElderry, 1988.

Lobel, A. *The Rose in My Garden*. New York: Greenwillow, 1984.

Martin, B. *Brown Bear, Brown Bear*. New York: Holt, Rinehart and Winston, 1970.

Martin, B. *Fire! Fire! Said Mrs. McGuire*. New York: Holt, Rinehart and Winston, 1970.

Martin, B., and Archambault, J. *The Braggin' Dragon*. Allen, Tex.: DLM, 1988.

Martin, B., and Archambault, J. *Good Night, Mr. Beetle*. Allen, Tex.: DLM, 1988.

Mayer, M. *What Do You Do with a Kangaroo?* New York: Scholastic, 1973.

Munsch, R. *Mud Puddle*. Scarborough, Ontario: Firefly, 1982.

Munsch, R. *Mortimer*. Scarborough, Ontario: Firefly, 1982.

Nelson, J. *Peanut Butter and Jelly*. Cleveland: Modern Curriculum Press, 1989.

Quackenbush, R. *She'll Be Coming 'Round the Mountain*. New York: Lippincott, 1973.

Ryan, P., and Pallotta, J. *The Crayon Counting Book*. Watertown, Mass.: Charlesbridge, 1996.

Sendak, M. *Pierre*. New York: Harper & Row, 1962.

Shaw, C. B. *It Looked Like Spilt Milk*. New York: Harper & Row, 1947.

Shaw, N. *Sheep on a Ship*. Boston: Houghton Mifflin, 1989.

Stevens, J. *The House that Jack Built*. New York: Holiday House, 1985.

Westcott, N. *I Know an Old Lady Who Swallowed a Fly*. New York: Little, Brown, 1980.

Wood, A. *King Bidgood's in the Bathtub*. New York: Harcourt Brace Jovanovich, 1985.

Wood, A. *The Napping House*. San Diego: Harcourt Brace Jovanovich, 1984.

Wood, D., and Wood, A. *The Little Mouse, the Red Ripe Strawberry, and the Big Hungry Bear*. New York: Scholastic, 1984.

Yolen, J. *Owl Moon*. New York: Philomel, 1987.

3

Word Recognition

SETTING OBJECTIVES

When you finish reading this chapter, you should be able to

▶ Describe some ways to help a child develop a sight vocabulary.

▶ Describe some activities for teaching use of context clues.

▶ Discuss the role of phonics in the reading program.

▶ Define each of the following terms: *consonant blend, consonant digraph, vowel digraph, diphthong.*

▶ Describe how to teach a child to associate a specific sound with a specific letter or group of letters.

▶ Discuss ways to teach the various facets of structural analysis.

▶ Identify the skills children need in order to use a dictionary as an aid in word recognition.

Pay close attention to these terms when they appear in the chapter.

analytic approach to
  phonics instruction

cloze procedure

context clues

homographs

inflectional endings

onset

phonemic awareness

phonics

rime

semantic clues

sight words

structural analysis

syntactic clues

synthetic approach to
  phonics instruciton

word configuration

In addition, pay close attention to the specific phonics terms discussed in this chapter.

Good readers differ from poor readers in both the size of sight vocabularies and the ability to decode words. Good readers tend to have larger sight vocabularies than poor readers, thereby decreasing their need to stop and analyze words. When they do have to analyze words, good readers often have a more flexible approach than poor readers do because they generally have been taught several strategies and have been encouraged to try a new one if one strategy fails (Jenkins et al., 1980). Poor readers frequently know only a single strategy for decoding words. No one strategy is appropriate for all words, however, and thus these children are at a disadvantage when they encounter words for which their strategy is not useful. Even if they have been taught several strategies, poor readers may have failed to learn a procedure that will allow them to decode unfamiliar words as efficiently as possible. "Research suggests that, no matter which strategies are used to introduce them to reading, the children who earn the best scores on reading comprehension tests in the second grade are the ones who made the most progress in fast and accurate word identification in the first grade" (Anderson et al., 1985, pp. 10–11).

Samuels (1988) sees word recognition skills as "a necessary prerequisite for comprehension and skilled reading" and points out that "we need a balanced reading program, one which combines decoding skills and the skills of reading in context" (pp. 757, 758). He has long supported the idea that accurate and automatic word recognition is necessary for reading fluency. This automaticity (application without conscious thought) in word recognition is achieved through extended practice. Repeated readings of the same passages can help move students from accuracy to automaticity in word recognition.

Adams (1991) also endorses the need for word recognition skills along with strategies for acquiring meaning. She encourages "thorough overlearning of letters, spelling patterns, and spelling-sound correspondences—and also of vocabulary, syntactic patterns, rhetorical devices, text structures, conceptual underpinnings, and modes of thought on which the full meaning of text depends." However, she denounces "'ponderous drills' on 'isolated skills'" (Adams, 1991, p. 394). She also emphasizes the need for automaticity in decoding to free students' attention for comprehension ("A Talk with Marilyn Adams," 1991).

This chapter presents a variety of methods of word recognition and stresses a flexible approach to unfamiliar words, encouraging application of those word recognition strategies that are most helpful at the moment. It also explains ways to show children how to use a number of word recognition strategies jointly to help in decoding words.

Word Recognition Strategies

Word recognition strategies and skills help a reader recognize written words. They include development of a store of words that can be recognized immediately on sight and the ability to use context clues, phonics, structural analysis, and dictionaries for word identification where each strategy is appropriate. The last four types are sometimes referred to as *word attack* strategies or skills.

Chapter 3 Organization

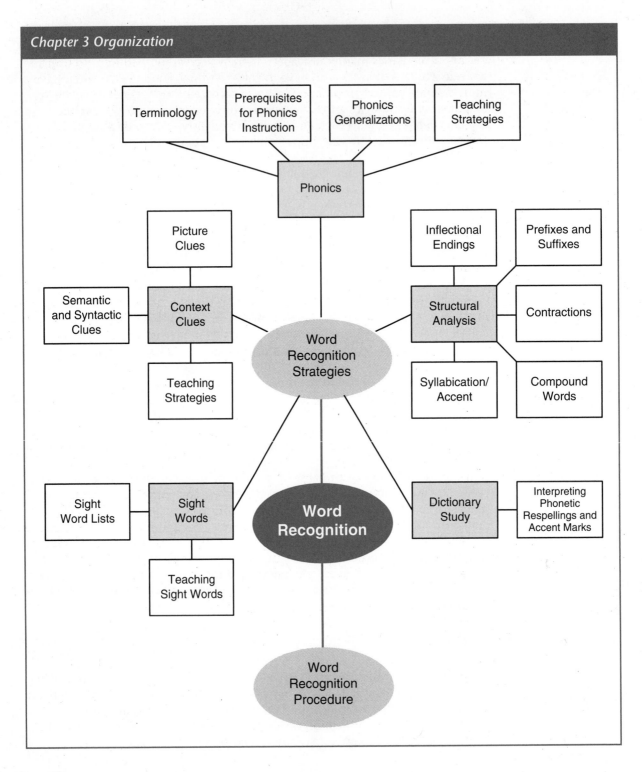

Children need to be able to perform all of the word recognition strategies because some will be more helpful than others in certain situations. Teaching a single approach to word identification is not wise, because children may be left without the proper tools for specific situations. In addition, depending on their individual abilities, children find some word recognition strategies easier to learn than others. A child who has a hearing loss, for example, may not become very skillful at using phonics but may learn sight words easily and profit greatly from the use of context clues.

Instruction in word recognition should not dominate reading time. Much time should be spent in reading connected text; Stahl (1992) suggests half of the time or more. Attention to comprehension instruction should also receive ample time.

Gill (1992, p. 450) warns that instruction in word recognition "hinders progress when it places the child in reading material on his frustration level," because this prevents the child from extracting information from patterns that he or she is capable of detecting in the text. When children are taught with materials that emphasize repetitions of spelling patterns, they tend to develop strategies based on alphabetic principles. To accomplish this, they need to be exposed to texts that contain unchanging patterns that they are able to detect. Some children also need assistance in detecting these patterns.

Sight Words

Young readers also need to develop a store of sight words, words that are recognized immediately without having to resort to analysis. The larger the store of sight words a reader has, the more rapidly and fluently he or she can read a selection. Comprehension and reading speed suffer if a reader has to pause too often to analyze unfamiliar words. The more mature and experienced a reader becomes, the larger his or her store of sight words becomes. (Most, if not all, of the words used in this textbook, for example, are a part of the sight vocabularies of college students.) Thus, one goal of reading instruction is to turn all the words students continuously need to recognize in print into sight words.

Artley (1996) suggests development of a basic stock of sight words first, then teaching of other methods of word recognition. This allows inductive reasoning about sound-symbol associations and other word elements, such as prefixes and suffixes. There are a number of reasons why sight words need to be taught:

1. The English language contains a multitude of irregularly spelled words, that is, words that are not spelled the way they sound. Many of these are among the most frequently used words in our language. The spellings of the following common words are highly irregular in their sound-symbol associations: *of, through, two, know, give, come,* and *once.* Rather than trying in vain to sound out these words, children need to learn to recognize them on sight as whole configurations.

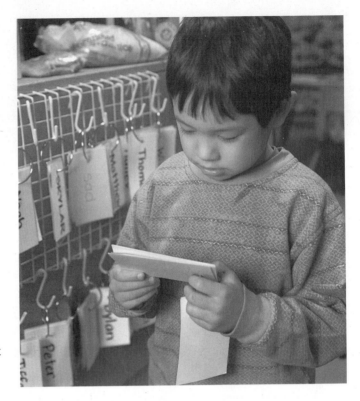

Young readers need to develop a store of sight words. (© *David Young Wolff/Photo Edit*)

2. Learning several sight words at the very beginning of reading instruction gives the child a chance to engage in a successful reading experience very early and consequently promotes a positive attitude toward reading.

3. Words have meaning for youngsters by the time they arrive at school, but single letters have no meaning for them. Therefore, presenting children with whole words at the beginning allows them to associate reading with meaning rather than with meaningless memorization.

4. After children have built up a small store of sight words, the teacher can begin phonics instruction with an analytic approach. (More about the analytic approach appears later in this chapter.)

Most children know some sight words when they first come to school. They have learned the names of some of their favorite fast-food restaurants and other businesses from signs, the names of some of their favorite foods and drinks from the packages or labels, or both categories of words, as well as others, from television commercials. Children who have been read stories while sitting on their parents' laps may well have picked up vocabulary from favorite stories that were repeatedly shared. Still, the sight vocabularies of beginning students are meager compared to those mature readers need.

A teacher must carefully choose which words to teach as sight words. Extremely common irregularly spelled words (*come, to, two*) and frequently used regularly spelled words (*at, it, and, am, go*) should be taught as sight words so that children can read connected sentences early in the program. The first sight words should be useful and meaningful. A child's name should be one of those words; days of the week, months of the year, and names of school subjects are other prime candidates. Words that stand for concepts unfamiliar to youngsters are poor choices. Before children learn *democracy* as a sight word, for example, they need to understand what a democracy is; therefore, this is not a good word to teach in the primary grades.

Teaching some words with regular spelling patterns as sight words is consistent with the beliefs of linguists who have become involved in developing reading materials (see Chapter 7 for further details). Words with regular spelling patterns are also a good base for teaching "word families" in phonics; the *an* family, for example, includes *ban, can, Dan, fan, man, Nan, pan, ran, tan,* and *van*.

Sight Word Lists

Lists of basic sight words may give teachers an indication of the words that are most frequently used in reading materials and therefore needed most frequently by students. The Dolch list of the 220 most common words in reading materials (excluding nouns), though first published in the 1930s, has repeatedly been found to be relevant and useful in more recent materials (Mangieri and Kahn, 1977; Palmer, 1985). Another well-known list of basic sight words is Fry's "Instant Words" (Fry, 1977). This list presents the words most frequently used in reading materials.

Teaching Sight Words

Before children begin to learn sight words, they must have developed visual discrimination skills; that is, they must be able to see likenesses and differences among printed words. It is also helpful, although not essential, for them to know the names of the letters of the alphabet, because this facilitates discussion of likenesses and differences among words. For example, a teacher could point out that, whereas *take* has a *k* before the *e, tale* has an *l* in the same position.

A potential sight word must initially be identified for learners. A teacher should show the children the printed word as he or she pronounces it, or pair the word with an identifying picture. Reading aloud to children as they follow along in the book is one way to identify vocabulary for children within a meaningful context. Regardless of the method of presentation, one factor is of paramount importance: the children must *look* at the printed word when it is identified in order to associate the letter configuration with the spoken word or picture. If children fail to look at the word when it is pronounced, they have no chance of remembering it when they next encounter it.

Teachers should also encourage children to pay attention to the details of the word by asking them to notice ascending letters (such as *b, d, h*), descending letters (such as *p, g, q*), word length, and particular letter combinations (such as double letters). Careful scrutiny of words can greatly aid retention.

The most natural, holistic approach to sight word instruction is reading to children as they follow along. Teachers may use this approach with groups of students when big books are available, allowing all children in the group to see the words. They may also read from books that are available in multiple copies in the classroom, with each child or pair of children following along on his or her own copy of the story. Books with accompanying tapes or records can promote sight vocabulary in a similar way.

Children learn early to recognize some sight words by their visual *configurations,* or shapes. Teachers should not overly stress this technique, because many words have similar shapes. But since many children seem to use the technique in the early stages of reading, regardless of the teacher's methods, a teacher can use configuration judiciously to develop early sight words. One way to call attention to shape is to have the children frame the words to be learned:

The limitation of configuration as a sight word recognition clue is demonstrated by the following words:

Teachers can call attention to word makeup through comparison and contrast, comparing a new word to a similar known word: *fan* may be compared to *can* if the children already have *can* in their sight vocabularies. Either the teacher can point out that the initial letters of the words are different and the other letters are the same, or the students can discover this on their own. The latter method is preferable, because the students are likely to remember their own discoveries longer than they will remember something the teacher has told them.

Few words are learned after a single presentation, although Ashton-Warner (1963) claims that children will instantly learn words that are extremely important to them. Generally, a number of repetitions are necessary before a word actually becomes a sight word.

Veatch (1996) asserts that Aston-Warner's Key Vocabulary approach, in which children pick words that have intense meaning for them, is efficient and reliable in developing sight vocabulary. The teacher writes on cards the words the children choose and gives them to the children. The children say the letters in the words, trace them (moving left to right), and use the words (to write stories, to play games, and so on).

The teacher should carefully plan practice with potential sight words. This practice should be varied and interesting, because children will more readily learn those things that interest them. Games are useful if they emphasize the words being learned rather than the rules of the game.

Practice with potential sight words should generally involve using the words *in context*. Children cannot pronounce many words out of context with certainty—for example, *read*. The following sentences indicate the importance of context:

I *read* that book yesterday.   I can't *read* without glasses.

Another reason for using context when presenting sight words is that many commonly used words have little meaning when they stand alone. Prime examples are *the, a,* and *an*. Context for words may be a sentence (*The* girl ate *a* pear and *an* apple.) or short phrases (*the* girl, *a* pear, *an* apple). Context is also useful if pronunciation is less clear than it should be. Children may confuse the word *thing* with *think* unless the teacher has presented context for the word: "I haven't done a useful thing all day."

McGill-Franzen (1993) points out the value of highly predictable books, such as those used in the Reading Recovery Program, for beginning readers. Peterson (1991) has arranged a continuum of Reading Recovery books from easy to more complex, based partially on the context provided. The books at the easiest levels are highly predictable from the pictures and repetitive sentence patterns. Saccardi (1996) also recommends the use of predictable books for many literacy activities and suggests particular books and appropriate uses for each.

The language experience approach, in which students' own language is written down and used as the basis for their reading material, is good for developing sight vocabulary. This approach (described in detail in Chapter 7) provides a meaningful context for learning sight words, and it can be used productively with individuals or groups. The word-bank activities associated with this approach are particularly helpful.

Teachers may also present words in conjunction with pictures or with the actual objects the words name, such as chairs and tables, calling attention to the fact that the labels name the items. These names can be written on the board so that youngsters can try to locate the items in the room by finding the matching labels.

Constructing picture dictionaries, in which children illustrate words and file the labeled pictures alphabetically in a notebook, is a good activity for helping younger children develop sight vocabulary. This procedure has been effective in helping children whose primary language is not English learn to read and understand English words.

Teachers can use labels to help children learn to recognize their own names and the names of some of their classmates. On the first day of school, the teacher can give each child a name tag and label each child's desk with his or her name.

The teacher may also label the area where the child is supposed to hang a coat or store supplies. The teacher should explain to the children that the letters written on the name tags, desks, and storage areas spell their own names and that no one else is supposed to use these areas. The children should be encouraged to look at the names carefully and try to remember them when locating their belongings. Although the children may initially use the name tags to match the labels on the desks and storage areas, by the time the name tags are worn out or lost, the children should be able to identify their printed names without assistance.

The teacher can generally accelerate this process by teaching children how to write their names. Children may first trace the name labels on their desks with their fingers. Next, they can try to copy the names on sheets of paper. At first, the teacher should label all students' work and drawings with the students' names, but as soon as the children are capable of writing their names, they should label their own papers. From the beginning, the children's names should be written in capital and lower-case letters, rather than all capitals, since this is the way names most commonly appear in print.

The days of the week can also be taught as sight words. Each morning, the teacher can write "Today is" on the chalkboard and fill in the name of the appropriate day. At first the teacher may read the sentence to the children at the beginning of each day, but soon some children will be able to read the sentence successfully without help.

Function words—words, such as *the* and *or,* that have only syntactic meaning rather than concrete content—are often particularly difficult for children to learn because they lack concrete meaning and because many of them are similar in physical features. These words need to be presented in context repeatedly so that the surrounding words can provide meaning (Hargis et al., 1988). Jolly (1981) suggests teaching these troublesome words by presenting only one word at a time of a pair of words that are likely to be confused (for example, *was* and *saw*). He also suggests teaching words with more obvious differences in features first, then those with subtler differences. For example, teach *that* with words like *for* and *is* before presenting it with *this* and *the*. Teachers can also delete the words from passages, leaving blanks for the students to fill in with the target words.

Much teaching of sight word recognition takes place as a part of basal reader lessons. The teacher frequently introduces the new words, possibly in one of the ways discussed here, before reading, discussing meanings at the same time. Then students have a guided silent reading period during which they read material containing the new words in order to answer questions asked by the teacher. Purposeful oral rereading activities offer another chance to use the new words. Afterward, teachers generally provide practice activities suggested in the teacher's manual of the basal reading series. Follow-up activities may include skill sheets, games, manipulative devices, and special audiovisual materials. Writing new words is helpful for some learners, especially for kinesthetic learners (those who learn through muscle movement).

Games such as word bingo are useful for practice with sight words. The teacher or a leader calls out a word, and the children who recognize that word on their cards cover it. When a child covers an entire card, he or she says, "Cover," and the teacher or leader checks the card to see if all the covered words were actually called.

Another technique is to list sight words on a circular piece of cardboard and have children paper-clip pictures to appropriate words. The teacher can make this activity self-scoring by printing the matching words on the backs of the pictures, as shown here.

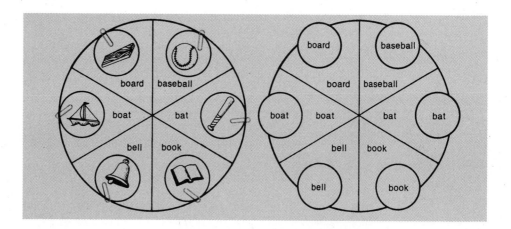

Dickerson (1982) compared the use of physically active games, passive games, and worksheets in an attempt to discover which would be most effective in increasing the sight vocabularies of remedial first graders. The physically active games proved to be most effective, followed by the passive games. Worksheets were the least effective, although the children who used the worksheets did gain some sight vocabulary. Teachers may consider increasing use of more active games, such as those in which children stand and act out action verbs. The Classroom Scenario that follows describes such an activity.

Classroom Scenario

Developing Sight Vocabulary

Mr. Barkley, a first-grade teacher, found that three children were having trouble remembering the action words in the stories they were reading. He called these children over to a corner of the room near the chalkboard and wrote these words on the board: *jump, walk, run.* He introduced the words by saying, "We have seen these words in our stories this week, but they have been hard for you to remember, so we are going to practice reading them as we play a game. This word is *jump.* Can you jump for me?" The children jumped. Then he said, "Good. Whenever you read the word *jump* for this game, I want you to jump just like that."

(continued)

Mr. Barkley introduced *walk* and *run* in the same way. The students readily demonstrated each one.

Then Mr. Barkley brought out a board game with a racetrack oval drawn on it. Each space in the path around the oval had a simple sentence containing either *jump, walk,* or *run* written on it. The children took turns spinning a spinner and moving the number of spaces indicated around the racetrack with a personally selected token (one of several different miniature race cars). A child who landed on a space had to read the sentence, tell what it meant, and perform the action in the sentence. For example, the child might read, "Mary can jump," and then say, "That means Mary can do this." Then the child would stand up and jump. If a child could not read the sentence or tell/show what it meant, another player could "steal his or her play" by reading the sentence and performing the action. The player who got to try this would be determined by having the opponents of the player who missed spin the spinner for a high number.

The first child around the track won the game, but all three children were actively involved with the action words and made progress in reading them correctly as the game continued.

Analysis of Scenario

Mr. Barkley used a physically active game to develop the children's sight vocabularies after more passive reading activities had failed to be effective with these children. He targeted the activity for the children who were having difficulty, not forcing the repetitive practice on those who had mastered the words. He presented the words in sentence contexts to encourage children to recognize the words in typical reading situations, rather than as isolated entities.

Ceprano (1981) reviewed research on methods of teaching sight words and found that no one method alone was best for every student. She found evidence that teaching the distinctive features of words helped children learn. She also found evidence that use of picture clues along with specific instruction to focus attention on the words facilitated learning. She reported, however, that some research indicates that teaching words in isolation or with pictures does not ensure the ability to read words in context. In fact, indications are that "most learners need directed experience with written context while learning words in order to perceive that reading is a language process and a meaning-getting process" (p. 321). Therefore, when teachers are working with sight-word instruction, it seems wise to present words in context rather than just in isolation.

Time for Reflection	Some people believe sight words should be taught in context. Others believe they should be taught in isolation. **What do *you* think?**

Context Clues

Context clues—the words, phrases, and sentences surrounding the words to be decoded—help readers determine what the unfamiliar words are. Here we will focus on the function of context clues as *word recognition* aids; Chapter 5 considers the function of context clues as *comprehension* aids.

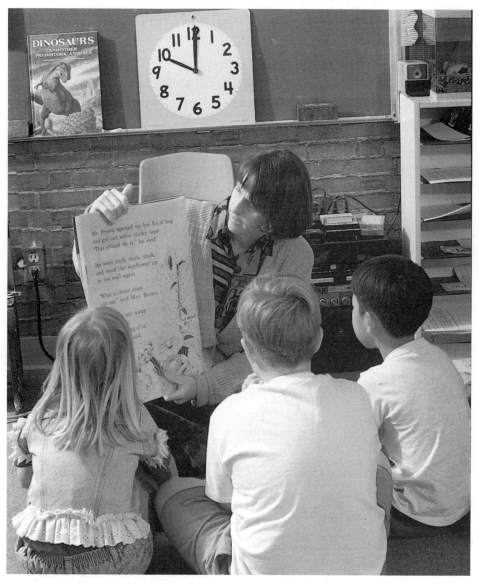

The teacher should carefully plan practice with potential sight words. (© *Tony Freeman/ Photo Edit*)

Since research has found that syntactic and semantic context influence readers' identification of words, it is important that word recognition skills be introduced and practiced in context (Jones, 1982). Much of the written material to which primary-level readers are introduced falls well within their comprehension as far as vocabulary and ideas are concerned, but these youngsters cannot always recognize in printed form the words that are familiar in oral form. Context clues can be extremely helpful in this process. Research also shows that context clues help younger and poorer readers recognize words more than they help older and better readers (Gough, 1984; Daneman, 1991).

Picture Clues

Picture clues are generally the earliest context clues children use. If children are exposed to many pictures of a character, such as one named Julie, in beginning reading materials, they may come to recognize the character instantly. When they are shown a page containing a picture of Julie and a single word, they may naturally assume that the word names the picture and that the word is *Julie*. If they do not relate the picture to the word in this manner, the teacher can ask a question such as "Who is in the picture?" to lead them toward understanding the relationship. If a child responds, "A girl," the teacher might ask, "What kind of letter is at the beginning of the word?" The response "A capital letter" would prompt the question "What kinds of words have we talked about that begin with capital letters?" After eliciting the answer "Names," the teacher can then ask, "What is the name of the girl in the picture?" This question should produce the response "Julie." Finally, the teacher asks, "Now what do you think the word is?" At this point, a correct response is extremely likely. The teacher should use a procedure that encourages the use of picture clues *along with,* rather than apart from, the clues available in the printed word.

Teachers should not overemphasize picture clues. These clues may be useful in the initial stages of instruction, but they become less useful as the child advances to more difficult material, which has a decreasing number of pictures and an increasing proportion of print. Encouraging too much reliance on pictures may result in too little time spent on developing word analysis skills.

Semantic and Syntactic Clues

As soon as possible, teachers should encourage first-grade children to use written context as a clue to unknown words. The idea of using context clues can be introduced by oral activities like the following Model Activity. The sentences can often be drawn from stories that have just been read or listened to in class.

In the sample sentences in the Model Activity, children can use both semantic (meaning) and syntactic (grammar) clues in choosing words to fill in the blanks. Youngsters generally use these two types of clues in combination, but to clarify their differences, we will consider them separately first.

Semantic clues are clues derived from the meanings of the words, phrases, and sentences surrounding the unknown word. In the examples just given, children

Model Activities

Use of Oral Context

Read sentences such as the following to the children, leaving out words as indicated by the blanks. Sentences can be drawn from books the teacher plans to share later in class. After reading each sentence, ask the children what word they could use to finish the sentence in a way that would make sense. The children will find that the sentences that have missing words at the end are easier. In some cases, the children may suggest several possi- bilities, all of which are appropriate. Accept all of these contributions with positive comments.

Sample sentences:

1. Jane went out to walk her _____ .
2. John was at home reading a _____ .
3. They were fighting like cats and _____ .
4. I want toast and _____ for breakfast.
5. Will you _____ football with me?

can ask themselves the following questions to decide what words would make sense:

Sentence 1. What are things that can be walked?

Sentence 2. What are things that can be read?

Sentence 3. What expression do I know about fighting that has *like cats and* in it?

Sentence 4. What food might be eaten with toast for breakfast?

Sentence 5. What things can you do with a football?

Various kinds of semantic clues exist, including the following:

1. *Definition clues.* A word may be directly defined in the context. If the child knows the word in oral form, he or she can recognize it in print through the definition.

    The *dictionary* is a book in which the meanings of words can be found.

2. *Appositive clues.* An appositive may offer a synonym or a description of the word that will cue its recognition. Children need to be taught that an appositive is a word or phrase that restates or identifies the word or expression it follows and that it is usually set off by commas, dashes, or parentheses.

    They are going to *harvest,* or gather in, the season's crops.

    That model is *obsolete* (outdated).

    The *rodents*—rats and mice—in the experiment learned to run a maze.

3. *Comparison clues.* A comparison of the unfamiliar word with a word the child knows may offer a clue. In the examples, the familiar words *sleepy* and *clothes* provide the clues for *drowsy* and *habit.*

Like her sleepy brother, Mary felt *drowsy.*

Like all the clothes she wore, her riding *habit* was very fashionable.

4. *Contrast clues.* A contrast of the unknown word with a familiar one may offer a clue. In the examples, the unfamiliar word *temporary* is contrasted with the familiar word *forever,* and the unfamiliar word *occasionally* is contrasted with the familiar word *regularly.*

It will not last forever; it is only *temporary.*

She doesn't visit regularly; she just comes by *occasionally.*

5. *Common-expression clues.* Familiarity with the word order in many commonly heard expressions, particularly figurative expressions, can lead children to the identity of an unknown word. In the context activity discussed earlier, children needed to know the expression "fighting like cats and dogs" to complete the sentence. Children with varied language backgrounds are more likely to be able to use figurative expressions to aid word recognition than are children with less developed backgrounds.

He was as quiet as a *mouse.*

Daryl charged around like a bull in a *china* shop.

6. *Example clues.* Sometimes examples are given for words that may be unfamiliar in print, and these examples can provide the clues needed for identification.

Mark was going to talk about *reptiles*—for example, snakes and lizards.

Andrea wants to play a *percussion* instrument, such as the snare drum or the bells.

Syntactic clues are provided by the grammar or syntax of our language. Certain types of words appear in certain positions in spoken English sentences. Thus, word order can give readers clues to the identity of an unfamiliar word. Because most children in schools in the United States have been speaking English since they were preschoolers, they have a feeling for the grammar or syntax of the language. Syntactic clues help them discover that the missing words in sentences 1 through 4 in the oral-context activity presented earlier in this section are nouns, or naming words, and that the missing word in sentence 5 is a verb, or action word.

Looking at each item, we see that in sentence 1 *her* is usually followed by a noun. *A* is usually followed by a singular noun, as in sentence 2. Sentences 3 and 4 both employ *and,* which usually connects words of the same type. In sentence 3, children are likely to insert a plural animal name because of the absence of an article (*a, an, the*). Similarly, in sentence 4 *and* will signal insertion of another food. Sentence 5 has the verb marker *will,* which is often found in the sequence "Will you (verb) . . . ?"

As we pointed out earlier, semantic and syntactic clues should be used *together* to unlock unknown words.

Teaching Strategies

Early exercises with context clues may resemble the oral-context exercise explained earlier. It is good practice for a teacher to introduce a new word in context and let children try to identify it, rather than simply telling them what the word is. Then children can use any phonics and structural analysis knowledge they have, along with context clues, to help them identify the word. The teacher should use a context in which the only unfamiliar word is the new word; for example, use the sentence "My *umbrella* keeps me from getting wet when it rains" to present the word *umbrella*. The children will thus have graphic examples of the value of context clues in identifying unfamiliar words.

When a child encounters an unfamiliar word when reading orally to the teacher, instead of supplying the word, the teacher can encourage the child to skip it for the time being and read on to the end of the sentence (or even to the next sentence) to see what word would make sense. The teacher can encourage use of the sound of the initial letter or cluster of letters, sounds of other letters in the word, or known structural components, along with context. In a sentence where *hurled* appears as an unknown word in the phrase *hurled the ball,* a child might guess *held* from the context. The teacher could encourage this child to notice the letters *ur* and try a word that contains those sounds and makes sense in the context. Of course, this approach will be effective only if the child knows the meaning of *hurled.* Encouraging the child to read subsequent sentences could also be helpful, since these sentences might disclose situations in which *held* would be inappropriate but *hurled* would fit.

A cloze passage, in which words have been systematically deleted and replaced with blanks of uniform length, can be a good way to work on context clue use. For this purpose, the teacher may delete certain types of words (nouns, verbs, adjectives, etc.) rather than using random deletion. The students should discuss their reasons for choosing the words to be inserted in the blanks, and the teacher should accept synonyms and sometimes nonsynonyms for which the students have a good rationale. The point of the exercise is to have the students think logically about what makes sense in the context. (Other uses for the *cloze procedure* and more details about it are found in Chapters 5, 10, and 12.)

Use of context clues can help children make educated guesses about the identities of unfamiliar words. Context clues are best used with phonics and structural analysis skills because they help identify words more quickly than phonics or structural analysis clues alone would. But without the confirmation of phonics and structural analysis, context clues provide only guesses. As we mentioned earlier, when a blank is substituted for a word in a sentence, students can often use several possibilities to complete the sentence and still have it make sense. When children encounter unknown words, they should make educated guesses based on the context and verify those guesses by using other word analysis skills.

A modified cloze procedure can be used with a story summary to develop children's skill in decoding in a meaningful context. The first letter of the deleted word is provided, helping children use their knowledge of sound-symbol relationships as well as choosing words that make sense in the context (Johnson and Louis, 1987).

DeSerres (1990) introduces basal reader stories' mastery vocabulary by presenting each word on the board in sentence context, having students write the word in another sentence or phrase context on 3" × 5" word cards for their word banks, and letting them share their sentences. Later she uses modified cloze stories (in which selected words, rather than regularly spaced words, are deleted) with the mastery words as the words chosen for omission. Students fill in the blanks by choosing from their word cards as the class reads the story together. Then they fill in the blanks on individual copies of the stories and read them to partners. Partners point out parts that do not make sense. Later, students produce their own stories. This procedure gives practice with using context.

A child who encountered the following sentence with a blank instead of a word at the end might fill in the blank with either *bat* or *glove*:

Frank said, "If I am going to play Little League baseball this year, I need a new ball and _____ ."

If the sentence indicated the initial sound of the missing word by presenting the initial letter *g,* the child would know that *glove,* rather than *bat,* was the appropriate word.

Frank said, "If I am going to play Little League baseball this year, I need a new ball and g_____ ."

Structural analysis clues can be used in the same way. In the following sentence, a child might insert such words as *stop* or *keep* in the blank.

I wouldn't want to _____ you from going on the trip.

The child who had the help of the familiar prefix *pre-* to guide his or her choice would choose neither. The word *prevent* would obviously be the proper choice.

I wouldn't want to pre_____ you from going on the trip.

Suffixes and ending sounds are also very useful in conjunction with context to help in word identification. Teachers can use exercises similar to the following to encourage children to use phonics and structural analysis clues along with context clues. Sample sentences can be drawn from stories that the children are about to read in class.

Word Identification

Model Activities

Write the following sentences on the board.

1. This package is too h _ _ _ y for me. Let someone else carry it.

2. I want to join the Navy and ride in a sub _ _ _ _ _ _ .

3. If you keep up that arguing, you will sp _ _ _ the party for everyone.

4. You can't hurt it. It's <u>in</u> _ _ <u>str</u> _ _ _ <u>ible</u>.

5. She lives in a <u>pent</u> _ _ _ _ _ apartment.

6. My grandmother has a home <u>r</u> _ _ _ <u>dy</u> for any disease.

Ask the children to read the sentences silently and to try to identify the incomplete words from the clues in the surrounding words and the letters or groups of

letters that have been supplied. Let volunteers go to the board and complete the incomplete words. Ask these volunteers if they can tell how the clues in the sentences helped them decide on the words to write. Encourage the students to use the same strategy to figure out other unfamiliar words in the story they are about to read.

Some words are difficult to pronounce unless they appear in context. *Homographs*—words that look alike but have different meanings and pronunciations, such as *row, wind, bow, read, content, rebel, minute, lead, record,* and *live*—are prime examples. Here are some sentences that demonstrate how context can clarify the pronunciations of such words:

1. The *wind* is blowing through the trees.
   Did you *wind* the clock last night?

2. She put a *bow* on the gift.
   You should *bow* to the audience when you finish your act.

3. Would you *rebel* against that law?
   I have always thought you were a *rebel*.

4. Did your father *record* his gas mileage?
   Suzanne broke Jill's *record* for the highest score in one game.

Although most of the examples in this section show only a single sentence as the context, children should be encouraged to look for clues in surrounding sentences as well as in the sentence in which the word occurs. Sometimes an entire paragraph will be useful in defining a term.

Phonics

Before you read this section, go to "Test Yourself" at the end of the chapter and take the multiple-choice phonics test. It will give you an idea of your present knowledge of phonics. After you study the text, go back and take the test again to see what you have learned.

Phonics is the association of speech sounds (*phonemes*) with printed symbols (*graphemes*). In some languages, this sound-symbol association is fairly regular, but not in English. A single letter or combination of letters in our alphabet may stand for many different sounds. For example, the letter *a* in each of the following words has a different sound: *cape, cat, car, father, soda.* On the other hand, a single sound may be represented by more than one letter or combination of letters. The long *e* sound is spelled differently in each of the following words: *me, mien, meal, seed,* and *seize.* To complicate matters further, the English language abounds with words that contain letters that stand for no sound, as in i*s*land, *knight*, *write*, lam*b*, *gnome*, *psalm*, and r*hyme*.

The existence of these spelling inconsistencies does not imply that phonics is not useful in helping children decode written English. We discuss inconsistencies to counteract the feeling of some teachers that phonics is an infallible guide to pronouncing words in written materials. Teaching phonics does not constitute a complete reading program; rather, phonics is a valuable aid to word recognition when used in conjunction with other skills, but it is only *one* useful skill among many. Mastering this skill, with the resulting ability to pronounce most unfamiliar words, should not be considered the primary goal of a reading program. Children can pronounce words without understanding them, and deriving *meaning* from the printed page should be the objective of all reading instruction.

Groff (1986) found that, if beginning readers can attain an approximate pronunciation of a written word by applying phonics generalizations, they can go on to infer the true pronunciation of the word. He found, for example, that "100% of the second graders tested could infer and produce the *o* of *from* as /u/ after first hearing it as /o/. The pronunciation /from/ was close enough to /frum/ for these young pupils to infer its correct pronunciation" (p. 921). Groff concluded that children need practice in making such inferences. First, they need to apply phonics generalizations to unfamiliar words, producing approximate pronunciations of the words. Then they can infer the real pronunciations of the words by thinking of words they know that are close in sound to the approximations achieved by the generalizations.

Skilled readers appear to identify unfamiliar words by finding similarities with known words (Anderson et al., 1985). For example, a reader might work out the pronunciation of the unknown word *lore* by comparing it with the known word *sore* and applying the knowledge of the sound of *l* in other known words, such as *lamp*. Cunningham (1978, 1979) suggests using a similar approach to identify polysyllabic words as well as single-syllable words.

Carnine (1977) studied the transfer effects of phonics and whole word approaches to reading instruction and found superior transfer to new words among the students who were taught phonics. The phonics group even had greater transfer to irregular words, although it was not extensive. Research with adults has been interpreted as indicating that teachers should present *several* sound-symbol correspondences for each grapheme rather than one-to-one correspondences, thereby providing their students with a set for diversity. If such a procedure had been used in this study, it might have produced more transfer to irregular words.

Phonics techniques are not intended to be ends in themselves; rather, they are means to the end of successful reading. Maclean (1988) sees phonics as "a catalyst which triggers the process of learning to read" (p. 517). It helps students pair spoken and written words and lays the groundwork for them to develop their own decoding routines, which may bear little resemblance to the rules used in phonics instruction. In order for the phonics catalyst to produce a reaction, children must be allowed to do large amounts of reading in appropriate materials.

The following Classroom Scenario shows one way that phonics principles begin to form in classes.

Classroom Scenario

Development of Phonics Knowledge

Marty, a first grader, was turning the pages of a calendar in his classroom, finding numbers that he recognized on each page. Suddenly he called to his teacher excitedly, "Mrs. Overholt, this is almost like my name!"

Mrs. Overholt joined Marty at his table. "Yes, it is," she replied. "Show me the part that is the same."

Marty pointed to the letters *M, a, r,* in sequence.

"That's right," Mrs. Overholt said. "Can you tell me what month this is?"

"No," Marty said.

"The month is March," said Mrs. Overholt. "Does it sound a little like your name, too?"

"Yes," Marty almost squealed. "The beginning of it sounds like the beginning of my name."

"You really listened carefully to hear that," Mrs. Overholt said. "Those letters stand for the same sounds in your name and in the word *March.* Keep your eyes open for other words like this. You may be able to figure out what they are by remembering what you found out about letters and sounds."

Analysis of Scenario

Mrs. Overholt used a teachable moment with Marty. He had made a discovery about words that excited him and his teacher helped him to expand it.

A good phonics program provides sufficient reinforcement for a skill that is being taught and offers a variety of reinforcement opportunities (Spiegel, 1990). The practice activities in this text offer some ideas for reinforcement opportunities. Although reinforcement in phonics instruction may include practice with single letters and sounds, it must include application of the strategy or skill with whole words and longer pieces of discourse, such as sentences and paragraphs. Spiegel (1990) suggests the following sequence: "auditory discrimination of the sound of interest, visual discrimination of the letter pattern, and then work with words, sentences, and short paragraphs" (p. 328). We believe this practice should be expanded to include work with whole selections, such as predictable books that contain the letter-sound association that is being emphasized. In fact, a whole selection, in the form of a big book, may be shared with the children orally, with children chiming in on the highly predictable parts wherever possible. From this beginning, the teacher may have students locate the letter representing the sound under consideration, listen for the sound as he or she reads portions of the story aloud again, and make their own generalizations about the relationship between the sound and the letter that represents it. The children will not state their personal generalizations in the same form as the rules that would be found in a reading text, but they will understand the connection more deeply and retain it better if they have discovered it themselves.

Morrow and Tracey (1997) found that preschool teachers often used context-based phonics instruction (teaching letter-sound associations in meaningful or functional contexts), whereas kindergarten, first-grade, and second-grade teachers used more explicit phonics instruction (sequential, systematic presentation of sound-symbol associations, employing direct instructional strategies in isolation from meaningful contexts). Few teachers at any of these levels used an approach that combined explicit instruction and context-based instruction, an approach that appears to have much merit. Lapp and Flood (1997) point out that when children are taught language skills and strategies in a context that includes the exploration of books, a balanced approach to literacy instruction has been attained.

Time for Reflection	Some people believe children should learn basic skills before they begin reading stories, but others believe they should learn skills as they encounter the need for them within stories. **What do *you* think?**

If students are to learn phonics associations effectively, they need to see a reason for doing so. The relevance of learning sound-symbol associations is much clearer when students can see the letters and sounds as a part of a meaning-bearing system, rather than as isolated bits of meaningless information.

If basal reading series consistently designed the stories and phonics instruction to support each other, the connection between the phonics instruction and achieving meaning when reading might be much clearer. Anderson and others (1985, p. 47) found that "a high proportion of the words in the earliest selections children read should conform to the phonics they have already been taught."

Adams sees the instructional goal of phonics as students' understanding of the alphabetic principle in written English. She points out that participating in language experience activities, writing with invented spelling, sharing books, and reading interesting texts can help in reaching this goal ("A Talk with Marilyn Adams," 1991).

Time for Reflection	Some people think phonics is all that a child needs for a word recognition program. Others think that several different word attack methods are needed. **What do *you* think?**

Terminology

To understand written material about phonics, teachers need to be familiar with the following terms.

Vowels. The letters *a, e, i, o,* and *u* represent vowel sounds, and the letters *w* and *y* take on the characteristics of vowels when they appear in the final position in a word or syllable. The letter *y* also has the characteristics of a vowel in the medial (middle) position in a word or syllable.

Consonants. Letters other than *a, e, i, o,* and *u* generally represent consonant sounds. *W* and *y* have the characteristics of consonants when they appear in the initial position in a word or syllable.

Consonant Blends (or Clusters). Two or more adjacent consonant letters whose sounds are blended together, with each individual sound retaining its identity, constitute a consonant blend. For example, although the first three sounds in the word *strike* are blended smoothly, listeners can detect the separate sounds of *s, t,* and *r* being produced in rapid succession. Other examples are the *fr* in *frame,* the *cl* in *click,* and the *br* in *bread,* to mention only a few. Many teaching materials refer to these letter combinations as consonant clusters rather than consonant blends.

Consonant Digraphs. Two adjacent consonant letters that represent a single speech sound constitute a consonant digraph. For example, *sh* is a consonant digraph in the word *shore* because it represents one sound and not a blend of the sounds of *s* and *h.* Additional examples of consonant digraphs appear on page 103.

Vowel Digraphs. Two adjacent vowel letters that represent a single speech sound constitute a vowel digraph. In the word *foot, oo* is a vowel digraph. Additional examples of vowel digraphs appear on page 104.

Diphthongs. Vowel sounds that are so closely blended that they can be treated as single vowel units for the purposes of word identification are called *diphthongs.* These sounds are actually vowel blends, since the vocal mechanism produces two sounds instead of one, as is the case with vowel digraphs. An example of a diphthong is the *ou* in *out.* Additional examples of diphthongs appear on page 104.

Prerequisites for Phonics Instruction

There seems to be agreement that good auditory and visual discrimination are prerequisites for learning sound-symbol relationships. We know that children must be able to distinguish one letter from another and one sound from another before they can associate a given letter with a given sound. *Visual discrimination* refers to the ability to distinguish likenesses and differences among forms, and *auditory discrimination* refers to the ability to distinguish likenesses and differences among sounds. To achieve these skills, children must first understand the concepts of *like* and *different.* Also, to achieve auditory discrimination, children must have *phonemic awareness,* or the awareness that speech is composed of separate sounds (phonemes). They must be able to hear sounds within words, or they will be unable to form mental connections between sounds and letters (Beck and Juel, 1995; Griffith and Olson, 1992; Juel, 1988, 1991; Ball and Blachman, 1991; Lundberg et al., 1988; Pearson, 1993; Adams, 1990; Gill, 1992). Training in phonemic awareness has been shown to be effective and to have a positive effect on reading acquisition (Lundberg et al., 1988; Yopp, 1992; Bradley and Bryant, 1983). Phonemic awareness activities may ask children "to match words by sounds, isolate a sound in a word, blend individual sounds to form a word, substitute sounds in a word, or segment a word into its constituent sounds" (Yopp, 1992, p. 699). Yopp (1992) points out that playful, gamelike activities such as riddles and guessing games are best because they engage children in the tasks.

Yopp (1995b, p. 20) says, "Most youngsters enter kindergarten lacking phonemic awareness. Indeed, few are conscious that sentences are made up of individual words, let alone that words can be segmented into phonemes." Use of read-aloud books is a way to work on phonemic awareness, because many books have rhyme, alliteration, assonance, and other features that allow children to play with the sounds of language (Yopp, 1995a; Yopp, 1992; Griffith and Olson, 1992).

Richgels, Poremba, and McGee (1996) suggest a "What Can You Show Us?" activity to develop phonemic awareness in a holistic context. They describe it as a "functional, contextualized, social literacy activity" (p. 641). It accompanies shared reading activities. Before shared reading, a *preparation* step involves selecting reading materials and displaying them appropriately; for example, if the text is copied onto a chart, the features in words that the teacher wants to emphasize can be highlighted in some way. The next step involves the children's *previewing* the text and being given a chance to discuss what they see. Next, *student demonstrations* of what they know about the text (for example, identifying letters or words) take place. The shared reading (teacher reading, joint reading, and student activities) comes next. During and after this activity the students apply what they know about the text. There may be further student demonstrations.

Phonemic awareness can be taught directly and may also "develop as a consequence of learning phonics, learning to read, or even learning to write, especially when teachers encourage students to use invented spellings" (Pearson, 1993, p. 507). In whole language classrooms, phonemic awareness and phonics may be learned through invented-spelling activities.

Activities requiring children to discriminate among letter and word forms are more useful to beginning readers than activities requiring them to identify similarities and differences among geometric forms (Sippola, 1985). Unless children need practice in developing the concepts of *like* and *different,* it is pointless to have them make distinctions among shapes and forms. Instead, they need practice with simultaneous and successive visual discrimination of letters and words. Simultaneous discrimination occurs when children match printed symbols that are alike while they can see both symbols. Successive discrimination occurs when children find a duplicate symbol after a stimulus card is no longer visible. Similarly, attention to general sounds in the environment has value only in teaching concepts of *like* and *different* (Sippola, 1985). Beginning readers need to focus primarily on observing similarities and differences in the initial sounds and rhyming sounds of words.

Introducing children to simple rhymes is a good way to sensitize them to the likenesses and differences in verbal sounds. The teacher can ask children to pick out the words that rhyme and to supply words to rhyme with a given word. This ability is fundamental to the construction of "word families." Children should also be able to hear similarities and differences in word endings and in middle vowels; for example, they should be able to tell whether *rub* and *rob,* or *hill* and *pit,* have the same middle sound. Finally, they should be able to listen to the pronunciation of a word sound by sound and mentally fuse or blend the sounds to recognize the intended word.

The following model activities should help children develop visual and auditory discrimination abilities.

Model Activities

Visual Discrimination

Write on the board some letters that are similar in appearance (*b, d,* and *p,* for example) Say to the children: "Let's look at these letters. Are any of them alike? How are the first two letters different? What is different about the other letter?"

Then say to them: "Now I am going to give you a copy of a page of the story that we read today. Look at the first letter on the board. (Point to the letter.) Then look at the page from the story. Every time you see this letter in the story, circle it with your green crayon. (Give them time to search for the letter *b* and mark their pages.) Now look at the second letter. (Point to it.) Every time you see this letter in the story, circle it with your red crayon. (Give them time to do this.) Now look at the third letter. (Point to it.) Every time you see this letter in the story, circle it in yellow. (Give them time to do this.) Then display a large copy of the story and let individuals come up and point to the letters that should have been circled in the different colors, while children check their own papers.

Repeat the activity with a set of words containing these letters, such as *big, pet,* and *dog.* Ask the same questions about the words. Then have the children perform a similar activity with the words, using fresh pages from the story so that their previous marks will not confuse them.

Model Activities

Auditory Discrimination

Name several puppets with double names to stress initial consonant sounds (Molly Mouse, Freddie Frog, Dolly Duck, and Bennie Bear). While holding a puppet, say: "I'd like you to meet Molly Mouse. Molly Mouse only likes things that begin the same way that her name begins. Molly Mouse likes milk, but she doesn't like water. I am going to name some things that Molly Mouse likes or doesn't like. You

(continued)

must listen closely to the way each word begins. Raise your hand if I say something that Molly Mouse likes. Keep your hand down if I say something that Molly Mouse doesn't like. Let's begin. Molly Mouse likes meat." The children should raise their hands. If they don't seem to understand why she likes meat, talk about the beginning sound and give additional examples. Then say: "Molly Mouse likes potatoes." The children should keep their hands down.

Activities

Additional Visual and Auditory Discrimination Activities

Visual Discrimination

1. Locate a page in a big book that has pairs of similar-looking letters close to each other, and help students discover how the letters are alike and how they differ. Examples of letter pairs to use: *d b, p q, m n.*

2. Choose a word that is frequently confused with a similarly shaped word from a big book story that is being shared. Write this word on the board once, along with several repetitions of the word with which it may be confused. Have the children find the word on the board that is different. Then have them locate the same word in the big book story. Read aloud the sentence in which the word appears. Example of words that could be used: *on on no on.*

Auditory Discrimination (beginning sounds)

1. Play a guessing game. Ask if there is anyone in the room whose name starts with the same sound as the beginning of the word *top.* The first child who replies whose name starts with this sound may give the next clue.

2. Find poems that repeat certain sounds. Examples: "Wee Willie Winkie," "Lucy Locket," "Bye-Baby Bunting," "Deedle, Deedle, Dumpling."

Auditory Discrimination (medial and final sounds, whole word)

1. Use riddles to relate sounds to words. For example, ask each child to guess what word, illustrated by the following riddle, begins with the same sound as *pig.*

   I am good to eat.
   I rhyme with *teach.*
   I am a fruit.
   What am I?

2. Let the children supply the missing rhyming word in a familiar verse.

Phonics Generalizations

Some teachers believe that good phonics instruction is merely the presentation of a series of principles that children are expected to internalize and use in the process of word identification. Difficulties arise from this conception, however.

First, pupils tend to internalize a phonics generalization more rapidly and effectively when they can arrive at it inductively. That is, by analyzing words to which a generalization applies and by deriving the generalization themselves from this analysis, children will understand it better and remember it longer.

Second, the irregularity of the English spelling system results in numerous exceptions to phonics generalizations. Children must be helped to see that generalizations help them to derive *probable* pronunciations rather than infallible results. When applying a generalization does not produce a word that makes sense in the context of the material, readers should try other reasonable sound possibilities. For example, in cases where a long vowel sound is likely according to a generalization but results in a nonsense word, the child should be taught to try other sounds, such as the short vowel sound, in the search for the correct pronunciation. Some words are so totally irregular in their spellings that even extreme flexibility in phonic analysis will not produce close approximations of the correct pronunciations. In such situations, the child should be taught to turn to the dictionary for help in word recognition. Further discussion of this approach to word recognition can be found later in this chapter.

Third, students can be so deluged with rules that they cannot memorize them all. This procedure may result in their failure to learn any generalization well.

Teachers can enhance a phonics program by presenting judiciously chosen phonics generalizations to youngsters, as long as they are taught, not as unvarying rules, but as guides to best guesses. Authorities vary on which generalizations to present (Bailey, 1967; Burmeister, 1968; Clymer, 1996; Emans, 1967), but they agree on some. Considering the findings of phonics studies and past teaching experience, we believe the following generalizations are among the most useful:

1. When the letters *c* and *g* are followed by *e, i,* or *y,* they generally have soft sounds: the *s* sound for the letter *c* and the *j* sound for the letter *g.* (Examples: *cent, city, cycle, gem, ginger, gypsy.*) When *c* and *g* are followed by *o, a,* or *u,* they generally have hard sounds: *g* has its own special sound, and *c* has the sound of *k.* (Examples: *cat, cake, cut, go, game, gum.*)

2. When two like consonants are next to each other, only one is sounded. (Examples: *hall, glass.*)

3. *Ch* usually has the sound heard in *church,* although it sometimes sounds like *sh* or *k.* (Examples of usual sound: *child, chill, china.* Examples of *sh* sound: *chef, chevron.* Examples of *k* sound: *chemistry, chord.*)

4. When *kn* are the first two letters in a word, the *k* is not sounded. (Examples: *know, knight.*)

5. When *wr* are the first two letters in a word, the *w* is not sounded. (Examples: *write, wrong.*)

6. When *ck* are the last two letters in a word, the sound of *k* is given. (Examples: *check, brick.*)

7. The sound of a vowel preceding *r* is usually neither long nor short. (Examples: *car, fir, her.*)

8. In the vowel combinations *oa, ee, ai,* and *ay,* the first vowel is generally long and the second one is not sounded. This may also apply to other double vowel combinations. (Examples: *boat, feet, rain, play.*)

9. The double vowels *oi, oy,* and *ou* usually form diphthongs. Whereas the *ow* combination frequently stands for the long *o* sound, it may also form a diphthong. (Examples: *boil, boy, out, now.*)

10. If a word has only one vowel and that vowel is at the end of the word, the vowel usually represents its long sound. (Examples: *me, go.*)

11. If a word has only one vowel and that vowel is *not* at the end of the word, the vowel usually represents its short sound. (Examples: *set, man, cut, hop, list.*)

12. If a word has two vowels and one is a final *e,* the first vowel is usually long and the final *e* is not sounded. (Examples: *cape, cute, cove, kite.*)

Rosso and Emans (1981) tried to determine whether knowledge of phonic generalizations helps children decode unrecognized words and whether children have to be able to state the generalizations to use them. They found statistically significant relationships between knowledge of phonic generalizations and reading achievement, but pointed out that this link does not necessarily indicate a cause-and-effect relationship. They also discovered that "inability to state a phonics rule did not seem to hinder these children's effort to analyze unfamiliar words . . . this study supports Piaget's theory that children in the concrete operations stage of development may encounter difficulty in describing verbally those actions they perform physically" (p. 657). Teachers may need to investigate techniques for teaching phonics generalizations that do not require children to verbalize the generalizations.

It is wise to teach only one generalization at a time, presenting a second only after students have thoroughly learned the first. The existence of exceptions to generalizations should be freely acknowledged, and children should be encouraged to treat the generalizations as *possible* rather than *infallible* clues to pronunciation.

In their summary of *Beginning to Read: Thinking and Learning about Print* by Adams (1990), Stahl, Osborn, and Lehr (1990) emphasize that rote knowledge of abstract generalizations will not produce a skillful decoder. They point out the importance of the connection of generalizations with experience. "Rules are intended to capture the patterns of spelling. But productive use of those patterns depends on relevant experience, not on rote memorization" (p. 83). They conclude that phonics generalizations have only temporary value; in fact, "Once a child has learned to read the spellings to which they pertain, they are superfluous" (p. 126).

Consonants. Although consonant letters are more consistent in the sounds they represent than vowel letters are, they are not perfectly consistent. The following list shows some examples of variations with which a child must contend.

Consonant	Variations	Consonant	Variations
b	board, lamb	n	never, drink
c	cable, city, scene	p	punt, psalm
d	dog, jumped	q(u)	antique, quit
f	fox, of	s	see, sure, his, pleasure, island
g	go, gem, gnat		
h	hit, hour	t	town, listen
j	just, hallelujah	w	work, wrist
k	kitten, knee	x	fox, anxiety, exit
l	lamp, calf	z	zoo, azure, quartz

Consider the cases in which *y* and *w* take on vowel characteristics. Both of these letters represent consonant sounds when they are in the initial position in a word or syllable, but they represent vowel sounds when they are in a final or medial position. For example, *y* represents a consonant sound in the word *yard,* but a vowel sound in the words *dye, myth,* and *baby.* Notice that actually three different vowel sounds are represented by *y* in these words. *W* represents a consonant sound in the word *watch,* but a vowel sound in the word *cow.*

Consonant Digraphs. Several consonant digraphs represent sounds not associated with either of the component parts. These are as follows:

Consonant Digraph	Example	Consonant Digraph	Example
th	then, thick	ph	telephone
ng	sing	gh	rough
sh	shout	ch	chief, chef, chaos

Other consonant digraphs generally represent the usual sound of one of the component parts, as in *write, pneumonia,* and *gnat.* Some sources consider one of the letters in each of these combinations as a "silent" letter and do not refer to these combinations as digraphs.

Vowels. The variability of the sounds represented by vowels has been emphasized before. Some examples of this variability are as follows:

Vowel Letter	Variations
a	ate, cat, want, ball, father, sofa
e	me, red, pretty, kitten, her, sergeant
i	ice, hit, fir, opportunity
o	go, hot, today, women, button, son, work, born
u	use, cut, put, circus, turn

In the examples here, the first variation listed for each vowel is a word in which the long vowel sound, the same as its letter name, is heard. In the second variation the short sound of the vowel is heard. These are generally the first two sounds taught for each vowel.

Another extremely common sound that children need to learn is the schwa sound, a very soft "uh" or grunt usually found in unaccented syllables. It is heard in the following words: sof*a*, kitt*e*n, opportun*i*ty, butt*o*n, circ*u*s. As you can see, each of the vowel letters can represent the schwa sound in some words.

Three types of markings represent the three types of vowel sounds we have discussed:

Marking	Name of Mark	Designation
ā, ē, ī, ō, ū	macron	long vowel sound
ă, ĕ, ĭ, ŏ, ŭ	breve	short vowel sound
ə	schwa	soft "uh" sound

Some dictionaries place no mark at all over a vowel letter that represents the short sound of the vowel.

Vowel Digraphs. Some vowel digraphs represent sounds not associated with either of the letters involved. These are as follows:

Vowel Digraph	Example
au	taught
aw	saw
oo	food, look

Other vowel digraphs generally represent the usual sound of one of the component parts, as in br*ea*k, br*ea*d, b*oa*t, s*ee*d, and *ai*m. Some sources treat one of the letters in these combinations as "silent" and do not refer to them as digraphs.

Diphthongs. There are four common diphthongs, or vowel blends.

Diphthong	Example	Diphthong	Example
oi	foil	ou	bound
oy	toy	ow	cow

Notice that the first two diphthongs listed (*oi* and *oy*) stand for identical sounds, as do the last two (*ou* and *ow*). Remember that the letter combinations *ow* and *ou* are *not always diphthongs*. In the words *snow* and *blow, ow* is a vowel digraph representing the long *o* sound. In the word *routine, ou* represents the $\overline{oo}$ sound, and in the word *shoulder, ou* represents the long *o* sound.

Teaching Strategies

There are two major approaches to phonics instruction: the synthetic and the analytic.

In the *synthetic approach*, the teacher first instructs children in the speech sounds that are associated with individual letters. Because letters and sounds have no inherent relationships, this task is generally accomplished by repeated drill on sound-symbol associations. The teacher may hold up a card on which the letter *b* appears and expect the children to respond with the sound ordinarily associated with that letter. The next step is to blend the sounds together to form words. The teacher encourages the children to pronounce the sounds associated with the letters in rapid succession so that they produce a word or an approximate pronunciation of a word, which they can then recognize and pronounce accurately. This blending process generally begins with two- and three-letter words and proceeds to much longer ones.

Although blending ability is a key factor in the success of a synthetic phonics approach, many commercial materials for reading instruction give little attention to its development. Research indicates that children must master both segmentation of words into their component sounds and blending before they are able to apply phonics skills to the decoding of unknown words and that the ability to segment is a prerequisite for successful blending. Research also indicates that a teacher cannot assume children will automatically transfer the skills they have been taught to unknown words. Direct instruction for transfer is needed to ensure that it will occur (Johnson and Baumann, 1984).

In the synthetic phonics approach, children are sometimes asked to pronounce nonsense syllables because these syllables will appear later in written materials as word parts. Reading words in context does not generally occur until these steps have been repeatedly carried out and the children have developed a moderate stock of words.

The *analytic approach* involves teaching some sight words, followed by teaching the sounds of the letters within those words. Many educators prefer this approach, and it is used in many basal reader series, partly because it avoids the distortion that occurs when consonants are pronounced in isolation. For example, trying to pronounce a *t* in isolation is likely to result in the sounds *tə*. Pronouncing a schwa sound following the consonant can adversely affect the child's blending because the word *tag* must be sounded as *tə-a-gə*. No matter how fast children make those sounds, they are unlikely to come very close to *tag*. With an analytic approach, the teacher would refer to "the sound you hear at the beginning of the word *top*," when cueing the first sound in *tag*. The same process may be used to introduce other consonants, consonant blends, consonant digraphs, vowels, diphthongs, and vowel digraphs in initial, medial, and final positions. One possible problem when using analytic phonics, however, is that children may not be able to extract an individual sound just from hearing it within a word. Partly for this reason and partly because some analytic phonics instruction is worded in a confusing manner, Adams's (1990) findings seem to indicate that even though trying to isolate phonemes can result in distortion, the advantages of asking students to produce phonemes in isolation can outweigh the disadvantages.

Trachtenburg (1990) suggests a procedure that is basically an analytic approach in which phonics instruction occurs within the context of reading quality children's literature. Here the progression is from the whole literature selection to the phonic element within the selection and back to another whole literature selection for application of the new knowledge. This procedure is consistent with Harp's (1989) statement: "While the process may be broken down to examine individual pieces, before the instruction ends the process should be 'put back together' so that the children see the relationship between the part and the whole" (p. 326).

Trachtenburg's method proceeds as follows:

- First, the teacher reads to the class a literature selection that contains many examples of the phonic element in question. Students may discuss or dramatize the story, when the teacher has finished.

- The teacher introduces the phonic element that is the target for the lesson (long *a, e, i, o,* or *u;* short *a, e, i, o,* or *u;* or some other element) by explaining that the children are going to learn one of the sounds for a specific letter or letter combination.

- Then the teacher writes a portion of the story that contains the target element on the chalkboard or a transparency. The teacher reads this portion of the story aloud, pausing to underline the words containing the target element.

- The teacher identifies the sound involved and asks the children to read the story portion with him or her and listen for the sound. The teacher may suggest a key word that will help them remember the sound in the future.

- The teacher guides practice with the new sound, using a mechanical device in which initial consonants can be varied while the medial vowel remains stationary or a similar device in which both initial and final consonants can be varied. An example of such a device is shown in Activity 3 (page 115) for phonics practice in this chapter. The teacher may also provide practice with a similar device that allows sentence parts to be substituted, which enables children to practice the sound in larger language chunks. For example, adjectives, verbs, or adverbs could be varied, as could prepositional phrases, verb phrases, or any other sentence part.

- Finally, the teacher presents another book that has numerous examples of the phonic element. Children may then be allowed to read this book independently, read it in unison from a big book, or read it with a partner, depending on their individual achievement levels.

Trachtenburg (1990) offers the following list of trade books that repeat long and short vowel sounds.

Short a

Flack, Marjorie. *Angus and the Cat.* Doubleday, 1931.

Griffith, Hellen. *Alex and the Cat.* Greenwillow, 1982.

Kent, Jack. *The Fat Cat.* Scholastic, 1971.

Most, Bernard. *There's an Ant in Anthony.* William Morrow, 1980.

Nodset, Joan. *Who Took the Farmer's Hat?* Harper & Row, 1963.

Robins, Joan. *Addie Meets Max.* Harper & Row, 1985.

Schmidt, Karen. *The Gingerbread Man.* Scholastic, 1985.

Seuss, Dr. *The Cat in the Hat.* Random House, 1957.

Long a

Aardema, Verna. *Bringing the Rain to Kapiti Plain.* Dial, 1981.

Bang, Molly. *The Paper Crane.* Greenwillow, 1985.

Blume, Judy. *The Pain and the Great One.* Bradbury, 1974.

Byars, Betsy. *The Lace Snail.* Viking, 1975.

Henkes, Kevin. *Sheila Rae, the Brave.* Greenwillow, 1987.

Hines, Anna G. *Taste the Raindrops.* Greenwillow, 1983.

Short and long a

Aliki. *Jack and Jake.* Greenwillow, 1986.

Slobodkina, Esphyr. *Caps for Sale.* Addison-Wesley, 1940.

Short e

Ets, Marie Hall. *Elephant in a Well.* Viking, 1972.

Galdone, Paul. *The Little Red Hen.* Scholastic, 1973.

Ness, Evaline. *Yeck Eck.* E. P. Dutton, 1974.

Shecter, Ben. *Hester the Jester.* Harper & Row, 1977.

Thayer, Jane. *I Don't Believe in Elves.* William Morrow, 1975.

Wing, Henry Ritchet. *Ten Pennies for Candy.* Holt, Rinehart & Winston, 1963.

Long e

Galdone, Paul. *Little Bo-Peep.* Clarion/Ticknor & Fields, 1986.

Keller, Holly. *Ten Sleepy Sheep.* Greenwillow, 1983.

Martin, Bill. *Brown Bear, Brown Bear, What Do You See?* Henry Holt, 1967.

Oppenheim, Joanne. *Have You Seen Trees?* Young Scott Books, 1967.

Soule, Jean C. *Never Tease a Weasel.* Parents' Magazine Press, 1964.

Thomas, Patricia. *"Stand Back," Said the Elephant, "I'm Going to Sneeze!"* Lothrop, Lee & Shepard, 1971.

Short i

Browne, Anthony. *Willy the Wimp*. Alfred A. Knopf, 1984.

Ets, Marie Hall. *Gilberto and the Wind*. Viking, 1966.

Hutchins, Pat. *Titch*. Macmillan, 1971.

Keats, Ezra Jack. *Whistle for Willie*. Viking, 1964.

Lewis, Thomas P. *Call for Mr. Sniff*. Harper & Row, 1981.

Lobel, Arnold. *Small Pig*. Harper & Row, 1969.

McPhail, David. *Fix-It*. E. P. Dutton, 1984.

Patrick, Gloria. *This Is . . .* Carolrhoda, 1970.

Robins, Joan. *My Brother, Will*. Greenwillow, 1986.

Long i

Berenstain, Stan and Jan. *The Bike Lesson*. Random House, 1964.

Cameron, John. *If Mice Could Fly*. Atheneum, 1979.

Cole, Sheila. *When the Tide Is Low*. Lothrop, Lee & Shepard, 1985.

Gelman, Rita. *Why Can't I Fly?* Scholastic, 1976.

Hazen, Barbara S. *Tight Times*. Viking, 1979.

Short o

Benchley, Nathaniel. *Oscar Otter*. Harper & Row, 1966.

Dunrea, Olivier. *Mogwogs on the March!* Holiday House, 1985.

Emberley, Barbara. *Drummer Hoff*. Prentice-Hall, 1967.

McKissack, Patricia C. *Flossie & the Fox*. Dial, 1986.

Miller, Patricia, and Iran Seligman. *Big Frogs, Little Frogs*. Holt, Rinehart & Winston, 1963.

Rice, Eve. "The Frog and the Ox" from *Once in a Wood*. Greenwillow, 1979.

Seuss, Dr. *Fox in Socks*. Random House, 1965.

Long o

Cole, Brock. *The Giant's Toe*. Farrar, Straus & Giroux, 1986.

Gerstein, Mordicai. *Roll Over!* Crown, 1984.

Johnston, Tony. *The Adventures of Mole and Troll*. G. P. Putnam's Sons, 1972.

Johnston, Tony. *Night Noises and Other Mole and Troll Stories*. G. P. Putnam's Sons, 1977.

Shulevitz, Uri. *One Monday Morning*. Charles Scribner's Sons, 1967.

Tresselt, Alvin. *White Snow, Bright Snow*. Lothrop, Lee & Shepard, 1947.

Short u

Carroll, Ruth. *Where's the Bunny?* Henry Z. Walck, 1950.

Cooney, Nancy E. *Donald Says Thumbs Down*. G. P. Putnam's Sons, 1987.

Friskey, Margaret. *Seven Little Ducks*. Children's Press, 1940.

Lorenz, Lee. *Big Gus and Little Gus*. Prentice-Hall, 1982.

Marshall, James. *The Cut-Ups*. Viking Kestrel, 1984.

Udry, Janice May. *Thump and Plunk*. Harper & Row, 1981.

Yashima, Taro. *Umbrella*. Viking Penguin, 1958.

Long u

Lobel, Anita. *The Troll Music*. Harper & Row, 1966.

Segal, Lore. *Tell Me a Trudy*. Farrar, Straus & Giroux, 1977.

Slobodkin, Louis. *"Excuse Me—Certainly!"* Vanguard Press, 1959.

Source: Phyllis M. Trachtenburg. "Using Children's Literature to Enhance Phonics Instruction," *The Reading Teacher* 43 (May 1990), 648–654. Reprinted with permission of Phyllis M. Trachtenburg and the International Reading Association. All rights reserved.

The following Focus on Strategies tells how a teacher introduced the long *e* sound in story context, thus using an analytic approach to phonics.

**Focus on
Strategies**

Teaching Phonics Through Literature

Ms. Mahan started her class by reading the predictable book *Peanut Butter and Jelly* (JoAnne Nelson, Modern Curriculum Press, 1989) to her first graders. By the time she got to page 13, the children were chiming in on the repeated line "But peanut butter and jelly is my favorite thing to eat," as she always encouraged the children to do when they discovered the predictable pattern. When the story had been completed, the teacher responded to requests to "read it again" by doing so. This time the children joined in on the repeated line from the beginning.

The children discussed the story, and Ms. Mahan made a list on the board of the children's personal favorite things to eat.

Then Ms. Mahan wrote the letter combination *ea* on the board. One of the words on the list of the children's favorite foods was *beans.* Another one was *peanuts.* She pronounced each of these words and pointed out that both contained a long *e* sound. Then she displayed transparencies of pages from the story *Peanut Butter and Jelly.* As she read page 5, she underlined the words *meat, peanut,* and *eat.* She then reread each underlined word and asked the children to listen to the sounds. She told the class that the letter combination *ea* often has the long *e* sound. Then she read the words again as they listened specifically for the long *e* sound.

She proceeded to display subsequent pages from the story, asking the children to watch for the *ea* combination in the words and raise their hands when they saw it. When hands were raised, she let the children identify the words with the *ea* combination. Then the children listened for the long *e* sound in each word. The following words from this story fit this pattern: *eat, meat, peanut, cream, wheat, treat, heat,* and *beat.* They also found the word *cereal* and recognized that they heard the long *e* sound. Since they had not yet had instruction on syllabication or schwa sounds, Ms. Mahan simply agreed that there was a long *e* sound after the *r* and went on to the next word. On page 18 they saw a word with the *ea* combination that did not have the long *e* sound: *bread.* The presence of this word allowed Ms. Mahan to point out that sounds are not always consistent and that the sound-letter clues only helped the children make "best guesses" about pronunciations, not absolute certainties.

Ms. Mahan then encouraged the children to play with the words that had been located. She wrote *eat* on the board and asked them how to turn it into *meat.* She let Tammy come to the board and add the needed letter. Then she wrote *eat* again and asked who could turn it into *wheat,* then *treat,* then *heat,* then *beat.* Finally, she branched out from words that were found directly in the story and let the children form *neat* and *seat.* She also let them transform *cream* into *team, seam,* and *dream* by removing the initial blend and replacing it with other letters.

(continued)

Then Ms. Mahan pointed out that sometimes there are several ways to spell a particular sound. She used the transparencies of the story again, encouraging the children to listen for the long *e* sound in words other than the ones already underlined. They located *sweet, street, beet, even,* and *cheese.* Ms. Mahan asked if they could suggest any other letter patterns that could spell the long *e* sound. They quickly identified the *ee* combination, and eventually Tommy said that the *e* by itself could also spell the sound.

Ms. Mahan then shared the books *Ten Sleepy Sheep* (Holly Keller, Greenwillow, 1983) and *Never Tease a Weasel* (Jean C. Soule, Parents' Magazine Press, 1964) with the children and put them in the reading center, along with *Peanut Butter and Jelly,* to be reread by the children independently or with partners.

The children were then given time to write their own stories about favorite foods. Ms. Mahan asked them to notice which words had the long *e* sound as they wrote. She let them share their stories orally with small groups of their peers.

The following two sample lesson plans further illustrate the analytic method. The first one is *inductive*: the children look at a number of specific examples related to a generalization and then derive the generalization. The second is *deductive*: the teacher states a generalization and then has the children apply the generalization in decoding unfamiliar words.

Analytic-Inductive Lesson Plan for Initial Consonant

Model Activities

Write on the chalkboard the following words, all of which the children have learned previously as sight words:

dog	did
daddy	donkey
do	Dan

Ask the children to listen carefully as you pronounce the words. Then ask: "Did any parts of these words sound the same?" If you receive an affirmative reply, ask: "What part sounded the same?" This should elicit the answer that the first sound in each word is the same or that the words sound alike at the beginning.

Next, ask the children to look carefully at the words written on the board. Ask: "Do you see any-thing that is the same in all these words?" This should elicit the answer that all of the words have the same first letter or all of the words start with *d*.

Then ask what the children can conclude about words that begin with the letter *d*. The expected answer is that words that begin with the letter *d* sound the same at the beginning as the word *dog* (or any other word on their list).

Next, invite the children to name other words that have the same beginning sound as *dog*. Write each word on the board. Ask the children to observe the words and draw another conclusion. They may say, "Words that sound the same at the beginning as the word *dog* begin with the letter *d*."

Ask the children to watch for words in their reading that begin with the letter *d* to check the accuracy of their conclusions.

Model Activities

Analytic-Deductive Lesson Plan for Soft Sound of *c*

Tell the children: "When the letter *c* is followed by *e, i,* or *y,* it generally has its soft sound, which is the sound you have learned for the letter *s.*" Write the following examples on the chalkboard: *city, cycle,* and *cent.* Point out that in *cycle* only the *c* that is followed by *y* has the soft sound. Follow this presentation with an activity designed to check the children's understanding of the generalization. The activity might involve a worksheet with items like this:

Directions: Place a check beside the words that contain a soft *c* sound.

_____ cite	_____ cider
_____ cape	_____ cord
_____ cede	_____ cymbal
_____ cut	_____ cod
_____ cell	

The soft *c* sound is the sound we have learned for the letter _____ .

An approach that has some aspects of both the synthetic and analytic approaches is the teaching of *onsets* and *rimes.* In this approach, the teacher breaks down a syllable into the part of the syllable before the vowel (onset) and the remainder of the syllable (rime) that begins with the vowel. In the past, these rimes were referred to as *phonograms.* (See Example 3.1.)

Example 3.1 *Onsets and Rimes*

Word	Onset	Rime
black	bl–	–ack
may	m–	–ay
am	—	am

In one rime-based instructional program, the Benchmark Word Identification Program, children compare an unknown word to familiar words in order to decode the words by analogy. Then they use context to check their predictions (Stahl, 1992; Gaskins et al., 1988; Gaskins et al., 1991; Gaskins et al., 1997). Such an approach is called an *analogy approach* or a *compare/contrast approach.* The children are taught an initial set of "key words," containing the phonograms or rimes. After comparing the unknown word to a known one and coming up with a tentative decision about the pronunciation of the unknown word, a child would be expected to check to see whether the new word produced made sense in the sentence in which it was found. According to Adams (1990), the letter-sound correspondences in rimes are more stable than the correspondences found when the letters are taken in isolation.

Gunning (1995) proposes a system for phonics instruction called Word Building that uses onsets and rimes. The class first builds words by adding onsets to rimes, then by adding rimes to onsets. This is followed by reading that allows practice with the patterns under consideration. Gunning also suggests having the students make words with magnetic letters, mix the letters up and reassemble the words, and then observe how each word changes as letters are added and removed, a process advocated by Clay (1993). Students are shown how to decode hard words by using phonic elements that they have learned. This approach can be used with multisyllabic words as well as with single-syllable words.

Gaskins and others (1991) found that direct instruction was useful in teaching phonics through the analogy approach. In every lesson, teachers inform the children about "*what* they are going to teach, *why* it is important, *when* it can be used, and *how* to use it" (p. 215). This explanation is followed by teacher modeling and group and individual guided practice for the students. Every-pupil response activities and teacher feedback are important program features. Key words are introduced through a structured language experience activity (the writing of a group story with the key words just presented). Phonemic awareness activities are also included to facilitate the learning of onsets such as the initial consonant *f* or the initial consonant blend *fr*. Gaskins and others (1996/1997; 1997) stress the need for students to be reflective and analytic about words and spelling patterns. They also emphasize that the students must learn the importance of analyzing all letters in a word and relating the letters to sounds so that they can retrieve the word later. Students do this by matching sounds to letters as they "stretch out" the pronunciation of the words. Self-talk about the procedure is encouraged. The following Model Activity shows use of an analogy or compare/contrast approach.

Analogy or Compare/Contrast Approach

Model Activities

The teacher writes the key words *be* and *rain* on the board and pronounces them. Then he or she writes: "The student hopes to remain in that group." The teacher verbalizes the thought pattern needed to decode the word in this way: "If this (pointing to *be*) is *be,* then this is probably *re.* If this (pointing to *rain*) is *rain,* then this is probably *main.*" (Note: The sounds of the initial consonants *r* and *m* must have been taught previously.) The teacher continues: "The word is *remain.* Does that make sense in the context?" After receiving an affir-

mative reply, the teacher says: "Yes, *remain* means to stay."

Then the teacher provides a list of key words the students have already studied and turned into sight words, as well as several paragraphs, preferably from a story they are about to read, with difficult words underlined. The teacher asks the students to decode these underlined words, using the key words and the strategy that has just been modeled. After the children have worked at this task independently, the teacher calls on several students to verbalize their strategies for the difficult words.

Spiegel (1990) recommends the commercial games *Road Race* (Carpenter, Curriculum Associates, 1987) and *Word Trek* (Collgrove, DLM, 1977) as educationally valid decoding games that work well with the compare/contrast, onset-rime, and word family approaches to phonics instruction.

Ehri and Robbins (1992) found that students needed some knowledge of phoneme-grapheme correspondences in order to be able to use onset-rime units. Bruck and Treiman (1992) discovered that beginning readers can use analogies, but tend to rely more on individual phoneme-grapheme correspondences to decode new words. Their findings suggest that students need instruction on individual phoneme-grapheme correspondences, especially for vowels, rather than just on relationships between groups of phonemes and groups of graphemes. They warn that rime instruction is not sufficient by itself.

Johnson and Baumann (1984) cite research indicating that "programs emphasizing a phonics or code approach to word identification produce superior word-calling ability when compared to programs applying an analytic phonics or meaning emphasis" (p. 590). But, they continue, "there seem to be distinct differences in the quality of error responses made by children instructed in the two general methodologies—readers' errors tend to be real words, meaningful, and syntactically appropriate when instruction emphasizes meaning, whereas code-emphasis word-identification instruction results in more nonword errors that are graphically and aurally like the mispronounced words" (p. 590). Because the goal of reading is comprehension, not word calling, the analytic approach, which uses meaning-emphasis techniques, seems to be the better choice for instruction.

Teachers should keep in mind a caution about the teaching of phonics generalizations that involve the use of such terms as *sound* and *word*. Studies by Reid and Downing indicate that young children (five year olds) have trouble understanding terms used to talk about language, such as *word, letter,* and *sound* (Downing, 1973), and Meltzer and Herse (1969) found that first-grade children do not always know where printed words begin and end. In addition, Tovey (1980) found that the group of second through sixth graders he studied had difficulty in dealing with abstract phonics terms such as *consonant, consonant blend, consonant digraph, vowel digraph, diphthong, possessive, inflectional ending,* and others. His study also showed that the children had learned sound-symbol associations without being able to define the phonics terms involved. Before teaching a lesson using linguistic terms, the teacher should check to be sure that students grasp such concepts. Technical terminology should be deemphasized when working with students who have not mastered the terms.

Cordts (1965) suggests using key words to help children learn the sounds associated with vowels, consonants, vowel digraphs, consonant digraphs, diphthongs, and consonant blends. In all cases, these words should already be part of the children's sight vocabularies. Cordts suggests that a key word for a vowel sound be one that contains that vowel sound and can be pictured, whereas a key word for a consonant sound should be one that can be pictured and has that consonant sound at the end. She believes that consonant sounds can be heard more clearly at the ends than at the beginnings of words.

Other authorities also encourage the use of key words, but most suggest using words with the consonant sounds at the beginning. The sounds may be harder to distinguish, but usable key words are much easier to find when initial sounds are used.

Key words are valuable in helping children remember sound-symbol associations that are not inherently meaningful. People remember new things through associations with things they already know. The more associations a person has for an abstract relationship, such as the letter *d* and the sound of *d*, the more quickly that person will learn to link the sound and the symbol. The person's retention of this connection will also be more accurate. Schell (1978) refers to a third-grade boy who chose as key words for the consonant blends *dr, fr,* and *sp* the character names *Dracula, Frankenstein,* and *Spiderman.* These associations were both concrete and personal for him. The characters were drawn on key-word cards to aid his memory of the associations.

Consonant substitution activities are useful for helping students see how their knowledge of some words helps them to decode other words. Following is a Model Activity for teaching consonant substitution.

Model Activities

Consonant Substitution

Write a known word, such as *pat,* on the board and ask the students to pronounce the word. Then write on the board a letter for which the sound has been taught (for example, *m*). If the letter sound can be pronounced in isolation without distortion, ask the students to do so; if not, ask for a word beginning with this sound. Then ask the students to leave the *p* sound off when they pronounce the word on the board. They will respond with *at.* Next, ask them to put the *m* sound in front of the *at,* and they will produce *mat.* The same process is followed with other sounds, such as *s, r,* and *b.*

This procedure is also useful with sounds at the ends of words or in medial positions. Vowel substitution activities, in which you may start with a known word and have the students omit the vowel sound and substitute a different one (for example: s*a*t, s*e*t, s*i*t; p*a*t, p*e*t, p*i*t, p*o*t), can also be helpful.

Cunningham and Cunningham (1992) suggest an activity called Making Words, which is a guided group invented-spelling instructional strategy designed to take advantage of the values of writing with invented spelling while offering a more direct instructional procedure. In it the children use the letters of a long word to spell short words of varying lengths, eventually trying to actually spell the long word from which the others were made. They then sort the words they have made according to a variety of patterns. This activity is designed to be used along with writing activities that involve invented spelling.

Oleneski (1992) used the jump rope rhyme "Teddy Bear" to teach sounds in an analytic manner with authentic material. She duplicated the rhyme, which the children knew well, and let them engage in activities such as reading it and sequencing its parts with sentence strips. Then she covered up certain words and had the children figure out what these words were. She then asked them to predict which letters would represent the beginning and ending sounds of the target words. Students continued to use the poem for reading and writing activities to keep the instruction on sounds in context. This procedure could be used with other jump-rope rhymes or ball-bouncing rhymes.

Drill on letter-sound associations need not be dull. Teachers can use many game activities, and activities that are more formal will not become boring if they are not overused. When planning games, teachers should always remember that, although competitive situations are motivational for some youngsters, other children are adversely affected by being placed in win/lose situations, especially if they have little hope of being winners at least part of the time. Game situations in which children cooperate or in which they compete with *their own previous records* rather than with one another are often more acceptable. Following are some practical examples of both competitive and noncompetitive games.

Activities

1. Give each child a sheet of paper that is blank except for a letter at the top. Have the children draw pictures of as many items as they can think of that have names beginning with the sound of the letter at the top of the page. Declare the child with the most correct responses the winner.

2. Make five decorated boxes, and label each box with a short vowel. Have the children locate pictures of objects whose names contain the short vowel sounds and file them in the appropriate boxes. Each day take out the pictures, ask the children to pronounce the names, and check to see if the appropriate sounds are present. Do the same thing with long vowel sounds, consonant sounds, consonant blends, digraphs, diphthongs, and rhyming words.

3. Place a familiar word ending on a cardboard disk like the one pictured here. Pull a strip of cardboard with initial consonants on it through an opening cut in the disk. Show the children how to pull the strip through the disk, pronouncing each word that is formed.

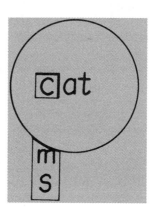

4. Divide the children into two groups. Give half of them initial consonant, consonant blend, or consonant digraph cards. Give the other half word-ending cards. Instruct the children to pair up with other children holding word parts that combine with their parts to form real words. Have each pair hold up their cards and pronounce the word they have made when they have located a combination. Then let them search for other possible combinations for their word parts.

5. Use riddles. For example: "I have in mind a word that rhymes with *far.* We ride in it. It's called a _____ ."

6. Let the children find a hidden picture by shading in all the spaces that contain words with long vowel sounds.

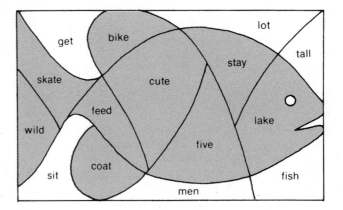

To be effective, practice exercises should always be preceded by instruction and followed by feedback on results. The absence of prior instruction may cause students to practice the wrong response. Feedback, which should come either directly from the teacher or through a self-correcting procedure (posted answers, for example), will inform students of errors immediately so that they do not learn incorrect responses. When students fail to see reasons for errors, the teacher will need to provide explanations and reteach the strategy or skill.

A phonics strategy or skill is a means to an end, not an end in itself. Readers who can recognize words without resorting to letter-by-letter sounding will recognize them more quickly than those who must sound out the words, and the process will interfere less with their train of thought than sounding out the words would have. When the words to be recognized are seen in context, as in most normal reading activities, the sound of the first letter alone may elicit recognition of the whole word. Context clues can provide a child with an idea about the word's identity, and the initial sound can be used to verify an educated guess. This procedure is efficient and is a good way to identify unfamiliar words quickly. Of course, the ultimate goal of instruction in phonics and other word identification skills is to turn initially unfamiliar words into automatically recognized sight words.

Structural Analysis

Structural analysis is closely related to phonics and has several significant facets:

1. Inflectional endings
2. Prefixes and suffixes
3. Contractions
4. Compound words
5. Syllabication and accents

Structural analysis strategies and skills enable children to decode unfamiliar words by using units larger than single graphemes; this procedure generally expedites the decoding process. Structural analysis can also help in understanding word meanings, a function discussed in Chapter 4.

Inflectional Endings

Inflectional endings are added to nouns to change number, case, or gender; added to verbs to change tense or person; and added to adjectives to change degree. They may also change a word's part of speech. Since inflectional endings are letters or groups of letters added to the endings of root words, some people call them *inflectional suffixes*. Here are some examples of words with inflectional endings.

Root Word	New Word	Change
boy	boys	Singular noun changed to plural noun
host	hostess	Gender of noun changed from masculine to feminine
Karen	Karen's	Proper noun altered to show possession (change of case)
look	looked	Verb changed from present tense to past tense
make	makes	Verb changed from first or second person singular to third person singular
mean	meaner	Simple form of adjective changed to the comparative form
happy	happily	Adjective changed to adverb

Generally, the first inflectional ending to which children are exposed is *-s*. This ending often appears in early reading materials and should be learned early in the first grade. Other inflectional endings children are likely to encounter in these early materials are *-ing* and *-ed*.

A child can be shown the effect of the addition of an *-s* to a singular noun through use of illustrations of single and multiple objects. An activity such as that shown in the following Model Activity: Recognizing Inflectional Ending *-s* can be used to practice this skill. A second Model Activity for various inflectional endings demonstrates further possibilities for practice with different inflectional endings.

Model Activities

Recognizing Inflectional Ending *-s*

Give the following practice sheet to the children.

Ask the children to read and follow the directions. Then go over the practice sheet with them orally, asking how each word that shows more than one thing looks different from the word that shows only one thing. They should come to the conclusion that *-s* at the ends of the words indicates more than one thing.

Directions: Circle the word that describes two things.

bell   bells

car   cars

dogs   dog

book   books

Model Activities

Recognizing Inflectional Endings

Write on the board sentences containing inflectional endings that have already been discussed, taken from a book that has been shared in class. Ask the children to read the sentences silently, looking for the inflectional endings they have studied in class. After the silent reading, let volunteers go to the board, circle the inflectional endings in the sentences, and tell how each ending affects word meaning or word use.

You may not wish to use all possible examples from the book in this activity. Instead, you can encourage students to go back to the book itself, either individually or in pairs, locate the inflectional endings under consideration, and make a list of the words they find. These words can be discussed later in a group discussion, with the students finding the words in the story and reading the sentences in which they appear.

As an example, *Ox-Cart Man* (Hall, Puffin Books, 1979) could be used for sentences containing the words *backed, filled, packed, sheared, spinning, pairs, mittens, candles, shingles, brooms, carved, borrowed, potatoes, counted, apples, honeycombs, turnips, cabbages, maples, tapped, boiled, feathers, collected, waved, walked, ox's, days, hills, valleys, streams, farms, villages, kissed, pockets, coins, pounds, candies, tucked, kettle's, waiting, stitching, whittling, cooked, sawed, embroidered, trees, knitted, planted, blossoms, bloomed, bees, starting, squawked, dropping,* and *clouds.* From this short book, you could effectively re- view the inflectional endings *-ed, -s, -'s,* and *-ing.* You may decide to handle each inflectional ending in a separate lesson.

Children in the primary grades are frequently exposed to the possessive case formed by *-'s.* Here is an activity designed for work with this inflectional ending.

**Model
Activities**

Using *-'s* for the Singular Possessive

Tell the children: "When I say, 'This is the book of my brother,' I mean that the book belongs to my brother. Another, shorter, way to say the same thing is 'This is my brother's book.' The *apos- trophe s* on the end of the word *brother* shows that the noun following *brother* (*book*) belongs to *brother.*"

Have the children examine stories they have read recently for examples of the use of *-'s.* Let them read the sentences they found that contained *-'s* and tell the meanings of the phrases in which it occurs.

Prefixes and Suffixes

Prefixes and suffixes are *affixes,* letters or sequences of letters that are added to root words to change their meanings and/or parts of speech. A *prefix* is placed be- fore a root word, and a *suffix* is placed after a root word.

Children can learn the pronunciations and meanings of some common pre- fixes and suffixes. Good readers learn to recognize common prefixes and suffixes instantly; this helps them recognize words more rapidly than they could if they had to resort to sounding each word letter by letter. Knowledge of prefixes and suffixes can help readers decipher the meanings as well as the pronunciations of unfamiliar words.

The suffixes *-ment, -ous, -tion,* and *-sion* have especially consistent pronuncia- tions and thus are particularly useful to know. The suffixes *-ment* and *-ous* generally have the pronunciations heard in the words *treatment* and *joyous.* The suffixes *-tion* and *-sion* have the sound of *shun,* as heard in the words *education* and *mission.*

Whereas prefixes simply modify the meanings of the root words, suffixes may change the parts of speech as well as modify the meanings. Some of the resulting modifications are listed here.

Root Word	Affix	New Word	New Meaning or Change
happy	un-	unhappy	not happy
amuse	-ment	amusement	verb is changed to noun
worth	-less	worthless	meaning is opposite of original meaning

Use activities like the two following Model Activities.

Model Activities

Recognition of Prefixes and Suffixes

After instruction in prefixes and suffixes, give the students duplicated sheets containing paragraphs from a story that has just been shared in class. Ask them to circle the prefixes and suffixes they see in the paragraphs, working independently. Then divide them into small groups and have them compare and discuss their responses. Each group should come to an agreement about the correct answers. Finally, check the group responses in a whole-class discussion, calling on small-group representatives to give each group's responses to various items.

For example, in *Nadia the Willful* (Alexander, Knopf, 1983), the following words appear: *stubbornness, willful, kindness, graciousness, return, emptiness, punishment, remind, uneasily, hardness, coldness, unhappiness, bitterness, inside, recall, recalled, unbidden, happiness, sharpness,* and *forward.* Some of the words occur several times. The paragraphs in which these words appear can be duplicated for this exercise.

Not all of the words need to be used in a single lesson. You may wish to use one prefix or suffix at a time.

Model Activities

Adding Prefixes and Suffixes

Write the following root words on the chalkboard.

1. agree   2. move   3. construct

Ask the children to write on their papers as many new words as they can by adding prefixes and suffixes to these root words. Then have the children form small groups and share the words they have formed with the other group members. Group members may question some of the words their classmates have

formed and may consult reference books or the teacher to confirm or discredit words formed. Then representatives from the small groups may share the groups' word collections with the rest of the class.

The children may then be encouraged to produce small-group or individual stories using some of the words they constructed. These stories can be shared orally or in written form (perhaps on the bulletin board or in a reading center) with the rest of the class.

In the third and fourth grades, children begin to encounter more words that contain prefixes, suffixes, or both (White, Sowell, and Yanagihara, 1989; Nagy and Anderson, 1984). White, Sowell, and Yanagihara (1989) have identified nine prefixes (*un-; re-; in-, im-, ir-* [meaning *not*]; *dis-; en-, em-; non-; in-, im-* [meaning *in* or *into*]; *over-* [meaning *too much*]; and *mis-*) that cover 76 percent of the prefixed words in the *Word Frequency Book* (Carroll, Davies, and Richman, 1971). They recommend that these prefixes be taught systematically during grades three through five, beginning with *un-,* which alone accounts for 26 percent of the prefixed words. An analysis of their word counts would lead us to add *sub-, pre-, inter-,* and *fore-* to the recommended list, since they occur as frequently as *over-* and *mis-,* thereby covering 88 percent of the prefixed words.

White, Sowell, and Yanagihara (1989) have identified ten suffixes and inflectional endings that are part of 85 percent of the suffixed words in the *Word Frequency Book:* *-s, -es; -ed; -ing; -ly; -er, -or* (agentive); *-ion, -tion, -ation, -ition; -ible, -able; -al, -ial; -y;* and *-ness.* The three inflectional endings *-s/-es, -ed,* and *-ing* alone account for 65 percent of the incidences of suffixed words in the sample.

Contractions

The apostrophe used in contractions indicates that one or more letters have been left out when two words were combined into one word. Children need to be able to recognize the original words from which the contractions were formed. The following are common contractions, with their meanings, that teachers should present to children:

can't/cannot	I'd/I had or I would	I'll/I will	shouldn't/should not
couldn't/could not	they'd/they had or they would	I'm/I am	we've/we have
didn't/did not		I've/I have	won't/will not
don't/do not	they'll/they will	isn't/is not	wouldn't/would not
hadn't/had not	they're/they are	let's/let us	you'll/you will
hasn't/has not	they've/they have	she'd/she would or she had	you're/you are
he'll/he will	wasn't/was not	she'll/she will	you've/you have
he's/he is or he has	we're/we are	she's/she is or she has	
	weren't/were not		

The teacher may wish to teach contractions in related groups—for example, those in which *not* is the reduced part, those in which *have* is the reduced part, and so on. Students should locate these contractions and their uncontracted referents in context and use them in writing to enhance their learning.

Compound Words

Compound words consist of two (or occasionally three) words that have been joined together to form a new word. The original pronunciations of the component words are usually maintained, and their meanings are connected to form the meaning of the new word: *dishpan,* for example, is a pan in which dishes are washed. Children can be asked to underline or circle component parts of compound words or to put together familiar compound words as practice activities. An exercise for compound words follows.

Model Activities

Recognizing Parts of Compound Words

Display a page from a big book (or a transparency made from a regular-size book) that contains several compound words. Let students come to the book (or the projected image) and point out the words that are made up of two or more words (for example, in *Song and Dance Man* [Acker-man, Knopf, 1988], the words *Grandpa, Grandma, cardboard, leather-trimmed, inside, half-moon, spotlight, woodpecker, somebody's, bathroom, gold-tipped,* and *stairway*). Write the words on the chalkboard. Let volunteers come to the board and circle the separate words that make up each compound word. Have a class discussion about the way to decide how to pronounce compound words.

Syllabication/Accent

Since many phonics generalizations apply not only to one-syllable words but also to syllables within longer words, many people believe that breaking words into syllables can help determine pronunciation. Some research indicates, however, that syllabication is usually done after the reader has recognized the word and that readers use the sounds to determine syllabication rather than syllabication to determine the sounds (Glass, 1967). If this procedure is the one children normally use in attacking words, syllabication would seem to be of little use in a word analysis program. On the other hand, many authorities firmly believe that syllabication is helpful in decoding words. For this reason, a textbook on reading methods would be incomplete without discussions of syllabication and a related topic, stress or accent.

A *syllable* is a letter or group of letters that forms a pronunciation unit. Every syllable contains a vowel sound. In fact, a vowel sound may form a syllable by itself (*a/mong*). Only in a syllable that contains a diphthong is there more than one vowel sound. Diphthongs are treated as single units, although they are actually vowel blends. While each syllable has only one vowel sound or diphthong, a syllable may have more than one vowel letter. Letters and sounds should not be confused. The word *peeve,* for example, has three vowel letters, but the only vowel sound is the long *e* sound. Therefore, *peeve* contains only one syllable.

There are two types of syllables: open and closed. Open syllables end in vowel sounds; closed syllables end in consonant sounds. Syllables may in turn be classified as accented (given greater stress) or unaccented (given little stress). Accent has much to do with the vowel sound we hear in a syllable. Multisyllabic words may have primary (strongest), secondary (second strongest), and even tertiary (third strongest) accents. The vowel sound of an open accented syllable is usually long (*mī' nus, bā' sin*); the second syllable of each of these example words is unaccented, and the vowel sound represented is the schwa, often found in unaccented syllables. A single vowel in a closed accented syllable generally has its short sound, unless it is influenced by another sound in that syllable (*căp' sule, cär' go*).

Following are several useful generalizations concerning syllabication and accent:

1. Words contain as many syllables as they have vowel sounds (counting diphthongs as a unit). Examples: *se/vere* (final *e* has no sound); *break* (*e* is not sounded); *so/lo* (both vowels are sounded); *oil* (diphthong is treated as a unit).

2. In a word with more than one sounded vowel, when the first vowel is followed by two consonants, the division is generally between the two consonants. Examples: *mar/ry, tim/ber.* If the two consonants are identical, the second one is not sounded.

3. Consonant blends and consonant digraphs are treated as units and are not divided. Examples: *ma/chine, a/bridge.*

4. In a word with more than one sounded vowel, when the first vowel is followed by only one consonant or consonant digraph, the division is generally after the vowel. Examples: *ma/jor, ri/val* (long initial vowel sounds). There are, however, many exceptions to this rule, which make it less useful. Examples: *rob/in, hab/it* (short initial vowel sounds).

5. When a word ends in *-le* preceded by a consonant, the preceding consonant plus *-le* constitute the final syllable of the word. This syllable is never accented, and the vowel sound heard in it is the schwa. Examples: *can/dle, ta/ble.*

6. Prefixes and suffixes generally form separate syllables. Examples: *dis/taste/ful, pre/dic/tion.*

7. A compound word is divided between the two words that form the compound, as well as between syllables within the component words. Examples: *snow/man, thun/der/storm.*

8. Prefixes and suffixes are usually not accented. Example: *dis/grace' ful.*

9. Words that can be used as both verbs and nouns are accented on the second syllable when used as verbs and on the first syllable when used as nouns. Examples: *pre/sent'* —verb; *pres' ent*—noun.

10. In two-syllable root words, the first syllable is usually accented, unless the second syllable has two vowel letters. Examples: *rock' et, pa/rade'.*

11. Words containing three or more syllables are likely to have secondary (and perhaps tertiary) accents, in addition to primary accents. Example: *reg' i/men/ta' tion.*

Readiness for learning syllabication includes the ability to hear syllables as pronunciation units. Here is an early exercise on syllabication.

**Model
Activities**

Syllabication

Teachers can have children as young as first graders listen to words and clap for every syllable heard. Ask the children to say words aloud and listen for the syllables. Let them clap once for each syllable as it is pronounced. Include both single-syllable and multisyllabic words in the exercise.

Some example words you may use are as follows:

1. rule
2. table
3. meaningful
4. middle
5. disagreement
6. person
7. fingertip
8. name

Generalizations about syllabication can be taught using the same process as that for phonic generalizations, described earlier in this chapter. The teacher can present many examples of a particular generalization and lead the children to state the generalization.

Waugh and Howell (1975) point out that in dictionaries it is the syllable divisions in the phonetic respellings, rather than the ones indicated in the boldface entry words, that are useful to students in pronouncing unfamiliar words. The divisions of the boldface entry words are a guide for hyphenations in writing, not for word pronunciation.

Accentuation generally is not taught until children have a good background in word attack skills and is often presented in conjunction with dictionary study as a tool for word attack. More will be said on this topic in the next section of this chapter.

Dictionary Study

Dictionaries are valuable tools that can help in completing many kinds of reading tasks. They can help students determine pronunciations, meanings, derivations, and parts of speech for words they encounter in reading activities. They can also help with word spellings, if children have some idea of how the words are spelled and need only to confirm the order of letters within the words. Picture dictionaries are used primarily for sight word recognition and spelling assistance. Children can be introduced to picture dictionaries as early as the first grade. They can learn how dictionaries are put together and how they function by making their own picture dictionaries. Intermediate-grade pupils can develop dictionaries of special terms like *My Science Dictionary* or *My Health Dictionary*. From these they can advance to beginning and intermediate dictionaries.

This section deals mainly with the role the dictionary plays in helping children with word recognition; Chapter 4 discusses the dictionary as an aid to comprehension of word meanings. Study skills related to dictionary use, such as use of guide words, are covered in Chapter 9.

Although the dictionary is undeniably useful in determining the pronunciation of unfamiliar words, students should turn to it only as a last resort for this purpose. They should consult it only after they have applied phonics and structural analysis clues along with knowledge of context clues. There are two major reasons for following this procedure. First, applying the appropriate word recognition skills immediately, without having to take the time to look up the word in the dictionary, is less of a disruption of the reader's train of thought and therefore less of a hindrance to comprehension. Second, a dictionary is not always readily available; thoroughly mastered word recognition skills, however, will always be there when they are needed.

When using other word attack skills has produced no useful or clear result, children should turn to the dictionary for help. Obviously, before children can use the dictionary for pronunciation, they must be able to locate words in it. This skill is discussed in Chapter 9.

After children have located particular words, they need two more skills to pronounce the words correctly: the ability to interpret phonetic respellings and to interpret accent marks.

Interpreting Phonetic Respellings and Accent Marks

The pronunciation key, along with knowledge of sounds ordinarily associated with single consonants, helps in interpreting phonetic respellings in dictionaries. A pronunciation key is present somewhere on every page spread of a good dictionary. Students should not be asked to memorize the diacritical (pronunciation) markings used in a given dictionary, because different dictionaries use different markings; learning the markings for one could cause confusion when students use another. The sounds ordinarily associated with relatively unvarying consonants may or may not be included in the pronunciation key. Because they are not always included, it is important that children have a knowledge of phonics.

Here are four activities related to interpretation of phonetic spellings.

Activities

1. Have the students locate a given word in their dictionaries (example: *cheat* [*chēt*]). Call attention to the phonetic respelling beside the entry word. Point out the location of the pronunciation key and explain its function. Have the children locate each successive sound-symbol in the key—*ch, ē, t*. (If necessary, explain why the *t* is not included in the key.) Have the children check the key word for each symbol to confirm its sound value. Then have them blend the three sounds together to form a word. Repeat with other words. (Start with short words and gradually work up to longer ones.)

2. Code an entire paragraph or a joke using phonetic respellings. Provide a pronunciation key. Let groups of children compete to see who can write the selection in the traditional way first. Let each group of students who believe they have done so come to your desk. Check their work. If it is correct, keep it and give it a number indicating the order in which it was finished. If it is incorrect, send the students back to work on it some more. Set a time limit for the activity. The activity may be carried out on a competitive or a noncompetitive basis.

3. Give the children a pronunciation key, and let them encode messages to friends. Check the accuracy of each message before it is passed on to the friends to be decoded.

4. Use an activity such as the following Model Activity.

Model Activities

Pronunciation Key

Write the following hypothetical pronunciation key on the board. Tell the children: "Pretend that this list of words is part of the pronunciation key for a dictionary. Choose the key word or words that would help you pronounce each of the words listed below it. Hold up your hand when you have written the number of the appropriate key word on your paper beside the number of each entry word." (You may form the list of words from a book the children are about to read, thereby giving them some advance preparation for the words that they will meet in the book.)

When all the children have made their choices, call on a volunteer to reply to each one, telling why he or she chose a particular answer.

Pronunciation Key: (1) cat, (2) āge, (3) fär, (4) sōfə, (5) sit

1. cape (kāp)
2. car (kär)
3. ago (ə/gō′)
4. aim (ām)
5. fad (fad)
6. race (rās)
7. rack (rak)
8. affix (ə/fiks′)

Some words will have only one accent mark, whereas others will have marks showing different degrees of accent within a single word. Children need to be able to translate the accent marks into proper stress when they speak the words. Here are two ideas for use in teaching accent marks.

Activities

1. Write several familiar multisyllabic words on the board. (*Bottle* and *apartment* are two good choices.) Explain that when words of more than one syllable are spoken, certain syllables are stressed or emphasized by the speaker's breath. Pronounce each of the example words, pointing out which part or parts of each word receive stress. Next, tell the class that the dictionary uses accent marks to indicate which parts of words receive stress. Look up each word in the dictionary, and write the dictionary divisions and accent marks for the word on the board. Pronounce each word again, showing how the accent marks indicate the parts of the words that you stress when you pronounce them. Then have the children complete the following Model Activity.

2. Introduce the concept of accent in the same way described in the first activity. Then distribute sheets of paper with a list of words such as the following.

(1) des′ ti na′ tion

(2) con′ sti tu′ tion

(3) mys′ ti fy′

(4) pen′ nant

(5) thun′ der storm

Ask volunteers to read the words, applying the accents properly. When they have done so, give them a list of unfamiliar words with both accent marks and diacritical (pronunciation) marks inserted. (Lists will vary according to the children's ability. Use of words from their classroom reading material is preferable to use of random words.) Once again, ask the children to read the words, applying their dictionary skills.

Model Activities

Accent Marks

Write the following words on the board.

1. truth ful   6. peo ple

2. lo co mo tion   7. gig gle

3. fric tion   8. emp ty

4. at ten tion   9. en e my

5. ad ven ture   10. ge og ra phy

Call on volunteers to pronounce these words and decide where the accent is placed in each one.

Have them come to the board and indicate placements of the accents by putting accent marks (′) after the syllables where they think the accents belong. Then have all the students look up the words in the dictionary and check the placements of the accents. Anyone who finds an incorrectly marked word can come to the board, make the correction, and pronounce the word with the accent correctly placed.

Word Recognition Procedure

It is helpful for children to know a strategy for decoding unfamiliar words independently. A child may discover the word at any point in the following procedure; he or she should then stop the procedure and continue reading. Sometimes it is necessary to try all of the steps.

Step 1. Apply context clues. This may involve reading to the end of the sentence or paragraph in which the word is found to intake enough context to draw a reasonable conclusion about the word.

Step 2. Try the sound of the initial consonant, vowel, or blend along with context clues.

Step 3. Check for structure clues (prefixes, suffixes, inflectional endings, compound words, or familiar syllables).

Step 4. Begin sounding out the word using known phonics generalizations. (Go only as far as necessary to determine the word.)

Step 5. Consult the dictionary.

A teacher may explain this five-step strategy in the following way:

1. First, try to decide what word might reasonably fit in the context in which you found the unfamiliar word. Ask yourself: "Will this word be a naming word? A word that describes? A word that shows action? A word that connects two ideas?" Also ask yourself: "What word will make sense in this place?" Do you have the answer? Are you sure of it? If so, continue to read. If not, go to Step 2.

2. Try the initial sound(s) along with the context clues. Does this help you decide? If you are sure you have the word now, continue reading. If not, go to Step 3.

3. Check to see if there are familiar word parts that will help you. Does the word have a prefix or suffix that you know? If this helps you decide on the word, continue reading. If not, go to Step 4.

4. Begin sounding out the word, using all of your phonics skills. If you discover the word, stop sounding and go back to your reading. If you have sounded out the whole word and it does not sound like a word you know, go to Step 5.

5. Look up the word in the dictionary. Use the pronunciation key to help you pronounce the word. If the word is one you have not heard before, check the meaning. Be sure to choose the meaning that fits the context.

For example, a reader who is confronted with the unfamiliar word *chamois* might apply the strategy in the following way:

1. "'He used a chamois to dry off the car.' I've never seen the word *c-h-a-m-o-i-s* before. Let's see. . . . Is it a naming word? . . . Yes, it is, because *a* comes before it. . . . What thing would make sense here? . . . It is something that can be used to dry a car. Could it be *towel*? . . . No, that doesn't have any of the right sounds. Maybe it is *cloth*? . . . No, *cloth* starts with *cl*."

2. "*Ch* usually sounds like the beginning of *choice*. . . . I can't think of anything that starts that way that would fit here. . . . Sometimes it sounds like *k*. . . . I can't think of a word that fits that either. . . . *Ch* even sounds like *sh* sometimes. . . . The only word I can think of that starts with the *sh* sound and fits in the sentence is *sheet,* and I can tell that none of the other sounds are right."

3. "I don't see a prefix, suffix, or root word that I recognize, either."

4. "Maybe I can sound it out. *Chămois*. No, that's not a word. *Kāmois*. That's not a word either. *Shămois*. I don't think so. . . . Maybe the *a* is long. *Chāmois*. No. *Kāmois*. No. *Shāmois*. No."

5. "I guess I'll have to use the dictionary. What? *Shăm′ ē*? Oh, I know what that is. I've seen Dad use one! Why is it spelled so funny? Oh, I see! It came from French."

A crucial point for teachers to remember is that children should not consider use of word recognition skills important *only* during reading classes. They should apply these skills whenever they encounter an unfamiliar word, whether it happens during reading class, science class, a free reading period, or in out-of-school situations. Teachers should emphasize to their students that the strategy explained here is applicable to *any* situation in which an unfamiliar word occurs.

Teachers should also encourage students to self-correct their reading errors when the words they read do not combine to make sense. This can be accomplished with some well-planned instruction. Taylor and Nosbush (1983) had children individually read orally from material at their instructional levels. They praised each child for things he or she did well when reading, especially any self-correcting behavior the student exhibited when miscues (unexpected responses) affected the meaning. They encouraged each student to try to make sure the material being read made sense. They also discussed some miscues that the student did not self-correct, particularly ones that did not make sense but for which good context clues were available. Students instructed in this way did better at self-correction than did students who read orally without being asked to pay attention to meaning.

Summary

Word recognition skills help readers identify words while reading. One skill is sight word recognition, the development of a store of words a person can recognize immediately on sight. Use of context clues to help in word identification involves using the surrounding words to decode an unfamiliar word. Both semantic and syntactic clues can be helpful. Phonics, the association of speech sounds (phonemes) with printed symbols (graphemes), is very helpful in identifying unfamiliar words, even though the sound-symbol associations in English are not completely consistent. Structural analysis skills enable readers to decode unfamiliar words using units larger than single graphemes. The process of structural analysis involves recognition of prefixes, suffixes, inflectional endings, contractions, and compound words, as well as syllabication and accent. Dictionaries can also be used for word identification. The dictionary respelling that appears in parentheses after the word supplies the word's pronunciation, but the reader has to know how to use the dictionary's pronunciation key to interpret the respellings appropriately.

Children need to learn to use all of the word recognition skills. Because they will need different skills for different situations, they must also learn to use the skills appropriately.

An overall strategy for decoding unfamiliar words is useful. The following five-step strategy is a good one to teach: (1) use context clues; (2) try the sound of the initial consonant, vowel, or blend in addition to context clues; (3) check for structure clues; (4) use phonics generalizations to sound out as much of the word as necessary; and (5) consult the dictionary.

Test Yourself

True or False

_____ 1. It is wise to teach only a single approach to word attack.

_____ 2. All word recognition strategies are learned with equal ease by all children.

_____ 3. Sight words are words that readers recognize immediately without needing to resort to analysis.

_____ 4. The English language is noted for the regularity of sound-symbol associations in its written words.

_____ 5. Teaching a small store of sight words can be the first step in implementing an analytic approach to phonics instruction.

_____ 6. Early choices for sight words to be taught should be words that are extremely useful and meaningful.

_____ 7. Games with complex rules are good ones to use for practice with sight words.

_____ 8. Most practice with sight words should involve the words in context.

_____ 9. If teachers teach phonics well, they do not need to bother with other word recognition strategies.

_____ 10. Consonant letters are more consistent in the sounds they represent than vowel letters are.

_____ 11. Phonics generalizations often have numerous exceptions.

_____ 12. It is impossible to teach too many phonics rules, since these rules are extremely valuable in decoding unfamiliar words.

_____ 13. In a word that has only one vowel letter at the end, the vowel letter usually represents its long sound.

_____ 14. It is wise to teach only one phonics generalization at a time.

_____ 15. Structural analysis skills include the ability to recognize prefixes and suffixes.

_____ 16. The addition of a prefix to a root word can change the word's meaning.

_____ 17. Inflectional endings can change verb tenses.

_____ 18. The apostrophe in a contraction indicates possession or ownership.

_____ 19. Every syllable contains a vowel sound.

_____ 20. There is only one vowel letter in each syllable.

_____ 21. Open syllables end in consonant sounds.

_____ 22. The vowel sound in an open accented syllable is usually long.

_____ 23. The schwa sound is often found in unaccented syllables.

_____ 24. When dividing words into syllables, we treat consonant blends and consonant digraphs as units and do not divide them.

_____ 25. Prefixes and suffixes generally form separate syllables.

_____ 26. Prefixes and suffixes are usually accented.

_____ 27. Picture clues are the most useful word recognition clues for sixth-grade students.

_____ 28. A comparison or contrast found in printed material may offer a clue to the identity of an unfamiliar word.

_____ 29. Context clues used by themselves provide only educated guesses about the identities of unfamiliar words.

_____ 30. Children should be expected to memorize the diacritical markings used in their dictionaries.

_____ 31. Accent marks indicate which syllables are stressed.

_____ 32. Some words have more than one accented syllable.

_____ 33. Writing new words is helpful to some learners in building sight vocabulary.

_____ 34. The language experience approach is good for developing sight vocabulary.

_____ 35. One method of teaching sight words is best for all students.

Multiple Choice

_____ 1. In the word _myth,_ the _y_
a. has the characteristics of a vowel.
b. is silent.
c. has the characteristics of a consonant.

_____ 2. When it occurs in the initial position in a syllable, the letter _w_
a. stands for a vowel sound.
b. is silent.
c. stands for a consonant sound.

_____ 3. In the word _strong,_ the letters _str_
a. represent a consonant blend.
b. are silent.
c. represent a single sound.

_____ 4. Consonant digraphs
    a. represent two blended speech sounds.
    b. represent a single speech sound.
    c. are always silent.

_____ 5. The word *sheep* is made up of
    a. five sounds.
    b. four sounds.
    c. three sounds.

_____ 6. In the word *boat*, the *oa* is a
    a. vowel digraph.
    b. diphthong.
    c. blend.

_____ 7. In the word *boy,* the *oy* is a
    a. vowel digraph.
    b. consonant digraph.
    c. diphthong.

_____ 8. The word *diphthong* contains
    a. three consonant blends.
    b. three consonant digraphs.
    c. a consonant digraph and two consonant blends.

_____ 9. In the word *know,* the *ow* is a
    a. diphthong.
    b. vowel digraph.
    c. consonant blend.

_____ 10. In the word *his,* the letter *s* has the sound usually associated with the letter(s)
    a. *s.*
    b. *z.*
    c. *sh.*

_____ 11. Which type of accent mark indicates the heaviest emphasis?
    a. Primary
    b. Secondary
    c. Tertiary

For your journal...

1. Write a description of how you would teach sight recognition of function words that do not represent concrete images, words such as *for* and *which.*

2. React to the following statement: "Going back to teaching basic phonics skills will cure all of our country's reading ills."

3. After observing a teacher teaching a synthetic phonics lesson and a teacher teaching an analytic phonics lesson, write an evaluation of the two approaches, based upon your observations. Be sure to evaluate the methods, not the instructors.

4. React to the following statement: "I do not believe in teaching children to use context clues. It just produces a group of guessers."

. . . And your portfolio

1. Plan a lesson to teach one or more word recognition strategies, using a popular picture book that contains appropriate examples of phonic and structural analysis elements.

2. Develop a collection of rhymes, riddles, and poems to use to promote auditory discrimination skills.

4

Meaning Vocabulary

SETTING OBJECTIVES

When you finish reading this chapter, you should be able to

▶ Discuss some factors involved in vocabulary development.

▶ Name and describe several techniques of vocabulary instruction.

▶ Identify some special types of words and explain how they can cause problems for children.

Meaning vocabulary (words for which meanings are understood) is essentially the set of labels for the clusters of concepts that people have learned through experience. These clusters of concepts, or knowledge structures, are called *schemata*. (Schemata are also discussed in detail in Chapter 5.) Because students must call on their existing schemata in order to comprehend, meaning vocabulary development is an important component of comprehension (Jones, 1982). Therefore, direct instruction in word meanings is a valuable part of reading instruction. Research indicates that preteaching new vocabulary terms can result in significant gains in comprehension (Roser and Juel, 1982; Carney et al., 1984) and that long-term vocabulary instruction, in which words are taught and reinforced over a period of time, enhances comprehension of materials containing those words (Beck, Perfetti, and McKeown, 1982; McKeown et al., 1983; Robinson et al., 1990).

In Chapter 3 we examined the importance of decoding words and developing a sight vocabulary, but these abilities have little value if students do not understand the words. Children's sight vocabularies should be built from words they already comprehend, words that are a part of their meaning vocabularies. This chapter focuses on the development of extensive meaning vocabularies and the difficulties that certain types of words may present to youngsters.

Vocabulary Development

It is difficult to pinpoint the age at which children learn the precise meanings of words. Early in the language development process, they learn to differentiate between antonyms (opposites), making more discriminating responses as they grow older. Sometimes they overgeneralize about word meanings: a very young child who learns the word *car*, for example, may apply it to any motor vehicle, making no discrimination among cars, trucks, vans, and other kinds of vehicles. Some children as old as nine years have trouble distinguishing between the meanings of *ask* and *tell*, and some children as old as ten years have not yet differentiated between the words *brother* and *boy* and the words *sister* and *girl* (McConaughy, 1978). As children mature, they learn more about choosing specific words.

Children increase their vocabularies at a rapid rate during the elementary school years. Vocabulary building is a complex process involving many kinds of words: words with *multiple meanings* (The candy is *sweet*. Mary has a *sweet* disposition.); words with *abstract definitions* (*Justice* must be served.); *homonyms* (She will take the *plane* to Lexington. He has on *plain* trousers.); *homographs* (I will *read* the newspapers. I have *read* the magazine.); *synonyms* (Marty was *sad* about leaving. Marty was *unhappy* about leaving.); and *antonyms* (Bill is a *slow* runner. Mary is a *fast* runner.). Children must also acquire meanings for a number of relational terms, such as *same/different, more/less, taller/shorter, older/younger, higher/lower,* and so on. In content area instruction, students must deal with *technical vocabulary* (words whose only meanings are specific to the content areas, for example, *photosynthesis*) and *specialized vocabulary* (words with general meanings as well as specialized meanings that are specific to the content area, for example, *pitch* in

Chapter 4 Organization

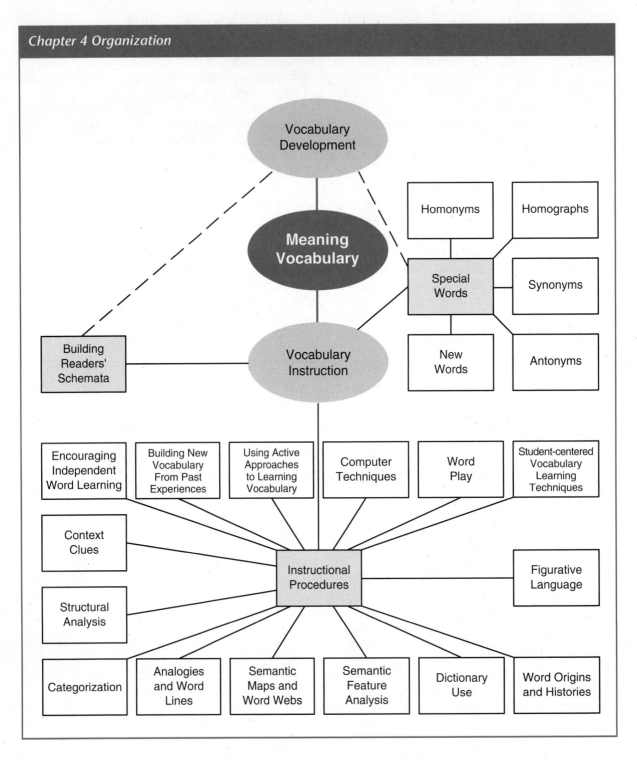

the area of music). Content area materials also abound with special *symbols* and *abbreviations* that children must master in order to read the materials successfully.

Vocabulary Instruction

Children learn much vocabulary by listening to the conversations of those around them. Therefore, a language-rich environment promotes vocabulary acquisition (Anderson and Nagy, 1991). Teachers can provide such environments in their classrooms. They can greatly influence children's vocabulary development simply by being good models of vocabulary use. For example, when teachers read aloud or give explanations to the class, they should discuss any new words used and encourage the children to use them. Teachers should not "talk down" to children but should use appropriate terminology in describing things to them and participating in discussions with them.

Learning new vocabulary may just involve acquisition of a new label for a concept that is already known. In this case, the teacher's task is simple. The teacher provides the new term (such as *journey*) and tells the children it means the same thing as a familiar term (such as *trip*) (Armbruster and Nagy, 1992).

Most teachers recognize the importance of vocabulary instruction as a part of reading and language arts classes. The importance of teaching word meanings and encouraging variety in word choice and exactness in expressing thoughts is generally accepted. Teachers therefore usually give attention to many aspects of vocabulary instruction—such as structural analysis; use of context clues; and use of reference books, such as dictionaries and thesauruses—during language classes. During these lessons, teachers also need to help the children understand the real-world purpose for building vocabulary: a rich vocabulary helps us to communicate effectively. The more words we know and use appropriately, the better we are able to communicate our knowledge and our feelings to others.

Vocabulary instruction should take place throughout the day, however, not just during the language arts or reading period. Vocabulary knowledge is important in all subject areas covered in the curriculum. Children need to develop their vocabularies in every subject area so that the specialized or technical words they encounter are not barriers to learning. Nelson-Herber (1986) suggests intensive direct teaching of vocabulary in specific content areas to help students read the content materials successfully. She endorses building from the known to the new, helping students understand the interrelationships among words in concept clusters (groups of related concepts), and encouraging students to use new words in reading, writing, and speaking. Construction of word meaning by the students from context, experience, and reasoning is basic to her approach. At times the students work in cooperative groups on vocabulary exercises, and they are involved with vocabulary learning before, during, and after reading of assigned material. The techniques described in this chapter and the ideas presented in Chapter 10 will help teachers plan effectively for vocabulary instruction in various content areas.

Whereas some teachers stress the need for vocabulary instruction throughout the day, others argue that such instruction logically belongs in a reading or language arts class. **What do *you* think?**

Choosing words to teach can be a problem for teachers. Blachowicz and Lee (1991) suggest choosing these terms from classroom reading materials. The terms should be central to the selections in which they appear. The teacher should activate prior knowledge related to the words before the reading begins and have students use the new vocabulary in postreading discussion. Words that students still do not understand well need further attention and elaboration. The students might use the words in retellings, dramatizations, or writings based on the story or selection for further experiences.

Teachers can approach vocabulary instruction in a variety of ways, but some vocabulary instructional techniques appear to be more effective than others. The most desirable instructional techniques are those that

1. Assist students in integrating the new words with their background knowledge.
2. Assist students in developing elaborated (expanded) word knowledge.
3. Actively involve students in learning new words.
4. Help students acquire strategies for independent vocabulary development.
5. Provide repetition of the words to build ready accessibility of their meanings.
6. Have students engage in meaningful use of the words (Carr and Wixson, 1986; Nagy, 1988; Blachowicz and Lee, 1991; Beck and McKeown, 1991).

We will now look at several common methods of vocabulary development.

Building Readers' Schemata

Vocabulary terms are labels for *schemata,* or the clusters of concepts each person develops through experience. Sometimes children cannot understand the terms they encounter in books because they do not know the concepts to which the terms refer. In this case, concept or schemata development involving the use of direct and vicarious experiences is necessary. Blachowicz (1985) affirms the importance of building a conceptual base for word learning.

A good technique for concept development is to offer as concrete an experience for the concept as possible. The class should then discuss the attributes of the concept. The teacher should give examples and nonexamples of the concept, pointing out the attributes that distinguish examples from nonexamples. Next, the students should try to identify other examples and nonexamples that the teacher supplies and give their reasons. Finally, the students should suggest additional examples and nonexamples.

For example, to develop the concept of *banjo,* the teacher could bring a banjo to class. The teacher would show it to the students, play it for them (or get someone to do so), and let them touch it and pluck or strum the strings. A discussion of its attributes would follow. The children might decide that a banjo has a circular body and a long neck, that it has a tightly stretched cover over the body, that it has strings, and that one can play music on it. The teacher might show the children pictures or real examples of a variety of banjos, some with five and some with four strings, and some with enclosed backs and some with open backs. Then the teacher might show the children a guitar, pointing out the differences in construction (different shape, different material forming the front of the instrument, different number of strings, etc.). The teacher might also show several other instruments, at first following the same procedure, then letting the students identify how they are different from and similar to banjos. The students can provide their own examples of banjos by bringing in pictures or actual instruments. They will note that, although there may be some variation in size and appearance, the essential attributes are present. They can also name and bring pictures or actual examples of instruments that are not banjos, such as harps, mandolins, or violins, and explain why these instruments do not fit the concept.

Concrete experiences for abstract concepts are difficult to provide, but the teacher can use approximations. For example, to develop the concept of *freedom,* the teacher can say, "You may play with any of the play equipment in the room for the next ten minutes, or you may choose not to play at all." After ten minutes have passed, the teacher can tell the class that they were given the freedom to choose their activity; that is, they were not kept from doing what they chose to do. The teacher may then offer several examples of freedom. One might be the freedom to choose friends. No one else tells the children who their friends have to be; they choose based on their own desires. The teacher should also offer several nonexamples of freedom, perhaps pointing out that during a game players are restrained by a set of rules and do not have the freedom to do anything they want to do. Then the teacher should ask the students to give examples of freedom and explain why these examples are appropriate. A student may suggest that the freedom we have in this country to say what we think about our leaders is a good example, because we are not punished for voicing our views. After several examples, the students will be asked for nonexamples. They may suggest that people in jail do not have freedom, because they cannot go where they wish or do what they wish. After students have offered a number of nonexamples, the teacher may ask them to be alert for examples and nonexamples of freedom in their everyday activities and to report their findings to the class. Some may discover that being "grounded" by their parents is a good nonexample of freedom.

Thelen (1986) indicates that meaningful learning is enhanced by teaching general concepts before specific concepts. In this way, the children have the schemata they need to incorporate new facts they encounter. Using this approach, the teacher presents the concept of *dog* before the concept of *poodle,* and the children thus have a prior pool of information to which they can relate the new information about *poodle.* Isabel Beck has stated that ownership of a word, or the ability to relate the word to an existing schema, is necessary for meaningful learning. In other words, students need to relate the word to information they already know. Semantic mapping and semantic feature analysis (discussed later in this chapter) are two particularly good methods for accomplishing this goal.

Firsthand experiences, such as field trips and demonstrations, can help students associate words with real situations. These experiences can be preceded and followed up by discussion of the new concepts, and written accounts of the experiences can help students gain control of the new vocabulary. For example, a field trip can be preceded by a discussion of the work that is done at the target location. During the field trip, each activity the students witness can be explained as they watch. This explanation should include the proper terms for the processes and personnel involved. After the trip, the students can discuss the experience. They can make graphic displays of the new terms (see the sections on semantic maps and word webs), classify the new terms (see the section on categorization), make comparison charts for the words (see the section on semantic feature analysis), analyze the structure of the words (see the section on structural analysis), or manipulate the new terms in some other way. They may write individual summaries of the experience or participate in writing a class summary. They may wish to use reference books to expand their knowledge about some of the new things they have seen. All of these activities will build both the children's concepts and their vocabularies, thereby enhancing their comprehension of material containing this vocabulary.

Vicarious experiences can also help to build concepts and vocabulary. Audiovisual aids, such as pictures, films, filmstrips, records, and videotapes, can be used to illustrate words that students have encountered in reading and provide other words for discussion. Books such as thesauruses, children's dictionaries, and trade books about words are also useful sources of information about words.

Storytelling and story reading are good ways to provide vicarious experiences. Studies by Roe (1985, 1986) and Pigg (1986) showed that a seven-week program of daily one-hour storytelling/story reading sessions with language follow-up activities could improve vocabulary skills of kindergarten, first-grade, and second-grade students. Students in the experimental groups in these studies produced more words in stories, more different words, and more multisyllabic words than students in the control groups did. Language follow-up activities included creative dramatics, creative writing (or dictation), retelling stories with the flannel board, and illustrating scenes from the stories and describing them to the teacher. The following Classroom Scenario is drawn from one of Roe's experiences.

**Classroom
Scenario**

Using Literature Selections to Develop Vocabulary

Dr. Roe (1985), a visiting teacher, was presenting the song "The Old Woman Who Swallowed a Fly" in a first-grade class. After she sang the line "How absurd to swallow a bird," she asked the students, "What does *absurd* mean?" None of them knew.

Dr. Roe told them that *absurd* meant *silly* or *ridiculous*. Then she asked them, "Would it be silly for a woman to swallow a bird?"

The children answered, "Yes," in unison.

"Would it be absurd for me to wear a flowerpot on my head to teach the class?" she then asked.

Again the children answered, "Yes!"

"What are some other absurd things that you can think of?" Dr. Roe finally asked.

Each child gave a reply. If the reply showed understanding of the term, Dr. Roe provided positive reinforcement. If it did not show understanding of the term, her questioning led the child to see why the thing mentioned was not absurd, and the child was given another chance to answer.

Weeks later, when these children encountered the word again in the story *Horton Hatches the Egg,* they remembered its meaning.

Analysis of Scenario

The children encountered a word in the context of a familiar song. The word's meaning was unclear to them, so the teacher supplied both a definition and other examples of the concept behind the term. To ensure that the children really understood the term, the teacher asked them to supply their own examples. This activity helped the children make the word their own through active involvement with it.

Instructional Procedures

Although procedures for vocabulary development vary widely, many of them have produced good results, and teachers should be familiar with a variety of approaches. A number of the programs described here combine several approaches, and good teachers will also use combinations of approaches in their classrooms. Graves and Prenn (1986) point out that "there is no one best method of teaching words . . . various methods have both their costs and their benefits and will be very appropriate and effective in some circumstances and less appropriate and effective in others" (p. 597).

Research on vocabulary instruction indicates that "extensive reading can increase vocabulary knowledge, but direct instruction that engages students in construction of word meaning, using context and prior knowledge, is effective for learning specific vocabulary and for improving comprehension of related materials" (Nelson-Herber, 1986, p. 627). McKeown and colleagues (1985) also offer support for this assessment.

Some research findings indicate that "vocabulary instruction improves comprehension only when both definitions and context are given, and has the largest effect when a number of different activities or examples using the word in context are used" (Stahl, 1986, p. 663). Techniques requiring students to think deeply about a term and its relationships to other terms are most effective. Class discussion seems to make students think more deeply about words as they make connections between their prior knowledge and new information. Multiple presentations of information about a word's meaning and multiple exposures to the word in varying contexts both benefit comprehension. In addition, the more time spent on vocabulary instruction, the better the results. Vocabulary programs that extend over a long period of time give students a chance to encounter the words in a number of contexts and to make use of them in their own language (Stahl, 1986).

When commercial materials are used, word meanings should be related to the students' own experiences through discussion. Then students should use the words in some way to demonstrate their understanding of the meanings. Because multiple experiences with each word are necessary for complete learning, the number of words presented should not be overwhelming. Spaced reviews of the words will enhance retention of the word meanings.

We will now look at a number of carefully researched instructional techniques and the studies related to them. Then we will describe several common methods of vocabulary development.

Using Active Approaches to Learning Vocabulary

Beck and McKeown (1983) described a program of vocabulary instruction that emphasized relating vocabulary to students' preexisting word knowledge and experiences. Students generated their own context for the terms being taught by answering questions about the words (for example, the teacher might say, "Tell about something you might want to *eavesdrop* on" [p. 624]). The program also helped students to further their word knowledge by introducing new words in global semantic categories, such as *people* or *places,* and by requiring the students to work with the relationships among words. The children were asked to differentiate among critical features of words and to generalize from one word to similar ones. They were also asked to complete analogies involving the words and to pantomime words. These activities were in keeping with suggestions 2 and 3 about vocabulary instruction presented in the list on page 138; the students were active participants in the activities described rather than passive observers. Students were given a number of exposures to each word in a variety of contexts. The final aspect of the program was development of rapid responses to words by using timed activities, some of which were gamelike. These activities kept the students actively involved and probably increased their interest as well.

The children involved in Beck and McKeown's program learned the words taught, developed speed and accuracy in making semantic decisions, showed comprehension of stories containing the target words superior to that of a control group, and evidently learned more than the specific words taught, as indicated by the size of their gains on a standardized measure of reading comprehension and vocabulary.

A closely related procedure, developed by Blachowicz (1986), also helps teachers focus on vocabulary instruction. First, teachers activate what the students know about the target words in the reading selection, using either exclusion brainstorming (in which students exclude unrelated words from a list of possible associated words) or knowledge rating (in which students indicate their degree of familiarity with the words). Then the teachers can elicit predictions about "connections between words or between words and the topic and structure of the selection" (p. 644), emphasizing the words' roles in semantic networks. (Word webs or semantic feature analysis, discussed later in this chapter, may be used.) Next, the students are asked to construct tentative definitions of the words. They read the text to test these definitions, refining them as they discover additional information. Finally, the students use the words in other reading and writing tasks to make them their own.

Blachowicz (1985, p. 877) points out that "the harder one works to process stimuli . . . the better one's retention." Blachowicz's approach causes the students to work harder by predicting and constructing definitions rather than merely memorizing the material presented.

Another active way to clarify word meanings by associating situations with them is dramatization of words. This technique is more effective than mere verbal explanations of terms. Under some circumstances, dramatization of words has proved to be more effective than use of context clues, structural analysis, or dictionaries (Duffelmeyer, 1980; Duffelmeyer and Duffelmeyer, 1979).

Davis (1990) has pairs of students construct "concept cards" for new vocabulary terms. On the cards they list definitions, synonyms, and examples for the terms. She has the students supplement their own knowledge by consulting dictionaries and thesauruses. Then she has them discuss the various connotations of the synonyms provided. Following the discussion, the class is divided into teams that compete to supply the most definitions, synonyms, or examples for words from the cards.

Cudd and Roberts (1993/1994) use sentence expansion activities to work on vocabulary. They create sentence stems composed of syntactic structures and vocabulary the children have encountered in classroom reading materials. Then they display the stems on the board and lead a discussion of them. Students supply endings for the sentences and then read the completed sentences. Students write their sentences based on the stems, working with peer-editing partners. Then they illustrate one or two of their sentences. In this way, students become actively involved in using the target vocabulary.

Petrick (1992) suggests the use of manipulatives to explain or demonstrate content area vocabulary. Teachers can use tape measures to show the meanings of certain lengths (*foot, yard,* etc.), use cotton balls and water to demonstrate *absorption,* or use a rubber band to demonstrate the concept of *elasticity.*

Stahl and Kapinus (1991) found a technique called Possible Sentences to be effective in teaching content area vocabulary. In this activity, the teacher chooses six to eight difficult words and four to six familiar words that are important to the selection. The teacher writes these words on the board and may offer a definition of each one. Students are asked to supply possible sentences for these terms that include at least two of the words. This causes them to think about the relationships among the terms. When all words are represented in the possible sentences, the students read the selection. After reading, each possible sentence is discussed and either accepted as true or changed to make it true. This technique requires much active processing of the vocabulary.

Iwicki and her colleagues (1992) found that they could enhance vocabulary learning through an activity called Vocabulary Connections. They put the vocabulary terms and definitions on wall charts, then asked students to relate to each term situations in the literature selection they were reading and situations in previously read books. For example, the word *pandemonium* is used in *Welcome Home, Jelly Bean* (Shyer, 1988). It can later be related to events in *The Black Stallion* (Farley, 1941). This activity can be motivational and can encourage use of higher-level thinking skills.

Primary-grade children can be asked to illustrate new vocabulary words to show their understanding. Then the children's illustrations can be shown to a small group of other class members, who try to identify the word being illustrated in each picture and record it on their papers. Finally, each artist tells which word each of his or her pictures represented. This procedure gets the children very actively involved with words (Baroni, 1987).

Building New Vocabulary from Past Experiences

Word meaning should be taught from an experience base, to prevent students' acquiring a store of words for which they have only superficial understanding. Duffelmeyer (1985) suggests four techniques to link word meaning and experience: use of synonyms and examples, use of positive and negative instances of the concepts, use of examples and definitions, and use of definitions together with sentence completion. His techniques are all teacher directed and involve verbal interaction between the teacher and the students.

Encouraging Independent Word Learning

Instruction that gradually moves the responsibility for determining new word meanings from the teacher to the student helps students become independent learners. Teachers can guide students to use context clues to define words independently by using a four-part procedure. First, students are given categorization tasks. Second, they practice determining meanings from complete contexts. Third, they practice determining meaning in incomplete contexts. Finally, they practice defining new vocabulary by means of context clues (Carr and Wixson, 1986).

Context Clues

In Chapter 3, we discussed the use of *context clues* to help children recognize words that are familiar in speech but not in print. Context clues can also key the meaning of an unfamiliar word by directly defining the word, providing an *appositive,* or comparing or contrasting the word with a known word. For example:

A *democracy* is a government run by the people being governed. (definition)

He made an effort to *alleviate,* or relieve, the child's pain until the doctor arrived. (appositive)

Rather than encountering hostile natives, as they had expected, many settlers found the natives to be *amicable.* (contrast)

Context can also offer clues in sentences other than the one in which the new word appears, so children should be encouraged to read surrounding sentences for clues to meaning. Sometimes an entire paragraph embodies the explanation of a term, as in the following example:

I've told you before that the flu is contagious! When Johnny had the flu, Beatrice played with him one afternoon, and soon Beatrice came down with it. Joey caught it from her, and now you tell me you have been to Joey's house. I hope you don't come down with the flu and have to miss the party on Saturday.

When introducing new words in context, teachers should use sentences that students can relate to their own experiences and that have only one unfamiliar word each. It is best not to use the new word at the very beginning of the sentence, since the children will not have had any of the facilitating context before they encounter it (Duffelmeyer, 1982).

Teachers can use a "think-aloud" strategy to help students see how to use context clues. Here is a sample activity that makes use of this strategy.

Model Activities

Intermediate-Level Lesson on Context Clues

Write one of the sentences mentioned previously on the board or display it using a transparency. Say: "Rather than encountering hostile natives, as they had expected, many settlers found the natives to be amicable. I wonder what *amicable* means? Let's see; the sentence says *'Rather than encountering hostile natives.'* That means the natives weren't hostile. *Hostile* means *unfriendly;* so maybe *amicable* means *friendly.*"

After several example "think-aloud" activities in which the teacher models the use of context clues, the teacher can ask student volunteers to "think aloud" the context clues to specific words. Students may work in pairs on a context clues worksheet and verbalize their context usage strategies to each other. Finally, the students should work alone to determine meanings from context clues.

Blachowicz (1993) suggests a procedure called *C(2)QU* to teach context use. The steps are as follows:

C1: *Context.*   A broad, meaningful context is provided for an unfamiliar word. Students hypothesize about the meaning.

C2: *Context.*   More explicit context is provided. Students orally analyze their original hypotheses.

Q: *Question.*   Students are asked a question involving the meaning of the word. They discuss the meaning.

U: *Use.*   Students are asked to use the word appropriately in oral or written sentences.

This procedure requires active participation by students, which should result in more effective learning.

Context clues are available in both text and illustrations in many trade books, such as *The Amazing Bone* by William Steig (Farrar, Straus & Giroux, 1976). *A Gaggle of Geese,* by Eve Merriam (Knopf, 1960), puts collective terminology for groups into an interesting context (Howell, 1987). Teaching use of context clues in these meaningful settings encourages students to use such clues in their independent reading.

Some researchers have found that use of closed-caption television programs to provide readers with both auditory and visual context was effective with below-average readers and bilingual students (Koskinen et al., 1993; Neuman and Koskinen, 1992). They found that such programs provided readers with print to read in a motivational format. Words could be discussed while the students were viewing video images. Later they could be read from handouts prepared with sentences drawn from the captioned video and finally from magazines and books on the same topic. They could also be used in written retellings of the viewed episode. Although the match between the audio and the captions seen was not exact, the captions were presented at a rapid rate for poor readers (about 120 words per minute), and the captions were in all capital letters, the results teachers obtained were impressive. Videotaping the programs allows repetition of the reading for different purposes and use of small segments (only a few minutes each) of video in a lesson. However, copyright laws must be studied to ensure that use is in compliance with these laws.

Edwards and Dermott (1989) select difficult words from material about to be assigned, take a quotation using each word in good context from the material, and provide written comments to the students to help them use appropriate context clues or other strategies (primarily structural analysis or dictionary use). The students try to use the clues available to decide on the meanings of the words before reading. Class discussion helps the students to think through the strategy use.

Gipe (1980) expanded a context method (in which students read new words in meaningful contexts) to include having children apply the words based on their own experiences and then studied the effectiveness of this method, compared to three other methods. The other methods were an association method (in which an unknown word is paired with a familiar synonym), a category method (in which students place words in categories), and a dictionary method (in which students look up the word, write a definition, and use the word in a sentence). The expanded context method was found to be the most effective of the four. The application of the new words may have been the most important aspect of the context method that Gipe used. After the students derived the meaning of the

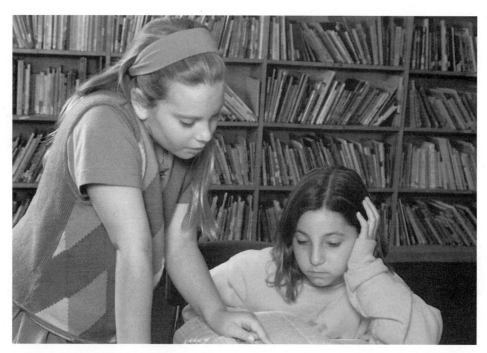

Students can consult dictionaries for meanings of words for which the context gives inadequate information. (© *Mary Kate Denny/Photo Edit*)

word from a variety of contexts, including a definition context, they *applied* the word to their personal experiences in a written response. Thus, the instruction follows the first desirable instructional technique for vocabulary listed earlier in this chapter: assisting students in integrating the new words with their background knowledge.

Teachers need to help students learn *why* and *when* to use context clues (Blachowicz and Zabroske, 1990). Context clues are useful when the context is explicit about word meaning, but they are less useful when the meaning is left unclear. If the clues are too vague, they may actually be misleading (Schwartz, 1988; Schatz and Baldwin, 1986). Furthermore, if the word is not important to understanding the passage, the explicitness of the context is not important. Teachers should model their decision-making processes about the importance of determining the meaning of the word, the usefulness of the context, and the kinds of clues available there through think-alouds. Students need to realize that the meanings they attribute to the words must pass the test inherent in the question "Does this make sense here?" They also need to realize that structural analysis clues may help them decide whether or not a meaning suggested by the context is reasonable.

It is estimated that average ten- to fourteen-year-old students could acquire from 750 to 8,250 new words each year through incidental, rather than directed, contextual learning (Schwartz, 1988; Herman et al., 1987; Nagy, Herman, and Anderson, 1985; Wysocki and Jenkins, 1987). Helping students learn to use context more efficiently should therefore greatly enhance their vocabulary learning.

Activities

Using a selection the students are about to read, take an unfamiliar word, put it into a title, and construct several sentences that offer clues to its meaning. Show the title on the overhead projector; then show one sentence at a time, letting the students guess the meaning of the word at each step (Kaplan and Tuchman, 1980).

Combining contextual and definitional approaches to vocabulary instruction is more effective than using a contextual approach alone. In fact, "it would be hard to justify a contextual approach in which the teacher did not finally provide an adequate definition of the word or help the class arrive at one" (Nagy, 1988, p. 8). In addition, teachers can have students apply context clues fruitfully in conjunction with structure clues, which we will discuss next.

Structural Analysis

Structural analysis, discussed in Chapter 3 as a word recognition skill, can also be used as an aid in discovering meanings of unknown words. Knowing meanings of common affixes and combining them with meanings of familiar root words can help students determine the meanings of many new words. For example, if a child knows the meaning of *joy* and knows that the suffix *-ous* means *full of,* he or she can conclude that the word *joyous* means *full of joy.* Students can often determine meanings of compound words by relating the meanings of the component parts to each other (*watchdog* means a *dog* that *watches*). After some practice, they can be led to see that the component parts of a compound word do not always have the same relationships to each other (*bookcase* means a *case* for *books*).

Children begin to learn about word structure very early. First, they deal with words in their simplest, most basic forms—as *morphemes,* the smallest units of meaning in a language. (The word *cat* is one morpheme.) Then they gradually learn to combine morphemes. If an *s* is added to form the plural, *cats,* the final *s* is also a morpheme, because it changes the word's meaning. There are two classes of morphemes, distinguished by function: *free* morphemes, which have independent meanings and can be used by themselves (*cat, man, son*), and *bound* morphemes, which must be combined with another morpheme to have meaning. Affixes and inflectional endings are bound morphemes; the *-er* in *singer* is an example.

Practice activities such as the following can help children see how prefixes and suffixes change meanings of words. *Un-* is the most common prefix appearing in the *Word Frequency Book* (Carroll, Davies, and Richman, 1971; White, Sowell, and Yanagihara, 1989).

**Model
Activities**

Prefix *un-*

Have the students read the book *Fortunately* by Remy Charlip (New York: Scholastic, 1964). Discuss with them the meanings of *fortunately* and *unfortunately,* using the situations from the book to make the discussion concrete and clear. When they have stated that *unfortunately* means *not fortunately* or *the opposite of fortunately,* have them decide what part of the word means *not.* After they identify the *un-* as the part that means *not,* have them name other words they know that begin with *un-*. Discuss the meanings of these words, pointing out that the prefix means *not* or *the opposite of* in each case in which the remainder of the word forms a root word, but not if the beginning two letters are not a prefix attached to a root word. Ask them to look in their reading assignments for words starting with *un-* in which *un-* is a prefix added to a root word. Have them use their knowledge of the meaning of *un-* to determine the meanings of each of these words.

White, Sowell, and Yanagihara (1989) caution teachers that prefixes may have more than one meaning. *Un-, re-, in-,* and *dis-,* the four most frequently used prefixes, have at least two meanings each. *Un-* and *dis-* may each mean either *not* or *do the opposite. In-* may mean either *not,* or *in,* or *into. Re-* may mean either *again* or *back.* Both the word parts and the context of the word should be considered in determining meanings of prefixed words.

The following Classroom Scenario shows another application of structural analysis in the classroom.

**Classroom
Scenario**

Use of Structural Analysis Skills

A middle school science textbook presented two theories of the solar system: a geocentric theory and a heliocentric theory. Two diagrams were provided to help the students visualize the two theories, but the diagrams were not labeled. Mrs. Brown, the teacher, asked the students, "Which diagram is related to each theory?"

Matt's hand quickly went up, and he accurately identified the two diagrams.

"How did you decide which was which?" asked Mrs. Brown.

"You told us that *geo-* means *earth. Centric* looks like it comes from *center.* This diagram has the earth in the center. So I decided it was geocentric. That would mean the other one was heliocentric. Since the sun is in the center in it, I guess *helio-* means *sun.*"

Analysis of Scenario

Mrs. Brown had taught an important science word part the first time it occurred in her class. She had encouraged her students to use their knowledge of word parts to figure out unfamiliar words. Matt followed her suggestions and managed to make decisions about key vocabulary based on his knowledge of word parts.

The students can study word cards that contain words derived from Latin or Greek word parts, such as *prescription* and *scripture*. They can be encouraged to think of other examples and asked to use the derived words in sentence context.

See the Focus on Strategies on Compound Words for an activity that can offer practice in determining meanings of compound words.

**Focus on
Strategies**

Compound Words

Mr. Clay based his lesson on the book *The Seal Mother* by Mordicai Gerstein (Dial, 1986). He introduced the story by saying that it was an old Scottish folktale. He wrote the word *folktale* on the board. Then he asked, "What can you tell me about this word?"

Bobby said, "It is made up of two words: *folk* and *tale.* That makes it a compound word."

"Good, Bobby," Mr. Clay responded. "What does that make you believe this word means?"

"A tale is a story," LaTonya replied.

"That's right," said Mr. Clay. "Can anyone add anything else to what we know about the word's meaning? What does *folk* mean?"

Carl answered tentatively, "A kind of music?"

"There is folk music, just as there are folktales, but we still need a meaning for the word *folk*," Mr. Clay responded.

After he got only shrugs, he explained, "A folktale is a tale, or story, told by the folk, or common people, of a country. Folktales were passed down orally from older people to younger ones over the years. See how both parts of the compound word give something to the meaning?

"Listen as I read this story to you. When I finish, we will try to retell the story by listing the main events."

The children listened intently. When he finished the story, Mr. Clay asked them to list the events in the story in order. As they suggested events, he wrote each one on the board. When he had listed all of the events they could remember, they discussed how to put some of the events in the proper order. Mr. Clay erased and moved the sentences around until the children were satisfied.

Then Mr. Clay asked the children, "Did you use any compound words to retell the story?"

Hands shot up all over the room. Mr. Clay called on them one by one, and they pointed out *fisherman, sealskin, without, oilcloth, inside, rayfish, everywhere, grandfather,* and *whenever.* The children who mentioned the words were allowed to go to the board and circle them, identify the two words that made up each compound, and try to define each compound word, using the meanings of the two component words. Other students helped in determining the definitions, and sometimes the dictionary was consulted.

Finally, the children were asked to copy the compound words from the board into their vocabulary study notebooks. "I'm putting three copies of *The Seal Mother* in the reading center for the rest of this week," Mr. Clay said. "When you have time, take your vocabulary notebook to the center and read the book to yourself or with a partner. Each time you find one of our compound words, put a checkmark by the word in your notebook. When you find a compound word that we didn't use in our retelling, copy it into your notebook, and write a definition for it, using the meanings of the two words and the context of the sentence in which you found it. We'll discuss the other words that you found on Friday."

On Friday, the children had found a number of words in the book that they hadn't used in their retelling, including *moonlit, moonlight, everything, wide-eyed, tiptoed, another,* and *into.* A discussion of the words and their meanings followed. Mr. Clay asked how use of some of these words added to the children's understanding of the story.

"*Moonlit* and *moonlight* give you a picture in your mind of the scene," Jared said.

"*Wide-eyed* lets us know how his parents' talk made the boy feel," Marissa added.

"*Tiptoed* showed us how he walked quietly," Tyrone said.

"Watch for compound words in other books that you read, and use the meanings of the two words in each compound to help you with meanings that you don't already know," Mr. Clay told them as he ended the lesson.

Categorization

Categorization is grouping together things or ideas that have common features. Classifying words into categories can be a good way to learn more about word meanings. Young children can begin learning how to place things into categories by grouping concrete objects according to their traits. Once the children have developed some sight vocabulary, it is a relatively small step for them to begin categorizing the words they see in print according to their meanings. Very early in their instruction, children will be able to look at the following list and classify the words into such teacher-supplied categories as "people," "things to play with," "things to eat," and "things to do."

Word List

doll	bicycle	ball	run	girl
candy	cookie	boy	baby	sit
toy	dig	sing	mother	banana

The children may discover that they want to put a word in more than one category. This desire will provide an opportunity for discussion about how a word may fit in two or more places for different reasons. The children should give reasons for all of their placements.

After the children become adept at classifying words into categories supplied by the teacher, they are ready for the more difficult task of generating the categories needed for classifying the words presented. The teacher may give them a list of words such as the following and ask them to place the words in groups of things that are alike and to name the trait the items have in common.

Word List

horse	cow	goose	stallion	foal
gosling	mare	filly	chick	calf
colt	gander	bull	hen	rooster

Children may offer several categories for these words: various families of animals; four-legged and two-legged animals; feathered and furred animals; winged and wingless animals; or male animals, female animals, or animals that might be either sex. They may also come up with a classification that the teacher has not considered. As long as the classification system makes sense and the animals are correctly classified according to the stated system, it should be considered correct. Teachers should encourage students to discover various possibilities for classifications.

Discussion of the different classification systems may help to extend the children's concepts about some of the animals on the list, and it may help some children develop concepts related to some of the animals for the first time. The classification system allows them to relate the new knowledge about some of the animals to the knowledge they already have about these animals or others. The usefulness of categorization activities is supported by research indicating that presenting words in semantically related clusters can lead to improvement in students' vocabulary knowledge and reading comprehension (Marzano, 1984).

A classification game such as the one in the next Model Activity provides an interesting way to work on categorization skills.

**Model
Activities**

Classification Game

Divide the children into groups of three or four, and make category sheets like the one shown here for each group. When you give a signal, the children start writing as many words as they can think of that fit in each category; when you signal that time is up, a child from each group reads the group's words to the class. Have the children compare their lists and discuss why they placed particular words in particular categories.

Appropriate categories other than the ones used below are meats, fruits, and vegetables; mammals, reptiles, and insects; or liquids, solids, and gases.

Cities	States	Countries

The ability to classify is a basic skill that applies to many areas of learning. Many of the other activities described in this chapter, including those for analogies, semantic maps, and semantic feature analysis, depend on categorization.

Analogies and Word Lines

Analogies compare two relationships and thereby provide a basis for building word knowledge. Educators may teach analogies by displaying examples of categories, relationships, and analogies; asking guiding questions about the examples; allowing students to discuss the questions; and applying the ideas that emerge (Bellows, 1980).

Students may need help in grouping items into categories and understanding relationships among items. For example, the teacher might write *nickel, dime,* and *quarter* on the board and ask, "How are these things related? What name could you give the entire group of items?" (Answer: *money.*) Teachers can use pictures instead of words in the primary grades; in either case, they can ask students to apply the skill by naming other things that would fit in the category (*penny* and *dollar*). Or the teacher could write *painter* and *brush* and ask, "What is the relationship between the two items?" (Answer: A *painter* works with a *brush.*) Teachers should remember to simplify their language for discussions with young children and to have students give other examples of the relationship (*dentist* and *drill*). After working through many examples such as these, the students should be ready for examples of simple analogies, such as "Light is to dark as day is to night," "Glove is to hand as sock is to foot," and "Round is to ball as square is to block." Students can discuss how analogies work: "How are the first two things related? How are the second two things related? How are these relationships alike?" They can then complete incomplete analogies, such as "Teacher is to classroom as pilot is to _____." Younger children should do this orally; older ones can understand the standard shorthand form of *come:go::live:die* if they are taught to read the colon (:) as *is to* and (::) as *as* (Bellows, 1980).

HuffBenkoski and Greenwood (1995) taught second graders how to use analogies. These authors modeled their reasoning processes for the students through think-alouds as they analyzed analogies. They also had students explain their reasoning processes. The children came up with a definition for *analogies*. Attention then was given to classification activities—choosing words that did or did not belong with a given set of words related to a theme study. Next, the children were asked to state the relationship between two words. Following that, students completed analogies that had one part missing. Finally, students produced their own analogies in groups and individually.

Teachers may use word lines to show the relationships among words, just as they use number lines for numbers. They can arrange related words on a graduated line that emphasizes their relationships. For young children, they can use pictures and words to match or ask them to locate or produce appropriate pictures. Upper-grade students can be asked to arrange a specified list of words on a word line themselves. Word lines can concretely show antonym, synonym, and degree analogies, as in this example:

enormous	large	medium	small	tiny

Analogies that students could develop include "enormous is to large as small is to tiny" (synonym); "enormous is to tiny as large is to small" (antonym); and "large is to medium as medium is to small" (degree). The teacher can have the children make their own word lines and analogies (Macey, 1981).

Dwyer (1988) suggests mapping analogies, as shown in Example 4.1. This map provides the relationship involved, a complete example, two incomplete examples for the students to complete, and one space for an example that comes entirely from the student.

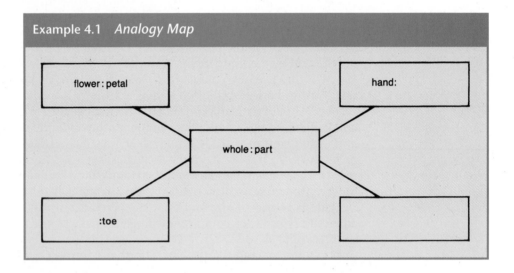

Example 4.1 *Analogy Map*

Semantic Maps and Word Webs

Semantic maps can be used to teach related concepts (Johnson and Pearson, 1984; Johnson, Pittelman, and Heimlich, 1986). "Semantic maps are diagrams that help students see how words are related to one another. . . . Students learn the meanings and uses of new words, see old words in a new light, and see relationships among words" (Heimlich and Pittelman, 1986).

To construct a semantic map with a class, the teacher writes on the board or a chart a word that represents a concept that is central to the topic under consideration. The teacher asks the students to name words related to this concept. The students' words are listed on the board or chart grouped in broad categories, and the students name the categories. They may also suggest additional categories. A discussion of the central concept, the listed words, the categories, and the interrelationships among the words follows.

The discussion step appears to be the key to the effectiveness of this method, because it allows the students to be actively involved in the learning. After the class has discussed the semantic map, the teacher can give an incomplete semantic map to the children and ask them to fill in the words from the map on the board or chart and add any categories or words that they wish. The children can work on their maps as they do the assigned reading related to the central concept. Further discussion can follow the reading, and more categories and words can be added to the maps. The final discussion and mapping allow the children to recall and graphically organize the information they gained from the reading (Johnson, Pittelman, and Heimlich, 1986; Stahl and Vancil, 1986). Example 4.2 shows a semantic map constructed by one class.

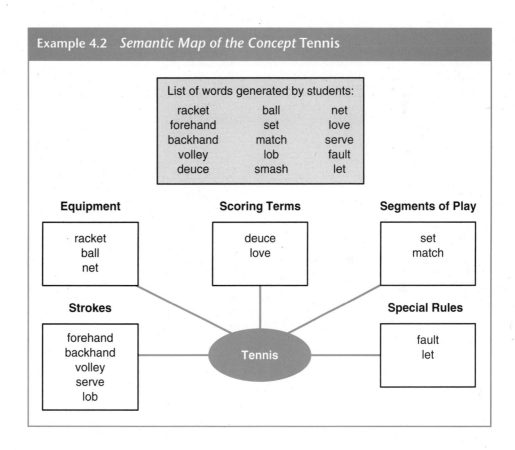

Example 4.2 *Semantic Map of the Concept* Tennis

List of words generated by students:

racket	ball	net
forehand	set	love
backhand	match	serve
volley	lob	fault
deuce	smash	let

Equipment
racket
ball
net

Scoring Terms
deuce
love

Segments of Play
set
match

Strokes
forehand
backhand
volley
serve
lob

Special Rules
fault
let

Tennis

Because a semantic map shows both familiar and new words under labeled categories, the process of constructing one helps students make connections between known and new concepts (Johnson, Pittelman, and Heimlich, 1986). The graphic display makes relationships among terms easier to see. Discussion of the map allows the teacher to assess the children's background knowledge, clarify concepts, and correct misunderstandings (Stahl and Vancil, 1986).

Schwartz and Raphael (1985) used a modified approach to semantic mapping to help students develop a concept of *definition*. The students learned what types of information are needed for a definition and learned how to use context clues and background knowledge to help them better understand words. Word maps are really graphic representations of definitions. The word maps Schwartz and Raphael used contained information about the general class to which the concept belonged, answering the question "What is it?"; the properties of the concept, answering the question "What is it like?"; and examples of the concept (see Example 4.3).

Example 4.3 *Word Map for Definition*

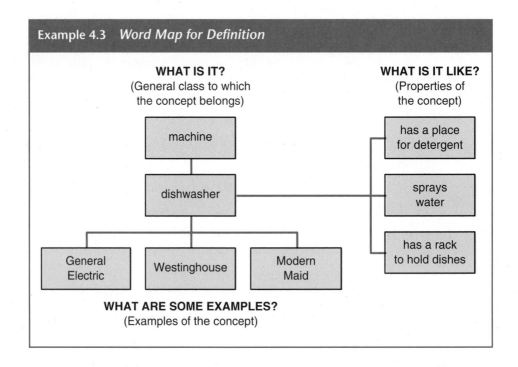

With the basic information contained in such a map, students have enough information to construct definitions. This procedure for understanding the concept of definition is effective from the fourth-grade level through college. The approach used by Schwartz and Raphael started with strong teacher involvement, but control was gradually transferred to the children. Children were led to search the context of a sentence in which the word occurred for the elements of definition needed to map a word. Eventually the teachers provided only partial context for the word, leading the children to go to outside sources, such as dictionaries, for information to complete the maps. Finally, teachers asked the students to write definitions, including all the features previously mapped, without actually mapping the word on paper. This activity helps bring meanings of unknown terms into focus through analogies and examples (Smith, 1990).

Word webs are another way to represent the relationships among words graphically. Students construct these diagrams by connecting related words with lines. The words used for the web may be taken from material students have read in class.

Semantic Feature Analysis

Semantic feature analysis is a technique that can help children understand the uniqueness of a word as well as its relationships to other words (Johnson and Pearson, 1984). To perform such an analysis, the teacher lists in a column on the board or a chart some known words with common properties. Then the children generate a list of features possessed by the various items in the list. A feature only needs to apply to one item to be listed. The teacher writes these features in a row across the top of the board or chart, and the students fill in the cells of the resulting matrix with pluses to indicate the presence of the feature and minuses to indicate its absence.

Example 4.4 shows a partial matrix developed by children for various buildings. "Walls" and "doors" were other features the children suggested for the matrix; they were omitted from the example only for space considerations. Both of these features received a plus for each building, emphasizing the similarities of the terms *jail, garage, museum,* and *church.*

Example 4.4   *Semantic Feature Analysis Chart*

	barred windows	exhibits	steeple	cross	cars	lift-up doors	guards	oil stains
jail	+	–	–	–	–	–	+	–
garage	?	–	–	–	+	+	–	+
museum	?	+	–	–	?	–	+	–
church	–	–	+	+	–	–	–	–

The children discussed the terms as they filled in the matrix. In the places where the question marks occur, the children said, "Sometimes it may have that, but not always. It doesn't have to have it." The group discussion brought out much information about each building listed and served to expand the children's existing schemata.

Students can continue to expand such a matrix after initially filling it out by adding words that share some of the listed features. For example, the children added *grocery store* to the list of buildings in Example 4.4 because it shared the walls and doors, and they added other features showing the differentiation, such as *food, clerks,* and *shopping carts.*

Johnson and Pearson (1984) suggest that after experience with these matrices, children may begin to realize that some words have different degrees of the same feature. At this time, the teacher may want to try using a numerical system of coding, using 0 for *none,* 1 for *some,* 2 for *much,* and 3 for *all.* Under the feature "fear," for example, *scared* might be coded with a 1, whereas *terrified* might be coded with a 3.

Anders and Bos (1986) suggest using semantic feature analysis with vocabulary needed for content area reading assignments. They believe that, because the analysis activates the students' prior knowledge through discussion and relates prior knowledge to new knowledge, students will have increased interest in the reading and therefore will learn more. This technique can be used before, during, and after the reading. A chart can be started in the background-building portion of the lesson, added to or modified by the students as they read the material, and refined further during the follow-up discussion of the material.

Metaphoric or figurative language (nonliteral language) can also be taught through a technique similar to semantic feature analysis (Thompson, 1986). A comparison chart can clarify differences and similarities between concepts that are not literally members of the same category. Finding similarities between essentially dissimilar things helps children understand the comparisons used in metaphoric language. For example, both *eyes* and *stars* might have the characteristic "shining" or "bright," leading to the source of the intended comparison in the expression "her eyes were like stars." (A detailed section on figurative language appears later in this chapter.)

Dictionary Use

The dictionary can be an excellent source for discovering meanings of unfamiliar words, particularly for determining the appropriate meanings of words that have multiple definitions or specific, technical definitions. In some instances, children may be familiar with several common meanings of a word, but not with a word's specialized meaning found in a content area textbook. For example, a child may understand a reference to a *base* in a baseball game but not a discussion of a military *base* (social studies material), a *base* that turns litmus paper blue (science material), or *base* motives of a character (literature). Words that have the greatest number of different meanings, such as *run* or *bank,* are frequently very common.

Dictionaries are not always used properly in schools, however. Teachers should instruct children to consider the context surrounding a word, read the different dictionary definitions, and choose the definition that makes the most sense in the context. Without such instruction, children have a strong tendency to read only the first dictionary definition and to try to force it into the context. The teacher should model the choice of the correct definition for the students so that they can see what the task is. Students will then need to practice the task under teacher supervision.

The following Model Activities, pages 159 and 160, are good to use for practice immediately following instruction in dictionary use and for later independent practice.

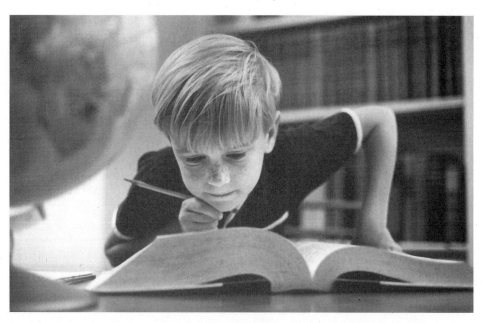

In order to use the dictionary properly for vocabulary development, students must be instructed to consider a word's context, to read the different definitions, and to choose a definition for the word in its specific context. (© *Ed Lettau/Photo Researchers*)

Students can also use dictionaries to study *etymology*, the origin and history of words. Dictionaries often give the origin of a word in brackets after the phonetic respelling (although not all dictionaries do this in the same way), and archaic or obsolete definitions are frequently given and labeled so that students can see how words have changed.

Model Activities

Appropriate Dictionary Definitions

Write the following sentences on the board. Ask the children to find the dictionary definition of *sharp* that fits each sentence. You may ask them to jot each definition down and have a whole-class or small-group discussion about each one after all meanings have been located, or you may wish to discuss each meaning as it is located. The students may read other definitions for *sharp* in the dictionary and generate sentences for these as well.

1. Katherine's knife was very sharp.

2. There is a sharp curve in the road up ahead.

3. Sam is a sharp businessman. That's why he has been so successful.

4. I hope that, when I am seventy, my mind is as sharp as my grandmother's is.

5. We are leaving at two o'clock sharp.

Model Activities

Multiple Meanings of Words

Give the students a list of sentences, drawn from their textbooks, that contain words with specialized meanings for that subject. Have them use the dictionary or the textbook's glossary to discover the specialized meanings that fit the context of the sentences. After the students have completed the task independently, go over the sentences with them and discuss reasons for right and wrong responses.

The material you give to the students may look something like this:

Directions: Some words mean different things in your textbooks from what they mean in everyday conversation. In each of the following sentences, find the special meanings for the words and write these meanings on the lines provided.

1. Frederick Smith has decided to *run* for mayor.
   _____

2. The park was near the *mouth* of the Little Bear River. _____
   _____

3. The management of the company was unable to avert a *strike.* _____
   _____

4. That song is hard to sing because of the high *pitch* of several notes. _____

5. That number is written in *base* two. _____
   _____

Teaching word meanings through dictionary use has been widely criticized, but it is nevertheless a useful technique for vocabulary development if it is applied properly. Research (e.g., Graves and Prenn, 1986) supports this view. Combining a definitional approach to vocabulary instruction with a contextual approach is more effective than using a definitional approach in isolation. Sentences that illustrate meanings and uses of the defined words can help immensely (Nagy, 1988).

Chapter 9 presents information about the mechanics of dictionary use. Chapter 3 discusses using the dictionary for word recognition.

Word Origins and Histories

As mentioned earlier, the study of word origins and histories is called *etymology.* Children in the intermediate grades will enjoy learning about the kinds of changes that have taken place in the English language by studying words and definitions that appear in very old dictionaries and by studying differences between American English and British English. Following is an additional useful source: Funk, Wilfred. *Word Origins & Their Romantic Stories.* Avenal, New Jersey: Outlet Book Company, 1992.

Teachers need to help children understand the different ways words can be formed. *Portmanteau* words are formed by merging the sounds and meanings of two different words (for example, *smog,* from *smoke* and *fog*). *Acronyms* are words formed from the initial letters of a name or by combining initial letters or parts from a series of words (for example, *radar,* from *r*adio *d*etecting *a*nd *r*anging). Some words are just shortened forms of other words (for example, *phone,* from *telephone; flu,* from *influenza;* and *piano,* from *pianoforte*). Both shortened forms and acronyms are ways our language has become more compact (Richler, 1996). Some words are borrowed from other languages (for example, *lasso,* from the Spanish *lazo*). The teacher can discuss the origins of such terms when they occur in students' reading materials. In addition, students should try to think of other words that have been formed in a similar manner. The teacher may also wish to contribute other examples from familiar sources.

Figurative Language

Figurative language, or nonliteral language, can be a barrier to understanding written selections. Children tend to interpret literally many expressions that have meanings different from the sums of the meanings of the individual words. For example, the expression "the teeth of the wind" does not mean that the wind actually has teeth, nor does "a blanket of fog" mean a conventional blanket. Context clues indicate the meanings of such phrases in the same ways that they cue the meanings of individual words.

Adults often assume children have had exposure to expressions that in fact are unfamiliar to them. Children need substantial help in order to comprehend figurative language. Even basal readers present many of these expressions. Some common figures of speech that cause trouble are

1. *Simile*—a comparison using *like* or *as*

2. *Metaphor*—a direct comparison without the words *like* or *as*

3. *Personification*—giving the attributes of a person to an inanimate object or abstract idea

4. *Hyperbole*—an extreme exaggeration

5. *Euphemism*—substitution of a less offensive term for an unpleasant term or expression

Teaching children to recognize and understand similes is usually not too difficult, because the cue words *like* and *as* help to show the presence of a comparison. Metaphors, however, may cause more serious problems. A metaphor is a comparison between two unlike things that share an attribute (Readence, Baldwin, and Head, 1986). Sometimes children do not realize that the language in metaphors is figurative; sometimes they do not have sufficient background knowledge about one or both of the things being compared; and sometimes they simply have not learned a process for interpreting metaphors.

The two things compared in a metaphor may seem to be incompatible, but readers must think of past experiences with each, searching for a match in attributes that could be the basis of comparison. Visual aids can be helpful in this process. Thompson (1986) suggests a comparison chart like the following.

Comparison Chart

Man	*Mouse*
—	small
—	squeaks
√	alive
—	four legs
√+	timid

—	indicates dissimilarity.
√	indicates similarity.
√+	indicates *important* similarity.

The teacher can "think aloud" about the operation of metaphors and their purposes, asking students questions related to the process being demonstrated. Group discussion of the comparison chart helps to activate students' prior knowledge about the items being compared, and the chart helps make similarities more obvious.

Readence, Baldwin, Rickelman, and Miller (1986) found specific word knowledge to be an important factor in interpreting metaphors. The traditional practice offered in many commercial materials may not be helpful to students in interpreting other metaphors not covered in the material. Readence, Baldwin, and Head (1986, 1987) suggest the following instructional sequence for teaching metaphorical interpretation:

1. The teacher can display a metaphor, such as "Her eyes were stars," together with the more explicit simile, "Her eyes were as bright as stars," and explain that metaphors have missing words that link the things being compared (such as *bright* does). Other sentence pairs can also be shown and explained.

2. Then the students can be asked to find the missing word in a new metaphor, such as "He is a mouse around his boss." They can offer guesses, explaining their reasons aloud.

3. The teacher can explain that people have lists of words related to different topics stored in their minds. Examples can be modeled by the teacher and then produced by the students. At this point, the students can try to select the attribute related to the new metaphor. If there are two incorrect guesses, the attribute *timid* can be supplied and the reason for this choice given. This process can then be repeated with another metaphor.

4. As more metaphors are presented, the teacher can do less modeling, turning over more and more control of the process to the students.

After explaining each type of figurative language, modeling its interpretation, and having students interpret it under supervision, the teacher may provide independent practice activities such as the following ones. Ideally, the teacher should take examples of figurative expressions from literature the children are currently reading and use these expressions in constructing practice activities.

Activities

1. Show students pictures of possible meanings for figurative expressions found in their reading materials, and ask them to accept or reject the accuracy of each picture. Have them look carefully at the context in which the expression was found before answering. (For example, if you illustrate the sentence "She worked like a horse" with a woman pulling a plow, children should reject the picture's accuracy.)

2. Give each child a copy of a poem that is filled with figures of speech, and have the class compete to see who can "dig up" all the figures of speech first. You may require students to label all figures of speech properly as to type and to explain them.

Teachers can also use an activity like the Model Activity below to illustrate figures of speech.

**Model
Activities**

Figures of Speech

Display the following cartoon on a transparency:

DENNIS THE MENACE® used by permission of Hank Ketcham and © by Field Enterprises, Inc.

Lead a discussion about the cartoon using the following questions as a guide.

1. What does "been through the mill" really mean, as Dennis's mother used it?

2. What does Dennis think it means?

3. How is the woman likely to react to Dennis's question?

4. How does Dennis's mother probably feel about the question?

5. Can misunderstanding figurative language cause trouble at times? Why do you say so?

Have the children suggest other figurative expressions that could produce misunderstandings. Then, as a follow-up activity, let them draw funny scenes in which the misunderstandings occur.

Also have the children look for other examples in newspaper comics. Ask them to cut out the examples and bring them to school for discussion.

Student-Centered Vocabulary Learning Techniques

Some vocabulary learning techniques focus on students and their individual needs and interests. Explanations of several of these techniques follow.

Vocabulary Self-Collection Strategy. Haggard (1986) suggests the following approach for general vocabulary development:

1. Ask each child to bring to class a word that the entire class should learn. (The teacher brings one, too.) Each child should determine the meaning of his or her word from its context, rather than looking it up in the dictionary.

2. Write the words on the board. Let each participant identify his or her word and tell where it was found, the context-derived meaning, and why the class should learn the word. The class should then discuss the meaning of the word, in order to clarify and extend it and to construct a definition on which the class agrees. The result may be checked against a dictionary definition, if desired.

3. Narrow the list down to a manageable number, and have the students record the final list of words and definitions in their vocabulary journals. Some students may want to put eliminated words on their personal lists.

4. Make study assignments for the words.

5. Test the students on the words at the end of the week.

Word Banks or Vocabulary Notebooks. Students can form their own word banks by writing on index cards words they have learned, their definitions, and sentences showing the words in meaningful contexts. They may also want to illustrate the words or include personal associations or reactions to the words. Students can carry their word banks around and practice the words in spare moments, such as while waiting for the bus or the dentist. In the classroom, the word banks can be used in word games and in classification and other instructional activities.

Vocabulary notebooks are useful for recording new words found in general reading or words heard in conversations or on radio or television. New words may be alphabetized in the notebooks and defined, illustrated, and processed in much the same way as word bank words.

Both word banks and vocabulary notebooks can help children maintain a record of their increasing vocabularies. Generally, word banks are used in primary grades and notebooks in intermediate grades and above, but there are no set limits for either technique.

Word Play

Word play is an enjoyable way to learn more about words. It can provide multiple exposures to words in different contexts that are important to complete word learning. Gale (1982, p. 220) states, "Children who play with words show a stronger grasp of meaning than those who do not. To create or comprehend a pun, one needs to be aware of the multiple meanings of a word."

The following activities present some other ways that teachers can engage children in word play.

Activities

1. Have students write words in ways that express their meanings; for example, they may write *backward* as *drawkcab,* or *up* slanting upward and *down* slanting downward.

2. Ask them silly questions containing new words. Example: "Would you have a terrarium for dinner? Why or why not?"

3. Discuss what puns are and give some examples. Then ask children to make up or find puns to bring to class. Let them explain the play on words to classmates who do not understand it. Example: "What is black and white and read all over?" Answer: A newspaper (word play on the homonyms *red* and *read*).

4. Use Hink Pinks, Hinky Pinkies, and Hinkety Pinketies—rhyming definitions for terms with one, two, and three syllables, respectively. Give a definition, tell whether it is a Hink Pink, Hinky Pinky, or Hinkety Pinkety, and let the children guess the expression. Then let the children make up their own terms. Several examples follow.

   Hink Pink: Unhappy father—Sad dad

   Hinky Pinky: Late group of celebrators—Tardy party

   Hinkety Pinkety: Yearly handbook—Annual manual

5. Give the students a list of clues ("means the same as . . . ," "is the opposite of . . . ," and so forth) to words in a reading selection, along with page numbers. Tell them to go on a scavenger hunt for the words and write the words beside the appropriate clues (Criscuolo, 1980).

6. Have students use what Ruddiman (1993) calls the "Vocab Game" to develop students' word knowledge. For this game, have each student bring in a word from real-life reading each week. Have the students try to stump you with their words, while other students try to figure out their classmates' words. In the process, affixes and roots are located, dictionary definitions checked, the contexts in which the words were found shared, synonyms and antonyms discussed, and analogies presented. The class can earn points by stumping you or by figuring out another student's word. Have a recorder keep a record of the information about the words, which you word process and duplicate for the class. Use cloze-type tests (teacher or student constructed) to check the learning of the vocabulary.

7. Students might also enjoy crossword puzzles or hidden-word puzzles that highlight new words in their textbooks or other instructional materials.

Riddles are a very effective form of word play. To use riddles, children must interact verbally with others; to create riddles, they have to organize information and decide on significant details. Riddles can help children move from the literal to the interpretive level of understanding (Gale, 1982). Tyson and Mountain (1982) point out that riddles provide both context clues and high-interest material. Both of these factors promote vocabulary learning.

Riddles can be classified into several categories: those based on homonyms, on rhyming words, on double meanings, and on figurative/literal meanings, for example. (See the section "Special Words" later in this chapter.) An example of a homonym riddle is: "What does a grizzly *bear* take on a trip? Only the *bare* essentials" (Tyson and Mountain, 1982, p. 170).

Riddles work best with children who are at least six years old (Gale, 1982), and they continue to be especially effective with children through eleven years of age. After that, interest in this form of word play wanes.

Time for Reflection	Some people think word play is a waste of time. Others say it aids vocabulary development. **What do *you* think?**

Computer Techniques

Computers are present in many elementary school classrooms in this age of high technology, and the software available includes many programs for vocabulary development. Although some of them are simply drill-and-practice programs, which are meant to provide practice with word meanings the teacher has already taught, some tutorial programs provide initial instruction in word meanings. (These programs may also include a drill-and-practice component.) Programs focusing on synonyms, antonyms, homonyms, and words with multiple meanings are available, as are programs providing work with classification and analogies.

Word-processing programs that have a find-and-replace function can be profitably used in vocabulary instruction. A child may be given a disk that has files containing paragraphs with certain words used repeatedly. The child may use the find-and-replace function to replace all instances of a chosen word with a synonym and then read the paragraph to see if the synonym makes sense in each place it appears. If it does not, the child can delete the synonym in the inappropriate places and choose more appropriate replacements for the original word or actually put the original word back into the file. Then the child can read the file again to see if the words chosen convey the correct meanings and if the variation in word choices makes the paragraph more interesting to read.

A paragraph such as the following one could be a starting place:

Shonda had to run to the store for her mother because, just before the party, her mother got a run in her pantyhose. Shonda had to listen to her mother run on and on about her run of bad luck that day before she was able to leave the house. When she arrived at the store, she saw her uncle, who told her he had decided to run for office, delaying her progress further. She finally bought the last pair of pantyhose in the store. There must have been a run on them earlier in the day.

See Chapter 11 for more information on computer use.

See Chapter 11 for more information on computer use.

Time for Reflection	Some teachers think that having students learn the dictionary definitions of weekly teacher-chosen vocabulary words is a good approach to vocabulary instruction. Others believe in using a variety of methods to help students acquire meaning vocabulary. **What do *you* think?**

Special Words

Special types of words, such as those discussed in the following sections, need to be given careful attention.

Homonyms

Homonyms (also known as *homophones*) can cause trouble for young readers because they are spelled differently but pronounced the same way. Some common homonyms are found in the following sentences.

I want to *be* a doctor.
That *bee* almost stung me.

She has *two* brothers.
Will you go *to* the show with me?
I have *too* much work to do.

I can *hear* the bird singing.
Maurice, you sit over *here*.

Mark has a *red* scarf.
Have you *read* that book?

I *ate* all of my supper.
We have *eight* dollars to spend.

Fred Gwynne's *A King Who Rained* (Windmill, 1970) and *A Chocolate Moose for Dinner* (Windmill/Dutton, 1976) both have homonyms in their titles, as well as throughout their texts (Howell, 1987). Pettersen (1988) suggests letting the students look for homonyms in all of their reading materials. Students can construct lists of homonym pairs that mean something to them because they discovered the qualifying words for at least one word in each pair themselves. This paragraph is a good one to use as a starter for such an exercise, if readers want to try it for themselves. (Hint: *all-awl* is a good start.) Expanding Pettersen's activity to require the use of each homonym in a meaningful sentence is a way to keep the focus on meaning.

Activities

1. Have children play a card game to work on meanings of homonyms. Print homonyms on cards and let the children take turns drawing from each other, as in the game of Old Maid. A child who has a pair of homonyms can put them down if he or she gives a correct sentence using each word. The child who claims the most pairs wins.

2. Have students web homonyms in the following way:

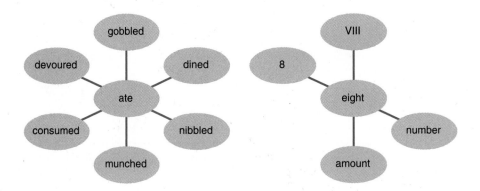

Homographs

Homographs are words that have identical spellings but not the same meanings. Their pronunciations may or may not be the same. Readers must use context clues to identify the correct pronunciations, parts of speech, and meanings of homographs. Examples include:

> I will *read* my newspaper. (pronounced *rēd)*
> I have *read* my newspaper. (pronounced *rĕd)*

> I have a *contract* signed by the president. (noun: pronounced *con' trakt;* means a document)
> I didn't know it would *contract* as it cooled. (verb: pronounced *cən/trakt';* means to reduce in size)

The books by Fred Gwynne mentioned in the section on homonyms are also rich sources of homographs.

Synonyms

Synonyms are words that have the same or very similar meanings. Work with synonyms can help expand children's vocabularies.

Study of the sports page of the newspaper for ways that writers express the ideas of *win* and *lose* can be a good way to introduce synonyms. The teacher should take this opportunity to show the students the different shadings of meaning that synonyms may have. For example, the headlines "Cats Maul Dogs" and "Cats Squeak By Dogs" both mean that the Cats beat the Dogs, but one indicates a win by a large margin, whereas the other indicates a close game. In addition, some synonyms are on varying levels of formality (for example, *dog* and *pooch*) (Breen, 1989).

Sylvester and the Magic Pebble by William Steig (Simon & Schuster, 1969) offers several good opportunities for discussion of synonyms used in describing the rain's cessation, the lion's movement, and the lion's feelings. In *Alexander and the Terrible, Horrible, No Good, Very Bad Day* by Judith Viorst (Atheneum, 1972), the synonyms are right there in the title, ready for discussion (Howell, 1987).

A teacher can also provide a stimulus word and have the students find as many synonyms as they can. The class can discuss the small differences in meaning of some words suggested as synonyms. For example, the teacher can ask, "Would you rather be called *pretty* or *beautiful*? Why?"

Antonyms

Antonyms are two words that have opposite meanings. Their meanings are not merely different; they are balanced against each other on a particular feature. In the continuum *cold, cool, tepid, warm,* and *hot,* for example, *cold* is the opposite of *hot,* being as close to the extreme in a negative direction as *hot* is in a positive direction. Thus, *cold* and *hot* are antonyms. *Tepid* and *hot* are different, but not opposites. *Cool* and *warm* are also antonyms. Similarly, *buy* and *sell* are antonyms because one is the reverse of the other. But *buy* and *give* are not antonyms, because no exchange of money is involved in the giving. The words are different, but not opposite. Powell (1986) points out that the use of opposition (citing antonyms) in defining terms can help to set the extremities of a word's meaning and provide its shadings and nuances. Research has shown that synonym production is helped by antonym production, but the reverse has not been shown to be true. Therefore, work with antonyms may enhance success in synonym exercises.

Frog and Toad Are Friends by Arnold Lobel (Harper & Row, 1970) provides students with examples of antonyms to discuss in an interesting context (Howell, 1987). Teachers may wish to locate other trade books that could be used for meaningful exposures to antonyms.

New Words

New words are constantly being coined to meet the changing needs of society and are possible sources of difficulty. Have students search for such words in their reading and television viewing and then compile a dictionary of words so new that they are not yet in standard dictionaries. The class may have to discuss these words to derive an accurate definition for each one, considering all the contexts in which the students have heard or seen it (Koeller and Khan, 1981). These new words may have been formed from Latin and Greek word elements, from current slang, or by shortening or combining older words (Richek, 1988).

Summary

Acquiring a meaning vocabulary involves developing labels for the schemata, or organized knowledge structures, that a person possesses. Because vocabulary is an important component of reading comprehension, direct instruction in vocabulary can enhance reading achievement. Although pinpointing the age at which children learn the precise meanings of words is difficult, children generally make more discriminating responses about word meanings as they grow older, and vocabulary generally grows with increasing age.

There are many ways to approach vocabulary instruction. The best techniques link new terms to the children's background knowledge, help them expand their word knowledge, actively involve them in learning, help them become independent in acquiring vocabulary, provide repetition of the words, and have them use the words meaningfully. Techniques that cause children to work harder to learn words tend to aid retention. Teachers may need to spend time on schema development before working with specific vocabulary terms.

Vocabulary development should be emphasized throughout the day, not just in reading and language classes; children can learn much vocabulary from the teacher's modeling of vocabulary use. Context clues, structural analysis, categorization, analogies and word lines, semantic maps and word webs, semantic feature analysis, dictionary use, study of word origins and histories, study of figurative language, a number of student-centered learning techniques, word play, and computer techniques can be helpful in vocabulary instruction.

Some special types of words can cause comprehension problems for children. They include homonyms, homographs, synonyms, antonyms, and newly coined words.

Test Yourself

True or False

_____ 1. Context clues are of little help in determining the meanings of unfamiliar words, although they are useful for recognizing familiar ones.

_____ 2. Structural analysis can help in determining meanings of new words containing familiar prefixes, suffixes, and root words.

_____ 3. When looking up a word in the dictionary to determine its meaning, a child needs to read only the first definition listed.

_____ 4. Homonyms are words that have identical, or almost identical, meanings.

_____ 5. Antonyms are words that have opposite meanings.

_____ 6. Word play is one good approach to building vocabulary.

_____ 7. Children sometimes make overgeneralizations in dealing with word meanings.

_____ 8. The development of vocabulary is essentially a child's development of labels for his or her schemata.

_____ 9. Work with analogies bolsters word knowledge.

_____ 10. Semantic mapping involves systematically deleting words from a printed passage.

_____ 11. Instruction in vocabulary that helps students relate new terms to their background knowledge is helpful.

_____ 12. Active involvement in vocabulary activities has little effect on vocabulary learning.

_____ 13. Pantomiming word meanings is one technique to produce active involvement in word learning.

_____ 14. Children should have multiple exposures to words they are expected to learn.

_____ 15. Working hard to learn words results in better retention.

_____ 16. There is no one best way to teach words.

_____ 17. Both concrete and vicarious experiences can help to build concepts.

_____ 18. Vocabulary instruction should receive attention during content area classes.

_____ 19. "Think-aloud" strategies can help students see how to use context clues.

_____ 20. Although use of categorization activities is motivational, according to current research findings it is not an effective approach.

_____ 21. Semantic mapping can help students develop a concept of definition.

_____ 22. Semantic feature analysis is the same thing as structural analysis.

_____ 23. Semantic feature analysis can help students see the uniqueness of each word studied.

_____ 24. The study of word origins is called _etymology._

_____ 25. Word banks can help students maintain a record of their increasing vocabularies.

_____ 26. At present no computer programs are available for vocabulary development.

_____ 27. A word-processing program can facilitate certain types of vocabulary instruction.

_____ 28. Children instinctively understand figures of speech; therefore, figurative language presents them with no special problems.

For your journal...

1. Reflect on the value of context clues for vocabulary development.
2. React to commercial computer software for vocabulary development that you have used. Include strengths and weaknesses of the programs.

...And your portfolio

1. Plan a lesson on dictionary use that requires the students to locate the meaning of a word that fits the context surrounding that word.
2. Plan a lesson designed to teach the concept of *justice* to a group of sixth grade students.
3. After collecting examples of figurative language from a variety of sources, use them as the basis for a lesson on interpreting figurative language.

Comprehension: Part 1

SETTING OBJECTIVES

When you finish reading this chapter, you should be able to

▶ Explain how schema theory relates to reading comprehension.

▶ Explain how a reader's purpose and other aspects of the rest of the situation in which reading takes place affect comprehension.

▶ Describe some characteristics of text that affect comprehension.

▶ Discuss some prereading, during-reading, and post-reading activities that can enhance comprehension.

Chapter 5 Organization

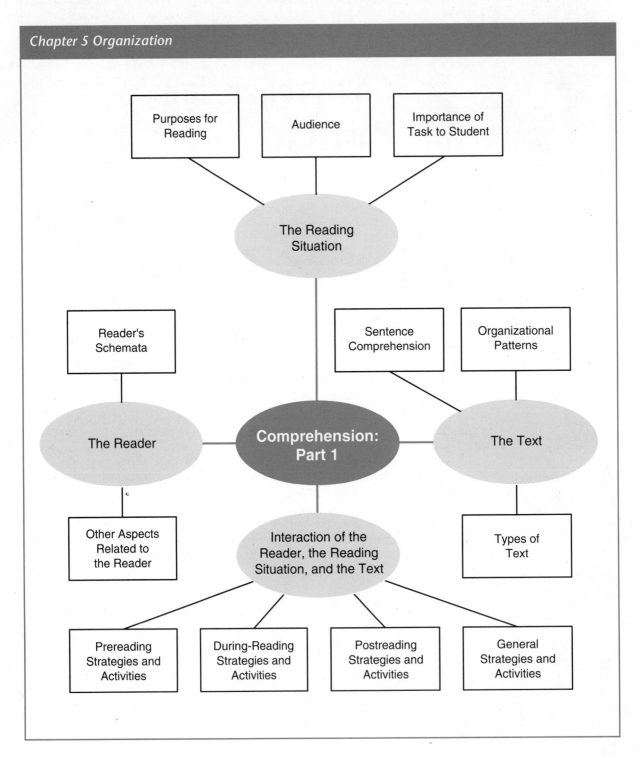

The objective of all readers is, or should be, comprehension of what they read. Shanklin and Rhodes (1989) see comprehension as an evolving process, often beginning before a book is opened, changing as the material is read, and continuing to change even after the book is completed. This developmental nature of comprehension is enhanced when the child interacts with others about aspects of the material after it has been read. Therefore, classroom interaction related to reading materials is important to comprehension development and should be planned carefully.

This chapter discusses the importance to comprehension of the interaction among the reader, the reading situation, and the text. It explores the importance of the reader's schemata, the reader's purposes for reading, audience for reading, and characteristics of the text to be read. It also presents strategies to be used before, during, and after reading.

As Pearson and Johnson (1978) point out, "reading comprehension is at once a unitary process and a set of discrete processes" (p. 227). We discuss the individual processes separately; yet teachers must not lose sight of the fact that there are many overlaps and interrelationships among the processes. Close relationships even exist between comprehension and decoding. Research has shown that good comprehenders are able to decode quickly and accurately (Eads, 1981; "A Talk with Marilyn Adams," 1991). Thus, developing decoding strategies to the automatic stage is important. Teachers should always keep in mind, however, that use of decoding strategies is merely a means of accessing the meaning of the written material. When good decoders have problems with comprehension, they need help in developing language proficiency and listening comprehension. This can be accomplished partly by increased reading at levels that currently yield good comprehension and partly by vocabulary and comprehension strategy instruction (Dymock, 1993).

Comprehension strategy instruction should make use of the students' own textbooks. The teacher should tell the students the strategy they are going to learn and how it will help them in their reading. Then the teacher should describe the strategy, model it, provide teacher-guided practice with it, and provide cooperative and independent practice opportunities (Roe, 1992).

This chapter is a logical continuation of Chapter 4, "Meaning Vocabulary," because vocabulary knowledge is a vital component of comprehension. Therefore, these chapters cannot truly be considered separately and are divided here only for convenience of presentation. Similarly, the coverage of the types of comprehension in Chapter 6 is a continuation of the topic that is separated for ease of treatment.

Readers approach a text with much background knowledge (many schemata) concerning their world, and they use this knowledge along with the text to construct the meanings represented by the printed material that meet their purposes for reading. To access the information supplied by the text, they must use word recognition strategies (covered in Chapter 3) and comprehension strategies (covered in Chapter 4, this chapter, and Chapter 6). They combine their existing knowledge with new information supplied by the text in order to achieve understanding of the material.

The Reader

This section discusses factors related to readers that affect their comprehension, including their schemata, sensory and perceptual abilities, thinking abilities, word recognition strategies, and affective aspects, such as attitudes, self-concepts, and interests.

Readers' Schemata

Educators have long believed that if a reader has not been exposed to a writer's language patterns or to the objects and concepts to which the writer refers, the reader's comprehension will at best be incomplete. This belief is supported by theories holding that reading comprehension involves relating textual information to preexisting knowledge structures, or *schemata* (Pearson et al., 1979). These schemata represent a person's organized clusters of concepts related to objects, places, actions, or events. Each schema a person has represents what the person knows about a particular concept and the interrelationships among the known pieces of information. For example, a schema for *car* may include a person's knowledge about the car's construction, its appearance, and its operation, as well as many other facts about it. Two people may have quite different schemata for the same basic concept; for example, a race-car driver's schema for *car* (or, to be more exact, his or her cluster of schemata about cars) will differ from that of a seven-year-old child.

Types of Schemata

People may have schemata for objects, events, abstract ideas, story structure, processes, emotions, roles, conventions of writing, and so forth. In fact, "schemata can represent knowledge at all levels—from ideologies and cultural truths . . . to knowledge about what patterns of excitations are associated with what letters of the alphabet" (Rumelhart, 1981, p. 13). Each schema a person has is incomplete, as though it contained empty slots that could be filled with information collected from new experiences. Reading of informational material is aided by the existing schemata and also fills in some of the empty slots in them (Durkin, 1981b).

Students need schemata of a variety of types to be successful readers. They must have concepts about the arrangement of print on a page, about the purpose of printed material (to convey ideas), and about the relationship of spoken language to written language. They need to be familiar with vocabulary and sentence patterns not generally found in oral language and with the different writing styles associated with various literary genres (Roney, 1984).

A *story schema* is a set of expectations about the internal structure of stories (Mandler and Johnson, 1977; Rand, 1984). Readers find well-structured stories easier to recall and summarize than unstructured passages. Possession of a story schema appears to have a positive effect on recall, and good readers seem to have a better grasp of text structure than poor readers. Having children retell stories is a good way to discover their grasp of a story schema (Rand, 1984).

Having many experiences with well-formed stories helps children develop a story schema. Storytelling and story reading appear to be excellent ways to develop children's schemata related to stories or other materials they will be expected to read. Hearing a variety of stories with standard structures helps children develop a story schema that allows them to anticipate or predict what will happen next. This ability enables children to become more involved in stories they read and better able to make and confirm or reject predictions—a process that fosters comprehension—effectively. The sentence structures in the stories told and read to children expose them to patterns they will encounter when they read literature on their own and will help make these patterns more understandable (Rand, 1984; Nessel, 1985; Pigg, 1986; Roe, 1985, 1986). Other ways to help develop children's story schemata include direct teaching of story structure and story grammars, covered later in this chapter in the section "Story Grammar Activities."

Perhaps the most important concept children need to have in their "reading schema" is the understanding that reading can be fun and can help them do things. They also need extensive background knowledge about the nature of the reading task and general background knowledge on the topics about which they are reading (Roney, 1984). Often children do not comprehend well because they know very little about their world (Cunningham, 1982b).

Research Findings About Schemata

Many research studies have supported schema theory. Anderson and colleagues, for example, discovered that recall and comprehension of passages with two possible interpretations (in one case, wrestling versus a prison break; in another, card playing versus a music rehearsal) were closely related to the readers' background knowledge and/or the testing environment (Pearson et al., 1979). Bransford and Johnson discovered that recall of obscure passages increased if a statement of the passage's topic or a picture related to the passage was provided.

Studies have shown that the provision of background information on a topic before reading is likely to enhance reading comprehension, especially inferential comprehension (Pearson et al., 1979; Stevens, 1982). These findings indicate that teachers should plan experiences that will give children background information to help them understand written material they are expected to read and to help them choose appropriate schemata to apply to the reading. When children have trouble using their experiential backgrounds to assist in reading comprehension, teachers need to find out whether the children lack the necessary schemata or whether they possess the needed schemata, but cannot use them effectively when

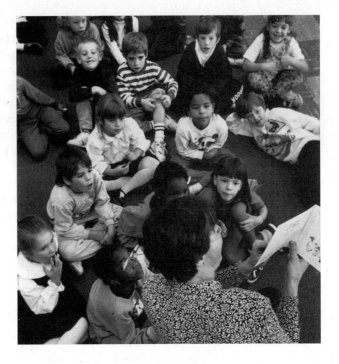

Story reading is an excellent way to develop children's schemata related to stories or other materials that they will be expected to read. (© *Bill Paxson/Courtesy of Des Moines Public Schools*)

reading (Jones, 1982). If the children lack the schemata, the teacher should plan direct and vicarious experiences to build them, such as having the children examine and discuss pictures that reveal information about the subject, introducing new terminology related to the subject, taking field trips, giving demonstrations, or having students read about particular topics in other books. Poor readers frequently need more help with concept development and more discussion time before reading than teachers provide (Bristow, 1985). If children already know about the subject, letting them share their knowledge, preview the material to be read, and predict what might happen can encourage them to draw on their existing schemata (Jones, 1982).

Readers vary in the relative degrees to which they emphasize two processes of comprehension (Spiro, 1979). *Text-based processes* are those in which the reader is primarily trying to extract information from the text. *Knowledge-based processes* are those in which the reader primarily brings prior knowledge and experiences to bear on the interpretation of the material. For example, consider this text: "The children were gathered around a table on which sat a beautiful cake with *Happy Birthday* written on it. Mrs. Jones said, 'Now, Maria, make a wish and blow out the candles.'" Readers must use a text-based process to answer the question "What was written on the cake?" because the information is directly stated in the material. They must use a knowledge-based process to answer the question "Whose birthday was it?" Prior experience will provide them with the answer, "Maria," because they have consistently seen candles blown out by the child who is celebrating the birthday at parties they have attended. Of course, before they use the knowledge-based process, they must use a text-based process to discover that Maria was told to blow out the candles.

Skilled readers may employ one type of process more than the other when the situation allows them to do this without affecting their comprehension. Less able readers may tend to rely too heavily on one type of processing in all situations, resulting in poorer comprehension. Unfortunately, some students have the idea that knowledge-based processing is not an appropriate reading activity, so they fail to use knowledge they have.

Rystrom presents a good argument that reading cannot be exclusively knowledge-based, or "top-down": if it were, two people reading the same material would rarely arrive at the same conclusions, and the probability that a person could learn anything from written material would be slight. Rystrom has an equally convincing argument that reading is not exclusively text-based, or "bottom-up": if it were, all people who read a written selection would agree about its meaning. It is far more likely that reading is interactive, involving both information supplied by the text and information brought to the text by the reader, which combine to produce a person's understanding of the material (Strange, 1980). (See Chapter 1 for a detailed discussion of this idea.) Example 5.1 illustrates this process.

Example 5.1   *Flow of Information During Reading*

Stored information brings meaning to text.

New information gained from text is stored in an organized manner.

A reader uses information stored in the brain in the form of schemata to help in understanding the message conveyed by the print. The new information gained from the page is then stored in the brain, connected in an organized manner to the schema that it enriched.

If reading performance results from interaction between information in the text and information the reader possesses, anything that increases a reader's background knowledge may also enhance reading performance. In general, students at schools with broad curricular scopes have been found to score higher on inferential reading comprehension than students at schools with narrow curricular scopes (Singer, McNeil, and Furse, 1984). Increased exposure to social studies, science, art, music, mathematics, and other content areas should therefore enhance reading achievement.

Helping Students Use Their Schemata

Background knowledge that students possess needs to be activated through discussion or by other means, just as related concepts students do not possess need to be developed before reading begins. Children need to realize that what they already know can help them understand the topics discussed in their reading materials (Wilson, 1983). Some techniques that may be used for schema activation include the prediction strategies in a Directed Reading-Thinking Activity (described in Chapters 7 and 10), the preview step of the SQ3R study method (described in Chapter 9), and the purpose questions of the Directed Reading Activity (described in Chapter 7).

Another good way to help children learn to activate schemata is for the teacher to "think aloud" for the students, modeling the activation of schemata for a passage while reading (Bristow, 1985). Of course, they cannot activate knowledge that they do not have.

Teachers should make sure the material students are asked to read is not too difficult for them. Difficult materials tend to work against students' use of meaning-seeking activities because they cause students to focus too much on decoding and not enough on comprehension.

Other Aspects Related to the Reader

The discussion in Chapter 1 of the many aspects of the reading process includes a number of aspects related to the reader that affect comprehension. Experiential background is the basis for readers' schemata, which were discussed in detail earlier. Other aspects of readers discussed in Chapter 1 under The Reading Process include their sensory and perceptual abilities, their thinking abilities, and affective aspects, such as self-concepts, attitudes, and interests. Readers' attitudes and interests affect motivation to read, and readers who are not motivated to read are not likely to give the reading task the degree of attention needed to result in high levels of comprehension. Facility with word recognition strategies also enhances comprehension because it releases the students' attention from the word recognition task and allows the students to apply it to the task of comprehension (Irwin, 1991). Some educators have been concerned that nonstandard dialects could be a major barrier to comprehension. Goodman and Buck (1997, p. 459) assert that "dialect-involved miscues do not interfere with the reading process or the construction of meaning, since they move to the readers' own language."

In recent years, attention has been directed to Howard Gardner's theory of multiple intelligences, which recognizes several distinct areas of potential that readers possess to different degrees (Gardner, 1983; Armstrong, 1994; Lazear, 1992). The areas of potential are discussed in Chapter 14. Lessons that incorporate use of more than one type of intelligence, or potential, are likely to be appropriate for more students than lessons that involve only one.

Gardner (1995, p. 202) defines an intelligence as follows: "an *intelligence* is a biological and psychological potential; that potential is capable of being realized to a greater or lesser extent as a consequence of the experiential, cultural, and motivational factors that affect a person." It is not the same as a learning style; it is applied to a more narrow range of activities. Gardner asserts that there is not one "right way" to use the multiple intelligences theory in education. Furthermore, he says that not every topic can be taught through all intelligences. Trying to teach every topic that way is a waste of time, and some efforts to force attention on particular intelligences are pointless. Playing music in the background while students work in areas other than music does not use musical intelligence, for example. He does believe that concepts should be taught in a variety of *appropriate* ways, so that more students will be reached (Gardner, 1995).

Time for Reflection	Gardner does not believe that every topic can be taught through all intelligences, yet some teachers disagree. Gardner, for example, doesn't believe that the mathematical skill of a person who is strong in musical intelligence is enhanced by music being played in the background while the person is doing math problems. **What do *you* think?**

The Reading Situation

The reading situation includes purposes for the reading, both self-constructed and teacher-directed; the audience for the reading; and the importance the reading task has for the individual.

Purposes for Reading

All of the reading that children do should be purposeful, because children who read with a purpose tend to *comprehend* what they read better than those who have no purpose. This result may occur because the children are attending to the material, rather than just calling words. For this reason teachers should set purposes for youngsters by providing them with pertinent objectives for the reading or help them set their own purposes by deciding on their own objectives. Objectives may include reading for enjoyment; to perfect oral reading performance or use of a particular strategy; to update knowledge about a topic, to link new information to that already known; to obtain information for an oral or written report; to confirm or reject predictions; to perform an experiment or apply information gained from the text in some other way; to learn about the structure of a text; or to answer specific questions (Blanton et al., 1990; Irwin, 1991).

Teacher-constructed purpose questions can help students focus on important information in the selection and should replace such assignments as "Read Chapter 7 for tomorrow." Providing specific purposes avoids presenting children with the insurmountable task of remembering everything they read and allows them to know that they are reading to determine main ideas, locate details, understand vocabulary terms, or meet some other well-defined goal. As a result, they can apply themselves to a specific, manageable task. However, if teachers always use the same types of purpose questions and do not guide children to set their own purposes, children may not develop the ability to read for a variety of purposes. Purpose-setting activities can help students activate their existing schemata about the topic of the material.

Cunningham and Wall (1994, p. 481) suggest always setting a purpose for student reading that is either "(a) a clear and precise statement of what the students are to focus on while they read or (b) a clear preview of the task they will be asked to perform after reading." This allows students to use the purpose to help them choose reading strategies. Cunningham and Wall suggest making purposes more specific for more difficult texts to guide the students to the important and challenging content.

Blanton and colleagues (1990) recommend setting a single purpose for reading, rather than multiple purposes, for maximum effectiveness. A single purpose may be especially effective for poor readers because it can help to avoid cognitive confusion from the overload of multiple purposes. The purpose should be one that is sustained throughout the entire selection, not met after reading only a small portion of the material; in other words, the purposes should be fairly broad in scope. Purposes should be formed carefully, because poor ones can actually misdirect the students' attention by focusing on information that is not essential to the passage and slighting important information. Purposes should help readers differentiate between relevant and irrelevant information.

When teachers set purposes for reading, they may then "think aloud" how the purpose was developed, thus modeling the purpose-setting procedure for later independent use by students. Even when teachers set purposes for students initially, responsibility for setting purposes should gradually shift from the teacher to the students. Students are capable of setting their own purposes, and they will be more committed to purposes they have set than to ones set by the teacher. Having students predict what will happen in a story or what information will be presented in an informational selection is a step in helping students set themselves the purpose of reading to find out if their predictions are accurate. Such purposes engage the students in the reading more than teacher-generated ones.

The Directed Reading-Thinking Activity, described further in Chapters 7 and 10, encourages such personal purpose setting through predictions on the part of the students. Fielding and colleagues (1990) found that prediction questions were more effective than traditional basal reader questions if the predictions were compared with the actual text after reading (Pearson and Fielding, 1991). Therefore, teachers should be sure to follow up on predictions if this type of purpose is used. Actually, all purposes should be discussed immediately after the reading is completed. Neglecting this procedure may cause students to ignore the purposes and merely try to pronounce all the words in the selection.

Commercial reading materials tend to offer a variety of types of purpose questions. However, teachers sometimes do not make use of these ready-made questions, or they may paraphrase them. If teachers are going to use self-constructed questions, they should give careful thought to the desired outcomes of the reading and the types of purpose questions most likely to lead to these outcomes.

Prereading questions should focus on predicting and relating text to prior knowledge. Students should be asked about the details that relate to problems, goals, attempts to solve problems, characters' reactions, resolutions, and themes (Pearson, 1985). (More about this type of questioning appears in the section "Story Grammar as a Basis for Questioning" in Chapter 6.)

Even when teachers do not provide purpose questions, children are often guided in the way they approach their reading assignments by the types of questions that teachers have used in the past on tests, using this knowledge to set their own purposes for reading. If a teacher tends to ask for factual recall of small details in test questions, children will concentrate on such details and perhaps overlook the main ideas entirely. In class discussion, the teacher may be bewildered by the fact that the children know many things that happened in a story without knowing what the basic theme was. Teachers need to be aware that their testing procedures affect the purposes for which children read content material in their classrooms.

Time for Reflection	Some teachers believe that students should always set their own purposes for reading. Others believe that teachers should set the purposes. Still others believe that sometimes it is appropriate for teachers to set purposes, but that much of the time, students should do the purpose setting. **What do *you* think?**

Audience

The audience for the reading may consist of only the reader, reading alone for personal or teacher-directed purposes. In this case, the reader is free to use his or her available reading strategies as needed to meet the purposes. The degree to which the reader has accepted the purposes as valid will affect his or her comprehension of the material.

Sometimes the audience for the reading is the teacher and sometimes it is other children. Mosenthal (1979) found that third- and sixth-grade students resolved contradictions in text differently when their audience was the teacher than when their audience was younger children. Third graders restructured text more to reduce contradictions for the younger children, whereas sixth graders restructured text more for the teacher. (Mosenthal and Na, 1980b; Mosenthal, 1984). Better readers and poorer readers may respond to the teacher as an audience differently because the teacher may encourage more use of a variety of strategies by students in higher reading groups than by those in lower ones. Teachers have been found to focus more on word recognition concerns with lower groups and more on meaning with higher groups (Irwin, 1991), a tendency that could be detrimental to the students in lower groups. Anderson and colleagues (1983) found that a meaning focus was more effective than a word recognition focus with both poor and good readers.

In school, a common audience is the reading group. Some children may comprehend less well when reading to perform in a reading group than when reading independently. They may even react differently to different groups of children, for example, younger students as opposed to students of their own age. Teachers should be aware of this possibility and assess reading comprehension in a variety of settings.

Importance of Task to Student

The degree to which students embrace the purposes for reading the material will affect the attention they give to the task and the perseverance with which they attempt it. The risk factor will have an additional effect on the results of the reading. Mosenthal and Na (1980a) found that students performed differently on reading tasks in high-risk situations, such as tests, than in low-risk situations, such as normal classroom lessons. In high-risk situations, low-ability and average-ability students tended to reproduce the text, whereas high-ability students tended to reproduce and embellish it. In low-risk situations, the students tended to respond according to their typical verbal interaction patterns with the teacher (Mosenthal and Na, 1980b).

The Text

Reading a text involves dealing with its specific characteristics and deriving information from it using word recognition and comprehension strategies. Texts are made up of words, sentences, paragraphs, and whole selections. Since vocabulary is one of the most important factors affecting comprehension, Chapter 4 was devoted to vocabulary instruction. Sentence difficulty and organizational patterns are other text characteristics. Although some suggestions in this section focus on comprehension of sentences or paragraphs, comprehension is a unitary act, and eventually all the procedures discussed here must work together for the reader to achieve comprehension of the whole selection.

People who choose texts and supplementary material for children must be aware of the difficulty of the material they choose, especially when students will use it independently. The directions provided for students and the instructional language used in such materials should be of high quality. The language of the directions should be clearer than the language of the exercises (Spiegel, 1990).

Sentence Comprehension

Children may find complicated sentences difficult to understand, so they need to know ways to derive sentence meanings. Research has shown that systematic instruction in sentence comprehension increases reading comprehension. For example, Weaver had students arrange cut-up sentences in the correct order by finding the action word first and then asking *who, what, where,* and *why* questions (Durkin, 1978–1979). This activity may work especially well when the sentences are drawn from literature selections the teacher has shared with the students. Another approach is to have children discover the essential parts of sentences by writing them in telegram form, as illustrated in the following Model Activity.

Model Activities

Telegram Sentences

Write a sentence like this one on the chalkboard: "The angry dog chased me down the street." Tell the children that you want to tell what happened in the fewest words possible because, when you send a telegram, each word used costs money. Then think aloud about the sentence: "Who did something in this sentence? Oh, the dog did. My sentence needs to include the dog. . . . What action did he perform? He chased. I'll need that action word, too. 'Dog chased. . . .' That doesn't make a complete thought, though. I'll have to tell whom he chased. He chased me. Now I have a complete message that leaves out the extra details. My telegram is: 'Dog chased me.'"

Then let the students write a telegram based on some story they have read or heard. For example, have them write the telegram that Little Red Riding Hood might have sent to her mother after the woodcutter rescued her and her grandmother. This telegram might contain several pared-down sentences.

Teachers should help children learn that sentences can be stated in different ways without changing their meanings. For example, some sentence parts can be moved around without affecting the meaning of the sentence, as in these two sentences:

On a pole in front of the school, the flag was flying.

The flag was flying on a pole in front of the school.

On the other hand, teachers should acknowledge that moving sentence parts *can* affect the meaning. For example, the following two sentences have distinctly different meanings:

Carla helped Teresa.

Teresa helped Carla.

Sentence Difficulty Factors

A number of types of sentences, including those with relative clauses, other complex sentences, those with missing words, those in the passive voice, and those expressing negation, have been found to be difficult for children to comprehend. Children understand material better when the syntax is like their oral language patterns, but the text in some primary-grade reading material is syntactically more complex than the students' oral language.

Relative clauses are among the syntactic patterns that do not appear regularly in young children's speech. Relative clauses either restrict the information in the main clause by adding information or simply add extra information. Both types may be troublesome. In the example "The man *who called my name* was my father," the relative clause indicates the specific man to designate as "my father" (Kachuck, 1981).

Teachers should ask questions that assess children's understanding of particular syntactic patterns in the reading material and, when misunderstanding is evident, they should point out the clues that can help children discover the correct meanings (Kachuck, 1981). Teachers may find it necessary to read aloud sentences from assigned passages to children and explain the functions of the relative clauses found in the sentences. Then they may give other examples of sentences with relative clauses and ask the children to explain the meanings of these clauses. Feedback on correctness or incorrectness and further explanation should be given at this point. Finally, teachers should provide children with independent practice activities to help them set the new skill in memory.

Students who need more work with relative clauses can be asked to turn two-clause sentences into two sentences (Kachuck, 1981). Teachers can model this activity also, as in the earlier example: "The man called my name. The man was my father." Supervised student practice with feedback and independent practice can follow, using progressively more difficult sentences. Students can move from this activity into sentence combining, which we will examine next. Finally, they should apply their understanding in reading whole passages (Kachuck, 1981). Until they have used the skill in interpreting connected discourse, it is impossible to be sure they have mastered it.

Sentence combining involves giving students two or more short sentences and asking them to combine the information into a single sentence. (For example, they might be asked to combine these two sentences: "Joe has a bicycle. It is red." Responses might include "Joe has a red bicycle." "Joe has a bicycle, and it is red." "Joe has a bicycle that is red." "Joe's bicycle is red.") Such activities bring out the important fact that there are always multiple ways of expressing an idea in English (Pearson and Camperell, 1981).

Discussion of a number of sentence combinations may bring out much about the children's syntactic knowledge. Wilkinson and Patty (1993) have found that students can learn to attend to elements of text related to connectives through sentence-combining practice, but not just through reading texts written by other students during sentence-combining practice activities.

Reading and writing specific sentence patterns is beneficial to students' literacy development. Reading patterned books not only helps the children read successfully because of their predictability, but also provides models for their writing efforts (Boyle and Peregoy, 1990).

Punctuation

Punctuation can greatly affect the meaning a sentence conveys; it represents pauses and pitch changes that would occur if the passage were read aloud. While punctuation marks represent the inflections in speech imperfectly, they greatly aid in turning written language into oral language.

Commas and dashes indicate pauses within sentences. Periods, question marks, and exclamation points all signal pauses between sentences and also alter the meaning:

He's a crook. (Making a statement)
He's a crook? (Asking a question)
He's a crook! (Showing surprise or dismay at the discovery)

To help students see how punctuation can affect the meaning of the material, use sentences such as the following:

Mother said, "Joe could do it."   We had ice cream and cake.
Mother said, "Joe could do it?"   We had ice, cream, and cake.
"Mother," said Joe, "could do it."   We had ice cream and cake?

Discuss the differences in meaning among the sentences in each set, highlighting the function of each punctuation mark.

Underlining and italics, which are frequently used to indicate that a word or group of words is to be stressed, are also clues to underlying meaning. Here are several stress patterns for a single sentence:

Pat ate one snail.
Pat *ate* one snail.
Pat ate *one* snail.
Pat ate one *snail*.

In the first pattern, the stress immediately indicates that Pat, and no one else, ate the snail. In the second variation, stressing the word *ate* shows that the act of eating the snail was of great importance. In the third variation, the writer indicates that only one snail was eaten. The last variation implies that eating a snail was unusual and that *snail* is more important than the other words in the sentence.

Teachers need to be sure that children are aware of the aids to comprehension that punctuation provides and that they practice interpreting punctuation marks. One possible practice activity follows:

> To spark interest in reading a class novel and make students more aware of mechanical elements such as quotation marks, periods, and commas, have students read the novel in parts (as in a play) with a narrator. (Carr, 1991)

Time for Reflection	Some teachers think there should be much work with sentence-level comprehension before moving on to whole selections. Others think they should address sentence-level comprehension only within the context of whole selections. **What do *you* think?**

Organizational Patterns

The internal organization of paragraphs in informational material can have a variety of patterns (for example, listing, chronological order, comparison and contrast, and cause and effect). In addition, paragraphs of each of these types also generally have an underlying organization that consists of the main idea plus supporting details. Whole selections contain these same organizational patterns and others, notably a topical pattern such as the one used in this textbook. Students' comprehension of informational material can be increased if they learn these organizational patterns. The Model Activities in this section show two examples of teaching procedures for paragraph patterns. Similar exercises may be constructed with longer selections as well, preferably ones drawn from books available for the children to read.

Model Activities

Chronological Order Paragraphs

Write the following paragraph on the chalkboard:

> Jonah wanted to make a peanut butter sandwich. First, he gathered the necessary materials—peanut butter, bread, and knife. Then he took two slices of bread out of the package and opened the peanut butter jar. Next, he dipped the knife into the peanut butter, scooping up some. Then he spread the peanut butter on one of the slices of bread. Finally, he placed the other slice of bread on the peanut butter he had spread, and he had a sandwich.

Discuss the features of this paragraph, pointing out the functions of the sequence words, such as *first, then, next*, and *finally*. Make a list on the board, showing the sequence of events, numbering the events appropriately, or numbering them directly above their positions in the paragraph. Next, using another passage of the same type, preferably from a literature or content area selection that the students have already read, have them discover the sequence under your direction. Sequence words should also receive attention during this discussion. Then have the students detect sequence in other paragraphs from literature or content area selections that you have duplicated for independent practice. Discuss these independent practice paragraphs in class after the students have completed the exercises. Finally, alert students to watch for sequence as they do their daily reading.

Model Activities

Cause-and-Effect Paragraphs

Write the following paragraph on the chalkboard:

Jean lifted the box and started for the door. Because she could not see where her feet were landing, she tripped on her brother's fire truck.

Discuss the cause-and-effect relationship presented in this paragraph by saying: "The effect is the thing that happened, and the cause is the reason for the effect. The thing that happened in this paragraph was that Jean tripped on the fire truck. The cause was that she could not see where her feet were landing. The word *because* helps me to see that cause."

Then lead class discussions related to the cause-and-effect paragraph pattern by using other cause-and-effect paragraphs with different key words (such as *since* or *as a result of*) or with no key words at all. These examples should preferably be chosen from the children's classroom reading materials.

Types of Text

Narrative (storylike) selections generally consist of a series of narrative paragraphs that present the unfolding of a plot. They have a number of elements (setting, characters, theme, and so on) that have been described in story grammars (discussed later in this chapter). Although they are usually arranged in chronological order, paragraphs may be flashbacks, or narrations of events from an earlier time, to provide readers with the background information they need to understand the current situation.

Expository (explanatory) selections are composed of a variety of types of paragraphs, usually beginning with one or more introductory paragraphs and composed primarily of a series of topical paragraphs, with transition paragraphs to indicate shifts from one line of thought to another and illustrative paragraphs to provide examples to clarify the ideas. These selections generally conclude with summary paragraphs.

Teaching students to make use of paragraphs that have specific functions can be beneficial. For example, students can be alerted to the fact that *introductory paragraphs* inform the reader about the topics a selection will cover. These paragraphs usually occur at the beginnings of whole selections or at major subdivisions of lengthy readings.

If children are searching for a discussion of a particular topic, they can check the introductory paragraph(s) of a selection to determine whether or not they need to read the entire selection. (The introductory sections that open each chapter in this book are suitable for use in this manner.) Introductory paragraphs can also help readers establish a proper mental set for the material to follow; they may offer a framework for categorizing the facts readers will encounter in the selection.

Summary paragraphs occur at the ends of whole selections or major subdivisions and summarize what has gone before, stating the main points of the selection in a concise manner and omitting explanatory material and supporting details. They offer a tool for rapid review of the material. Students should be encouraged to use these paragraphs to check their memories for the important points in the selection.

To carry the reader through the author's presentation of an idea or a process, the topical paragraphs within an expository selection are logically arranged in one of the organizational patterns discussed earlier in this chapter. The writer's purpose will dictate the order in which he or she arranges the material—for example, chronologically or in a cause-and-effect arrangement. A history textbook may present the causes of the Civil War and lead the reader to see that the war was the effect of these causes. At times, a writer may use more than one form of organization in a single selection, such as combining chronological order and cause-and-effect organization in history materials.

One way to work on recognition of text patterns is to write examples of text patterns on index cards and give them to small, cooperative groups of students to sort into the patterns represented. Discussion of the reasons for the classifications takes place in a whole-class setting. Students move from this activity to locating the patterns in their content textbooks (Kuta, 1992).

Regardless of the approach, attention needs to be given to text structure. Pearson and Fielding (1991, p. 832) state, "It appears that any sort of systematic attention to clues that reveal how authors attempt to relate ideas to one another or any sort of systematic attempt to impose structure upon a text . . . facilitates comprehension as well as both short-term and long-term memory for the text."

Chapter 10 discusses various text patterns in more detail.

Interaction of the Reader, the Reading Situation, and the Text

Factors related to the reader, the reading situation, and the text all interact as the student reads in instructional settings. To encourage comprehension of whole selections, teachers usually incorporate prereading, during-reading, and postreading activities into lessons. Some techniques are more general and include activities for more than one of these lesson parts. Example 5.2 shows some techniques applicable to various parts of a lesson.

Prereading Strategies and Activities

Prereading activities are often intended to activate students' problem-solving behavior and their motivation to examine the material (Tierney and Cunningham,

Example 5.2 *Interaction of Reader, Reading Situation, and Text*

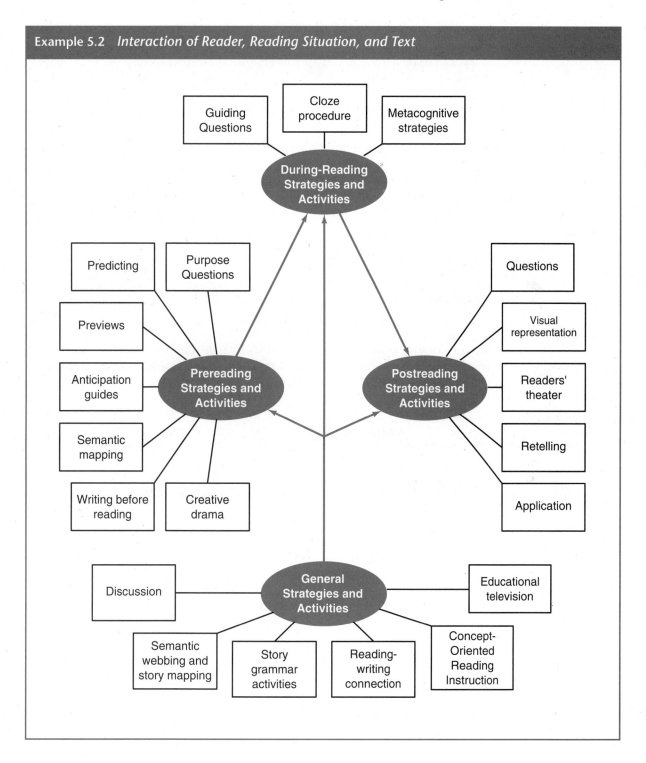

1984). The making of predictions in the Directed Reading-Thinking Activity described in Chapter 7 is a good example of this type of activity. Use of purpose questions as described earlier in this chapter is another example. The following activities can also serve to activate schemata related to the subject or type of text to be read to enhance comprehension of the material, and they can actually be used to build background for topics covered by the reading material.

Previews

Story previews, which contain information related to story content, can benefit comprehension. Research has shown that having students read story previews designed partially to build background knowledge about the stories increases students' learning from the selections impressively and that story previews can help students make inferences when they read. The previews help children to activate their prior knowledge and to focus their attention before reading (Tierney and Cunningham, 1984).

Anticipation Guides

Anticipation guides can be useful prereading devices. Designed to stimulate thinking, they consist of declarative statements, some of which may not be true, related to the material about to be read. Before the children read the story, they respond to the statements according to their own experiences and discuss them (Wiesendanger, 1985). The value of anticipation guides can be extended into the postreading part of the lesson by repeating the process after reading, considering the input from the reading, resulting in a combination anticipation/reaction guide. (See the next Classroom Scenario for an example of an anticipation/reaction guide.) Following is an anticipation guide for the story *The Little Red Hen*.

Anticipation Guide

Directions: Read each statement below and make a checkmark on the line under *Yes* if you agree with the statement or on the line under *No* if you disagree with the statement.

Yes   *No*

_____ _____ 1. You should have to work for your rewards.

_____ _____ 2. You should be generous to others with your possessions.

_____ _____ 3. It is important to cooperate to get work done in the fastest and easiest way.

_____ _____ 4. Some people should work to support others who do not want to work.

Merkley (1996/1997) suggests adding an "I'm Not Sure" column to anticipation guides. She thinks it causes students who choose this option to attend more carefully to the text to discover the answer.

Classroom Scenario

Use of Anticipation/Reaction Guide

Ms. Bucholtz's sixth-grade class had been studying the many cultures that make up the United States culture. To introduce the Chinese culture to a group of children who had no Chinese-American classmates, she decided to have them read *Child of the Owl* by Laurence Yep, a book for which she had a classroom set. She had prepared an anticipation/reaction guide that was designed to help them banish stereotypes and see the commonalties among all people.

Ms. Bucholtz began the lesson by holding up the book. She said, "Look at the cover of the book I have just given to you. From what you see on the cover, what do you think the book will be about?"

Blake said, "Maybe it will be about a baby owl."

Krystal looked at him disdainfully and said, "Oh, don't be silly. The picture is of a Chinese girl and an owl necklace. She's in front of a Chinese store. I think it's about her getting that necklace."

Ms. Bucholtz looked at Krystal and said, "Your prediction is reasonable, but you shouldn't say someone else's is silly. We don't have enough information yet to know if live owls will be in the story."

"I'm sorry, Blake," Krystal said. "Sometimes the cover does fool you, and it almost looks like an owl is flying behind her."

"That looks like a ghost owl. It looks spooky," said DeRon. "Maybe this is a ghost story."

"*Yep* sounds Chinese," Marie said.

"It is," Pete replied. "This guy wrote *Dragonwings* too, and it was great. It was about Chinese who came to America. I guess this one will be too, but the main character will be a girl in this one."

"You'll have to read the book to see if your predictions are right," said Ms. Bucholtz, "but first I want you to turn over that paper I put on your desk."

The children turned over the following anticipation/reaction guide:

Anticipation/Reaction Guide

Directions: As you read *Child of the Owl* by Laurence Yep, you will find out some things about Chinese and Chinese-American people and some things about people in general. Before you read the book, write *Yes, No,* or *Sometimes* on the line under the word *Before* to show what you believe to be true at this time. After you read the book, write *Yes, No,* or *Sometimes* on the line under the word *After* to show what you believe then.

Before   *After*

_____   _____   1. Chinese-Americans can speak Chinese.

_____   _____   2. Chinese-Americans can write Chinese.

_____   _____   3. Chinese-Americans live in Chinatowns.

(continued)

Before   *After*

_____   _____   4. Chinese-Americans are very close to family members and take care of them when they need help.

_____   _____   5. Chinese-Americans live just like other Americans.

_____   _____   6. Chinese-Americans are wealthy.

_____   _____   7. All it takes to fit in in Chinatown is to look Chinese.

_____   _____   8. Chinese owls are supposed to be evil.

_____   _____   9. Chinese-Americans eat with chopsticks, instead of forks and knives.

_____   _____   10. People can hurt people whom they care about.

_____   _____   11. The way people look and act on the outside is the way they are inside.

_____   _____   12. Chinese-Americans have feelings that are like other Americans' feelings.

_____   _____   13. People make sacrifices for people whom they love.

_____   _____   14. Chinese-Americans have been treated fairly since they came to this country.

"Bryan, read the directions for us," Ms. Bucholtz requested.

Bryan read the directions.

Then Ms. Bucholtz said, "Please follow the directions and fill in the *Before* column now. Then break into your cooperative groups and discuss the reasons for your answers with your classmates. When all of you have discussed your answers, you may begin reading. A few minutes before the period ends today, I'll stop you and let you discuss your predictions with your group and set new ones if your old ones no longer seem likely. You'll be reading this book all week. We'll discuss and revise predictions every day and jot down our new predictions. When you finish reading, fill in the *After* column on your guide. You may want to look back in the book for evidence for your responses to share later. When your entire group is finished, discuss those responses with your classmates. Then we'll talk about the guide as a whole class. Happy reading!"

The children quickly read and completed the guide, but their small-group discussions were filled with uncertainty about the items that specified Chinese-Americans, since none of the children knew any. Statements such as the following were heard: "Of course, a person who looked Chinese would fit in in Chinatown. I'd stick out like a sore thumb, though." "The Chinese in that book I read weren't wealthy, but that was a long time ago." "Sure, they do; they always have chopsticks in Chinese restaurants." "They can speak Chinese, because we can speak American." They were quick to support the answers they had given for more general categories with statements such as the following: "Mr. Woolly looks mean, but he gives us candy when we are in his store." "But Mr. Lynn looks nice, and he is super." "Guess that means 'Sometimes,' right?" "Yeah, 'Sometimes.'" "My Mom bought me a boom box with her new dress money because she felt sorry for me." "My brother spent *all* of his paycheck to buy flowers for this girl he is crazy about, even though he couldn't go to the ballgame with his friends after he did it."

Predictions were quickly revised after the day's reading, and they continued to be revised every day.

On Friday, the children independently filled out the *After* column on the guide, some of them mumbling about how wrong they had been. Their discussions of the responses in their small groups were lively, with reading from the text to support many points. Some of the comments were as follows: "*Casey* couldn't even speak Chinese." "Her Uncle Phil and his family were wealthy, but her grandmother wasn't. So 'Sometimes.'" "Look at how different Gilbert was than he seemed to be." (This was followed by the reading of several example passages.) The whole-class discussion was rich, featuring comments such as the following: "People are a lot alike in how they feel, even if they look different on the outside." "I felt like she did when her grandmother was in the hospital when my Dad got hurt on the job." "Gilbert is like my cousin. He wants to act cool, too."

Ms. Bucholtz ended the focus on the book by inviting the children to read individually other books about the Chinese or Chinese-American culture for comparisons and contrasts with this book next week.

Analysis of Scenario

Ms. Bucholtz began the lessons by eliciting from the students predictions, based on the book cover, that activated the schemata they had for the story. Then she gave them an anticipation/reaction guide that elicited further predictions and led them to commit their predictions to paper. The small-group discussions of the predictions and adjustment of predictions throughout the week kept the students involved in the reading. Returning to the anticipation/reaction guide at the end caused them to revise predictions based on the reading. They were encouraged to be ready to defend their answers with evidence.

Semantic Mapping

Semantic mapping is a good prereading strategy because it introduces important vocabulary that students will encounter in the passage and activates their schemata related to the topic of the reading assignment. This makes it possible for them to connect new information in the assignment to their prior knowledge. The procedure may also motivate them to read the selection (Johnson et al., 1986). Semantic mapping is discussed in Chapter 4.

Writing Before Reading

Hamann and her colleagues (1991) found that having students write about relevant personal experiences before they read a selection resulted in more on-task behavior, more sophisticated responses to characters, and more positive reactions to the selections. This helped the students become more involved with their reading.

Creative Drama

Although creative drama is most often used as a postreading activity, it also may be used *before* a story is read to enhance comprehension. The teacher may describe the situation developed in the story and let the children act out their own solutions. Then they can read the story to see how their solutions compared with the actual story. The teacher can take the parts of various characters to help move the drama along and to pose questions related to setting, characters, emotions, and critical analysis (Flynn and Carr, 1994).

During-Reading Strategies and Activities

Some strategies and activities can be used during reading to promote comprehension.

Metacognitive Strategies

Recently much attention has been given to students' use of metacognitive strategies during reading. Certainly, effective use of metacognitive techniques has a positive effect on comprehension. Since learning metacognitive strategies enhances study skills, this topic will be covered in detail in Chapter 9. Some information related to the use of metacognitive skills during reading as an aid to comprehension is included here to show the interrelationships of these two aspects of reading.

Metacognition refers to a person's knowledge of the intellectual functioning of his or her own mind and that person's conscious efforts to monitor or control this functioning. It involves analyzing the way thinking takes place. In reading tasks, the reader who displays metacognition selects skills and reading techniques that fit the particular reading task (Babbs and Moe, 1983).

Part of the metacognitive process is deciding what type of task is needed to achieve understanding. The reader needs to ask:

1. Is the answer I need stated directly? (If so, the reader looks for the author's exact words for an answer.)

2. Does the text imply the answer by giving strong clues that help determine it? (If so, the reader searches for clues related to the question and reasons about the information provided to determine an answer.)

3. Does the answer have to come from my own knowledge and ideas as they relate to the story? (If so, the reader relates what he or she knows and thinks about the topic to the information given and includes both sources of information in the reasoning process in order to come to a decision about an answer.)

Teacher modeling is a good way to teach metacognitive strategies. When modeling cognitive activities, teachers need to help students see their reasoning. It is not possible, however, to reduce the mental processes associated with strategic reading to a fixed set of steps, because "what an expert reader does when encountering an unknown affixed word in one text situation may differ from what is done when an unknown affixed word is met in another textual situation" (Duffy et al., 1988, p. 765). Poor readers often do not grasp the need for variation from situation to situation.

Teachers can help poor readers become more strategic through direct instruction in which they model reasoning processes for the students to help them understand how reading works. Teachers may then ask the students to explain how they made sense of material they have read, and they may provide additional help if the students' responses indicate the need (Herrmann, 1988). Teaching students to combine the two metacognitive strategies of self-questioning and prediction can result in better comprehension scores for middle school students reading below grade level than using only a self-questioning strategy or traditional vocabulary instruction. This may be because the combination strategy causes them to monitor the information more actively as they read to confirm predictions (Nolan, 1991).

Good readers monitor their comprehension constantly and take steps to correct situations when they fail to comprehend. They may reread passages or adjust their reading techniques or rates. Poor readers, on the other hand, often fail to monitor their understanding of the text. They make fewer spontaneous corrections in oral reading than good readers do and also correct miscues that affect meaning less frequently than do good readers. They seem to regard reading as a decoding process, whereas good readers see it as a comprehension-seeking process (Bristow, 1985).

Studies have shown that gifted students tend to be more efficient in the use of strategies, learn new strategies more easily, are more apt to transfer them to new situations, and are better at discussing their understanding of their cognitive processes than average students. There are indications that gifted students, like other students, can benefit from metacognitive instruction (Borkowski and Kurtz, 1987; Cheng, 1993).

Baumann and his colleagues (1993) advocate using *think-alouds* to enhance children's comprehension monitoring: "Think alouds involve the overt, verbal expression of the normally covert mental processes readers engage in when constructing meaning from texts" (p. 185). Baumann and colleagues used think-alouds to model for the students the asking of questions about the material, accessing prior knowledge about the topic, asking if the selection is making sense, making predictions and verifying them, making inferences, retelling what they have already read, and rereading or reading further to clear up confusion. They had the students use think-alouds as they applied the strategies to their reading. At times, the students were divided into small groups or pairs to apply the think-alouds, and this collaborative activity appeared to be especially helpful. Interest was built by comparing the students as readers to reporters: they interview writers as they read, just as reporters interview people. The instructional format used was to tell the students *what* the strategy was, *why* it was important and helpful for them to know, *how* it functions, and *when* it should be used (Baumann and Schmitt, 1986).

Focus on Strategies

Think-Aloud Session

Mr. Barr's fourth-grade class was beginning a unit on elderly people. Mr. Barr had assembled a number of books featuring elderly characters for the unit study. The books covered a wide range of reading levels, and some presented complex or unfamiliar concepts. Mr. Barr wanted to encourage students to use their metacognitive skills as they read from this collection of books. He decided to use one book, *The Hundred Penny Box* by Sharon Bell Mathis, for which he had a class set, to model his own metacognitive processes when reading texts.

First he read the title, author's name, and illustrators' names from the book cover. "I'll bet this will be a good book," he said. "I've read other books by this author, and they were good books. These illustrators are always good too. I loved their illustrations in *Why Mosquitoes Buzz in People's Ears*. Let's see what this book is likely to be about. The picture shows a little boy looking into a box and either getting a penny out or putting one in, while an elderly woman sits in a chair in the background. That box must be the one mentioned in the title. I guess it has a hundred pennies in it. I wonder if they belong to the boy or to the woman, and I wonder if the woman is his grandmother. Maybe she has saved the pennies for him. I'll have to read to find out."

Opening the book to the first page of text, Mr. Barr remarked about the facing page, "I liked the picture on the front better than this one. This one looks a little depressing. I wonder if the book is going to be sad."

Then Mr. Barr read the first paragraph of the text aloud and said, "If Michael is sitting on the bed 'that used to be his' in the room with his great-great-aunt, he probably had to let her have his room. She must have moved in with his family. I wonder how he felt about giving up his bed? . . . Great-great-aunt. . . . A great-aunt is the sister of a grandparent, so a great-great-aunt must be the sister of a great-grandparent. Aunt Dew must be pretty old."

Mr. Barr read the next paragraph and said, "I guess the hundred penny box is Aunt Dew's, and she lets Michael play with it sometimes. . . . Sometimes she would forget who Michael was. I had an elderly uncle who forgot who we were sometimes. He called me by my daddy's name. . . . I wonder what the song has to do with forgetting."

After he read the third and fourth paragraphs, he said, "She called him by his daddy's name too. I think it irritated Michael's mother."

Mr. Barr continued to model his thinking for the children for several more pages. Then he said, "So far it seems that Michael's mother is frustrated with trying to take care of Aunt Dew, but Michael likes to get her to play with him with the box. I think that there is going to be trouble between Michael's mother and Aunt Dew, and I think it will have something to do with that box. I'll have to read on if I want to find out." ˙

Then Mr. Barr asked for a volunteer to read and think aloud about the next part. After reading the second paragraph on page 14, Susan said in alarm, "Is Michael stealing the box? He didn't seem like he would steal from his aunt. I don't think that's it. I'll read on to see."

Several paragraphs later, Susan exclaimed, "Oh, no! His mother is going to burn the box!"

After the next paragraph, Susan said, "But Michael won't let her have it. Is he protecting it from her, or does he want it for himself? I think he's protecting it."

After the next paragraph, Susan said with more assurance, "He *is* protecting it. But I can't believe his mother burned someone else's things up. He's been helping Aunt Dew hide some of her other stuff. Maybe he was going to hide the box. But, if he was, why did he go in the kitchen with it? I'm confused. I'll have to read more."

Mr. Barr stopped her there. He asked her to make a prediction about what would happen next, and she replied, "I think he will run away with the box and save it."

Then Mr. Barr told the class to break up into pre-established groups of four and complete reading the book aloud, taking turns reading and thinking aloud about it as they read. At the end of each person's turn (about two pages each time), that person would summarize the situation and make a prediction about what would happen next.

Impatient to read on, the children quickly formed their groups and began to read. The book was short enough to be completed that day.

The next day the children were reminded of the questioning, predicting, connecting to prior knowledge, and summarizing that they had done in the think-alouds the day before. Mr. Barr encouraged them to continue to do these things silently as they read their individually chosen selections for that day.

Englot-Mash (1991) helps students learn to tie strategies together in a usable manner by presenting them with the flow chart in Example 5.3.

This chart helps the students to think about their fix-up strategies in a concrete way.

Palincsar and Brown (1986) suggest *reciprocal teaching* as a means to promote comprehension and comprehension monitoring. In this technique, the teacher and the students take turns being the "teacher." The "teacher" leads the discussion of material the students are reading. The participants have four common goals: "predicting, question generating, summarizing, and clarifying" (p. 772).

Example 5.3 *Strategy Use*

Example: A Skilled Reader's Possible "Flow Chart"

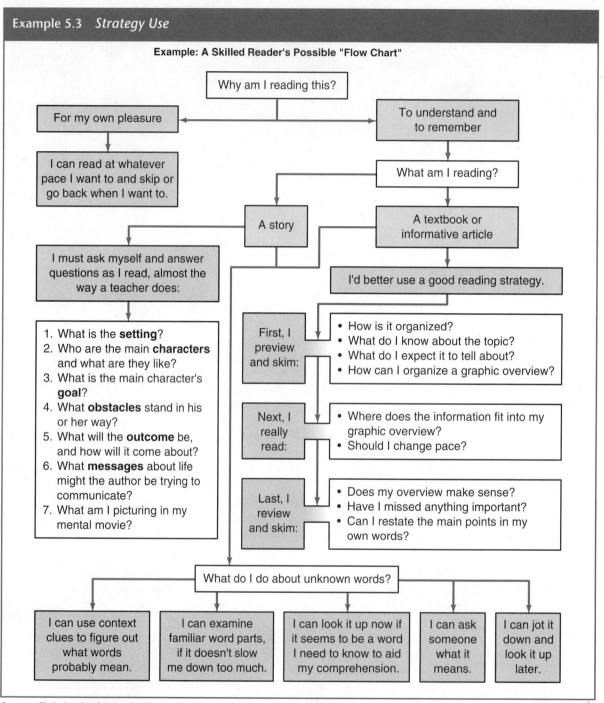

Source: Christine Englot-Mash. "Tying Together Reading Strategies," *Journal of Reading*, 35 (October 1991), 151. Reprinted with permission of the International Reading Association. All rights reserved.

1. Predictions made by the students provide them with a purpose for reading: to test their predictions. Text features such as headings and subheadings help students form predictions.

2. Generating questions provides a basis for self-testing and interaction with others in the group.

3. Summarizing, which can be a joint effort, helps students to integrate the information presented.

4. Clarifying calls attention to reasons the material may be hard to understand. Students are encouraged to reread or ask for help when their need for clarification becomes obvious.

When using reciprocal teaching, the teacher must explain to the students each component strategy and the reason for it. Instruction in each strategy is important. At first, the teacher leads the discussion, modeling the strategies for the children. The children add their predictions, clarifications, and comments on the teacher's summaries and respond to the teacher's questions. Gradually the responsibility for the process is transferred from the teacher to the students. The teacher participates, but the students take on the "teacher" role, too. The interactive aspect of this procedure is very important. Rosenshine and Meister (1994) reviewed research on reciprocal teaching and concluded that such instruction should be incorporated into ongoing practice.

Richards and Gipe (1992) describe another very active during-reading strategy. They suggest asking students to consider after each paragraph an idea they know about, appreciate, or understand and an idea they dislike, dispute, or don't understand. They must also give reasons for these reactions. They may share their responses with other students as they go or record them to share after the entire selection has been read. For each paragraph, students may also indicate a connection with their own experiences by telling what the paragraph reminds them of. All of these activities help students connect their knowledge to the text and expand comprehension.

The following Classroom Scenario shows how one child used her metacognitive skills.

**Classroom
Scenario**

Metacognition

As Ina Maxwell works at her desk one January morning, a student comes by to share a discovery about her reading. The girl is currently reading *Dark Hour of Noon*.

"*Dark Hour of Noon* reminds me of *Number the Stars,* that book we read last fall," she says. "In *Number the Stars,* the Nazis came and told the Jews to move to camps. They took butter and other foods. The Nazis were killing Jews. Adolf Hitler was in charge of the Germans."

(continued)

Analysis of Scenario

Ms. Maxwell encourages her students to make connections with life experiences and previous reading material as they read. Her encouragement and openness to students' comments lead students to share these connections with her, even when they are unsolicited.

Guiding Questions

During reading, guiding questions are often used to enhance comprehension. Research indicates that questions posed by the teacher when students are reading seem to facilitate comprehension (Tierney and Cunningham, 1984). Some authorities have suggested that extensive use of self-questioning while reading also will facilitate comprehension. Teaching students to turn each factual statement they need to remember into a *why* question that they attempt to answer enhances their learning of the factual information. (For example: "Why did Davy Crockett leave Tennessee to fight at the Alamo?") Better answers to the *why* questions result in better memory for the facts (Menke and Pressley, 1994).

Shoop (1986) describes the Investigative Questioning Procedure (*InQuest*), a comprehension strategy that encourages reader interaction with text. In this technique, which combines student questioning with creative drama, the teacher stops the reading at a critical point in the story. One student takes the role of a major character, and other students take the roles of investigative reporters "on the scene." The reporters ask the character interpretive and evaluative questions about story events. More than one character may be interviewed to delve into different viewpoints. Then the children resume reading, although the teacher may interrupt their reading several more times for other "news conferences." When first introducing the procedure, the teacher may occasionally participate as a story character or a reporter, in order to model the processes involved. The class should evaluate the process when the entire story has been covered.

InQuest lets students monitor comprehension. They actively keep up with "what is known." Before this procedure can be effective, however, students must have had some training in generating questions. One means to accomplish this training is to give students opportunities to view and evaluate actual questioning sessions on news shows. They need to learn to ask questions that produce information, evaluations, and predictions, and they need to ask a variety of types of questions and to use *why* questions judiciously to elicit in-depth responses.

Cloze Procedure

The *cloze procedure* is sometimes used as a strategy for teaching comprehension. In using the cloze procedure, the teacher deletes some information from a passage and asks students to fill it in as they read, drawing on their knowledge of syntax, semantics, and graphic clues. Cloze tasks can involve deletions of letters, word parts, whole words, phrases, clauses, or whole sentences. In macrocloze activities, entire story parts are deleted. The deletions are generally made for specific purposes to focus on particular skills. When a whole word is deleted and a standard-sized blank is left, the readers must use semantic and syntactic clues to decide on a replacement. If the blanks vary in length according to word length, word recognition skill also can be incorporated. If a short underline is provided for each letter, additional clues become available, and the task of exact replacement becomes easier. However, the discussion of alternatives when standard-sized blanks are used can be extremely beneficial in developing comprehension skills.

Although either random or regularly spaced deletions can lead students to make predictions and confirm predictions based on their language knowledge, such systems of deletion will not focus on a particular skill. Teachers should always elicit reasons for particular choices and give positive reinforcement for good reasoning.

In preparing a cloze passage designed for teaching, rather than testing, teachers should leave the initial and final sentences of the selection intact and delete no more than 10 percent of the words. They can choose passages of any length (Schoenfeld, 1980).

When multiple-choice answers are provided for completing passages, the task is not a true cloze procedure, but is referred to as a *maze* procedure. Maze techniques are probably less effective in encouraging learners to use their linguistic resources (Valmont, 1983). However, they may simplify the task for readers who need scaffolding and may prepare students for participating in cloze activities.

Postreading Strategies and Activities

Postreading strategies help students integrate new information into existing schemata. They also allow students to elaborate upon the learning that has taken place. Students should be given an opportunity to decide what further information they would like to have about the topic and where they can find out more (Crafton, 1982). They may read about the topic and share their findings with the class.

Questions

Whereas prereading questions may focus children's learning more than postreading questions do, research indicates that postreading questions may facilitate learning for all information in the text. There appears to be an advantage to using higher-level, application-type, and structurally important questions. Children obtain greater gains from postreading questions if feedback on answers is provided, especially feedback on incorrect answers (Tierney and Cunningham, 1984).

Visual Representation

After reading, students may be asked to sketch or paint what they learned from the text or what it made them think about and then share their sketches with a group, explaining how the sketches relate to the text. The sharing can extend the comprehension of all participants (Shanklin and Rhodes, 1989).

Quiocho (1997) had students work in groups. One student would read a section of a text aloud while other group members made sketches based on what they were hearing. Group members discussed the accuracy of each sketch, and the sketches were revised on the basis of the discussion.

Readers' Theater

Readers' theater is another way to enhance comprehension of text. In this approach, after the students read a story, it is transformed into a readers' theater script. The students then take specific parts and practice reading the script together. Finally, they read the script for an audience (Shanklin and Rhodes, 1989).

Retelling

Talking about reading material has been shown to have a positive effect on reading comprehension. Therefore, an appropriate comprehension enhancement technique is *retelling* of the important aspects of the material read. To retell a story or selection, the reader must organize the material for the presentation. Students are generally paired with partners for this activity. After silent reading of a section from the text, one child retells what has been read, while the other listens. Tellers and listeners alternate. This technique has been used with fourth graders, resulting in better comprehension than did producing illustrations or answering questions about the text.

Teachers should introduce the retelling technique by explaining that it will help the children become better storytellers, in the case of presentation of narrative retellings, and help them see how well they understand the reading selections. They should model a good retelling for the students, provide guided practice, and then allow independent practice. Prereading and postreading discussions of the story frequently help students improve the retelling. The teacher may wish to tape retellings and play them back to allow students to identify their strengths and weaknesses. Short, well-constructed materials should be chosen when the procedure is first used (Koskinen et al., 1988; Morrow, 1989).

Children can retell stories for teachers, classmates, or younger children in the school, or they can retell stories into a tape recorder. Story retellings can be done unaided or with the assistance of the pictures in the book. Retellings can also be done with flannel boards, with props (for example, stuffed animals), as chalk talks, or as sound stories in which sound effects are added to the telling of the story. These retellings make children more familiar with the use of "book language" (Morrow, 1989).

Application

A good postreading activity for use with content area selections that explain how to do something (for example, how to work a certain type of math problem or how to perform a science experiment) is to have the students perform the task, applying the information that was read. Postreading activities that are often appropriate for social studies reading are constructing time lines of events included in the reading selection and constructing maps of areas discussed. Many of the activities described in the section "Creative Reading" in Chapter 6 are good postreading activities that ask the students to go beyond the material just read and create something new based on the reading.

Time for Reflection	Some teachers think there should be comprehension instruction based on workbook activities. Others believe that comprehension strategies are best learned when they are integrated into authentic learning situations across the curriculum. **What do *you* think?**

General Strategies and Activities

Some types of strategies are useful throughout the reading process. Several of these are discussed next.

Discussion

Goldenberg (1992/1993) advocates what he calls "instructional conversations." Basically these are highly interactive discussions among the teacher and the students. Students focus on a topic chosen by the teacher and are gently guided by the teacher's questions and probing for elaboration and for text support for their positions, but they are not dominated by the teacher. Students are encouraged to use their background knowledge to contribute to the discussion, and, in some cases, the teacher provides needed background information that the students do not have. Sometimes the teacher offers direct teaching of a needed skill or concept.

The discussions generally center on questions for which a number of correct answers may exist. The teacher encourages participation from the students, but does not determine the order of speaking. Ideas are built on previously shared ones, and the teacher is responsive to students' contributions. Students are provided with a positive climate for attempting to construct meaning. Recording points that students make on the board, in a list, or on a semantic map, can be helpful. Having students write about the topic after the discussion can show what they have learned.

Another way to foster student discussion is through use of informational storybooks, which present facts through fictional situations. These books were found to enhance discussion more than books that were all fiction or all fact (Leal, 1993). The children discussed these books more, made more predictions about them, and connected more outside information to them.

Cornett (1997) allows only students who have read the material to participate in story discussions. Before the discussion, students think of parts that are exciting or puzzling or that connect to their lives to read aloud or discuss. They also list questions they have about the book, to ask the others. They look for special language in the book and decide what truths the book holds. Then they meet with three to five other students for student-led discussions.

Semantic Webbing and Story Mapping

Semantic webbing is a way of organizing terms into categories and showing their relationships through visual displays that can help students integrate concepts. Each web consists of a core question, strands, strand supports, and strand ties. The teacher chooses the core question, which becomes the center of the web, to which the entire web is related. The students' answers are web strands; facts and inferences taken from the story and students' experiences are the strand supports; and the relationships of the strands to one another are strand ties (Freedman and Reynolds, 1980).

Example 5.4 shows a semantic web based on *Prince Caspian* by C. S. Lewis. This web was developed by Winter Howard, a sixth grader. Before constructing webs like this one, the children in Winter's class read a portion of the book to a point where the hero found himself in a difficult situation. At this point the teacher, Natalie Knox, asked the children to predict what would happen next. The core question ("What will the Old Narnians do with or to Prince Caspian?") focuses on this prediction. Students answered the question individually, and their answers became web strands (for example, "Nikabrik will try to kill Caspian"). Support for strands was drawn from the story and from students' experiences. Then the strands were related through strand ties (shown with broken lines in the example). The webs were then used as a basis for reading the end of the story to see what really happened.

Instruction in story structure can benefit reading comprehension, since mental representations of story structures can aid comprehension (Fitzgerald, 1989; Gordon and Pearson, 1983; Davis and McPherson, 1989). A *story map* is "a graphic representation of all or part of the elements of a story and the relationships between them" (Davis and McPherson, 1989, p. 232). In addition to representing plots, settings, characterizations, and themes of stories visually, these maps (sometimes called *literature webs*) can emphasize the authors' writing patterns in predictable books. They "provide an instructional scaffolding for prediction, discussion, and language extension activities using children's trade books" (Reutzel and Fawson, 1989, p. 208).

Some webs are based on plot structure or story grammar, but some are more like structured overviews. One way to construct story maps is to put the theme in the center and arrange main events or settings sequentially in a second level of circles. Circles with characters, events, and actions may be connected to these second-level circles, and each may have additional circles attached to them, arranged in a clockwise order. Teaching readers to fill in story structure compo-

Example 5.4 *Semantic Web*

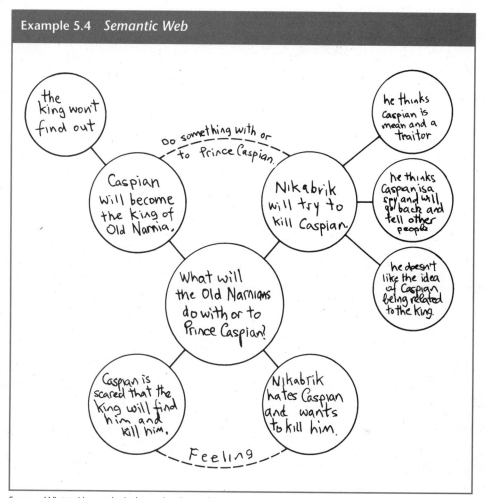

Source: Winter Howard, sixth grade, Central Intermediate School, Harriman, Tennessee.

nents on story maps while reading is beneficial to the students' comprehension (Davis and McPherson, 1989). Primary-grade students can learn about basic story elements from story mapping, first with pictures and later with written phrases (Felber, 1989; Munson, 1989). Example 5.5 shows an example of mapping of just the characters in a story by a first grader.

Story maps resemble semantic maps or webs. They help readers perceive the way their reading material is organized. They can be used to activate schemata for a story that is about to be read or as a means to focus postreading discussion. When the story map is used to activate schemata, the students may try to predict the contents of the story from it and then read to confirm or reject their predictions. Students may also refer to the map as reading progresses to help them keep their thoughts organized. After reading, the students can try to reconstruct the

Example 5.5 *Semantic Mapping of the Characters in a Story*

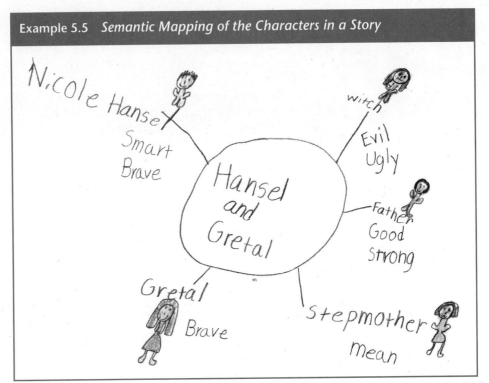

Source: Tiffany Nicole Reagan, Bethany Vincent Frady's first grade, Mary V. Wheeler Elementary School, Pikeville, Tennessee.

map from memory or can simply discuss it and its relationship to the story events. Using maps can help improve comprehension of both narrative and expository text (Reutzel, 1985).

Miller (1996) suggests using an activity that is similar to mapping. She has students develop a "seeing stick," a kind of visual time line or collection of evidence about a topic. A seeing stick is a vertical set of boxes that contain a record of events or information, with one picture or written description in each box.

Story Grammar Activities

A *story schema* is a person's mental representation of story structures and the way they are related. Knowledge of such structures appears to facilitate both comprehension and recall of stories. Children's written stories can serve as a source for understanding their concepts of story, and their retellings of stories also reveal story knowledge (Golden, 1984).

A *story grammar* provides rules that define these story structures. Jean Mandler and Nancy Johnson developed a story grammar that includes six major structures: setting, beginning, reaction, attempt, outcome, and ending (Whaley, 1981).

In a simplified version of Perry Thorndike's story grammar, the structures are setting, characters, theme, plot, and resolution (McGee and Tompkins, 1981). Teachers may be able to help students develop a concept of story by using these or other story grammars.

Teachers can use many activities to develop the concept of story. For instance, they can read stories and talk about the structure in terms children understand (folktales and fairy tales make good choices because they have easily identifiable parts), or they can have children retell stories. Reading or listening to stories and predicting what comes next is a good activity, as is discussion of the predicted parts. Teachers may give students stories in which whole sections are left out, indicated by blank lines in place of the material (macrocloze activity), and ask students to supply the missing material and then discuss the appropriateness of their answers. By dividing a story into different categories and scrambling the parts, teachers can give students the opportunity to rearrange the parts to form a good story. Or they can give the children all of the sentences in the story on strips of paper and ask them to put together the ones that fit together (Whaley, 1981).

An enjoyable activity for working on the concept of story has each student start by writing a setting for a story. Then each paper is passed to a classmate, who adds a beginning and passes the paper to another classmate. Reactions, attempts, outcomes, and endings, respectively, are added as the papers are passed to each successive student. When the stories are complete, they are read aloud to the class (Spiegel and Fitzgerald, 1986).

Fowler (1982) suggests the use of *story frames* to provide a structure for organizing a reader's understandings about the material. Frames are sequences of blanks linked by transition words that reflect a line of thought. Frames like the ones in Example 5.6 can be used with a variety of selections. Oja (1996, p. 129) says, "Using story frames along with basic elements of story grammar directs both students' and teachers' attention to the actual structure of the story and how the content fits that structure."

The frames can be the basis for the postreading class discussion of a story. Because the frames are open ended, the discussion will include much varied input. The teacher should stress that the information used in subsequent blanks should relate logically to the material that came before it. Students may use frames independently after the process has been modeled and practiced in class, and the class may also discuss the results. This technique is especially useful with primary-grade students and remedial reading students (Fowler, 1982).

Norton (1992) suggests acting out stories through creative drama, drawing plot diagrams, identifying the plot structures of wordless books, and writing stories based on wordless books as ways to work with younger students' understanding of plot structures. Acting out nursery rhymes that have logical sequences (for example, "Little Miss Muffett") allows students to identify characters, action, and sequence in a simplified setting. By asking the students to try to act out the story in a different order, the teacher can show them how changing the order of events destroys the story.

Example 5.6 *Sample Story Frames*

Frame 1: Setting

The setting for the story is _____ _____.
     (where)   (when)

I could tell where the story took place because the story said "_____

_____."

I could tell when it took place because the story said "_____

_____."

Frame 2: Characters

The main character in this story is _____.
                    (name)

I could tell that _____ was _____
           (name)   (trait)

because the story said "_____."

I could tell that _____ was _____
           (name)   (another trait)

because the story said "_____."

Creative dramatics can help young students comprehend stories. Dramatics can activate schemata, improve readiness, enhance vocabulary development, encourage use of metacognitive strategies, and improve oral reading skills of students in kindergarten through junior high school. The active reconstruction of a story through drama focuses children's minds on the characters, setting, and plot of a story. Interpretation conflicts can be resolved through discussion. Stories with a lot of dialogue are good for use with drama. As students read these stories, they must use their knowledge of such print features as quotation marks to interpret what each speaker is saying (Miller and Mason, 1983; Bidwell, 1992).

Older students also benefit from drawing plot diagrams and relating these diagrams to characterizations and themes. The plot diagram of *Mufaro's Beautiful Daughter* (Steptoe, 1987) in Example 5.7 shows how the plot relates to the characters of the two daughters and to the overall theme that kindness and generosity are good and will be rewarded, whereas greed and selfishness are bad and will be punished (Norton, 1992).

Teachers can improve understanding of story features such as plots, themes, characters, and setting by using movies, a medium in which students generally have high interest. For example, they can list types of plots that movies may have

Example 5.7 *Plot Diagram of* Mufaro's Beautiful Daughter

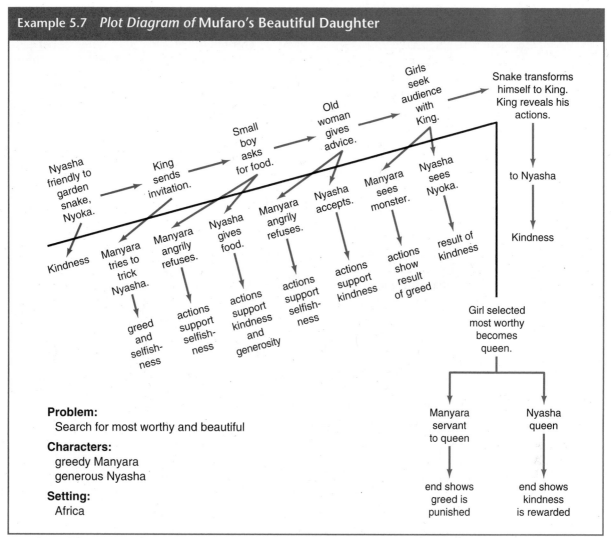

Problem:
Search for most worthy and beautiful

Characters:
greedy Manyara
generous Nyasha

Setting:
Africa

and let the students match movies to plots (Sawyer 1994). This understanding can then be transferred to stories in books through parallel techniques.

Settings may serve simply as backdrops for stories, or they may be integral to the narrative, influencing characters, action, and theme. Use of sensory imagery by the author helps to make the setting clear. Pictures in the book also enhance the effect of the words in the text in clarifying setting (Watson, 1991).

To fully comprehend a story, the readers must understand the characters. Preadolescents often focus on what is happening in a story rather than on the reasons behind the actions. They may assume that story characters think and feel the same way they do, even if the characters come from very different back-grounds. Younger children may focus on only part of a story and consider only the perspective of the main character. Story maps that include character perspec-tives that go with each story event can help students understand stories more fully (Emery, 1996). Having students create a collage of words describing a char-acter's traits, drawn from both text and pictures and superimposed on a drawing of the character, can also be helpful (Golden et al., 1992). Use of character inter-rogations, in which one student plays the character and other students question him or her, is another valuable way to work on understanding characterization, as is use of character journals, discussed in the next section (Van Horn, 1997).

Awareness of story characters' emotions is particularly helpful in understand-ing cause-and-effect relationships in the stories. Students need instruction in un-derstanding emotional words and finding clues to characters' emotional states, and they need to realize that story characters may experience several emotions si-multaneously (Barton, 1996).

Word lines, such as those described in Chapter 4, and word webs can be used to show the relationships among the words. Barton (1996) uses the categories of "strong," "moderate," and "mild" to organize related emotion words in word webs. For example, *ecstatic* would be placed under "strong" in a web for the word *happiness*.

Teachers can ask students questions to help them make connections between their own emotions and those of story characters. One question Barton (1996, p. 25) suggests is: "Has anyone ever treated you like this character is being treated by the people around him/her? How did it feel?" Teachers can also alert students to clues authors supply about characters' emotions, such as explicit character statements and actions, explicit plot events, text features, and emotional words. Implicit clues that need attention may come from the setting, the characters' thoughts, the story mood, or the author's style (Barton, 1996).

Students need to be able to identify themes. Au (1992, p. 106) states that "themes are often implicit and emerge gradually as the story unfolds." The theme is "an idea that encompasses the text as a whole." (Some stories may have several themes.) The teacher can offer support through questions and comments as stu-dents work at constructing the theme of a story. Gradually, the students can take more responsibility for the construction. Students learn from opportunities to discuss themes with peers.

To help children comprehend stories that start and end at the same place, with a series of events in between, the *circle story* can be effective (Jett-Simpson, 1981; Smith and Bean, 1983). The teacher draws a circle on a large sheet of paper and divides it into a number of pie-shaped sections corresponding to the number of events in the story. The teacher reads the story to the children, who then de-cide which events need to be pictured in each section of the circle. Circle story completion can be done in small groups, with each child responsible for illustrat-ing a different event. If the paper is large enough, all of the children can work at the same time.

Even though there is much interest among educators in the use of story grammars, questions about this technique remain. Results of studies on the effectiveness of story grammar instruction in increasing reading comprehension have been contradictory (Dreher and Singer, 1980; Greenewald and Rossing, 1986; Sebesta et al., 1982; Spiegel and Fitzgerald, 1986). Some have shown positive effects, and others have shown no benefits. It must be remembered that story grammars describe only a limited set of relatively short, simple stories, ones derived from a fairy tale or folktale tradition, and are unable to describe stories that have characters with simultaneously competing goals (Fitzgerald, 1989; Mandler, 1984; Schmitt and O'Brien, 1986).

Reading-Writing Connection

Composition and comprehension both involve planning, composing, and revising. Although these steps may seem clear in composition, their equivalents in reading may be less obvious. Teachers may need to think of the prereading activities related to background building, schema activation, and prediction as the planning phase in comprehension; developing tentative meanings while reading as the composing phase; and revising the meanings when new information is acquired as the revision phase.

Many writing activities that accompany comprehension instruction are composition activities (Pearson, 1985). Writing story predictions based on questioning or prereading word webs is an example of writing in the prereading phase. Note taking during reading may be in the form of outlines or series of summary statements (another obvious link between reading and writing activities). Macrocloze activities related to story grammars and the use of story frames are other ways to use writing to enhance reading. Interpretive reading activities, such as rewriting sentences containing figurative expressions into literal forms and rewriting sentences containing pronouns by using their referents instead, are composition activities. Many writing activities are a part of creative reading instruction. Several of these activities are mentioned in Chapter 8 and the section on creative reading in Chapter 6.

A *character journal* involves writing diary entries from the viewpoint of a character in a story. Students can be asked to write a diary entry for each chapter in a book. The entries are written in the first-person voice. Students are encouraged to write as the character might have written, without concern for mechanics and spelling. Personal comments not in the voice of the character can be allowed, but they should be put in parentheses or brackets to set them apart from regular entries. Teacher responses to the entries can help encourage the students and reassure them about their competence. When students are asked to compose diary entries for characters in the literature they are reading, they become more intensely involved in the reading. To accomplish this, the students must get inside the character's head and experience the events through his or her eyes. This perspective produces improved comprehension (Hancock, 1993).

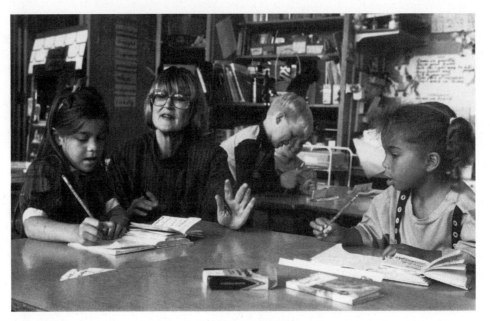

Composition and comprehension both involve planning, composing, and revising.
(© *Elizabeth Crews*)

Writing comments about reading may be facilitated through use of a computer. Bernhardt (1994) suggests putting a reading passage on the computer and allowing students to interact with it by breaking it into meaningful or difficult chunks. Then they mark, number, or reorder these chunks and intersperse their own comments and questions in the text. Comments are written in all capital letters so that they stand out from the original text. The active involvement with the text can promote better understanding.

Cooperative groups work well for helping students understand characterization in a story. After students have read a selection, the teacher can give each group a character to describe. He or she can instruct the children to first web the characters' characteristics and evidence from the story and then write character descriptions based on the web (Avery and Avery, 1994).

More on the reading-writing connection appears in Chapters 1, 7, 8, and 10.

Concept-Oriented Reading Instruction (CORI)

Concept-Oriented Reading Instruction (CORI) is designed to increase motivation. It is an instructional framework defined by seven themes: "real-world observation, conceptual theory, strategy instruction, self-directed learning, collaboration, self-expression, and coherence" (Guthrie, Alao, and Rinehart, 1997, pp. 440–441).

Real-world observation, managed through such activities as field trips and exhibits, motivates students to read to answer questions focused on particular concepts. The teacher offers strategy instruction as needed, while the students locate reference materials and collect information. Work in teams takes place as the students share findings, evaluate information, and integrate information from several sources. Team members decide how to share their findings with the rest of the class. Since the reading and writing the students do are centered around content concepts, there is coherence and connectivity in the instructional program (Guthrie, Alao, and Rinehart, 1997).

Educational Television

"Reading Rainbow" is a television program that presents books to children. It regularly tries to relate the topics in featured books to children's experiences, a procedure that facilitates comprehension. This modeling of a solid comprehension strategy may help students apply the strategy in their later reading. Comprehension monitoring and summarizing of material also are modeled on this program (Wood and Duke, 1997).

Summary

The central factor in reading is comprehension. Since reading is an interactive process that involves the information brought to the text by readers, the information supplied by the text, and the reading situation, good comprehension depends on many factors. Among them are readers' backgrounds of experience, sensory and perceptual abilities, thinking abilities, and word recognition strategies, as well as their purposes for reading, their audience for the reading, the importance of the reading to them, and their facility with various comprehension strategies that will help them unlock the meanings within the text. Children's schemata, built through background experiences, aid comprehension of printed material and are themselves modified by input from this material.

Having a purpose for reading enhances comprehension. Teachers should learn how to set good purposes for children's reading assignments and discover how to help them learn to set their own purposes.

The audience for reading affects the reading strategies used. The audience may be the reader himself or herself, the teacher, or other children.

The importance the reading has for the reader is also a factor. High-risk reading for a test may be done differently from low-risk reading in the classroom setting.

Features of the text itself also affect comprehension. Sentences that are complex, contain relative clauses, are in the passive voice, have missing words, or express negation may need special attention because students may have difficulty comprehending them. The meaning conveyed by punctuation in sentences should receive attention. Students also need help in understanding the functions of paragraphs and the organizational patterns of paragraphs and whole selections.

Prereading, during-reading, and postreading activities can foster children's comprehension of reading selections. Prereading activities such as previews, anticipation guides, semantic mapping, writing before reading, and creative drama can be helpful. Metacognitive strategies, questioning, and the cloze procedure are among the techniques that can be used during reading. Postreading activities usually involve questioning, making visual representations, using readers' theater, retelling, and application of concepts. Some activities—such as semantic webbing and story mapping, story grammar and story frame activities, other story structure techniques, writing activities related to reading, Concept-Oriented Reading Instruction, and educational television—may be involved in prereading, during-reading, and postreading activities at various times.

Test Yourself

True or False

_____ 1. Each schema that a person has represents what the person knows about a particular concept and the interrelationships among the known pieces of information.

_____ 2. Anything that increases a reader's background knowledge may also increase comprehension.

_____ 3. Previews for stories that build background related to the stories have a positive effect on comprehension.

_____ 4. Punctuation marks are clues to pauses and pitch changes.

_____ 5. Character journals are journals filled with character sketches.

_____ 6. Comprehension-monitoring techniques are metacognitive strategies.

_____ 7. Punctuation marks do not function as clues to sentence meaning.

_____ 8. Reading comprehension involves relating textual information to preexisting knowledge structures.

_____ 9. Comprehension strategies should be taught in a way that emphasizes their application when students are actually reading connected discourse.

_____ 10. Less able readers may rely too heavily on either text-based or knowledge-based processing.

_____ 11. Richard Rystrom argues that reading is exclusively a top-down process.

_____ 12. InQuest combines student questioning with creative drama.

_____ 13. Story grammar activities can increase children's understanding of story structure and serve as a basis for questioning.

_____ 14. Relative clauses cause few comprehension problems for children.

_____ 15. Semantic webbing involves systematically deleting words from a printed passage.

_____ 16. Think-alouds are useless in teaching metacognitive strategies.

_____ 17. Concept-Oriented Reading Instruction is designed to increase motivation.

_____ 18. An intelligence is the same as a learning style.

For your journal...

1. Choose a short selection about an uncommon subject. Question your classmates to find out how complete their schemata on this topic are, and give them copies of the selection to read. Later, discuss the difficulties that some of them had because of inadequate prior knowledge. In your journal, write your observations about this activity and indicate what you could have done to develop schemata before the reading took place.

2. Read Margaret Egan's article "Capitalizing on the Reader's Strengths: An Activity Using Schema" (*Journal of Reading*, 37 [May 1994], pp. 636–640), and try the check activity "Travail in Nova Scotia" with a group of middle or upper elementary students. Write your results in your journal.

...And your portfolio

1. Construct a time line for a chapter in a social studies text that has a chronological-order organizational pattern. Write a description of how you could use the time line with children to teach this organizational pattern.

2. Construct an anticipation guide for a well-known folktale.

3. Construct a story map for a story.

4. Read Egan's article, cited in item 2 of "For your journal . . . ," and compose a check story to use with students in a specific grade.

6

Comprehension: Part 2

SETTING OBJECTIVES

When you finish reading this chapter, you should be able to

▶ Describe ways to promote reading for literal meanings.

▶ Explain the importance of being able to make inferences.

▶ Discuss some of the things a critical reader must know.

▶ Explain what *creative reading* means.

▶ Explain how to construct questions for discussions and assessments.

Whereas Chapter 5 emphasized the role of the reader, the text, and the reading situation, as well as some comprehension strategies, Chapter 6 examines two types of comprehension—literal and high-order—and describes approaches for developing each type. In addition, this chapter explains questioning techniques that can be used to guide reading, enhance comprehension and retention, and assess comprehension. Three important activities related to effective questioning are discussed: preparing questions, helping students answer questions, and helping students question. Although the two chapters look at different aspects of comprehension, the material in both chapters is necessary to understanding the overall process.

Types of Comprehension

Readers employ different types of comprehension in order to understand fully what they read. To take in ideas that are directly stated is *literal comprehension*; this is the most basic type. Higher-order comprehension includes interpretive, critical, and creative comprehension. To read between the lines is *interpretive reading*; to read for evaluation is *critical reading*; and to read beyond the lines is *creative reading*. Example 6.1 shows these types of comprehension and their elements.

Perhaps because literal comprehension is the easiest to deal with in the classroom, teachers have given it a disproportionate amount of attention; but children need to achieve higher-order reading comprehension to become thoughtful and effective citizens.

Literal Comprehension

Reading for literal comprehension, or acquiring information that is directly stated in a selection, is important in and of itself and is also a prerequisite for higher-level comprehension. Recognizing *stated* information is the basis of literal comprehension. The specific, explicitly stated parts of a paragraph or passage that contain the basic information are the details on which main ideas, cause-and-effect relationships, inferences, and so on are built. For example, in the sentence "The man wore a red hat," the fact that a *red* hat was being worn is one detail that readers can note. To locate details effectively, students may need some direction about the types of details signaled by specific questions. For example, a *who* question asks for the name or identification of a person, or sometimes an animal; a *what* question asks for a thing or an event; a *where* question asks for a place; a *when* question asks for a time; a *how* question asks for the way something is or was accomplished; and a *why* question asks for the reason for something. After discussing these question words and their meanings, the teacher can model for the students the locations of answers to each type of

Chapter 6 Organization

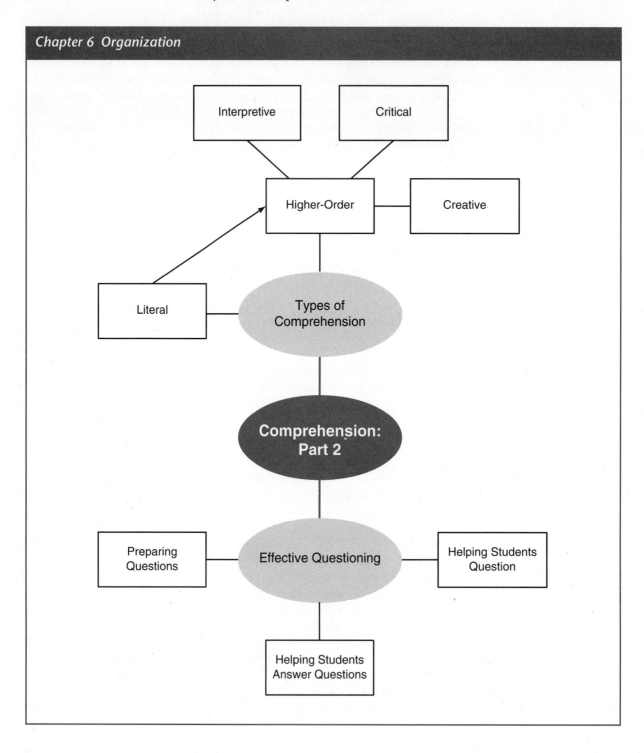

question in a passage displayed on the chalkboard or a transparency. Then the students can participate in an activity such as the following one to practice the skill. Newspaper articles are good for practice of this sort, since lead paragraphs tend to include information about *who, what, where, when, why,* and *how.* The teacher should provide feedback on the correctness of responses as soon as possible after the students complete the activity.

Model Activities

Locating Details in a Newspaper Story

Have the students read the following newspaper article and answer the questions in small groups, making sure that every group member agrees to each answer chosen.

Jane and John Stone, owners of Stone's Grocery, had $100 stolen from them as they left the store last night at eleven o'clock. The robber stepped from behind a shrub outside the door of the grocery store and pulled a gun from his pocket, saying, "Hand over that cash sack!" Stone handed the robber the sack of money he had just removed from the cash register, and the man turned and fled, leaving both Mr. and Mrs. Stone unharmed.

1. Who was involved in this event?
2. What took place?
3. Where did it take place?
4. When did it take place?
5. How or why did it take place?

Have a whole-class discussion of the article, with members from the different groups giving their groups' answers and reasons for their answers.

Sequence, the order in which events in a paragraph or passage occur, is signaled by time-order words such as *now, before, when, while, yet, after,* and so on. Children must learn to recognize straightforward chronological sequence, as well as flashbacks and other devices that describe events "out of order."

Teachers must model the process of finding the correct sequence of events in a passage before expecting students to locate such sequences independently. Helpful time-order words should be discussed and pointed out in selections. Then students need to engage in practice activities related to this skill.

The ability to read and follow directions is a prerequisite for virtually all successful schoolwork. It involves understanding details and sequence.

The teacher should take a set of directions for performing a task and model following these directions carefully, reading the directions aloud as each step is completed and commenting on the meaning of each instruction. Then he or she should follow the directions again, leaving out a vital step. Class discussion about the results of not following directions carefully should follow. After several modeling episodes, the teacher should consistently refer children to written directions

Example 6.1　*Types of Comprehension*

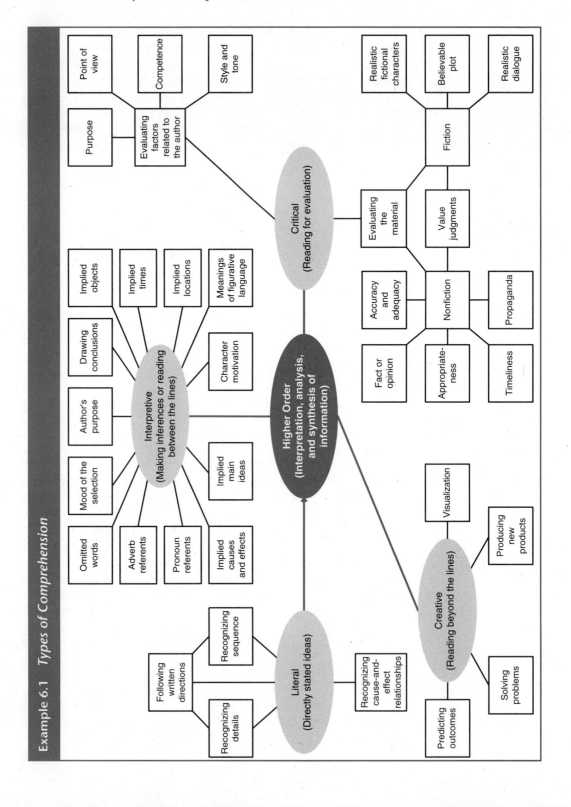

instead of telling them how to do everything orally. Children can be asked to read the directions silently and then repeat them in their own words.

Recognizing and understanding a cause-and-effect relationship in a written passage is an important reading skill. It is considered a literal skill when the relationship is explicitly stated ("Bill stayed out *because* he was ill"); it is considered an interpretive skill if the relationship is implied.

Following are some activities for developing literal comprehension.

Activities

1. After students have read a paragraph, preferably from a book they have chosen to read, ask them questions whose answers are directly stated in the paragraph, as shown in the following example. Have them show where they found the answers in the paragraph.

   Tom's favorite toy was his dump truck. Although Tom was usually a generous boy, he never offered to let anyone else play with the truck. He had had the truck for three years, and it was still as good as new. Tom was afraid that other children would be careless with his toy.

   a. What was Tom's favorite toy?
   b. What was the condition of Tom's toy?
   c. How long had Tom had his favorite toy?

2. Give the children a set of directions for a task that they need to complete, and have them number the important details (or steps), as has been done in the following example. Go through one or more examples before you ask them to work alone or cooperatively, with partners or in small groups.

   To make a good bowl of chili, first (1) sauté the onions for about ten minutes. Then (2) add the ground beef and brown it. (3) Stir the mixture frequently so that it will not burn. Finally, (4) add the tomatoes, tomato sauce, Mexican-style beans, salt, pepper, and chili powder. (5) Cook over low heat for forty-five minutes to one hour.

3. Make some copies of a menu. After showing students how to locate items and prices, ask them to read it and answer specific questions such as these:

   a. What is the price of a soft drink?
   b. Can you order a baked potato separately? If so, under what heading is it found?
   c. What else do you get when you order a rib steak?
   d. How many desserts are available?

4. Using a description like the following one and reading each step aloud, draw an object on the board. Then give the children a written description of another object and ask them to draw it.

The flower has five oval petals. The petals are red. The center, at which the petals meet, is brown. The flower has a long green stem. At the bottom of the stem are overlapping blade-shaped leaves, which are half as tall as the stem.

5. Display (by writing on the board or by showing a transparency) a paragraph from a book the students have read that contains a cause-and-effect relationship. Model the process of locating the cause and the effect. Point out clue words, such as *because,* if they are present, but make sure the children know they cannot always expect such clues to be present. Then show the children another paragraph from the same book or another one. State the cause of the action, and have them identify the effect. Discuss the children's responses. A paragraph similar to the following one could be used for instruction.

Bobby, Jill, Leon, and Peggy were playing softball in Bobby's yard. Peggy was up at bat and hit the ball squarely in the direction of Bobby's bedroom window. As the group watched in horror, the softball crashed through the window, shattering the glass.

Question: What happened when the softball hit the window?
or
What caused the window to break?

6. Have the children read a selection such as the folktale "Lazy Jack." Then list the events in the story out of sequence, and show students how to reorder them. Using another selection, like that in the Model Activity "Placing Story Events in Order," ask the children to list the events in sequence. (Use shorter selections for younger children.)

7. Discuss with the children the functions of such key words as *first, next, last,* and *finally.* Then give them a paragraph containing these words, and ask them to underline the words that help to show the order of events.

8. Use an activity similar to the Model Activity "Following Directions" on pages 225-226.

9. Teach the children the meanings of words commonly encountered in written directions, such as *underline, circle, divide, color, example, left, right, below, over,* and *match.*

10. Write directions for an activity, and have the students perform it. Construction and cooking projects, as well as science experiments and magic tricks, can be used. Discussion can center on the results that occur if the correct sequence is not followed. Directions can be cut apart, scrambled, and reconstructed to show comprehension of the necessary sequence.

**Model
Activities**

Placing Story Events in Order

Discuss the meaning of sequence with the children. Give an example of the sequence in a very familiar story such as "The Three Little Pigs." Then ask the children to read the following story and place the list of events in order.

We were all excited on Friday morning because we were going to go to the circus. We had trouble concentrating on eating breakfast, but Mother wouldn't allow us to leave the table before we were finished.

Immediately after breakfast, we piled into the station wagon. Everyone was talking at once and bouncing around on the seats as Dad started the car and backed out of the driveway. We were making so much noise and moving around so much that Dad didn't hear or see the truck turn the corner. The truck driver honked his horn, but it was too late. Dad backed right into the side of the truck.

The angry driver jumped out of his truck, but when he saw the crowd of us in the station wagon, he calmed down. He and Dad talked to each other awhile, staring at the damaged side of the truck oc-

casionally. Then they went into the house to report the accident to the police.

Mother recovered from the shock and told us to get out of the car. "We'll have a long wait before we will be able to leave," she said.

Story Events

The family got into the station wagon.

The truck driver honked his horn.

The family ate breakfast.

Dad backed out of the driveway.

Dad and the truck driver talked.

Mother told the children to get out of the car.

Dad backed into the side of the truck.

Dad and the truck driver went into the house.

The driver jumped out of his truck.

After everyone has finished the exercise independently, discuss the children's results in class. Be sure to have the children give the reasons for their decisions.

**Model
Activities**

Following Directions

Give the students handouts with the following information printed on them.

Directions: Read all the items before you begin to carry out each instruction. Work as quickly as you can; you have five minutes to finish this activity.

1. Write your name at the top of the paper.

2. Turn the paper over and add 15 and 25. Write the answer you get on this line: _____ .

3. Stand up and clap your hands three times.

4. Count the number of times the word *the* is written on this page. Put the answer on this line: _____ .

5. Go to the board and write your name.

6. Count the people in this room. Put the answer under your name at the top of the page.

7. Now that you have read all of the directions, take your paper to the teacher. It should have no marks on it.

After the children have finished the exercise, hold a discussion about why some of them made marks on the paper that they should not have made. Emphasize the importance of reading and following directions carefully to avoid errors.

Higher-Order Comprehension

Higher-order reading comprehension goes beyond literal understanding of a text. It is based on the higher-order thinking processes of interpretation, analysis, and synthesis of information.

Knowledge is necessary to higher-order thinking, but students do not always use the knowledge they possess to think inferentially, critically, and creatively (Beck, 1989). They may have the background knowledge needed for comprehending a text but may fail to use it, or they may have misconceptions about certain topics that are more detrimental to comprehension than no background knowledge at all. All groups of students, regardless of socioeconomic level or ethnic origin, vary in background knowledge. Semantic mapping accompanied by group discussion can help students with little individual knowledge about a topic pool their information and expand their knowledge (Maria, 1989).

Making *predictions* about reading material is an important higher-order reading skill. Predicting what will happen in a story or other reading selection engages students' interest and leads them to organize their thinking. A hypothesis-testing process is initiated in which students make predictions and then read to confirm or reject them. If the predictions must be rejected, the students revise them. In all cases, they must be ready to explain why they made the predictions and why they believe the predictions can be accepted or must be rejected.

Students need to realize that *any* evidence that refutes a prediction is enough to show the prediction is not valid, but even a great deal of supporting evidence in favor of a prediction may not conclusively prove that it is true. They also need to realize that just because a prediction has not been refuted at one point in the reading does not mean that evidence to refute it will not appear later. People often tend to overlook refuting evidence while noticing confirming evidence, and students must be taught to avoid doing this. By refuting unsupportable predictions, students reduce uncertainty about the story's outcome. Teachers should ask students if their predictions have been proven wrong yet and ask other, similar questions to encourage them to search for refuting evidence (Garrison and Hoskisson, 1989).

Asking for predictions when the text offers clues about what will happen helps make students aware of the usefulness of text information in making inferences. Asking for predictions when there are no text clues about what will happen encourages creative thinking on the part of the children. Both types of prediction activities are good to include in lessons over time (Beck, 1989).

Ollmann (1996) tried seven types of open-ended reading response formats with her middle-school students: literary letters to the teacher; reading response questions; two-column responses, in which quotations from the book are written on one side and personal responses to the quotations on the other; letters to the author with questions about the development of the book; hexagonal essays, in which students respond to the book from the perspective of each of the six levels of Bloom's Taxonomy; buddy journals, in which partners who have read the same book write about it in a journal and respond to each other's entries; and character journals, in which students write first-person diary entries as a main character in the book. The hexagonal essay worked best at promoting higher-order thinking: with it, students "summarize the plot, make a personal association with text, analyze the theme, analyze literary techniques, compare and contrast with other literature, and evaluate the work as a whole" (Ollmann, 1996, p. 579). The two-column response format also did well. Character journals led to development of empathy with the characters.

Interpretive Reading

Interpretive reading is reading between the lines or *making inferences*. It is the process of deriving ideas that are implied rather than directly stated. Interpretive reading includes making inferences about main ideas of passages, cause-and-effect relationships that are not directly stated, referents of pronouns, referents of adverbs, and omitted words. It also includes detecting the mood of a passage, detecting the author's purpose in writing a selection, drawing conclusions, and interpreting figurative language.

No text is ever fully explicit. Some relationships among events, motivations of characters, and other factors are left out, with the expectation that readers will figure them out on their own. Readers, therefore, must play an active role in constructing the meanings represented by the text. They must infer the implied information by combining the information in the text with their background knowledge of the world. Stories that require more inferences are more difficult to read (Carr, 1983; Pearson, 1985).

Lange (1981) has pointed out that "readers make inferences consistent with their schemata" (p. 443), but it is important to realize that children have less prior knowledge than adults do and do not always make inferences spontaneously, even when they possess the necessary background knowledge. Even very young children can, during their daily activities, make inferences by connecting new information to information they already possess, but they do not necessarily apply this skill to reading without teacher direction. Active involvement with the printed message enhances students' abilities to make inferences related to it.

Comparing events in students' own lives with events that might occur in stories they are about to read is one way to help them see the thinking processes they should use when they read. Even poor readers show the ability to make inferences about the material they are reading when such a procedure is used (Hansen and Hubbard, 1984). Having young children listen to one another's experiences related to a story, listen to one another's predictions about the story, and write down their own experiences and predictions can enhance their ability to make inferences about the story (Hansen, 1981b). In addition, providing practice in answering inferential questions is an effective method for helping the children improve in this skill (Hansen, 1981a; McCormick and Hill, 1984).

McIntosh (1985) suggests that teachers should ask first graders to make inferences based only on pieces of information located close together in the text. When the information is not adjacent in the text, the teacher can use guiding questions to lead students to it. This type of instruction helps students become aware of the need to search actively for the meanings of written passages. Older children grow in their ability to make inferences, possibly because of their increased knowledge of the world.

Students are expected to make inferences about a number of things: locations, people who act in certain ways, time, actions, devices or instruments, categories, objects, causes and/or effects, solutions to problems, and feelings. To make these inferences, they can relate important vocabulary in the reading material to their backgrounds of experience. First, the teacher should explain how important words in a passage can help in making a particular inference about the passage. Then the teacher should have students practice and apply this procedure. During the application phase, students are asked to make an inference based on the first sentence and then retain, modify, or reject it as each subsequent sentence is read (Johnson and Johnson, 1986). Such instruction is needed because some students will make hypotheses about the reading material but will fail to modify them when additional information shows them to be incorrect. Instead, they may distort subsequent information in an attempt to make it conform to their original hypotheses. These children may have problems with passages that present one idea and follow it with a contrasting idea or passages that present an idea and subsequently refute it. They may also have difficulty with passages that give examples of a topic, followed by a topic statement, or with passages that give no topic statement (Kimmel and MacGinitie, 1985).

Using a passage that contains a word with multiple meanings, asking for possible meanings for the word based on initial sentences, and then reading to confirm or disprove these predictions about meanings can be a good way to help students learn to revise hypotheses when reading. Reading stories written from unusual points of view can also help; for example, *The True Story of the 3 Little Pigs*, as told to Jon Scieszka (Viking Kestrel), is written from the wolf's point of view (Kimmel and MacGinitie, 1985).

Pearson (1985) succinctly describes a method related to teaching inference skills that was developed by Gordon and Pearson (1983): "(1) ask the inference question, (2) answer it, (3) find clues in the text to support the inference, and (4) tell how to get from the clues to the answer (i.e., give a 'line of reasoning')" (Pearson, 1985, p. 731). First, the teacher models all four steps; then the teacher performs steps 1 and 2, while requiring the students to complete steps 3 and 4; then the teacher performs steps 1 and 3, requiring the students to complete steps 2 and 4; and finally the teacher asks the question (step 1) and the students perform all the other steps. The responsibility for the task is thus gradually transferred from teacher to students. This is an excellent procedure and can be used for other skills as well.

Interpreting anaphora is another task that requires students to make inferences. *Anaphora* refers to the use of one word or phrase to replace another one (Irwin, 1991). Examples are using pronouns in place of nouns (*he* for a noun like *Bill*), using adverbs for nouns or noun phrases (*here* for a phrase like *in the kitchen*), letting adjectives stand for the nouns that would have followed them (*several* for *several people*), using a superordinate term to stand for a subordinate one (*reptile* for *rattlesnake*), using an inclusive term to stand for an extended section of text (*This* for *a disturbance in the neighborhood* presented in an earlier sentence), and letting referents in another sentence or clause represent deleted items (*I will too,* following *Mom will bake brownies for the sale. Bake brownies for the sale* is "understood").

At some point, teachers will probably need to address in class all forms of anaphora, but the approaches used can be similar. Modeling of the thought processes used is important. Since children frequently have trouble identifying the noun to which a pronoun refers, they need practice in deciding to whom or to what pronouns refer. The Classroom Scenario on pronoun referents in the next

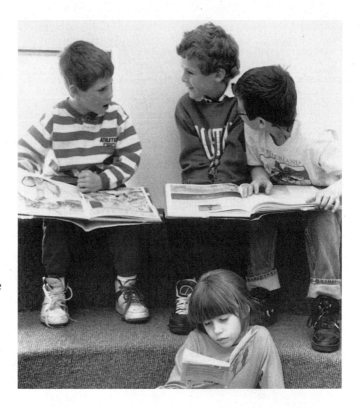

Readers employ literal comprehension as well as higher-order comprehension (interpretive comprehension, critical reading, creative reading) to understand fully what they read. (© *Jean Claude Lejeune/Stock Boston*)

section offers ideas for instruction about and practice with pronouns. Some other forms of anaphora are discussed in subsequent sections.

Pronoun Referents. A piece of writing seldom, if ever, explicitly states the connection between a pronoun and its referent (an anaphoric relationship), so the task of determining the referent is an inferential one. Students recall structures in which the referent is a noun or a noun phrase more easily after reading than structures in which the referent is a clause or a sentence (Barnitz, 1979).

Mark wanted an ice cream cone but did not have enough money for it. (noun phrase referent)

Mike plays the guitar for fun, but he does not do it often. (sentence referent)

Similarly, children find it easier to remember structures in which the pronoun follows its referent than ones in which the pronoun comes first (Barnitz, 1979).

Because it was pretty, Marcia wanted the blouse.

Marcia wanted the blouse because it was pretty.

Teachers should give attention to the structures just described. They should use stories or content selections the students are currently reading and explain the connections between the pronouns and referents in a number of examples before asking students to determine the relationships themselves. See the following Classroom Scenario for an example of such a procedure.

**Classroom
Scenario**

Pronoun Referents

Mr. Stevens wrote the following sentence on the chalkboard: "Joan put the license plate on her bicycle." Then he read it to the class. After reading the sentence, he modeled the process involved in determining the referent in the sentence by saying, "*Her* is a pronoun that stands for a noun (or, with younger children, 'a person, place, or thing'). The noun usually comes before the pronoun that stands for it. The two nouns in this sentence that come before *her* are *Joan* and *plate*. *Her* indicates a woman or a girl. A plate isn't a woman or a girl, so *her* probably stands for *Joan*."

Then he wrote this second sentence on the chalkboard: "Since the book was old, it was hard to replace." He asked the children to determine the referent for *it* in this sentence in the way he had determined the referent for *her* in the other sentence.

Ronnie said, "*It* refers to *book*."

Mr. Stevens asked Ronnie, "How did you know?"

"You told us that *it* refers to a thing, and the book is the only thing mentioned in the sentence," Ronnie responded.

"That's good thinking," Mr. Stevens replied, as he wrote a new sentence on the board for further guided practice. After another student successfully dealt with this sentence, Mr. Stevens gave the students a handout that included several para-graphs from a book they were reading in class. Each paragraph included pronouns and referents. He asked the students to draw an arrow from each pronoun to its ref-erent and be ready to explain their choices later in the day in small-group sessions.

Analysis of Scenario
Mr. Stevens followed a good instructional plan by first modeling the skill of deter-mining pronoun referents, then offering the students guided practice in which they were asked to support their responses with reasons, and finally having students prac-tice independently, using other sentences chosen from material they were currently reading.

Time for Reflection

Some people believe that children intuitively know the referents for pronouns. Oth-ers say children need instruction to help them recognize referents. **What do you think?**

Adverb Referents. At times adverbs refer to other words or groups of words with-out an explicitly stated relationship. Teachers can explain these relationships, us-ing examples such as the following, and then let children practice making the connections independently.

> I'll stay at home, and you come here after you finish. (The adverb *here* refers to *home.*)

> I enjoy the swimming pool, even if you do not like to go there. (The adverb *there* refers to *swimming pool.*)

Omitted Words. Sometimes words are omitted and said to be "understood," a structure known as *ellipsis.* Ellipsis can cause problems for some students, so again teachers should provide examples, explain the structure, and then give children practice in interpreting sentences.

> Are you going to the library? Yes, I am. (In the second sentence, the words *going to the library* are understood.)

> Who is going with you? Bobby. (The words *is going with me* are understood.)

> I have my books. Where are yours? (Here the second sentence is a shortened form of *Where are your books?*)

After this structure has been thoroughly discussed, students may practice by re-stating the sentences, filling in the deleted words.

Main Ideas. The main idea of a paragraph is the central thought around which the whole paragraph is organized. It is often, but not always, expressed in a *topic sentence* in expository writing; in narrative writing, even fewer topic sentences will be found.

To understand written selections fully and to summarize long selections, children must be able to determine the main ideas in their reading materials. Teachers should provide them with opportunities to practice recognizing main ideas and help them to realize the following facts:

1. A topic sentence often states the main idea of the paragraph.

2. The topic sentence is often, though not always, the first sentence in the paragraph; sometimes it appears at the end or in the middle.

3. Not all paragraphs have topic sentences.

4. The main idea is supported by all of the details in a well-written paragraph.

5. When the main idea is not directly stated, readers can determine it by discovering the topic to which all the stated details are related.

6. The main idea of a whole selection may be determined by examining the main ideas of the individual paragraphs and deciding to what topic they are all related.

The teacher should model the thought process students need to follow in deciding on the main idea of a selection before asking them to try this task independently. For paragraphs with topic sentences, the teacher can show students that the topic sentence is the main idea and that the other sentences in the paragraph relate to it by taking a paragraph, locating the topic sentence, and showing the relationship of each of the other sentences to the topic sentence. Then the teacher can give the students paragraphs and ask them to underline the topic sentences and tell how each of the other sentences relates to each topic sentence.

Activities such as those illustrated in the following Focus on Strategies and described in the Model Activity on inferring unstated main ideas can give pupils practice in locating main ideas in paragraphs.

**Focus on
Strategies**

Finding Main Ideas

Mrs. Braswell wrote the following paragraph on the chalkboard:

Edward Fong is a good family man. He is well educated, and he keeps his knowledge of governmental processes current. He has served our city well as a mayor for the past two years, exhibiting his outstanding skills as an administrator. Edward Fong has qualities that make him an excellent choice as our party's candidate for governor.

She said: "I am going to try to locate the topic sentence, the one to which all of the other sentences are related. The topic sentence provides one type of main idea for the paragraph. . . . Now, let's see, is it the first sentence? No. None of the other sentences appear to support his being a good family man. . . . Is it the second sentence? No. It isn't supported by the first sentence. . . . Is it the third sentence? No. It may be supported by the second sentence, but not by the others. . . . Is it the fourth sentence? Yes, I think it is. A candidate for governor would do well to be a good family man, be well educated and knowledgeable about government, and have experience as a city administrator. All the other sentences support the last one, which is broad enough in its meaning to include the ideas expressed in the other sentences."

After this demonstration, Mrs. Braswell let one student "think aloud" the reasoning behind his or her choice of a topic sentence for another paragraph. Finally, she had students work on this process in pairs, "thinking aloud" to each other.

A topic merely identifies the subject matter; a main idea also includes the type of information given about the topic. For example, a topic of a paragraph or selection might be "football," whereas the main idea might be "There are several different ways to score in football."

Duffelmeyer and Duffelmeyer (1991) suggest the use of gamelike activities to show students that a topic and a statement about the topic combine to make a main idea statement. They encourage following these activities with modeling of the writing of details to support the main idea statements formed, followed by guided practice for the students in performing this task.

To give students a concrete analogy for main ideas and details, a teacher can use a familiar object such as a bicycle. The bicycle can be identified as the main idea, and the handlebars, seat, pedals, gears, wheels, and chain can represent the supporting details that together make up the main idea.

Finding the main idea in whole selections of nonfiction generally is a categorizing process in which the topic is located and the information given about the topic is then examined (Moldofsky, 1983). In fiction, however, there is not a "topic" but a central problem, which is rarely stated explicitly.

Individual teachers mean different things when they request main ideas from students, and, when students are asked to give the main idea of a passage, some produce topics, some topic sentences, and some brief summaries. A description of the task expected, however, may be all students need to lead them to produce the desired response (Moore and Cunningham, 1984).

In many selections, readers must infer the main idea from related details. Even in selections in which the main idea is directly stated, readers generally must make inferences about which sentence states the main idea. The teacher can help develop students' readiness to make such inferences by asking them to locate the main ideas of pictures first. Then the teacher can ask them to listen for main ideas as he or she reads to them. Finally, the teacher can have them look for main ideas of passages they read.

Showing students how to infer unstated main ideas is a more difficult process than showing them how to decide which stated sentence represents the main idea. In the following Model Activity, the teacher could compare each of the possible choices to the details in the selection, rejecting those that fail to encompass the details. As students practice and become more proficient at identifying implied main ideas, the teacher should omit the choices and ask them to state the main idea in their own words (Moore and Readence, 1980). Teachers can also increase passage length as the children gain proficiency, beginning with paragraphs that have directly stated topic sentences, moving to paragraphs that do not have directly stated topic sentences, and finally moving gradually to entire selections. Because of their obvious morals, Aesop's fables are good for teaching implied main ideas. The teacher can give students a fable and ask them to state the moral, then compare the actual morals to the ones stated, discuss any variations, and examine reasoning processes. Children may have fun using Arnold Lobel's *Fables* (Harper & Row, 1980) with this activity as well.

Inferring Unstated Main Ideas

**Model
Activities**

Model the generation of a main idea for a paragraph from one of the students' textbooks that has an unstated main idea. Be sure to show how each sentence in the paragraph supports the main idea you generated. Then display a copy of the following paragraph (or a similar one from one of their textbooks) and main idea choices on the chalkboard or a transparency.

The mayor of this town has always conducted his political campaigns as name-calling battles. Never once has he approached the basic issues of a campaign. Nevertheless, he builds himself up as a great statesman, ignoring the irregularities that have been discovered during his terms of office. Do you want a person like this to be reelected?

The main idea of this selection is:

1. The current mayor is not a good person to reelect to office.

2. The mayor doesn't say nice things about his opponents.

3. The mayor is a crook.

4. The mayor should be reelected.

Say: "In this selection, the main idea is implied but not directly stated. Choose the correct main idea from the list of possible ones. Try to use a thinking process similar to the one I used in the example that I gave for you. Be ready to explain the reason for your choice to your classmates."

Eventually the students should be given a paragraph and asked to construct a main idea statement with no choices provided.

Finding main ideas in fiction is a somewhat different process. To help students learn to locate a central problem in a fictional work, the teacher should first activate their schemata for problems and solutions, perhaps by talking about background experiences or stories previously read. Then the class may identify and categorize types of problems. Finally, the teacher should model the process of identifying a central story problem with a familiar, brief story. Pauses during reading to hypothesize about the central problem and to confirm or modify hypotheses can show the students how to search for the thing the central character wants, needs, or feels—the thing that provides the story's problem. The teacher should let the children see how the story's events affect the hypotheses they have made. Events of a story may be listed on the board to be analyzed for the needs or desires of the main character (Moldofsky, 1983).

Activities

1. Gather old newspapers and cardboard for mounting. Cut from the newspapers a number of articles that you think will interest the children, and separate the text of each article from its headline. Mount each article and title on cardboard. The children's task is to read each article and locate the most suitable headline for it. To make the task easier, have them begin by matching captions to pictures, use very short articles, or use articles that are completely different in subject matter. Have the children discuss the reasons for their choices. Make the activity self-checking by coding articles and headlines. To follow up, you might use these ideas: (a) have children make pictures and captions to share in the reading center, or (b) have them try to match advertisements to pictures or captions to cartoons.

2. Collect newspaper articles and cut off headlines. Then have students construct titles using the information in the lead paragraph. Show them how to do this before you ask them to work on the task alone.

Cause and Effect. Sometimes a reader needs to infer a cause or an effect that has been implied in the material. Cause-and-effect relationships can be taught using cause-and-effect chains in real life and in stories. Brainstorming out loud about causes and effects may help children develop more skill in this area. The teacher can ask: "What could be the effect when a person falls into the lake? What could be the cause of a crying baby?" Then the teacher should elicit the reasoning behind children's answers. The following Classroom Scenario describes a practice activity for this skill.

Classroom Scenario

Inferring Cause-and-Effect Relationships

Mrs. Taylor stacked three books on the edge of her desk as the children watched. Then she said, "Cover your eyes or put your heads down on your desks so that you can't see the books anymore. Don't peek."

When all eyes were covered, Mrs. Taylor knocked the books off of the desk. Then she said, "You can open your eyes now."

The children opened their eyes and saw the books on the floor.

"What caused the books to be on the floor?" Mrs. Taylor asked.

Rob immediately responded, "You knocked them off."

"How do you know that I knocked them off?" Mrs. Taylor persisted. "You didn't see me do it."

"Nobody except you was up there," Rob replied.

(continued)

"How do you know that I didn't just lay them gently on the floor?" the teacher then asked.

"Because they made such a loud noise," Rob answered. "If you had put them down gently, there wouldn't have been much noise."

"Excellent thinking, Rob!" said Mrs. Taylor. "You used clues to figure out something that you didn't actually see. When you read, you can use that skill, too. Sometimes the author leaves clues about what he wants you to know, but he doesn't come right out and say it. You have to use clues he gives and 'read between the lines' to find out what happened. We're going to try doing that right now."

Mrs. Taylor passed out a handout with the following paragraphs on it. She said, "Read the following paragraphs and answer the question."

> Jody refused to go to bed when the babysitter told her it was time. "This is a special occasion," she said. "Mom and Dad said I could stay up two hours later tonight."
>
> Reluctantly, the babysitter allowed Jody to sit through two more hour-long TV shows. Although her eyelids drooped, she stubbornly stayed up until the end of the second show.
>
> This morning Jody found it hard to get out of bed. All day there was evidence that she was not very alert. "What is wrong with me?" she wondered.
>
> Question: What caused Jody to feel the way she did today?

When everyone had finished reading and had answered the question independently, Mrs. Taylor had one child answer the question aloud. The other children verified the answer, and several pointed out the clues in the material that helped them to decide on the answer.

Analysis of Scenario

Mrs. Taylor used a concrete experience to show the children how they made inferences about experiences every day. Then she had them try to apply the same kind of thinking to a reading experience, analyzing their thinking and pointing out the clues they used, so that classmates who were having trouble with the skill could see how they processed the information.

Detecting Mood. Certain words and ways of using words tend to set a mood for a story, poem, or other literary work. Teachers should have children discuss how certain words trigger certain moods—for example, *ghostly, deserted, haunted,* and *howling* convey a scary mood; *lilting, sparkling, shining,* and *laughing* project a happy mood; *downcast, sobbing,* and *dejected* indicate a sad mood. They should model for the children the process of locating mood words in a paragraph and using these words to determine the mood of the paragraph. Then they can give the children copies of selections in which they have underlined words that set the mood and let them decide what the mood is, based on the underlined words. Finally, teachers can give the students a passage such as the one provided in the following Classroom Scenario and tell them to underline the words that set the mood. After the students complete the practice activity, they should discuss the mood that the words established.

**Classroom
Scenario**

Detecting Mood

Mrs. Vaden read the following excerpt from *Homesick: My Own Story* by Jean Fritz (Dell, 1982, p. 138) to her class.

> By the time we were at the bottom of the hill and had parked beside the house, my grandmother, my grandfather, and Aunt Margaret were all outside, looking exactly the way they had in the calendar picture. I ran right into my grandmother's arms as if I'd been doing this every day.
>
> "Welcome home! Oh, welcome home!" my grandmother cried.
>
> I hadn't known it but this was exactly what I'd wanted her to say. I needed to hear it said out loud. I was home.

Mrs. Vaden said, "In this passage, the mood of happiness is effectively developed by describing the girl running into her grandmother's arms, the cries of 'welcome' from her grandmother, and the statement 'I was home.' All these things combine to help us feel the happy mood. Some authors carefully choose words to help readers feel the mood they want to share. Read the paragraph on the board, decide what mood the author wanted to set, and be ready to tell the class which words helped you to decide about the mood."

The following paragraph was on the board:

> Jay turned dejectedly away from the busy scene made by the movers as they carried his family's furniture from the house. "We're going away forever," he thought sadly. "I'll never see my friends again." And a tear rolled slowly down Jay's cheek, further smudging his unhappy face.

Steve raised his hand. When the teacher called on him, he said, "The mood is sad."

"That's right," Mrs. Vaden responded. "What clues did you use to decide that?"

"*Sadly, tear,* and *unhappy,*" he replied.

Sharon chimed in, "I see another one. *Dejected* is a sad word, too."

"Very good," said Mrs. Vaden. "You both found clues to the mood of this paragraph. Next, we will look for the mood as we begin to read our story for this week. Jot down the clue words as you find them to help you decide on the mood."

Analysis of Scenario

Mrs. Vaden first showed the children how she decided about the mood of a passage in a literature selection with which they were familiar. Then she gave them an opportunity to determine the mood for another selection, under her supervision. Finally, she asked them to apply the skill in further purposeful reading activities.

Detecting the Author's Purpose. Writers always have a purpose for writing: to inform, to entertain, to persuade, or to accomplish something else. Teachers should encourage their students to ask, "Why was this written?" by presenting them with a series of stories and explaining the purpose of each one, then giving them other stories and asking them to identify the purposes. The class should discuss reasons for the answers. The following Model Activity gives students practice in detecting purpose.

Model Activities

Detecting the Author's Purpose

Display the following list of reading selections on the board, or display the actual books. Ask the children to consider the selections and decide for each selection whether the author was trying to inform, entertain, or persuade.

This Is the Way It Works: A Collection of Machines by Robert Gardner. New York: Doubleday, 1980.

The Long Road to Gettysburg by Jim Murphy. New York: Scholastic, 1992.

The Good, the Bad, and the Goofy by Jon Scieszka. New York: The Trumpet Club, 1992.

A Book of Puzzlements: Play and Invention with Language by Herbert Kohl. New York: Schocken, 1981.

"Put Safety First." A pamphlet.

After each child has had time to make a decision about each selection, ask volunteers to share their responses and the reasons for each one. Clear up any misconceptions through discussion.

Drawing Conclusions. To draw conclusions, a reader must put together information gathered from several sources or places within the same source. Students may develop readiness for this skill by studying pictures and drawing conclusions from them. Answering questions like the following may also help. The teacher should model the process before having the students attempt it.

1. What is taking place here?

2. What happened just before this picture was taken?

3. What are the people in the picture preparing to do?

Cartoons may be used to good advantage in developing this comprehension skill. The teacher can show the students a cartoon like the following one and ask a question that leads them to draw a conclusion, such as "What kind of news does Dennis have for his father?" Putting together the ideas that an event happened today and that Dennis's father needs to be relaxed to hear about it enables students to conclude that Dennis was involved in some mischief or accident that is likely to upset his father. The teacher can model the necessary thinking process by pointing out each clue and relating it to personal knowledge about how parents react. Then students can practice on other cartoons.

DENNIS the MENACE

"LET ME KNOW WHEN YOU'RE RELAXED ENOUGH TO
HEAR ABOUT SOMETHIN' THAT HAPPENED TODAY."

DENNIS THE MENACE® used by permission of Hank Ketcham and © by Field Enterprises, Inc.

In the early grades, riddles such as "I have a face and two hands. I go tick-tock. What am I?" offer good practice in drawing conclusions. Commercial riddle books, which allow readers to answer riddles and explain the reasoning behind their answers, may also be used for developing this skill.

Another way to help children draw conclusions is to ask questions about sentences that imply certain information. For example, the teacher can write on the chalkboard, "The two men in uniforms removed a stretcher from the back of their vehicle." Then the teacher can ask: "What kind of vehicle were these men driving? What are your reasons for your answers?" Even though the sentence does not directly state that the vehicle is an ambulance, the details lead to this conclusion. With help, children can become adept at detecting such clues to implied meanings. The following Model Activity offers practice with this skill.

**Model
Activities**

Drawing Conclusions

Divide the children into small co-operative groups. Give each group a copy of a handout containing the following two paragraphs. Tell the children: "Read each paragraph and answer the question that follows it. After each person in your group has finished, discuss the answers with the members of your group and explain why you answered as you did. Modify your answers if you believe your thinking was wrong originally. Be ready to share your decisions with the rest of the class."

Ray went through the line, piling his plate high with food. He then carried his plate over to a table, where a server was waiting to find out what he wanted to drink. Where was Ray?

_____

_____

Cindy awoke with pleasure, remembering where she was. She hurried to dress so that she could help feed the chickens and watch her uncle milk the cows. Then she would go down to the field, catch Ginger, and take a ride through the woods. Where was Cindy?

_____

_____

Hold a whole-class discussion in which representatives from each small group share their groups' answers.

To draw conclusions about characters' motives in stories, children must have some knowledge about how people react in social situations. This knowledge comes from their backgrounds of experience. Teachers' questions can encourage inferences by requiring students to consider events from the viewpoints of different characters; to think about the characters' likely thoughts, feelings, and motives; and to anticipate consequences of the actions of various characters (Moss and Oden, 1983).

Interpreting Figurative Language. Interpreting figurative language is an inferential task. Idioms abound in the English language. An *idiom* is a phrase that has a meaning different from its literal meaning. A person who "pays through the nose," for example, does not make use of that body part but does pay a great deal. Idioms make language more difficult to comprehend, but they also add color and interest (Bromley, 1984).

Students who are not part of the mainstream culture often lack the backgrounds of experience with the culture to help them interpret idioms. They may be confused over the idea that a word or phrase has different meanings in different contexts, and its meaning in an idiomatic context may be very different from any of its denotative meanings.

It may be helpful to teach idioms by defining and explaining them when they occur in reading materials or in oral activities. Studying the origins of the expressions may also be helpful. After an idiom's meaning has been clarified, students need to use it in class activities. They may rewrite sentences to include newly learned idioms or replace these idioms with more literal language. Deaton (1992) found that doing writing that makes use of idioms can help students better understand the meanings. Illustrating idioms is another helpful activity. Students can also listen for idioms in class discussion or try using them. Creative writing about possible origins of idioms may elicit interest in discovering their real origins (Bromley, 1984).

One of the best ways to teach figurative language, as well as all interpretive reading strategies and skills, is through think-alouds. The following Focus on Strategies includes excerpts from a think-aloud used by a primary-grade classroom teacher in which she emphasized the figurative language in the selection and shows how she followed up the think-aloud to focus attention specifically on personification.

More extensive coverage of figurative expressions appears in Chapter 4. That discussion identifies different types of figures of speech and offers teaching suggestions.

**Focus on
Strategies**

Figurative Language Instruction

Evelyn Forbes was reading aloud from the story "The Big Green Umbrella" by Elizabeth Coatsworth while the students followed along in their books. As she read the paragraph of text that said that "the umbrella seemed to grow tired of keeping the rain off the Thomases on rainy days and standing in the dark corner. . . . It had heard the talk of the winds . . . whispering of raindrops, which had seen all the world. . . . the umbrella acted," she stopped and inserted her thoughts about the text. "Wind can't really talk, and raindrops can't whisper," she mused. "Umbrellas can't grow, hear, or act. People do. Why is the author making the umbrella have the characteristics of a person?" At this point she paused and discussed personification with the students, connecting it to previous reading they had done. After the discussion, she drew the following diagram on the board and had the children suggest the characteristics given to the umbrella that were characteristics of a person. She wrote these characteristics on the raindrops falling from the umbrella.   *(continued)*

Reading further, Mrs. Forbes came to the statement that "it soared upward like a kite" and "turned head-over-heels like a child at play." She repeated the similes and said, "These words paint a picture in my head of kites flying in a blue sky while children turn somersaults in the grass. What pictures are in your heads?" Then she called the children's attention to the use of *like* to compare the umbrella with things that she knew about that she could picture.

Later in the paragraph, the umbrella was said to be "dancing and bowing above the river," and the children were able to apply their knowledge of personification once more. Mrs. Forbes stopped reading after a few more paragraphs in which the story characters have speculated about the plight of the umbrella. She said, "Mr. Thomas is wrong about the umbrella. What do you think is going to happen?" The students' predictions ended the lesson for that day, leaving them eager for reading time the next day, when they would discover whether or not their predictions were right.

Critical Reading

Critical reading is evaluating written material—comparing the ideas discovered in the material with known standards and drawing conclusions about their accuracy, appropriateness, and timeliness. The critical reader must be an active reader, questioning, searching for facts, and suspending judgment until he or she has considered all the material. Critical reading depends on both literal and interpretive comprehension, and grasping implied ideas is especially important.

People must read critically to make intelligent decisions based on the material they read, such as which political candidate to support, which products to buy, which movies to attend, which television programs to watch, and so on. Since children face many of these decisions early in life, they should receive early instruction in critical reading.

Teachers can begin promoting critical reading in the first grade, or even kindergarten, by encouraging critical thinking. When reading a story to the class, they can ask, "Do you think this story is real or make-believe? Why do you think so?" If the children have difficulty in answering, questions such as "Could the things in this story really have happened? Do you know of any children who can fly? Have you ever heard of any *real* children who can fly? Have you ever heard of anyone who stayed the same age all of the time? Do all people grow up after enough years have passed?" can be helpful. By asking "Can animals really talk? Have you ever heard an animal talk?" teachers can help children understand how to judge the reality or fantasy in a story.

Critical thinking can also be promoted at an early stage through critical reading of pictures. If children are shown pictures that contain inaccuracies (for example, a car with a square wheel), they can identify the mistakes. Children's magazines often contain activities of this type, and illustrators of books often inadvertently include incorrect content. After the children have read (or have been read) a story containing such a picture, ask them to identify what is wrong in the picture, according to the story.

Critical listening instruction and critical reading instruction have been effective with students in grades one through six, regardless of whether or not they have already mastered basic decoding skills, and such instruction is appropriate for remedial, as well as developmental, readers. Instruction in critical listening has been shown to improve critical reading and general reading comprehension for remedial readers in grades four through six (Boodt, 1984).

Critical reading is closely related to revision in writing. Both activities require critical thinking. Students must evaluate their own writing to improve it, just as they evaluate the writing of others as they read.

Group thinking conferences can help students become better critical readers. In these small-group conferences, students read their own written materials aloud. After a piece has been read, the teacher motivates discussion by asking what the piece was about, what the students liked about it, and what questions or suggestions the students might have for the author. The students revise their own pieces after the group conferences. The same type of conference can be held about a published text by a professional author. This process gives student writers insight into what readers expect of writers. If students fail to respond in ways that alert their classmates to missing or inappropriate aspects of the written pieces, the teacher can ask questions aimed at helping them make these discoveries (Fitzgerald, 1989).

As Robertson and Rane-Szostak (1996) have done with older students, middle-school teachers can use short written dialogues between two people who have different positions on the issue being discussed to help students develop critical thinking skills. The students, in collaborative learning groups, can be asked to evaluate the dialogues by identifying each person's viewpoint, biases in the presentations, evidence for positions, evidence that was excluded, misstated facts, and mistaken reasoning. The groups then can choose the most reasonable position. Each group can act out its dialogue and explain its decision. The other class members can then add to the analysis.

To foster critical reading skills in the classroom, teachers can encourage pupils to read with a questioning attitude and can lead them to ask questions such as the following when they are reading nonfiction:

1. Why did the author write this material?

2. Does the author know what he or she is writing about? Is he or she likely to be biased? Why or why not?

3. Is the material up to date?

4. Is the author approaching the material logically or emotionally? What emotional words does he or she use?

5. Is the author employing any undesirable propaganda techniques? If so, which ones? How does he or she use them?

Fiction can also be read critically, but the questions that apply are a little different.

1. Could this story really have happened?

2. Are the characters believable within the setting furnished by the story? Are they consistent in their actions?

3. Is the dialogue realistic?

4. Did the plot hold your interest? What was it that kept your interest?

5. Was the ending reasonable or believable? Why or why not?

6. Was the title well chosen? Why or why not?

Groups may be used for discussion of the reading material, whether all of the children have read the same selection or some of them have read different selections on a common topic or from a common genre. The children compose questions to be discussed by the group, with the group making the decision about which questions to consider. When questions have been selected, the children prepare for the group meeting by reading and/or rereading material to answer the questions, taking notes about their findings, and marking (with paper markers) passages in the book that support their answers. The group discussions that ensue are just that: children discuss without holding up their hands for a turn or being called on. They respond to the comments and questions of the other group members (Reardon, 1988). In this activity, analysis of the material is meaningful to the students: they decide what is significant in the material, and they relate the material to matters of importance to them, for example, how the author's use of language affects the story.

Careful questioning by the teacher to extend limited and stereotyped depictions of people in reading materials can help children develop expertise in critical reading. Children must be encouraged to relate their personal experiences to the materials. Children can examine stereotyped language in relation to stories in which it occurs, and teachers can point out the problems caused by looking at people and ideas in a stereotyped way (Zimet, 1983). For example, some books give the impression that certain nationalities have particular personality characteristics, but it should be easy to demonstrate that not all people of that nationality are alike, just as not all Americans are alike. Multicultural literature can be a vehicle through which teachers can create awareness of cultural variations and of negative biases that exist toward some groups, allowing progress to be made toward elimination of these biases (Barta and Grindler, 1996).

Critical thinking is often important to the interpretation of humor (Whitmer, 1986). Therefore, humorous literature can be an enjoyable vehicle for teaching critical reading skills. It is especially good for determining the author's purpose (often to entertain, but sometimes also to convince through humor) and for evaluating content (especially distinguishing fact from fantasy and recognizing assumptions).

Many excellent books for children are filled with themes of honesty and dishonesty, sharing and selfishness, courage and cowardliness, and many others. Discussion of these themes in the context of the stories' characters, with consideration of alternatives available to them and of the appropriateness or inappropriateness of their actions, can build skill in critical reading (McMillan and Gentile, 1988). The students can be asked to compare the actions of the characters to standards of behavior set by the law, the school, parents, and so forth.

Resnick (1987) points out that "[h]igher order thinking often yields multiple solutions, each with costs and benefits, rather than unique solutions" and that "[h]igher order thinking involves imposing meaning, finding structure in apparent disorder" (p. 3). Literature analysis can help students become skillful in performing these tasks. One critical reading activity is to have children evaluate the evidence that Chicken Little had that the sky was falling and decide whether or not the other animals were right to just take her word for it. They can also be asked if the Little Red Hen used good strategies to elicit help from the other animals and what else she might have done (Beck, 1989).

To analyze characterization in literature selections, students must be able to make inferences about characters. Norton (1992) believes teachers need to model the process of making inferences about characters for the students. They can read examples from a text, pause and verbalize a question that requires an inference, and answer the question, using supporting data from the text and making their reasoning process clear to the students. They can tell how their prior knowledge and beliefs affected the answer. Then students can be asked to attempt these same steps. Norton suggests the story *Shiloh* (Naylor, 1991) as a good one for helping students learn to make inferences about characters.

Norton (1992, p. 65) says that students must understand that making inferences involves going beyond the information stated in the text and that "they must use clues from the text to hypothesize about a character's emotions, beliefs, actions, hopes, and fears. Students must also be aware that authors develop characters through dialogue, narration, thoughts, and actions." This activity leads directly into character analysis.

Commeyras (1989) suggests the use of literature selections and a grid developed by Ashby-Davis (1986) to help students learn about character analysis. Example 6.2 shows a completed grid based on the character of Tom Sawyer. Such a grid leads students to collect evidence about a character, interpret the evidence, and make a generalization about the evidence after all of it has been collected. Looking for commonalities and discrepancies in the data and considering the amount of evidence available for a conclusion drawn are important to good critical analysis. When readers draw evidence from reactions of other characters in the story, they must evaluate the credibility of the sources before accepting the evidence.

Santino (1991) suggests having students compare different versions of folktales with Venn diagrams and comparison charts to improve comprehension and

Example 6.2 *Sample Grid on* **Tom Sawyer**

	External clues	Student's interpretation

(1) Frequent kinds of statements made by this character

A. Fibs — A. Tom gets his way.

B. Commands — B. Tom is confident.

My summary of these interpretations of statements:

Tom is bold and daring.

(2) Frequent actions of the character

A. Mischievous — A. Tom likes to fool around.

B. Heroic — B. Tom isn't afraid.

My summary of these interpretations of actions:

Tom's good deeds are more important than his misbehavior.

(3) Frequent ways of thinking by this character:

A. He schemes. — A. Tom finds solutions.

B. He's optimistic. — B. Tom has confidence.

My summary of these interpretations of thought:

Tom is smart.

(4) What do others frequently say to the character:

A. What have you done? — A. Tom is unpredictable.

B. This is fun! — B. Tom has good ideas.

Summary of my interpretations of these statements:

Tom is independent in his actions.

(5) What do others do to this character:

A. They get mad at him. — A. Tom upsets people.

B. They follow his lead. — B. Tom gets respect.

Summary of my interpretation:

Tom gets to people one way or another.

(6) What do others say about the character:

A. He's stubborn. — A. Tom doesn't give up.

B. He's brave. — B. Tom helps others.

Summary of my interpretation:

Tom isn't all good or all bad.

My final generalization concerning the personality of Tom Sawyer:

Tom Sawyer is a boy who gets into trouble, but ends up doing the right thing in the end.

Source: Michelle Commeyras, "Using Literature to Teach Critical Thinking," *Journal of Reading,* 32 (May 1989), 703–707. Reprinted with permission of Michelle Commeyras and the International Reading Association. All rights reserved.

see commonalities in stories from different cultures. Example 6.3 shows a comparison of a Russian folktale with an Appalachian one.

Teachers can also encourage students to think critically by having them compare film versions of stories with the text versions. Analysis of the dramatic interpretation of a story can also provide students with a model of creative response to the narrative (Duncan, 1993). See Chapter 11 for a Classroom Scenario involving comparisons of text and film versions of stories.

If the children have adequate schemata for understanding the text, it is better to have them read the text before seeing the film. Sometimes the children may be exposed to the story on film, but only a portion of the text version may be used in instruction. Then some students may be motivated to finish the text on their own. Most film versions are necessarily abbreviated versions. However, seeing an abbreviated presentation of a story that provides a knowledge of its basic structure may provide needed support for disabled readers, giving them confidence to attempt to read the text (Duncan, 1993).

Students can use Venn diagrams to show how characters were alike and different in film and text versions of stories. They can also write film reviews, including notes about how true the film was to the book. *Sarah, Plain and Tall*; *Where the Red Fern Grows*; *The Secret Garden*; *Bridge to Terabithia*; and *Tuck Everlasting* are books that have film versions available for comparison.

Commeyras (1993) suggests using Dialogical-Thinking Reading Lessons (D-TRLs) to promote critical thinking among students. She explains, "D-TRLs encourage students to (a) return to the text to verify or clarify information; (b) consider multiple interpretations; (c) identify reasons to support interpretations; and (d) evaluate the acceptability and relevance of competing or alternative interpretations" (p. 487).

A story that contains an issue that can be considered from more than one perspective is chosen for the D-TRL. During the reading phase of the D-TRL, the reading may be guided or independent, depending on the students' capabilities. During the discussion phase, the central question is introduced, along with two hypothetical conclusions about the answer. The children are invited to take one of the positions or announce that they are undecided. This helps to engage students in the search for information. Then the students search the text for support for each conclusion. The teacher lists all suggestions on the board. After reasons have been listed, the students should evaluate each one. Criteria for evaluation should include: (1) Is the reason based on verifiable information (either from the text, prior knowledge, or logic)? (2) Is the reason relevant to the conclusion? Then the students attempt to draw final conclusions from the entire discussion. Some may believe they were correct initially; some may still be undecided; and some may have changed their positions, depending on the evidence brought out in the discussion. After students can do all of this well, they can generate their own hypothetical conclusions in subsequent lessons and, eventually, their own central questions.

Evaluating Factors Related to the Author. Krieger (1990) found that middle-school students were not aware of the authors of the material they read and the

Example 6.3 *Comparison of Folktales*

Comparison of Two Stories

	Hardy Hardhead	Fool of the World and the Flying Ship
QUEST	To break enchantment and marry King's daughter	To provide flying ship to Czar and marry Czar's daughter
CHARACTERS	Two older brothers (Tom & Will) favored by parents	Two older brothers favored by parents
	Younger brother (Jack) – thought to be foolish	Younger brother – Fool of the World
	Old Man ← Tom and Will didn't share / Jack shared food / Gave Jack a flying ship and money (Take in everyone)	Old man ← Fool shared food / Showed Fool how to get flying ship (Take in everyone)
	[1]Hardy Hardhead [2]Eatwell [3]Drinkwell [4]Runwell [5]Harkwell	[4]Man with bread [5]Man walking around lake [3]Man on one leg (other tied to head) [1]Man listening to all that is being done in the world
	[6]Seewell [7]Shootwell	[2]Man with gun [6]Man with wood on shoulders [7]Man with sack of straw
ACTION	Each person Jack picked up helped Jack win a bet with the witch.	Each person the Fool picked up helped him perform a seemingly impossible task for the Czar.
RESOLUTION	Jack paid back old man and kept ship. Enchantment on King's girl was broken.	Fool married princess. They fell in love with each other.

Character Comparison

Hardy Hardhead
Seewell

Two Older Brothers
Foolish Younger Brother
Old Man
Big Eater
Big Drinker
Fast Runner
Man with Good Hearing
Good Marksman

Man with Wood
Man with Straw

devices the authors used (flashbacks, foreshadowing, and so forth) for special purposes. She read to these students, modeling her thinking processes concerning why the author included certain details as she read. She asked them to make predictions about what might happen next from clues left by the author. Outside assignments based on the material read allowed for further thinking about the story or the author by the students; students might be asked to keep listening journals with reactions to the stories, for example. Through this listening experience, Krieger opens the students' minds to the ways authors express ideas, making it more likely that they will be able to read stories with understanding later.

McKeown and her colleagues (1993) have developed a technique called Questioning the Author to help children access ideas in a text. They point out that someone wrote the ideas in the text and that some people do not write as clearly as others. Students are invited to figure out the ideas behind the author's words, determine the author's reasons for presenting the particular information and decide whether the author has presented the ideas clearly. Then students are asked to state confusing material in a clearer way. Teachers should model this process for students before asking them to do it independently.

The mature critical reader must consider and evaluate factors related to the person who wrote the material, taking into account the following four categories.

Author's purpose. The critical reader will try to determine whether the author wrote the material to inform, to entertain, to persuade, or for some other purpose. This is an interpretive reading skill.

Author's point of view. The critical reader will want to know if the writer belonged to a group, lived in an area, or held a strong view that would tend to bias any opinions about a subject in one way or another. Two accounts of the Revolutionary War might be very different if one author was from Canada and the other from the United States.

Students can learn more about point of view by writing letters or essays about issues from different points of view. For example, they might take the point of view of an elementary school student, a concerned parent, or a principal when a school dress code is being considered.

Author's style and tone. The author's style is the manner in which he or she uses vocabulary (vividness, precision, inclusion of emotional words, use of figurative language) and sentence structure (the order within the language). Special attention should be given to use of *figurative language,* language that is not meant to be taken literally, and use of emotional words, which do much to sway the reader toward or away from a point of view or attitude. Note the effects of these two sentences:

Author 1: Next we heard the *heart-rending* cry of the wounded tiger.

Author 2: When the tiger was shot, it let out a *vicious* roar.

Teachers should be aware of undesirable aspects of the style or tone of some writers of material for youngsters. A condescending tone, for example, will be quickly sensed and resented.

Author's competence. The reliability of written material is affected by the author's competence to write about the subject in question. If background information shows that a star football player has written an article on the nation's foreign policy, intermediate-grade youngsters will have little trouble determining that the reliability of the statements in this article is likely to be lower than the reliability of a similar article written by an experienced diplomat.

To determine an author's competence, students should consider his or her education and experience, referring to books such as *Current Biography Yearbook: 1997* (H. W. Wilson, 1997) and *Seventh Book of Junior Authors and Illustrators* (H. W. Wilson, 1996) or to book jacket flaps to find such information. Teachers can give students a topic and ask them to name people who might write about it. Students can discuss which people might be most qualified, or they can compare two authors of books on the same subject and decide which one is better qualified. Students who are knowledgeable about a topic and others who are not can write reports on that topic, while the remaining students predict which people are likely to have the most accurate reports. The students can follow up with a comparison for accuracy (Ross, 1981).

Evaluating the Material.   Besides comprehending the material literally, the critical reader needs to be able to determine and evaluate the following factors.

Timeliness. The critical reader will wish to check the date the material was published, because the timeliness of an article or a book can make a crucial difference in a rapidly changing world. An outdated social studies book, for example, may show incorrect boundaries for countries or fail to show some countries that now exist; similarly, an outdated science book may refer to a disease as incurable when a cure has recently been found. A history book with a 1985 copyright date would contain no information about Operation Desert Storm.

Accuracy and adequacy. Nonfiction material should be approached with this question in mind: "Are the statements presented here true?" The importance of a good background of experience becomes evident in this situation. A reader who has had previous experience with the material will have a basis of comparison not available to one lacking such experience. A person with only a little knowledge of a particular field can often spot such indications of inadequacy as exaggerated statements, one-sided presentations, and opinion offered as fact. Obviously, readers can check reference books to see if the statements in the material are supported elsewhere.

Appropriateness. Critical readers must be able to determine whether the material is suitable for their purposes. A book or an article can be completely accurate and not be applicable to the problem or topic under consideration. For example, a child looking for information for a paper entitled "Cherokee Ceremonies" needs to realize that an article on the invention of the Cherokee alphabet is irrelevant to the task at hand.

Inquiry Charts can be constructed in order to promote use of critical reading strategies (Hoffman, 1992). First, the class identifies a topic and formulates the questions that will be the basis of the inquiry. The teacher records these on a large I-Chart (See Example 6.4 for a sample I-Chart). Materials, such as textbook selections, trade books, encyclopedia articles, and magazine articles, that pertain to the topic are also collected and listed on the I-Chart as they are used.

Example 6.4   I-Chart

I - CHART
GUIDING QUESTIONS

TOPIC: Columbus	1. Why did Columbus sail?	2. What did he find?	3. What important things did he do when he got there?	4. How was Columbus regarded by others?	Other Interesting Facts & Figures	New Questions
WHAT WE KNOW	to prove the world was round	America	... not sure	He was a hero	He sailed in 1492. He was Spanish	Did he have a family?
SOURCES 1. Meet Christopher Columbus, de Kay New York; Random House, 1969	He was trying to find a new route to the Indies	He found friendly Indians... some pieces of gold... different islands. He found America	He named the islands. He claimed the land for Queen Isabella and King Ferdinand. He brought back gold for Isabella	At the beginning people regarded him as a normal person. Later, when he got back, they thought he was a great man.	C.C. had asked the King of Portugal for ships. He was turned down. When he came back he landed in Portugal and was taken to the king. The king was mad that he didn't help him.	Whatever happened to his son?
2. The World Book Encyclopedia World Book Childcraft, Inc. 1979	to find riches... and a shorter route to the Indies. He wanted to be famous... to be known as a great sailor and explorer.	He found America. Indians... new islands.	He named the islands. He captured some Indians as slaves. He became the governor.	He was an "understanding... dreamy" person. It sounds like he had a lot of friends	In other books I've read he wasn't very popular. He had 2 sons, not 1. Six brothers and a sister. He was born in Italy.	Whatever happened to his sons?
3. Where do You Think You're Going Christopher Columbus? Jean Fritz. New York: G.P. Putnam's Sons, 1980	Because he liked to travel and explore, they said they would give a big reward for finding a new route to the Indies	He found Indians... Some small hunks of gold	He talked to the Indians. He asked for directions to the Palace of the Khan. He named the islands	Before he went he was wealthy because he had married a rich woman. He was famous after he sailed, but a couple of years later, everyone forgot about him.	Columbus sounded greedy in this book. He said he saw land first and claimed the prize money. He claimed that all of this was God's work.	Was he really cruel to the Indians? Whatever happened to the slaves he brought back to Spain?
SUMMARY	To find a new route to the Indies... He hoped to find riches and become famous as an explorer. He already knew the world was round.	He found America and the Indians living there. He found a little gold.	He claimed the new land for Spain. He named the islands. He met with the Indians. He took some back to Spain as slaves. He became Governor.	Before he sailed he was normal;... a dreamer. After he came back he was famous and a hero. He seemed greedy. Everyone forgot about him after a while.	He claimed he was doing God's work. His family supported him. He tried to get money for his voyage from lots of people. He was born an Italian.	Find out more about his family and what happened to them. Was he cruel to the Indians? What happened to the slaves?

Source: James V. Hoffman. "Critical Reading/Thinking across the Curriculum: Using I-Charts to Support Learning." *Language Arts,* February 1992. Copyright 1992 by the National Council of Teachers of English. Reprinted with permission.

Next, the teacher questions the students to discover their prior knowledge about the topic and enters their responses, whether correct or incorrect, on the I-Chart under the identified questions. Information the students have that is not related to the identified questions is recorded under "Other Interesting Facts and Figures." If students have other questions that have not been identified, these are listed under "New Questions." Then the students read the source material independently or in a group, or the teacher reads it to them. Each source is discussed, and decisions are made about the appropriateness of the information in answering the identified questions. Information pertinent to the questions is recorded in the proper spaces. More "Interesting Facts" and "New Questions" may also be added.

After all sources have been read and information from them recorded, the students write summary statements to answer each question, considering the information from all of the sources. They also summarize the "Interesting Facts." Then the students compare what they had listed as prior knowledge with the newly acquired information and note the differences, clarifying any misconceptions previously held. Unanswered "New Questions" are researched further by individuals or small groups, who must decide about appropriate sources for the information, and findings are reported to the class.

Differentiation of fact from opinion. This skill is vital for good critical reading. People often unquestioningly accept as fact anything they see in print, even though printed material is often composed of statements of opinion. Some authors intermingle facts and opinions, giving little indication that they are presenting anything but pure fact. Also, many readers are not alert to clues that signal opinions. By pointing out these clues and providing practice in discrimination, teachers can promote the ability to discriminate between facts and opinions.

Some readers have trouble reading critically because they lack a clear idea of what constitutes a fact. *Facts* are statements that can be verified through direct observation, consultation of official records of past events, or scientific experimentation. The statement "General Lee surrendered to General Grant at Appomattox" is a fact that can be verified by checking historical records. For various reasons, *opinions* cannot be directly verified. For example, the statement "She is the most beautiful girl in the world" is unverifiable and is therefore an opinion. Even if every girl in the world could be assembled for comparison, people's standards of beauty differ and a scale of relative beauty would be impossible to construct.

Knowledge of key words that signal opinions, such as *believe, think, seems, may, appears, probably, likely,* and *possibly,* can be extremely helpful to readers. Teachers often find that pointing out such indicators to children and giving the children practice in locating them is highly beneficial.

Children must also understand that not all opinions are of equal value, since some have been based on facts, whereas others are unsupported. Critical readers try to determine the relative merit of opinions as well as to separate the opinions from the facts.

Newspaper editorials offer one good way for children to practice distinguishing fact from opinion, especially in the intermediate grades. Students can underline each sentence in the editorial with colored pencils, one color for facts and another for opinions. They can then be encouraged to discuss which opinions are best supported by facts.

Furleigh (1991) has students read and analyze an editorial for the subject or main idea, the writer's opinion about the subject, and their own opinions about the subject. The teacher or peers then evaluate the answers each student provides. When peers do the evaluations, the evaluations become additional practice sessions for them.

Activities similar to the following Model Activity may also be used to help children make this difficult differentiation.

Model Activities

Fact and Opinion

Give the students copies of the following paragraph, which opens the book *Homesick: My Own Story* by Jean Fritz (Dell, 1982, p. 9):

In my father's study there was a large globe with all the countries of the world running around it. I could put my finger on the exact spot where I was and had been ever since I'd been born. And I was on the wrong side of the globe. I was in China in a city named Hankow, a dot on a crooked line that seemed to break the country right in two. The line was really the Yangtse River, but who would know by looking at a map what the Yangtse River really was?

Ask students to read this opening paragraph carefully, underlining any part or parts that are statements of opinion. Ask them to decide what they can tell about the main character from both the facts and the opinions revealed in this opening paragraph. Then have them decide how the located opinion or opinions are likely to affect the story about to be read.

Let the students share their reactions to this opening passage before they begin to read the book. After they have finished reading the book, have them discuss whether or not their initial reactions were accurate.

Recognition of propaganda techniques. Elementary school children, like adults, are constantly deluged with writing that attempts to influence their thinking and actions. Some of these materials may be used for good purposes and some for bad ones. For example, most people would consider propaganda designed to persuade people to protect their health as "good" and propaganda intended to persuade people to do things that are harmful to their health as "bad." Since *propaganda techniques* are often used to sway people toward or away from a cause or point of view, children should be made aware of these techniques so that they can avoid being unduly influenced by them.

The Institute for Propaganda Awareness has identified seven undesirable propaganda techniques that good critical readers should know about:

1. Name calling—using derogatory labels (*reactionary, troublemaker*) to create negative reactions toward a person without providing evidence to support such impressions.

2. Glittering generalities—using vague phrases to influence a point of view without providing necessary specifics.

3. Transfer technique—associating a respected organization or symbol with a particular person, project, product, or idea, thus transferring that respect to the person or thing being promoted.

4. Plain-folks talk—relating a person (for example, a politician) or a proposed program to the "common people" in order to gain their support.

5. Testimonial technique—using a highly popular or respected person to endorse a product or proposal.

6. Bandwagon technique—playing on the urge to do what others are doing by giving the impression that everyone else is participating in a particular activity.

7. Card stacking—telling only one side of a story by ignoring information that favors the opposing point of view.

Teachers should describe propaganda techniques to the class and model the process of locating these techniques in printed materials such as advertisements. Then the children should practice this skill. Children can learn to detect propaganda techniques by analyzing newspaper and magazine advertisements, printed political campaign material, and requests for donations to various organizations.

Making value judgments. Readers need to be able to determine whether the actions of both fictional and real-life characters are reasonable or unreasonable. To help children develop this ability, teachers may ask questions such as the following:

Was the Little Red Hen justified in eating all the bread she made, refusing to share with the other animals? Why or why not?

Was it a good thing for Heidi to save bread from the Sessmans' table to take back to the grandmother? Why or why not?

Readers draw on their schemata related to right and wrong actions in order to complete this type of activity. Because of their varying schemata, not all children will answer in the same way.

Activities like the following ones can be used to provide children with practice in critical reading strategies.

Activities

1. Have a propaganda hunt. Label boxes with the names of the seven propaganda techniques listed earlier. Then ask children to find examples of these techniques in a variety of sources and drop their examples into the boxes. As a class activity, evaluate each example for appropriateness to the category in which it was placed.

2. Use computer simulation programs for practice in making critical judgments. These programs provide simulated models of real-life experiences with which students can experiment in a risk-free manner.

3. Ask students to compare two biographies of a well-known person by answering questions such as "How do they differ in their treatment of the subject? Is either of the authors likely to be biased for or against the subject? Are there contradictory statements in the two works? If so, which one seems most likely to be correct? Could the truth be different from both accounts?"

4. Have students compare editorials from two newspapers with different viewpoints or from different areas. Have them decide why differences exist and which stand, if either, is more reasonable, based on facts.

5. Ask students to examine newspaper articles for typographical errors and to determine whether or not each typographical error changed the message of the article.

6. Have the class interpret political cartoons from various newspapers.

7. Ask students to examine the headlines of news stories and decide whether or not the headlines fit the stories.

8. Ask students to write editorials about topics of interest, including facts, their own opinions, and their reasons for the opinions.

9. Locate old science or geography books containing statements that are no longer true, and use them to show the importance of using current sources. Let students compare old and new books to find the differences (new material included, "facts" that have changed, etc.), and discuss what types of material are most and least likely to be dependent on recent copyright dates for accuracy (Ross, 1981).

10. Direct students to write material that will persuade their classmates to do something. Then examine the material for the techniques they used.

11. Discuss the nutritional aspects of sugar and chemical food additives and the foods that contain them. Then have students examine the ingredient lists from popular snacks, asking themselves what food value various snacks have, according to their labels (Neville, 1982).

Some teachers tell students that they should believe certain things "because it says so in the book." Others tell them, "Don't believe everything that you read." **What do *you* think?**

Creative Reading

Creative reading involves going beyond the material presented by the author. Like critical reading, creative reading requires readers to think as they read, and it also requires them to use their imaginations. Such reading results in the production of new ideas.

Teachers must carefully nurture creative reading, trying not to ask only questions that have absolute answers, since such questions may discourage the diverse processes characteristic of creative reading. To go beyond the material in the text, readers must make use of their background schemata, combining this prior knowledge with ideas from the text to produce a new response based on, but not completely dictated by, the text. Creative readers must be skilled in the following areas.

Predicting Outcomes. Predicting outcomes, discussed earlier as a good purpose-setting technique, is a creative reading skill. In order to predict outcomes, readers must put together available information and note trends, then project the trends into the future, making decisions about what events might logically follow. A creative reader is constantly predicting what will happen next in a story, reacting to the events he or she is reading about and drawing conclusions about their results.

An enjoyable way to work on this skill is to have students read one of the action comic strips in the newspaper for several weeks and then predict what will happen next, based on their knowledge of what has occurred until that time. The teacher can record these predictions on paper and file them; later, students can compare the actual ending of the adventure with their predictions. The teacher should be sure students can present reasons to justify what they predict. When judging their theories, the teacher should point out that some predictions may seem as good a way to end the story as the one the comic strip artist used. Other predictions may not make sense, based on the evidence, and reasons for this should be made clear.

Another way to work on prediction is to stop students at particular points in their reading of a literature selection and let them predict what will happen next. In the story "Stone Soup," for example, the teacher would stop before the first townsperson contributed food to the soup and ask what the students think will happen next. A similar pause and request for a prediction after the point in the story at which the first contribution was made to the soup would then be appropriate.

To help students acquire the skill of reading creatively, teachers should model the thought process involved. After the students practice on various texts, the teacher can ask them to explain their reasons for thinking as they did. Some questions they might answer for *Heidi,* for example, are as follows:

What would have happened in the book if Peter had not pushed Klara's wheelchair down the side of the mountain?

What would have happened if Herr Sessman had refused to send Heidi back to the Alm, even though the doctor advised it?

Visualization. *Visualization* is seeing pictures in the mind, and readers draw on their existing schemata to accomplish this. By vividly visualizing the events depicted by the author's words, creative readers allow themselves to become a part of the story; they see the colors, hear the sounds, feel the textures, taste the flavors, and smell the odors the writer describes. They will find that they are living the story as they read. By doing this, they will enjoy the story more and understand it more deeply.

Guided imagery has been shown to enhance comprehension, but training in visualization may be less effective with very young children, who may not be able to form images on command, than with third- through sixth-grade students (Tierney and Cunningham, 1984). It can be used before reading, during reading, or after reading. Students can be told to see pictures in their minds as they read silently. This can help them with later recall of events read. Guided imagery activities before reading a story can help readers draw on their past experiences to visualize events, places, and things in a story. Creating such images before reading has been shown to result in better literal comprehension than is produced by creating the images after reading (Harp, 1988; Fredericks, 1986).

Dee Mundell suggests four steps for helping children develop techniques for visualization. First, teachers should lead students to visualize concrete objects after they have seen and closely examined them in the classroom. Then teachers can ask children to visualize objects or experiences outside the classroom. They can draw concrete objects they visualize and compare their drawings to the actual objects later. Next, teachers can read high-imagery stories to the children, letting individuals share their mental images with the group and having small groups illustrate the stories after the reading. Finally, teachers should encourage students to visualize as they read independently (Fredericks, 1986).

Open-ended questions can aid development of imagery (Fredericks, 1986). For example, if a child says she sees a house, the teacher can ask, "What does it look like?" If she replies that it is white with green trim, the teacher may ask, "What is the yard like?"

Following are activities that encourage visualization.

Activities

1. Give students copies of a paragraph from a children's book that vividly describes a scene or a situation, and have them illustrate the scene or situation in a painting or a three-dimensional art project.

2. Using a paragraph or statement that contains almost no description, ask students questions about details they would need in order to picture the scene in their minds. An example follows.

The dog ran toward Jane and Susan. Jane held out her hands toward it and smiled.

Questions: What kind of dog was it? How big was it? Why was it running toward the girls? What happened when the dog reached the girls? Where did this action take place? Was the dog on a leash, behind a fence, or running free?

3. Have the children dramatize a story they have read, such as the folktale "Caps for Sale."

4. Compare the characters, action, and scenery in a movie with mental images formed from reading a book or story (Rasinski, 1988).

Solving Problems. Creative readers relate the things they read to their own personal problems, sometimes applying the solution of a problem they encounter in a story to a different situation. For instance, after reading the chapter in *Tom Sawyer* in which Tom tricks his friends into painting a fence for him, a child may use a similar ruse to persuade a sibling to take over his or her chores or homework.

To work on developing this problem-solving skill, teachers need to use books in which different types of problems are solved, choosing an appropriate one to read or to let the children read. Then the teacher can ask the children questions such as the following:

1. What problem did the character(s) in the story face?

THE FAMILY CIRCUS   **By Bil Keane**

"I like reading. It turns on pictures in your head."

Reprinted with special permission of King Features Syndicate, Inc.

2. How was the problem handled?

3. Was the solution a good one?

4. What other possible solutions can you think of?

5. Would you prefer the solution in the book or one of the others?

Literature selections abound with characters trying to solve problems in efficient and inefficient ways. Children can analyze these problem-solving situations. Problems in a story can be identified as they occur. Discussion of the situation can take place at each problem occurrence. Some element of the story can be changed, and the children can then be asked how the character would have handled the new situation (Beck, 1989). *Encyclopedia Brown* and *Nate the Great* mysteries offer good problem-solving opportunities for children in intermediate and primary grades, respectively (Flynn, 1989). Any of the *Amelia Bedelia* books would also work well for this activity.

Bransford and Stein's IDEAL approach to problem solving is good to use in conjunction with cooperative learning techniques (Bransford and Stein, 1984; Flynn, 1989). The *I* stands for *identifying* the problem, the *D* for *defining* the problem more clearly, the *E* for *exploration* of the problem, the *A* for *acting* on ideas, and the *L* for *looking* for the effects. Cooperative learning techniques encourage the development of problem-solving skills through discussion, negotiation, clarification of ideas, and evaluation of the ideas of classmates. These activities lead to meeting group and individual goals.

Producing New Creations. Art, drama, and dance can be useful in elaborating on what students read. By creating a new ending for a story, adding a new character, changing some aspect of a character, or adding an additional adventure within the framework of the existing story, students approach reading creatively. Following are some possible activities; some of them involve responding to literature through writing. (More on the reading-writing connection appears in Chapter 8.)

Activities

1. Ask students to illustrate a story they have read, using a series of pictures or three-dimensional scenes.

2. Have students write plays or poems based on works of fiction they have read and enjoyed.

3. Have the students write prose narratives based on a poem they have read.

4. After the children have read several stories of a certain type (such as *Just So Stories*), ask each of them to write an original story of the same type.

5. Have the students transfer the story of Heidi to the Rocky Mountains or to Appalachia.

Some teachers think that only literal-level thinking should be expected of young children when these children read. Others believe that the children can and should do higher-order thinking about their reading. **What do** *you* **think?**

Effective Questioning

Whether teachers prepare only test questions or both purpose and test questions, all teachers use both written and oral questions as a part of class activities. Regardless of when they are used, questions have been found to foster increased comprehension, apparently because readers give more time to the material related to answering them (Durkin, 1981b). Research indicates that simply asking more inference questions during and after reading stories results in improved inferential comprehension (Hansen, 1981a; Hansen and Pearson, 1983; Pearson, 1985). Thus, the types of questions that teachers ask about selections affect the type of information that students recall about selections, and students remember best information about which they have been directly questioned (Wixson, 1983). For this reason, teachers need to understand thoroughly the process of preparing questions.

Farrar (1984a) asserts that the phrasing of questions should depend on the amount of challenge individual children need. Questions can be phrased differently and still address the same content. The phrasing can make questions easier or harder to answer and can require simple or complex answers. It may take several questions requiring simple responses to elicit all the information obtainable from one question that requires a complex response.

Another related problem is some children's lack of familiarity with the question-answer-feedback sequence often used for instructional purposes. Some children have not been exposed to this language pattern at home and find it strange and confusing that the teacher is asking for information he or she already knows. Teachers may need to actively teach the question-answer-feedback strategy in oral and written situations so that students will respond appropriately (Farrar, 1984b). Teacher modeling of the answers to questions is helpful. In the process, the teacher can explain how to interpret the question, how and where to find the information, and how to construct the answer after the information is located (Armbruster, 1992).

Preparing Questions

Teachers often ask questions that are devised on the spur of the moment. This practice no doubt results from the pressure of the many different tasks a teacher must perform during the day, but it is a poor one for at least two reasons. First, questions developed hastily, without close attention to the material involved, tend to be detail questions ("What color was the car? Where were they going?"), since detail questions are much easier to construct than most other types. But detail questions fail to measure more than simple recall. Second, many hastily constructed questions tend to be poorly worded, vague in intent, and misleading to students. Example 6.5 shows some options on which to base questioning.

Example 6.5   *Options for Questioning*

Questions Based on Comprehension Factors

1. Main idea—identify central theme or idea of selection
2. Detail—identify directly stated facts
3. Vocabulary—define words to fit the context of the selection
4. Sequence—identify order of events in selection
5. Inference—infer information implied by the author
6. Evaluation—judge ideas presented, based on a standard
7. Creative response—go beyond the material and create new ideas based on the material read

Questions Based on Source of Answers

1. Textually explicit—answers directly stated in the text
2. Textually implicit—answers implied by the text that require inferences on the part of the reader
3. Scriptually implicit—answers come from the reader's background knowledge

Questions Based on Story Grammar

1. Setting—when and where story took place and who was involved
2. Initiating event—event that started story sequence
3. Reaction—main character's reaction to the initiating event
4. Action—main character's actions caused by the initiating event and subsequent events
5. Consequence—result of main character's actions

Questions Based on Comprehension Factors

One basis for planning questioning strategies is to try to construct specific types of questions to tap different types of comprehension and different factors related to comprehension. Seven major types of questions are generally useful in guiding reading: main idea, detail, vocabulary, sequence, inference, evaluation, and creative response.

Main Idea Questions. Main idea questions ask the children to identify the central theme of the selection. These questions may give children some direction toward the nature of the answer. The question "What caused Susie to act so excited?" could direct readers toward the main idea of a passage in which Susie was very excited because she had a secret. An example of a question that offers no clues to the main idea is "What is a sentence that explains what this selection is about?" Main idea questions help children to become aware of the relationships among details.

Detail Questions. Detail questions ask for bits of information covered by the material. They ask for information such as "Who was coming to play with Maria? What was Betty bringing with her? What happened to Betty on the way to Maria's house? When did Betty finally arrive? Where had Betty left her bicycle?" Whereas it is important for students to assimilate the information these questions cover, very little depth of comprehension is necessary to answer them all correctly. Therefore, even though these questions are easy to construct, they should not constitute the bulk of the questions the teacher asks.

Vocabulary Questions. Vocabulary questions check children's understanding of word meanings, generally as used in a particular selection. For discussion purposes, a teacher might ask children to produce as many meanings of a specific word as they can, but purpose questions and test questions should ask for the meaning of a word as it is used in the selection being read.

Sequence Questions. Sequence questions check the child's knowledge of the order in which events occurred in the story. The question "What did Alex and Robbie do when their parents left the house?" is not a sequence question, since children are free to list the events in any order they choose. The question "What three things did Alex and Robbie do, in order, when their parents left the house?" requires children to display their grasp of the sequence of events.

Inference Questions. Inference questions ask for information that is implied but not directly stated in the material. These questions require some reading between the lines. The following is an example.

> Margie and Jan were sitting on the couch listening to Boyz II Men CDs. Their father walked in and announced, "I hear that there is a Boyz II Men concert at the Municipal Auditorium next week." Both girls jumped up and ran toward their father. "Can we go? Can we go?" they begged.

> Question: Do you think Margie and Jan liked to hear the music of Boyz II Men? Why or why not?

Evaluation Questions. Evaluation questions require children to make judgments about the material. Although these judgments are inferences, they depend on

The types of questions that teachers ask about selections affect the type of information that students recall about selections, and students remember best information about which they have been directly questioned. (© *Joel Gordon*)

more than the information implied or stated by the story; the children must have enough experience related to the situations involved to establish standards for comparison. An example of an evaluation question is "Was the method Kim used to rescue Dana wise? Why or why not?" These questions are excellent for open-ended class discussion but hard to grade as test questions.

Creative Response Questions. Creative response questions ask children to go beyond the material and create new ideas based on the ideas they have read. Questions requiring creative response are also good for class discussions. As a means of testing comprehension of a passage, however, they are not desirable, since almost any response could be considered correct. Examples of creative response questions include "If the story stopped after Jimmy lost his money, what ending would you write for it?" and "If Meg had not gone to school that day, what do you think might have happened?"

Other Categorizations of Question Types

Pearson and Johnson (1978) suggest three question types. They label questions as *textually explicit* when they have answers that are directly stated in the text, *textually implicit* when they have implied answers (but the text contains clues for making the necessary inference), and *scriptually implicit* when the reader must answer them from his or her background knowledge.

The reader's own characteristics interact with the text and the question to determine the actual demands of the question-answering task. A reader's interest, background knowledge, and reading skill affect the difficulty and type of question for each reader. The structure of a question may lead a teacher to expect a textually explicit response, whereas the student's background may cause him or her to give a scriptually implicit response (Wixson, 1983). For example, if the text tells readers how to construct a kite, a child who has actually made a kite before reading the material may answer the question on the basis of direct experience, rather than from information presented in the text.

Inability to take the perspective of another person can affect comprehension. Students who can take the perspective of another person do better on scriptually implicit questions than those who cannot (Gardner and Smith, 1987).

Story Grammar as a Basis for Questioning

Another basis for questioning deserves attention: use of story grammar. A story is a series of events that are related to one another in particular ways. As people hear and read many stories, they develop expectations, sometimes called *story schemata,* about the types of things they will encounter; these help them organize information. Related story schemata are described by a *story grammar.* As Sadow (1982) suggests, questions based on a story grammar may help children develop story schemata. The questions should be chosen to reflect the logical sequence of events.

David Rumelhart proposed a simple story grammar that "describes a story as consisting of a setting and one or more episodes" (Sadow, 1982, p. 519). The setting includes the main characters and the time and location of the events, and each episode contains an initiating event, the main character's reaction to it, an action of the main character caused by this reaction, and a consequence of the action, which may act as an initiating event for a subsequent episode. (Sometimes some of the elements of an episode are not directly stated.) Sadow suggests the following five generic questions as appropriate types to ask about a story:

1. Where and when did the events in the story take place, and who was involved in them? (setting)
2. What started the chain of events in the story? (initiating event)
3. What was the main character's reaction to this event? (reaction)
4. What did the main character do about it? (action)
5. What happened as a result of what the main character did? (consequence) (Sadow, 1982, p. 520)

Such questions can help students see the underlying order of ideas in a story, but of course teachers should reword them to fit the story and the particular children. For example, Question 1 can be broken into three questions (*where, when, who*), and the teacher can provide appropriate focus by using words or phrases from the story. After students address these story grammar questions, which establish the essential facts, they should answer questions that help them relate the story to their experiences and knowledge (Sadow, 1982).

Marshall (1983) has also suggested using story grammar as a basis for developing comprehension questions and for evaluating student retellings, which can sometimes be used instead of questions. A checklist for story retellings can indicate if story parts were included and whether they were included with or without prompts. In Marshall's questioning scheme, *theme* questions are similar to main idea questions and ask about the major point or moral of the story. As in Sadow's questioning scheme, *setting* questions are *where* and *when* questions. *Character* questions ask about the main character and/or other characters. *Initiating events* questions often ask about a problem faced by a particular character. *Attempts* questions ask what a character did about a situation or what he or she will do. *Resolution* questions ask how a character solved the problem or what the reader would do to solve the problem. *Reaction* questions focus on what a character felt, the reasons for a character's actions or feelings, or the feelings of the reader.

Guidelines for Preparation

Some guidelines for preparing questions may be useful to teachers who wish to improve their questioning techniques. The following suggestions may help teachers avoid some pitfalls that other educators have detected:

1. In trying to determine overall comprehension skills, ask a variety of questions designed to reflect different types of comprehension. *Avoid overloading the evaluation with a single type of question.*

2. Don't ask questions about obscure or insignificant portions of the selection. Such questions may make a test harder, but they don't convey realistic indications of comprehension. *"Hard" tests and "good" tests are not necessarily synonymous.*

3. Avoid ambiguous or tricky questions. *If a question has two or more possible interpretations, more than one answer for it has to be acceptable.*

4. Questions that a person who has not read the material can answer correctly offer you no valuable information about comprehension. *Avoid useless questions.*

5. Don't ask questions in language that is more difficult than the language of the selection the question is about. *Sometimes you can word questions in a way that prevents a child who knows the answer from responding appropriately.*

6. Make sure the answers to sequence questions require knowledge of the *order* of events. *Don't confuse questions that simply ask for lists with sequence questions.*

7. Don't ask for unsupported opinions when you are testing for comprehension. Have children give support for their opinions, by asking, "Why do you think that?" or "What in the story made you think that?" *If you ask for an unsupported opinion, any answer will be correct.*

8. Don't ask for opinions if you want facts. *Ask for the type of information you want to receive.*

9. Avoid questions that give away information. Instead of asking, "What makes you believe the boy was angry?" ask, "How do you think the boy felt? Why?" *Questions may lead students to the answers by supplying too much information.*

10. Use precise terms in phrasing questions related to reading. *Ask students to compare or contrast, to predict, or to draw conclusions about the reading* (Smith, 1989).

Helping Students Answer Questions

Raphael and Pearson (1982) taught students three types of Question-Answer Relationships (QARs). QAR instruction encourages students to consider both information in the text and their own background knowledge when answering questions (Raphael, 1986). The relationship for questions with answers directly stated in the text in one sentence was called "Right There." The students looked for the words in the question and read the sentence containing those words to locate the answer. The relationship for questions with an answer in the story that required information from multiple sentences or paragraphs was called "Think and Search," and the relationship for questions for which answers had to come from the reader's own knowledge was called "On My Own" (Raphael and Pearson, 1982). Modeling the decision about question-answer relationships and correct answers based on them was an important part of the teaching. Supervised practice following the modeling, with immediate feedback on student responses, was also important. The practice involved gradually increased passage lengths, progressing from simpler to more difficult tasks (Raphael, 1982). Learning the three types of QARs enhanced students' success in answering questions. The training appeared to help average- and low-ability students most (Raphael, 1984). Primary-grade children needed more repetition to learn QARs than intermediate-grade children did (Raphael, 1986).

Raphael (1986) subsequently modified QAR instruction to include four categories, clustered under two headings. Example 6.6 illustrates this modification.

In the modified scheme, the "In My Head" category is divided into questions that involve both the text information and the reader's background of experiences (Author and You) and those that can be answered from the reader's experience without information from the story (On My Own) (Raphael, 1986).

Discussing the use of the QAR categorization to plan questioning strategies, Raphael (1986) states:

> Questions asked prior to reading are usually On My Own QARs. They are designed to help students think about what they already know and how it relates to the upcoming story or content text. In creating guided reading questions, it is important to balance text-based and inference questions. For these, Think and Search QARs

Example 6.6   *Question-Answer Relationships (QARs)*

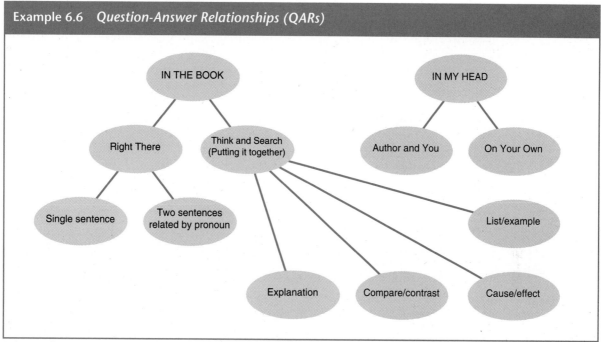

Source: Taffy E. Raphael. "Teaching Question Answer Relationships, Revisited," *The Reading Teacher,* 39 (February 1986), 516–522. Reprinted with permission of Taffy E. Raphael and the International Reading Association. All rights reserved.

should dominate, since they require integration of information and should build to the asking of Author and You QARs. Finally, for extension activities, teachers will want to create primarily On My Own or Author and You QARs, focusing again on students' background information as it pertains to the text. (p. 521)

Helping Students Question

Active readers constantly question the text. As they construct meaning, they ask themselves, "Does this make sense?" Many authorities advocate teaching the reader to generate questions throughout the reading process to enhance comprehension, and such training has proven to be effective. Students who are trained to ask literal questions about material being read have learned to discriminate questions from nonquestions and good literal questions from poor ones. After they practiced the production of good literal questions for paragraphs and then for stories that they read to answer the questions, their comprehension improved (Cohen, 1983). Other students who were taught (through modeling, with gradual phasing out of teacher involvement) to generate their own questions based on a story grammar also had enhanced comprehension (Nolte and Singer, 1985). Bristow (1985) believes that provision of interspersed questions in the text to provide a transition from teacher questioning to self-questioning may be helpful.

Student-generated questions can motivate peers to respond and cause the questioner to have more interest in the response. Both Commeyras (1994, p. 519) and Simpson (1996, p. 124) conclude that "good discussion questions are the ones students *want* to discuss." Questioning and sharing responses in small groups can help children improve critical insights into texts.

Busching and Slesinger (1995) led students to ask their own questions about their readings. The students wrote, in their reading response journals or notebooks, questions that selections raised. This preserved the questions for ongoing reflection. Busching and Slesinger (1995, p. 344) discovered that "[w]hether a question is about facts or concepts is less important than whether a question is a part of something significant. The outward form of the question may have little to do with the level, the depth, or the importance of thinking that has occurred." When reading *Rose Blanche*, middle-school students first raised factual questions because of their limited backgrounds of experience. Later, more of their questions were on higher levels. Some of their questions became "What if . . ." questions.

Kitagawa (1982, p. 43) encouraged children to become questioners by asking questions that had to be answered by a question, such as "What question did the author mainly answer in the passage we just read?" She also encouraged them to develop questions they wished to have answered through educational activities, such as field trips, and to construct preview questions, based on titles and pictures, for reading selections. Students were asked what questions they would ask the author of a selection or a character, if they could, and they were asked to predict the questions that would be answered next in the selection.

| **Time for Reflection** | Some teachers believe that they must do all of the questioning in the classroom. Others believe that the students need to learn to ask their own questions. **What do *you* think?** |

Summary

This chapter examines types of reading comprehension. Literal comprehension results from reading for directly stated ideas. Higher-order comprehension goes beyond literal comprehension to include interpretive, critical, and creative reading. Interpretive reading is reading for implied ideas; critical reading is reading for evaluation; and creative reading is reading beyond the lines. Teachers can generally teach strategies in all of these areas most effectively through explanation and modeling, guided student practice, and independent student practice.

Questioning techniques are important to instruction because teachers use questions to provide purposes for reading, elicit and focus discussion, and check comprehension of material read. Questions may be based on comprehension factors or story structure. Students may need to be taught how to approach answering questions. Self-questioning by the reader is also a valuable comprehension and comprehension-monitoring technique. Teachers can help students develop the skill of self-questioning.

True or False

_____ 1. Literal comprehension involves acquiring information that is directly stated in a selection.

_____ 2. Students must attend to details when they follow directions.

_____ 3. Critical reading is reading for evaluation.

_____ 4. Critical reading strategies are easier to teach than literal reading strategies.

_____ 5. Higher-order comprehension may involve determining the author's purpose.

_____ 6. Critical readers are not interested in copyright dates of material they read.

_____ 7. An inference is an idea that is implied in the material, rather than being directly stated.

_____ 8. Elementary school children are too young to be able to recognize propaganda techniques.

_____ 9. A bandwagon approach takes advantage of the desires of people to conform to the crowd.

_____ 10. Critical thinking skills should first be given attention in the intermediate grades.

_____ 11. Critical readers read with a questioning attitude.

_____ 12. Creative reading involves going beyond the material presented by the author.

_____ 13. Teachers should give little class time to creative reading because it is not practical.

_____ 14. In composing comprehension questions for testing purposes, teachers should use several types of questions.

_____ 15. A good test is a hard test, and vice versa.

_____ 16. Listing questions and sequence questions are the same thing.

_____ 17. The main idea of a paragraph is always stated in the form of a topic sentence.

_____ 18. Children make inferences that are consistent with their schemata.

_____ 19. Some children have difficulty determining referents of pronouns and adverbs.

_____ 20. Young children are unable to make inferences.

_____ 21. Hexagonal essays promote higher-order thinking.

For your journal...

1. Using the seven question types based on comprehension factors that are described in this chapter, compose some questions about the content of this chapter or of another chapter in this book. Answer the questions.

2. After you have read a novel written for children, write story grammar–based questions about the story. Answer the questions.

...And your portfolio

1. Make a board or folder game based on a favorite children's book for a grade of your choice.

2. Make a file of examples of each propaganda technique listed in the chapter. Describe instructional uses for your file.

Major Approaches and Materials for Reading Instruction

Key Vocabulary

Pay close attention to these terms when they appear in the chapter.

computer-assisted instruction

computer-managed instruction

directed reading activity

directed reading-thinking activity

eclectic approaches

individualized reading approach

language experience approach

linguistics

literature-based approaches

minimally contrasting spelling patterns

programmed instruction

trade books

word bank

SETTING OBJECTIVES

When you finish reading this chapter, you should be able to

▶ Discuss the characteristics of different types of published reading series.

▶ Compare and contrast a directed reading activity with a directed reading-thinking activity.

▶ Discuss the characteristics of literature-based approaches to reading instruction.

▶ Explain the rationale behind the language experience approach.

▶ Discuss the place of computers in reading instructional programs.

▶ Discuss how a teacher might use elements of several approaches in a single classroom.

Chapter 7 Organization

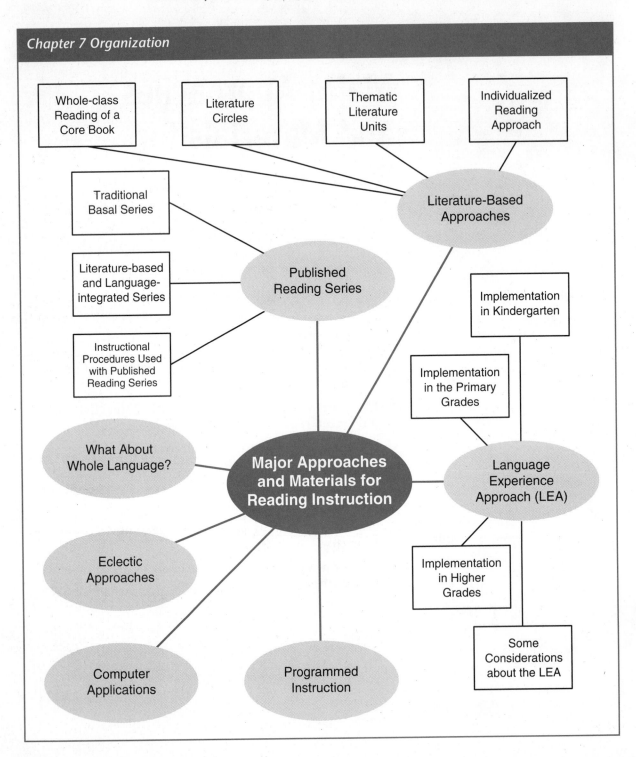

Over the years, educators have developed many approaches to teaching reading. This chapter discusses some of the more widely accepted approaches. These approaches are not mutually exclusive; many teachers use more than one method simultaneously. They often select the best techniques and materials from a number of approaches to meet the varied needs of individual students in their classrooms. We take the position that no one approach is best for all students or all teachers. Therefore, we attempt to acquaint teachers with the characteristics of different approaches so that they will be able to choose intelligently the procedures to be used in their classrooms.

Just as there are many approaches, there are many types of materials that can be used for reading instruction, varying from chalkboards and charts to published reading series, library books, and computers. All are tools to help teachers present reading instruction effectively.

Because whole language is a philosophy (see Chapter 1), we do not present it as an approach in this chapter. Some of the approaches given here, however, are consistent with the whole language philosophy, and teachers can use most instructional materials holistically.

Published Reading Series

Many schools depend on published reading series for materials to support reading instruction. For many years, the published reading series have been like the traditional basal series described here. These series have evolved over time. Recently, publishers have been moving toward more literature-based and language-integrated series as they try to take into account both the criticisms of the traditional series and the current theory and research in reading.

Traditional Basal Series

For many years, basal reader series have been the most widely used materials for teaching reading in the elementary schools of the United States. They begin with prereading materials and provide materials for development and practice of reading strategies in each grade. These series generally have consisted of one or more readiness books, some preprimers, a primer, a first reader, and one or two readers for each successive grade level through grade six or eight.

In addition to the student books, basal reader series include teacher's manuals with detailed lesson plans to help teachers use the readers effectively. Teachers who follow these plans use what is called a *directed reading activity (DRA)*, described later in this chapter. Basal reader series also include workbooks and/or blackline duplicating masters of skill sheets that children can use to practice skills and strategies they have previously learned in class. Workbooks are not designed to teach the skills and strategies and should not be used for this purpose. Many publishing companies offer other supplementary materials to be used in conjunction with basal series, such as "big books" (chart-sized versions of books); student

Basal readers are anthologies of stories, content area selections, poems, and plays.
(© *Carol Palmer/The Picture Cube*)

journals; read-aloud libraries for the teacher; unit tests; puppets to go with some early stories; computer management, reinforcement, and/or enrichment activities; and various other items. Big books are important tools in holistic teaching. They are discussed in detail in Chapter 2.

Basal reading series are quite useful for elementary school teachers. They provide anthologies of stories, content area selections, poems, plays, and so on that can be the basis for enriching classroom reading activities. Many of these pieces are whole selections or excerpts from high-quality literature. The new basals contain much literature because the publishers are trying to provide material that teachers want (Cullinan, 1992). Many newer basal reading programs are presenting integrated, thematic approaches to reading, but not all of these programs provide teachers with theme-level goals and objectives. Many of the cross-curricular activities have weak relations to the theme and the other curricular areas and therefore lack sufficient focus and connections, although they are improvements on previous basal units (Lipson et al., 1993).

The teacher's manuals offer many valuable suggestions for teaching reading lessons and thus can save much lesson preparation time. Such suggestions are becoming less skill driven and more language oriented in many series and offer positive guidance for teachers, helping them to include all aspects of reading (word recognition, comprehension, oral reading, silent reading, reading for information, and reading for enjoyment) in their reading lessons. Manuals allow for systematic teaching and reteaching of skills and strategies and systematic review. They also offer ways to monitor the success of the instruction (Wiggins, 1994).

As Wiggins (1994) points out, when a basal reading program is used, teachers have an idea of what the students have been taught in past years. This can aid in curricular planning.

Some people equate basal readers with the overly simplified texts that have received so much media attention. Many publishers today, however, consider factors other than readability formulas to aid in placement, and vocabulary control may be more often accomplished by using traditional stories with repetitive lines and predictable formats than by changing the stories to fit vocabulary goals.

The wealth of material offered in the teacher's manuals allows teachers to choose from among the offered suggestions those that fit their needs and discard the ones that do not. If, however, teachers try to do everything suggested, they may use valuable time for activities that are inappropriate for some groups of children, leaving inadequate time for appropriate ones. Teachers should not use basal readers from front to back in their entirety without considering the special needs of the children in their classes. A teacher might use one set of activities from the basal one year and a different set the next year to accommodate the different needs of the two classes.

Publishers of basal readers are continually working to improve them. To provide stories with high quality, limited vocabulary, and extensive repetition, they include unaltered folktales in some of the early readers. They also include other good literature, often without adaptation, as well as more content area material. Unlike the language in earlier basal readers, the language in today's basal readers is more natural and conversational. These readers have diversified characters, including people of various racial and ethnic groups, elderly people, and people with disabilities, and depict them in less stereotyped ways than in the past. Women are portrayed in roles other than the traditional ones.

Some educators have complained that basal reader workbook pages often fail to relate directly to the story in the reader and give insufficient attention to higher-level comprehension skills. Therefore, teachers may wish to have students write responses to the selections in reading logs and let students discuss the selections in literature circles or use a variety of other literary response activities, such as drama, art, and storytelling, rather than depending on workbook activities that are unrelated to the stories or that cover comprehension superficially.

Basal publishers have put many research findings about reading into practice in basal lessons within the context of the pressures classroom teachers face. Basal readers address considerations from diagnosis to reading appreciation and offer suggestions for both instructional techniques and guided practice. Teachers should make their instructional needs known to publishers. Publishers have been responsive to user reactions in the past and are likely to continue to be responsive.

Hoffman and McCarthey (1995) report that studies of the first grade materials of old and new basals of five companies show that the new materials are very different from the old ones. The new materials have less vocabulary control, more diversity of genre, minimal adaptations, higher literary quality, increased predictability, and decreased decodability. These findings are encouraging.

Uses and Misuses of Basal Materials

Much of the criticism of basal readers has focused on less than desirable uses of the materials. Teachers have a responsibility to plan the use of all materials in their classrooms, including the basal readers, regardless of the presence or absence of guiding suggestions accompanying the materials.

If teachers perceive basals as *total* reading programs, they may fail to provide the variety of experiences children need for a balanced program. Basals can never provide all of the reading situations a student needs to encounter.

Some teachers form basal reading groups based on achievement. They place the best readers in the top group, the average readers in a middle group or groups, and the poorest readers in the lowest group. In this way, these teachers believe they can provide all of the children with basal materials that are appropriate for their reading levels. In actuality, however, the match of materials with children is not always good. Forell (1985) has pointed out that good readers are often placed in comfortable reading materials in which word recognition problems are not frequent and attention can be given to meaning, using context clues to advantage. Poor readers, however, are often placed in "challenging" material that causes frustration and is not conducive to comprehension, because so much attention is needed for word recognition—an arrangement that denies them a chance for fluent reading. All readers should be given material that is comfortable enough to allow reasonable application of comprehension skills. Teachers may be reluctant to place students in materials at as low a level as they need in order to allow this to happen, but doing so can be beneficial in the long run.

Wiggins (1994) suggests a different way to use the basal that could alleviate the problems created by some current grouping practices. He recommends teaching core basal reader lessons with the whole class and forming small groups for follow-up activities. The composition of the small groups would be flexible, clustering students with common weaknesses and strengths, and would be based on the needs for that particular day. All students would start at the beginning of the on-grade-level book, and instruction, rather than materials, would be adjusted. Although vocabulary would be introduced, prior knowledge assessed, purposes developed for reading, and discussions of reading held in a whole-class setting, differentiated reinforcement activities would be provided in small groups, according to the specific needs. Some small groups might be teacher-directed; others might be cooperative. Center work could also provide reinforcement. The reading center might involve independent reading, shared reading, peer tutoring, or co-operative learning activities.

Blanton, Moorman, and Wood (1986) suggest that teachers use direct instruction in basal reader skill lessons by assessing the students' background knowledge related to the skill; explaining the skill in detail, including when it is needed and why it is important; having the students explain the skill in their own words; modeling the use of the skill for the students and then providing them with guided practice with the skill; having students apply the skill in regular reading materials; and leading the students in discussion of real-world encounters with the skill. Some of these steps may already be included in basal manual instructions. Teachers can add the other steps for more complete skills lessons. Of course, teachers need to provide much time for actual reading of connected text.

Teachers may ask students to illustrate scenes from the story, write questions to be answered by other class members, write other adventures for story characters, read books by the author of the story or books related to the story, or engage in many other activities that encourage active participation and interaction with the selection (Weiss, 1987; Fuhler, 1990).

Educators have expressed considerable concern about the misuse of workbooks that accompany basal readers; some teachers use them to keep children busy while they meet with other children or do paperwork. Wiggins (1994) decries the fact that some teachers assign all pages sequentially to all students, regardless of appropriateness to the individual child's needs. It is important to note that the fault here is with the teachers' procedures and not with the workbooks. Workbook activities should always be purposeful, and teachers should never assign workbook pages simply to keep students occupied. Teachers should also grade and return completed workbook assignments promptly, since children need to have correct responses reinforced immediately and need to be informed about incorrect responses so that they will not continue to make them. One way by which teachers can increase the effectiveness of their use of workbooks is to use the every-pupil-response technique, having all students respond to instructions at the same time (Schachter, 1981).

In summary, teachers do not have to follow all suggestions in the manuals—or, indeed, *any* of the suggestions—in order to use basal materials to provide children with a variety of reading materials that would not otherwise be available in many schools. Likewise, they are not limited to using only the suggestions in the manuals. The manner in which basal materials are used, not the basals themselves, has often been the main concern about basal programs.

| Time for Reflection | Some teachers believe that all students should complete all workbook pages, to ensure learning. Others believe that students should be assigned only pages that fit their particular needs. **What do *you* think?** |

Types of Basal Reading Programs

Although the preceding discussion of basal reading programs contained some generalizations about them, the intention is not to imply that all basal reader series are alike. On the contrary, these series differ in basic philosophies, order of presentation of strategies and skills, degree and type of vocabulary control, types of selections, and number and types of practice activities provided. Some supplement workbook/skill sheet material with student journals that call for more varied responses. Most are eclectic in approach, but some emphasize a single method, such as a linguistic or an intensive phonics approach.

Linguistics is the scientific study of human speech. Linguistic scientists (also called *linguists*), such as Leonard Bloomfield, have provided principles that have affected development of reading instructional materials. A number of these principles have been applied to many of the basal reading series. Some series have been based specifically on Bloomfield's ideas and have incorporated a number of his beliefs, including the following:

1. Beginning readers should be presented with material that uses only a single sound for a letter at a time. Other sounds for the letter should not be presented until the first association is mastered.

2. Irregularly spelled words should be avoided in beginning reading material, although some (for example, *a* and *the*) must be used to construct sentences that have relatively normal patterns.

3. Word-attack skills should be taught by presenting *minimally contrasting spelling patterns*, words that vary by a single letter. For example, one lesson might contain the words *can, tan, man, ban, fan, ran*, and *pan*. This exposure to minimally contrasting patterns is designed to help the child understand the difference a certain letter makes in the pronunciation of a word.

4. Sounds should not be isolated from words, however, because when sounds are pronounced outside the environment of a word, they are distorted. This is particularly true of isolated consonant sounds; *buh, duh*, and *puh* are sounds incorrectly associated with the letters *b, d*, and *p*.

These materials emphasize reading orally. Reading is looked on as turning writing back into spoken language. (See Bloomfield and Barnhart [1961], for a discussion of Bloomfield's approach.)

Series that focus on intensive phonics use a synthetic phonics approach to phonics instruction. (See Chapter 3 for a description of this approach.) The materials often look similar to the ones found in a linguistic series, but the sounds are not isolated from the words in a linguistic approach, whereas they are taught in isolation and then blended into words in a synthetic phonics approach.

Teachers should be aware of the differences among basal series. Before a school system adopts a basal series, teachers should examine many series and select the one that best fits their own student population and supports their philosophy regarding reading instruction.

Changes Occurring in Basal Reader Programs

Traditional basal reader programs focused primarily on reading instruction, rather than on the integration of language skills. Generally they contained much specially written material and/or many adapted stories in order to fit grade-level readability standards. All lessons tended to be teacher directed, with little time allocated for independent reading by the students. Generally only one teaching procedure was suggested, although enough enrichment suggestions were often included to give teachers some choice in individualizing their class presentations. The series' skill instruction and practice components often included mainly work with isolated words, sentences, and paragraphs, and they often had numerous skill activities to be completed in each lesson.

In general, current series have moved away from this traditional mold. They are offering integrated reading and language instruction, providing literature selections or excerpts that have not been modified heavily (or at all), and offering practice activities that go beyond worksheets alone. They are explicitly giving the teacher greater decision-making power in using the materials and are including more independent student activities. Publishers are incorporating the newer techniques to different degrees. One of the most common variations among series lies in the approaches taken to the skill instruction and practice. Most publishers have tried to retain the positive features of their previous programs, while offering more literature and integrated activities. The offerings of basal reader series, finally, can be seen as a continuum from the rigidly controlled and teacher-directed materials of yesterday to the more open-ended, diverse, and student-centered materials of today. Some publishers have moved so far in the new directions that they now refer to their materials as *literature-based* and *language-integrated* series to reflect the newer philosophy.

Literature-Based and Language-Integrated Series

One of the most widely heralded moves recently made by educational publishers is the creation of *literature-based* reading series. These programs offer quality literature selections for students to read, often in their entirety and without adaptation. In addition, some series are integrating instruction involving all the language arts, including listening, speaking, and writing activities to accompany the literature selections that make the lessons true communication experiences. Example 7.1 shows excerpts from a literature-based series selection.

The story presented is the fourth one in a thematic unit of five related stories about "Experiences." The major outcome expected from the unit is that the "students read, understand, and share personal narratives" (p. 173B). Page 173E shows an overview of how the theme can be taught in relation to *Barrio Boy*. Pages 174B–174C offer information about prereading activities and theme goals. Page 174D (not shown here) is about three ongoing theme activities. They include independent reading and writing, a theme project, and a writing center

Example 7.1   *Literature-Based Series Example*

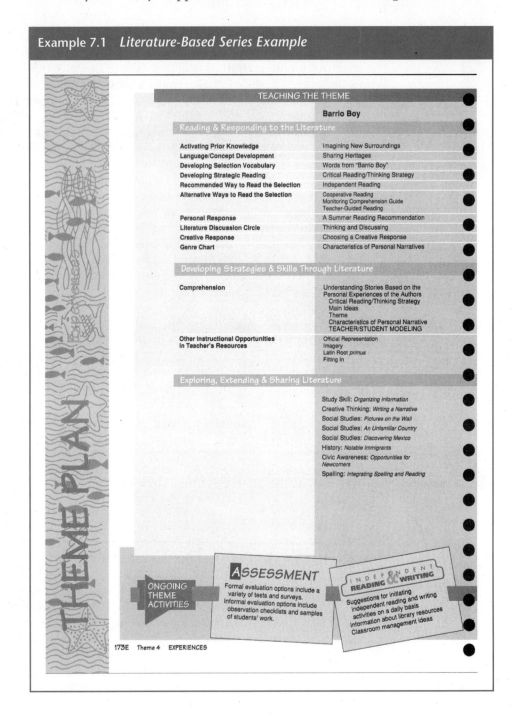

TEACHING THE THEME

Barrio Boy

Reading & Responding to the Literature

Activating Prior Knowledge	Imagining New Surroundings
Language/Concept Development	Sharing Heritages
Developing Selection Vocabulary	Words from "Barrio Boy"
Developing Strategic Reading	Critical Reading/Thinking Strategy
Recommended Way to Read the Selection	Independent Reading
Alternative Ways to Read the Selection	Cooperative Reading
	Monitoring Comprehension Guide
	Teacher-Guided Reading
Personal Response	A Summer Reading Recommendation
Literature Discussion Circle	Thinking and Discussing
Creative Response	Choosing a Creative Response
Genre Chart	Characteristics of Personal Narratives

Developing Strategies & Skills Through Literature

Comprehension	Understanding Stories Based on the Personal Experiences of the Authors
	Critical Reading/Thinking Strategy
	Main Ideas
	Theme
	Characteristics of Personal Narrative
	TEACHER/STUDENT MODELING
Other Instructional Opportunities in Teacher's Resources	Official Representation
	Imagery
	Latin Root *primus*
	Fitting In

Exploring, Extending & Sharing Literature

Study Skill: *Organizing Information*

Creative Thinking: *Writing a Narrative*

Social Studies: *Pictures on the Wall*

Social Studies: *An Unfamiliar Country*

Social Studies: *Discovering Mexico*

History: *Notable Immigrants*

Civic Awareness: *Opportunities for Newcomers*

Spelling: *Integrating Spelling and Reading*

ONGOING THEME ACTIVITIES

ASSESSMENT
Formal evaluation options include a variety of tests and surveys. Informal evaluation options include observation checklists and samples of students' work.

INDEPENDENT READING & WRITING
Suggestions for initiating independent reading and writing activities on a daily basis. Information about library resources. Classroom management ideas.

173E   Theme 4   EXPERIENCES

THEME PLAN

Example 7.1 *Literature-Based Series Example (cont.)*

DISCUSSING EXPERIENCES

■ Anthology, pages 172-173, or Theme Poster 4

ACTIVATING PRIOR KNOWLEDGE Use the Anthology or the Theme Poster to engage students in a discussion of memorable experiences in their lives and of personal narrative as a type of writing. You may wish to ask the following questions:

• What events in your life might make good stories?

• What stories have you heard other people tell that involve particularly memorable characters or unusual events?

Home-School Connection
PARENT RESOURCES
■ Newsletter 4

PREVIEWING THE LITERATURE

■ Anthology, pages 172-239

BUILDING BACKGROUND Have students turn to pages 172-173. Point out the title and the genre label. Explain that in this theme students will be reading five personal narratives (stories about things that have happened in the authors' lives).

Have students read the table of contents on page 174. Then have them preview each story. The following can be used to initiate a discussion.

• Do you think "The Figgerin' of Aunt Wilma" will be humorous or serious? Why?

• What kinds of experiences do you think Gary Soto tells about in "Summer School"?

• What kind of information might you expect to learn about the Reverend Martin Luther King, Jr., in a personal narrative written by his daughter?

• What might have seemed strange or confusing to Ernesto Galarza when he first came to the United States from Mexico?

• How do you think Jean Fritz felt about coming to the United States in 1927?

Example 7.1 *Literature-Based Series Example (cont.)*

Barrio Boy

TTAS: Choose from these activities to relate content to students' interests and experiences.

Reading & Responding to the Literature

Building Background from Diverse Perspectives

Choose from the activities below to prepare students to read "Barrio Boy."

1Bii Speaking to Express Oneself

Imagining New Surroundings
ACTIVATING PRIOR KNOWLEDGE

■ Journal, page 81

The next selection is Ernesto Galarza's personal narrative about his childhood experiences settling with his family in the United States after having left Mexico. Ask students to think of a time that they themselves went somewhere they had never been before. Encourage volunteers to describe their experiences and what they learned. You may want to share similar experiences from your life, such as your first days at college or teaching at a new school. Have students share their ideas about the ways people grow and change in response to new situations by completing the activity on Journal page 81.

Sharing Heritages
LANGUAGE/CONCEPT DEVELOPMENT

STUDENTS ACQUIRING ENGLISH

To help students relate to the author's immigrant experience, invite class members to share where they or some of their ancestors emigrated from when they came to the United States. Guide students in locating on a world map or globe the countries or regions mentioned; invite students to share stories about the immigration experiences of family members.

You may also want to lead students in a discussion of family customs that can be traced back to former homelands. These customs might include speaking their native language, celebrating holidays of one's own culture and eating traditional foods, and belonging to organizations that have as members many people from the same culture. Point out that keeping such traditions alive not only can help a family feel comfortable when the members first immigrate, but can also add richness to family life generations after their arrival.

2Dii Appreciating Cultural Diversity

▼ *2Civ Use Graphic Sources*

▼ *TAAS Obj 5: Use to help students practice using graphic sources.*

▼ *2A Developing Vocabulary*

Words from "Barrio Boy"
DEVELOPING SELECTION VOCABULARY

■ Transparency 4/4

■ Journal, page 81

Key Words: *boisterous, compassion, demonstration, interpret, reassuring*

Display Transparency 4/4. Have students use the Reading New Words Strategy to figure out the meanings and pronunciations of the underlined words.

USING SUFFIXES You might point out that two of the words end with the *-ion* suffix that is used to create noun forms, and one ends with the *-ous* suffix that is used to create adjective forms.

TRANSPARENCY 4/4

boisterous   compassion   demonstration
interpret   reassuring

Read the passage from a travel guide below and think about the meanings of the italicized words. What words or phrases in the context are clues to the vocabulary words? If you need help with any of the words, check the Glossary.

Once you arrive in this exotic city, go to the marketplace to enjoy the boisterous bargaining and conversation of these noisy, spirited people. You may feel compassion for the street merchants of this country, but their joy, enthusiasm, and pride are reassuring. If you do not speak the local language, you may have to hire someone to interpret for you as you bargain to purchase souvenirs. Be sure to see a demonstration of the local craft of rug weaving at the northern corner of the market near the main square.

Answer the questions below.

Do you enjoy being boisterous?
What makes you feel compassion?
Give an example of something you find reassuring.
Could you interpret for someone? Explain.
What kind of demonstration could you give?

Theme 4 EXPERIENCES Barrio Boy **205J**

Example 7.1 Literature-Based Series Example (cont.)

Use prompts such as the following to check students' understanding of the vocabulary words.

- Why might people in a library stare at a *boisterous* person?
- When might a friend need you to show *compassion*?
- What kinds of *demonstrations* have you seen in science classes?
- What could help you *interpret* a message written hundreds of years ago?
- Why might a favorite stuffed animal be *reassuring* to a young child away from home?

INDEPENDENT PRACTICE Ask students to complete the vocabulary activity on Journal page 81. Call on volunteers to read the completed postcard when students have finished.

ADDITIONAL SUPPORT

- Teacher's Book, page 239F
- Student Resource Book, Theme 4

For students who may benefit from additional vocabulary support, a lesson and practice page using the words focused on in the above activity as well as the following additional words from the selection are provided.

Additional Words: alien, taunts

Reading the Literature

Developing Strategic Reading
CRITICAL READING/THINKING STRATEGY 2D Appreciating Literature

- Anthology, pages 206–219
- Journal, page 82

STUDENT MODELING Ask students to explain the Critical Reading/Thinking Strategy for fiction and why it is useful. If necessary, refer students to the summary of this strategy on page 228 of their Journal Handbook.

Have students tell how they know the selection is a personal narrative and explain what they know about this type of story. Invite volunteers to model how to preview "Barrio Boy." Direct students' attention to page 206, which shows part of a map of Mexico and California, and the pictures on pages 212 and 216, which represent Ernesto's classroom and schoolmates. Ask students what they expect the story to be about, on the basis of their preview.

Then have students turn to the author's biography on page 236, and have a volunteer read the information. Remind students that another part of being critical readers is asking themselves from what point of view the author is writing. Ask students what the author's bias, or attitude toward the subject, is likely to be. Encourage them to explain how they arrived at their conclusions. Then have them record on Journal page 82 the kinds of events they expect to read about.

205K Theme 4 EXPERIENCES Barrio Boy

Barrio Boy

▼ *TAAS Obj 1: Use to help students practice using prefixes and suffixes.*

▼ *2Ai Structural Analysis*

TTAS: Use the Additional Support to reteach.

JOURNAL PAGE 82

▼ *TAAS Obj 5: Use to help students practice using graphic sources.*

▼ *2Civ Use Graphic Sources*

▼ *TAAS Obj 6: Use to help students practice recognizing author's point of view.*

Example 7.1 *Literature-Based Series Example (cont.)*

From Jalcocotán, a mountain village in Mexico, Ernesto's family moves many times, seeking work and safety from the Mexican Revolution. Ernesto and his mother, Doña Henriqueta, finally settle in a barrio, a Spanish-speaking neighborhood, in Sacramento, California. The ways of Americans, or gringos, seem strange to the new immigrants. But this land offers many new possibilities for Ernesto, possibilities that could brighten his future.

We found the Americans as strange in their customs as they probably found us. Immediately we discovered that there were no *mercados* and that when shopping you did not put the groceries in a *chiquihuite*. Instead everything was in cans or in cardboard boxes or each item was put in a brown paper bag. There were neighborhood grocery stores at the corners and some big ones uptown, but no *mercado*. The grocers did not give children a *pilón*, they did not stand at the door and coax you to come in and buy, as they did in Mazatlán. The fruits and vegetables were displayed on counters instead of being piled up on the floor. The stores smelled of fly spray and oiled floors, not of fresh pineapple and limes.

Neither was there a plaza, only parks which had no bandstands, no concerts every Thursday, and no promenades of boys going one way and girls the other. There were no parks in the *barrio*; and the ones uptown were cold and rainy in winter, and in summer

Illustrated by B. J. Johnson   207

---

1 ⬛ **Personal Narrative** ▼ *2Diii*
POINT OF VIEW
Ask students who the word *we* refers to in the first sentence. (the narrator and his family) Point out that since the author is telling about a time in his life in this selection, it is a personal narrative.

2 ⬛ **Reading Strategy** ▼ *2Ai*
READING NEW WORDS
Point out to students the words *mercados* and *chiquihuite*. If any students in your class speak Spanish, you may wish to have them pronounce these words for the class and explain their meanings. Then invite other students to point out context clues that would help them figure out the general meaning of each of these terms.

3 ⬛ **Major Skill** ▼ *2Biii*
STORY DETAILS: MAIN IDEA
Explain that the main idea of this part of the narrative is that differences between the familiar culture of Mexico and the unfamiliar one of the United States at first made life difficult for Ernesto and his family.

▼ *TAAS Obj 3: Use to help students practice identifying implied main idea. (Annotation 3)*
▼ *2Diii Understanding Story Elements*
▼ *2Ai Context Clues*
▼ *2Biii Identifying Main Idea*

⬛ **TEACHER'S RESOURCES**

⬛ **Anthology, pages 206–211**
Review with students the characteristics of personal narrative:
• Written in first-person narration
• Describes events in the author's life

• May be told in the form of a story, with such elements as setting, characters, dialogue, plot, mood, and theme

Suggest that students use Journal page 82 to help them evaluate and appreciate the selection. Remind students to use the Reading New Words Strategy if they come across an unfamiliar word. Have students read up to the last full paragraph on page 211. After students finish reading this section, use the prompts to lead students in a discussion of this part of the narrative.

2D Appreciating Literature

Theme 4   EXPERIENCES   Barrio Boy   *207*

Example 7.1   *Literature-Based Series Example (cont.)*

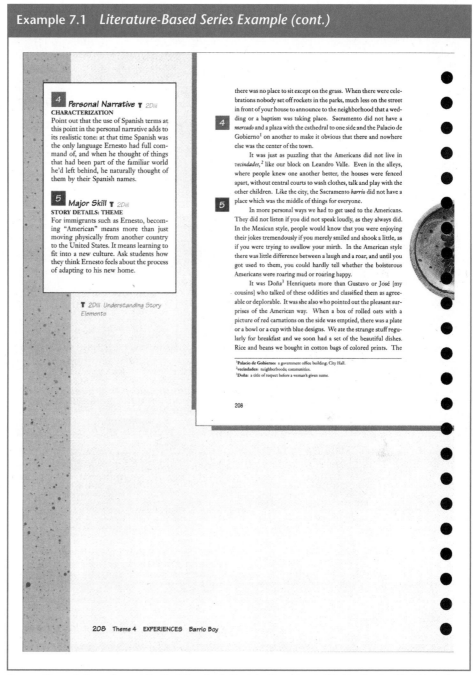

4 *Personal Narrative* ▼ *2Diii*
CHARACTERIZATION
Point out that the use of Spanish terms at this point in the personal narrative adds to its realistic tone: at that time Spanish was the only language Ernesto had full command of, and when he thought of things that had been part of the familiar world he'd left behind, he naturally thought of them by their Spanish names.

5 *Major Skill* ▼ *2Diii*
STORY DETAILS: THEME
For immigrants such as Ernesto, becoming "American" means more than just moving physically from another country to the United States. It means learning to fit into a new culture. Ask students how they think Ernesto feels about the process of adapting to his new home.

▼ *2Diii Understanding Story Elements*

there was no place to sit except on the grass. When there were celebrations nobody set off rockets in the parks, much less on the street in front of your house to announce to the neighborhood that a wedding or a baptism was taking place. Sacramento did not have a *mercado* and a plaza with the cathedral to one side and the Palacio de Gobierno[1] on another to make it obvious that there and nowhere else was the center of the town.

It was just as puzzling that the Americans did not live in *vecindades*,[2] like our block on Leandro Valle. Even in the alleys, where people knew one another better, the houses were fenced apart, without central courts to wash clothes, talk and play with the other children. Like the city, the Sacramento *barrio* did not have a place which was the middle of things for everyone.

In more personal ways we had to get used to the Americans. They did not listen if you did not speak loudly, as they always did. In the Mexican style, people would know that you were enjoying their jokes tremendously if you merely smiled and shook a little, as if you were trying to swallow your mirth. In the American style there was little difference between a laugh and a roar, and until you got used to them, you could hardly tell whether the boisterous Americans were roaring mad or roaring happy.

It was Doña[3] Henriqueta more than Gustavo or José [my cousins] who talked of these oddities and classified them as agreeable or deplorable. It was she also who pointed out the pleasant surprises of the American way. When a box of rolled oats with a picture of red carnations on the side was emptied, there was a plate or a bowl or a cup with blue designs. We ate the strange stuff regularly for breakfast and we soon had a set of the beautiful dishes. Rice and beans we bought in cotton bags of colored prints. The

[1]**Palacio de Gobierno:** a government office building; City Hall.
[2]**vecindades:** neighborhoods; communities.
[3]**Doña:** a title of respect before a woman's given name.

208

208   Theme 4   EXPERIENCES   Barrio Boy

project. Pages 205J–205K offer teachers a variety of activities from which to choose when introducing the story. Pages 205K–205L give ideas for reading strategically and ways to read the story. (Only page 205K is reproduced here.) This range of choices encourages teachers to make independent decisions about the lesson, based on the characteristics of their individual classes. The story pages from the student book are found on pages 207–219 of this teacher's manual, reduced in size, with instructional notes and resources included on the sides and bottoms of the pages. Pages 207–208 of this material are reproduced here to show how the various parts of the story are connected to instructional suggestions for the teacher. Other lesson pages contain suggestions for student responses to *Barrio Boy*, including discussion ideas, ideas for creative response, writing activities, oral rereading, and ideas for exploration of language; suggestions for developing comprehension strategies and skills through the literature; and ideas for exploring, extending, and sharing the story. Teachers are encouraged to select from the suggested activities and different ways of reading the selection the ones that meet the needs and interests of the students in the particular class.

Instructional Procedures Used with Published Reading Series

A number of instructional procedures can be used with published reading series. Some are built into the manuals included in the series, and some can be easily adapted to use with these materials.

Directed Reading Activity (DRA)

The *directed reading activity (DRA)* is a teaching strategy used to extend and strengthen a child's reading abilities. It can be used with a story from a published reading series or with any other reading selection, including content area materials or trade books. The DRA is the strategy that is generally built into basal reading series' teacher's manuals. Following are five components often included in the DRA:

1. *Motivation and development of background.* The teacher attempts to interest students in reading about the topic by helping them associate the subject matter with their own experiences or by using audiovisual aids to arouse interest in unfamiliar areas. It may not be necessary to work on motivation for all stories.

    At this point, the teacher can determine whether the children have the backgrounds of experience and language needed for understanding the story, and, if necessary, he or she can develop new concepts and vocabulary before they read the story.

2. *Directed story reading (silent and oral).* Before children read the story silently, the teacher provides them with purpose questions (or a study guide) or helps them to set their own purposes (by questioning or predicting) to direct their

reading (on a section-by-section basis at lower grade levels). Following the silent reading, the teacher may ask children to read aloud their answers to the purpose or study-guide questions, read aloud to prove or reject their predictions, or read orally for a new purpose. Oral reading is not always included in upper-grade lessons. This section of the lesson is designed to aid children's comprehension and retention of the material.

3. *Strategy- or skill-building activities.* At some point during the lesson, the teacher provides direct instruction in one or more word recognition or comprehension strategies or skills.

4. *Follow-up practice.* Children practice strategies and skills they have already been taught, frequently by doing workbook exercises.

5. *Enrichment activities.* These activities may connect the story with art, music, or creative writing or may lead the children to read additional material on the same topic or by the same author. Creative drama is often included as an enrichment activity, linking the reading with speaking and listening.

Although the steps may vary from series to series, most basal reading lessons have parts that correspond to this list of components. Directed reading of a story generally involves the teacher asking questions and the children reading to find the answers, or the teacher asking the children to make predictions and read to confirm or reject them. Traditional basal readers tend to give the teacher responsibility for purpose setting. Literature-based and language-integrated series, in contrast, have moved toward giving students more responsibility for purpose setting and stress the making and confirming of predictions.

Adaptations of the DRA. Rearranging a basal reading lesson so that the activities labeled *enrichment activities* are completed before, rather than after, the story is read, can produce better results than presentation in the traditional order. These activities help the students build and integrate background knowledge (Reutzel, 1985; Prince and Mancus, 1987; Thames and Readence, 1988; Pearson and Fielding, 1991).

Comprehension monitoring (metacognitive activities) can be made a natural part of a DRA by using student *predictions*, rather than teacher questions, as the purpose-setting vehicle for the lessons, using the title, pictures, and children's background information about the general topic that has been activated as a basis for the predictions. The predictions are revised as necessary as the children read the material, much as is done in a directed reading-thinking activity, discussed in the next section. *Self-questioning* before and during the reading is encouraged. In addition, stops at logical story breaks can be made to allow *summarization* of main points as a check for continuing comprehension. Summarization of the entire selection can follow completion of the reading. The students may ask classmates questions they have generated about story features (Schmitt and Baumann, 1986). Some basal series incorporate some of these activities into their teacher's manual suggestions, and the newer literature-based and language-integrated readers tend to use the predicting and confirming techniques regularly.

The Directed Reading-Thinking Activity (DRTA)

One alternative to the DRA is the *directed reading-thinking activity (DRTA)*. The DRTA fits into a whole language philosophy better than does the DRA because it focuses on student control instead of primarily teacher guidance of the reading. The DRTA is a general plan for directing children's reading of either stories in published reading series, trade books, or content area selections and for encouraging children to think as they read and to make predictions and check their accuracy. Stauffer (1968) offered some background for understanding the DRTA:

> Children are by nature curious and inquiring, and they will be so in school if they are permitted to inquire. It is possible to direct the reading-thinking process in such a way that children will be encouraged to think when reading—to speculate, to search, to evaluate, and to use. (p. 348)

Stauffer (1969) further pointed out that teachers can motivate students' effort and concentration by involving them intellectually and encouraging them to formulate questions and hypotheses, to process information, and to evaluate tentative solutions. The DRTA is directed toward accomplishing these goals. The teacher observes the children as they read, in order to diagnose difficulties and offer help (kidwatching time). Perhaps because the student is interacting with the material during reading, the DRTA is extremely useful for improving children's comprehension of selections. After the reading, skill-building activities take place.

The lesson plan in Example 7.2 illustrates the steps in the directed reading-thinking activity. It is designed for use with the reading selection *Barrio Boy*, excerpted in Example 7.1. The strategy and skill-building activities in the basal teacher's manual can be used with this instructional procedure.

Making predictions about what will occur in a text encourages children to think about the text's message. In making predictions, students use their background knowledge about the topic and their knowledge of text organizational patterns. This step provides purposes for reading: trying to confirm one or more predictions from others in the group and to confirm or reject their own. It also encourages students to apply metacognitive skills as they think through their lines of reasoning. When students are unable to make predictions as requested, the teacher can model his or her thinking in making a prediction, using a think-aloud, or provide several possible predictions for the student to choose from and ask for the reason a particular one is chosen. The teacher should accept all predictions and encourage the students to reflect on their accuracy later. If students are new at making predictions, the teacher can use highly predictable materials, such as folktales, to encourage success. It may help to have the students summarize what has happened before making predictions (Johnston, 1993).

In preparing a DRTA, the teacher should select points at which to pause so that the children can make predictions. These points should probably be ones where the story line changes, points of high suspense, or other logical spots, and there should be no more than four or five stops in a story (Haggard, 1988). During pauses, the teacher may use one or more open-ended questions to elicit student predictions about the next part of the story (Blachowicz, 1983). Smyers (1987) suggests that at each stopping point the students should be asked to write

---

Example 7.2   *DRTA Plan for a Reading Selection from a Published Series*

[Note: Page numbers mentioned in this DRTA plan refer to pages in the selection excerpted in Example 7.1. Not all of the story is reproduced there, but it can be found in *Beyond the Reef.*]

Step 1: Making Predictions From Title Clues

Write the title of the story or chapter to be studied on the chalkboard, and have a child read it. For this selection, write "Barrio Boy." Ask the children, "What do you think this story will be about?" Give them time to consider the question thoroughly, and let each child have an opportunity to make predictions. All student predictions should be accepted, regardless of how reasonable or unreasonable they may seem, but the teacher should not make any predictions during this discussion period.

Step 2: Making Predictions From Picture Clues

Have the students open their books to the beginning of the selection. Ask them to examine carefully the picture on the first page. After they have examined it, ask them to revise the predictions they made earlier, based on the additional information in the picture.

Step 3: Reading the Material

Have the students read the italicized paragraph that introduces the story on page 207 to check the accuracy of their predictions.

Step 4: Assessing the Accuracy of Predictions and Adjusting Predictions

When all of the children have read the italicized paragraph, lead a discussion by asking such questions as "Who correctly predicted what the story was going to be about?" Ask the children who believe they were right to read orally to the class the parts of the paragraph that support their predictions. Children who were wrong can tell why they believe they were wrong. Let them revise their predictions, if necessary, and then ask them, "Now what do you think the story will tell about Ernesto's and his mother's experiences?"

Example 7.2 *(cont.)*

**Step 5: Repeating the Procedure Until All Parts of the Lesson
Have Been Covered**

Have the children read pages 207–211 (end of the second complete paragraph) to
check the accuracy of their predictions. Have them read selected parts orally to justify the predictions they think were correct and tell why they believe other predictions were incorrect. Have them revise or adjust their predictions, based on their
reading. Then pose the question "What do you think will happen when Ernesto
enrolls in school?" and have them read pages 211–213 (end of second paragraph)
to check their predictions. After a discussion of the accuracy of the predictions and
revisions of predictions, ask them, "How do you think Ernesto will adjust to school?
Do you think he will have problems? If so, what kinds? Will he overcome the problems?" Have them read to the end of the story to check their predictions for the
final time.

---

questions, particularly prediction-eliciting questions. This procedure helps to balance the student-teacher exchanges in class, increasing the students' share. (See
Chapter 10 for an example of the DRTA applied to a content area lesson.)

**Time for
Reflection**

Some teachers think a DRA is too prescriptive to use, but consider a DRTA acceptable
because it gives students some control over their own learning. Other teachers believe
that there is a place for each technique. **What do *you* think?**

Literature-Based Approaches

Many educators, including those who embrace the whole language philosophy
and those who favor more structured approaches, recognize the value of using
quality literature as a basis for reading instruction. Teachers need to understand
theoretical perspectives on literature and reading and also need to know reasons
for using a particular book and a particular instructional approach (McGee and
Tompkins, 1995). Wordless picture books, for example, provide materials for the
emerging literacy of young children. These children can learn to follow a plot
without having to decode words, and they can learn to provide their own interpretations of the author's ideas. Patterned books can provide another level of literary exposure for beginning readers. Books of all types may be read aloud to
students or be made available in reading corners for students to read independently. Activities such as retelling stories with or without flannel boards, writing

reactions to books, and conversing about books with the teacher and other students may take place.

A literature-based approach places emphasis on connecting the stories to the children's personal background knowledge, analyzing stories and selections for particular elements, and monitoring students' understanding of the reading materials. In addition, "good literature offers readers opportunities to engage in life experiences that they would otherwise miss" (Barone, Eeds, and Mason, 1995, p. 31). Essential reading skills and strategies can be taught within the context of material the children are actively involved in reading. The writers' styles can be studied and used as models for children's personal writing (Aiex, 1988; Fuhler, 1990). For example, Lunsford (1997) found that minilessons based on literature enhanced her writing workshops.

Obviously, given these priorities, the foundation of a literature-based program must be *trade books*, that is, books not written primarily for instructional purposes. Most teachers have always made use of trade books for children in their classrooms. They have read aloud to the children from these books, urged students to read the books in the classroom reading center or to check them out from the school library for recreational reading, and used them as supplements to basal instruction. In a literature-based program that is built on a whole language perspective, the teacher uses knowledge of students' backgrounds and attempts to "hook" them on reading selections. He or she has a clear instructional plan and clear goals and expectations for students. The students' strategy use is monitored by both teacher and students, who share in responsibility for learning (Ruddell, 1992).

Literature-based programs may be conducted in a number of ways, and combinations of these approaches are common in most literature-based classrooms. Four such approaches are whole-class reading of a core book, use of literature circles with multiple copies of several books, use of thematic literature units, and individualized reading approaches (Henke, 1988; Zarillo, 1989; Hiebert and Colt, 1989). Each of these approaches will be discussed in turn. A common adjunct to all of them is Sustained Silent Reading (SSR), in which students and teachers alike are allowed time to read materials of their own choice without interruption (Tunnell and Jacobs, 1989). Hilbert (1992/1993) suggests holding student-led discussion groups every five to eight weeks to allow children to share and compare the plots, themes, and characters of books they have read during SSR. Later, groups may report their decisions to the whole class. Reading may also be shared through puppet shows, puppet displays, or posters. SSR is described in detail in Chapter 8.

Literature-based instruction has been successful with a wide range of students. Zuker (1993) found that a literature-based whole language teaching/learning philosophy applied in classes with students who had language and learning disabilities resulted in positive gains in listening, speaking, reading, and writing. Stewart and others (1996, p. 476) found that literature-based developmental reading programs resulted in improved reading performance by seventh and eighth graders. They believe that "choice leads to interest and ownership, interest and ownership to practice, and practice to speed and fluency. Speed and fluency result in increased comprehension and retention (i.e., reading proficiency)." Time for reading is, of course, necessary for this model to work.

On the other hand, Scharer and Detwiler (1992) point out some concerns regarding literature-based instruction. When it is used, teachers find it hard to be sure all needed strategies and skills are being covered, hard to know how to assess progress, and hard to know how to handle the poorer readers. Certainly teachers need to be well prepared as language teachers to use the approaches effectively.

Whole-Class Reading of a Core Book

Generally, core books used for whole-class reading are acquired in classroom sets so that every student has a personal copy. Teachers usually select these books for the quality of the material and sometimes because they fit into the overall classroom curriculum by relating to studies in other curricular areas, such as social studies and science. It is a further advantage if the teacher personally likes the book, for the teacher's attitude is communicated to the children as the reading progresses. It is important that the books selected provide something significant to talk about (Egawa, 1990).

Before a book is presented to the class, there may be prereading activities in which the students share personal experiences related to the book's content and activate information they possess about the topics or themes covered in it. (See Chapter 5 for information about techniques for schema activation.) The teacher may also present a minilesson on some literary element that is important in the book, such as characterization or flashbacks (Atwell, 1987). Purposes for listening to or reading the material are often set by having students predict what will happen in the story, based on the title and possibly on the picture on the book's cover or the first page of the story. At other times, purposes may be set by having students generate questions about the story that they expect to answer from reading. Occasionally the teacher may suggest some purpose question that will focus the readers on a key element in the book, such as "How is the setting of the story important to its plot?"

Sometimes the teacher first presents the book to the students by reading aloud part or all of it, depending on the students' reading abilities and the difficulty of the book. A chapter book may be read in installments over a period of days. After the teacher's oral reading, silent reading of the book by the students generally follows. At other times, the students may read the book silently first. Sometimes some students may present the book or a portion of it in a readers' theater as an introduction for other students.

At strategic points in the initial reading or independent rereading, there are usually pauses for small-group or whole-class discussion of the material. If predictions were made initially, these discussions may focus on the predictions, which can be evaluated, retained for the time being, altered slightly, or changed completely, based on the new information. The discussion may also focus on the purpose questions that were generated or on students' personal reactions to the story. To guide these discussions, the teacher may design questions that help the children to relate the story to their own experiences and to think critically and creatively about the material.

Between reading sessions, students may write reactions to the story in literature logs. The literature logs may be written just for the individual students, to help them think through what they are reading; or they may be dialogue logs, addressed to the teacher or a buddy. If the logs are a part of a written dialogue with the teacher, the teacher must respond to each entry with his or her own reaction to the story and/or to the student's reaction. Students should be free to write any honest response to the material without concern for negative teacher reaction. For example, a student who is bored by the story should feel free to say so in the log. Thus, the teacher's comments should be encouraging, thought provoking, and nonjudgmental. The teacher should not be looking for predetermined responses, but should respond with genuine interest in the students' comments (Wollman-Bonilla, 1989; Fuhler, 1994). Students should be encouraged to link the reading material with personal experiences. The teacher should model such entries for students by sharing his or her personal log entries orally. Students should also be encouraged to note phrases and expressions that appealed to them, statements expressing personal confusion, and predictions about what will happen next. Many different learning goals may be met through this student-teacher interaction (Flitterman-King, 1988; McWhirter, 1990). An example of one type of literature log is presented in Example 7.3. Another type is presented in Chapter 8.

Follow-up activities should be used after the book has been read to extend the children's understanding and help them elaborate on the ideas they gained from the shared book. These activities often involve writing, for example, composing another episode for the characters in the story, another story of the same genre, or a character sketch of a favorite character. Retelling the story in various ways is a good follow-up activity, especially for young children. They may simply retell the story to a partner, who may ask questions about missing events or ideas; they may retell the story using a flannel board and appropriate pieces; or they may act out the story through creative dramatics or puppetry. Illustrating the story sequence or selected parts of the story is a good follow-up activity that causes the students to reflect on the story and provides the teacher with insight into the students' degrees of comprehension of the story. The students may construct group or individual story maps after the reading. The maps can be displayed in the classroom or shared during discussions or oral presentations. Students may apply information learned in the story (for example, how to do origami), or they may read related materials because of aroused interest in the topic.

Teachers have made many individual modifications of the procedures for close reading of a book by a class. Shaw (1988) had fifth graders keep narrative journals in which they wrote after reading each chapter of their book, taking the perspective of the main character to relate that character's adventures. Through this activity, they learned much about summarizing and the first-person narrative form. Journal writing is a powerful way to reflect and discover insights about material read. It encourages active reading and gives the teacher a glimpse of the students' personal transactions with the story (Fuhler, 1994).

Example 7.3 *Literature Log*

EIGHT COUSINS   Read to 53
10-8-86
        Each time I read this book it seems to get easier to read.
I guess it is because I'm getting used to the proper English used.
I enjoy it a lot and feel so carried off when I read it. So far the
story is very good and I just want to always know what's going
to happen next.
                                                        Anita

Anita,
      I haven't read *Eight Cousins*, but I sure would like to after
reading your enthusiastic responses. I must confess that Louisa
May Alcott is one author I've never read. I think I'll read *Eight
Cousins* and give her a try.
      Can you discover what or how the author is creating such
a wonderful feeling for you?
                                                        Mrs. H.

Source: Jill Dillard, "Lit Logs: A Reading and Writing Activity for the Library/Media Center and the Classroom." Reprinted with permission of the author and the Ohio Educational Library/Media Association's *Ohio Media Spectrum* journal, from the Winter 1989 issue, Vol. 41, No. 4, p. 39.

Wertheim (1988) created a personal teaching guide for the novels she had her students read by listing difficult vocabulary at the beginning of each chapter; underlining important vocabulary in the text; writing discussion questions on the pages to which they pertained (coded as literal, inferential, and critical); writing other, more inclusive, questions at ends of chapters; and listing follow-up activities at the end of the book. This plan appears to be very practical and efficient.

The following Focus on Strategies describes one way to do close reading of a core book. This example is not a prescribed procedure; many variations are possible.

**Focus on
Strategies**

Whole-Class Reading of a Core Book

In this lesson, the teacher has chosen the book *Patchwork Quilt* because of the way it shows relationships among the characters. This book is good for use with younger readers; for older readers, teachers would probably choose chapter books, with the discussion times coming at the ends of chapters.

The teacher opens with a minilesson on character development, leading the children to see how authors reveal characterization through the things the character says and does, the things other characters say about the character, and the ways they react to him or her.

Next, the teacher asks the students to brainstorm their personal associations for the words *Grandma, quilt,* and *masterpiece*. Webs of these associations are written on the board or on a chart.

Now the teacher invites the children to predict what the story will be about. They write down their predictions or share them orally with partners or the whole group. The teacher tells the children that as they read the story they should look for clues that will either confirm or disprove their predictions, and they should also look for the characteristics of the characters (noticing what is said about and to them, what they say, and what they do).

The teacher may ask the students to read just the first two pages of the story and stop to discuss these questions with others at their tables:

What is the relationship between Tanya and her grandmother like?

Do you have a relationship like that with some older person?

Now students may read the rest of the story, with the number of pages read each time varying with the maturity of the students. Some possible stopping points and questions for discussion in the small groups include the following.

After two more pages:

Did Tanya's mother understand why Grandma wanted to make the quilt?

How did the reaction of Tanya's mother to the quilt make Grandma feel? How could you tell?

After five more pages:

What did Grandma mean when she said, "A quilt won't forget. It can tell your life story."?

Can a quilt really tell stories? If so, how?

Did Mama find out what Grandma meant about the quilt telling stories? How do you know?

After four more pages:

When Grandma got sick, why didn't she tell the others at first?

How did she feel about leaving her quilt unfinished? How could you tell?

Why did each person who worked on the quilt do what he or she did?

Would you have wanted to work on it if you had been one of them? Why or why not?

After the next page:

Was Tanya right to take squares out of Grandma's old quilt without asking permission? Why did she do it? What will Grandma think of it?

(continued)

After the story is finished:

How did Grandma feel about her quilt pieces going into the quilt?

What did she say and do that makes you believe that?

Why did they give Tanya the quilt?

How will Tanya feel about this quilt when she is older?

Do you have anything that you feel that way about?

Follow-up activities for after the reading may include some of the following:

1. Find another book that tells about a relationship between a child and a grandparent or another older person. Compare and contrast the stories.

2. Design a get-well card that Tanya might have made for her grandmother when she was sick.

3. Write a diary entry that Tanya might have made on the third day after she saw how sick her grandmother was. Have Tanya tell her diary how she felt about her grandmother's illness.

4. Pick a character and describe him or her. List his or her characteristics and why you did or did not like him or her.

5. Make a small patchwork quilt for the classroom. (Students provide material scraps for it. The children design the quilt pattern after looking at books about quilts and pictures of quilts, then cut out the pieces, and sew them together.) The quilting may be done by a volunteer parent or group of parents, or a resource person may show quilts and demonstrate quilting.

Literature Circles

In literature circles, the teacher chooses several books for which multiple copies are available, introduces each one, lets children choose which book to read, presents the books to the children if they are unable to read them independently first, has children hold discussions about the books, may participate as a member in group discussions, has students respond in logs, and lets the children help decide about ways to share the experience of the books (Egawa, 1990; Heald-Taylor, 1996). In these groups, students initiate and sustain discussion topics, connect literature selections to their lives, compare literature selections and authors with each other, note authors' styles, and consider authors' intents. The structured book choices lead them to try books in a variety of genres and by a variety of authors (Keegan and Shrake, 1991; Samway et al., 1991). Personal responses to literature replace "correct" answers to questions about the stories. Participation in an interpretive community of readers allows half-formed ideas to be explored from different perspectives. Students are required to provide substantiation for their contributions to the group. They should be receptive to the interpretations of their classmates, but they should also feel free to disagree (Spiegel, 1996).

Reading response journals allow the collection of reactions to the reading throughout the reading process, not just at the end, and can be the basis for small-group discussions. Supportive comments by the teacher can encourage students to react honestly to the material and persevere in the reading. Sometimes students may need encouragement to be more specific in their entries (Hancock, 1992; Raphael et al., 1992; Fuhler, 1994). To provide such encouragement, Berger (1996, p. 381) had her students respond to these questions: "What do you notice? . . . What do you question? . . . What do you feel? . . . What do you relate to?" These questions led the students to do more than just summarize the reading.

Moore (1991) had teachers in a graduate methods course take part in electronic dialogue journals with fifth-grade students (using computers and modems). The partners discussed the book *Superfudge* by Judy Blume. The teachers modeled good discussions of characters and setting through their entries, and the quality of students' entries improved. Both groups enjoyed the interaction. Roe conducted a smiliar project (Roe and Smith, 1997). (See Chapter 11 for more detail about the project.)

Hancock (1992) believes awareness of typical response patterns in literature response journals can help teachers encourage extensions of response types. Some possible response types involve interaction with the characters, empathy with the characters, prediction and validation of predictions, personal experiences that relate to the reading, and philosophical reflections. Since spelling and grammar are not checked in any way, the students feel freer to communicate.

This approach is described in more detail in Chapter 8.

Thematic Literature Units

Thematic literature units center around themes, based on topics such as homes, families, survival, taking care of our earth, wild animals, pets, specific geographic regions (for example, South America), or specific groups of people (for example, Japanese); genres, such as biography, science fiction, or folktales; or authors, such as Cynthia Voigt, Judith Viorst, or Maurice Sendak. Thematic units allow students to delve more deeply into ideas and thus develop deeper understandings and see connections between ideas. Shanahan, Robinson, and Schneider (1995, p. 718) urge development of units around such themes as "We all should try to make the world a better place," rather than just topics, such as "lupines." With themes, students can support or challenge a position and think more deeply about it. Themes can help teachers and learners focus on meaning making. A theme offers a *focus* for instruction and activities, making it easier for students to see the reason for classroom activities, acquire an integrated knowledge base, achieve depth and breadth of learning, and connect with real audiences. The variety of materials used allows for these accomplishments (Lipson et al., 1993; Bergeron, 1996).

There are other values as well. The reflection involved in studying themes can enhance metacognition, but perhaps the biggest advantage of thematic teaching is the promotion of positive attitudes toward reading and writing. The range of topics covered and the opportunity for self-selection promote student interest and positive attitudes. Another advantage is that time is less fragmented in a classroom in which the teacher uses thematic units. The number of subjects to be taught is reduced by embedding one subject in another one (Lipson et al., 1993).

Evans (1994) describes a bilingual thematic unit on fear, composed of scary stories from English and Spanish cultures. The focus can be on understanding fear and overcoming it. Since fear is a universal emotion, its use as a topic allows for cultural comparisons of literary treatments of the topic. *Great Scary Imaginings* (Humanities Software) is a computer program that could be used with such a unit. It is designed to go with Mercer Mayer's *There's a Nightmare in My Closet* (The Dial Press, 1968). It contains a database of activities to encourage the children to write about the story with a compatible word-processing program. Other print books, such as Mayer's *You're the Scaredy Cat* (Four Winds Press, 1974) or his *Terrible Troll* (The Dial Press, 1968) can be used for a unit on scary things along with the computer program *Monsters & Make-Believe* (Pelican). This is a talking word processor with graphics capabilities that allows students to create pictures of monsters using various body parts supplied by the program (Wepner, 1993). Layering instruction in different books exposes students to a variety of viewpoints about a topic (Strickland, 1994/1995).

A story can be used as the focus for curricular integration (Lauritzen, Jaeger, and Davenport, 1996). White and Lawrence (1992) describe building a thematic unit on the literature selection *Why Mosquitoes Buzz in People's Ears* by Verna Aardema. Related readings and activities were chosen to complement and elaborate on this selection.

The teacher collects a variety of related books (a *textset*) for the children to read during the unit. The organization of the unit provides the mental set for the children to see connections among the literature selections (Roser, Hoffman, and Farest, 1990; Lipson et al., 1993). Roser and colleagues (1992) incorporated literature comparison charts (which they called *language charts*) into thematic units to facilitate the making of connections among the stories. The charts seemed to enhance the students' reactions to the literature.

Textsets are books that have the same author, theme, topic, genre, or some other characteristic. They can set the stage for critical thinking by students as they look for connections. Textsets encourage discussion and varied interpretations (Heine, 1991). A textset on Katherine Paterson's books might include *Bridge to Terabithia, Lyddie, The Great Gilly Hopkins, Jacob Have I Loved,* and *The Sign of the Chrysanthemum*. Textsets are available for computers on CD-ROM, as well. *Stories and More* (IBM) is a primary-level, literature-based, read-aloud program. It provides voice-supported reading as well as interactive computer activities for some of the stories (Wepner, 1992). Obviously, use of textsets allows small-group discussion in which students can compare and contrast a variety of related books and write in response journals about the relationships they have discovered.

Gallagher (1995) suggests hooking the interest of adolescent readers with one or more young adult novels, then presenting a classic that is related in some way to the young adult literature. The connections made between or among the books can enrich the reading. For example, Katherine Paterson's *Park's Quest* could lead to the reading of Charles Dickens's *Great Expectations*. Both books are concerned with a young man's search for his own identity. S. E. Hinton's *The Outsiders* could also be paired with *Great Expectations*, since Ponyboy says he feels like Pip. Joan Lowery Nixon's *The Name of the Game Was Murder* could be paired with Agatha Christie's *And Then There Were None* (Pavonetti, 1996). Books may be paired according to theme, setting, mood, or some other element.

Thematic units are often opened with prereading activities for developing background, such as those mentioned earlier for the core book, in which children discuss what they already know about the focus of the unit. Students may brainstorm terms they associate with the theme, and these terms may be organized into a semantic web. (See Chapters 4, 5, and 8 for more on semantic webs and literature webs.)

The teacher may read aloud one or more books that fit the focus of the unit before allowing students to form small groups to read from multiple copies of other related books. One fifth-grade teacher read aloud *Lincoln: A Photobiography* at the beginning of a unit based on the genre of biography and let the students form small groups to read such books as *What's the Big Idea, Ben Franklin?; Eleanor Roosevelt: First Lady of the World; A Weed Is a Flower: The Life of George Washington Carver;* and others for which she had secured multiple copies. Single copies of other biographies were also available for independent reading, as well as short biographies in basal readers, anthologies, and periodicals (Zarrillo, 1989).

Some unit activities should be designed for whole-group participation (for example, the read-alouds), some for small-group participation (for example, activities related to the multiple-copy books), and some for independent work (for example, literature logs about books read individually). Many books need to be available in single and multiple copies to meet the varied needs of the students and to allow students who work quickly to choose additional books to read.

The teacher may read aloud to the entire class the selection or selections chosen to open the unit. Some selections may be presented through videotapes or audiotapes. Each reading should be accompanied by or followed by discussion of the material, writing in literature logs, and other activities, such as those listed for follow-up activities in the section on whole-class reading of a core book.

The teacher may then give book talks about the books that are available in multiple copies to help children make decisions about the groups in which they will work. Students should have choices regarding these books, although it may be necessary to let them give their top three choices and be assigned a book from these choices because of the limited number of copies available for each book. Book talks may also be given for some of the single-copy books. In addition, as students finish reading certain books, they may give book talks to entice their classmates to read these books.

Whole-group activities are likely to include minilessons related to the reading that the children are doing. These minilessons may focus on literary elements or reading strategies.

When small groups meet about the books they are reading in common, activities such as those described in the section "Literature Circles" in Chapter 8 can be used. As small-group and independent reading progresses, students may continue to build on the webs they started during the introductory activities. At the end of the unit, culminating activities may include comparing and contrasting the books read and some elements of the books, such as characters, settings, plots, and themes; construction of time lines related to the unit theme; creative dramatics based on readings; writing related to the theme; and so on. For example, students may cooperatively write a story with the same theme that appears in the books they have read in the unit (Marzano, 1990).

Some commercial materials are available to help teachers plan activities for thematic literature units. *Bookshelf, Stage 1* (Scholastic) contains six copies each of eighteen different books. Thirteen themes and a variety of genres are included. The kit also contains big books, audiocassettes, and a teacher's resource book. The resource book provides a wide choice of suggestions for using each literature selection. Spiegel (1990) recommends this set of materials for young readers because of its many positive attributes. She recommends *Reading Beyond the Basics Plus* (Perfection Form) for grades four through six. This is a set of resource books for ten high-quality children's novels. Each resource book provides a variety of activity choices for use with one of the novels.

Example 7.4 shows one type of thematic literature unit plan.

Individualized Reading Approach

The *individualized reading approach* encourages children to move at their own paces through reading material they have chosen, rather than requiring them to move through teacher-prescribed material at the same pace as other children placed in the same group for reading instruction. With the individualized reading approach, which is designed to encourage independent reading, each child receives assistance in improving performance when need for such assistance becomes apparent.

Characteristics of an individualized reading approach include the following:

1. *Self-selection.* Children are allowed to choose material they are interested in reading. Each child may choose a different book. The teacher may offer suggestions or give help if it is requested, but the decision ultimately rests with the child. Thus, an individualized reading approach has built-in motivation: children want to read the material because they have chosen it themselves.

2. *Self-pacing.* Each child reads the material at his or her own pace. Slower students are not rushed through material in order to keep up with the faster ones, and faster children are not held back until others have caught up with them.

Example 7.4 *Thematic Literature Unit Plan*

Pam Petty, a second-grade teacher at Carthage Elementary School in Carthage, Tennessee, developed a thematic unit around the reading of *Freckle Juice* by Judy Blume (Dell, 1971).

Related Poetry and Songs

Poems:
- "Freckles" by Watts
- "Everybody Says" by Aldis
- "Freckles" by Fisher
- "Millions of People" by Krows
- "Extraordinary Me" by Hajdusiewicz

Song:
- "I Love Myself"

Math
- Problem solving
- Student generated problems
- Dealing with money
- Calculations with time
- Graphing
- Addition
- Subtraction
- Liquid measure
- Measuring for recipe

Reading
- Story elements
- Characterization
- Vocabulary development
- Cause/effect pattern
- Prediction
- Rhyming words
- Descriptive language
- Contractions
- Plurals

Health
- Self-esteem
- Reading ingredients on food labels

Art
- Drawing or modeling Andrew's face

Music
- Singing

Book: *Freckle Juice*, by Judy Blume
Focus: Self-esteem and diversity of people
Grade: Second

Writing
- Reading response journal
- Writing advertisements
- Writing recipes for personal traits
- Creative writing about themselves

Grammar and Usage

Parts of speech
- Nouns
- Verbs

Teacher References
- *Meet the Authors and Illustrators*
- *Poetry Place Anthology*
- *Poetry Works!*

Related Books
- *People*, by Peter Spier
- *Pondlarker*, by Fred Gwynne
- *Thunder Cake*, by Patricia Polacco

Oral Language Arts

Listening and speaking
- Poetry reading
- Discussions
- Readers' theater

Example 7.4 *Thematic Literature Unit Plan (cont.)*

Pam's unit plan also uses other literature selections as it focuses on self-esteem and diversity among people. It has cross-curricular connections with a number of content areas: listening/speaking, reading, writing, health, math, art, and music, as shown in the diagram.

The unit covers ten days of instruction, as follows:

Day 1

The children are introduced to Judy Blume, the author. The teacher shares information gleaned from Scholastic's *Meet the Authors and Illustrators* by Deborah Kovacs and James Preller. Other books by Judy Blume are displayed. The children examine the book for information such as title, author, copyright date, and publisher. They are asked to look at the cover picture and the picture at the beginning of Chapter 1 and make predictions based on the title and pictures.

Day 2

The students read Chapter 1. They keep a word log of "neat" words and unknown words found in the chapter. In the search for "neat" words, students look for interesting language usage. (This activity is repeated for each chapter.) The class begins to construct a story map on the board. The teacher diagrams the elements of the story as the students dictate. The students use the map to fill in data about the story on a story-frame handout that asks for main characters, setting, problem, and solution. They copy the map on the board onto the back of their story-frame handout.

The poems "Freckles" by Mabel Watts, "Everybody Says" by Dorothy Aldis, and "Freckles" by Aileen Fisher (found in *Poetry Place Anthology*, Scholastic, 1983) are used for choral reading. Then they are examined for rhyming words, plurals, nouns, verbs, and contractions. The words in the poems are used to stimulate brainstorming about other words that share the same characteristics.

The students begin a reading response journal in which they respond each day to the reading. They also discuss their entries in small groups.

For each chapter (Chapter 1 on this day), on a cause-and-effect chart, one main action is chosen as the cause and entered on the left side of the chart, and the result or effect of this action is entered on the right side.

Day 3

The students read Chapter 2. They read the poem "Millions of People" by Jane W. Krows (*Poetry Place Anthology*), which is useful for promoting self-esteem. They also examine the poem for plurals, nouns, and rhyming words.

Example 7.4   *Thematic Literature Unit Plan (cont.)*

The students sing "I Love Myself" (Affective Enterprises).

The students do creative writing on "The Best Things About Me" or "What I Would Like to Change about Myself (and Why)," or they design flyers advertising Freckle Juice for sale.

Day 4

The students read Chapter 3.

The teacher reads aloud the book *People* by Peter Spier (Doubleday, 1980). This book shows global diversity among people.

The children write original recipes for curls, blue eyes, height, or other traits.

Day 5

The students take one card per character and list that character's name, description, and traits on one side of the card. They draw a picture of the character on the back. Students hold up character cards to respond to questions in class.

For art, the students draw Andrew's face or make it out of clay and glue on popcorn or other materials for freckles.

Day 6

The students read Chapter 4. They do choral reading of the poem "Extraordinary Me" by Babs Bell Hajdusiewicz (*Poetry Works!*, Modern Curriculum Press, 1990). The students use the descriptive language to draw a picture of the person. Then they compare their pictures with the one on the poem chart.

The students make lists of words to describe themselves. Classmates read the lists and try to guess who is being described.

Day 7

The students read Chapter 5. They finish the story map and story frame.

The teacher gives the students a handout with a boy's face on it, laminating film, and markers. The students listen to the teacher read descriptions of three story events: being embarrassed at school, drawing blue spots on face, and being sad and sick after drinking juice. The students color laminating film and hold it on the boy's picture to show which event is being read about.

Day 8

The students do math problems related to Andrew's allowance and saving to buy the juice, problems related to telling time (connected with events in the story),

Example 7.4 *Thematic Literature Unit Plan (cont.)*

problems about adding or multiplying quantities of liquid (quarts of freckle juice), and problems related to making and reading graphs. The teacher reads *Pondlarker* by Fred Gwynne to the students to further stimulate discussion of self-esteem.

Day 9

The students retell the story or perform it through readers' theater.
The teacher reads *Thunder Cake* by Patricia Polacco to the children. This book involves both self-esteem and a recipe.

Day 10

The teacher shows students cans and boxes of food or juice and tells them to write down the expected ingredients for Thunder Cake. Then the class follows the recipe for Thunder Cake and compares the actual list of ingredients to the students' expected list. The students discuss "surprise" ingredients (such as tomatoes).

3. *Strategy and skill instruction.* The teacher helps students, either on an individual basis or in groups, develop their word recognition and comprehension strategies and skills as needed.

4. *Recordkeeping.* The teacher keeps records of each child's progress. He or she must know the levels of a child's reading performance to know which books the child can read independently, which are too difficult or frustrating, and which can be read with the teacher's assistance. The teacher must also be aware of a student's reading strengths and weaknesses and should keep a record of the strategies and skills help the child has received. Each child should keep records of books read, new words encountered, and new strategies learned.

5. *Student-teacher conferences.* One or two times a week, the teacher schedules a conference with each child, varying from three to fifteen minutes depending on the purpose.

6. *Sharing activities.* The teacher plans some time each week for the children to share books they have read individually. The children may share with the entire class or with a small group. Sharing can sometimes take the form of book auctions in which the children bid with play money on the opportunity to read a book next. The "auctioneer" tries to interest the students in bidding by telling about the book (Bagford, 1985).

7. *Independent work.* The children do a great deal of independent work at their seats, rather than spending most of the assigned reading period in a group

with the teacher. Better readers and older children can benefit more from time spent in individualized reading than can poorer readers and younger students, who need more teacher direction (Bagford, 1985).

Since exposure to different types of literature can help children build schemata for these types and should thus increase their efficiency in processing texts, the individualized reading approach is congruent with schema theory (Hacker, 1980). In addition, the variety of material students read provides them with vicarious experiences that help build other schemata and thus enhance future comprehension. Children encounter words in a variety of meaningful contexts, thus extending their vocabulary knowledge (Bagford, 1985).

Individualized reading helps students realize that reading is enjoyable. At the same time, reading books at comfortable reading levels develops fluency and can contribute to improved reading rates (Bagford, 1985).

To set up an individualized reading program, a teacher must have available a large supply of books, magazines, newspapers, and other reading materials, covering a variety of reading levels and many different interest areas. This collection will need to be supplemented continuously after the program begins, for many children will quickly read all the books that are appropriate for them.

The teacher should have read a large number of the books available to the children, since doing so makes it much easier to check the students' comprehension. Starting a file of comprehension questions and answers for books being used in the program is a good idea; these questions will be available year after year and will help refresh the teacher's memory of the books. The teacher will also find it convenient to have a file of strategy- and skill-developing activities, covering the entire spectrum of word recognition and comprehension strategies and skills and a wide range of difficulty levels.

When starting an individualized program, the teacher should determine the children's reading levels and interests in order to choose books for the program that cover a sufficiently broad range of topics and difficulty levels. Before initiating an individualized program, the teacher can plan routines to follow in the classroom, considering questions such as: (1) How are books to be checked out? (2) How will conferences be set up? (3) What should children who are working independently at their desks do when they need assistance? The room arrangement can also be planned in advance to allow for good traffic flow. If books are categorized and located in a number of places instead of bunched together in a single location, students will have less trouble finding them, and the potential noise level in the room will be lower.

The teacher may find that having a file folder for each child helps in organizing and recordkeeping. Each file folder can contain both checklists on which to record strategy and skill strengths and weaknesses and a form noting conference dates and instructional help given. Students can keep their own records in file folders that are accessible to both them and the teacher. These records will have different content and more or fewer specific details, depending on the maturity of the children.

Student-teacher conferences serve a variety of purposes, including the following:

1. *To help with book choices.* Teachers should spend some time showing children how to choose appropriate books. Teachers can encourage them to read one or two pages of the books they think might appeal to them and consider the number of unfamiliar words they encounter. If there are more than five unfamiliar words per page, the book might be too difficult, whereas if there are no unfamiliar words, the child should consider the possibility that he or she could read more difficult material. A teacher can suggest potentially interesting books to students who find it hard to make a choice. Student-written book reviews may be provided for students who are having trouble deciding about books. Students can learn to write good reviews by examining models of written reviews and receiving assistance from the teacher or librarian (Jenks and Roberts, 1990).

2. *To check comprehension.* Conferences help determine how well the children are comprehending the books and other materials they are reading. Much of the time, the teacher and students may have authentic discussions about issues in the book during the conferences. Sometimes, however, the teacher may ask a student to retell all or part of the story or ask a variety of types of comprehension questions. (See Chapter 6 for information on question types.)

3. *To check word recognition strategies and oral reading skills.* The teacher can ask a child to read orally, observing his or her methods of attacking unfamiliar words and using oral reading skills, such as appropriate phrasing and good oral expression.

4. *To give strategy and skill assistance.* If a child is the only one in the room who needs help with a particular strategy or skill, the teacher can help that child on a one-to-one basis during a conference.

5. *To plan for sharing.* Some conferences are designed to help children prepare for sharing their reading experiences with others. If a child wishes to read a portion of a book to the class, the teacher might use a conference to listen to the child practice audience reading and to give help with the presentation.

There is nothing contradictory about using group instruction in an individualized reading program. A teacher can group children with similar skill difficulties to give help. The important thing is to be sure that all children get the instruction they need when they need it and are not forced to sit through instruction they do not need.

In an individualized reading program, each child is expected to be involved in independent silent reading a great deal of the time. This time should not be interrupted by noisy surroundings or non-task-oriented activities. The teacher should make the rules for the reading time very clear and indicate acceptable activities, such as taking part in student-teacher conferences, selecting a book, reading silently, giving or receiving specific reading assistance, taking part in a reading group, completing a strategy or skill-development practice activity, or keeping records concerned with reading activity.

Individualizing a reading program is a huge undertaking, but such a program can be introduced gradually by using it only one day a week while using the basal program the other four days, and increasing time spent in the individualized program one day at a time over a period of weeks until all five days of the week are devoted to it, or by introducing the program to one reading group at a time while the remaining groups continue the basal program. After one group has become familiar with the approach, other groups can be introduced to it, until the entire class is participating in the individualized reading program. Teachers whom Harris (1996) worked with thought that using the basal for part of the week and literature-based instruction for the other part of the week would be a good way to start.

The main advantages of an individualized reading approach follow.

1. Children have built-in motivation to read books they have chosen themselves.

2. Children are not compared negatively with one another because every child has a different book and the books are primarily trade books, which have no visible grade designations.

3. Each child has an opportunity to learn to read at his or her own rate.

4. Student-teacher conferences create a great deal of personal contact between the teacher and students.

Characteristics of this approach that some educators have considered to be disadvantages are the following:

1. The teacher must amass and continually replenish a large quantity of reading material.

2. The need to schedule many individual conferences and small-group meetings can create time difficulties.

3. An enormous amount of bookkeeping is necessary.

4. The program lacks a sequential approach to strategy and skill development.

Focus on Strategies

Individualized Reading Approach

Mr. Neal is sitting at a table with Paul, a student who has been reading the book *Maniac McGee*. They are having a lively discussion about which characters in the story value reading and how they show that they do. Mr. Neal is able to tell from this discussion how well Paul has comprehended aspects of the book, but he is also engaged in a valid discussion of the content about which he has a personal opinion with a boy who has his own opinion, feels free to share it, and knows how to use events from the book to back up his ideas.

(continued)

In the meantime, most of the other class members are reading from self-selected books at their desks or on the carpeted area of the reading center. When Megan has problems with a word in her book, she quietly leans over and asks for assistance from her assigned buddy, Tracy. When Tracy fails to be of help, Megan lists the word, page, and paragraph and reads on in her book.

Trey, who has a great deal of trouble sustaining independent reading over a period of time, is sitting at the computer, reading from a book on CD-ROM that allows him to click on words he doesn't know to obtain both pronunciations and definitions. With this assistance, Trey is able to remain focused on his reading for the entire period.

Jason and Joshua are sitting close together discussing the mock interview they plan to use during the book-sharing time on Friday. Both have read *Hatchet* and have decided to share with the rest of the class by having Jason play a reporter and Joshua play Brian. They are intently listing interview questions and answers to use for this purpose.

As Mr. Neal finishes the conference with Paul, he asks who needs some help. Megan and Mark hold up their hands, and Mr. Neal moves to their desks to offer assistance. Then he returns to the conference table and calls Michael, who is scheduled for the next conference, to come up. Michael has been having difficulty with word recognition skills, and Mr. Neal asks him to read orally from some new material in the book he is currently reading, in order to assess the particular difficulties that he is having.

After Michael's conference, Mr. Neal will meet with a small group of students who need help in making inferences when they read. He will model the process for them and have them engage in some directed practice activities.

Each student in Mr. Neal's class has self-selected material to read when he or she is not involved in a teacher-student conference, a peer-planning session, or a needs-group session. The students know the procedures to use when they have trouble, and they know they can receive individual attention during conferences or at intervals during class time if they follow accepted procedures. The fact that they have chosen their reading material heightens their motivation to read it and makes student engagement more likely.

Time for Reflection	Some teachers believe that literature-based instruction using trade books should completely replace use of published reading series that contain anthologies of literature. Others believe that use of both will result in the best instruction. **What do *you* think?**

Language Experience Approach (LEA)

The *language experience approach* interrelates the different language arts and uses the children's experiences as the basis for reading materials. The rationale for this approach has been stated very concisely by one of its leading proponents, R. V. Allen:

What I can think about, I can talk about.

What I can say, I can write—or someone can write for me.

What I write, I can read.

I can read what I write, and what other people can write for me to read (1973, p. 158).

This approach to reading is obviously not new, although its implementation has changed over the years. Today the experience charts used in the approach may be either group or individual compositions; stories about field trips, school activities, or personal experiences outside school; or charts that contain directions, special words, observations, job assignments, questions to be answered, imaginative stories or poems, or class rules. Current applications are often found in whole language classrooms, since this approach allows the children control over the content and language used in the stories.

Because the stories used in the language experience approach are developed by the children, they are motivational, and because they use the language of the children, the reading material is meaningful to the children. The language experience approach has been used effectively with students who speak English as a second language, providing material for reading instruction that they can understand (Moustafa and Penrose, 1985; Moustafa, 1987).

A child's background may be limited, but every child has experiences that can be converted into stories. In addition, the teacher can plan interesting firsthand experiences that can result in reading material that is meaningful for all students.

The language experience approach is consistent with schema theory. Because it uses the child's experiences as the basis for written language, the child necessarily has adequate schemata to comprehend the material and can thus develop a schema for reading that includes the idea that written words have meaning (Hacker, 1980). The language patterns found in stories composed by children are often much more mature than those found in basal readers, since children use compound and complex sentences and a wide vocabulary. Nevertheless, children seem to find their own language patterns much easier to read than those in basal readers, probably because clues in a familiar context are easier to use. In fact, students often pick up the long, unusual words in experience stories faster than many of the short service words, probably because the distinctive configurations of these words contribute to recognition.

With the language experience approach, reading grows out of natural, ongoing activities. Children can see the relationships between reading and their oral language. This approach offers good opportunities for developing the concepts of *writing, word,* and *sentence.* During the language experience process, children see the transformation from oral language to print take place, including directionality, spacing between words, and punctuation and capitalization. Framing

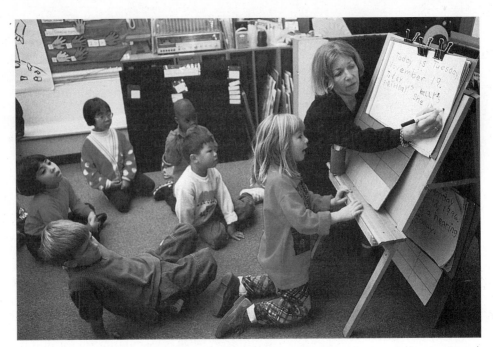

During the creation of a language experience chart, children see the transformation from oral language to print taking place. (© *Elizabeth Crews*)

the individual language units with the hands also helps to illustrate their meanings (Blass, Jurenka, and Zirzow, 1981). Another benefit is that observations made during dictation and reading of a language experience story and during the follow-up activities can provide the teacher with diagnostic insights into children's reading difficulties (Waugh, 1993).

Implementation in Kindergarten

Chapter 2 describes the use of language experience charts in kindergarten and also provides an example of a chart. At this level, teachers often use the charts to emphasize that oral language can be recorded and reconstructed, rather than focusing on having the children read the charts. Others, such as Karnowski (1989), involve kindergarten students in activities more like those described for the primary grades in the next section. Karnowski's approach uses the language experience approach with process writing, having the children choose their topics for writing from among their previous experiences. Discussion and sometimes dramatic play and/or drawing precede the writing of the story. The initial dictation of the story is revised and edited according to the children's direction, to show that first drafts are not the only drafts. The teacher reads and rereads charts before the children read them independently. Then the teacher uses the charts to teach vocabulary, decoding, and comprehension skills. Of course, the charts are "published" for reading by the children and their peers. This approach fits perfectly with the current belief in emergent literacy.

Individual stories may be solicited by asking the children to write something they want the class to know, a kind of written show-and-tell. The writing should include invented spellings such as the ones described in Chapter 2 (Coate and Castle, 1989).

Those children who have started to recognize many words may move into a program similar to the one described next for use in the primary grades.

Implementation in the Primary Grades

Implementation of the language experience approach with a group of primary-grade students may take a number of forms, but the following steps are common:

1. Participating in a common experience
2. Discussing the experience
3. Cooperative writing of the story on a chart, the board, or a computer
4. Participating in extension activities related to the story

After the children have participated in a common experience and have talked it over thoroughly, they are ready to compose a group experience story. First, the teacher may ask for suggestions for a title, allowing the students to select their favorite by voting. Then the teacher records the title on the chalkboard or a transparency. Each child offers details to add to the story, which the teacher also records. She or he may write "Joan said" by Joan's contribution or may simply write the sentence, calling attention to capitalization and punctuation while doing so. After recording each idea, the teacher reads it aloud. After all contributions have been recorded, the teacher reads the entire story to the class, sweeping his or her hand under each line to emphasize the left-to-right progression. Then the teacher asks the class to read the story with him or her as he or she moves a hand under the words. Under cover of the group, no child will stand out if he or she does not know a word.

If the children have had numerous experiences with this type of activity, the teacher may proceed to other activities involving the story. If this is a very early reading experience for the group, the teacher will probably stop at this point until the next day. On the second day, the class can be divided into three or four groups with which the teacher can work separately. To begin each group session, the teacher rereads the story to the children, using a master chart made the day before. Then the group rereads it with him or her. Next, a volunteer may read the story with the teacher, filling in the words he or she knows while the teacher supplies the rest. After each child in the group has had a chance to read, the teacher asks students to find certain words on the chart. The teacher may also show the children sentence strips (also prepared the day before) and have them match these strips with the lines on the chart, either letting volunteers reconstruct the entire chart from the sentence strips or using this as a learning-center activity to be completed individually while other groups are meeting. Group charts can be useful in developing many skills and are commonly used for lessons in word endings, compound words, long and short vowels, rhyming words, initial consonants, capitalization, punctuation, and other areas.

If the teacher makes a copy of the story for each student, it is possible to underline on that copy the words that the student recognizes while reading the story. The teacher may then make word cards of these words, which serve as the beginnings of the children's *word banks*. (Word cards containing the words a child has used in stories can eventually be used to practice sight vocabulary, work on word recognition skills, and develop comprehension skills.) As a group of students finishes meeting with the teacher, the students may be given the opportunity to illustrate their stories individually.

After this first attempt, students will write most experience stories in small groups, sometimes working on a story together and sometimes producing and sharing individual stories. At times, some children may dictate their stories to helpers from higher grades. Some teachers use tape recorders for dictation.

Class stories do not always have to be in the same format. They may take the form of reports, newspaper articles, descriptive essays, or letters, or they can be creative in content while using a particular writing style to which the children have been exposed. For example, after reading predictable books to the children, the teacher can encourage the children to produce the same kind of story. The repetition and predictability in the stories make sharing these child-developed books with classmates a profitable way to provide extensive practice in reading familiar words and language structures (Reimer, 1983).

It is important that teachers use the children's own language in language experience stories, even if the children's language does not fit the teacher's idea of basic words and sentence patterns for reading. If they do not do so, students are not likely to reap the full benefits of this approach.

Computers can be useful in a language experience lesson. The teacher can type into the computer student-dictated material and modify it as the students direct. A large monitor or projection device is needed for this approach. The students may use one beginning and develop different endings, then print out the various versions for comparison. The teacher can give students individual printed copies to illustrate and/or expand (Grabe and Grabe, 1985).

At some point the students may be able to enter their stories into the computer themselves. Several word-processing programs are easy enough for even primary students to learn to use.

Children can write stories on the computer most effectively when several students work together. The group of children can collectively decide what to say, taking turns entering sentences as they are composed, or some students can be in charge of keyboarding and others in charge of content and mechanics, spelling, and grammar.

Sharing stories, whether orally or in written form, is very important, since group members will soon see that certain words occur over and over again and that they can read the stories their classmates write. The experience stories written by the group as a whole may be gathered into a booklet under a general title chosen by the group, and individuals may also bind their stories into booklets. Children will enjoy reading one another's booklets, and a collection of their own stories provides both a record of their activities and evidence of their growth in reading and writing.

In some schools students write language experience stories, illustrate them, make them into books, and set them up in a classroom library with library pockets and checkout cards, as they might have in a regular library. Children assume jobs as librarians.

As time passes and the children learn to write and spell, they may wish to write experience stories by themselves, asking the teacher or turning to their word banks or dictionaries for help in spelling. Teachers should allow children to use invented spellings when they are writing, since they can go back and correct spelling and rewrite the story in a neater form later if others are to read it.

Rereading and editing require children to make judgments about syntax, semantics, and the topic and about whether or not others will understand the written account. These activities provide ways to emphasize comprehension when using language experience stories. At first this should be done with extensive teacher guidance; later children can work more independently (Sulzby, 1980). The following Classroom Scenario presents the language experience approach in a primary-grade classroom.

**Classroom
Scenario**

Language Experience Approach

A lifelike raccoon puppet was shown to the children in a first-grade classroom. The presenter introduced the puppet as Rocky Raccoon and proceeded to tell them about his personality, including his preferences (for example, Rocky Road ice cream and rock music). The children looked at Rocky, touched his fur, and discussed him thoroughly. Then they dictated the following story:

Rocky Raccoon
Rocky is beautiful. Rocky is soft. Rocky is funny. Rocky is a nice raccoon. Rocky can do tricks. Rocky is cuddly. Rocky is fluffy.

The presenter read the story to the class and allowed them to read it with her. Then she posed this question: "Does your story sound like the ones that you have been listening to your teacher read to you?"

After thinking about it, the children said it did not sound like the books they had heard being read. The presenter then asked them, "What could you do to the story to make it sound more like the stories in books?"

Several children said, "Not repeat *Rocky* so many times. Use longer sentences. Put stuff from sentences together."

(continued)

Step by step, the presenter questioned them about which *Rocky* mentions to change and what to change them to and which sentences went together and how they should be combined. The children's revisions were recorded one at a time, and the story was reread each time to see if they liked it better. They also decided to add a sentence. The final version that met with their approval went like this:

Rocky Raccoon

Rocky is beautiful. He is soft. He is funny. Rocky is a nice raccoon. He can do tricks. He is cuddly and fluffy. Rocky looks like he is wearing a mask.

Analysis of Scenario

This activity was the children's first experience with revising their own writing. They liked the fact that they could change the writing around to make it sound better to them. Even though they did not end up with classic literature, they had taken a step in their literacy development.

Word banks offer many opportunities for instructional activities. When children have accumulated a sufficient number of word cards in their word banks, they can use them to compose new stories or to play word-matching or visual and auditory discrimination games. To develop comprehension skills, a teacher can use classification games, asking questions such as "How many of you have a color word? A word that shows action? A word that names a place?" When each student has as many as ten word cards, the children can begin to alphabetize them by the first letter, which gives them a practical reason to learn alphabetical order. They can also develop picture dictionaries representing the words on their cards, or they can search for their words in newspapers and magazines. After they recognize that their words appear in books, they will realize they can read the books. The uses for word banks seem to be limited only by the teachers' and children's imaginations.

Implementation in Higher Grades

The language experience approach has many applications above the primary grades. These applications are often in content area instruction: writing the results of scientific experiments; comparing and contrasting people, things, or events; writing directions for performing a task; and so forth.

Many computer applications lend themselves to upper-grade activities, for they allow children to enter their stories easily and provide ease of revision without the drudgery of recopying. A good computer application is the production of a newspaper based on experiences around the school. Programs are available that make the production of a nice-looking newspaper relatively easy for children. Children can be reporters, who initially enter the stories into the computer; editors, who edit the work of the reporters; and "typesetters," who format the edited material (Mason, 1984).

Text structures found in content area textbooks, such as comparison-and-contrast patterns, can initially be taught through language experience activities. Then students will be more likely to understand these structures when they encounter them in content materials. First, the teacher can present children with two items and ask them how these items are alike. Then the teacher can ask how the items are different. The class can construct a chart of these likenesses and differences during the discussion. After the discussion, the children can dictate a language experience story based on the information listed on their chart. The teacher can encourage them to write first about likenesses and then about differences. Practice activities with the completed story may include matching the two parts of a contrast, for example, matching "a marble is round," with "a jack has points." Parts of the story can be scrambled, and then the story can be rearranged with the comparisons and contrasts lined up appropriately (Kinney, 1985).

Heller (1988) has pointed out that direct teaching of story structure during language experience activities that are used with older remedial learners can be helpful. She also emphasizes the inclusion of revision and editing as natural extensions of experience story writing.

Some Considerations About the LEA

The language experience approach offers something for children regardless of the modes through which they learn best because it incorporates all modes. For instance, the learners use the auditory mode when stories are dictated or read aloud, the kinesthetic (motor) mode when they write stories, and the visual mode when they read stories.

The language experience approach promotes a good self-concept. It shows children that what they have to say is important enough to write down and that others are interested in it. It also promotes close contact between teachers and students. Finally, this approach has been highly successful as a remedial technique in the upper grades, allowing low-achieving readers to read material that interests them rather than lower-level materials that they quickly recognize as being designed for younger children.

If the LEA is the only reading approach used, development of reading skills in a predetermined sequence is not likely. However, there is no single correct sequence for presenting reading skills, and children learn from a variety of programs that provide different skill sequences.

Using only the LEA would also result in lack of systematic repetition of new words and lack of vocabulary control in general. Still, structure words, which are important and need to be learned in context, are generally repeated quite often.

With the LEA as the exclusive approach to reading instruction, the limitations of the children's backgrounds of experience might drastically limit reading content, and the materials used in reading would also rarely be of good literary quality. However, since the LEA is generally used along with other approaches, such problems are unlikely to develop.

| Time for Reflection | Some teachers think the language experience approach is too unstructured in relation to skill development to be useful. Others think it is valuable, but only as a supplement to other approaches. Still others think it can serve as an exclusive approach in the beginning stages of reading instruction. **What do *you* think?** |

Programmed Instruction

Programmed instruction is sometimes used to offer individualized instruction. Programmed materials instruct in small, sequential steps, each of which is referred to as a *frame*. The student is required to respond in some way to each frame and is instantly informed of the correctness of his or her response (given immediate reinforcement). Because the instruction is presented to an individual child, rather than to a group, each child moves through the material at his or her own pace, thereby benefiting from some individualization. Branching programs provide an even greater degree of individualization by offering review material to children who respond incorrectly to frames, thereby indicating that they have not mastered the skills being presented.

Programmed instruction can also provide follow-up reinforcement for instruction presented by the teacher, freeing the teacher from many drill activities and allowing him or her more time to spend on complex teaching tasks. The programmed materials are designed to be self-instructional and do not require direct teacher supervision.

On the other hand, programmed instruction does not lend itself to teaching many complex comprehension skills, such as those involving analysis and interpretation, nor does it promote flexibility of reading rate. It also does not encourage student-to-student interaction (Wood, 1989). Word analysis and vocabulary-building skills are most prominently treated in programmed materials, so teachers may wish to use other materials (for example, basal texts) or techniques (for example, semantic webbing) to present and provide practice in the complex comprehension skills. Materials used with programmed instruction may consist of print materials such as programmed texts, or they may exist in electronic format, presented on computers.

Computer Applications

Computers are valuable tools for the reading teacher. Through software available for computer-assisted instruction (CAI), computer-managed instruction (CMI), word processing, database applications, and literature presentation, teachers can plan many meaningful learning experiences for students. Because of the interactive characteristics of the computer—it can provide immediate responses to input from student users—teachers find that it is a good tool for individualizing instruction. Because of its ability to repeat instructions patiently without showing irritation or judging students negatively, it is also useful for remedial instruction. Word-processing programs allow teachers and students alike to easily revise and edit their written products, which can be printed in neat form to be read by class members. Its utility for enhancing the use of the language experience approach has already been covered in the section on that approach. Database programs are valuable research tools and can be used to help students organize data for writing reports.

Much writing is exchanged among classrooms when networks and electronic mail systems are available (Newman, 1989; DeGroff, 1990). Use of such experiences has resulted in more lengthy writing and improved attitudes and performance in reading and writing for middle-grade students (Riel, 1989; Moore, 1991). Newman (1989) found similar advantages for older students in length of text produced, attitudes toward writing, and language development (Moore, 1991).

Many literature programs present literature in an interactive format, and some software is specifically designed to build reading comprehension. *Super Solvers Midnight Rescue!* (The Learning Company) is a game in which students must read letters, diaries, newsletters, and excerpts from classics to collect clues and solve a mystery. The program features animation and sound effects (Larson, 1994).

Some teachers wonder if computers have a place in whole language and literature-based classrooms. DeGroff (1989, 1990) and many others say "yes." Whole language and literature-oriented teachers often use computer programs, such as interactive fiction programs, that are more open-ended than drill-and-practice programs. Also especially popular are programs that allow construction of semantic maps, story maps, and interactive branching stories, as well as programs that offer onscreen activities tied in with popular trade books. *Story Club* (Davidson) is a program designed to fit into a whole-language classroom. This program has students listening, speaking, reading, and writing. One component is a talking word processor combined with a paint program. Web browsers that give students access to information on the Internet can be powerful research tools in both whole-language and more traditional classrooms.

When pairs of students are allowed to work together at the computer, the language interactions are rich, whether the students are reading an interactive fiction story, using a simulation program, or writing a story together. The computer screen appears to be a stimulus for interaction as children pass by or wait for turns (DeGroff, 1990; Cochran-Smith, 1988). The computer offers opportunities for reading meaningful material such as messages, directions, stories, informational articles, and their own writing and that of other students (DeGroff, 1990).

Some computer-based programs for teaching reading employ a multisensory approach. The IBM *Writing to Read* program, for example, attempts to teach reading through an approach that involves tactile, visual, and auditory senses.

Hypertext and hypermedia applications offer many mutlisensory experiences, as well (Dillner, 1993/1994).

Additional information about the applications covered in this section can be found in Chapter 11.

Eclectic Approaches

Eclectic approaches combine the desirable aspects of a number of different methods rather than strictly adhering to a single one. Teachers often take an eclectic approach in choosing instructional materials and techniques to fit their unique situations and provide a variety of reading experiences for children. The following examples are only possibilities, and teachers should remember that the only limitations are school resources and their own imaginations.

1. Language experience stories can be based on characters, events, or ideas in either trade books or basal stories. The teacher can plan an experience related to the story, lead a discussion of the experience, and record the students' dictated account. If an experience such as this is used prior to reading the book or basal story, it can help to activate the children's schemata related to the story. It will also probably involve use of some of the same vocabulary in the story, providing an introduction to this vocabulary in context. The story may also be used as a basis for skills instruction suggested in the basal reader (Jones and Nessel, 1985).

2. Grabe (1981) also suggests having the teacher supplement the basal reader approach by having children write "books about the book": they dictate stories about the basal selection using the new vocabulary. This approach has been found to enhance comprehension and vocabulary skills.

3. Teachers may use basal readers for up to 50 percent of the reading time. The remainder of the time can be spent on shared reading of trade books. This practice allows the teachers a wide range of choice and control over decisions about reading instruction in their classrooms. In some classrooms, the basal stories may simply be used as they fit into thematic units being taught (Henke, 1988).

4. In a class in which whole-class reading of a core book is taking place, language experience stories can be written, based on material from the particular book being read. For example, if the core book is *The Cay* by Theodore Taylor (Avon, 1969), the experience might be to try to weave a mat while blindfolded. The students could write a story about the experience and, in the process, develop a better understanding of the difficulty Phillip had when Timothy asked him to weave a mat, even though he was blind.

5. Computer-assisted instruction can be used with any approach. The use of the word-processing function of the computer makes the computer a natural tool for implementation of the language experience approach. Children who

tend to produce only short stories because of difficulties in writing are freed to write more extensively with the ease of editing the computer offers.

6. Teachers can use the individualized reading approach for two or three days each week and the basal program for the rest of the week, or they can alternate weeks with the individualized reading approach and the basal. They may supplement either or both with occasional language experience activities, either on or off of the computer.

7. Teachers can use a thematic literature unit approach to reading instruction, making use of pertinent basal reader stories as they are available and using language experience activities as appropriate to the planned curriculum. They may use database software to store information about the unit on the computer in an organized way, and they may use word-processing software to produce written reports about aspects of the theme.

8. Walker-Dalhouse and others (1997) conducted a literature-based reading program that employed basal themes with middle-school students. Some of the selections were from the Houghton Mifflin literature-based reading program; others were theme-related trade books. Writing, language, oral reading, and independent reading were taught in the communications area. Writing and grammar lessons were related to the literature theme, although a grammar textbook was used. Oral reading groups read a common book and discussed it. Students also chose independent books from a group designated by the teachers, and the teachers developed instructional packets for each group. Students chose books, completed the activities in the packets, and had conferences with the teachers about the reading. Students responded well to the program.

Classroom Scenario

An Eclectic Approach

Ms. Gray, a teacher who embraces an eclectic approach to reading instruction, is working with one reading group in a corner of the room during her scheduled reading time. At the same time, children from another reading group are illustrating a language experience story that they wrote on the previous day. As they finish their illustrations, pairs of children from this group are forming sentences with their word-bank words. Several other children are busy reading self-selected library books at their seats.

Three children have returned to the room from the library and have seated themselves together to discuss some research reading they have been doing on space travel. One of them is holding the printout from a database query she had made during the library trip.

(continued)

In another corner of the room, two girls are reading an interactive text story on a computer, discussing each decision and coming to a consensus about it before indicating their choices through keyboard commands.

Analysis of Scenario
In this classroom, all of the students are busy at reading tasks, but the tasks involve many different approaches to reading instruction. The teacher has chosen activities that fit the children's individual instructional needs.

Time for Reflection

Some teachers believe that they should stay with a single approach to reading instruction. Others believe that using the best ideas from all approaches is preferable. What do *you* think?

What About Whole Language?

Some readers may be wondering why whole language is not featured as a section of this chapter. As mentioned at the beginning of the chapter, we have not included it in this way because whole language is not an *approach* to reading instruction. Rather, it is a curricular philosophy, or belief system, as described in Chapter 1.

Many of the approaches mentioned in this chapter are frequently used by whole language teachers: the language experience approach, use of thematic literature units, use of literature circles, some variations of whole-class reading of a core book, the individualized reading approach, and some computer applications.

Some educators even say that teachers can use a whole language philosophy and blend the instructional activities with systematic direct instruction (Spiegel, 1992; Yatvin, 1991). Spiegel (1992) sees direct instruction as teaching children strategies to be used flexibly to meet reading needs and suggests blending the best of whole language and systematic direct instruction in reading strategies to assist all children in reaching their full literacy potential. Strategies may be taught and then practiced using authentic materials, rather than worksheets or other forms of isolated drill. This position will likely be heavily debated for some time to come.

Summary

Published reading series are the most widely used materials for teaching reading in elementary schools in this country. Basal readers have been improved in recent years and provide teachers with anthologies of reading materials, detailed teacher's manuals, and many supplementary materials. Some published series are being called literature-based and/or language-integrated series because of their greater focus on quality literature selections and integration of other types of language activities with the reading. Many new series are also giving teachers and students more decision-making power and control over the lessons. Literature-based and language-integrated series focus on more prediction making by the students and more instructional options for the teacher than are found in traditional basal reader manuals.

The directed reading activity (DRA) is the teaching strategy presented in traditional basal manuals. This strategy can be used with other reading materials as well. Teachers can use the *enrichment activities* of the DRA before the story to help build and integrate background. Comprehension monitoring can also be made a natural part of a DRA. An alternative to the DRA is the directed reading-thinking activity (DRTA).

Literature-based reading approaches include whole-class reading of a core book, literature circles reading several books for which there are multiple copies, thematic literature units, and the individualized reading approach. Whole-class reading of a core book, thematic literature units, and the individualized reading approach all include use of minilessons. Thematic literature units center around a theme, a genre, or an author. All of these approaches include various types of responses to literature. The individualized reading approach allows children to move at their own paces through reading material that they have chosen. Student-teacher conferences help the teacher monitor progress and build rapport with the students. Sharing activities allow group interaction.

The language experience approach interrelates the different language arts and uses children's experiences as the basis for reading materials. This approach has many advantages: it incorporates the visual, auditory, and kinesthetic modes of learning; it promotes a positive self-concept and fosters close contact between teachers and students; and it serves as an effective remedial technique in the upper grades. This approach can be introduced in kindergarten, but it continues to have applications for all students in higher grades, especially in conjunction with content area activities.

Some approaches are particularly helpful for individualizing instruction. Among these are programmed instruction and computer approaches, in addition to the individualized reading approach. Programmed instruction is administered through materials that present information in small, sequential steps. The student responds at each step and receives immediate feedback about the correctness of the response. Students are allowed to learn at their own paces. Computer approaches include computer-assisted instruction (CAI) and computer-managed instruction (CMI), in which the computer takes care of such tasks as recordkeeping, diagnosis, and prescription of individualized assignments. Many computer applications have been found to be appropriate for use in whole language classrooms. Computer-managed instruction can help teachers keep track of student performance.

An eclectic approach combines desirable aspects of a number of different methods. The only limitation to possible combinations is the teacher's imagination.

Whole language has not been discussed extensively in this chapter because it is a philosophy, rather than an approach. However, many of the approaches described in this chapter are congruent with a whole language philosophy. Chapters 1, 2, and 8 present additional information related to this philosophy.

Test Yourself

True or False

_____ 1. All published reading series are alike.

_____ 2. Teacher's manuals in basal reading series generally provide detailed lesson plans for teaching each story in a basal reader.

_____ 3. Basal reader workbooks are designed to teach reading skills and do not require teacher intervention.

_____ 4. Workbook activities are useful only for keeping children busy while the teacher is engaged in other activities.

_____ 5. Published literature-based reading series have moved toward offering teachers more decision-making opportunities than traditional basal readers generally offered.

_____ 6. The language experience approach (LEA) uses child-created material for reading instruction.

_____ 7. A word bank is a collection of words that the teacher believes children should learn.

_____ 8. The language experience approach promotes a better self-concept in many children.

_____ 9. The individualized reading approach utilizes self-selection and self-pacing.

_____ 10. The individualized reading approach involves no direct skills instruction.

_____ 11. Student-teacher conferences are an integral part of the individualized reading approach.

_____ 12. When literature-based reading programs are used, children interact with texts in meaningful ways.

_____ 13. Close reading of core books, discussion, and writing related to the reading take place in many literature-based classrooms.

_____ 14. Thematic literature units involve the reading of a single book by all class members and writing of a book report on the book.

_____ 15. Programmed instruction presents instructional material in small, sequential steps.

_____ 16. An eclectic approach combines features from a number of different approaches.

_____ 17. The language experience approach is not consistent with schema theory.

_____ 18. Open-ended computer applications, such as word-processing and database programs, do not fit in whole language classrooms as well as do drill-and-practice programs.

_____ 19. The directed reading-thinking activity is a good alternative to the directed reading activity to provide a more student-centered experience.

_____ 20. Word processing on the computer is useful for writing language experience stories.

_____ 21. The language experience approach is not useful above first grade.

_____ 22. Whole language instruction is a well-defined approach to teaching reading, complete with standard activities and materials.

For your journal...

1. Visit an elementary school classroom and then write about the instructional materials used in the reading program.

2. Visit a school and watch an experienced teacher use a DRA. Write your reactions.

...And your portfolio

1. Plan an individualized reading approach for a specific group of children. Explain what materials will be used (include reading levels and interest areas of the materials) and where they will be obtained. Outline the recordkeeping procedures; explain how conferences will be scheduled and the uses to which they will be put; and describe the routines children will follow for selecting books, checking out books, and receiving help while reading.

2. Develop a directed reading-thinking activity (DRTA) for a trade book.

3. Choose a basal reader for a grade level you might teach. Examine it for variety of writing types (narrative, expository, poetry). Make a chart showing the frequency of the various types. Note also the frequency of different types of content (language skills, social studies, science, art, mathematics, music, and so on).

4. Plan a thematic literature unit for a grade level of your choice. Think about ways that you can actively involve the children with the books.

8

Language and Literature

Key Vocabulary

SETTING OBJECTIVES

When you finish reading this chapter, you should be able to

▶ Discuss some basic principles of whole language.

▶ Explain the importance of integrating the language arts and of integrating language across the curriculum.

▶ Identify some relationships between reading and writing.

▶ Understand how to implement the writing process and list the major steps in this process.

▶ Discuss procedures for using journals and for implementing writing and reading workshops.

▶ Design a classroom environment conducive to reading and writing.

▶ Select appropriate literature of good quality and high interest and read or tell stories expressively.

▶ Discuss a variety of ways to respond to literature.

▶ Identify ways to use children's literature in different areas of the curriculum and to create thematic units.

Pay close attention to these terms when they appear in the chapter.

Caldecott Award

genre

journal

literature circles

Newbery Award

readers' theater

reading and writing workshops

Sustained Silent Reading (SSR)

thematic unit

webbing

whole language

writing process

This chapter opens with a brief discussion of some principles for facilitating language development, which are the basis for many of the strategies and procedures that follow. The chapter also presents reasons for connecting the language arts, particularly reading and writing, and discusses the value of literature for integrating the curriculum. Reading-writing connections are demonstrated through discussions of process writing, journal writing, and reading and writing workshops. The chapter also supports the concept of student-centered learning, which enables students to make choices and assume responsibility for their learning.

The second part of the chapter focuses on the use of literature to integrate the curriculum. It provides ideas for enabling the teacher to create a classroom environment where children support one another's efforts and experience a sense of ownership in their reading and writing. That section also offers suggestions for selecting appropriate literature for children, as well as for helping children choose books for themselves. Many ways to respond to literature, including literature circles, oral interpretation, drama, written expression, art, and music, are presented. Trade books may be used in all areas of the curriculum, and suggestions are given for creating thematic units focusing on specific books, genres, themes, and authors.

Facilitating Language Development

Instead of limiting language instruction to workbooks and practice sheets, many teachers today encourage children to use language in authentic, integrated situations. Learning is centered on the child, and the child learns communication skills through verbal interaction with others. Some basic tenets for facilitating language development are given here. These guiding principles are congruent with the *Standards for the English Language Arts* (1996) and also represent the whole language philosophy discussed in Chapters 1, 7, and 13.

- *Learning is integrated.* Students learn more effectively when they can see connections and relationships among ideas and subjects than when they learn bits and pieces of information in isolation.

- *Tasks are authentic.* Authentic activities relate to real-world tasks such as writing letters and reading for information. When students can see the purpose and meaning of the work they do, they understand why it is important to do it.

- *Learning is social.* The purpose of language is to communicate with others. Students therefore learn to use language by sharing ideas, working cooperatively, and becoming part of a community of learners.

- *Classrooms are learner centered.* To feel a commitment to learning language, students need to be actively involved in the learning process by accepting such responsibilities as making choices, taking part in negotiating decisions regarding procedures and curriculum, and self-evaluation.

Chapter 8 Organization

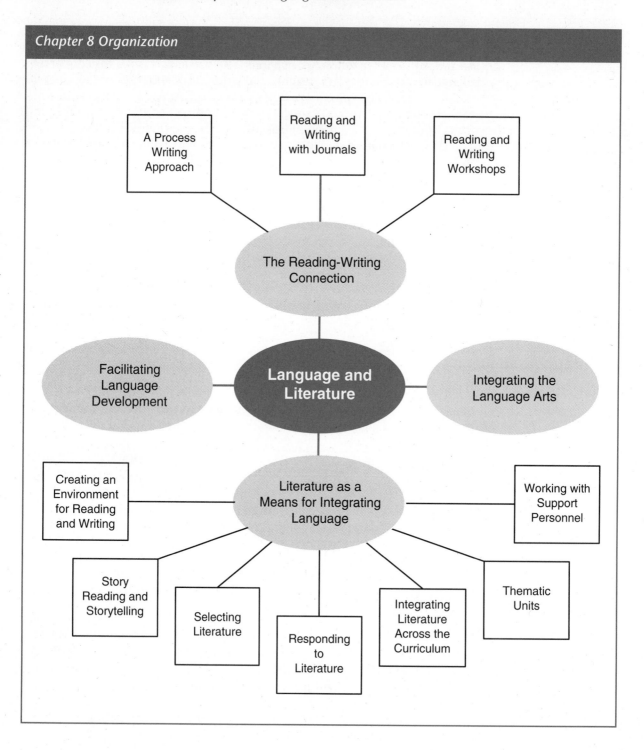

- *Learning is whole to part.* Reading skills and strategies are learned in meaningful context. For example, instead of learning phonics by filling out worksheets, children learn phonics by observing letter-sound patterns during shared reading.

- *Literature is an integral part of the curriculum.* Since a widely accepted premise is that children learn to read by reading, classrooms should offer a wide variety of books and related materials. Good books can be used across the curriculum as sources of information and pleasure.

Integrating the Language Arts

Listening, speaking, reading, and writing have long been accepted as the language arts, but developers of the *Standards for the English Language Arts* have expanded the concept to include visual language, consisting of viewing and visually representing. "Being literate in contemporary society means being active, critical, and creative users not only of print and spoken language but also of the visual language of film and television, commercial and political advertising, photography, and more" (*Standards*, 1996, p. 5). As teachers challenge students to integrate visual communication with other language forms, students are learning to use, interpret, and create such visual texts as illustrations, graphs, charts, videos, and electronic displays.

The integration of language arts in the classroom is not a new idea; indeed, curriculum designers have advocated it from time to time for decades (Jensen and Roser, 1990). In many classrooms, however, the practice of scheduling a specific amount of time for spelling, handwriting, reading groups, grammar, and so forth has prevailed. Such segmentation of the language arts interferes with children's natural, purposeful use of language in real situations, and it may result in their failure to apply what they already know about oral language to reading and writing.

For the classroom teacher, integration may mean setting aside a large block of time for language arts. This time period allows for flexible scheduling and freedom to fully develop special projects. Integration means coordinating activities so that children can see the natural connections among the various forms of language as they work to achieve goals. During this extended time period, children may engage in a variety of language activities, such as pursuing research projects, responding creatively to stories, preparing a school newspaper, or working at a poetry center. With a little guidance from the teacher, they become aware of the interrelationships among the language arts. They see, for instance, how the stories they read can serve as models for the stories they want to write, how the information they need for writing reports can be found by using research materials, or why good handwriting and correct spelling are important for publishing their own books.

Although a time period may be allocated for language arts instruction, integrated language experiences extend throughout the day into every area of the curriculum. For example, reading, writing, speaking, listening, and viewing are essential for learning about ideas that have changed history and science concepts that have resulted in new discoveries. In the following activity, the teacher provides an integrated language arts lesson by reading a book and then allowing the students to pursue their natural curiosity. During this lesson, children become involved in listening, speaking, reading, writing, and problem solving.

Integrated Language Arts Lesson

Model Activities

After reading Katherine Paterson's *Park's Quest* to the class, ask: "What do you think the title means? What is a quest?" If the students wish to pursue various aspects of the book, form groups to investigate topics that interest them. These topics may lead to such activities as a debate over the United States' involvement in the Vietnam War, a student-made book that connects the quest of King Arthur with that of Park, a diary in which students write from Park's perspective after each day on the farm, a report on the causes and effects of a stroke on a person's health, and an annotated bibliography of books about the Vietnam War.

The Focus on Strategies shows how a single book can become a theme for learning in many areas. As seen here, the teacher may introduce a book that so intrigues the students that they assume an active role in developing meaningful related activities. They contribute their own ideas so that their investigation is truly learner centered rather than teacher directed.

Focus on Strategies

Developing a Literature-Based, Student-Centered Theme That Integrates the Language Arts

Ms. Brison introduced Chris Van Allsburg's *The Wretched Stone* to her students by asking them to listen for clues that tell what the stone represents. This story was one of her favorites, and she hoped the students would like it too. When she finished reading it aloud, the students eagerly raised their hands to tell what they thought the stone really was. Isaac, the class scientist, thought it was malachite, and Katrina knew it must be a mirror (not a bad guess!). Others thought it was an object from outer space.

The students begged Ms. Brison to reread the story, and she agreed to do so if they would listen again for clues. This time Janis solemnly said, "I believe it's a television because that's how television makes some people act." The others quickly agreed as they noted the similarities between a television set and the stone in the story.

Still fascinated, the students wanted to know more about the story, so Ms. Brison asked them what they would like to do with it. Mike suggested finding other books by Chris Van Allsburg to read, and Beth wanted to learn more about the way sailors lived and worked long ago. Tim said he could teach a group how to make sailor's knots, and Molly said they could write logs as if they were sailors on the ship.

Ms. Brison recorded the ideas on the chalkboard, then placed each idea at the top of a piece of chart paper. She wrote *Other* at the top of one chart to allow the students to come up with other creative responses. She told the students to think about what they would like to do and then sign up to work on a topic. Those responsible for finding other books by Van Allsburg first checked the school library and the neighborhood branch library. Tim's dad took him to the downtown library, where he found *The Widow's Broom*. Susie knew someone who had a copy of *The Stranger* that she was able to borrow, and Ms. Brison located *Two Bad Ants* at the Teacher Center. Each day she read a different story until the children became quite familiar with Van Allsburg's style. "His books always have something mysterious in them," Jack said. "Yes," Connie continued, "and they start like it's for real, and then something happens that makes you know it has to be fantasy."

As their projects neared completion, the students decided to put their work at a center so that they could see what others were doing. The students who signed up to research the lives of sailors years ago collected books about sailing, took notes, and compiled an illustrated informational book that told of the hardships of sea travel—the food sailors ate, the length of their journeys, weather signs, the consequences of storms at sea, and the stars they used to chart their courses. Some students, intrigued by pirates on the high seas, found stories and legends about pirates, particularly Blackbeard. Another group dramatized the story for the class next door, and students who had read *Jumanji* decided to make their own board game with penalties and rewards. Van Allsburg's detailed illustrations intrigued many children, who compared his black-and-white drawings in earlier books with the colored ones in more recent books.

"I guess I didn't have to wonder if the students would like *The Wretched Stone*," Ms. Brison thought. "I can't believe how enthusiastic they were, and all I really had to do was introduce the book. They took it from there."

Ms. Brison realized that while the students were having fun investigating Chris Van Allsburg, they were actually learning a great deal about language and literature. She got out her curriculum guide and checked off several language skills for her grade level: making inferences, differentiating reality from fantasy, recognizing an author's style, locating information, and using reference materials. Of course, there were other skills as well.

This had been a truly integrated language arts theme: the thoughtful listening as the students tried to identify the elements of mystery, the well-supported points they made while defending their views about Van Allsburg's use of fantasy, the reading of related storybooks and reference materials, and the incredible informational book they wrote that portrayed the harsh life at sea. Perhaps the logs they wrote as sailors impressed Ms. Brison most of all. The students had used such vivid descriptive words to express their feelings as they moved from being lively, active sailors to entranced viewers of the stone.

(continued)

Ms. Brison chuckled to herself as she realized how her teaching had changed over the years. Instead of planning a theme herself and providing all the resource materials, she had students accepting this responsibility with a little guidance from her. Instead of learning discrete skills and using workbooks, the students were using authentic language strategies that had evolved from an intriguing book. Not a bad arrangement, she thought, as she glanced over the books on her shelf and pulled out Lynne Cherry's *The Great Kapok Tree*. I wonder what they will do with this one!

Time for Reflection

Some teachers believe they need to teach each language art separately (i.e., fifteen minutes for handwriting, twenty minutes for spelling, etc.) each day in order to be sure to cover each subject. Other teachers feel that integration of the language arts is more meaningful and that eventually every subject will be covered. **What do *you* think?**

The Reading-Writing Connection

In recent years, many educators have viewed both reading and writing as composing processes (Butler and Turbill, 1987; Flood and Lapp, 1987; Squire, 1983). Based on prior knowledge, attitudes, and experiences, the reader constructs meaning from text and the writer composes meaningful text. Both reading and writing require the use of similar thinking skills, such as analyzing, selecting and organizing, inferencing, evaluating, problem solving, and making comparisons. Tierney and Shanahan (1991, p. 275) state that "reading and writing, to be understood and appreciated fully, should be viewed together, learned together, and used together."

Reading and writing tend to reinforce each other. According to Smith (1983), children must learn to read like writers in order to write like writers. By offering a model, good literature instructs young authors through example and inspires them to try their hand at creating stories of their own (Lancia, 1997). Children quickly detect patterns in predictable and repetitive books, which they imitate as they write themselves (Saccardi, 1996). By carefully observing an author's use of dialogue while reading a story, a child begins to learn how to create dialogue when writing a story. Or in trying to write a description of the setting for a piece of writing, a child reads and rereads the setting from another selection to get ideas.

Table 8.1 shows examples of links between reading and writing (based on Butler and Turbill, 1987; Hornsby, Sukarna, and Parry, 1986). Stotsky (1983) warns, however, that although similarities exist in the ways in which reading and writing are learned, research shows there are sufficient differences to warrant attention to each independently, as well as in combination.

Educators have explored many ways of implementing the linkage between reading and writing in purposeful ways. Teachers and children have used message

Table 8.1   *Links Between Reader and Writer*

Reader	Writer
Brings, uses prior knowledge about topic	Brings, uses prior knowledge about topic
Reconstructs another's meaning	Constructs own meaning
Predicts what comes next	Predicts what should come next
Has expectations for text based on experiences	Has expectations for how text might develop
Modifies comprehension of text as reading continues	Develops and changes meaning while writing
Engages in "draft reading"—skimming, making sense	Engages in "draft writing"—getting ideas, writing notes
Rereads to clarify	Rewrites to clarify
Uses writer's cues to help make sense of reading	Uses writing conventions to assist reader
Responds by talking, doing, and/or writing	Gets response from readers

boards, or centrally located bulletin boards, for sending and receiving messages (Boyd, 1985; Harste, Short, and Burke, 1988), and some students correspond with other students through pen-pal programs. Several types of young authors' programs exist for various purposes, including encouraging children to write illustrated bound books and to share their writing with other authors outside their schools (Harris-Sharples, Kearns, and Miller, 1989). Following are some class activities for combining writing with reading.

Activities

1. Let the students write a class newspaper on one of these themes: (a) news stories that are modern adaptations of fairy tales and Mother Goose rhymes, (b) a newspaper written at the same time and place as the setting of the book the teacher is reading to the class, or (c) a literary digest of news about books. Children may compose advertisements for favorite books to place in the newspaper.

2. Encourage students to write a radio or television script based on a story they have read. (First, they should read some plays to become familiar with directions for staging and appropriate writing style for dialogue.)

3. Arrange for students to write to pen pals from other regions of the country. As they correspond, they are likely to become interested in those geographical areas, so provide resource materials for them to read about their pen pals' homes.

4. Hold a young authors' conference in which children display and read from books they have published. The conference could take place among classes within a single school, or it could be districtwide.

5. As children become involved in a thematic unit, let them find places to write for information. They will need to describe their needs and ask for appropriate resource material. When they receive the material, they will need to read it to be able to decide how to use it for their projects.

A Process Writing Approach

A *process writing approach* is a child-centered approach to writing in which children create their own pieces of writing based on their choice of topic, their awareness of audience, and their development of ideas from initial stages through revisions to final publication. The process is ongoing and recursive, with writing in some form generally occurring every day and with pieces in various stages of development.

Cross-grade process writing programs provide opportunities for older students to act as literary advisors and/or attentive audiences for younger children and for younger children to act as audiences for older writers. One of the authors of this text (Roe, 1990) conducted a program in which fifth graders from Austin Hamby's class served as partners for Ann Norris's second graders, as described in the following Classroom Scenario.

**Classroom
Scenario**

Cross-Grade Process Writing

During the second/fifth grade partnership at Crossville Elementary School, the fifth graders were preparing to give their completed books to their second-grade partners. It was their first attempt at process writing, and most of them were somewhat amazed at how well their stories had developed with input from classmates and teachers during conferences. One boy said, "This is a good story. I'd really like to keep it for myself." Nevertheless, he gave his book to his partner, who was delighted with it and told the story to anyone who would listen. A couple of times fifth graders excitedly showed the program director their writing, saying, "Look what I wrote for my partner! It wasn't part of an assignment; I just wanted to do it."

Analysis of Scenario
Awareness of their audience for the stories caused students to devote much attention to the development process. The students were much more concerned about revising their stories to improve them and copying them neatly for their partners than they had been about polishing stories that were written before the project began. The fifth graders produced whole books for their young partners, complete with title pages, copyright dates, dedications, and "about the author" sections. Writing for authentic purposes obviously made a difference in the quality of these students' writing.

Stages of the Writing Process

The *writing process* consists of the following major stages: prewriting, drafting, revising, editing, and publishing and/or sharing. These stages may be used at any grade level, although, of course, first graders' writing will be very simple, and their bookmaking will require a great deal of guidance from the teacher. In fact, in some cases the teacher may write stories from student dictation. As children progress through the grades, they will be capable of producing more complex, more carefully edited works. The stages of the writing process may be briefly described as follows.

Prewriting. The author prepares for writing by talking, drawing, reading, and thinking about the piece and by organizing ideas and developing a plan.

Drafting. The author sets ideas on paper without regard for neatness or mechanics.

Revising. After getting suggestions from others, the author may wish to make some changes in the initial draft. These changes may include adding dialogue, deleting repetitive parts, adding depth to a character, clarifying meaning, providing needed information, or changing the ending of the story.

Editing. With careful proofreading and the help of peers and the teacher, the author corrects spelling and mechanics.

Sharing and Publishing. After careful revisions, the authors are eager to share finished pieces with real audiences. Pages can be fastened with brads, taped together, sewn, or professionally bound. Finished books may be kept in the classroom or taken to the school library, fitted with pockets, and checked out.

Computers simplify the writing process. A word-processing program enables students to enter rough drafts quickly, revise frequently, and print their final copies. Students revise by inserting or deleting material and moving chunks of text, and they edit by correcting spelling and mechanics.

Reading and Writing with Journals

Students write in journals to reflect on and record their thoughts and ideas, without concern for correctness of form or mechanics. Writers determine the audience, for sometimes journals or designated pages within them are personal, and other times they are meant to be shared. Journals may be spiral notebooks or simply papers stapled together with student-decorated construction-paper covers. Students must have time for journal writing, preferably on a daily basis, so that they can rehearse what they want to write. A child of any age can do journal writing, with younger children using invented spellings and pictures to express their ideas.

To introduce students to journal writing, the teacher might discuss diary writing and read books written in letter or journal form, such as Joan Blos's *A Gathering of Days: A New England Girl's Journal, 1830–32* or Beverly Cleary's *Dear Mr. Henshaw*. The teacher should write in a journal along with the children to model the importance of recording thoughts and ideas. If students have trouble finding topics, the teacher might offer such suggestions as an important event, a perplexing problem, or a really good friend. Writers should understand that journals are a place where they can complain, ask questions, or express their true feelings.

Journal writing can take many forms. Dialogue journals are interactive, with the teacher or other reader responding to the student's writing. The responder should never correct the student's writing but can model proper spelling and writing conventions in the response. Reading or literary journals enable students to write responses to what they have read and receive the teacher's supportive feedback as a guide for further reading (Wollman-Bonilla, 1989). In buddy journals (see Example 8.1), student pairs "converse" in writing on a continuing basis, thus engaging in a meaningful writing and reading exchange (Bromley, 1989).

A double entry journal enables the student to respond to a passage of particular interest. The student writes what the author says on one side of the page and enters a personal response on the other side. Responses may be drawings, opinions, questions, reflections, or connections to personal experiences (Popp, 1997). In Example 8.2, sixth grader Madyson Burgess responds to *The Westing Game* by Ellen Raskin.

Time for Reflection	Although journals are generally considered to be places that children can write freely without regard for mechanical accuracy, some people believe that teachers should correct errors in spelling or punctuation when they read journals. **What do *you* think?**

Reading and Writing Workshops

Reading and writing workshops provide opportunities for teachers to teach specific strategies directly during brief minilessons and for students to spend most of their time actually reading and writing. These workshops operate in the manner described here (Ross, 1996).

Writing workshops consist of four steps: a minilesson, a status-of-the-class report, the actual writing workshop, and sharing time (Atwell, 1987). The minilesson lasts only a few minutes and deals with issues related to following procedures, writing realistic dialogue, using mechanics correctly, starting with good leads, or similar ones (Clemmons and Laase, 1995). The status-of-the-class check is made as the teacher calls each student's name and records what the student will be doing during the workshop. The writing workshop, when most students write and/or confer, consumes most of the class time. Group share occurs during the last few minutes when students share their writing, try out ideas, and respond to one another's writing.

Although formats differ, most reading workshops operate in a similar manner, beginning with a minilesson that might be about comprehension strategies,

Example 8.1 *Buddy Journal Entries*

Fri, 16, Feb, 1990

Erin,
    You are a very good reader. You are going to be a better reader if you keep practicing.
    do you like school? What is your favorite subject? My favorite subject is spelling.
                        Your partner,
                        Lesley Ann Richards

Wed. 21, 1990

Lesley,
    I do not like school very much. My favorite subject is scisce.
            do you like school?
                        Your Partner,
                        Erin Young

Source: Leslie Ann Richards and Erin Young, Crossville Elementary School, Crossville, Tennessee.

literary appreciation, or genres. After the teacher records student-selected tasks on the status-of-the-class record sheet, students spend most of their time with self-selected reading and responses. During this time, the teacher may hold conferences with some of the students. Before the end of class, students spend five to ten minutes sharing their activities, books, or projects with one another (Atwell, 1985, 1987; Reutzel and Cooter, 1991). Such workshops promote inquiry by letting students reflect on literature, interpret it, seek deeper meanings for it, and respond to it in various ways (Heald-Taylor, 1996).

The following Classroom Scenario, taken from Holly Martin's sixth-grade class, illustrates what happens during a typical writing workshop.

Example 8.2   Double Entry Journal

Quote	My Opinion
"He found Madame Hoo in their rear fourth-floor apartment kneeling before her bamboo trunk, fingering mementoes from her childhood in China".	This in my opinion is saying Madame Hoo is missing her home in China or maybe she is missing her childhood.

Source: Madyson Burgess, Prescott Central Middle School, Cookeville, Tennessee, 1997. Used with permission.

Classroom Scenario

Writing Workshop

Holly Martin begins by asking the students to recall what their four options are during writing workshop. They reply that they can read, write, think, and write in journals. She reminds them that good writers "take the time" and "make the effort," and then says she will be asking some of them to conference with her during class. She asks them to brainstorm what to write, and they respond with letters to pen pals in other schools, Writer's Showcase, poetry to submit to a magazine, and essays for special friends. After checking with students about what they plan to do, she lets them pursue their writing. Some move to the alcove where trade books are shelved, select their books, and sprawl on the floor to read them. Others pick up their writing folders to begin work on a piece. Still others begin writing in their journals. Holly calls on one student, and he discusses with her some problems he is having in completing his story. She asks a few questions that lead him to consider some options, takes notes on what occurred, and then moves on to the next student. As the class continues, students move about, finding the materials they need, talking quietly with other students, and continuing their writing.

Analysis of Scenario
These students understand their purposes for writing (to correspond with pen pals, enter contests, write newspaper articles, etc.) and are free to make choices about what they need to do to meet their objectives.

Time for Reflection

In reading/writing workshops, teachers present skills and strategies during five- or ten-minute minilessons, then allow students to actually read or write during remaining class time. Some teachers spend an entire class period (forty-five minutes or so) teaching skills and strategies, believing they need this much time to provide instruction. What do *you* think?

Literature as a Means for Integrating Language

Literature can be the basis for learning to read and write and for developing positive attitudes toward further language learning. Teachers who integrate literature with language arts give children purposes and opportunities for reading and writing throughout the day and across all areas of the curriculum. They read aloud to students daily from various genres of children's literature and provide a variety of good books for classroom library shelves.

Creating an Environment for Reading and Writing

The classroom environment should be supportive and free from the risks that inhibit honest expression. Children should feel a sense of ownership in the reading they do by choosing the books they want to read and deciding where and how to read them, how to respond, and how their own related work is to be displayed or published. They may sit in an author's chair to read their own writing or favorite stories by professional authors to their friends.

In a supportive classroom, teachers encourage children to read by arranging portable, freestanding bulletin boards and chalkboards, sets of shelves, and other furniture to create nooks and crannies for reading. They provide carpet scraps and cushions that allow children to read comfortably and privately. Bookshelves and containers filled with books should be within easy reach. Writing materials, including lined and unlined paper, pencils with erasers, colored pens for revising and editing, and folders for completed work, are readily available. Backs of furniture become spaces for showing children's work and creating inviting displays about books. Teachers set up writing centers with activities that encourage children to make written responses to books, and provide enough time for such reading and writing to take place. Working together, teacher and students can design bulletin boards and arrange displays that center around a theme, represent a genre (such as poetry or biography), or focus on books by a popular author.

For an international theme, place book jackets or photocopies of book covers around a wall map of the world with strands of yarn that reach from the book jacket to the place on the map that is the setting for the book. Examples include Katherine Paterson's *Jacob Have I Loved* for Chesapeake Bay, Lois Lowry's *Number the Stars* for Denmark, Jean Craighead George's *Julie of the Wolves* for the Arctic tundra, and Paula Fox's *Lily and the Lost Boy* for Greece (see Example 8.3).

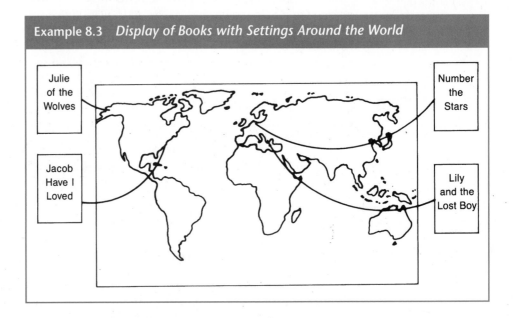

Example 8.3 *Display of Books with Settings Around the World*

Sustained Silent Reading (SSR), or Drop Everything and Read (DEAR), occurs in classrooms where children are given time, a wide selection of books, and encouragement to read. The teacher sets aside a period of time each day, usually from fifteen to thirty minutes, for silent reading. SSR can be used by a single classroom or by the entire school (students and staff). The teacher also reads to model the value of reading even for adults. Since there is no formal reporting or assessment at the conclusion of SSR periods, students feel no pressure as they read. SSR can be effective with kindergartners and first graders, but it consists mostly of looking at books and pretend reading, and it tends to be noisier (with children reading aloud to themselves) and of shorter duration (five to ten minutes) (Kaisen, 1987; McCracken and McCracken, 1986). Extensive standardized testing of reading skills has shown that students who have been engaging in SSR and who have teachers who read to them score significantly higher than students who are deprived of these benefits (Trelease, 1995).

Story Reading and Storytelling

Reading aloud to children of all ages fulfills many purposes. Good oral reading by the teacher serves as a model and allows students to experience literature they might not be able or inclined to read for themselves. It can whet their appetites to read more on their own, since an exciting chapter or section of a book often stimulates children to read the entire book themselves. Besides providing exposure to specific books, reading to children can introduce them to creative and colorful use of language in prose and poetry, present new vocabulary and concepts, and acquaint them with the variety of language patterns found in written communication.

Teachers approach read-aloud events in different ways (Barrentine, 1996). Some limit interactions during story reading and focus on reflective after-reading discussions. These discussions enable students to connect stories to their lives, explore layers of meaning, develop knowledge about literary elements, and personalize story meanings. Other teachers read stories interactively, encouraging children to respond verbally to their peers, to the text, and to the teacher as they listen. During interactive read-alouds, teachers ask questions to guide students in constructing meaning and making personal reponses.

Just before reading aloud to the class, the teacher might ask students to listen to how the author uses a lead sentence to create interest in the story or uses dialogue to develop characterization. During the story, the teacher can stop occasionally to point out a literary technique or to ask students to close their eyes and visualize a descriptive passage. After completing the story or chapter, the teacher might ask students what they specifically liked or disliked about the way the author wrote. When the teacher points out such features to the class, students learn to evaluate material, thus making them more critical readers and improving their writing abilities as well. The following Classroom Scenario shows how one teacher reads aloud to her third graders.

**Classroom
Scenario**

Reading Aloud to Students

Kim Yunker calls her students to a corner of the classroom that has been set up to resemble a room in pioneer days. She asks a child to turn off the lights while she lights a kerosene lamp. Seated in a rocker, she chooses a book from many that relate to the unit theme, "Little House in the Big Woods." She introduces Cynthia Rylant's *When I Was Young in the Mountains* and then begins reading aloud. Occasionally she interjects questions such as "What is okra?" and "What do you think a johnny house is?" After she finishes the book, she asks questions about life in pioneer days, and the children browse quietly through some of the other books. As the children leave, they return to illustrating spelling words related to the unit (e.g., *maple, wagon, slate*) or building a fort from Lincoln Logs.

(continued)

Analysis of Scenario
In Kim Yunker's class, story reading is integrated with the theme so that children are able to make connections between the stories and the work they are doing in other subjects.

Research supports the benefits of reading aloud to students. In *Becoming a Nation of Readers*, Anderson and colleagues (1985) conclude, "The single most important activity for building the knowledge required for eventual success in reading is reading aloud to children" (p. 23). In addition, Michener (1988) finds research support for the following benefits of reading aloud to students:

1. Helps them get off to a better start in reading.
2. Improves their listening skills.
3. Increases their ability to read independently.
4. Expands their vocabularies.
5. Improves their reading comprehension.
6. Helps them to become better speakers.
7. Improves their abilities as writers.
8. Improves the quantity and quality of independent reading.

Teachers should read in natural tones and with expression, providing time for sharing the illustrations, exploring key words and phrases, and evaluating reactions. The best stories to read aloud are those that children cannot easily read by themselves, that the teacher personally likes and is thoroughly familiar with, and that possess the qualities characteristic of the best literature. Jim Trelease's *The New Read-Aloud Handbook* (1995) is an excellent source of information about how and what to read aloud to children.

Although teachers typically choose fiction to read aloud, Doiron (1994) recommends reading nonfiction as well for a balanced reading program. When reading nonfiction, teachers can respond to children's special interests, relate books to thematic units, probe into student-initiated inquiries, read high-interest excerpts selectively, and expand students' knowledge of a variety of topics. As children listen to informational books and discuss ideas from them, they may find it easier and more natural to read expository text for their own pleasure.

Similarly, teacher storytelling acquaints children with literature and provides good listening experiences. With no book between the storyteller and the audience, listeners focus on each word and gesture. They visualize the story to suit themselves because there are no illustrations (Nessel, 1985), and they develop their imaginations and move toward higher levels of thinking (Aiex, 1988). Folktales are especially good for telling because they were told and told again long before they were captured in print.

Students as storytellers develop fluency and expression in oral language. By preparing and telling stories, they also develop poise and build self-esteem. As storytellers, students must be aware of pitch, volume, timing, and gesture, as well as the responsiveness of the audience. A logical progression is for students to move from hearing, reading, and telling stories to writing original stories, which are often based on literary patterns they already know (Peck, 1989).

Selecting Literature

From the thousands of books published annually for children, teachers and media specialists must select good-quality literature that they think children will want to read. Making such decisions is a challenge and a responsibility. Teachers can assess children's personal reading interests by simply asking them to list three things that interest them or by administering an interest inventory. A useful source in selecting children's books is a listing of Newbery and Caldecott Award winners. The John Newbery Award is presented annually to the author whose book is selected by a special committee as the year's most distinguished contribution to American literature for children. Excellence in illustration is the criterion used in granting the annual Randolph Caldecott Award.

Some educators advocate classics, quality books that have endured for a generation or more, as the foundation for reading. Not all classics are popular with students, however, so it is important to choose appropriate works and avoid those that may discourage students from reading. Some favorite classics are *Charlotte's Web; The Borrowers; The Lion, the Witch, and the Wardrobe*; and *Little House in the Big Woods* (Wilson and Abrahamson, 1988).

Another consideration in choosing books is their social significance in relation to human values, cultural pluralism, and aesthetic standards (Norton, 1995). For minority children, multicultural literature based on familiar traditions and values can be a mirror that reflects and validates their own cultural experiences. For mainstream children, such books can be revealing windows into less familiar cultures (Cox and Galda, 1990). See Chapter 14, Appendix A, for a list of multiethnic books.

Despite adult critics' recommendations, many children prefer to make their own choices. Each year, the International Reading Association–Children's Book Council Joint Committee publishes an annotated list of "Children's Choices," which appears in the October issue of *The Reading Teacher*. Each list is compiled by approximately 10,000 children who, working in teams, read new books and vote for their favorites. Since children are the ultimate critics of their literature, teachers and librarians should consider their choices seriously when purchasing and recommending books.

In helping children select books, teachers need to know both the books that are available and their children's needs and interests. Teachers can guide children's choices by helping them locate books on special topics, sampling new books to pique their interest, allowing time for children to browse in the library, and suggesting titles on occasion. Regardless of this assistance, however, most children will value the freedom to choose their own books.

Selecting appropriate poetry for children is especially difficult. Poorly chosen poems can prejudice children against poetry, whereas a suitable poem will amuse, inspire, emotionally move, or intellectually interest them. Children prefer poems with rhyme, rhythm, humor, and narration; works by Shel Silverstein (*Where the Sidewalk Ends, Light in the Attic*) and Jack Prelutsky (*The New Kid on the Block, Something Big Has Been Here*) are natural favorites. The humor they use comes from alliteration, plays on words, or highly exaggerated situations, as in "Sarah Cynthia Sylvia Stout Who Would Not Take the Garbage Out" (from *Where the Sidewalk Ends*). Kupiter and Wilson (1993) contend, however, that teachers must sensitively cultivate an interest in poetry that goes beyond Silverstein and Prelutsky; they must build bridges from these popular poems to the rich array of diverse poetry waiting to be tapped.

Not to be overlooked are the intriguing nonficton selections that can supplement textbooks or even substitute for them. So many appealing, well-illustrated informational books on nearly any topic are available that choosing the best books can be difficult. Considerations in making selections include content that is accurate and current, organization and layout that facilitate easy use, cohesive text in which ideas are arranged logically, specialized vocabulary that is clearly defined, and attention-grabbing content and illustrations (Sudol and King, 1996).

Because informational books can be read or viewed at varying levels, most are appropriate for many ages. Young readers can pore over illustrations in David Macaulay's *Cathedral* and *Pyramid*, for example, whereas more mature students can read to find out how these structures were built. Worthy (1996) found that nonfiction selections, particularly those dealing with sports, animals, drawing, or cars, are popular with reluctant readers. Joanna Cole's Magic School Bus series, a mixture of fact and fiction, appeals to children who enjoy the characters and their escapades, as well as to children seeking information. Fascinating books about animals—books useful for enriching a thematic unit—include *Summer Ice: Life along the Antarctic Peninsula*, a combination of text and photographs about animal life in Antarctica; *Raptor Rescue: An Eagle Flies Free*, detailing the work of Minnesota's Raptor Center in rehabilitating injured raptors, and *Dolphin Man: Exploring the World of Dolphins*, a photobiography of Randy Wells, an authority on dolphins.

Many teachers prefer paperback books, because multiple copies of one book cost the same as a single library edition, allowing teachers to order enough for small groups of children to read and use in follow-up activities and discussions. Paperback books are often available at special reduced rates through book clubs such as Scholastic, Troll, and Trumpet.

Many good children's magazines and newspapers are available for different reading levels and different areas of interest. These periodicals are excellent classroom resources and offer several benefits for the reading program: (1) the material is current and relevant; (2) the reading range varies in levels of difficulty and content presented; (3) several genres usually appear in a single issue; (4) language activities, such as crossword puzzles, contests, and children's writings, are often included; (5) the illustrations and photographs are excellent and can improve comprehension; (6) their low cost makes them easily accessible; and (7) they are popular with reluctant readers (Seminoff, 1986; Worthy, 1996). Classroom subscriptions to two or three favorites will enrich the reading program. Some popu-

With teacher guidance, children read and respond to information found in a weekly news-paper. (© *Elizabeth Crews/Stock Boston*)

lar choices are listed in Appendix B to this chapter, and a more complete listing is available in Stoll's *Magazines for Kids and Teens* (1997).

Responding to Literature

According to reader response theory, readers are actively constructing meaning as they read. Since each reader differs in terms of background experiences and pre-formed attitudes, each interprets the text somewhat differently. Thus, no text has a single correct meaning (Cox, 1997).

Rosenblatt (1978) proposed that any text can be read efferently (for informa-tion) and/or aesthetically (as a lived-through experience), as has been explained in Chapter 1 of this textbook. Usually readers move back and forth along a contin-uum between an efferent stance and an aesthetic stance until they settle on a sin-gle predominant stance (Cox, 1997). They may be getting information as they read, but they may also be experiencing the emotions of the characters, the mood of the story as the plot unfolds, or a sense of morality toward an episode in his-tory. For example, Lloyd Alexander's *The King's Fountain* gives a historical perspec-tive of village life, but the courageous poor man's efforts to save his village tug at the heart. Both types of responses are important, but teachers tend to ask ques-tions that call for efferent responses (Zarillo and Cox, 1992), even though aesthetic responses may be more meaningful and more enduring. Students need to be able to choose their types of responses and have adequate time for reflecting on and responding to books (Cox and Many, 1992; Hickman, 1995).

Teachers can prepare generic questions to encourage children to respond thoughtfully to literature. These questions may be used during conferences, for written responses, for group activities, or during class discussions. Questions should be open-ended, not limited to a single correct answer. Popp (1997) suggests four categories of questions, which are given here with sample prompts for each category.

Evaluation

What did you like or dislike about this book? Why?

Why do you think the main character acted in such a way?

Connection

How did a character make you think of someone you know?

Has anyone you know faced a similar challenge? What was it?

Comprehension

What is a theme of this story?

What does this story mean to you?

Strategy

How did you figure out an unfamiliar word in this story?

What special features helped you understand the story?

Time for Reflection

Some teacher's manuals—and often teachers themselves—identify a single theme or a single correct interpretation for a literary selection. Should teachers accept as correct other themes or interpretations that students discover for themselves? Can more than one answer be acceptable? **What do *you* think?**

Literature Circles

An organized way of responding to literature is through *literature circles* (Bell, 1990; Gilles, 1989; Harste, Short, and Burke, 1988; Strickland et al., 1989; Strube, 1996; Zogby, 1990). These groups give students opportunities to read and respond to good literature, engage in high-level thinking about books, and do extensive and intensive reading.

Groups are formed after the teacher and students have established rapport so that they feel comfortable exchanging thoughts and ideas. Usually there are four or five groups in a class, each consisting of four to six members. Groups generally meet daily or two or three times a week, with each group lasting about two to three weeks. Exact procedures for groups vary, but the following practices are typical:

1. Have available multiple copies of several good books by the same author, or with a common theme. Briefly introduce these books to the students, and ask the students to write their names and their first and second choices on slips of paper. Form groups based on student selections, not achievement levels.

2. Explain literature logs, in which students write their reflections about what they read (see Example 8.4).

3. Have students meet in groups, look through their books, decide how far to read each time (it must be a reasonable "chunk"), and begin reading. With younger children, read the book to them and then place the book, along with a tape, at the listening center.

4. During group sessions, have a student leader conduct the activities, which may consist of silent reading, writing in and sharing literature logs, asking open-ended questions, discussing what was read, and doing extension activities.

5. Encourage students to create extension projects individually, in pairs, or as a group. Examples include reading a similar book or a book by the same author, creating a drama, and writing an epilogue for the story.

6. Have students evaluate their own performances by using a checklist similar to the following one. Discuss the evaluation with each student, item by item.

   _____ Used reading time wisely.

   _____ Completed assigned number of pages each time group met.

   _____ Participated in discussion.

   _____ Listened to others attentively.

   _____ Wrote something in literature log each time.

   _____ Helped plan and carry out extension activity.

7. Keep your own checklist for each student. Use one form for each group each time groups meet. (See Chapter 12 for a teacher's checklist for literature circles.)

When writing in their literature logs, students record personal interpretations, strategies for constructing meaning, questions that arise, and issues they may want to discuss with others (Popp, 1997). From reading these entries, teachers not only become aware of ways that students are reacting to literature, but also gain insight into each student's literacy processes (Handloff and Golden, 1995).

Literature circles provide students with many opportunities for developing social skills and taking responsibility. Students make decisions about how to manage the circles, solve problems that arise in groups, monitor their own progress, and pursue personal inquiry (Heald-Taylor, 1996). Literature discussions arising from student questions generate more excitement and transfer more responsibilty for learning to the students than do teacher-posed questions (Commeyras and Sumner, 1996). In order for groups to function well, however, the teacher needs

Example 8.4   *Literature Log*

Part 1

Amaroq, the Wolf

NAME: *Katie Smith*
DATE: *September 11*

TITLE OF BOOK: *Julie of the wolves*
PAGE STARTED: 20
PAGE STOPPED: 45

RETELL:

Miyax is still looking for food. No matter what she will not give up. Now she is communicating with the wolves. She talks and acts like them.

Jello, one of the wolves, brings food back from the hunt and Miyax gets offered some.

COMMENTS:

- p. 20 How many wolves? Have I missed missed something?
- p. 22 Does Miyax think the wolves can understand her? Can they?
- p. 23 Eelie? Excitement = Eelie?
- p. 24 Why does she try to make the wolves get food for her when she has an ulo?
- p. 25 Sunny Night?
- p. 27 "learn about her family" Does that mean her wolf family?

REACTION:

Exciting!

to demonstrate in advance what might occur during literature circles and prepare students to interact effectively (Short and Kauffman, 1995).

Oral Interpretation of Literature

Fluent oral reading with intonation and phrasing that accurately reflect the mood and tone of the story or poem is another way to respond to literature. Oral reading is more difficult than silent reading because, in order to convey the author's message to an audience, the reader must pronounce words correctly, phrase appropriately, enunciate distinctly, use proper intonation, and pace the reading appropriately. To accomplish these goals, the oral reader should have an opportunity to read silently first to become acquainted with the author's style of writing, determine the author's message, and check the correct pronunciation of unfamiliar words. If the passage is particularly difficult, the reader may need to practice it aloud to ensure proper phrasing and intonation.

Oral reading skills require special attention. The teacher may demonstrate good and poor oral reading, let the children analyze these performances, and then help students draw up a list of standards or guidelines like the following:

1. Be sure you can pronounce each word correctly before you read your selection to an audience. If you are not sure of a pronunciation, check the dictionary or ask for help.

2. Say each word clearly and distinctly. Don't run words together, and take care not to leave out word parts or add parts to words.

3. Pause in the right places. Pay attention to punctuation clues.

4. Emphasize important words. Help the audience understand the meaning of the selection by the way you read it. Read slowly enough to allow for adequate expression, and speak loudly enough to be easily heard.

5. Prepare carefully before you read to an audience.

When well-rehearsed oral reading occurs, there should be one or more people with whom the reader is attempting to communicate through reading. Audience members should not have access to the book from which the performer is reading so they cannot follow the reading with their eyes. Instead, they should listen to the reader to grasp the author's meaning or, if the reader is reading to prove a point, to agree or disagree. The reader must attempt to hold the audience's attention through oral interpretation of the author's words. A stumbling performance will lead to a restless, impatient audience and a poor listening situation.

Some examples of purposes for audience reading include

1. Confirming an answer to a question by reading the portion of the selection in which the answer is found.

2. Reading a news story in which the class should be interested or background information for a topic of discussion from a reference or trade book.

3. Making announcements or issuing invitations.

4. Sharing a part of a published story, a poem (poems are written to be read aloud), or an experience story that the reader has enjoyed.

5. Participating in choral reading or readers' theater.

6. Reading aloud directions for a group activity, such as performing an experiment, making a model, or playing a game.

7. Sharing riddles, jokes, and tongue twisters to entertain classmates.

8. Reading stories aloud to children in lower grades.

9. Reading the part of a character in a play or the narration for a play or other dramatic presentation.

Books by Paul Fleischman contain poems for two voices that invite students or groups of students to collaborate in reading aloud. Sometimes passages are to be read singly and sometimes in unison, but students must read expressively and fluently to achieve the proper effect. *Joyful Noise* contains poems about insects that think and act as humans; *I Am Phoenix* consists of poems that celebrate a variety of birds.

Responses Through Drama

Dramatic interpretations of literature evoke aesthetic responses, and they help children find success because there are no right or wrong answers (Fennessey, 1995). Through drama children can deepen their responses to literature and discover underlying meanings. Drama helps children become aware of different points of view and develops imagination and critical thinking.

Drama can take many forms. In *pantomime*, children speak no lines but show what is happening through their gestures and body movements. Simple nursery rhymes and fables are good for pantomiming. *Characterization* focuses on revealing the way characters feel, act, and relate to other characters in the story, and children attempt to speak, to move, and to modify their facial expressions as they become the story characters. *Improvisation* or *creative dramatics* means acting out a story without using a script, and *choral speaking* or *choral reading* is the dramatic interpretation of poetry or other literature with two or more voices. In *readers' theater*, students read aloud in dramatic style from scripts; no sets, costumes, or props are necessary, and the emphasis is on interpretive oral reading (Cullinan and Galda, 1994; Savage, 1994).

Responses Through Written Expression

Traditional written book reports in which students merely summarize plots of stories have in many cases been replaced by more authentic responses to literature. Students are encouraged to react thoughtfully to what they read by writing in literature logs or critically reviewing books on note cards that are filed for other students to read. In one class, students place minireviews of favorite books they want to recommend on a bulletin board. Example 8.5 is a sample of a child's recommendation.

Example 8.5   *Book Recommendation*

<u>Hatchet</u> by Gary Paulsen (1988)

A really great survival story! You can almost see inside Brian's mind as he tries to figure out what to do to stay alive. He has so many problems— a bear, a tornado, no food. It's amazing the way he solves his problems. Very exciting!

Several ideas for activities that combine reading and writing were presented earlier in this chapter. Here are some additional activities that focus on written responses to literature.

Activities

1. Ask students to collect as many Newbery Award books and Honor books (runners-up to Award books) as they can find, read several of them, and ask their friends to read others. After making up and filling out an evaluation checklist for each book, including such criteria as characterization, author's style, authenticity of setting, and plot development, they may add to the checklist comments about the merit of each book.

2. Let each student read a biography of a famous person from history and write a story about what would happen if that person lived today—for example, how he or she would bring peace to the world, solve medical problems, or protect the environment. The popular *Lincoln: A Photobiography*, by Russell Freedman, would be a good choice.

3. Choose an environmental book, such as Chris Van Allsburg's *Just a Dream*, and have students discuss the issues. Ask them each to choose one issue that especially concerns them and write letters to their congressperson describing the issue and recommending solutions.

4. Read Byrd Baylor's *I'm in Charge of Celebrations*, and discuss the meaning of *celebration* as used in this book. Then ask the children to keep journals of their own special celebration days over a period of two or three months. Students may wish to share their celebrations by reading from their journals.

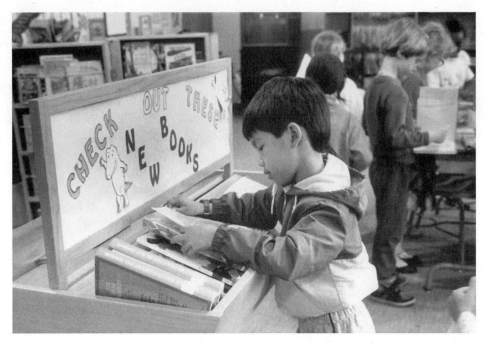

Lively responses to literature are likely to occur in classrooms with nurturing environments that provide an abundance of fine-quality books, opportunities for library visits, adequate time for selecting and reading, introductions of new books, daily reading aloud, book discussions, and creative experiences with literature. (© *Elizabeth Crews/Stock Boston*)

5. Read Mem Fox's *Wilfred Gordon McDonald Partridge* or a similar book about elderly people to the class, and discuss both the contributions and special needs of older people. Ask each child to identify an elderly person to whom he or she can write a letter or send a story. Help the children follow through with their plans.

Responses Through Art and Music

Many children who have difficulty expressing themselves with words prefer to respond to literature in other ways (Hoyt, 1992). Art and music offer creative options for these children.

Through exposure to well-illustrated picture books, children learn to appreciate the artists' work and begin to see themselves as illustrators capable of creating their own art (Galda and Short, 1993). They can interpret stories through many art media, including clay, paint, papier-mâché, scraps of felt and ribbon, colored pencils and pens, and three-dimensional objects. Using such media, they create collages and montages, dioramas and puppet figures, mobiles and stabiles, and illustrations for their own storybooks (Russell, 1994).

Children have a natural tendency to respond to the rhythm and melody of music, so it makes sense to combine music with literature and language (Kolb, 1996). More picture books of children's story songs and singing games are available than ever before, and these books help children connect the words they sing with the words they see in print (Beaty, 1994). Some examples are

> *The Wheels on the Bus* by Maryann Kovalski (Boston: Little, Brown, 1987). An action song with movements and sounds that accompany the wheels, wipers, horns, and so forth.

> *Old McDonald Had a Farm* by Glen Rounds (New York: Holiday House, 1989). A familiar song with repetitive phrases such as "With a MOO-MOO here" and a chorus of "EE-AY, EE-AY, OH."

> *Abiyoyo* by Pete Seeger; Michael Hays, illustrator (New York: Macmillan, 1986). A story song based on a South African lullaby in which a little boy and his father make a monster disappear.

By picturing the instruments and simulating the sounds of a marching band, Lois Ehlert's *THUMP, THUMP, Rat-a-Tat-Tat* (Singapore: Harper & Row, 1989) can provide the stimulus for creating a rhythm band.

Integrating Literature Across the Curriculum

For students who find textbooks difficult or dull, supplementary trade books from a variety of genres offer a viable option for learning content area material.

In social studies, award-winning trade books can be found for nearly every period of history. Elizabeth Speare's *The Bronze Bow* is a novel about a boy who encounters Jesus in Rome; Marguerite De Angeli's *The Door in the Wall* treats the situation of a crippled boy in fourteenth-century England; *The Courage of Sarah Noble*, by Alice Dalgliesh, describes a young girl who must face the difficulties of living in Connecticut in early pioneer days; *The Sign of the Beaver*, by Elizabeth Speare, is the story of a boy's struggle to survive in the Maine wilderness in the 1700s; Carol Brink's *Caddie Woodlawn* brings the reader into the excitement of living on the Wisconsin frontier during the last half of the nineteenth century; Paula Fox's *The Slave Dancer* tells about a boy who becomes involved in the slave trade with Africa during pre–Civil War days; and Patricia MacLachlan's *Sarah, Plain and Tall* unites a woman from the East with a motherless family on a prairie farm during pioneer days. Biographies of famous people who lived during different historical periods also add spice to textbook accounts.

Teachers can use trade books to develop mathematical concepts as well. Starting with simple counting books such as the vividly illustrated *Brian Wildsmith's 1, 2, 3's*, teachers can use books to expand concepts dealing with shapes, comparative size, and ordinal numbers. Through the humorous and provocative situations in Rod Clement's *Counting on Frank*, the reader begins to think like a mathematician—experimenting, calculating, and estimating. Two books by

David Schwartz, *How Much Is a Million?* and *If You Made a Million*, use ridiculous situations to help the reader conceptualize the enormity of large numbers like one million.

Vocabulary lessons are lively and fun when the class uses trade books for word play and for learning interesting features of words. In the Amelia Bedelia books by Peggy Parish, Amelia takes everything literally, with disastrous results: her sponge cake is made of sponges! Fred Gwynne's *A Chocolate Moose for Dinner* illustrates figurative expressions and words with multiple meanings as a child might visualize them. William Steig's *CDB* uses letters of the alphabet to represent words for silly sayings.

An area of special concern today is the environment, which is well represented in children's literature (Galda, 1991; Galda and MacGregor, 1992; Pierce and Short, 1994). Lynne Cherry's beautifully illustrated *A River Ran Wild: An Environmental History* documents the story of the Nashua River—its pollution and revitalization—and her *The Great Kapok Tree* relates how the animals of a Brazilian rain forest convince a man not to cut down their home. Jeannie Baker has also written two thought-provoking environmental books: *Window*, which shows how a wilderness evolves into a crowded city, and *Where the Forest Meets the Sea*, in which a boy explores a prehistoric rain forest and ponders its future. In Chris Van Allsburg's *Just a Dream*, Walter's dream helps him realize the importance of caring for the environment.

The following list of activities combines various types of responses to literature. The value of using different forms of literature to integrate the curriculum becomes obvious as students study history by reading biographies of famous people, learn geography by comparing viewpoints of books about different countries, see relationships by examining concept books, understand current issues by reading books about the environment, gain insights into literature by discussing character development and story conflicts, and so on.

Activities

1. When more than one student reads the same book, try the following suggestions: dramatize a scene from the story; set up a puppet show and tape-record the voices of the characters; or compare views about character development, conflicts in the story, and the ending of the book.

2. For biographies, have students discuss the childhoods of famous people, what influences caused them to become famous, and what struggles they faced to accomplish their goals.

3. When students have read biographies of creative people, ask them to include examples of the subjects' famous works in their reviews: playing a recording by a well-known composer, showing an art print by a painter, or displaying a product of an inventor.

4. For realistic fiction, encourage students to identify the problems of the characters and how they are solved, relate the situation in the book to the students' own environments, or propose alternate solutions for the characters' problems.

5. Arrange a panel discussion in which several students who have read different books by the same author talk about similarities and differences in the books along with the writer's strengths and weaknesses, general philosophy, and change in style over time.

Thematic Units

Thematic units can be used within literature-centered instruction as an effective means of both integrating literature across the curriculum and extending knowledge. (See also the discussions of thematic units in Chapters 7, 10, and 13.) Four ways to develop themes are around a book, a topic, a genre, and an author. Example 8.6 is a graphic portrayal of a literature web with Faith Ringgold's *Tar Beach*, a Caldecott Honor Book that tells of Cassie Lightfoot's dream to be free. A web for Lois Lowry's *Number the Stars*, a Newbery Award winner, is shown in Example 8.7. This book deals with a Danish girl's heroic efforts to smuggle Jews to safety during World War II. Both books offer rich opportunities to integrate the curriculum.

Webbing is a technique that connects a central topic, or in these cases a book, to related ideas. A web is a framework that cuts across curricular areas. Emphasizing that no two webs are alike, Huck, Hepler, and Hickman (1997) recommend webbing as a plan for literature study that grows out of students' interests and the strengths of the books. During the process of creating a web, teachers become aware of the many directions in which books can lead children. Although the teacher uses the web as an overall plan, students contribute their own ideas as the theme unfolds so that the study becomes learner centered.

Also endorsing the use of webbing, Norton (1993) suggests a procedure for developing a unit. The first step is to identify a theme that can be enriched with literature. Then the teacher and students construct a web with subtopics that become the subjects of study for groups of students. They locate books and other resources that will help them investigate their subjects, then share their findings creatively with the rest of the class. Example 8.8 shows another way to develop a literature-based, learner-centered thematic unit that is based on the K-W-L procedure (Ogle, 1989) described in Chapter 10. The topic is immigrants.

Any *genre*, or classification of literature, can be a focus for study (Tompkins and McGee, 1993). In Example 8.9 the genre is folktales. Other viable genres are poetry, historical fiction, biography, and fantasy, each of which may be divided into subtopics. For instance, types of fantasy that may be studied are (1) modern literary tales based on folktales, (2) fantastic stories, which are basically realistic but contain elements of fantasy, (3) science fiction, or (4) high fantasy with heroes and heroines who confront evil for the sake of humanity.

A fourth type of thematic unit is based on a popular children's author. Knowing something about the real person behind their favorite books and *how* and *why* stories were written helps children develop author awareness and appreciation (Savage, 1994). Good choices of authors are Eric Carle, Tomie DePaola, Steven Kellogg, and Leo Lionni for younger children and Katherine Paterson, Gary

Example 8.6   *Literature Web*

African-American Folklore Listen to stories about African–Americans. What is special about these stories? (Virginia Hamilton's *The People Could Fly* is a good source.)	**Quilts** As a class make a story about what your class did this year. Each of you choose one part of the story. Draw a picture on a square of fabric. Put all the squares together to make a story quilt.	**Vocabulary** Learn some new words: *skyscraper, tar beach, union, factory, steel girders, cables,* and *floodlight* from this book. Use the words in a story about city life.
Art Look at the pictures in this book. What kinds of colors and designs are these? Compare these illustrations with those in other picture storybooks.		**Bridges** Find out about the George Washington Bridge. What are some other types of bridges? What do they look like? How are they built?
Nutrition Learn about the food pyramid. Have a picnic with your class. Plan a healthful menu, figure the cost, prepare the food, and send invitations.	*Tar Beach,* Faith Ringgold Crown, 1991	**Inner-City Living** Learn about living in a big city. Where do children play? Where do people work? Look at some books about cities to find the answers.
Creative Writing If you could fly over something to make it your own, what would it be? Draw a picture and write a story about it.	**Freedom** What does it mean to be free? Who is not free? Discuss freedom in class and listen to stories about how people became free.	**History/Drama** Find out what it was like to be a slave. Learn how slaves became free. Act out some scenes about being a slave and being free.

Source: Web based on *Tar Beach* by Faith Ringgold. New York: Crown, 1991.

Paulsen, Beverly Cleary, and Lois Lowry for older ones. Most children's libraries contain references on children's authors, such as the *Seventh Book of Junior Authors and Illustrators* (1996), published by the H. W. Wilson Company.

Example 8.7 *Literature Web*

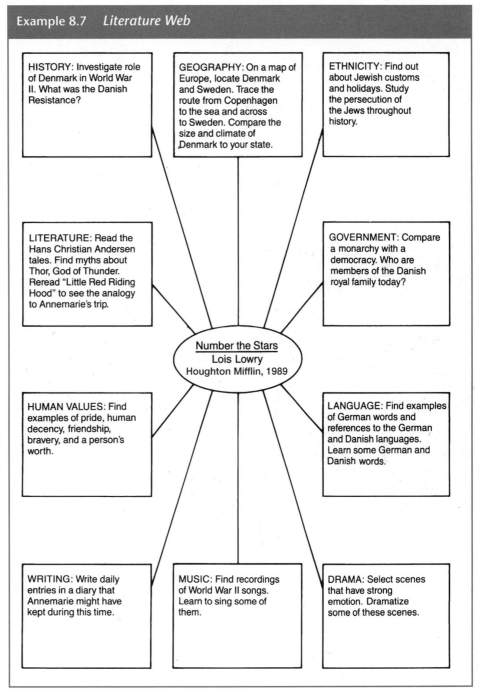

HISTORY: Investigate role of Denmark in World War II. What was the Danish Resistance?

GEOGRAPHY: On a map of Europe, locate Denmark and Sweden. Trace the route from Copenhagen to the sea and across to Sweden. Compare the size and climate of Denmark to your state.

ETHNICITY: Find out about Jewish customs and holidays. Study the persecution of the Jews throughout history.

LITERATURE: Read the Hans Christian Andersen tales. Find myths about Thor, God of Thunder. Reread "Little Red Riding Hood" to see the analogy to Annemarie's trip.

GOVERNMENT: Compare a monarchy with a democracy. Who are members of the Danish royal family today?

Number the Stars
Lois Lowry
Houghton Mifflin, 1989

HUMAN VALUES: Find examples of pride, human decency, friendship, bravery, and a person's worth.

LANGUAGE: Find examples of German words and references to the German and Danish languages. Learn some German and Danish words.

WRITING: Write daily entries in a diary that Annemarie might have kept during this time.

MUSIC: Find recordings of World War II songs. Learn to sing some of them.

DRAMA: Select scenes that have strong emotion. Dramatize some of these scenes.

Source: Web based on *Number the Stars* by Lois Lowry. Boston: Houghton Mifflin, 1989.

Example 8.8 *Thematic Unit: Immigrants*

Topic: Immigrants (adapted from the curriculum framework theme of multicultural studies)

Goal: To understand how immigrants adjust to a new environment

Initiating Activity: Read Allen Say's Caldecott winner *Grandfather's Journey* (Houghton Mifflin, 1993), the story of the author's grandfather, who lived in both Japan and the United States. Follow the reading with a discussion of how it feels to belong to two countries, and introduce the word *immigrant.*

What We Know: Ask the children what they know about immigrants. They respond by saying:

People come to the United States from all over the world.

Many of them speak different languages.

They have special customs.

What We Want to Learn: Ask the children what they want to learn. They respond by saying:

How do immigrants get to be citizens?

How do they feel about leaving their homes?

What are some problems they face in a new land?

How We Can Find Out: Ask the children how they will find the answers. They respond by saying:

Read books about people who are immigrants.

Invite an immigrant to speak to the class.

Ask our families where we came from.

Resource Materials: With your help and that of the librarian, the children collect trade books and reference sources to learn about immigrants. Some of their favorites are

Immigrant Kids by Russell Freedman (New York: Scholastic, 1980). Photographs tell the story of immigrant children at home, school, work, and play.

The Lotus Seed by Sherry Garland (Orlando: Harcourt Brace Jovanovich, 1993). A Vietnamese family flees its homeland to escape a war and takes along a precious lotus seed.

Molly's Pilgrim by Barbara Cohen (New York: Lothrop, 1983). A Jewish girl takes a doll to school dressed as her mother was dressed when she left Russia.

Refugees by Carole Seymour-Jones (New York: New Discovery Books, 1992). People who believe they must leave their country face problems in the new land.

> ### Example 8.8   *Thematic Unit: Immigrants (cont.)*
>
> *How My Family Lives in America* by Susan Kuklin (New York: Bradbury, 1992). Children of parents born in other countries tell what makes their families special.
>
> **Activities:** The children
>
> 1. inquire about their family backgrounds and find books about their own cultures.
> 2. use reference books to discover how immigrants become U.S. citizens.
> 3. read independently each day from a theme-related book.
> 4. make displays of books that feature different cultures.
> 5. write travel diaries of their journeys to the new land.
> 6. discuss which prized possessions they would take with them.
> 7. choose one nationality that represents many of the children and divide into groups to study the contributions of that culture (prominent people, inventions and discoveries, songs and dances, folklore, games, foods, vocabulary words, and customs).
> 8. meet in groups to prepare projects on these topics.
> 9. write a play about emigrating to the United States based on experiences and feelings understood from books read.
>
> **Culminating Activity:** The children invite another class to attend their play, view their book displays, and observe or participate in their group projects.
>
> **What We Learned:** Ask the children what they learned. They will give many answers, including these:
>
> About our own heritages
>
> Contributions of different nationalities
>
> Some of the problems immigrants face

Working with Support Personnel

Teachers and librarians should work together to use the library's resources both to reinforce subject matter and encourage students to read for pleasure. Teachers work with librarians by suggesting books and materials that will complement units of study and relate to the interests of their students. Librarians cooperate with teachers by introducing new books, presenting stories to the class, and showing students how to use the library.

Example 8.9 *Thematic Unit on Folklore*

1. Let children read and compare folktale variants, beginning with the Brothers Grimm tales and moving toward contemporary versions. (Reference source: *Household Stories* [New York: McGraw-Hill, 1966]).

2. Encourage children to tell stories, repeating familiar favorites or creating new tales.

3. Read and/or tell classic folktales to the students.

4. Provide opportunities for discovering word origins and literary allusions, especially in myths (e.g., echo, Pandora's box, Mercury, Atlas).

5. Let children dramatize folktales using puppets, pantomime, readers' theater, and creative dramatics.

6. Encourage children to write creatively. Have them

    a. study the characteristics of a fable (brevity, animal characters, a moral) and create new fables.

    b. write modern versions of fairy tales.

    c. make up a ballad based on folklore and set it to music.

    d. make up original *pourquoi* tales, such as "Why the Rabbit Has Long Ears."

    e. write new endings for folktales after changing major events in the stories, such as having the First Little Pig build his house out of stone and the Third Little Pig build his house out of spaghetti.

    f. select a newspaper story, find a moral for it (e.g., "theft doesn't pay"), and write a fable about this moral.

7. Help students find out how folktales were originally communicated and how they came to be written.

8. Invite storytellers for children to hear. Ask students to interview the storytellers about techniques and about the origins of the tales they tell.

9. Encourage students to compare similarities in characters and motifs of folktales from around the world (e.g., the Jackal in India, the Weasel in Africa, and Brer Rabbit in the United States).

10. Have students locate the origins of various versions of folktales on a map.

11. Ask students to compare the artwork used to illustrate folktales (e.g., the illustrations in Walt Disney's version of *Snow White and the Seven Dwarfs* with Nancy Burkert's illustrations).

12. Provide tapes of music and dance based on folktales, such as selections from Stephen Sondheim's *Into the Woods.*

> **Example 8.9** *Thematic Unit on Folklore (cont.)*
>
> 13. Ask students to consider the moral values depicted in folklore and compare them with values in today's literature.
>
> 14. Have students create a time line that shows the approximate times when various types of folklore originated.

Parents and the community should also be part of a school's literature program. If they realize the value of literature in their children's reading program, parents can encourage them to read for pleasure. Parent-teacher organizations can sponsor programs to review children's books and magazines that may be unfamiliar to parents and to suggest ways parents can provide a home atmosphere that promotes interest in reading. Parents or members of the community might also like to join children during an SSR or storytelling session; some nonschool personnel may be excellent storytellers or have books they are willing to contribute. The school, the home, and the community can work together to encourage language learning and love of literature.

Summary

Some basic principles for facilitating language development are that learning is integrated, tasks are authentic, learning is social, classrooms are learner centered, learning is whole to part, and literature is an integral part of the curriculum. Applications of these principles are found throughout the text.

Instead of separating the language arts into discrete time periods, teachers should integrate instruction in reading, writing, listening, and speaking. When children learn language as an integrated whole, they are likely to view reading and writing as meaningful events.

Many similarities exist between reading and writing. Both are composing processes in which meaning is constructed. Teachers can use this natural connection by guiding children into activities that call for both reading and writing. Process writing is a child-centered approach to writing that consists of five steps: prewriting, drafting, revising, editing, and publishing. Journal writing and reading enable students to record their ideas and, in many cases, read responses from their teacher. Writing and reading workshops provide minilessons and large blocks of time for students to concentrate on actual writing and reading.

Literature is useful for integrating language. Story reading and storytelling provide multiple benefits by enticing children to read and providing them with knowledge. Teachers should consider both literary merit and children's interests when helping children choose books, and they should establish environments with an abundance of interesting books and attractive displays that create interest in reading.

Children may respond to literature aesthetically (by living through the experience) or efferently (by seeking information). Their responses may take the following forms: literature circles, oral reading, drama, written expression, art, and music. Literature spans the curriculum by offering a wide variety of books on various subjects, and teachers can make literature the core of thematic units. These units may focus on books, themes, genres, or authors. Support personnel from the media center, home, and community contribute to the school's language and literature program.

Test Yourself

True or False

_____ 1. Ideally, the language arts should be integrated throughout the curriculum.

_____ 2. Reading and writing are both composing processes.

_____ 3. The *writing process* refers to the way children use punctuation, grammar, and spelling.

_____ 4. Children generally prefer poems with thoughtful, serious themes.

_____ 5. During the drafting stage, students must be careful to observe correct use of spelling and mechanics.

_____ 6. Children must work alone when doing revisions.

_____ 7. In dialogue journals, usually the student writes some thoughts and the teacher responds in writing.

_____ 8. Journal writing is a good opportunity for teachers to correct students' handwriting, spelling, and grammar.

_____ 9. In writing and reading workshops, students complete workbook exercises.

_____ 10. Elementary students are capable of using word processors to write and edit compositions.

_____ 11. Literature can be an effective way to integrate the language arts across the curriculum.

_____ 12. When readers take an aesthetic stance as they respond to literature, they read to gain information.

_____ 13. When reading aloud, teachers should speak in natural tones and with expression.

_____ 14. In a double entry journal, the student writes on one side of the page and the teacher writes on the other.

_____ 15. The Newbery Award is given for excellence in illustration.

_____ 16. Many good children's magazines are being published.

_____ 17. Silent reading is more difficult than oral reading.

_____ 18. Performers in readers' theater memorize their parts.

_____ 19. Members of literature circles make entries in literature logs.

_____ 20. When writing responses to literature, a child's first priority should be the mechanics of writing.

_____ 21. There is no need for teachers to read aloud to children after children learn to read for themselves.

_____ 22. Award-winning trade books can be found for nearly every period in history.

_____ 23. A literature web may have a book at the center with related subjects radiating from it.

_____ 24. Parents, media specialists, and the community should join to support the reading program.

For your journal...

1. Read a junior novel, such as *Little House in the Big Woods* or *The Sign of the Beaver*, and respond to it either aesthetically or efferently.

2. If you could choose, how would you prefer to respond to literature—through writing, oral expression, art, music, drama, or in some other way? Why?

3. How does it make you feel when you discover your personal meaning of a text, and the teacher tells you that you are wrong and the real meaning is something else?

...And your portfolio

1. Begin an annotated list of books you would like to have in your classroom library, and add to the list as you find other selections you wish to include.

2. When you are visiting schools, jot down literature-related ideas that you see teachers using. These might include bulletin-board displays, classroom library corners, theme-related book collections, and children's responses to literature.

3. As you come across books you might like to use during thematic units, copy the bibliographic information and brainstorm ways to connect each book to different areas of the curriculum.

**Chapter
Appendix A**

Children's Books Cited in Chapter 8

Alexander, Lloyd. *The King's Fountain.* New York: Dutton, 1989.

Baker, Jeannie. *Where the Forest Meets the Sea.* London: Walker Books, 1987.

Baker, Jeannie. *Window.* New York: Greenwillow, 1991.

Baylor, Byrd. *I'm in Charge of Celebrations.* New York: Scribner's, 1986.

Blos, Joan W. *A Gathering of Days: A New England Girl's Journal, 1830–32.* New York: Scribner's, 1979.

Brink, Carol. *Caddie Woodlawn.* New York: Macmillan, 1936.

Cherry, Lynne. *The Great Kapok Tree.* San Diego: Harcourt Brace Jovanovich, 1990.

Cherry, Lynne. *A River Ran Wild: An Environmental History.* San Diego: Harcourt Brace Jovanovich, 1992.

Clement, Rod. *Counting on Frank.* New South Wales, Australia: Collins/Angus and Robertson, 1990.

Cleary, Beverly. *Dear Mr. Henshaw.* New York: Morrow, 1983.

Dalgliesh, Alice. *The Courage of Sarah Noble.* New York: Charles Scribner's Sons, 1954.

De Angeli, Marguerite. *The Door in the Wall.* New York: Doubleday, 1949.

Fleischman, Paul. *I Am Phoenix.* New York: Harper & Row, 1988.

Fleischman, Paul. *Joyful Noise.* New York: Harper & Row, 1988.

Fox, Mem. *Wilfred Gordon McDonald Partridge.* Brooklyn: Kane/Miller, 1985.

Fox, Paula. *Lily and the Lost Boy.* New York: Yearling, 1987.

Fox, Paula. *The Slave Dancer.* Scarsdale, N.Y.: Bradbury, 1974.

Freedman, Russell. *Lincoln: A Photobiography.* New York: Clarion, 1987.

George, Jean. *Julie of the Wolves.* New York: Harper & Row, 1973.

Gwynne, Fred. *A Chocolate Moose for Dinner.* New York: Dutton, 1973.

Johnson, Sylvia. *Raptor Rescue: An Eagle Flies Free.* New York: Dutton, 1995.

Lewis, C. S. *The Lion, the Witch, and the Wardrobe.* New York: Macmillan, 1950.

Lowry, Lois. *Number the Stars.* Boston: Houghton Mifflin, 1989.

Macaulay, David. *Cathedral: The Story of Its Construction.* Boston: Houghton Mifflin, 1973.

Macaulay, David. *Pyramid.* Boston: Houghton Mifflin, 1975.

MacLachlan, Patricia. *Sarah, Plain and Tall.* New York: Harper & Row, 1985.

McMillan, Bruce. *Summer Ice: Life along the Antarctic Peninsula.* Boston: Houghton Mifflin, 1995.

Norton, Mary. *The Borrowers.* San Diego: Harcourt Brace Jovanovich, 1952.

Parish, Peggy. *Amelia Bedelia.* New York: Harper & Row, 1963.

Paterson, Katherine. *Jacob Have I Loved.* New York: Crowell, 1981.

Paterson, Katherine. *Park's Quest.* New York: Puffin, 1989.

Paulsen, Gary. *Hatchet.* New York: Bradbury, 1987.

Prelutsky, Jack. *The New Kid on the Block.* New York: Greenwillow, 1984.

Prelutsky, Jack. *Something Big Has Been Here.* New York: Greenwillow, 1990.

Pringle, Laurence. *Dolphin Man: Exploring the World of Dolphins.* New York: Atheneum, 1995.

Rylant, Cynthia. *When I Was Young in the Mountains.* New York: Dutton, 1983.

Schwartz, David M. *How Much Is a Million?* New York: Scholastic, 1985.

Schwartz, David M. *If You Made a Million.* New York: Scholastic, 1985.

Silverstein, Shel. *The Light in the Attic.* New York: Harper & Row, 1981.

Silverstein, Shel. *Where the Sidewalk Ends.* New York: Harper & Row, 1974.
Speare, Elizabeth. *The Bronze Bow.* Boston: Houghton Mifflin, 1961.
Speare, Elizabeth. *The Sign of the Beaver.* Boston: Houghton Mifflin, 1983.
Steig, William. *CDB.* New York: Simon & Schuster, 1968.
Van Allsburg, Chris. *Jumanji.* Boston: Houghton Mifflin, 1981.
Van Allsburg, Chris. *Just a Dream.* Boston: Houghton Mifflin, 1990.
Van Allsburg, Chris. *The Stranger.* Boston: Houghton Mifflin, 1986.
Van Allsburg, Chris. *Two Bad Ants.* Boston: Houghton Mifflin, 1988.
Van Allsburg, Chris. *The Widow's Broom.* Boston: Houghton Mifflin, 1992.
Van Allsburg, Chris. *The Wretched Stone.* Boston: Houghton Mifflin, 1991.
White, E. B. *Charlotte's Web.* New York: Harper & Row, 1952.
Wilder, Laura Ingalls. *Little House in the Big Woods.* New York: Harper & Row, 1932.
Wildsmith, Brian. *Brian Wildsmith's 1, 2, 3's.* New York: Franklin Watts, 1965.

Chapter Appendix B

Children's Periodicals

Boys' Life (1325 Walnut Hill Lane, P.O. Box 15079, Irving, TX 75015–2079). Age range 7–17. Boys in Scouting, general interest.
Chickadee (25 Boxwood Lane, Buffalo, NY 14227–2780). Age range 3–9. Science and nature.
Child Life (P.O. Box 7133, Red Oak, IA 51591–0133). Age range 9–11. Safety, health, fitness, nutrition; general interest.
Children's Digest (Children's Better Health Institute, 1100 Waterway Blvd., P.O. Box 567, Indianapolis, IN 46206). Age range preteen. Fitness, sports, general interest.
Children's Playmate (Children's Better Health Institute, 1100 Waterway Blvd., P.O. Box 567, Indianapolis, IN 46206). Age range 6–8. Safety, health, and nutrition; general interest.
Cobblestone (Cobblestone Publishing Co., 7 School Street, Peterborough, NH 03458). Age range 8–15. American history.
Creative Kids (Prufrock Press, P.O. Box 8813, Waco, TX 76714–8813). Ages 8–14. Literature.
Cricket (P.O. Box 7433, Red Oak, IA 51591–4433). Ages 9–14. Fiction, nonfiction, and art.
Faces (7 School Street, Peterborough, NH 03458). Age range 8–14. World cultures.
Highlights for Children (P.O. Box 269, Columbus, OH 43272–0002). Age range 2–12. General interest.
Humpty Dumpty's Magazine (1100 Waterway Blvd., P.O. Box 567, Indianapolis, IN 46206). Age range 4–6. General interest, health.
Jack and Jill (P.O. Box 10003, Des Moines, IA 50340). Age range 7–10. Health and fitness; general interest.
Ladybug: The Magazine for Young Children. (P.O. Box 7436, Red Oak, IA 51591–4486). Age range 2–7. General interest.
National Geographic World (P.O. Box 2330, Washington, DC 20013–2330). Age range 8–14. Natural history, science, outdoor adventures, young achievers.

Odyssey (Cobblestone Publishing, 7 School St., Peterborough, NH 03458). Age range 8–14. Astronomy and space science.

Owl (25 Boxwood Lane, Buffalo, NY 14227–2780). Age range 8+. Science, nature, and environment.

Ranger Rick (National Wildlife Federation, 8925 Leesburg Pike, Vienna, VA 22184–0001). Age range 6–12. Nature, environment, outdoors.

Scholastic Magazines (several options) (2931 E. McCarty St., P.O. Box 3710, Jefferson City, MO 65102–3710). Ages 6–18. Language arts, math, current events, home economics, and social studies.

Stone Soup: The Magazine by Young Writers and Artists. (Children's Art Foundation, P.O. Box 83, Santa Cruz, CA 95063). Age range 6–13. Writing and art by children.

3–2–1 Contact (Box 51177, Boulder, CO 80322). Age range 8–12. Science, nature, and technology.

Your Big Backyard (National Wildlife Federation, 8925 Leesburg Pike, Vienna, VA 22184). Age range 3–6. Nature and conservation.

Zillions—The Consumer Reports for Kids (P.O. Box 51777, Boulder, CO 80321–1777). Age range 8–14. Consumer education.

Reading/Study Techniques

Key Vocabulary

Pay close attention to these terms when they appear in the chapter.

bar graphs

circle or pie graphs

database

guide words

legend

line graphs

metacognition

picture graphs

reading rate

reading/study techniques

scale

SQRQCQ

SQ3R

SETTING OBJECTIVES

When you finish reading this chapter, you should be able to

▶ Discuss the features of the SQ3R study method.

▶ Explain the importance of developing flexible reading habits.

▶ Name some skills a child needs in order to locate information in books, libraries or media centers, or computer databases.

▶ Describe how to help a child learn to take good notes, make a good outline, and write a good summary.

▶ Discuss the metacognitive strategies children need.

▶ Explain how to teach a child to use graphic aids in textbooks.

Chapter 9 Organization

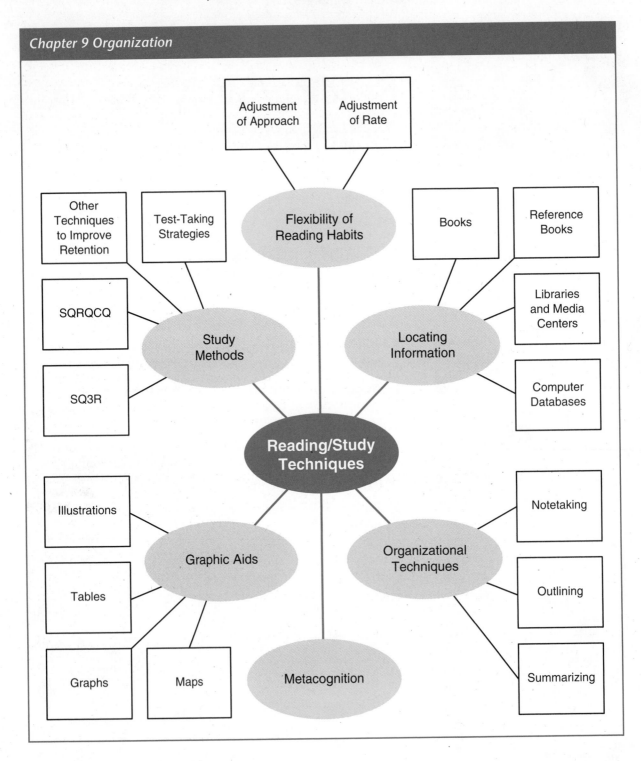

Reading/study techniques are strategies that enhance comprehension and retention of information in printed material and thus help children cope successfully with reading assignments in content area classes and with informational reading throughout their lives. Students need to develop the ability to use good study methods that can help them retain material they read, the ability to take tests effectively, flexibility of reading habits, the ability to locate and organize information effectively, and the ability to use metacognitive strategies when studying. They also need to learn the skills necessary to derive information from graphic aids (maps, graphs, tables, and illustrations) in content area reading materials.

Teaching study techniques is not exclusively the job of the intermediate-grade teacher, although the need for such instruction is more obvious at this level than at the primary level. Primary-grade teachers must lay the foundation for this instruction and make the children aware of the need for study skills. They can do this in a number of ways. They can have the children begin to keep assignment books in which to record all school assignments with related instructions and due dates. Teachers can introduce children to such activities as making free-form outlines related to stories they have heard or read and occasionally writing group

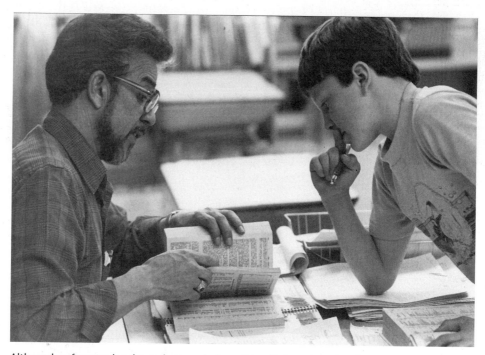

Although reference books such as encyclopedias, dictionaries, almanacs, and atlases can be helpful tools, teachers should use caution in assigning work from these books because their readability level is often high. (© *Mimi Forsyth/Monkmeyer Press Photo Service*)

experience charts in outline form. They can also let the children see them using indexes and tables of contents of books to find needed information, encourage the children to watch them use the card catalog to help locate books, and read aloud information related to content area study from a variety of reference books. Primary teachers can begin actual study skill instruction in the use of some parts of books (tables of contents, glossaries), dictionary use (alphabetical order, use of picture dictionaries), library use (location of the easy-to-read books, check-in and check-out procedures), map reading (titles, directional indicators, legends), graph reading (picture graphs, circle graphs, simple bar graphs), and picture reading.

Since some children are ready for more advanced techniques (such as note taking) much sooner than others, intermediate-grade teachers should determine the readiness of individual children for instruction in study techniques and offer instruction to fit their capabilities. Those children who are ready for more advanced techniques should be helped to develop these strategies as early as possible, because study techniques help children succeed in all subjects.

Teachers may present study techniques during a content class when the need arises or during a reading class, but they should be sure the strategies are applied to content soon after the reading class. Children will retain study techniques longer if they apply them, and they will see these skills as useful tools, rather than busywork exercises. They are more likely to apply their new knowledge if they practice the techniques in the context in which they will use them. Therefore, a teacher may find it very effective to set aside time during a content class to teach a study strategy that students will need to use immediately in that class.

Study Methods

Study methods are techniques that help students study written material in a way that enhances comprehension and retention. Unlike the directed reading activities (DRAs) found in teacher's manuals in basal reading series, study methods are student directed, rather than teacher directed. (See Chapter 7 for a description of a DRA.)

SQ3R

Probably the best-known study method is Robinson's *SQ3R* method: Survey, Question, Read, Recite, Review (Robinson, 1961). For this method, the steps given to the students are as follows:

- *Survey*. As you approach a reading assignment you should notice the chapter title and main headings, read the introductory and summary paragraphs, and inspect any visual aids such as maps, graphs, or illustrations. This initial survey provides a framework for organizing the facts you later derive from the reading.

- *Question*. Formulate a list of questions you expect to be answered in the reading. The headings may give you some clues.

- *Read.* Read the selection in order to answer the questions you have formulated. Since this is purposeful reading, making brief notes may be helpful.

- *Recite.* After reading the selection, try to answer each of the questions you formulated earlier without looking back at the material.

- *Review.* Reread to verify or correct your recited answers and to make sure that you have the main points of the selection in mind and that you understand the relationships among the various points.

Using a study method such as SQ3R will help a student remember content material better than simply reading the material would. Consequently, it is worthwhile to take time in class to show students how to go through the various steps. Teachers should have group practice sessions on SQ3R, or on any study method, before expecting the children to perform the steps independently.

Material chosen for SQ3R instruction should be content material on which the students should normally use the method. The teacher should ask all the students to survey the selection together—reading aloud the title and main headings and the introductory and summary paragraphs, and discussing the visual aids—in the first practice session.

The step that needs most explanation by the teacher is the Question step. The teacher can show children how to take a heading, such as "Brazil's Exports," and turn it into a question: "What are Brazil's exports?" This question should be answered in the section, and trying to find the answer provides a good purpose for reading. A chapter heading, such as "The Westward Movement," may elicit a variety of possible questions: "What is the Westward Movement?" "When did it take place?" "Where did it take place?" "Why did it take place?" "Who was involved?" The teacher can encourage children to generate questions like these in a class discussion during initial practice sessions.

After they have formulated questions, students read to find the answers. The teacher might make brief notes on the chalkboard to model behavior the children can follow. Then he or she can have students practice the Recite step by asking each child to respond orally to one of the purpose questions, with the book closed. During the Review step, the children reread to check all the answers they have just heard.

In subsequent practice sessions, the teacher can merely alert the children to perform each step and have them all perform the step silently at the same time. It will probably take several practice sessions before the steps are thoroughly set in the students' memories.

SQ3R is probably the best-known study method, but it is not the only one. Another useful method is explained in the following section.

SQRQCQ

Another method that seems simple enough to use with good results at the elementary level is one developed especially for use with mathematics materials: SQRQCQ (Fay, 1965). *SQRQCQ* stands for Survey, Question, Read, Question,

Compute, Question. This approach may be beneficial because youngsters frequently have great difficulty reading statement problems in mathematics textbooks. For this method, the steps given to the students are as follows:

- *Survey*. Read through the problem quickly to gain an idea of its general nature.

- *Question*. Ask, "What is being asked in the problem?"

- *Read*. Read the problem carefully, paying attention to specific details and relationships.

- *Question*. Make a decision about the mathematical operations to be carried out and, in some cases, the order in which they are to be performed.

- *Compute*. Do the computations you decided on in the preceding step.

- *Question*. Decide whether or not the answer seems to be correct, asking, "Is this a reasonable answer? Have I accurately performed the computations?"

As with SQ3R, the teacher should have the whole class practice the SQRQCQ method before expecting students to use it independently. Teaching the method takes little extra time, since it is a good way to manage mathematics instruction. (You may wish to refer to this section again as you read the section in Chapter 10 on mathematics materials.)

Other Techniques to Improve Retention

In addition to providing students with a good study method, a teacher can improve their ability to retain content material by following these suggestions:

1. Conduct discussions about all assigned reading material. Talking about ideas they have read helps to fix these ideas in students' memories.

2. Teach students to read assignments critically. Have them constantly evaluate the material they read, and avoid giving them the idea that something is true "because the book says so" by encouraging them to challenge any statement in the book if they can find evidence to the contrary. The active involvement with the material that is necessary in critical reading aids retention. (See Chapter 6 for a thorough discussion of critical reading.)

3. Encourage students to apply the ideas about which they have read. For example, after reading about parliamentary procedure, students can conduct a club meeting; after reading about a simple science experiment, they can actually conduct the experiment. Children learn those things they have applied in real life better than those about which they have only read.

4. Always be certain that students have in mind a purpose for reading before beginning each reading assignment, since this increases their ability to retain material. You may supply them with purpose questions or encourage them to state their own purposes. (Information about purpose questions is found in Chapters 5 and 6.)

5. Use audiovisual aids to reinforce concepts presented in the reading material.

6. Read background material to students to give them a frame of reference to which they can relate the ideas they read.

7. Prepare study guides for content area assignments. Study guides help children retain their content area concepts by setting purposes for reading and providing appropriate frameworks for organizing material. (Study guides receive extensive attention in Chapter 10.)

8. Teach students to look for the author's organization. Have them outline the material or construct a diagram of the organizational pattern.

9. Encourage children to picture the ideas the author is describing. Visualizing information will help them remember it longer. Some children will find it helpful to draw, graph, or chart the ideas they visualize. Semantic webs are particularly useful. (See Chapter 10 for a description of the use of webs with content material.)

10. Teach note-taking procedures and encourage note taking. Writing down information often helps children retain it.

11. After children have read the material, have them summarize it in their own words in either written or oral form.

12. Have children use spaced practice (a number of short practice sessions extended over a period of time) rather than massed practice (one long practice session) for material you wish them to retain over a long period of time.

13. Encourage *overlearning* (continuing to practice a skill for a while after it has been initially mastered) of material you wish students to retain for long periods of time.

14. When appropriate, teach some simple mnemonic devices (short phrases or verses used as memory aids)—for example, "there is a rat in the middle of separate."

15. Offer positive reinforcement for correct responses to questions during discussion and review sessions.

16. Encourage students to look for words and ideas that are mentioned repeatedly, because they are likely to be important ones.

17. Encourage students to study more difficult and less interesting material when they are most alert (Memory and Yoder, 1988).

18. Teach students to ask and answer *why* questions about each factual statement in an informational passage (Menke and Pressley, 1994).

Test-Taking Strategies

Students need to retain what they have read in order to do well on tests, but sometimes students who know the material fail to do as well as they could because they lack good test-taking strategies. Students may study in the same way for essay tests and objective tests, for example. Helping them understand how to study for and take different types of tests can improve their performances.

Teachers can help students prepare for taking essay tests by helping them understand the meanings of certain words, such as *compare, contrast, describe,* and *explain,* that frequently appear in essay questions. The teacher can state a potential question using one of these terms and then model the answer to the question, explaining what is important to include in the answer. If a contrast is requested, the differences in the two things or ideas should be explained. If a comparison is requested, likenesses should be included.

Preparation for objective tests can include learning important terms and their definitions, studying for types of questions that have been asked in the past, and learning to use mnemonic devices to help in memorizing lists. Teachers should encourage students to use all of these techniques.

Teachers can also encourage students to consider the words *always, never,* and *not* carefully when answering true-false questions, since these words have a powerful effect on the meaning. They can make sure students realize that if any part of a true-false statement is false, the answer must be false. They can also caution students to read and consider all answers to a multiple-choice question before choosing an answer.

Children can also be helped to perform better on standardized tests through focused instruction. Teachers should discuss with the children the purpose of the tests and the special rules that apply during testing well before the standardized tests are to be given. They should provide practice in completing test items within specified time limits. A practice test with directions, time limits, and item formats as similar as possible to those of the actual test should be given to familiarize the children with the overall testing environment (Stewart and Green, 1983).

Children need to learn to follow the directions for testing exactly, including those related to recording answers. They should learn to answer first those items they can answer quickly and to check answers if they have time left. They need to realize the importance of reading all answers before choosing the best one and to understand that they should guess rather than leave an answer blank if there is not a severe penalty for guessing.

Flexibility of Reading Habits

Flexible readers adjust their approaches and rates to fit the materials they are reading. Good readers continually adjust their reading approaches and rates without being aware of it.

Adjustment of Approach

Flexible readers approach printed material according to their *purposes for reading* and the *type of material.* For example, they may read poetry aloud to savor the beauty of the words, or they may read novels for relaxation in a leisurely fashion, giving attention to descriptive passages that evoke visual imagery and taking time to think about the characters and their traits. If they are reading novels simply to be able to converse with friends about the story lines, they may read less carefully, wishing only to discover the novels' main ideas and basic plots.

Flexible readers approach informational reading with the goal of separating the important facts from the unimportant ones and paying careful attention in order to retain what they need from the material. Rereading is often necessary if the material contains a high density of facts or very difficult concepts and inter-relationships. With such material, reading every word may be highly important, whereas it is less important with material containing few facts or less difficult concepts. Flexible readers approach material for which they have little background with greater concentration than material for which their background is extensive.

Some reading purposes do not demand the reading of every word in a passage. Sometimes *skimming* (reading selectively to pick up main ideas and general impressions about the material) or *scanning* (moving the eyes rapidly over the selection to locate a specific bit of information, such as a name or a date) is sufficient. Skimming is the process used in the Survey step of SQ3R, when students are trying to orient themselves to the organization and general focus of the material. Scanning is useful when searching for names in telephone books or entries in dictionaries or indexes.

Adjustment of Rate

Children often make the mistake of trying to read everything at the same rate. Some of them read short stories as slowly and carefully as they read science experiments, and they will probably never enjoy recreational reading because they have to work so hard and it takes them so long to read a story. Other children read everything rapidly, often failing to grasp essential details in content area reading assignments even though they complete the reading. Reading rate should not be considered as separate from comprehension. The optimum rate for reading a particular piece is the fastest rate at which the reader maintains an acceptable level of comprehension.

Students will use study time more efficiently if they are taught to vary their rates to fit the reading *purposes* and *materials*. A student should read light fiction for enjoyment much faster than a mathematics problem that must be solved. When reading to find isolated facts such as names and dates, the student will do better to scan a page rapidly for key words than to read every word of the material. When reading to determine main ideas or organization of a selection, he or she will find skimming more practical than reading each word of the selection.

One way to help children fit appropriate rates to materials is to give them various types of materials and purposes, allow them to try different rates, and then encourage them to discuss the effectiveness of different rates for different purposes and materials. This will be particularly helpful if regular classroom materials are used for the practice. Emphasis on increasing reading speed is best left until children have well-developed basic word recognition and comprehension skills. By the time they reach the intermediate grades, some will be ready for help in increasing their reading rates. It is important to remember that speed without comprehension is useless, so the teacher must be sure students maintain comprehension levels as they keep working to increase their reading rates. Techniques teachers can use with students to help them increase their reading rates include the following.

Activities

1. To encourage students to try consciously to increase their reading rates, time their reading for three minutes. At the end of that period, have the students count the total words read, divide by three, and record the resulting number as their rate in average words per minute. To ensure that they are focusing on understanding, follow the timed reading with a comprehension check. The students can graph the results of these timed readings over a period of time, along with the comprehension results. Ideally, students will see their rates increase without a decrease in comprehension. If the children's comprehension does decrease, encourage them to slow down enough to regain an appropriate comprehension level.

2. To help children cut down on unnecessary regressions (going back to reread), have them use markers to move down the page, covering the lines just read.

3. To help decrease children's anxiety about comprehension that could impede their progress, give them easy material for practice in building their reading rates.

Time for Reflection

Some teachers spend some time on development of reading rate, but do not address flexibility. Other teachers address flexibility, but give litttle attention to increasing rate. Some teachers work on both aspects. Still others dismiss rate considerations entirely, as inappropriate for elementary school instruction. **What do *you* think?**

Locating Information

To engage in many study activities, students need to be able to locate the necessary reading material. A teacher can help by pointing out the location aids in textbooks, reference books, and libraries and by showing them how to access databases.

Books

Most books offer students several special features that are helpful for locating needed information, including prefaces, tables of contents, indexes, appendices, glossaries, footnotes, and bibliographies. Teachers should not assume that children can adjust from the basal reader or trade book format to the format of content subject books without assistance. Basal readers have a great deal of narrative (storylike) material that, unlike most content material, is not packed with facts to be learned. When the trade books used in a program are primarily fiction, they will also be narrative in format. Although most basals have a table of contents and a glossary, they contain fewer of the special features just mentioned than do content textbooks; and, although some nonfiction trade books have tables of contents and/or glossaries, not all do. Therefore, teachers should present content textbooks to children carefully.

Preface/Introduction

When presenting a new textbook to students in the intermediate or upper grades, the teacher can ask them to read the preface or introduction to get an idea of why the book was written and of the manner in which the author or authors plan to present the material.

Table of Contents

On the day a new textbook is distributed, the teacher can also lead students in an examination of its table of contents. Even primary-level students can learn that the table of contents lists the topics the book discusses and the pages on which they appear, making it unnecessary to look through the entire book to find a specific section. The teacher can help students discover information about their new textbooks by asking questions such as the following:

What topics are covered in this book?

What is the first topic discussed?

On what page does the discussion about ＿＿＿＿ begin? (This question can be repeated several times with different topics inserted in the blank.)

Indexes

Students in the intermediate and upper grades should become familiar with indexes. They should understand that an index is an alphabetical list of items and names mentioned in a book and the pages where these items or names appear, and that some books contain one general index and some contain subject and author indexes as well as other specialized ones (for example, a first-line index in a music or poetry book). Most indexes contain both main headings and subheadings, and students should be given opportunities to practice using these headings to locate information within their books. The teacher can lead children to examine the index of a book to make inferences about which topics the author considers to be important, based on the amount of space devoted to them. The following Focus on Strategies shows use of the index to locate information.

Focus on Strategies

Using the Index to Locate Information

Several children in Ms. Rand's class needed to find out how to check addition problems the day before, but had trouble locating the part of the book they wanted and spent too much time on the task. Ms. Rand noticed that none of the children used the index to find the pages. When she questioned a couple of them, she found out that they had only a hazy concept that the index was in the back of the book, and they didn't know how to use it.

The next day, Ms. Rand set out to remedy this situation. "Turn to page 315 of your math books," she told her class. "Tell me what you find there."

Here is a portion of what the children found:

Sample Index

Addition
    checking, 50–54
    meaning of, 4
    on number line, 10–16, 25–26
    number sentences, 18–19
    regrouping in, 80–91, 103–104
Checking
    addition, 50–54
    subtraction, 120–125
Circle, 204–206
Counting, 2–4
Difference, 111–112
Dollar, 35
Dozen, 42
Graph, 300–306
    bar, 303–306
    picture, 300–303

"It's called the *index*," Tommy replied, as he located the page.

"Right, Tommy," said Ms. Rand. "The index is a part of the book that can help you find information that you need to locate in the book. It lists the topics in the book in alphabetical order, and after the topic it has the pages on which the topic is discussed in the book. For example, in your index, information about graphs is found on pages 300 through 306. The dash shows that all the pages in between 300 and 306 are about graphs too. If it had been written this way—(*She writes on chalkboard.*) 300, 306—that would mean the information would just be on those two pages. Who can tell me which pages talk about circles?"

"Pages 204 and 206," Tamara said.

"What about page 205?" asked Ms. Rand.

Ramon broke in: "It is about circles, too. You said the dash meant all of the pages between the ones listed."

"Oh, yeah," agreed Tamara, "205 is part of it, too."

"Very good," Ms. Rand replied. "Now look under the listing for Graph, and notice that there are some words indented there. These are types of graphs, and the particular types are listed with their own page numbers. When there is a list of indented terms under the main term, those terms are related to the main term, but they are there to help you find more specific topics. If I wanted to find out about bar graphs, I could look on pages 303 through 306. I wouldn't have to look at the other pages about graphs, because bar graphs wouldn't be discussed there. What if I wanted to read about picture graphs?"

"You would read pages 300 through 303," Penny replied.

"Right! And what if I wanted to find out about regrouping in addition?" Ms. Rand asked.

"Pages 80 through 104," said Morgan.

"All of them?" asked Ms. Rand.

"Well, there are dashes," Morgan replied.

"What else do you see besides the dashes?" Ms. Rand asked.

"There is a comma between the 91 and the 103," Morgan reported.

"What do you think that tells you?" Ms. Rand asked.

"I guess that 92 through 102 don't have anything about regrouping on them," Morgan answered hesitantly.

"Good thinking," Ms. Rand replied. "You are getting that punctuation figured out."

Then she told the class, "Now get in your math work groups and see if you can answer the questions on this sheet about the index in your math text."

The sheet contained the following questions:

1. On what pages would you look to find out how to check addition problems? Under what main topics and subheadings do you have to look to discover these page numbers?

2. On what page will you find *dollar* mentioned?

3. On what pages would you look to find out how to add using a number line? What main heading did you look under to discover this? What subheading did you look under?

4. Is there information about addition on a number line on pages 10 and 16? Is information about this topic on any other pages?

After the small groups had all reached agreement on the answers, the whole class discussed the items to ensure that everyone had been successful in understanding the process.

At the end of the lesson, Ms. Rand said, "Find the meaning of *addition* and read it to me."

Mark did so.

"Did you look in the index to find the page number?" she asked.

"Yes, I did," Mark said proudly.

(continued)

"Do you think you found it more quickly by looking in the index than you would have by turning through the book to find it?"

"Yes," Mark replied.

"When you need to look things up in your textbooks, remember that the index can be helpful to you," Ms. Rand reminded the group as the lesson ended.

In using an index, thinking skills become important when the word being sought is not listed. Readers must then think of synonyms for the word or another form of the word that might be listed. Brainstorming possibilities for alternative listings for a variety of terms could be a helpful class activity to prepare students to be flexible when such situations occur.

Appendices

Students can also be shown that the appendices of books contain supplementary information that may be helpful to them, for example, bibliographies or tabular material.

Glossaries

Primary-grade children can be shown that glossaries, which are often included in their textbooks, are similar to dictionaries but include only the words presented in the book in which they are found. Textbooks often contain glossaries of technical terms that can greatly aid students in understanding the book's content. The skills necessary for proper use of a glossary are the same as those needed for using a dictionary. (See Chapters 3 and 4 for discussions of dictionary use.)

Footnotes and Bibliographies

Footnotes and bibliographies refer students to other sources of information about the subject being discussed in a book, and teachers should encourage students to turn to these sources for clarification, for additional information on a topic for a report, or simply for their own satisfaction.

Reference Books

Elementary school children often need to find information in such reference books as encyclopedias, dictionaries, almanacs, and atlases. Unfortunately, many students reach high school still unable to use such aids effectively. Though some skills related to the use of reference books can be taught in the primary grades (for example, use of picture dictionaries), the bulk of the responsibility for teaching use of reference books rests with the intermediate-grade teacher.

Important skills for effective use of reference books include the following:

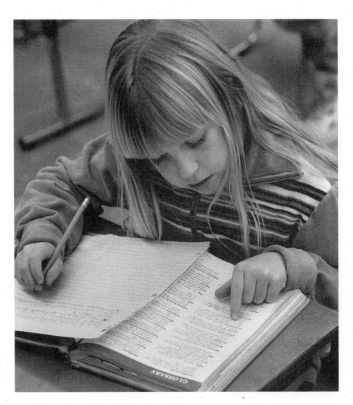

Glossaries are similar to dictionaries. (© *Kalman/ The Image Works*)

General
1. Knowledge of alphabetical order and understanding that encyclopedias, dictionaries, and some atlases are arranged in alphabetical order

2. Ability to use guide words, knowledge of their location on a page, and understanding that they represent the first and last entry words on a dictionary or encyclopedia page

3. Ability to determine key words under which related information can be found.

Encyclopedias
1. Ability to use cross-references

2. Ability to determine which volume of a set of encyclopedias will contain the information needed

Dictionaries
1. Ability to use pronunciation keys

2. Ability to choose from several possible word meanings the one that most closely fits the context in which a word is found

Atlases
1. Ability to interpret the legend of a map

2. Ability to interpret the scale of a map

3. Ability to locate directions on maps

Because encyclopedias, almanacs, and atlases are often written at much higher readability levels than other materials used in the classroom, teachers must use caution when assigning work in these reference books. Children are not likely to profit from looking up material in books that are too hard for them to read; when asked to do so, they tend to copy the material word for word without trying to understand it.

However, teachers should keep in mind the difference between *assigning* students to use a particular reference work and letting the students *choose* to use any work that interests them. Readers can handle much more difficult levels of high-interest material than of low-interest material. Therefore, a student who is intensely interested in the subject matter of an encyclopedia article may be able to glean much information from it, even if his or her usual reading level for school materials is lower. For this reason, teachers should never forbid students to try to use material that *may be* too difficult for them. They should, however, avoid *forcing* students to struggle with material that is clearly beyond their range of understanding.

Many skills related to the use of an atlas are included in the section on map reading in this chapter. Some factors related to dictionary and encyclopedia use are discussed in the following sections.

Dictionaries

Before a child can use a dictionary for any of its major functions, he or she must be able to locate a designated word with some ease. Three important skills are necessary to do this: using alphabetical order, using guide words, and locating variants and derivatives.

Using Alphabetical Order. Since the words in a dictionary are arranged in alphabetical order, children must learn to use alphabetical order to find the words they seek. Beginning with the first letter of the word, they gradually learn alphabetization by the first two or three letters, discovering that sometimes it is necessary to work through every letter in a word in the process.

The following Model Activity offers an idea for developing and strengthening students' knowledge of alphabetical order.

**Model
Activities**

Alphabetizing for a Picture Dictionary

Have first graders who are studying a science or social studies topic make a picture dictionary of words related to the topic that they encounter. For example, if the class is studying animals in science, the children might construct a picture dictionary that includes *bears, deer, lions, tigers, elephants,* and so on. The teacher can list each animal that enters the study on the board, and a child can find a picture of the animal, write the word on a page for the picture dictionary, and illustrate the page. The students can also write or dictate a factual statement about each animal. After a number of pages have been constructed, a small group of students can alphabetize them and place them in a looseleaf notebook. As more animals are studied, pages can be added for each one, constructed by one child and alphabetized in the class picture dictionary by another one. Of course, throughout the study, all students can use the picture dictionary for spelling help or just to browse.

Using Guide Words. Children need to learn that the guide words at the top of a dictionary page tell them the first and last words on that page. If they are proficient in using alphabetical order, they should be able to decide whether or not a word will be found on a certain page by checking to see if the word falls alphabetically between the two guide words.

Here is another suggestion for practice with guide words.

**Model
Activities**

Guide Words

Divide the group into two or more teams. Write the word pair *BRACE—BUBBLE* on the chalkboard or a chart. Ask the children to pretend that these words are the guide words for a page of the dictionary. Explain that you would expect the word *brick* to be on this page because *bri* comes after *bra* and *r* comes before *u*. Then write words, one at a time, from the following list on the board below the word pair. Let each team in turn tell you if the word would be found on the page with the designated guide words. Ask them to tell why they answered as they did. The team gets a point if the members can answer the questions correctly. The next team gets a chance to answer if they cannot. The reason for the answer is the most important part of the response.

1. beaker
2. boil
3. break
4. braid
5. bud
6. buy
7. brave
8. border
9. bypass
10. brag
11. bring
12. brother

Variation: Write four guide words and the two dictionary pages on which they appear on the chalkboard or a chart. For example, you could write

Page 300 *RAINBOW—RAPID*

Page 301 *RAPPORT—RAVEN*

Write the words from the following list below the two sets of guide words, one at a time. Ask each team in turn to indicate on which page the displayed word would be found, or if the word would be found on neither page. Have them tell why they answered as they did. (Of course, you would model the decision-making process for them, as described earlier, before the activity starts.) If the team answers the questions about a word correctly, it is awarded a point. If the team answers incorrectly, the next team gets a chance to answer.

1. rare
2. ramble
3. ranch
4. rabbit
5. rash
6. razor
7. rave
8. ratio
9. range
10. raw
11. rank
12. raincoat

Locating Variants and Derivatives. Variants and derivatives are sometimes entered alphabetically in a dictionary, but more often they are either not listed or are listed in conjunction with their root words. If they are not listed, the reader must find the pronunciation of the root word and combine the sounds of the added parts with that pronunciation. This procedure requires advanced skills in word analysis and blending.

Here is an exercise on determining the correct entry word in the dictionary.

Determining the Correct Entry Word

Model Activities

As the students are reading a story that contains many words with affixes, call their attention to the affixed words as they occur in the text. Tell the students that, if they wanted to look up the words in the dictionary, they might not be able to find them listed separately. These words have prefixes, suffixes, and inflectional endings added to root words, so students might need to locate their root words to find them. Choose one word from the text, perhaps *happily*. Point to the word, and say: "I recognize the *-ly* ending here. The rest of the word is almost like *happy*. The *y* was changed to *i* when the ending was added. So the root word is *happy*." Repeat this procedure for one or two other words from the text.

Later, as a follow-up activity, write on the board the list of words presented below. Then, for each word, ask the students to find the root word and tell about the other word parts that made the root word hard to find. They may also discuss the spelling changes made in the root word when endings were added.

1. directness
2. commonly
3. earliness
4. opposed
5. undeniable
6. gnarled
7. customs
8. cuter
9. joyfully
10. computable
11. comradeship
12. concentrating

Using Electronic Dictionaries. Some dictionaries are available on computer diskettes or CD-ROMs. They may provide definitions, spellings, pronunciations, and idioms. Some feature interactive multimedia. Users may be able to hear words pronounced when they click on them with the mouse, hear sound effects related to the words, and play word games. There may be color illustrations for many words, in addition to the standard definitions, sentences using the words, syllabic breakdowns, spellings, pronunciations, and plural forms (Johnson, 1994). Other aspects of dictionary use are discussed in Chapters 3 and 4.

Encyclopedia Use

Since encyclopedias vary in content and arrangement, students should be exposed to several different sets. Teachers should have them compare the entries from different encyclopedias on a specified list of topics. The following Model Activity can provide children with instruction and practice in the use of the encyclopedia as they work on a thematic unit on the Revolutionary War.

Model Activities

Encyclopedia Skills

Have students find the correct volume for each of the following topics, without opening the volume:

Revolutionary War

George Washington

Declaration of Independence

Muskets

British Parliament

Battle of Bunker Hill

Have them check their choices by actually looking up the terms. If they fail to find a term in the volume where they expected to find it, ask them to think of other places to look. Let them check these possibilities also. Continue the process until each term has been located. Here is a possible dialogue between teacher and student:

Teacher: In which volume of the encyclopedia would you find a discussion of George Washington?

Student: In Volume 23.

Teacher: Why did you choose Volume 23?

Student: Because *W* is in Volume 23.

Teacher: Why didn't you choose Volume 7 for the *G*s?

Student: Because people are listed under their last names.

Teacher: Look up the term and check to see if your decision was correct.

Student: It was. I found "George Washington" on page 58.

Teacher: Very good. Now tell me where you would find a description of the Battle of Bunker Hill.

Student: In Volume 2 under "Battle."

Teacher: Check your decision by looking it up.

Student: It's not here. It must be under "Bunker."

Teacher: Good idea.

Student: Here it is. It's under "Bunker Hill, Battle of."

Encyclopedia articles are often very difficult for many intermediate-grade readers to comprehend. This difficulty makes putting the information they find into their own words harder. To encourage appropriate encyclopedia use, the teacher can work with the students to construct a list of things the students should look for about their topics, and the students can list what they already know about each category of information. Next, the children can examine the graphic aids in the encyclopedia article to gather information. Then they can skim the written material to gather main ideas. Finally, they should read the material carefully and put it into their own words. They should be encouraged to consult other sources to check their facts and obtain additional information.

Electronic encyclopedias have become widely available and are located in some school settings. These encyclopedias are available in a CD-ROM format that is accessed by a computer. Some of these encyclopedias have text, pictures, sound, and animation. They can be searched through use of key words and phrases, alphabetical title searches, and topical searches. They are motivational and easy to use (Rickelman et al., 1991). These encyclopedias may not be available in many individual classrooms, but schools often provide them in the library or media center (Wepner, Seminoff, and Blanchard, 1995; Krushenisky, 1993; Melnick, 1991).

Other Reference Materials

Children are often asked to use materials other than books, such as newspapers, magazines, catalogues, transportation schedules, and pamphlets and brochures, as reference sources. For a thematic unit on pollution, for example, students might search through newspapers, magazines, and government pamphlets for stories and information about pollution and groups that are trying to do something about it, in addition to using trade books related to this problem. Similarly, a class studying Alaska might look in the newspaper to find out about the current weather in Alaska; in encyclopedias for information about weather patterns, clothing worn in different areas and/or seasons, geographical data, and points of interest; in travel brochures for methods of transportation to and within the state and prices for such transportation from various locations; in airline brochures for travel schedules; in magazines for feature stories about Alaska; and in catalogues to locate appropriate clothing for a trip to a particular part of Alaska in a certain month. All of these sources would supplement information gathered from nonfiction and fiction trade books about Alaska.

To help youngsters learn to locate information in newspapers, teachers can alert them to the function of headlines and teach them how to use the newspaper's index. Teachers also should devote some class time to explaining journalistic terms, which can help children better understand the material in the newspaper, and to explaining the functions of news stories, editorials, columns, and feature stories. Some of this instruction could actually be a part of a thematic unit on the newspaper. Children are often fascinated by the procedures involved in publishing a newspaper and the techniques used to design and produce a good newspaper. Activities such as the one on using a newspaper's index would be appropriate. Whenever possible, use real newspapers as a basis for activities similar to the one shown.

Other instruction could take place as an integral part of other units being used in the classroom. For example, before the students search the newspaper for information on pollution for the unit mentioned earlier, the teacher could introduce activities related to developing the concept of *main idea* (see Chapter 6) to sensitize youngsters to the function of headlines. This could help make their newspaper searches more efficient and meaningful.

In helping children to obtain information from magazines, teachers can call attention to the table of contents and give the children practice in using it, just as they do with textbooks. Distinguishing between informational and fictional materials is important in reading magazines, as is analyzing advertisements to detect propaganda. Chapter 6 contains activities related to these critical reading skills.

Model Activities

Using a Newspaper's Index

Hand out copies of the following newspaper index, or write the example on the board or a chart.

	Index
Classified Ads	B-5-10
Comics	B-11-12
Crossword	B-11
Editorials	A-2-3
Entertainment	B-3-4
Finance	A-4-7
Horoscope	A-8
Humor columns	A-8-9
Obituaries	A-11

Have a class discussion based on the following questions:

1. Where in the newspaper would you find information about the stock market? Why would you look there?

2. In what section would you look to find a movie that you would like to see or to find the television schedule? How did you know to look there?

3. On what page is the crossword puzzle found? How did you know?

4. How many pages have comics on them? How did you know?

5. Where would you look to find out which people have died recently? How did you know to look there?

To obtain information from catalogues, children again need to be able to use indexes. Activities suggested in this chapter for using indexes in newspapers and textbooks can be profitably used here also. The ability to read charts giving information about sizes and about shipping and handling charges may also be important in reading catalogues.

A variety of transportation schedules, pamphlets, and brochures may be used as reference sources in social studies activities. Since their formats may vary greatly, teachers will need to provide practice in reading the specific materials they intend to use in their classes.

Libraries and Media Centers

For whole language and literature-based classrooms, as well as for more traditional ones, school libraries or media centers are key locations. Teachers and librarians/media specialists should work together as teams to develop the skills that students need to use libraries effectively. (The librarian/media specialist will hereafter be referred to as *librarian* for the sake of easy reference, but the expanded role this person plays in dealing with multimedia should be kept in mind.)

Librarians can be helpful in many ways. They can show students the locations of books and journals, card catalogs, and reference materials (such as dictionaries, encyclopedias, atlases, and the *Reader's Guide to Periodical Literature*) in the library; explain the procedures for checking books in and out; and describe the rules and regulations regarding behavior in the library. Demonstrations of the use of the card catalog and the *Reader's Guide* and explanations of the arrangement of books in libraries are also worthwhile. Prominently displayed posters can remind children to observe checkout procedures and library rules. Currently, librarians are more frequently using library periods not only to help children locate and select books, but also to share literature with them (Walmsley, 1992).

Librarians may also introduce students to book reviews that can guide them in their selection of materials. The children can also be guided to write reviews that they can share with other students (Jenks and Roberts, 1990).

By familiarizing children with reasons for using the library and explaining to them why they may need to use such aids as manual and computerized card catalogs and the *Reader's Guide*, teachers can prepare students for a visit to the library. While they are still in the classroom, the children can learn that cards in the manual card catalog are arranged alphabetically and that the card catalog contains subject, author, and title cards. Sample cards of each type can be drawn on posters and placed on the bulletin board. In addition, fifth and sixth graders will benefit from a lesson that explains the use of cross-reference cards.

If the school has a computerized card catalog, students will be able to search for books by title, author, and subject, just as they do with the manual card catalog. They can choose the type of search they need, type in the key words necessary for the search, and view a list of the available books on the monitor. In Example 9.1 the student chose an author search, then typed in *Cherry*. The author search, shown at the top of the example, showed three books written or illustrated by Lynne Cherry. The student chose number *2* from this list and received the full record display for *A River Ran Wild: An Environmental History*.

Here are two other suggestions for practice with library skills:

1. The teacher can send the children on a scavenger hunt that requires using the library by dividing the class into teams and giving the teams statements to complete or questions to answer. (Example: The author of *The Secret Garden* is ——————— .)

2. The teacher can give students questions and ask them to show on a map of the library where they would go to find the answers (Muller and Savage, 1982).

The Classroom Scenario on locating information shows how one class puts their research skills to work.

The librarian is an important ally for the teacher as thematic units are planned, for no unit will be successful if the needed reading materials are not available in a reasonable supply. Both books and other media are needed for these units, and the books need to be on a variety of levels. The librarian is also a valuable helper as children search the library for this related material as the unit progresses. Librarians have useful input for teachers and students alike about books that are good for reading aloud, for sustained silent reading, and for reference sources. Cooperative planning between teachers and librarians can ensure that what goes on in the library and in the classroom are connected (Lamme and Ledbetter, 1990; Hughes, 1993). Schools in which a whole language philosophy is

Example 9.1 *Computerized Card Catalog Output*

	Author Search	Thu Mar 16 6:00 PM

·1. Cherry, Lynne, Ill.   Item No.: 3ACPL000236885
    Chipmunk song/by Joanne Ryder; pictures by Lynne Cherry.
    Call Number: E RYD   Date: c1987   Type: BK

2. Cherry, Lynne.   Item No.: 5ACPL000005272
    A river ran wild: an environmental history/Lynne Cherry.
    Call Number: J 974.4 CHE   Date: c1992   Type: BK

3. Cherry, Lynne, Ill.   Item No.: 3ACPL000234724
    When I'm sleepy/by Jane R. Howard; illustrated by Lynne Cherry.
    Call Number: E HOW   Date: c1985   Type: BK

4. Cherry, Sheldon H.   Item No.: 12334
    Planning ahead for pregnancy: health, fitness, and fertility/Sheldon…
    Call Number: 618.24 C   Date: 1987   Type: BK

5. Cherryh, C. J.   Item No.: 7CANE000000471
    Chanur's legacy
    Call Number: F CHE   Date: Type: NEO

"*" – Indicates All Copies Are Out
Enter A Number For The Full Record Display
) Scroll Up/Down   F9) Help   Esc) End Search

```
        TITLE:  A river ran wild: an environmental history/Lynne Cherry.
        COPIES: 2 – 2 Available For Loan
   CALL NUMBER: J 974.4 CHE
    SYSTEM NO.: 8054
        AUTHOR: Cherry, Lynne.
       EDITION: 1st ed.
 PLACE OF PUB:  San Diego:
     PUBLISHER: Harcourt Brace Jovanovich,
   DATE OF PUB: c1992
   DESCRIPTION: [34 p.]: col. ill., col. maps; 24 x 29 cm.
         NOTES: "A Gulliver Green book."
         NOTES: An environmental history of the Nashua River, from its discovery by Indians
                through the polluting years of the Industrial Revolution to the ambitious clean-up
                that revitalized it.
       SUBJECT: WATER QUALITY — NASHUA RIVER (MASS. AND N.H.) — HISTORY —
                JUVENILE LITERATURE.
       SUBJECT: MAN — INFLUENCE ON NATURE — NASHUA RIVER (MASS. AND N.H.) —
                HISTORY — JUVENILE LITERATURE.
       SUBJECT: INDIANS OF NORTH AMERICA — NASHUA RIVER (MASS. AND N.H.) —
                HISTORY — JUVENILE LITERATURE.
       SUBJECT: MAN — INFLUENCE ON NATURE.
       SUBJECT: NASHUA RIVER (MASS. AND N.H.) — HISTORY — JUVENILE LITERATURE
       SUBJECT: NASHUA RIVER VALLEY (MASS. AND N.H.) — HISTORY — JUVENILE
                LITERATURE.
       SUBJECT: NASHUA RIVER (MASS. AND N.H.) — HISTORY.
   LC CARD NBR: 91–012892 /AC
          ISBN: 0152005420 :
      LOCATION: ACL*
       COPY NO.: 1–2
```

**Classroom
Scenario**

Locating Information

Students in a fifth-grade classroom are about to begin a study of World War II. They have formed into groups, each of which will research a different topic related to the war. One group is going to research transportation methods for troops.

When the children in Keith's group meet, Keith says, "First we need to know the different types of transportation that were used. I think we can find that in the encyclopedia under 'World War II.' Who would like to check that out?"

"I will," replies Elaine. "I'll look in all of the different encyclopedias and see if they all have the same information or if they have different stuff. That will help us when we divide up jobs later."

"Good," Keith says. "Then we can make a list of the types of transportation, and each one of us can look up one or two of them and get more details. We can use the dictionary for a basic definition and the encyclopedia for more details on the type of transportation we are looking for, like 'jeeps.' Where else will we get information?"

"We can check the card catalog," Tammy suggests. "The subject cards on 'World War II' and things like 'jeeps' would give us some leads."

"I have a book at home on airplanes," Randy says. "Some of them were from World War II. Can I draw some for our report?"

"Great!" Keith says. "We need some visuals for our report, and you are better at drawing than the rest of us. We'll want some drawings of those planes and tanks and probably some other stuff. We'll all be on the lookout for examples that you can use for models. I'll also ask my Great Uncle Joe about it. He was in the Army in World War II."

Analysis of Scenario

These students have received instruction that made them aware of places to find information for class studies, and they are putting that information to use as they work in their research group. Randy does not have ideas about where to find things in the library, but he recognizes that he has a valuable personal resource and offers it for the study. The children have been taught that there are sources of information other than school materials, and they freely plan to use personal books and even primary sources.

embraced have children moving in and out of the library all the time. The library is used as "an extension of the classroom" (Hughes, 1993, p. 294). Many children use the library to find books, to read, to write, and to interact with classmates about books. Many use it to do research on questions they need to answer, and their research is specific and of personal interest. Many children use location aids in books more adeptly and at an earlier age than they did before the advent of whole language instruction (Hughes, 1993).

Valenza (1996) points out that since multimedia production is a research process, it belongs in the school library, where audiovisual and print resources are located, most schools have Internet connections, and librarians are available. When students need a research skill, librarians now often teach it or direct them to other students who can help with that skill. The library frequently remains open to students all day, allowing access when need exists (Hansen, 1993). (See Chapter 11 for more information on multimedia production.)

Time for Reflection	Some teachers think that the librarian should have the complete responsibility for teaching library skills. Others think the teaching of library skills should be a team effort. **What do** *you* **think?**

Computer Databases

In today's schools, students need to be able to locate and retrieve information from *computer databases*, in addition to performing more traditional activities. A computer database is a collection of related information that has been organized to facilitate retrieval through an electronic search. Each database is somewhat like a filing cabinet or several filing cabinets, with separate file folders for the different articles in the database. The information is categorized and indexed for easy retrieval. Users may create their own databases or use existing ones. Using databases, students pose questions, decide on key words to access the data, read, follow directions, collect and categorize data, summarize material, and make comparisons and contrasts (Layton and Irwin, 1989). The electronic encyclopedias discussed earlier are examples of databases that are available in some schools. In addition, many databases can be accessed through such online services as the Internet. For example, computer users can access LOCIS (Library of Congress Information System) through this service ("Open to Suggestion," 1994).

Smith (1991) found that HyperCard allowed students to create large databases with text, attractive graphics, and pleasing controls. Smith's students made a "Fantastic Fiction" HyperCard stack on which they shared their reactions to books they had read. They also developed stacks recreating the Algonquin myth "Why the Lynx Has a Short Tail" and a stack about the causes, battles, and results of the War of 1812.

Organizational Techniques

When engaging in such activities as writing reports, elementary school students need to organize the ideas they encounter in their reading. Too often teachers at the elementary level give little attention to organizational techniques such as note taking, outlining, and summarizing, and too many students enter secondary school without knowing how to perform these tasks.

Note Taking

Teachers may present note-taking techniques in a functional setting when children are preparing written reports on materials they have read. Children should be taught

1. To include key words and phrases in their notes.
2. To include enough of the context to make the notes understandable after a period of time has elapsed.
3. To include a bibliographical reference (source) with each note.
4. To copy direct quotations exactly.
5. To indicate carefully which notes are direct quotations and which are reworded.

Key words—the words that carry the important information in a sentence—are generally nouns and verbs, but they may include important modifiers. Example 9.2 shows a sample paragraph and a possible set of notes based on this paragraph. Laase (1997) suggests using sample paragraphs and an overhead projector to model note taking. Seitz (1997) also uses the overhead projector to model note taking for his middle-school students.

Example 9.2 *Sample Paragraph and Notes*

A restaurant is not as easy a business to run as it may appear to be to some people, since the problem of obtaining good help is ever-present. Cooks, dishwashers, and servers are necessary personnel. Cooks must be able to prepare the food offered by the restaurant. Dishwashers need to be dependable and thorough. Servers need to be able to carry out their duties politely and efficiently. Poorly prepared food, inadequately cleaned dishes, and rude help can be the downfall of a restaurant, so restaurant owners and managers must hire with care.

SAMPLE NOTE CARD

> Problem for restaurant owner or manager—good help: good cooks; dependable, thorough dishwashers; polite, efficient servers. Hire with care.

After reading the paragraph shown in Example 9.2, the note taker first thinks, "What kind of information is given here?" The answer, "Problem for restaurant owner or manager—good help," is the first note. Then the note taker searches for key words to describe the kind of help needed. For example, cooks who "are able to prepare the food offered by the restaurant" can be described as "good cooks"—ten words condensed into two that carry the idea. In the case of the nouns *dishwasher* and *servers*, descriptive words related to them are added; condensation of phrases is not necessary (although the *ands* between the adjectives may be left out) because the key words needed are found directly in the selection. The last part of the paragraph can be summed up in the warning "Hire with care." It is easy to see that key-word notes carry the message of the passage in a very condensed or abbreviated form.

A teacher can go through an example like this one with the children, telling them what key words to choose and why, and then provide another example, letting the children decide as a group which key words to write down and having them give reasons for their choices. Finally, each child can do a selection individually. After completing the individual note taking, the children can compare their notes and discuss reasons for choices.

Students can take notes in outline form, in sentences, or in paragraphs. Beginners may even benefit from taking notes in the form of semantic webs or maps. (See Chapters 4, 5, and 10 for elaboration of these techniques.)

Outlining

Teachers can lead children to understand that outlining is writing down information from the material they read in a way that shows the relationships among the main ideas and the supporting details, although, of course, the children must already know how to recognize main ideas and details. Two types of outlines that are important for children to understand are the *sentence* outline, in which each point is a complete sentence, and the *topic* outline, which is composed of key words and phrases. Since choosing key words and phrases is in itself a difficult task for many youngsters, it is wise to present sentence outlines first.

The first step in forming an outline is to extract the main ideas from the material and to list these ideas beside Roman numerals in the order in which they occur. Supporting details are listed beside capital letters below the main idea they support and are slightly indented to indicate their subordination. Details that are subordinate to the main details designated by capital letters are indented still further and preceded by Arabic numerals. The next level of subordination is indicated by lower-case letters, although elementary students will rarely need to make an outline that goes beyond the level of Arabic numerals.

A model outline form like the one shown in Example 9.3 may help students understand how to write an outline in proper form.

The teacher can supply students with partially completed outlines of chapters in their content textbooks and ask them to fill in the missing parts, gradually leaving out more and more details until the students are doing the complete outline alone. To develop students' readiness for outlining, the teacher can use the Model Activity on the next page.

Example 9.3 *Sample Outline*

TITLE
I. Main idea
   A. Detail supporting I
   B. Detail supporting I
      1. Detail supporting B
      2. Detail supporting B
         a. Detail supporting 2
         b. Detail supporting 2
      3. Detail supporting B
   C. Detail supporting I
II. Main idea
   A. Detail supporting II
   B. Detail supporting II
   C. Detail supporting II

Model Activities

Readiness for Outlining

1. Provide the children with a set of items to be categorized.

2. Ask them to place the items in categories. More than one arrangement may be possible; let them try several.

3. Provide the children with a blank outline form of this type:

4. Have the children fill in the outline.

   Example:

   a. Provide plastic animals: horse, cow, chicken, pig, elephant, lion, sea gull, rooster, tiger.

b. Give them time to categorize.

c. Provide this outline:

d. Possible solution:

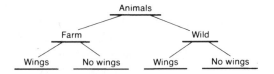

This activity can be used as a first step in teaching the concept of outlining to first and second graders. The next step might be to have the students make free-form outlines, or story webs, in which they use words, lines, and arrows to arrange key words and phrases from the story in a way that shows their relationships. Simple, very familiar stories allow children to concentrate on arranging the terms logically rather than on locating the details. Example 9.4 shows a web based on the familiar story "The Three Little Pigs." (See Chapter 5 for more information on webbing or mapping stories.)

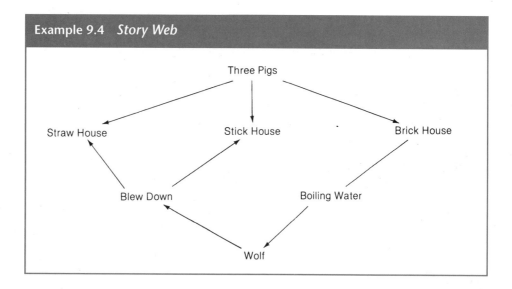

Example 9.4   *Story Web*

Teacher modeling of web construction should come first. Then one or more story webs may be constructed cooperatively by the whole class. The teacher may need to provide the key words and phrases in early experiences with webbing. The children can then cooperatively develop webs in small groups with help from the teacher's probing questions about connecting lines, directions of arrows, and positions of phrases. The children may also ask the teacher questions about their decisions. As they develop proficiency with the task, the teacher can allow them to choose key words and phrases themselves, at first with assistance and then independently. After mastering this step, the children can move on to forming webs without assistance (Hansell, 1978).

Children can obtain outlining practice by outlining material the teacher has entered into a computer file. The children can move phrases and headings around with a word-processing program and create an outline in relatively painless fashion.

| Time for Reflection | Some teachers believe in teaching only formal outlining. Others think students can benefit from organizational techniques such as webs. **What do *you* think?** |

Summarizing

In a summary, a student is expected to restate what the author has said in a more concise form. Main ideas of selections should be preserved, but illustrative materials and statements that merely elaborate on the main ideas should not be included.

Children should be led to see that, when making summaries, they should delete trivial and redundant material. Superordinate terms can be used to replace lists of similar items or actions (for example, *people* for *men, women, and children*). Steps in an action may be replaced by a superordinate action (*baked a cake* for *took flour, butter, . . . and then placed it in an oven*). Each paragraph can be represented with its topic sentence or implied main idea sentence (Brown and Day, 1983; Brown, Day, and Jones, 1983; Recht, 1984).

The teacher should model the deletion of nonessential material when constructing summaries and then should have students practice this activity under supervision. Choosing superordinate terms and actions and choosing or constructing topic sentences should also be modeled and practiced. Easy material should be used for beginning instruction, and paragraphs should be used before proceeding to longer passages (Recht, 1984).

One possible way the teacher can build children's experience with summarizing is to give them a long passage to read and three or four summaries of the passage. The teacher can let the students examine the summaries and decide which one is best and why each of the others was not satisfactory. The teacher can help in this exploration process by asking appropriate questions if the students appear confused about what to consider. For example, the teacher may ask, "Does this sentence tell something different, or is it just an example?" After the children have been successful in differentiating between the satisfactory and unsatisfactory summaries, the teacher can refer them to a passage in one of their textbooks, along with several possible summaries, and have them choose the best summary and tell why they did not choose each of the others. In addition, the Model Activity on single sentence summaries can provide practice with summarizing.

Model Activities

Single-Sentence Summaries

Have the children read a short passage like the following one and try to summarize its content in a single sentence.

Sometimes your hair makes a noise when you comb it. The noise is really made by static electricity. Static electricity collects in one place. Then it jumps to another place. Rub your feet on a rug. Now touch something. What happens? Static electricity collects on your body, but it can jump from your finger to other places. Sometimes you can see a spark and hear a noise.

Have students compare their answers and revise them as they discuss the merits of different answers.

Metacognition

Metacognitive strategies (strategies involving the ability to examine one's intellectual functioning) are important in reading for meaning and in reading for retention. Comprehension monitoring and taking steps to ensure comprehension when deficiencies are discovered are associated with reading for meaning. Students who monitor their comprehension and use fix-up strategies such as rereading, self-questioning, retelling, predicting and verifying, and reading further while withholding judgment are more likely to comprehend and retain the information read. Recognizing important ideas, checking mastery of the information read, and developing effective strategies for study are metacognitive techniques involved in reading for retention (Paris, Wasik, and Turner, 1991; Baumann, Jones, and Seifert-Kessell, 1993; Baker and Brown, 1984).

Metacognition involves knowing what is already known, knowing when understanding of new material has been accomplished, knowing how the understanding was reached, and knowing why something is or is not known. Children have shown some awareness of these aspects of learning (Guthrie, 1983).

Research indicates that comprehension monitoring is a developmental skill that is not fully developed until adolescence. Ann Brown and Sandra Smiley discovered that low-ability students did not always benefit from monitoring strategies. These strategies may be beneficial only if students possess the background and understanding to use them effectively. With attention to students' levels of maturity, however, aspects of comprehension monitoring can be taught. It is important for teachers to guide students toward actually using these strategies, rather than just teaching them *about* the strategies (Meir, 1984).

To help children develop metacognitive strategies, the teacher must convince them of the need to become active learners. Children need to learn to set goals for their reading tasks, to plan how they will meet their goals, to monitor their success in meeting their goals, and to remedy the situation when they do not meet their goals.

To plan ways to meet their goals, children need to know certain techniques, such as relating new information to their background knowledge, previewing material to be read, paraphrasing ideas presented, and identifying the organizational pattern or patterns of the text. Students should learn the value of periodically questioning themselves about the ideas in the material to see if they are meeting their goals (Babbs and Moe, 1983). They need to learn to ask if the information they have read makes sense. If it does not make sense, they need to learn to ask why it does not make sense. They should decide if they have a problem with decoding a word, understanding what a word means, understanding what a sentence is saying, understanding how a sentence relates to the rest of the passage, or grasping the focus or purpose of the passage (Wilson, 1983). If they have not met their goals because they did not recognize certain words, they need to use context clues, structural analysis, phonics, and possibly the dictionary. If word meaning is the problem, they can again use any of these techniques (except phonics). If sentence structure or sentence relationships are the problem, they can try identifying key words, breaking down sentences into separate meaning units, locating antecedents for pronouns, and other such techniques.

Teachers should teach specific strategies for students to use when they do not comprehend material. Moderately difficult material should be used for this instruction so that they will have some actual comprehension problems to confront, although it should not be too difficult to be useful. Teachers should present background information before the children read, so that they have the information needed to apply comprehension strategies (Fitzgerald, 1983).

The teacher can model strategies for monitoring comprehension by reading a passage aloud and "thinking aloud" about his or her own monitoring behaviors and hypotheses. Noting things that are currently known and unknown and modifying these notes as more information is added can be helpful. Students should be drawn into the process in subsequent lessons by using the "think-aloud" strategy. Eventually they need to apply the monitoring strategy independently (Fitzgerald, 1983). "Think alouds require a reader to stop periodically, reflect on how a text is being processed and understood, and relate orally what reading strategies are being employed" (Baumann, Jones, and Seifert-Kessell, 1993, p. 185). Teacher modeling and student practice of think-alouds can help students learn metacognitive strategies. Students have to be told what each strategy is and why it is important. Then modeling by the teacher through think-alouds and guided and independent practice by the students are needed (Baumann, Jones, and Seifert-Kessell, 1993).

Teachers can ask students to read difficult passages and then ask questions about them. The children write their answers and indicate their degree of confidence in the answers. Incorrect answers should have low confidence ratings and correct answers should have high ratings in order to indicate good comprehension monitoring (Fitzgerald, 1983).

Miholic (1994) has developed an inventory to encourage students to think about what they do as they read. The results of such an inventory also provide teachers with insights into students' strategy use.

More information on metacognition appears in Chapter 5.

| Time for Reflection | Some teachers begin work on comprehension monitoring in the primary grades. Others believe that it is best taught beginning in the intermediate grades. **What do** *you* **think?** |

Graphic Aids

Textbooks contain numerous reading aids that children often disregard because they have had no training in how to use them. We have already discussed glossaries, footnotes, bibliographies, and appendices in this chapter, but we also need to consider graphic aids such as maps, graphs, tables, and illustrations. Teachers should explain how these aids function, model their use for the students, and provide students with supervised practice in extracting information from them. Actually making graphic aids is also a good technique to help students develop their communication abilities.

Maps

Many maps appear in social studies textbooks, and they are also sometimes found in science, mathematics, and literature books. As early as the first grade, children can begin developing skills in map reading, which they will use increasingly as they progress through school and maps appear with greater frequency in reading materials.

A first step in map reading is to examine the title (for example, "Annual Rainfall in the United States") to determine what area is being represented and what type of information is being given about the area. The teacher should emphasize the importance of determining the information conveyed by the title before moving on to a more detailed study of the map. The next step is to teach children how to determine directions by helping them to locate directional indicators on maps and to use these indicators to identify the four cardinal directions.

Interpreting the map's *legend* is the next reading task. The legend contains an explanation of each symbol used on the map, and, unless a reader can interpret these symbols, he or she will be unable to understand the information the map contains.

Learning to apply a map's *scale* is fairly difficult. Because it would be highly impractical to draw a map to the actual size of the area represented (for instance, the United States), maps show areas greatly reduced in size. The scale shows the relationship of a given distance on the map to the same distance on the earth.

Upper-elementary school students can be helped to understand about latitude and longitude, the Tropic of Cancer and the Tropic of Capricorn, the north and south poles, and the equator. Students should also become acquainted with map terms such as *hemisphere, peninsula, continent, isthmus, gulf, bay*, and many others.

Each time children look at a map of an area, the teacher should encourage them to relate it to a map of a larger area—for example, to relate a map of Tennessee to a map of the United States. This points out the position of Tennessee within the entire United States.

Students need practice in thinking critically about the information that maps can provide (Mosenthal and Kirsch, 1990). For example, the teacher may provide students with a map of the United States in the early 1800s that shows waterways, bodies of water, and population distributions and ask the students to draw conclusions about the population distributions. The effect of the bodies of water should be evident to the children.

Some suggestions for teaching map-reading skills follow. These skills are best taught when the students need to read maps for a purpose in one or more of their classes. Map skills should be immediately applied to these authentic materials after instruction takes place.

Activities

1. To teach children to apply a map's scale, help them construct a map of their classroom to a specified scale. Provide step-by-step guidance.

2. Model the use of a map's legend. Then have the children practice using the map's legend by asking them questions such as the following:
   Where is there a railroad on this map?
   Where is the state capital located?
   Where do you see a symbol for a college?
   Are there any national monuments in this area? If so, where are they?

3. Give the children a map of their county or city, and let them locate their homes on the map.

4. Give the children maps such as the one presented in Example 9.5, and have them answer questions about them.

Graphs

Graphs often appear in social studies, science, and mathematics books to clarify written explanations. Four basic types of graphs are described as follows and are illustrated in Example 9.6.

1. *Picture* graphs express quantities through pictures.

2. *Circle* or *pie* graphs show relationships of individual parts to the whole.

3. *Bar* graphs use vertical or horizontal bars to compare quantities. (Vertical bar graphs are easier to read than horizontal ones.)

4. *Line* graphs show changes in amounts.

Students can learn to discover from the graph's title what comparison is being made or information is being given (for example, time spent in various activities during the day or populations of various counties in a state), to interpret the legend of a picture graph, and to derive needed information accurately from a graph.

One of the best ways to help children learn to read graphs is to have them construct meaningful graphs (Hadaway and Young, 1994). Following are some examples of graph construction activities:

1. A picture graph showing the number of festival tickets sold by each class. One picture of a ticket could equal five tickets.

2. A circle graph showing the percentage of each day that a child spends sleeping, eating, studying, and playing.

Example 9.5 *Sample Map and Questions: Number of American Indians by Counties of the U.S., 1970*

AMERICAN INDIAN POPULATION

- 10,000 and over
- 2,500–9,999
- 100–2,499
- under 100

Questions

1. What is this map about?
   a. American Indian Tribes of the United States
   b. Number of American Indians in United States counties in 1970
   c. Number of American Indians in United States counties today

2. The example shows a main map and two inset maps. What is true about these three maps?
   a. They are all drawn to the same scale.
   b. Two of them are drawn to the same scale.
   c. They are all drawn to different scales.

3. What indicates the densest population?
   a. Solid white

   b. Gray and white stripes
   c. Solid black

4. What was the Indian population in most of Tennessee?
   a. Under 100
   b. 100–2,499
   c. 2,500–9,999

5. The Indian population in Nevada varied from what to what?
   a. 100–2,499
   b. 2,500–10,000
   c. Under 100–10,000 and over

6. In what portion of the United States was there the largest concentration of Indians?
   a. Southwest
   b. Southeast
   c. Northeast

Map Source: Rand McNally and Company. Reprinted with permission.

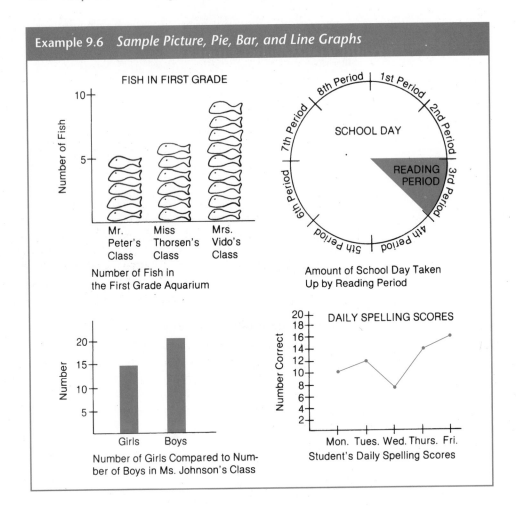

Example 9.6 *Sample Picture, Pie, Bar, and Line Graphs*

FISH IN FIRST GRADE

Number of Fish in the First Grade Aquarium

SCHOOL DAY

READING PERIOD

Amount of School Day Taken Up by Reading Period

Number of Girls Compared to Number of Boys in Ms. Johnson's Class

DAILY SPELLING SCORES

Student's Daily Spelling Scores

3. A bar graph showing the number of books read by class members each week for six weeks.

4. A line graph showing the weekly arithmetic or spelling test scores of one child over a six-week period.

Tables

Tables, which may appear in reading materials of all subject areas, may present a problem because children have trouble extracting specific facts from a large mass of available information. The great amount of information provided in the small amount of space on tables can confuse children unless the teacher provides a procedure for reading tables.

Just as the titles of maps and graphs contain information about their content, so do the titles of tables. In addition, since tables are arranged in columns and rows, the headings can provide information. To discover specific information, students must locate the intersection of an appropriate column with an appropriate row. The teacher can model reading tables, verbalizing the mental processes involved in locating the information. Then the children can be asked to read a table, such as the multiplication table shown in Example 9.7, and answer related questions. Some sample questions are provided.

Example 9.7   *Sample Table and Questions*

Questions

Multiplication Table

	1	2	3	4	5	6	7	8	9
1	1	2	3	4	5	6	7	8	9
2	2	4	6	8	10	12	14	16	18
3	3	6	9	12	15	18	21	24	27
4	4	8	12	16	20	24	28	32	36
5	5	10	15	20	25	30	35	40	45
6	6	12	18	24	30	36	42	48	54
7	7	14	21	28	35	42	49	56	63
8	8	16	24	32	40	48	56	64	72
9	9	18	27	36	45	54	63	72	81

1. What is the product of 5×6?
2. What is the product of 9×3?
3. Is the product of 5×4 the same as the product of 4×5?
4. Which number is greater: the product of 3×8 or the product of 4×7?
5. When a number is multiplied by 1, what will the product always be?
6. Why is 24 where the 4 row and the 6 column meet?
7. How do the numbers in the 2 row compare with the numbers in the 4 row?

Illustrations

Various types of illustrations, ranging from photographs to schematic diagrams, are found in textbooks. Too often children see illustrations merely as space fillers, reducing the amount of reading they will have to do on a page. As a result, they tend to pay little attention to illustrations even though illustrations are a very good source of information. A picture of a jungle, for example, may add considerably to a child's understanding of that term; a picture of an Arabian nomad may illuminate the term *Bedouin* in a history class. Diagrams of bones within the body can show a child things that cannot readily be observed firsthand.

Summary

Reading/study techniques enhance students' comprehension and retention of printed material. Study methods, such as SQ3R and SQRQCQ, can help students retain material that they read. A number of other techniques can also help children with retention.

Developing test-taking strategies can allow students to show teachers more accurately what they have learned. Students need strategies for taking objective and essay tests, and they need special strategies for standardized testing situations.

Flexible reading habits can help children study more effectively. Children need to be able to adjust their approaches to the reading and adjust their reading rates.

Children need to learn strategies for locating information in library books and textbooks, using the important parts of the books; in reference books, such as dictionaries and encyclopedias; in the library; and in computer databases. They also need to learn how to organize the information when they find it and to learn how to monitor their comprehension and retention of material (metacognition).

In addition, students need to know how to obtain information from the graphic aids found in textbooks. They must be able to read and understand maps, graphs, tables, and illustrations.

Test Yourself

True or False

_____ 1. SQ3R stands for Stimulate, Question, Read, Reason, React.

_____ 2. SQ3R is a study method useful in reading social studies and science materials.

_____ 3. SQRQCQ is a study method designed for use with mathematics textbooks.

_____ 4. Students remember material better if they are given opportunities to discuss it.

_____ 5. Study guides are of little help to retention.

_____ 6. Writing information often helps children to fix it in their memories.

_____ 7. Massed practice is preferable to spaced practice for encouraging long-term retention.

_____ 8. Students should read all reading materials at the same speed.

_____ 9. Rereading is often necessary for materials that contain a high density of facts.

_____ 10. Many content area textbooks offer glossaries of technical terms as reading aids.

_____ 11. Index practice is most effective when children use their own textbooks rather than a worksheet index that has no obvious function.

_____ 12. Elementary school students have no need to learn how to take notes, since they are not asked to use this skill until secondary school.

_____ 13. Subordination in outlines is indicated by lettering, numbering, and indentation.

_____ 14. The legend of a map tells the history of the area represented.

_____ 15. A good way to help children develop an understanding of graphs is to help them construct their own meaningful graphs.

_____ 16. Children may use newspapers, magazines, catalogues, and brochures as reference sources.

_____ 17. Teachers do not need to teach journalistic terms to elementary-level youngsters; this is a higher-level activity.

_____ 18. Using catalogues requires the ability to read charts.

_____ 19. Key words are the words that carry the important information in a sentence.

_____ 20. The ability to recognize main ideas is a prerequisite skill for outlining.

_____ 21. Guide words indicate the first two words on a dictionary page.

_____ 22. When making summaries, redundant material should be retained.

_____ 23. Some children fail to do well on essay tests because they do not understand terms like _compare_ and _contrast_.

_____ 24. Children need to practice under standardized testing conditions so that they will be familiar with the testing situation when they take a standardized test.

_____ 25. Comprehension monitoring is a skill that can be fully developed in first grade.

_____ 26. Rereading can be a useful metacognitive strategy.

For your journal...

1. Visit an elementary school library and listen as the librarian explains the reference materials and library procedures to students. In your journal, evaluate the presentation and decide how you might change it if you were responsible for it.

2. Choose a textbook from a subject area and grade level of your choice. Examine closely the material on twenty consecutive pages, and list the study skills needed to obtain information from these pages effectively.

. . . And your portfolio

1. Using materials of widely varying types, develop a procedure to help elementary students learn to be flexible in their rates of reading.

2. Choose a content area textbook at the elementary level, and plan procedures to familiarize children with the parts of the book and the reading aids the book offers.

3. Collect materials that youngsters can use as supplementary reference sources (newspapers, magazines, catalogues, brochures, etc.), and develop several short lessons to help the children read these materials effectively.

4. Make a variety of types of graphs into a display that you could use in a unit on reading graphs.

5. Collect pictures and diagrams that present information. Ask several children to study these pictures and extract as much information from them as possible. Then analyze the results.

Reading in the Content Areas

Key Vocabulary

Pay close attention to these terms when they appear in the chapter.

cloze test

content area textbook

Directed Reading-Thinking Activity (DRTA)

expository style

figurative language

frustration level

guided reading procedure (GRP)

independent level

instructional level

K-W-L teaching model

language arts

language experience approach (LEA)

narrative style

readability

study guide

SETTING OBJECTIVES

When you finish reading this chapter, you should be able to

▶ Use a cloze test to determine the difficulty of written materials.

▶ Identify some readability formulas that you can use to assess the difficulty of written materials.

▶ Describe several general techniques for helping students read content area materials.

▶ Describe some procedures and materials that are helpful in presenting material in language arts, social studies, mathematics, and science and health books.

Chapter 10 Organization

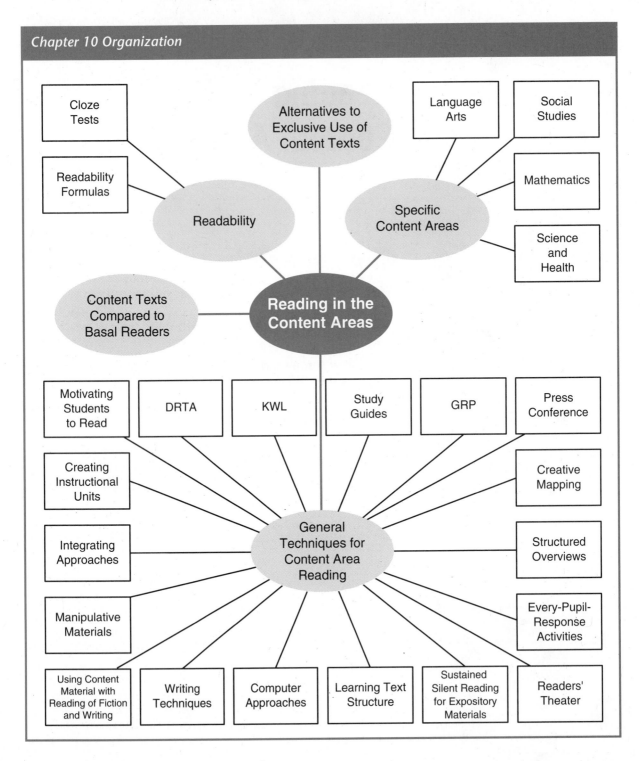

Reading in content area textbooks, such as those for social studies, science, mathematics, and other curricular areas, is often difficult for students. Content textbooks contain *expository* (explanatory) material that can be harder for children to read than *narrative* (story) material. They also contain many new concepts (Olson and Gee, 1991).

To read well in content area textbooks, children need good general reading strategies, including word recognition and comprehension, and reading/study strategies. If they cannot recognize the words they encounter, they will be unable to take in the information from the material. Without good literal, interpretive, critical, and creative reading comprehension strategies, they will not understand the textbook's message. And if they lack good reading/study strategies, they will be less likely to comprehend and retain the material.

Reading strategies are often initially acquired in reading class. Because content area books present special reading problems, however, teachers should be aware that simply offering their students instruction in basal readers during reading class, even though today's basal readers contain more content-oriented text, is not sufficient if the children are to read well in content area texts and nonfiction trade books. These trade books (library books) are used to supplement the curriculum in some classes and as the core of the curriculum in others. Special help with content area reading, at the time children are expected to do such reading, is important, for this is when children most effectively learn how to apply the strategies and techniques. Classrooms in which the teachers integrate learning activities across the curriculum (as in whole language classrooms), rather than scheduling separate periods for language, science, social studies, and so on, will offer opportunities throughout the day to help children read and comprehend the expository texts generally used in content areas.

Because of the special challenges posed by reading in content area textbooks, teachers often use concrete manipulatives (such as maps and pictures) to develop concepts, require retellings of text material, and have students summarize the material to check understanding. The teachers encourage students to visualize information and brainstorm about the topics, and they often provide narratives on the same topic and use audio or computer materials to aid comprehension. Semantic mapping of the main topic, use of the K-W-L procedure, and use of expository paragraph frames are other good techniques (Olson and Gee, 1991).

This chapter examines several content areas—language arts, social studies, mathematics, and science and health—along with their specific reading difficulties and activities to promote readiness and good comprehension. In addition, it presents general content area reading strategies to use in conjunction with the many strategies already described in Chapters 5 and 6 as comprehension aids in reading content area material.

Content Texts Compared to Basal Readers

Large portions of basal readers are written in a narrative style that describes the actions of people in particular situations. They do not present the density of ideas typical of content textbooks, which are generally written in an expository style, with heavy concentrations of facts. Children find narrative material easier to read than expository material. Basal reader selections often have entertaining plots that children can read for enjoyment. Content selections rarely offer this enticement.

Many children are unfamiliar with the organizational structures of expository texts. Therefore, students are left without a predictable structure to use when they are asked to read such materials (Beck and McKeown, 1991).

Students must give attention to each sentence in a content book, for nearly every one will carry important information that they must acquire before they can understand later passages. This is rarely true of basal readers, in which each selection is generally a discrete entity.

Not only are content textbooks (with the exception of many literature books) generally more difficult to read than basal readers, but in content areas teachers and students use many supplementary materials, some of which have been prepared as trade books, not textbooks. Whereas basal readers often have planned repetition of key words to encourage their acquisition, content area texts present many new concepts and vocabulary terms with little planned repetition. All of the content areas have specialized and technical vocabularies that students must acquire. Generally, basal readers contain little specialized or technical vocabulary. (See Chapter 4 for a discussion of specialized and technical vocabulary.)

Content textbooks contain a large number of graphic aids that students must interpret, whereas basal readers contain much smaller numbers of these aids. The illustrations in basal readers above first-grade level are included primarily for interest value, but those in content books are designed to help clarify concepts and need to be studied carefully.

Whereas content area textbooks have abundant headings that signal the organization of the selection, few such headings are used in basal readers, and the ones that are used are less informative than those in the content books. In reading content books, children should be helped to see that in many cases the headings outline the material for them, indicating main ideas and supporting details.

Readability

The teacher's first step in helping children to read content material is to be aware of the level of difficulty of the textbook assignments they make. Teachers must adjust their expectations for each student according to that student's reading ability, so that no child is assigned work in a book on his or her *frustration level*—that is, the level at which the material is so difficult that it will immediately be frustrating and the student will be unable to comprehend it. Trying to read from a book that is too hard for them can prevent students from learning the content. If children are forced to try to read a book at this difficulty level, they may develop negative attitudes toward the subject, the teacher, and even school in general. Students will probably learn best from printed material that is written on their *independent levels*, or the levels at which they read with ease and comprehension. They can also learn from textbooks written on their *instructional levels*, or the levels at which they read with understanding when given sufficient help by the teacher. (See Chapter 12 for further discussion of independent, instructional, and frustration levels.)

Cloze Tests

One way for the teacher to estimate the suitability of a textbook for students is to construct and administer a *cloze test*. The procedure for doing this follows:

1. Select a passage of approximately 250 consecutive words from the textbook. The passage should be one the students have not read, or tried to read, before.

2. Type the passage, leaving the first sentence intact and deleting every fifth word thereafter. In place of deleted words, substitute blanks of uniform length.

3. Give students the passage and tell them to fill in the blanks. Allow them all the time they need.

4. Score the test by counting as correct only the exact words that were in the original text. Determine each student's percentage of correct answers. If a student had less than 44 percent of the answers correct, the material is probably at his or her frustration level and is therefore too difficult. Thus, you should offer alternative ways of learning the material. If the student had from 44 to 57 percent of the answers correct, the material is probably at that student's instructional level, and he or she will be able to learn from the text if you provide careful guidance in the reading by developing readiness, helping with new concepts and unfamiliar vocabulary, and providing reading purposes to aid comprehension. If the student had more than 57 percent of the answers correct, the material is probably at that student's independent level, and he or she should be able to benefit from the material when reading it independently (Bormuth, 1968).

A teacher using the percentages given here must count *only* exact words as correct, since the percentages were derived using only exact words. Synonyms must be counted as incorrect, along with obviously wrong answers and unfilled blanks.

Because all the material in a given textbook is unlikely to be written on the same level, teachers should choose several samples for a cloze test from several places in the book in order to determine the book's suitability for a particular child.

Example 10.1 shows a cloze passage for a social studies textbook. This passage contains 283 words. No words have been deleted from the first sentence in order to give the student an opportunity to develop an appropriate mental set for the material that follows, and the entire paragraph in which the fiftieth blank occurs has been included in order to complete the thought that was in progress. A score of fewer than 22 correct responses indicates that the material is too difficult; a score of 22 to 28 indicates that the child can manage the material if the teacher gives assistance; and a score of more than 28 indicates that the child can read the material independently.

Some authorities prefer cloze tests to informal reading inventories, or IRIs (see Chapter 12 for a discussion of IRIs), for matching textbooks to students because these tests put the child in direct contact with the author's language without having the teacher as a mediator (through the written questions). Frequently a child can understand the text but not the teacher's questions related to it, which can cause the teacher to underestimate the child's comprehension of the material. On the other hand, some children react with frustration to cloze materials; these children would fare better if tested with an IRI. Children should have experience with cloze-type exercises before teachers use this procedure to help match students with the appropriate levels of textbooks.

Example 10.1   *Cloze Passage*

Directions: Read the following passage and fill in each blank with a word that makes sense in the sentence.

The first battle in July 1861 began like a holiday outing. Union supporters packed picnic _____ and (1)
followed soldiers from _____, D.C., into Virginia. Newspaper _____ also came to get _____ story. (2) (3) (4)
Armies from the _____ and the South met _____ a stream called Bull _____, about 25 miles (5) (6) (7)
from _____, D.C. At first Confederates _____ the Union soldiers back. _____ the Confederates (8) (9) (10)
attacked. Fierce _____ broke out, and the _____ army won the battle. (11) (12)

_____ Battle of Bull Run _____ the North that it _____ not win the war _____. Congress (13) (14) (15) (16)
passed laws calling _____ troops to serve three _____. President Lincoln's generals had _____ plan (17) (18) (19)
to save the _____. The Union's "anaconda plan" _____ named for the snake _____ squeezes its (20) (21) (22)
prey to _____. The Union planned to _____ the strength out of _____ South by a blockade, (23) (24) (25)
_____ closing of southern ocean _____. Union ships would stop _____ and keep Southerners from (26) (27) (28)
_____ money by selling cotton _____ other countries. (29) (30)

Under the _____ plan, Union ships would _____ control of the Mississippi _____. Confederate (31) (32) (33)
states would then _____ unable to send boats _____ supplies and soldiers to _____ Confederate (34) (35) (36)
states. Finally, Union _____ would try to capture _____, the Confederate capital. (37) (38)

Example 10.1 *Cloze Passage (cont.)*

The _____ also had plans. One _____ to destroy Union ships. _____1862, the South sent
(39)   (40)   (41)
_____ iron-sided steamship, *Merrimack*, up _____James River. (The South _____ the ship the
(42)   (43)   (44)
Virginia.) _____ *Merrimack* was far stronger _____ the Union's wooden ships. _____ Union ships
(45)   (46)   (47)
fired at _____, the cannonballs could not _____ the ship's sides.
(48)   (49)

The _____ day, the Union sent its own iron ship, the *Monitor*, to attack the *Merrimack*. The two ships
(50)

battled, with no clear winner.

Answers: (1) lunches (2) Washington (3) reporters (4) the (5) North (6) near (7) Run (8) Washington
(9) held (10) Then (11) fighting (12) Confederate (13) The (14) showed (15) would (16) easily (17) for
(18) years (19) a (20) Union (21) was (22) that (23) death (24) squeeze (25) the (26) or (27) ports
(28) supplies (29) earning (30) to (31) anaconda (32) take (33) River (34) be (35) with (36) other
(37) forces (38) Richmond (39) South (40) was (41) In (42) its (43) the (44) renamed (45) The (46) than
(47) When (48) it (49) pierce (50) next

After determining each student's ability to benefit from the class textbook, the teacher has the information needed to make instructional decisions. Those students who are on the independent level will be able to read textbook assignments and prepare for class discussion independently and will often be able to set their own purpose questions to direct their reading. Those who are at an instructional level will need to have the teacher introduce material carefully, build concepts and vocabulary gradually, and assign purpose questions. Those who are at a frustration level on the material will need to be introduced to the subject and, in order to understand the concepts and information involved, be given some simpler materials with a lower readability level than that of the text.

All students can participate together in discussing the material, and the teacher can record significant contributions on the board in the same way as in recording a language experience story. (Detailed discussions of the language experience approach appear later in this chapter and in Chapter 7.) When the teacher asks students to read the contributions from the board at the end of the discussion period, even poor readers may be able to read fairly difficult contributions because they have heard the sentences being dictated and have seen them being written down. Before the next class, the teacher can duplicate the class summary for each student to use in reviewing for tests. During study periods, he or she can help the children who are at their frustration levels to reread the notes, emphasizing the new words and concepts.

Readability Formulas

When teachers have determined the students' reading levels with tests, they can obtain an approximate idea of whether a textbook is appropriate by testing it with a standard measure of readability. Among widely used readability formulas, the *Spache Readability Formula* is designed for primary-grade books (Spache, 1966), the *Dale-Chall Readability Formula* is designed for materials from the fourth-grade through college levels (Dale and Chall, 1948), and the *Fry Readability Graph* (Fry, 1977) can be used on material at all levels.

Because readability formulas are strictly text based, they do not give information related to the interactive nature of reading. For example, they cannot gauge a reader's background knowledge about the topic, motivation to read the material, or interest in the topic, although these are important factors in determining the difficulty of a text for a particular child. In addition, they cannot separate reasonable prose from a series of unconnected words (Rush, 1985). They cannot measure the effects of an author's writing style or the complexity of concepts presented, and they do not consider the format of the material (typeface and type size, spacing, amount of white space on the page, and so on). For these reasons, no formula offers more than an approximation of level of difficulty for material. Formulas do, however, generally give reliable information about the relative difficulty levels of textbook passages and other printed materials, and this information can be extremely helpful to teachers. Example 10.2 shows a quick way to estimate readability.

Computer programs designed to test readability can ease the burden of making calculations by hand. A number of grammar and style checkers, such as *Grammatik* (Reference Software International), run several formulas.

Not only are many content area textbooks written at much higher readability levels than basal readers for the corresponding grades, but subject matter textbooks also often vary in difficulty from chapter to chapter. If teachers are aware of various levels of difficulty within a text, they can adjust teaching methods to help students gain the most from each portion of the book, perhaps by teaching easier chapters earlier in the year and more difficult chapters later on. Of course, this technique is not advisable for teaching material in which the concepts in an early, difficult chapter are necessary for understanding a later, easier chapter.

A good way to decrease the readability levels of content passages for students is to teach the content vocabulary thoroughly before the material containing that vocabulary is assigned to be read. The more unfamiliar content vocabulary is a major factor in the higher difficulty levels of many content area materials.

| Time for Reflection | Some teachers feel that because readability formulas do not take into consideration all factors involved in determining the difficulty of a text, they are not useful. Others feel that being able to determine relative difficulty of various passages is useful in planning instruction. What do *you* think? |

Example 10.2 *Graph for Estimating Readability*

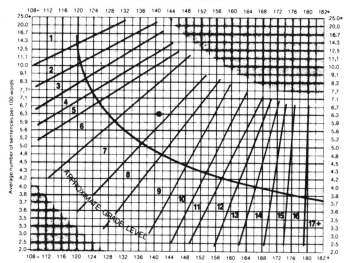

Expanded Directions for Working Readability Graph

1. Randomly select three (3) sample passages and count out exactly 100 words each, beginning with the beginning of a sentence. Do count proper nouns, initializations, and numerals.
2. Count the number of sentences in the hundred words, estimating length of the fraction of the last sentence to the nearest one-tenth.
3. Count the total number of syllables in the 100-word passage. If you don't have a hand counter available, an easy way is to simply put a mark above every syllable over one in each word, then when you get to the end of the passage, count the number of marks and add 100. Small calculators can also be used as counters by pushing numeral 1, then push the + sign for each word or syllable when counting.
4. Enter graph with *average* sentence length and *average* number of syllables; plot dot where the two lines intersect. Area where dot is plotted will give you the approximate grade level.
5. If a great deal of variability is found in syllable count or sentence count, putting more samples into the average is desirable.
6. A word is defined as a group of symbols with a space on either side; thus, *Joe, IRA, 1945,* and *&* are each one word.
7. A syllable is defined as a phonetic syllable. Generally, there are as many syllables as vowel sounds. For example, *stopped* is one syllable and *wanted* is two syllables. When counting syllables for numerals and initializations, count one syllable for each symbol. For example, *1945* is four syllables, *IRA* is three syllables, and *&* is one syllable.

Note: This "extended graph" does not outmode or render the earlier (1968) version inoperative or inaccurate; it is an extension. (REPRODUCTION PERMITTED—NO COPYRIGHT)

Source: "Fry's Readability Graph: Clarifications, Validity, and Extension to Level 17," *Journal of Reading,* 21 (December 1977), 249.

Alternatives to Exclusive Use of Content Texts

Some students find textbooks difficult to read or are unmotivated to read them because they find them dull and dry. For such students, supplementary trade books offer one viable option for learning content area material (Moss, 1991). Many children experience their first serious difficulties with reading as they begin reading textbooks, but the continued use of high-interest trade books along with textbooks may ease the transition. In selecting and using appropriate trade books, teachers should follow certain steps: identify concepts for further development; locate suitable trade books to help teach these concepts; present books to students by reading them aloud or making copies available for independent reading prior to textbook assignments; use trade books during and after reading of the text to extend concept acquisition; and provide follow-up activities in the forms of creative writing, drama, and interviewing (Brozo and Tomlinson, 1986).

By using nonfiction trade books to enhance the study of topics in the students' textbooks, regardless of whether or not the students have trouble reading the textbooks, teachers can help students learn more about the content. This practice is common in whole language classrooms, as well as many others. Trade books can be chosen to coincide with students' reading levels, easing one typical problem. These books can be visually appealing to students and, therefore, can arouse their interest. They can also cover a topic in greater depth than the length limits of a textbook would allow, and they frequently have very coherent organizational patterns. Newer books ensure access to timely information (Moss, 1991).

General Techniques for Content Area Reading

When working with students who are reading in the content areas, teachers should do many of the things suggested in earlier chapters for directing the reading of any material, such as developing vocabulary knowledge, activating background knowledge about the topic, and providing purposes for reading. They should also suggest use of a study method, such as SQ3R or another appropriate one, encourage note taking, and provide suggestions to promote retention of the material. (Information about these activities appears in Chapters 4, 5, 6, and 9.) Teachers may also use a number of other techniques, such as the ones in this section, to help their students read in content areas more effectively.

Motivating Students to Read

Mathison (1989) has found that teachers can stimulate interest in reading content area materials in a number of ways. Two strategies are using analogies to help give new ideas familiar connections and telling personal anecdotes that can help personalize reading material. For example, study of arteries and veins in a sixth-grade class could be motivated by drawing an analogy to roads leading into the downtown area; or, in a study of a particular climate, the teacher might share a personal anecdote about a camping trip in such a climate. Teachers should examine each reading assignment for possibilities for motivational introductions. Glynn (1996) also suggests ways to use analogies in science instruction.

Stories can help children see the connections that exist among people across time and from different places because of common needs people share. The participation in storytelling sessions helps the students develop shared experiences that create bonds among classmates (Combs and Beach, 1994). Such bonds allow the students to cooperate more freely as they work toward common goals in the classroom.

Directed Reading-Thinking Activity (DRTA)

The *Directed Reading-Thinking Activity (DRTA)* can be used to direct children's reading of either basal reader stories or content area selections. (A complete discussion of the DRTA is found in Chapter 7.) As Harp (1989) points out, in this activity students predict, read, and prove predictions as the teacher asks them what they think, why they think that, and how they can prove their points.

K-W-L Teaching Model

Ogle (1986, 1989) has devised what she calls the *K-W-L teaching model* for expository text. The *K* stands for "What I *Know*," the *W* for "What I *Want* to Learn," and the *L* for "What I *Learned*." In the first step the teacher and the students discuss what the group already knows about the topic of the reading material. The teacher may ask the students where they learned what they know or how they could verify the information. Students may also be asked to think of categories of information that they expect to find in the material they are about to read. The second step involves class discussion of what the students want to learn. The teacher may point out disagreements about the things that the students think they already know and may call attention to gaps in their knowledge. Then each student writes down personal questions to be answered by the reading. Students then read the material. After they have finished reading, they record what they have learned from the reading. If the reading did not answer all of their personal questions, students can be directed to other sources for the answers. (Example 10.3 shows a K-W-L study sheet that was filled out by a fourth-grade girl who was working with teacher Gail Hyder.) Weissman (1996) adapts paragraph frames (as described in the section "Learning Text Structure" in this chapter) to help her first graders complete the "What I Learned" step of the K-W-L, and Sippola (1995) adds a column labeled "What I Still Need to Learn" to the original three columns.

Study Guides

Study guides are prepared by the teacher to guide expository reading in content fields. They can set purposes for reading, as well as provide aids for interpreting

Example 10.3 *Completed K-W-L Sheet*

K - W - L   Welcome to the Green House   by: Jane Yolen

What I <u>Know</u>	What I <u>Want</u> to Know	What I <u>Learned</u>
a lot of animal live there.	What kind of animal live there.	butter flys, snakes, frogs, bats, fish, bees,
Plant live there.	What kind of plants grow there.	wild pigs, tamarin toucan, herons, Ocelot, lizirds,
A Green house is very hot.	How hot it is in there.	humingbirds, sloth.
		<u>flowers</u>
		crimson,
		orchid
		trees, vines
		lianas, very hot
		A wet house,

Source: Stephanie Hunsucker, fourth grade, Crossville, Tennessee.

material through suggestions about how to apply reading strategies. These guides also serve as vehicles for group discussions and cooperative learning activities. Discussion of the questions or items after reading the material is very important to the learning process. Mikel (1993) believes that teaching content subjects through use of cooperative learning groups increases the students' learning. There are many kinds of study guides, and the nature of the material and the reason for reading it can help teachers determine which kind to use.

Content-process guides, as shown in Example 10.4, focus on both the content and process aspects of reading. The study guide in Example 10.4 directs students' reading in the following way. First, the overview question offers an overall purpose for the reading, helping students read the material with the appropriate mental set. The first item after the overview question gives students content purposes for reading the first section. Notice that the questions are phrased to elicit thought about the information in the passage. Following the purposes are two

Example 10.4   *Sample Selection and Study Guide*

[Note: The material in this passage is part of a discussion of the Seven Years' War.]

The Proclamation of 1763   With the French defeat, many colonists eagerly prepared to move across the Appalachian Mountains. However, the British were worried. They knew that new settlements would anger the Iroquois, Delaware, Shawnee, and other Indian tribes who already lived there. To prevent fighting, the British issued the Proclamation of 1763. This act saved all land west of the Appalachians for Indians. Colonists could not settle there.

The Proclamation upset many colonists. Earlier, the French had blocked new settlements. The French had been defeated. Now, though, the British also stopped people from moving west. Many colonists wondered why they had fought the war.

The Cost of Victory   Colonial anger at Britain's Proclamation of 1763 was just one hardship the war caused. The British, the Indians, and the colonists each faced new troubles.

In Britain, the war had caused the government to borrow money. Between 1754 and 1763, the money Britain owed doubled. The country needed money to pay back its many loans.

Britain also had to pay the 10,000 soldiers it sent to North America. These troops were needed to protect the large new British empire. Britain now had to spend three times as much to defend its American empire as it did before the war.

For many Indian tribes, the war brought a loss of power. They could no longer use the French to help them against the British. And even 10,000 British soldiers could not stop settlers from moving onto Indian lands.

In the colonies, the war caused great suffering. Boston, a city of about 2,200 families, lost 700 men during the war. These deaths left many widows and orphans who needed help just to buy food.

Source: From *America Will Be* in *Houghton Mifflin Social Studies* by Armento, et al. Copyright 1994 by Houghton Mifflin Company. Reprinted by permission of Houghton Mifflin Company. All rights reserved.

Study Guide

Overview Question: What were the effects of the war on the people of America and Great Britain?

   1. Read the section titled "The Proclamation of 1763" to find out what effect this action had on the colonists. Were the colonists pleased with the effect? How can you tell?

       What is a settlement? What is a proclamation? If you don't know, locate the root words to help you figure this out.

Example 10.4 *Sample Selection and Study Guide (cont.)*

---

2. Read the section titled "The Cost of Victory" to discover other hardships the war caused. Look for hardships faced by the British, the Indian tribes, and the people of the colonies.

What is a synonym for *hardship*? Look for a context clue to this word's meaning.

---

questions about vocabulary meanings. The students are encouraged to use their skills in structural analysis to help them understand the vocabulary presented. This is process guidance. The second item offers purposes for reading the second main section. Notice that it specifies the groups under consideration. It is followed by a vocabulary question and a process suggestion to use context clues.

Pattern guides are study guides that stress the relationship among the organizational structure, the reading/thinking skills needed for comprehension, and the important concepts in the material. The first step in constructing such a guide is to identify the important concepts in the material. Then information about each concept must be located within the selection, and the author's organizational pattern must be identified. The teacher then integrates the identified concepts, the writing pattern, and the skills necessary for reading the material with understanding in a guide that offers as much direction as specific students need— whether it be the section of text in which the information is located; the page number; or the page, paragraph, and line numbers.

Conrad (1989) found that her students were able to work more effectively with cause-and-effect relationships if the effects were listed on the left side of the page and the causes on the right side. She believed this was because students tend to want to tell what happened and then add a *because* phrase. Example 10.5 shows a completed complex cause-and-effect pattern guide that also has an implicit comparison-contrast element, since effects on three populations are compared. This pattern guide is based on the text selection in Example 10.4. The guide had the two causes listed for the students, and they had to fill in the multiple effects.

Anticipation guides, which are used before reading a selection, require students to react to a series of statements related to the selection to be read. The children can react to the anticipation guide again when they have finished reading to see the differences, if any, between their initial opinions and the correct responses. When the teacher asks for responses both before and after reading, the guide is often referred to as an anticipation/reaction guide.

The statements in an anticipation guide should relate to major concepts and significant details in the reading material. They may reflect common misconceptions about the topic, challenging students' beliefs. They should link students' prior knowledge with text concepts, and they should be general (Duffelmeyer,

Example 10.5 *Cause-and-Effect Pattern Guide*			
Causes	**Effects**		
	On British	**On Indians**	**On Colonists**
Proclamation of 1763	Drew colonists' anger	Land west of Appalachians saved for them	Denied right to settle on land west of Appalachians
Seven Years' War	Needed money to pay back loans Had to pay larger numbers of soldiers	Loss of power Not enough British soldiers to keep settlers off of their lands	Widows and orphans who needed help to buy food

1994). The guide may be used in a group setting, with students discussing and justifying their responses (Wood and Mateja, 1983). See Chapter 5 for an example of an anticipation/reaction guide.

Duffelmeyer and Baum (1992) suggest extending the anticipation guide by having students decide if the text supported each of their choices and having them indicate why their choices were correct or incorrect by citing evidence from the text. This seems to be a good addition to the procedure. Merkley (1996/1997) suggests adding a prereading "I'm Not Sure" option to the "True and False" or "Yes and No" choices if the questions involve factual information. In postreading use of the items, "I'm Not Sure" should no longer be an option.

Guided Reading Procedure

Anthony Manzo's *guided reading procedure (GRP)*, designed to help readers improve organizational skills, comprehension, and recall, is appropriate for content area reading at any level. The steps in the procedure follow:

1. Set a purpose for reading a selection of about 500 words, and tell the children to remember all they can. Tell them to close their books when they finish reading.

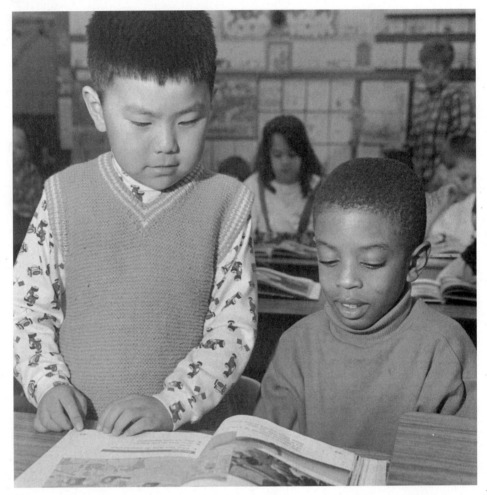

These first graders, who are looking at a book about Martin Luther King, illustrate how even young children become involved in content area reading. (© *Joseph Schuyler/ Stock Boston*)

2. Have the students tell everything they remember from the material, and record this information on the board.

3. Ask students to look at the selection again to correct or add to the information they have already offered.

4. Direct the children to organize the information in an outline (see Chapter 9), semantic web (see Chapter 5), or some other arrangement.

5. Ask synthesizing questions to help students integrate the new material with previously acquired information.

6. Give a test immediately to check on the children's short-term recall.

7. Give another form of the test later to check medium- or long-term recall (Ankney and McClurg, 1981).

Press Conference

Press Conference is a strategy in which some students take the parts of characters in material that has been read (literature, science, social studies, current events) and others take the parts of reporters interviewing the characters. The interviews must have carefully planned questions, and the interviewers must take detailed notes from which they compose news stories about the interviewees and/or the events in which they have been involved. These stories are taken through a process writing approach, and the final versions are published in a class newspaper (Dever, 1992).

Creative Mapping

Naughton (1993/1994) suggests *creative mapping* to enhance content area reading. Creative mapping combines semantic mapping with pictures to display material in a way that helps students see relationships and also helps them recall it.

First, a picture that represents the topic or main idea is drawn. Then supporting details are arranged on or around the image in an organized manner. Students draw on background knowledge and the text to complete the map.

Structured Overviews

Structured overviews of the vocabulary from a content area reading assignment can help students learn the terms and concepts. At first, the teacher can present an overview on an overhead projector, with students answering questions about how the vocabulary is related to the concepts in the assignment as the overview is developed in front of them, or the overview can be placed on strips on the bulletin board. Later the students can work cooperatively in small groups to form overviews or they can make individual overviews from a chapter they read (Wolfe and Lopez, 1992/1993).

Every-Pupil-Response Activities

Gaskins and her colleagues (1994) found that use of *every-pupil-response activities*, such as engaging in written responses to text, facilitated participation in discussion about the text. These responses were not graded, but were used to help students assess their own understanding of the text and sometimes of its organizational structure. Partner discussions followed the writing and in turn were followed by whole-class discussions. The students helped one another to clarify their understandings and to see alternate interpretations.

Teachers reminded the students to support their positions with evidence from the text. Teachers also presented the students with real-life problems to which they could apply information from the text, eliciting enthusiastic small-group discussions. They talked about the strategies that would best fit the solution of the particular problem, why these strategies should help, when they should be used, and how to use them. Teachers modeled strategy use for the students before asking them to participate in guided practice.

Readers' Theater

Young and Vardell (1993) suggest using *readers' theater* (a dramatic reading of a text in parts by two or more readers) with nonfiction trade books to increase active involvement with the material and add to enjoyment of it. Books with dialogue are especially easy to adapt to readers' theater scripts. Some other types of text may be rewritten as dialogue, or multiple narrators may be assigned. Prologues may be added to introduce the material in the scripts, and/or postscripts may be added to bring some scripts to a close. Students should have an active part in developing the scripts, making their production as much of a learning experience as the performances. Suggestions of books to use include David M. Schwartz's *How Much Is a Million?* for math; Joanna Cole's books about the magic school bus for science; and Joan Anderson's *The First Thanksgiving Feast*, Russell Freedman's *Buffalo Hunt*, and Jean Fritz's *And Then What Happened, Paul Revere?* for social studies.

Sustained Silent Reading (SSR) for Expository Materials

In regular sustained silent reading periods, children have free choice of materials to read, and they generally choose narrative materials. Joranko (1990) has a separate SSR period for her intermediate-grade students for reading in expository materials, to expose them to these materials in a self-selection situation on a regular basis. This approach should help students become familiar with many expository text structures without the pressure that accompanies assigned reading.

Learning Text Structure

Many students do not use text structure to help them comprehend and retain information from content area textbooks, but research has shown that text structure can be taught (McGee and Richgels, 1985). Systematic attention to clues about the organizational structure of a text and creation of visual representations of the relationships among ideas aid both comprehension and retention (Pearson and Fielding, 1991). Five of the more common expository text structures are cause/effect, comparison/contrast, problem/solution, description, and collection. Use of description and use of collection (a series of descriptions about a topic presented together) are more common in elementary-level texts than are the other three types.

Using graphic organizers (such as webs), teachers can show how passages with the same text structure can have different content. Then they can prepare a graphic organizer for each structure to be taught. Focusing on one structure at a time, they can present students with the graphic organizer for a passage and have them construct a passage based on this organizer (see the section "Webs Plus Writing" in this chapter), which will include appropriate clue words, such as *because, different from,* and so forth. Teachers should emphasize how the clue words help both readers and writers. After revising and refining their passages, students can compare them with the passage on which the graphic organizer was based (McGee and Richgels, 1985).

Hadaway and Young (1994) encourage the use of visual representations to help students grasp organization and content. They suggest the use of index cards to assist in the construction of time lines, especially when multiple sources are used. Venn diagrams can help students see common elements of concepts and can help them visualize similarities and differences in order to make comparisons and contrasts. Flow charts help students visualize a sequence of events, such as the sequence of steps in a science experiment.

Maps of the content may be used before, during, and/or after students read it. (See Chapter 5 for a discussion and some examples of semantic mapping.) Sometimes the teacher can construct the maps, and at other times students can do so (Flood, 1986). The teacher should also ask appropriate questions before, during, and after reading. (See Chapter 6 for a discussion of questioning techniques.)

Another way to work on students' knowledge of text structure is through use of expository paragraph frames. *Expository paragraph frames* are similar to the story frames described in Chapter 5. They provide sentence starters that include signal words or phrases to fit the paragraph organization. The sequential pattern appears to be an easy one for young children to recognize and use (Cudd and Roberts, 1989). The teacher can write a sequential paragraph that uses the cue words for sequence: *first, next, then, finally.* The sentences can be copied on sentence strips, the sequential nature of the material can be discussed in the group, and the students can be asked to arrange the sentences in sequential order in a pocket chart. The children can read the arranged sentences together. Then they can arrange the sentences individually and copy them on their papers in paragraph form. Finally, they can illustrate the information. The teacher can show the children a frame with the signal words and model filling in the frame with responses elicited from students. At this point, the meanings of signal words can be clarified.

Any expository structure can be used with appropriate frames. Cudd and Roberts (1989) suggest the use of two types of reaction frames that are elaborations of enumeration frames. One type leads the children to tie prior knowledge to new information; for example,

Before I started reading about trucks, I knew _____

_____ .

In the book I read, I learned that _____ .

I also learned _____ . The thing that surprised

me most was _____ .

Cairney (1990) says that these frames provide probes that encourage text recall. Lewis and her colleagues (1994) have found sequential, enumeration, comparison, contrast, and reaction frames to work well. They also have had success with getting children to draw pictures depicting sequential text after they read, but before they write about the material; having them transform the information in the text into a graphic form (for example, a chart or a map); and having them rewrite material in another genre, such as a job advertisement.

Computer Approaches

Dowd and Sinatra (1990) point out that there are three kinds of computer software designed to help students learn about text structure. One type models the different text structures, then has the students write something based on the model. Another type includes interactive/prompt tutorials on particular types of discourse. Some of these allow students to write working outlines for papers; and others allow students to process a complete draft, revise it, and edit it. The last type lets students use their knowledge of text structure to do real-life activities requiring use of that knowledge, such as writing a class newspaper.

World Classroom is a global online computer education network over which students can discuss curricular projects for the content areas with peers around the world. There are projects for science, social studies, language arts, and world events. To subscribe to this resource, a teacher needs a modem, communications software, and access to a telephone line (Wepner, 1993).

Wepner (1992) has described cross-curricular units on endangered species, which use books, software, magazines, and musical recordings. Some teachers overlook software when planning thematic units. Wepner (1992) makes suggestions for using technology with a variety of content area units.

Writing Techniques

A number of writing techniques may be used to advantage in helping students learn to read effectively in the content areas. Probably the best known is the language experience approach. Others include feature analysis plus writing, webs plus writing, and keeping learning logs.

Language Experience Approach (LEA)

The *language experience approach (LEA)* is a good basic method to use in content area teaching (Jones and Nessel, 1985). Expository text structure can be taught through the LEA (Kinney, 1985). For example, a teacher who wishes to have students learn the comparison-and-contrast pattern of writing can have them discuss how two objects are alike and different, make a chart showing the likenesses and differences, and dictate a story based on the chart. The teacher can ask first for likenesses and then for differences as the dictation takes place. Then the children can use their own story to locate the two related parts of a contrast and do other activities related to the structure. (This chapter contains several examples of applying the language experience approach to specific content areas to promote learning of the content.)

In social studies and science classes, students can be encouraged to observe things around them, record their observations (in pictures or writing), and associate what they observe with their past experiences and prior knowledge. When students keep observation notebooks, the teacher can lead them to draw conclusions about word parts in words chosen from their notebooks, thereby allowing them to work with words they can already identify. This enhances students' decoding skills while they are engaged in content learning (Sullivan, 1986).

Feature Analysis Plus Writing

A *feature matrix* can be helpful for gathering, comparing, and contrasting information about several items in the same category (Cunningham and Cunningham, 1987). The teacher first reads through the material and selects the members of the category and some features that some, all, or none of them have. Then he or she forms them into a matrix like the one in Example 10.6 and displays the matrix to the class. The students fill in the matrix in the same way that the semantic feature analysis chart in Chapter 4 was completed, leaving blanks when they are unsure about a feature. Then the students read the assigned material to confirm or revise their original markings and to fill in any empty spaces. They are encouraged to erase and change marks if the information they read refutes initial ideas. During class discussion following the reading, the students and teacher complete the class matrix cooperatively. If there is disagreement, students return to the text to find support for their positions. Some points may require library research.

Example 10.6 *Semantic Feature Matrix for Geometric Shapes*

	Straight lines	Curved lines	Four sides	Three sides	All sides must be equal in length
Triangle Rectangle Circle Square					

The information on the feature matrix can then be used as a basis for writing about the reading material. For instance, in Example 10.6, the teacher can choose one geometric shape and can model the writing of a paragraph about it. Students and teacher can then cooperatively write another paragraph about another shape. Then each student or small group of students may choose other shapes to write about. (Note that the matrix can be expanded to include many more shapes and features.) Using the information from a feature matrix for paragraph writing promotes retention of information covered in the matrix.

Webs Plus Writing

Webs are useful organizers in the content areas (Cunningham and Cunningham, 1987). Before the reading of the content material, the teacher records the information the students think they know about the topic of the chapter in the form of a web like the one shown in Example 10.7.

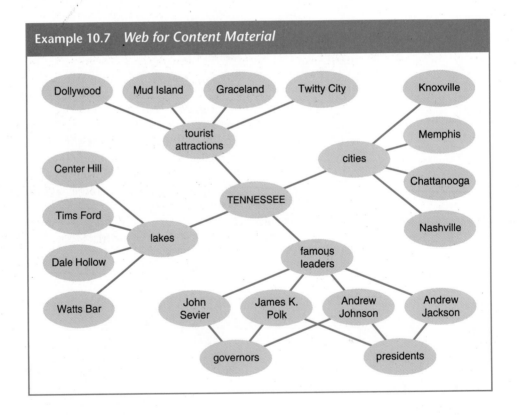

Example 10.7 *Web for Content Material*

The students may make individual webs, containing only the points they think are correct. Then they read the material, checking the information on the web and adding the new information they find. In class discussion following the reading, the class web is revised and disagreements are settled by consulting the text. The class can write paragraphs about different strands of the web—for example, about famous leaders from Tennessee.

Keeping Learning Logs

Using *learning logs* or journals to promote content area learning is a very effective technique. Students can follow the reading or discussion of a content topic with written summaries, comments, or questions related to the reading or class discussion. The content teacher can read the comments and adjust future lessons in response to the degree of understanding or confusion reflected in the logs (Gauthier, 1991).

Using Content Material with Reading of Fiction and Writing

Ollmann (1991) suggests using content material in the prereading phase to prepare students for reading literature that involves content concepts. The prereading of factual material may be accompanied by attention to the strategies needed to read the preliminary factual material that will help students understand the literature selection. Encyclopedia articles, travel magazines and brochures, *National Geographic*, or other material can often provide background information related to the setting or to scientific concepts involved in the stories. When the prereading material is being examined, the teacher can emphasize such strategies as skimming, scanning, use of alphabetical order and guide words, and others in a realistic setting.

Besides reading factual content material, students can read poems and other literature related to the content, think about the content from an aesthetic perspective, and write poetry related to the topic. For example, they can read poems like Heide's "Rocks" and McCord's "This Is My Rock" and Peters's book *The Sun, the Wind, and the Rain* when they are studying geology. Then they can write in descriptive or poetic form about the things they have discovered from the more factual books (McClure and Zitlow, 1991). Long (1993) suggests using acrostic poems, rather than formal written reports, to share information gained from researching a topic. She found that they worked well for third graders.

Manipulative Materials

Teachers can use *manipulative* learning materials to teach both content objectives and the reading skills necessary to attain these objectives. An example of manipulative materials would be puzzles that require matching content vocabulary terms with pictures representing the terms. After introducing and demonstrating these materials in whole-class sessions, the teacher should place them in learning centers for students to use independently. The materials should have directions for easy reference, and should have a way for the students to determine the accuracy of their answers or to receive reinforcement. If activities call for divergent thought, reinforcement is usually provided through sharing of a report or project. Activities include matching technical vocabulary terms with illustrations of their meanings in a puzzle format, matching causes with effects, and following directions to produce an art product (Morrow, 1982).

Integrating Approaches

Because no single technique will enable all students to deal with the many demands of content material, a teacher must know many approaches, teach them directly, and let the students know why they help. Children need to be able to pick out an appropriate approach for a particular assignment.

To begin, the teacher should present to the class some content and process (reading/study strategy) *objectives* for each lesson, then move on to *vocabulary* by presenting and teaching words through context clues or by relating the words to ones the children already know. Next comes a discussion designed to *supply background information, motivate the students, and relate the material to things they already know.* Then the teacher asks the students to *survey the material and predict* what it is going to tell. *Purposes for reading* are set, either through the predictions or by other techniques. The teacher should *guide the reading* through use of a study guide; reading to verify hypotheses; reading to answer *who, what, when, where, how,* and *why* questions; or selective reading to discover important information. Then the teacher should plan activities that guide students to *synthesize and reorganize information*—for example, use the guided reading procedure, construct main-idea statements, take notes, write a content-based language experience story on the material (first in groups, then individually), or make graphic representations of the content (graphs, charts, diagrams). Students need to be given opportunities to *apply* in some way the concepts they have read about (Gaskins, 1981).

Creating Instructional Units

Two types of instructional units used in conjunction with content instruction are thematic units, in which the theme is a concept or a topic, and literature-based units across the curriculum, in which a piece of literature is the central factor. Literature should be an integral part of both types. Smith and Johnson (1994) say, "Literature can become the lens through which content is viewed." It puts the content into context and perspective. In all classrooms, but especially in whole language classrooms, reading aloud or Sustained Silent Reading, paired reading and discussion, guided reading, and literature circles are becoming a part of much content area instruction. The following Classroom Scenario shows students working in a small group on a thematic unit.

**Classroom
Scenario**

Thematic Unit on Survival

The children in Ms. Parker's sixth-grade class had been reading books related to the theme of *survival*. Several of them were seated around a table, preparing to discuss how their books related to the theme.

"In *Julie of the Wolves*, Miyax has to survive by herself on the Alaskan tundra," Tonya began.

"In *Hatchet*, Brian has to survive by himself after his plane crashes in the Canadian wilderness," David said.

"Karana was left alone on an island off the coast of California," Zack said, referring to the main character in *Island of the Blue Dolphins*.

"Well, Phillip wasn't all alone on the Caribbean island in *The Cay* at first, but he did need help because he was blind after the blow to his head," David said. "Timothy, the black man, was really the one who made sure Phillip would survive. He used a lot of survival techniques."

"Let's list the survival techniques the characters used," Bruce said. "We could web them like Ms. Parker had us do with settings last month. We could use headings like 'Food' and 'Clothing.'"

"That's a good idea!" Tonya chimed in. "How about 'Shelter' for another heading?"

"Karana ate abalones and scallops from the sea," Zack said, "and she made herself a fenced-in house and a shelter in a cave."

"That's a good start," said Tonya. "Let's get that down on paper before we go on." She went to the storage shelf and returned with a piece of drawing paper and a black marker. She handed the materials to Bruce, the group member with the best handwriting skills. "Put your ideas and Zack's down before we forget them," she said. "Then we'll add more things from other people."

As Bruce began to write on the drawing paper, several other children began to take notes on their own papers about contributions they wanted to make.

Analysis of Scenario

The children in Ms. Parker's class had worked in discussion groups many times and were ready to participate when they came to the table. Tonya acted the part of a good leader by getting the discussion started and by collecting materials for the webbing and delegating the task of actually constructing the web to another student. Ms. Parker had taught a valuable skill, webbing, in earlier lessons, and these children remembered it and put it to use.

Thematic Content Units

The use of thematic units was discussed as one approach to literature-based reading instruction in Chapter 7. The same concept can apply to teaching content units (Crook and Lehman, 1991). Thematic content units involve linking reading of fiction and nonfiction about a content topic in order to help the children obtain a more complete picture of the topic. As Doiron (1994) points out, facts can be embedded in fiction, and narrative structures can be used to convey facts presented in nonfiction. Thus, both types of books are useful, and children need to be able to read both types. Some thematic units are related to a single discipline; some are interdisciplinary, linking content and skills from different disciplines through authentic tasks; and some are integrative, in which the theme is the focus and lines between the disciplines are not evident (Smith and Johnson, 1994). (Students may collaborate with the teacher in theme selection, or the content may be mandated by the school district.) Teachers should choose broad themes that lend themselves to good instructional activities (Lapp and Flood, 1994). A web of the content topic can be elaborated with fiction and nonfiction selections, textbooks, magazines, newspapers, videos, and software for use with each subtopic.

Teachers should not overlook the possible value of picture books in content units for the upper grades. These books are often relegated to the primary grades, but many are appropriate for older students, and they add motivation and variety to lessons (Danielson, 1992). Eve Bunting has written a number of books that would be appropriate for these students, although they can be used with younger students, as well. They include *How Many Days to America?* (Clarion, 1988), *Terrible Things* (The Jewish Publication Society, 1989), and *The Wall* (Clarion, 1990). Thematically focused alphabet books by Jerry Pallotta, George Ella Lyon, Gisela Jernigan, Abbie Zabar, Malka Drucker, and John Agard are also good. They cover a variety of topics, with many focusing on science and social studies concepts. For example, books by Zabar, Drucker, Red Hawk, and Agard introduce other cultures. Many of Pallotta's books have science and social studies themes (Chaney, 1993; Thompson, 1992). See Example 10.8.

After resources have been located and organized, the classroom activities to be used in the unit can be planned, with the web as a helpful reference, for it is not a complete plan. Teachers must decide on goals and objectives for their units, because not all concepts presented in all of the sources can possibly be used. Then they must choose instructional procedures and related activities to meet these goals, gather related materials, schedule unit activities, and decide how to assess the outcomes.

Thematic units connect information from language arts, science, social studies, math, art, music, and drama. Text sets (sets of books on one topic, by the same author, of the same genre, about the same culture, etc.) are useful in unit instruction. After students read the related texts, they can share and extend their understanding of each text in a different way than would have been possible if they had read only one text (Harste, Short, and Burke, 1988). Literature focuses can range from such topics as the Holocaust (Zack, 1991) to life long ago contrasted with life today (Rosenbloom, 1991). Nonfiction trade books need to be available on a number of difficulty levels, and teachers need to show students how to locate them and use them to find information. Assignments involving these books should require synthesis and critical thinking (Palmer and Stewart, 1997).

Example 10.8   *Page from Thematic Alphabet Book*

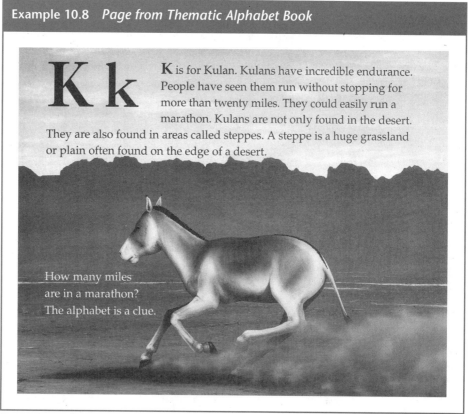

K k

K is for Kulan. Kulans have incredible endurance. People have seen them run without stopping for more than twenty miles. They could easily run a marathon. Kulans are not only found in the desert. They are also found in areas called steppes. A steppe is a huge grassland or plain often found on the edge of a desert.

How many miles are in a marathon? The alphabet is a clue.

Source: Jerry Pallotta, *The Desert Alphabet Book* (Watertown, Mass.: Charlesbridge Publishing, 1994). Copyright © 1994 by Jerry Pallotta. Illustration copyright © 1994 by Mark Astrella. Used with permission by Charlesbridge Publishing.

To set reading purposes, students can brainstorm questions about a topic. The children learn to read selectively to answer their questions. They can sort their questions into categories, discovering that by doing so they can find answers to more than one question at a time by locating the proper sections of books and becoming aware of the organization of nonfiction. When they share information with the class, they may refer to the text to prove points (Hess, 1991).

Literature-Based Units Across the Curriculum

A single piece of literature can be the basis of a unit that will include activities from many curricular areas. Related science, social studies, math, art, and music content may be taught with the piece of literature as the focal point. Language learning can take place along with reading, discussion, and writing done in relation to the literature selection. Example 10.9 shows one such unit for a sixth-grade class.

Example 10.9   Literature-Based Unit Across the Curriculum

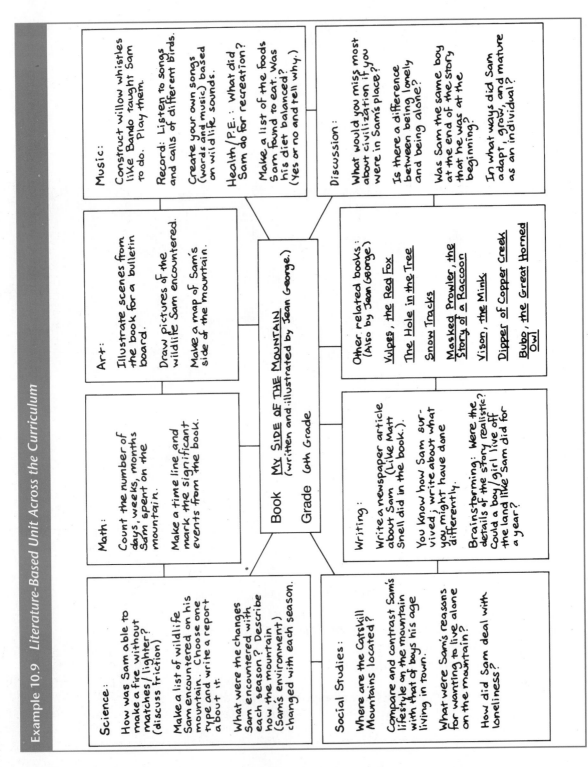

Book MY SIDE OF THE MOUNTAIN
(written and illustrated by Jean George.)

Grade 6th Grade

Science:

How was Sam able to make a fire without matches/lighter? (discuss friction)

Make a list of wildlife Sam encountered on his mountain. Choose one type and write a report about it.

What were the changes Sam encountered with each season? Describe how the mountain (Sam's environment) changed with each season.

Math:

Count the number of days, weeks, months Sam spent on the mountain.

Make a time line and mark the significant events from the book.

Art:

Illustrate scenes from the book for a bulletin board.

Draw pictures of the wildlife Sam encountered.

Make a map of Sam's side of the mountain.

Music:

Construct willow whistles like Bando taught Sam to do. Play them.

Record: Listen to songs and calls of different birds.

Create your own songs (words and music) based on wildlife sounds.

Health/P.E.: what did Sam do for recreation?

Make a list of the foods Sam found to eat. Was his diet balanced? (Yes or no and tell why.)

Social Studies:

Where are the Catskill Mountains located?

Compare and contrast Sam's lifestyle on the mountain with that of boys his age living in town.

What were Sam's reasons for wanting to live alone on the mountain?

How did Sam deal with loneliness?

Writing:

Write a newspaper article about Sam (Like Matt Snell did in the book.).

You know how Sam survived; write about what you might have done differently.

Brainstorming: Were the details of the story realistic? Could a boy/girl live off the land like Sam did for a year?

Other related books: (Also by Jean George)

Vulpes, the Red Fox

The Hole in the Tree

Snow Tracks

Masked Prowler, the Story of a Raccoon

Vison, the Mink

Dipper of Copper Creek

Bubo, the Great Horned Owl

Discussion:

What would you miss most about civilization if you were in Sam's place?

Is there a difference between being lonely and being alone?

Was Sam the same boy at the end of the story that he was at the beginning?

In what ways did Sam adapt, grow, and mature as an individual?

Source: Steve Gunter, graduate student, Tennessee Technological University, Cookeville, Tennessee.

Specific Content Areas

Special reading challenges are associated with each of the content areas. It is best to teach skills for handling these challenges when students need the skills in order to read their assignments.

Language Arts

The language arts block of the elementary school curriculum involves listening, speaking, reading, and writing instruction. It includes the subjects of reading, literature, and English. Since basal readers that may be used during reading class were discussed in other chapters in this textbook, they will not be considered here. Although literature is treated briefly in this chapter, more thorough coverage is found in Chapter 8.

Literature

Ideally, a literature program should encourage students to learn about their literary heritage, expand their imaginations, develop reading preferences, evaluate literature, increase their awareness of language, and grow socially, emotionally, and intellectually. These goals can be reached through a well-planned program in which the teacher reads aloud to students daily and provides them with opportunities to read and respond to literature. Teachers may teach literary skills directly through a unit on poetry or a novel, or they may integrate these skills with basal reader and language arts lessons.

Teaching Literature Skills. When developing literature programs, teachers should plan diversity in children's exposure to literature, rather than allowing students to have only random encounters with books (Stewig, 1980). They can organize instruction by genres (forms or categories), literary elements, or topics in order to vary students' experiences, and they should introduce students to the specialized vocabulary and skills they need to develop an appreciation of literature.

In literature classes, children are asked to read and understand many literary forms, including short stories, novels, plays, poetry, biographies, and autobiographies. One characteristic of all these forms is the frequent occurrence of *figurative* or nonliteral language, which is sometimes a barrier to understanding. Children tend to interpret such language literally. Chapter 4 covers teaching children to deal with figurative expressions.

Literary Elements. To understand literary passages, children need to be able to recognize and analyze plots, themes, characterization, settings, and authors' styles. The *plot* is the overall plan for the story; the *theme* is the main idea the writer wishes to convey; and *characterization* is the way in which the writer makes the reader aware of the characteristics and motives of each person in the story. The *setting* consists of time and place, and the *style* is the writer's mode of expressing thoughts. Teacher-directed questioning can make students aware of these literary elements and help children understand the interrelationships among them. Following are some points related to major story elements:

1. *Setting.* Teachers should point out how time and place affect the plot, characterization, and mood of a story. Stories must be true to their settings; characters behave differently today from the way they behaved a hundred years ago, and city life involves situations different from those that occur in country life. All of these facts make understanding the setting of a story important. *Madeline* by Ludwig Bemelmans is a good book to use in helping children see the importance of setting (Sharp, 1984).

2. *Characterization.* Children who examine literature with strong characterization find that writers develop their characters through dialogue, actions, interactions with others, and insights into their thoughts and feelings, as well as through description. Looking for these clues will make the children more attuned to the characters and should increase their overall understanding of the piece of literature. Children can also take note of how characters grow and change as the story progresses (Galda, 1989). The characterizations in Cynthia Voigt's *Dicey's Song* make good discussion material. In addition, the children can read *Miss Nelson Is Missing* by Harry Allard and James Marshall and compare and contrast the two identities of Miss Nelson. They could write dialogue for "Miss Nelson" and "Miss Swamp" and use this dialogue in a puppet show, imitating the way each character would speak, as well as using appropriate lines (Dreher, 1989).

3. *Plot.* Children may analyze short, simple stories to see how writers introduce their stories, develop them through a series of incidents, create interest and suspense, and reach satisfying conclusions. Awareness of the ways plots are developed can increase understanding of narratives. Picture books with predictable plots are good places to start. Mem Fox's *Hattie and the Fox* is a good choice for picture-book plot analysis (Galda, Carr, and Cox, 1989). *Doctor Desoto* by William Steig is another good book for examining plot with children (Sharp, 1984).

4. *Style.* Children should examine written material to analyze the authors' choices of words, sentence patterns, and manners of expression. The styles of writing in Maurice Sendak's *Chicken Soup with Rice*, Cynthia Rylant's *When I Was Young in the Mountains*, and Patricia MacLachlan's *Sarah, Plain and Tall* could be discussed and compared.

5. *Theme.* The concept of *theme* is abstract. Smit (1990) suggests selecting two stories that have the same theme but different settings, plots, and other elements to allow students to see how the same theme can be developed in different ways. She suggests *Why the Chimes Rang* by Raymond MacDonald Alden and *The Grateful Statues*, a Japanese folktale, for helping the students discover the theme of *giving*.

One way that teachers may work on these elements is through journal writing (Au and Scheu, 1989). (See Chapters 7 and 8 for more on journal writing.) The children may be asked to respond to a story by selecting a character from the story and writing a journal entry as though that character were writing it. The entries can be dated according to the time in which the book takes place. The journal writers can leave clues in their entries to the identities of the characters doing the writing. These entries can be shared orally, with the other children trying to decide which character wrote each entry. Such an activity encourages attention to characterization, point of view, and mood (Jossart, 1988).

Webbing literary elements related to a story can help students clarify their concepts of these elements. The teacher can read the story and have the students listen for the elements that need to be added to the web (Norton, 1993).

Literary Forms. Children's literature consists of a variety of genres or literary forms, including historical and realistic fiction, biographies, poetry, plays, informational books, and fantasy and folklore. Historical fiction, biographies, and informational books are all useful for integrating with content areas, whereas good realistic fiction serves as a model for helping children to understand others and solve problems in their own lives. Poetry encourages children to explore their emotions, and plays offer the pleasure of acting out favorite stories. Both modern fantasy and folklore allow children to escape into worlds of imaginary characters and events. Teachers should use all of these forms in their literature programs, and they can enhance children's understanding of them by reading literature of all forms aloud and pointing out the characteristics of each genre.

Folklore presents many possibilities for introducing different literary forms. Intermediate-grade children especially enjoy tall tales, and they can try to locate the exaggerations in the stories. Another form of folklore is the fable, which is usually characterized by brevity, a moral, and use of animal characters. Students can practice identifying the morals of the fables before they read the ones stated in the books. Myths, *pourquoi* ("why") tales, some Native American folklore, and Rudyard Kipling's *Just So Stories* provide explanations for universal origins. These stories are excellent for helping children to understand different cultures and become familiar with literary classics.

Teachers can introduce children to poetry by reading them poetry of all kinds and asking them to respond freely and with feeling. The children should then have opportunities to read much poetry for themselves and to participate in choral reading/speaking of poetry. Galda (1989) suggests following the reading of poems to which children respond positively with a focus on rhythm and rhyme, alliteration and onomatopoeia, and metaphors and imagery, to name only a few elements.

Spiegel (1991) suggests *Poetry Please!* (The Magic Library Series, TV Ontario) for introducing children to poetry as a genre. This program is a fifteen-minute video that explores what poetry is through examples and discussion. Stop-tape questions and a read-along activity get students actively involved. A teacher's guide suggests a variety of activities to use with the tape. *Poetry Works!* (Modern Curriculum Press) is a kit for kindergarten through grade three that includes poetry posters and an extensive teacher's guide that provides related poems and activities to be used with each poem. The thematic arrangement of the poems allows easy integration with social studies and science.

Play reading is quite different from reading the narrative and expository material discussed previously. Reading plays can help students see the relationship between print and spoken language (Manna, 1984). "A play's script, consisting mostly of dialogue, the sequence of events, and a limited description of the setting, stimulates children to pay close attention to textual details and helps them develop language skills basic to interpretive reading" (p. 712). Bringing the play to life involves many interpretive and creative decisions about the setting, action, and characters. Discussion about the way dialogue should be delivered makes the students sensitive to language styles and usages that fit the context and the characters.

Comparisons of narrative and script versions of the same stories can help students see the differences in the writing styles and help them learn to look for information in the right places (Manna, 1984). Many plays based on children's stories are readily available. Basal readers often include such plays, as do some trade books.

Both creative dramatizations of plays and dramatized reading, such as readers' theater, can be used in elementary classrooms. Tape-recording rehearsals for later evaluation and having children produce their own scripts for plays from narratives they have read are also valuable procedures (Manna, 1984).

English

English textbooks cover the areas of listening, speaking, and writing and generally consist of a series of sections of instructional material followed by practice exercises. The technical vocabulary includes such terms as *determiner, noun, pronoun, manuscript, cursive,* and *parliamentary procedure.* The concepts presented in the informational sections are densely packed; each sentence is usually important for understanding, and examples are abundant. Children need to be encouraged to study the examples because they help to clarify the information presented in the narrative portion of the textbook.

Teachers are wise to plan oral activities in class to accompany the listening and speaking portions of the English textbook, since such practice allows students to apply the concepts immediately and helps them retain the material. Similarly, it is wise to ask students to apply the concepts encountered in the writing section as soon as possible in relevant situations to aid retention.

Composition instruction can form the basis for reading activities. Children read to obtain information to include in their compositions, and they read to learn different styles of writing. For example, they read poems to absorb the style of writing before attempting to write poetry. Children can also read their own material in order to revise it to enhance clarity or ensure correct use of language conventions. They may read it aloud to peers for constructive criticism, or their peers may read it themselves (Dionisio, 1983).

Much of a student's formal vocabulary instruction takes place in English classes. Trade books can be the basis for vocabulary lessons. Fred Gwynne's *The*

King Who Rained offers good examples of figurative expressions and words with multiple meanings that can be used to interest students in word study. Emily Hanlon's *How a Horse Grew Hoarse on the Site Where He Sighted a Bare Bear* offers examples of homonyms in nonsense verses.

Social Studies

In social studies reading, youngsters encounter such technical terms as *democracy, tropics, hemisphere, decade*, and *century*, as well as many words with meanings that differ from their meanings in general conversation. When children first hear that a candidate is going to *run* for office, they may picture a foot race, an illusion that is furthered if they read that a candidate has decided to enter the *race* for governor. If the term *race* is applied to people in their texts, the children may become even more confused. Children who know that you *strike* a match or make a *strike* when bowling may not understand a labor union *strike*. Discussions about the *mouth* of a river could bring unusual pictures to the minds of youngsters. The teacher is responsible for seeing that the students understand the concepts these terms represent.

Social studies materials also present children with maps, charts, and graphs to read. Ways of teaching the use of such reading aids have been suggested in Chapter 9. Social studies materials must be read critically. Students should be taught to check copyright dates to determine timeliness and to be alert for such problems as outdated geography materials that show incorrect boundaries or place names.

Social studies texts in particular have been criticized for being difficult to read, often requiring more reading ability than prospective readers have, and varying four or more years in difficulty from passage to passage. Social studies texts have often been found to assume unrealistic levels of background knowledge on the part of the students and to lack coherence (Stetson and Williams, 1992; Beck and McKeown, 1991), interest, and meaning for them (Guzzetti, Kowalinski, and McGowan, 1992).

Trade books can be used to enhance the social studies program. They provide causal relationships between concepts and give students a chance to answer their own questions about the content from their reading. Trade books offer opportunities to meet curricular objectives for both reading and social studies simultaneously. Maps in trade books can be used to teach map-reading skills, to locate the places being studied and to identify the features of the land in these places, for example. When using such books, brainstorming about prior knowledge and forming semantic maps can be helpful. Then teachers can have students use think sheets on which they list their questions about a central question posed by the teacher, their ideas about how the questions would be answered, and how the texts answered the questions. They may eventually produce their own question-and-answer books about the topic (Guzzetti, Kowalinski, and McGowan, 1992).

The five fundamental themes in geography are location (where a story takes place and why); place (what the place is like); relationships within places (including human/environmental relationships); movement of people, materials, and ideas (descriptions and consequences); and regions (including how they change) (Norton, 1993; Committee on Geographic Education, 1983; *GEONews Handbook*, 1990). Norton (1993) shows how the books *People of the Breaking Day* by Marcia Sewell (Atheneum, 1990), *Christopher Columbus: Voyager to the Unknown* by Nancy Smiler Levinson (Lodestar, 1990), *Encounter* by Jane Yolen (Harcourt Brace Jovanovich, 1992), and *The Other Fourteen Ninety-Two: Jewish Settlement in the New World* by Norman H. Funkelstein (Scribner's, 1989) can help students learn about these five themes in the context of literature rather than textbook discussions. This treatment, supplemented with other books about the period, offers diverse perspectives on the geographic concepts being studied.

Picture books can be valuable for presenting many social studies concepts to middle and upper elementary students. These books elaborate on topics that would otherwise get limited attention. Sensitive issues that are ignored in textbooks can often be treated effectively in fictional accounts. Children become emotionally involved with other people and historical situations through these books (Farris and Fuhler, 1994).

Fictionalized biographies and diaries used for social studies instruction are excellent for teaching children to evaluate the accuracy and authenticity of material, since authors have invented dialogue and thoughts for the characters to make the material seem more realistic. Teachers should lead children to see that these stories try to add life to facts but are not completely factual, perhaps by having them check reference books for accuracy of dates, places, and names. Sometimes, reading an author's foreword or postscript will offer clues to the fictional aspects of a story; for example, at times only the historical events mentioned are true. Students should also be aware that authors use first-person narrative accounts to make the action seem more personal, but that in reality the supposed speaker is not the person who did the writing. Also, any first-person account offers a limited perspective, because the person speaking cannot know everything that all the characters in the story do or everything that is happening at one time. Teachers should alert students to look for the author's bias and ask them to check to see how much the author depended on actual documents if a bibliography of sources is given (Storey, 1982; Zarnowski, 1988).

Another approach to reading biographical material is to have students choose a famous person; read that person's biography; do additional research on the person, using multiple sources; make time lines of events in the person's life; and take on the role of that person in role-playing sessions. Since reading research strategies should be taught in context (McAloon, 1993), this procedure would provide a fertile ground for such teaching. Such studies can also naturally link social studies with science and language.

Use of biographies can help students think about social issues and individuals' involvement with them, assessing the importance of events and understanding the objective and subjective dimensions of the events. This can lead to lessons on determining fact and opinion (Miller, Clegg, and Vanderhoff, 1992).

Children can also be drawn into historical periods and issues through historical fiction. Historical fiction transforms a series of events into an interpretation of these events, providing humanizing details. It can help students understand the times in which historical events occurred. Children are able to become emotionally involved with people from the past. As they identify with the actual historical characters in the books they read, they face conflicting viewpoints that require them to do critical thinking. They read to interpret the moral and ethical issues faced during these events. They see multiple perspectives and can make informed judgments (Johnson and Ebert, 1992; Levstick, 1990). As students study these materials, teachers can read related materials to them to build background. Then the students can do activities such as making time lines based on their readings, marking maps to show where events in the reading occurred, classifying characters as to beliefs or allegiances, producing mock newspapers from the times, illustrating events and places described, writing diaries for characters in the reading, or writing letters to characters with comments and advice (Johnson and Ebert, 1992).

Social studies materials are generally written in a very precise and highly compact expository style in which many ideas are expressed in a few lines of print. Authors may discuss a hundred-year span in a single page or even a single paragraph or may cover complex issues in a few paragraphs, even though whole books could be devoted to these issues. Study guides are recommended for helping students read social studies materials with understanding and purpose.

Social studies materials are organized in a variety of ways, including cause-and-effect relationships, chronological order, comparisons and/or contrasts, and topical order (for example, by regions, such as Asia and North America, or by concepts, such as transportation and communication). The content selection in Example 10.4 is an example of the cause/effect pattern, but it also offers comparisons and contrasts of the effects of the war on different groups. To help children deal with cause-and-effect and chronological order arrangements, teachers can use the ideas found in Chapter 6 for helping students determine such relationships and sequences. Drawing time lines is one good way to work with chronological order, and pattern guides such as the one in Example 10.5 are ways to work on cause/effect or comparison/contrast relationships. Knowing the organizational pattern of the selection allows children to approach the reading with an appropriate mental set, which aids greatly in comprehension of the material.

Social studies materials are frequently written in a very impersonal style and may be concerned with unfamiliar people or events that are often remote in time or place. Students may also lack interest in the subject. For these reasons, teachers should use many interesting trade books to personalize the content and to expand on topics that are covered very briefly in the textbook. Biographies of famous people who lived during different historical periods add spice to textbook accounts, and use of literature about different peoples is one way to approach multicultural issues (Rasinski and Padak, 1990; Martinez and Nash, 1990; Pugh and Garcia, 1990). Walker-Dalhouse (1992) believes the use of multiethnic literature can decrease negative stereotyping of people from other cultures. (See Chapter 14, Appendix A, for a multiethnic book list.)

Using the Newspaper

Teachers may use special student newspapers or regular newspapers in class. The newspaper is a living textbook for social studies through which youngsters learn about tomorrow's history as it is happening today. Different parts of the newspaper require different reading skills, as noted here:

1. *News stories*—identifying main ideas and supporting details (who, what, where, when, why, how), determining sequence, recognizing cause-and-effect relationships, making inferences, drawing conclusions

2. *Editorials*—discriminating between fact and opinion, discovering the author's point of view, detecting author bias and propaganda techniques, making inferences, drawing conclusions

3. *Comics*—interpreting figurative language and idiomatic expressions, recognizing sequence of events, making inferences, detecting cause-and-effect relationships, drawing conclusions, making predictions

4. *Advertisements*—detecting propaganda, making inferences, drawing conclusions, distinguishing between fact and opinion

5. *Entertainment section*—reading charts (TV schedule and the like), evaluating material presented

6. *Weather*—reading maps

Each of these skills is discussed fully in either Chapter 6 or Chapter 9.

Following are several activities for practice in reading newspapers more effectively.

Activities

1. Have students locate the *who, what, where, when, why,* and *how* in news stories.

2. Using news stories with the headlines cut off, have students write their own headlines and compare them with the actual headlines.

3. Give children copies of news stories about the same event from two different newspapers. Then ask them to point out and discuss likenesses and differences.

4. Using copies of conflicting editorials, have students underline facts in one color and opinions in another color and discuss the results. Also, have them locate emotional language and propaganda techniques in each editorial.

5. Discuss the symbolism and the message conveyed by each of several editorial cartoons. Then ask students to draw their own editorial cartoons.

6. Have students compare an editorial and a news story on the same topic. Discuss differences in approach.

7. Tell students to locate comics that are funny. Then ask them to explain why they are funny.

8. Have students study the entertainment section and decide which movies or plays would be most interesting to them or locate time slots for certain television programs.

9. Encourage children to try to solve crossword puzzles.

10. Have students compare human interest features with straight news stories to discover which type of writing is more objective, which has more descriptive terms, and so on. Have them dramatize appropriate ones.

11. Ask students to search grocery advertisements from several stores for the best buy on a specified item or to study the classified advertisements to decide what job they would most like to have and why. Then ask them to write their own classified ads.

12. Have the youngsters study the display advertisements for examples of propaganda techniques.

13. Ask students to use the index of the paper to tell what page to look on for the television schedule, weather report, and so on.

14. Ask the children to search through the newspaper for typographical errors. Then discuss the effects of these errors on the material in which they appear.

15. Have students search the sports page for synonyms for the terms *won* and *lost*. Ask them why these synonyms are used.

Mathematics

Reading in mathematics poses special difficulties. First is the technical and specialized vocabulary. Young children have to learn terms like *plus, minus, sum*, and *subtraction*, whereas older children encounter such terms as *perimeter* and *diameter*. Words with multiple meanings also appear frequently. Discussions about *planes, figures*, or raising a number to the third *power* can confuse children who know other, more common meanings for these words. Nevertheless, many mathematics terms have root words, prefixes, or suffixes that children can use in determining their meanings. (For example, *triangle* means "three angles.")

Mountain (1993) suggests constructing stories that require the use of math synonyms in context to help students build concepts. Here is an example:

Mother needed *one yard* of material to make the cover.

"Mr. Huffer sells the material by the foot," Jamie complained.

"Then buy *three feet* of material," said Mother. "You're lucky he doesn't sell it by the inch. Then you'd have to remember to get *thirty-six* inches."

Some of the synonyms in the story can be provided and others left out, to be filled in by the students from the context. Whitin and Whitin (1997) encourage teachers to postpone the use of technical mathematics vocabulary until students have had a chance to explain significant concepts in their own words.

Difficulties with words are not the only problems children have with math textbooks. They are also required to understand a different symbol system and to read numerals as well as words, which involves understanding place value. Children must be able to interpret such symbols as plus and minus signs, multiplication and division signs, symbols for union and intersection, equal signs and signs indicating inequalities, and many others, as well as abbreviations such as *ft., lb., in., qt., mm, cm,* and so on.

Symbols are often particularly troublesome to children, perhaps partly because some symbols mean other things in other contexts; for example, − means *minus* in math but is a dash or a hyphen in regular print. Matching exercises such as the one described in the Model Activity below encourage youngsters to learn the meanings of symbols.

Model Activities

Matching Activity for Symbols

Place the symbols =, ≠, >, <, −, +, and ÷ on separate index cards. Write *equals, is not equal to, is greater than, is less than, minus, plus,* and *divided by* on other individual cards. Shuffle the cards and give them out randomly to students. Then let one student with a symbol card go to the front of the room and hold up his or her card. The student with the matching card should go up to join the first student. If nobody moves, the students with the definition cards all hold them up where the first student can see them, and he or she calls the student with the matching card to the front. If the student at the front cannot choose correctly, a student without a card may volunteer to make the match. After the match is made, the pair, or the trio if outside help was used, watches as other matches are made. Then each pair or trio thus formed makes up a math problem using its own symbol for the rest of the class to solve. These problems are written on the chalkboard. All students go to their seats and work the problems on their own papers. Then students who were not involved in constructing the problems volunteer to work them on the board, with the original pairs or trios acting as verifiers.

To read numbers, students must understand place value. They must note, for example, that the number 312.8 has three places to the left of the decimal point (which they must discriminate from a period), which means that the leftmost numeral indicates a particular number of hundreds, the next numeral tells how many tens, and the next numeral tells how many ones (in this case, three hundreds, one ten, and two ones, or three hundred twelve). To determine the value to the right of the decimal, they must realize that the first place is tenths, the second place is hundredths, and so forth. In this example, there are eight tenths; therefore, the entire number is three hundred twelve and eight tenths. This is obviously a complex procedure, involving not merely reading from left to right but also reading back and forth.

Mathematical sentences also present reading problems. Children must recognize numbers and symbols and translate them into verbal sentences, reading 9 ÷ 3 = 3, for example, as "nine divided by three equals three."

Students will need help in reading and analyzing word problems as well. Teachers should arrange such problems according to difficulty and avoid assigning too many at one time (Schell, 1982). Story problems can present special comprehension difficulties. They require the basic comprehension skills (determining main ideas and details, seeing relationships among details, making inferences, drawing conclusions, analyzing critically, and following directions). Chapter 9 contains a description of the SQRQCQ study method for mathematics, which takes these requirements into account.

Sometimes children find it useful to draw a picture of the situation a problem describes or to manipulate actual objects, and teachers should encourage such approaches to problem solving when they are appropriate. Teachers should watch their students solve word problems and decide where they need the most help: with computation, with problem interpretation (understanding of problems that they are not required to read for themselves), with reading, or with integration of the three skills in order to reach a solution. Small groups of students who need help in different areas of problem solving can be formed (Cunningham and Ballew, 1983).

Since story problems are not written in a narrative style, children often lack the familiarity with the text structure needed for ease of comprehension. The pattern of writing for story problems is procedural, with important details at the beginning and the topic sentence near the end. This pattern fails to offer children an early purpose for their reading (Reutzel, 1983).

Braselton and Decker (1994) suggest that teachers have students think of the word problems as short stories that they could comprehend by using their prior knowledge. They suggest the use of a graphic organizer to help students visualize the steps in problem solution. The use of the organizer can be taught through modeling by the teacher, followed by guided practice and independent practice by the students.

Collier and Redmond (1974) point out that mathematics material is very concise and abstract in nature and involves complex relationships. A high density of ideas per page appears in this kind of material, and understanding each word is very important, for one word may be the key to understanding an entire section. Yet elementary teachers too often approach a math lesson in terms of developing only computational skill, apparently not realizing that reading skills can be advanced during arithmetic lessons or that arithmetic statement problems would be more comprehensible if attention were given to reading skills.

Hadaway and Young (1994) suggest that children will benefit from creating story problems related to their own experiences after a group language experience approach with classroom-related math problems. A research study showed that students who made up their own math story problems to solve performed better on tests of application skills than did those who practiced textbook word problems. Children are likely to interpret a story problem more successfully if they have constructed a similar problem (Ferguson and Fairburn, 1985). Fortescue (1994, p. 576) says, "To write about a mathematical problem, one must separate the problem into a series of steps that lead to a solution. So, in writing about math problems or activities, students become familiar with analytical writing while gaining and displaying a deeper understanding of the math concept."

Students may be given a reaction guide composed of statements about the mathematics material that are either true or false and, working in cooperative groupings, they can complete the guide by agreeing or disagreeing with each statement and providing the reason (Wood, 1992).

Fortescue (1994) gave third graders math task cards and asked them to complete the activities on the cards, record the results, and describe what they did during the activity. Each activity and the way to talk and write about it were modeled for the whole group before the activity was completed by the students. The students completed the activities, talked to one another about them, and then wrote about them. They had other students and then the teacher read their descriptions to verify that they were clear. These activities clarified their thinking about math processes.

Teachers can use literature to help them teach mathematical material. Counting books, for example, can provide material for teaching addition and subtraction. Bell (October 1988) suggests the books *Animals One to Ten* by Deborah Manley, and *Anno's Counting House* by Mitsumasa Anno for working with addition and subtraction. An excellent book for developing concepts of large numbers is *How Much Is a Million?* by David M. Schwartz, and a good one for encouraging them to work with division is *The Doorbell Rang* by Pat Hutchins. This book can also be used for addition with younger children. Children's literature can also help students learn to tell time. Bell (November 1988) suggests using *The Scarecrow Clock* by George Mendoze for this purpose and the book *Chicken Soup with Rice* by Maurice Sendak for motivating children to learn to read the calendar. The following Focus on Strategies section shows a mathematics lesson that is based on literature.

Focus on Strategies

Mathematics Lesson Based on Literature

Ms. Barnes opened the class by displaying the book *The Doorbell Rang* by Pat Hutchins. "From the picture on the cover of this book and the title *The Doorbell Rang*, what do you think it will be about?" she asked the children.

"There are lots of people in the picture," Sammy said. "I think a lot of people have come to visit. The doorbell rings every time somebody comes. We have a doorbell that people ring when they come."

"What else does the picture make you think?" Ms. Barnes asked.

"They've tracked up the kitchen," said Monica. "The mom is going to have to clean it up. She'll send them all out."

"Does anybody else have something to add?" Ms. Barnes asked.

"The children don't look happy. Maybe she is running them out," Tasha suggested.

"They are looking out the slot in the door. Maybe the person that just rang the bell is someone they don't like," Jimmy said.

"Or maybe the kids don't want anyone else to come," Don added.

"Listen carefully as I read the story to see if your predictions were right," Ms. Barnes said. "Also listen to see what this book has to do with math."

Ms. Barnes read the story. When she finished, she asked, "Were your predictions right?"

"I was right that lots of people came and the bell rang every time," Sammy said.

"Mom didn't send them out of the kitchen, so Tasha and I were wrong," Monica said.

"I was wrong," Jimmy said. "They acted like they liked the people who came."

"But I'll bet they really didn't want all of those people to come and share the cookies. I think I was right, even though they don't act bad about it," Don said.

"How does all of this fit into a math problem?" asked Ms. Barnes.

"They have to decide how many cookies to give each person," Don replied.

"That's right. Now we are going to see how they figured it all out," Ms. Barnes said as she handed out stacks of plastic chips to each set of math partners in the room.

"Now," she said, "listen carefully and use your chips to answer my questions as I go back through the story."

She read the first two pages. "How many children were there?" she asked.

"Two," the children chorused.

"How many cookies did each one get?" she asked.

"Six," answered the children.

"We need to know how many cookies there were in all," she said. "What do we do to get this answer?"

"We add them," answered Joey.

"Who can write out an addition problem on the board that we have to solve?" she asked.

Benny went to the board and wrote "$6 + 6 =$ ".

"Now solve the problem," she told them.

The children, who had used the chips to solve problems before, worked with their partners to form two rows of six chips each and count them. Soon hands were up all over the room. When all were finished, Ms. Barnes called on Billy, who proudly answered "Twelve."

"Did anyone get any other answer?" she asked. A sea of shaking heads answered her. "Good job," she said. She let Sean go to the board and write the answer to the problem after the equals sign. Then she read further in the book.

"How many children were there after Tom and Hannah came?" she asked. Hands went up immediately, without use of the chips.

Ms. Barnes let Sammy give the answer, "four," and go to the board and write the entire problem and answer: "$2 + 2 = 4$."

(continued)

"Show with your chips how Sam and Victoria knew that each one would get three cookies," Ms. Barnes directed. The children arranged their chips into four rows of three chips each.

"Now write an addition problem to show how putting these cookies back on the plate would give us the twelve we started with," she told them. Children wrote on their own papers and consulted with their partners before holding up their hands. Ms. Barnes let Laticia write "3 + 3 + 3 + 3 = 12" on the board. She asked if everyone agreed, and they did.

She repeated the above procedure for the entrance of Peter and his brother and again for the entrance of Joy and Simon and their four cousins, with the added step of asking how many people were at the door when Joy and Simon came. The children quickly did the addition of two plus four without the aid of chips.

At the end of the lesson, the children counted the cookies on the tray that Grandma brought, added the number to twelve by combining the chips from several sets of partners, and put the total number of chips into twelve rows to see how many each one would have before they let in that last person at the door.

A whole language approach to teaching mathematics would include presenting mathematics content in ways that are like real-life uses—in other words, as a problem-finding social activity that is a tool with which to make sense out of life. Therefore, the mathematics program in a whole language setting would have problems related to students' everyday experiences, and, because students help to shape the curriculum in such classrooms, the problems would be written by teachers and students (Winograd and Higgins, 1994/1995). Language and mathematics strategy lessons would be interwoven as children worked on such tasks as conducting surveys and constructing graphs (Jongsma, 1991).

Donna Strohauer uses a technique called "mathematician's circle" in which students (one at a time) share problems they have generated with a group and invite other students to solve the problems. Answers and explanations of answers follow, and peers of the students presenting the problems are asked to make suggestions about the problems (Winograd and Higgins, 1994/1995).

Graphs, maps, charts, and tables, which often occur in mathematics materials, were discussed in Chapter 9. Students need help with these graphic aids in order to perform well on many mathematical assignments.

Science and Health

Extremely heavy use of technical vocabulary is typical in science and health textbooks, in which students will encounter terms like *lever, extinct, rodent, pollen, stamen, bacteria, inoculation,* and *electron*. Again, some of the words that have technical meanings also have more common meanings, for example, *shot, matter, solution,* and *pitch*. In these classes, as in all content area classes, the teacher is responsible for seeing that students understand the concepts represented by the technical and specialized terms in their subjects. For example, a science teacher might bring in a flower to explain what the *stamens* are and where they are located. Although diagrams are also useful, a diagram is still a step removed from the actual object, and the more concrete an experience students have with a concept, the more likely it is that they will develop a complete understanding of the concept.

Comprehension strategies, such as recognizing main ideas and details, making inferences, drawing conclusions, recognizing cause-and-effect relationships, classifying items, recognizing sequence, and following directions, are important in reading science and health materials, as are critical reading strategies. Students must determine the author's purpose for writing, check the completeness and timeliness of the information presented, and check the accuracy of the material (Casteel and Isom, 1994). Because material can rapidly become outdated, it is very important that students be aware of the copyright dates of these materials. The scientist's inquiring attitude is exactly the same as that of the critical reader. The ability to use such reading aids as maps, tables, charts, and graphs is also necessary.

Armbruster (1992/1993) points out that students need to learn how to read scientific material in order to obtain valid scientific information. She says, "The same skills that make good scientists also make good readers" (p. 347). Casteel and Isom (1994) have clearly illustrated the relationship of literacy processes to understanding of scientific material. The literacy processes form the root system that supports the branches that represent the parts of the scientific method, which in turn support the scientific facts, concepts, laws, and theories of science. (See Example 10.10.)

Science and health materials must be read slowly and deliberately, and rereading may be necessary to fully grasp the information presented (Mallow, 1991). These materials, like social studies materials, are written in a highly compact, expository style that often involves classification, explanations, and cause-and-effect relationships. The suggestions in Chapter 9 for teaching outlining skills can be especially useful in working with classification, which involves arranging information under main headings and subheadings.

Explanations in science and health materials often describe processes, such as pasteurization of milk, that may be illustrated by pictures, charts, or diagrams designed to clarify the textual material. Teachers might apply the material in Chapter 9 on reading diagrams and illustrations or the material in Chapter 6 on detecting sequence, since a process is generally explained in sequence. Similarly, the suggestions given in Chapter 6 for recognizing cause-and-effect relationships will help children handle this type of arrangement when it occurs in science textbooks.

Science textbooks often contain instructions for performing experiments. Readers must be able to comprehend the purpose of an experiment, read the list of materials to determine what must be assembled in order to perform the experiment, and determine the order of steps to be followed. The suggestions in Chapter 6 on locating main ideas, details, and sequential order and learning to follow

---

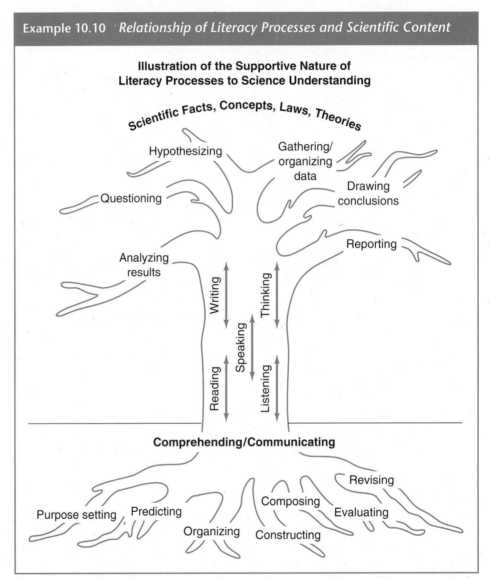

Example 10.10 *Relationship of Literacy Processes and Scientific Content*

**Illustration of the Supportive Nature of
Literacy Processes to Science Understanding**

Scientific Facts, Concepts, Laws, Theories

Hypothesizing

Gathering/
organizing
data

Questioning

Drawing
conclusions

Reporting

Analyzing
results

Writing

Thinking

Reading

Speaking

Listening

Comprehending/Communicating

Revising

Composing

Purpose setting Predicting

Evaluating

Organizing Constructing

Source: Carolyn P. Casteel and Bess A. Isom, "Reciprocal Processes in Science and Literacy Learning," *The Reading Teacher*, 47 (April 1994), 540. Reprinted with permission of Carolyn P. Casteel and the International Reading Association. All rights reserved.

directions should be useful when reading material of this nature. Before they perform an experiment, children should attempt to predict the outcome, based on their prior knowledge. Afterward they should compare their predicted results with the actual results, investigating the reasons for differences. Did they perform each step correctly? Can they check special references to find out what actually should have happened?

Because science textbooks are often written at higher difficulty levels than the basal readers for the same grade level, some children will need alternate materials for science instruction. Trade books are available on all levels of difficulty to meet this need.

Teachers can use children's trade books that deal with scientific concepts to help students distinguish between real and make-believe situations. Discussion of the books offers children a chance to ask questions, share their opinions and background knowledge, make predictions, and engage in inferential and critical thinking. Smardo (1982) suggests books that can be useful for particular scientific concepts, including the following:

Carle, Eric. *The Very Hungry Caterpillar*. New York: Philomel, 1969. (animal changes)

DeRegniers, Beatrice. *Shadow Book*. New York: Harcourt Brace Jovanovich, 1960. (shadows)

Provensen, Alice, and Martin Provensen. *A Year at Maple Hill Farm*. New York: Atheneum, 1978. (seasons)

Presenting scientific ideas and common misconceptions in story format, rather than in a straight expository format, as the books cited above do, helps students learn scientific information (Maric and Johnson, 1990; Schumm, 1991).

Science informational books, such as Laurence Pringle's *Into the Woods: Exploring the Forest Ecosystem*, help children understand the laws of nature. The color photographs and realistic illustrations found in many science books increase a child's enjoyment and understanding (Norton, 1995). *Tree of Life: The World of the African Baobab* by Barbara Bash and *The Hidden Life of the Desert* by Thomas Wiewandt emphasize the interrelatedness of plant and animal life. Another type of ecosystem is explored in *Life in a Tidal Pool* by Alvin and Virginia Silverstein (Martinez and Nash, 1990). Animal life in general is depicted in Doris Gove's *A Water Snake's Year*, Miriam Schleiss's *Squirrel Watching*, and Jan Sterling's *Bears* (Galda and MacGregor, 1992).

Endangered species are discussed in *No Dodos: A Counting Book of Endangered Animals* by Amanda Wallwork; *Saving Endangered Mammals: A Field Guide to Some of the Earth's Rarest Animals* by Thane Maynard; *The Endangered Florida Panther* by Margaret Goff Clark; and *On the Brink of Extinction: The California Condor* by Caroline Arnold. *Four Against the Odds: The Struggle to Save Our Environment* by Stephen Krensky and *The Fire Bug Connection* by Jean Craighead George are biographies of environmental activists. *Earthways: Simple Environmental Activities for Children* by Carol Petrash and *What To Do about Pollution* by Anne Shelby contain environmental activities for children (Pierce and Short, 1993/1994). Rule and Atkinson (1994) have analyzed books about ecology to help teachers choose wisely books that show realistic ecology problems, address possible solutions, have positive tones, avoid stereotypes, and are appropriate for the intended audience.

Keeping a science log or journal is a traditional practice for scientists and makes a natural connection to language instruction. Children can enter a short

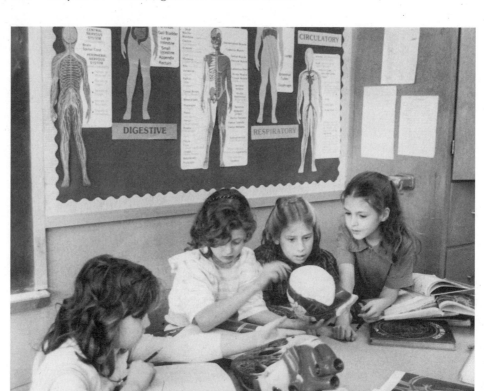

These students use many diverse reading and study skills in their science class as they follow directions, interpret diagrams, and relate text exposition and description to scientific materials and models. (© *David S. Strickler/The Picture Cube*)

science-related passage in a journal each day. The passage can vary from a single sentence about a nature observation to a complete explanation of an experiment and its results. Students can also write reports on science projects, detailing the procedures and the findings. These reports may be taken through initial drafts and revisions to the finished products (Rubino, 1991).

Science activities that involve direct experiences, such as using manipulative materials, doing experiments, or making observations of phenomena, can be used as the basis for language experience stories or charts that will provide reading material in science (Barrow, Kristo, and Andrew, 1984). The experience is accompanied and/or followed by class discussion, after which the children produce a chart or a story about the experience. Reading of related concept books, such as the ones just mentioned, may provide children with material to use in expanding their stories.

Having students brainstorm questions about material read in the science text, categorize the questions, and work as cooperative groups to answer them resulted in children interacting with the text as a group and sharing information (Sampson, Sampson, and Linek, 1994/1995). Such active involvement tends to facilitate learning.

Science centers in the primary grades can involve students in learning vocabulary, recording observational data, illustrating factual material, reconstructing factual materials, listening to and writing stories, and writing nonfiction books. All of these are active ways to learn the material (Piech, 1991).

Time for Reflection

Some teachers believe that literacy instruction should take place only during reading or language arts classes. Others believe it should also take place whenever students need literacy skills in content areas. **What do *you* think?**

Summary

Teachers must be aware that basal reading instruction alone is not likely to prepare children thoroughly to read in the content areas. Students need to learn reading skills that are appropriate to specific subject areas, as well as general techniques that are helpful in reading expository text. Content texts present more reading difficulties than do basal reader materials. They have a greater density of ideas presented, and they lack the narrative style that is most familiar to the children. They may also contain many graphic aids that have to be interpreted.

Teachers need to be aware of the readability levels of the materials they give children to read, and they must adjust their expectations and reading assignments based on the students' reading levels in relation to the readability of available instructional materials. Cloze tests and informal reading inventories can be used to predict how well children can read particular texts. Teachers can also use readability formulas in conjunction with the children's reading test scores to estimate the appropriate materials for specific children. Although readability formulas have the drawback of being completely text based, they can help teachers assess the relative difficulty of material with reasonable accuracy. Computer programs can help teachers apply readability formulas.

Many techniques can be used to help children read content area materials more effectively. Among them are the Directed Reading-Thinking Activity, the guided reading procedure, Press Conference, the language experience approach, feature analysis plus writing, keeping learning logs, webbing, creative mapping, structured overviews, every-pupil-response activities, readers' theater, the K-W-L teaching model, use of study guides, use of manipulative materials, computer approaches, integrated approaches, thematic content units, and literature-based units across the curriculum.

Each content area presents special reading challenges, such as specialized vocabulary. Reading in literature involves comprehending many literary forms, including short stories, novels, plays, poetry, biographies, and autobiographies. English textbooks cover the areas of listening, speaking, reading, and writing. The techniques presented in these areas need to be practiced through authentic oral and written experiences. Social studies materials abound with graphic aids to be interpreted and require much application of critical reading skills. The newspaper is a good teaching aid for the social studies area. Mathematics has a special symbol system to be learned, but perhaps the greatest difficulty in this content area is the reading of story problems. Children need to learn a procedure for approaching the reading of such problems. Science and health materials contain many graphic aids. They also often include instructions for performing experiments, which must be read carefully to ensure accurate results.

Use of literature selections to work with content area concepts is effective in every content area. In addition, including real-life activities and connections to the students' backgrounds of experiences enhances learning.

Test Yourself

True or False

_____ 1. Content area textbooks are carefully graded in terms of difficulty and are generally appropriate to the grade levels for which they are designed.

_____ 2. One difficulty encountered in all content areas is specialized vocabulary, especially common words that have additional specialized meanings.

_____ 3. The cloze technique can be used to help determine whether or not a textbook is suitable for a specific child.

_____ 4. All children in the fifth grade can benefit from the use of a single textbook designated for the fifth grade.

_____ 5. Readability formulas are too complicated for classroom teachers to use.

_____ 6. Students often must acquire early concepts and vocabulary in content textbooks before they can understand later content passages.

_____ 7. Offering youngsters instruction in basal readers is sufficient to teach reading skills needed in content area textbooks.

_____ 8. Story problems in mathematics are generally extremely easy to read.

_____ 9. Mathematics materials require a child to learn a new symbol system.

_____ 10. Concrete examples are helpful in building an understanding of new concepts.

———— 11. Science materials need not be read critically, since they are written by experts in the field.

———— 12. An expository style of writing is very precise and highly compact.

———— 13. The cause-and-effect pattern of organization is found in social studies and science and health materials.

———— 14. Social studies materials frequently have a chronological organization.

———— 15. All parts of the newspaper require identical reading skills.

———— 16. Study guides may set purposes for reading.

———— 17. The Directed Reading-Thinking Activity is a general plan for teaching either basal reader stories or content area selections.

———— 18. Readability formulas take into account the interactive nature of reading.

———— 19. Expository text structure can be taught through the language experience approach.

———— 20. Anticipation guides are used before reading a selection and can be the basis for discussion after reading has taken place.

———— 21. Children's literature can be used to teach social studies and science concepts.

———— 22. Real-life mathematics problems produced by children are effective teaching tools.

———— 23. Expository paragraph frames can scaffold children's attempts to write about content area topics.

———— 24. Passages using math synonyms can help students build concepts.

———— 25. Use of picture books should be avoided above the third grade.

For your journal...

1. Write about the usefulness of newspaper reading in your particular content area.

2. Describe how you can make use of trade books in a particular content area.

...And your portfolio

1. Develop a Directed Reading-Thinking Activity (DRTA) for a content area lesson. Then try it out in an elementary school classroom, and write an evaluation of its effectiveness.

2. Develop a lesson for teaching students the multiple meanings of words encountered in science and health, social studies, mathematics, or literature. Try the lesson out in an elementary school classroom, and write an evaluation of its effectiveness.

3. Select a passage from a social studies or science textbook. Prepare a study guide for children to use in reading/studying the passage.

4. Develop a bibliography of trade books that youngsters who are unable to read a particular content area textbook could use.

5. Prepare a comparison/contrast chart for some topic in your content area.

Use of Technology for Literacy Learning

Key Vocabulary

Pay close attention to these terms when they appear in the chapter.

CD-ROM

computer-assisted instruction (CAI)

computer-managed instruction (CMI)

database

database programs

desktop publishing

electronic bulletin boards

electronic mail

electronic mailing lists

hypermedia

hypertext

Internet

multimedia

newsgroups

spreadsheets

videoconferencing

videodisc

word-processing software

World Wide Web (WWW)

SETTING OBJECTIVES

When you finish reading this chapter, you should be able to

▶ Describe the teacher's role in choosing and using technology in literacy instruction.

▶ Identify a variety of technological tools for literacy instruction.

▶ Explain literacy applications for each of the technological tools.

▶ Describe how to integrate the use of technology into the regular literacy curriculum.

Chapter 11 Organization

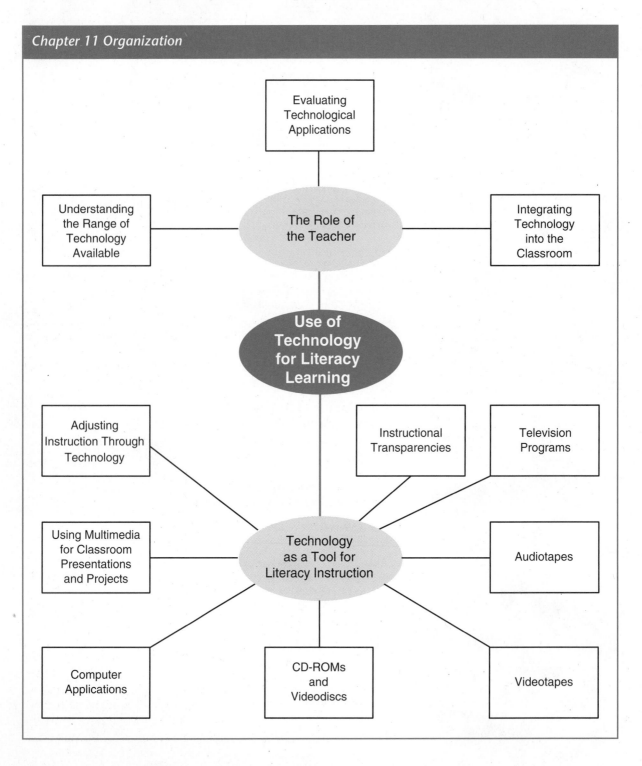

The days of a teacher standing in front of a class with only his or her voice, chalk, and chalkboard to use in instruction are over. Today classrooms are likely to be filled with technology that can enhance instruction in all subjects, including literacy instruction. Some of this technology has become familiar and comfortable to teachers with use over the years. Some emergent technology is so complex and unfamiliar that it intimidates many teachers—yet teachers should realize that all of the now-familiar technologies were once new and strange to some teachers. It is also important for teachers to realize that the older technological tools still have many valuable instructional uses and should not be cast aside just because a flashier or more stylish application is available.

Indeed, teachers must learn what technological tools exist to help them with their literacy instruction, what strengths and weaknesses each of these tools has, and how best to integrate their use into the literacy curriculum. No application should be chosen just because it is novel or popular. Each one must serve a legitimate purpose in the classroom.

Used properly, technological tools can offer students instruction in a range of literacy activities, from low-level drill-and-practice to higher-order thinking activities involved in simulations. They can serve as vehicles for presenting material in class, for providing instruction, and for recording class activities for the purpose of evaluation. They can be used with whole classes or with individuals, and they can be used to individualize instruction.

The Role of the Teacher

The teacher has a critical role to play in the application of technology to literacy instruction. He or she is the decision maker about the technological tools that will be used, but a teacher cannot make valid decisions about the best technological applications for classroom use without knowing which ones are available.

Understanding the Range of Technology Available

Overhead projectors, televisions, and audiotape recorders are so commonly available in classrooms that sometimes they are overlooked and sit unused when they would actually be ideal for particular teaching applications. Videotape recorders, CD-ROM and videodisc players, and computers are less pervasive in schools; most schools have them, but not in the quantities that would make them be considered standard classroom equipment. In some situations, they have to be checked out of the media center; in the case of computers, some schools require that students go to scheduled labs to access the equipment. The situation is improving yearly, but by no means do all classrooms have all of this equipment. Teachers need to know what is available in their schools, not only in the way of hardware, but also in the materials to use with it: a videodisc player, for example, is useless without appropriate discs. Computer software must be available for the particular type of computer (IBM-compatible or Macintosh, for example) in the classroom and also must be compatible with the computer's operating system.

Evaluating Technological Applications

All applications of technology in the classroom need to be evaluated for appropriateness and effectiveness, just as other materials should be. Teachers should not decide to use material or equipment simply because it is there. Example 11.1 shows some questions that a teacher may wish to ask about any potential application of technology in the curriculum.

Example 11.1   *Evaluation of Technological Applications*

To evaluate technological applications for your classroom, answer the following questions:

Does the application

1. address content that is needed in this curriculum?
2. motivate students to learn the content?
3. clarify the concept for the student in some way?
4. lend itself to use in your classroom structure?

Is the application

1. easy to implement?
2. instructionally sound?
3. cost-effective?
4. more effective than other possible approaches to the task?

Teachers have been evaluating use of transparencies with overhead projectors, television programs, audiotapes, and films for a long time. Videotape and some videodisc evaluations are similar to those for films. There are, however, some more specific concerns in evaluating computer software, such as the ones in Example 11.2.

Some of the considerations in Example 11.2 are appropriate only for software that would be considered computer-assisted instructional software, but most of them apply to any software. The best practice is to try out software before purchasing it, if possible, because some pedagogically unsound, user-*un*friendly, and inflexible software is available, along with the many good programs.

Example 11.2 *Evaluating Computer Software*

When evaluating computer software, ask the following questions.

1. Is the program compatible with the available hardware and operating system?
2. Does the program meet a curricular need better than another approach would?
3. Is the program well documented?
   a. Are the objectives of the program clearly presented?
   b. Are steps for initiating and running the program clearly stated?
   c. Are hardware requirements for the program clearly specified, and is this hardware available?
   d. Are time requirements for program use described, and are they reasonable for classroom use? (If a program can be saved at any time and re-entered at the same place, some of the problems with time are alleviated.)
4. Is the program user-friendly?
5. Is there a management system that keeps up with a student's performance on the program, if that would be appropriate?
6. Are the screens well designed and readable?
7. Is the program essentially crash-proof?
8. Is feedback about performance offered to the students? Is the feedback appropriate for them?
9. Do the students have control over the
   a. speed of the program presentation?
   b. level of difficulty of the program?
   c. degree of prompting offered by the program (including seeing instructions for use)?
   d. sequence of presentation of material?
10. Is the program highly interactive, requiring more of the student than just page-turning?
11. Is sound used appropriately, if at all? Can the sound be turned off without destroying the effectiveness of the program?
12. Is color used effectively, if at all?
13. Is the program adaptable for a variety of levels of students? Are your students within this range?
14. Is the material free of stereotypes and bias?
15. Is there a way that the teacher can modify the program for a particular class, set of data, or student? Is this procedure protected against student tampering?
16. Is information presented in the program accurate and presented clearly and in grammatically correct form?

Reviews in periodicals such as *Electronic Learning* and *The Reading Teacher* can be helpful. The Minnesota Educational Computing Consortium (MECC), a large distributor of educational software with an extensive catalogue of offerings, may also be a useful resource.

Integrating Technology into the Classroom

Any application of technology—whether it is a television program, a videotape, or a computer program—should fit seamlessly into the teacher's curricular structure, or it should not be used. The application should present, reinforce, or teach a concept; offer tools for recording, collecting, and retrieving data; motivate students in their study; or provide assessment opportunities. The content should be appropriate to the subject area, grade level, and maturity level of the students. The presentation format should fit into the classroom organizational structure, and the use should be adaptable to the time available. Teachers must decide which applications fit these criteria and which do not. Use of the evaluation questions found in Example 11.2, along with their knowledge of the students and the curriculum, can help teachers with this decision making.

Various technological applications are ideal for use with individual students, small groups, or whole classes (Lapp, Flood, and Lungren, 1995). Teachers can choose the best applications for particular circumstances. Some people have the erroneous belief that working at a computer has to be a solitary activity; but, on the contrary, students' social interactions while working on some types of computer projects can be highly beneficial. Students in those situations have had a tendency to help each other spontaneously (Dwyer, 1994).

Integration can take place across the curriculum. Morden (1994) reports an interdisciplinary simulation project in which she and a colleague involved students with literature selections about traveling, followed by the use of simulation software, such as *Oregon Trail* (MECC) and *Country Canada* (Didatech). Students chose travel destinations and gathered information about them, using letter writing with word processors and communication with people all over the world through *WorldClassroom*, a curriculum-based educational telecommunications network. Databases were used as organizational tools, and CD-ROMs and laserdiscs were viewed. Students had a budget, and they had to use a spreadsheet to plan an itinerary, staying within the budget. They "earned" money by doing jobs for the class or winning test review games. They planned a bon voyage party and even made invitations with *Print Shop* (Broderbund). As they "traveled" to their destinations, they collected information from people in those locations through telecommunications, CD-ROMs, laserdiscs, and even traditional print. They kept logs of their travels, one year on paper and the next year on audiotape, and used *HyperCard* to develop a multimedia scrapbook.

Students should use technological tools to complete authentic tasks that involve both basic and advanced skills. They can work collaboratively, with the teacher monitoring and assisting in the activities. The work may take place over a period of time, as is true in unit studies. Means and Olson (1994) have described one such example of integration. A summary is found in the following Classroom Scenario.

Classroom Scenario

Integrating Technology into Classroom Activities

Students in a fifth-grade class in California needed funds to go to a science camp, and they also needed appropriate materials, on easy reading levels, about Hispanic leaders. They decided on a multimedia project to develop their own materials, not only about local Hispanic heroes, but also about African-American and Vietnamese-American community leaders as well. They planned to sell the materials to others to raise funds for science camp.

The fifth-graders identified people that they wished to interview; planned, conducted, and videotaped the interviews; and wrote up the main points from each one.

The students carried out their plans by first studying existing interviews of famous people to help them construct their questions; then they formed groups and practiced interviewing skills on each other. The actual interviews were conducted by collaborative groups, with one student videotaping, one asking questions, and one taking notes. The interviews were critiqued and transcribed, and the key points were summarized. This task involved much proofreading and editing. The teacher, Cliff Gilkey, moved from group to group, monitoring progress and offering assistance.

Analysis of Scenario

The students were working on an authentic task to meet two real-life needs. The technology was used as a tool to help meet these needs. The process involved a number of important literacy skills as the students read interviews, composed questions, took notes, summarized material, and proofread and edited material. Cliff Gilkey was a coach and a facilitator of learning.

Time for Reflection

Some people think that only "cutting edge" technology should be used in today's classrooms. They would discard applications that have been around a long time, referring to them as "antiquated." Others consider it possible to embrace newer technologies without casting aside older ones that accomplish curricular goals effectively. What do *you* think?

Technology as a Tool for Literacy Instruction

This chapter, of course, is concerned primarily with the application of technology as a tool for literacy instruction, rather than for instruction in general. Following are ways that many types of technology can be used for this purpose.

Instructional Transparencies

Use of transparencies displayed on overhead projectors allows teachers who are not artistically inclined to present in an attractive way some material that they may have avoided showing in the past because some illustration was needed. Primary teachers, for example, might present sentences containing rebuses (pictures that represent words or syllables) to facilitate the reading of more advanced sentences early in the instructional program.

Writing on blank transparencies as they present new material allows teachers to provide visual clarification or presentation of ideas without turning their backs to their classes, a plus for maintaining control. This use of transparencies is effective before reading a story or content selection when teachers want to record semantic webs of prior knowledge about a topic or entries for the *K* and *W* portions of a K-W-L chart. After reading, students can use transparencies to expand the web or to fill in the *L* portion of the K-W-L chart. (See Chapter 10 for more about these charts, including an example of one such chart.)

When describing the steps in a process, such as the steps in the process writing approach (See Chapter 8), the teacher can use a series of transparencies with overlays that show each step as it is mentioned. In the process writing approach, a blank transparency can be used to record the results of a brainstorming session. Students, individually or in groups, may organize the results of the brainstorming on other blank transparencies for display and discussion. Current student work can be displayed on transparencies, and students can discuss possible needs for revision, if the permission of the creators is obtained; or anonymous student work from previous classes may be used for this purpose.

Television Programs

Many classrooms are equipped with televisions, making possible the incorporation of educational programming. Some shows, such as "Reading Rainbow," fit naturally into the literacy curriculum. In "Reading Rainbow" programs, books are read, illustrations are shared, and related activities are incorporated into the program to make the book presentations more meaningful. Other shows have less obvious connections, but any show that covers content currently being studied in a thematic unit would be likely to provide background information that would make reading and writing about that topic easier for students. If scheduling to fit the unit's prescribed time slot is a problem, it may be possible to videotape the program for later use, but teachers must be careful to adhere to copyright laws.

Taking notes on television programs is also a way for students to apply literacy skills. The notes may provide source material for reports that will be written later or projects that are being undertaken as a part of unit study. Movies that have pertinent content may be viewed, and students may then write reviews related to their accuracy and effectiveness. Some movies are based on children's books and can serve as an introduction or follow-up to the reading of those books.

Audiotapes

Sometimes a teacher may wish to use prerecorded audiotapes that provide information about something being studied in class. Prerecorded books on tape for read-alongs or prerecorded music that goes along with poetry that is being read may also be used. (This may be done using listening stations at which several children can listen to the same tape at the same time.) Students who are having difficulty reading the material can listen to the tape as they read, building sight vocabulary as they hear a fluent reader's correct phrasing and pronunciation. Teachers may tape the read-alouds that they do for the class and make them available to students who missed the reading or who wish to read along with the tapes. However, teachers most often use audiotape recorders to tape class activities. Tapes of group discussions or class presentations can be used for later evaluation of the activities. Audiotapes of a child reading orally over a period of time can be used as portfolio items for evaluation, since they provide convincing evidence of progress.

Many students have personal audiotape recorders. They may use these to tape themselves reading aloud or practicing an oral presentation and listen to the tapes to decide if they are ready to perform for the class. They may also tape class lectures and discussions to review before tests or to use for note taking in a less stressful situation, with the time pressure removed.

Videotapes

Many classrooms are equipped with videotape recorders, and others have them available for checkout from the media center. Videotapes are available for purchase, for checkout from school and public libraries, and for rental from video stores. They have almost completely replaced films and filmstrips as educational tools in most classrooms. Videotape recorders are easier to operate than most film projectors, and they make returning to a part to view it again much easier.

Videotapes are available on most topics that are included in the school curriculum, and they are good for the following:

- Introducing new topics for discussion

- Making new concepts seem more concrete as they are presented in the context of real-life situations

- Providing a focus for follow-up discussion at the end of a unit of study

They are particularly useful in illustrating text materials for less proficient readers or students with limited experiential backgrounds. They may help to bring a literary selection to life for students or help them understand a process that is described in a content-area textbook.

Movies based on children's books are often available on videotape or may be videotaped from television for use in the classroom. If the students have already read the book, they may compare and contrast the book and the movie. If they have not already read the book, they may view the movie first; and then students who choose to do so as an individual project may read the book and do the comparison.

Focus on Strategies

Use of Videotapes

Two classes of middle-school students read the book *Bridge to Terabithia* and then viewed a videotape of a movie based on the book. They compared and contrasted the book and the video, coming out firmly in favor of the book. The students felt that the movie at times differed from the book "for no reason at all," although they saw that some changes had been made because of time constraints. They commented, too, that many important details had been left out of the movie, making the character portrayals weaker.

These classes later read the book *Tuck Everlasting* and then viewed a videotape of a movie based on it. Once again they compared and contrasted the movie and the book, with similar results. They found many changes to be unnecessary and inexplicable and even decided that the impact of the plot, as it unfolded, was lessened because the movie contained some foreshadowing that was not in the book (Roe and Smith, 1997).

Videotapes are available on most topics that are included in the school curriculum.
(© Elizabeth Crews/Stock Boston)

A good application of videotape recorders in the classroom is having students make their own videotapes of class presentations or field trips. They can write scripts for skits or plays, do the casting, rehearse for the performances, videotape the productions, and edit the tapes until they have polished products. Creative drama and readers' theater performances can also be videotaped. Simulated newscasts can be written, cast, and videotaped, with editing as a final step. These activities involve many technological and higher-order thinking skills.

Today prices of camcorders (videocameras) are dropping significantly, and their size is also decreasing, making them easier for small hands to manipulate. Special editing equipment still may not be available, but connecting two videotape recorders makes basic editing possible.

CD-ROMs and Videodiscs

CD-ROMs and videodiscs can store large amounts of text, audio, and video information in relatively little space. They may be used to provide information for unit study, as videotapes do. They also generally offer high-quality images and sound. Some are interactive, allowing students to select words to be pronounced, defined, or pictured, for example. CD-ROMs have the advantage over videotapes of holding much more information—whole reference books or works of fiction can be stored on them. Unlike videotapes, CD-ROMs and videodiscs make it easy for the user to access information from them in a non-linear fashion, with the particular information being selected through keystrokes or mouse clicks with a CD-ROM or by a remote control unit or a bar code reader with a videodisc. Actually both CD-ROMs and videodiscs can be under the control of a computer, and both are good instructional tools. Relatively few classrooms are routinely supplied with videodisc players, and not all computers come with CD-ROM drives, however; therefore, this technology may not be accessible for all teachers.

Windows on Science (Optical Data Corporation) is an elementary videodisc program that integrates the use of videodiscs, reading, and writing. The videodiscs offer photographs, movie clips, animations, and diagrams to reinforce the science concepts. There are lesson plans to be used in conjunction with the discs (Rock and Cummings, 1994).

Among the most common materials available on CD-ROM are electronic books. Some simply show the book pages on the screen, and the user "turns pages" by clicking a mouse or touching a key. These programs have little to recommend them over books, which are more portable and do not require hardware. For some students, they may add some motivation to read, but others find reading from the screen more of a strain and less satisfying than reading from a printed page. Other books on CD-ROM take better advantage of the capabilities of computers. (See the next section, on computer applications, for more about CD-ROMs.)

Computer Applications

The computer generation is indeed here. Today's children expect to use computers, which now pervade every aspect of life. Computers are found more frequently in classrooms today than they were in the past, although they still are not available in large enough quantities to offer every elementary school student substantial computer time each day. Even though not all classrooms have computers, however, most classes have some access, either through resident computers, computers on carts that can be checked out from a central location, or a computer lab that has scheduled times for use by various classes.

Even when only one computer is available in the classroom, there are many possible applications. With a projection device, it can be used for recording language experience stories (see Chapter 7) or any cooperative writing, including creative writing and report writing. These writing efforts can be printed for use by individual students or small groups. The computer can be used to display simulation programs, with children making joint decisions about required choices and a designated student entering data. It can be used to record in databases project information that can be printed out for class use. Or students can work in small groups to prepare sections of a multimedia presentation, which are then combined for sharing with the whole class and other classes.

When computers must be checked out of a media center for use in the classroom, careful preplanning and completion of off-computer preparation activities before the computers are brought to the classroom can facilitate effective use. Paper-and-pencil rough drafts may be developed for written products before students start using a word-processing or desktop-publishing program, for example.

Time for Reflection	Some teachers believe that little can be accomplished when only one computer is available for a whole class. Others think there are many useful applications for a single computer. What do *you* think?

Some teachers use authoring software or programming languages to produce their own programs. This option is extremely time-consuming, especially if programming languages are used, but authoring systems demand less computer expertise, and teachers can learn to use them within a shorter time frame to produce computer-based courseware. Some authoring systems are fairly user-friendly, containing English statements and menus, prompts, and help options to guide the teacher in choosing programming actions in a step-by-step manner. They provide, for example, lesson outlines that the teacher fills in with text, questions, answers, feedback, and prompts.

Teachers should not feel pressured to construct courseware in order to use the computer. Much commercial material is available, and evaluation skills may be more valuable than development skills (Isaak and Joseph, 1989; Geisert and Futrell, 1995). Multimedia authoring tools, such as *HyperCard* (Apple) and *HyperStudio* (Roger Wagner) may be used to combine text, graphics, and sound to present information. The products may be made basically linear or highly interactive. Both teachers and students can use these tools for developing materials (Grabe and Grabe, 1998).

Hypertext, Hypermedia, and Multimedia

Hypertext refers to information that is linked in a nonsequential manner, allowing students to choose the paths they will take through the information (Downes and Fatouros, 1995). With *hypermedia*, a variety of media—including text, full motion video, sound clips, graphics, and still images—can be viewed and/or heard in an order chosen by the user (Dillner, 1993/1994; Poole, 1997). *Multimedia* refers to the mixing of different media. Multimedia computer systems generally have interactive capabilities. For example, when reading an entry from a multimedia encyclopedia, a student may click on a word or symbol to view a picture, see a definition, see a video clip, or hear an audio clip related to the topic.

Hypertext allows enhancements to text that assist comprehension; with hypertext and hypermedia applications, for example, a student can use a mouse pointer and click when the cursor is over boldfaced words in the material. This may cause the program to display a glossary text that defines the word or provides a picture, and/or to read the word aloud. (The books on CD-ROM discussed earlier in this chapter are examples of hypertext and hypermedia applications.) Hypertext applications may also provide graphic organizers or interspersed questions. They may offer options for taking notes as the reading progresses and printing out notes for review or as a basis for developing essays. Although some applications of hypertext to reading are currently available, many require a level of hardware resources that some classrooms lack, such as CD-ROM drives. Use of Internet resources (discussed later in this section) involves students in hypertext experiences on the World Wide Web.

Hypertext materials present new reading challenges. Readers may continue to click on keywords that lead them further away from the original text; then they may have trouble returning to their points of origin, a situation referred to as a "navigational problem" (Reinking, 1997). There is also the danger that hypertext and hypermedia lead students to read about an extensive number of topics superficially, rather than reading in depth about any single topic (Leu, 1996).

Hypermedia applications may require laserdiscs/videodiscs/compact disks and players, as well as high-resolution color monitors. Some examples of reading applications include *The Manhole* and *Cosmic Osmo* (Activision). These programs include text, graphics, sound effects, and speech (Anderson-Inman et al., 1994; Blanchard and Rottenberg, 1990).

Word Processing

One of the most obvious applications of computers to literacy instruction is the use of word-processing software for both creative writing and writing of a functional nature, such as the writing of research reports. This software takes much of the dreaded labor out of editing and revising written products. Since words, sentences, and longer passages can be moved around with a few clicks of a mouse (or with some older software, a few keystrokes), students are less reluctant to reconsider the content, organization, and mechanical aspects of their papers and to make needed changes. Freedom from recopying an entire document is a definite plus, especially for younger students who may still be laboring to perfect their handwriting. There are word-processing programs on many different levels of difficulty, so it is possible to find tools easy enough for primary students and tools powerful enough to meet the needs of older ones. Roe (1987) has found that students who are allowed to do their creative writing on the computer, rather than with paper and pencil, tend to write longer pieces and to feel less resentful of making changes.

Butler and Cox (1992) found that when first graders are allowed to work in pairs to compose stories on a computer, they discuss language usage, spelling, and punctuation, as well as the mechanics of computer use. They reread what they have written frequently, as a springboard to adding new text, as both contribute to the story line. The full facilitative effects of word processing on the quality of student writing may not be evident until students become proficient in the use of the program and the equipment (Owston, Murphy, and Wideman, 1992; Schumm and Saumell, 1993). Peer assistance with computer tasks can help alleviate any problems with use of programs and equipment. It often appears to occur spontaneously, but teachers can capitalize on students' expertise by assigning peer tutors. There are particular advantages when lower-achieving students get the chance to be the experts (Sandholtz, Ringstaff, and Dwyer, 1997).

Use of spelling checkers and grammar checkers alerts students to words that *may* be misspelled or constructions that *may* need modification, but the checkers do not make the decisions about what will actually be done. Students have to look at each comment and decide upon its merits. This is a critical reading activity that is a natural part of the writing process.

Many word-processing programs include dictionaries and thesauruses, which students can use to help them make decisions about their word choices. The dictionary can be used in deciding if a word has the correct meaning for the context; the thesaurus can be used in choosing a synonym when a word has been overused in a selection or to pick a word that fits the situation exactly (Grabe and Grabe, 1998).

In addition to writing stories and research papers, students can produce class newspapers and magazines with word-processing software. Many teachers, however, go to desktop-publishing programs (discussed in the next section) or multimedia programs such as *HyperStudio* (Roger Wagner) for these activities. With *HyperStudio*, students can include audio or video clips of their presentations, artwork, and buttons to lead to information about the authors (Robinette, 1995).

Example 11.3 shows software that can be used for student writing (Wepner, 1992a; Wepner, 1993a; Lee, 1994; Larson, 1994).

Edinger (1994) reports that her school supplied inexpensive word processors (Tandy WP2s) for each child in her fourth-grade writing workshop. She found

---

Example 11.3 *Software for Student Writing*

Author! Author! (Mindplay), a program that allows children to write scripts for plays and create stages with movable graphics of characters and props

Great Beginnings (Teacher Support Software), a talking word-processing program with graphics and stimulus words related to four themes

Kid Works 2 (Davidson & Associates), a talking word-processing program with icons for nouns, verbs, and adjectives, along with a paint option for creating illustrations

Kids Media Magic (Humanities Software), a program for grades PreK–4 that includes word processing, rebus writing, and multimedia

Magic Media Slate (Sunburst), a program for grades 3–10 that not only provides a full-featured word processor, but also allows animation, sound, Quick-Time movies, drawings, clip art, and laser disc movie clips

MediaWeaver (Humanities Software), a multimedia word-processing program for grades 3–12

The Scholastic Process Writer (Scholastic), a program that offers a word processor, a computer-based writing coach, and postwriting tools

Story Book Weaver (MECC), a story-writing program with a wealth of objects to use in illustrating the stories

Student Writing Center (The Learning Center), a program for grades 4–adult that can be used for both word processing and desktop publishing, with tools such as the bibliography maker, spelling checker, and thesaurus

Write Away! (Sunburst), a word processor adaptable to four levels of students, from an easy picture-button interface for younger students to a full word processor for advanced ones

---

that the children were more willing to revise and to do multiple drafts of research papers and that use of the spelling checker helped weak spellers find and correct spelling errors, with the aid of a conventional dictionary. Students polished work more than they had in the past, and many began to write enthusiastically for the first time, with the aid of the word processors.

Teachers can also benefit from using word-processing software that enables them to produce handouts, tests, and letters to parents with relative ease. Using large monitors or projection devices that allow an entire group to see the material on the computer screens, teachers can write language experience stories on the computer, instead of on a chart or chalkboard.

There are many appropriate applications for computers in literary instruction.
(© *Elizabeth Crews*)

Desktop-Publishing Programs

Teachers use desktop-publishing programs in order to integrate text and graphics in a document (Heide and Henderson, 1994). With these programs it is generally possible to flow text around graphics, format text into columns, use a number of styles and sizes of type, and set up special formats for such applications as banners and greeting cards. Very attractive class newsletters, magazines, posters, and flyers can be produced. The programs may have clip art that can be used for illustrations, and students may be able to create their own illustrations or modify the available clip art. *The Print Shop Deluxe* (Broderbund) allows students to produce signs, posters, and banners, as well as to combine text and graphics to customize reports. With *Imagination Express* (EdMark), students can make electronic books with sound effects and animation (Robinette, 1995). *Creative Writer* (Microsoft Corp.) is a creative-writing and desktop-publishing program, and *Classroom Publisher* (Staz Software) is an easy-to-use desktop-publishing program suitable for grades 3 and up (Cowan, 1996).

Databases and Electronic Reference Works

Databases are organized collections of data that have the information filed so that it can be retrieved by category. They are usually created and searched by special database programs.

Database programs allow the categorization, storage, and orderly retrieval of data collected during research reading. When using databases, students perform such tasks as reading and following directions, taking notes, gathering and categorizing data, summarizing, posing questions, predicting outcomes, making comparisons and contrasts using collected information, using reference materials, identifying keywords for efficient data access, and testing hypotheses. All of these activities require them to be active, purposeful readers (Layton and Irwin, 1989). When creating databases, students must analyze and synthesize large amounts of information (Heide and Henderson, 1994).

Some libraries now have their holdings listed in computer databases that can be searched by author, title, and subject. Many elementary schools, however, still have traditional card catalogs.

Electronic reference works, such as electronic dictionaries, thesauruses, and encyclopedias, are elaborate databases that are searchable by keywords and categories. Such reference works take some of the manual labor out of library research, but still require the same cognitive skills for location of information. Electronic reference works are available at different levels of difficulty. Teachers need to check the intended age groups for these tools when purchases are made. Example 11.4 shows a screen from an electronic reference work.

Example 11.4   Microsoft® Encarta® 98 Encyclopedia, Deluxe Edition *Screen*

Source: Screen shot reprinted with permission from Microsoft Corporation. Microsoft® and Encarta® are trademarks of Microsoft Corporation.

Spreadsheets

Spreadsheets are specifically designed for working with numerical data. The data are entered in rows and columns, and formulas can be applied to the data, allowing calculations to be carried out rapidly and revised as the data are revised. Students may make use of spreadsheets in some data-collection projects for content-area subjects, and some teachers use spreadsheets to keep up with and average students' grades.

Electronic Books

The Living Books series from Broderbund offers many familiar children's books on CD-ROM, as well as some new selections. The pages contain text and illustrations, just as are found in printed books, but offer the reader a variety of options. The reader can choose to have the story read in English, Spanish, or Japanese. The child can read the story independently or have the computer read it aloud. In addition, the reader can click on objects in the pictures with the mouse and some of the picture elements will become animated and sometimes produce sound effects. This interactivity makes the books highly motivational, but students may be distracted from actual reading by the special effects (Willis, Stephens, and Matthew, 1996).

The Discis Books series is also available on CD-ROM. Students can click on words to get pronunciations, sound effects, syllable divisions, and explanations. The words that students click on for more information are saved in recall lists that the teacher can check. Students can also click on pictures to see labels, hear pronunciations, hear sound effects, and get syllable divisions. Words or phrases can be highlighted as the book is read; this helps to build word recognition. Students can hear the word pronounced in a second language, if they wish. Online audio help is available to the user. Activity guides accompany the CD-ROMs to give teachers ideas for story preparation, story connections, and story extensions.

The Internet

The Internet is a "network of networks" encompassing a multitude of computers throughout the world. Each of these server computers supplies different information or services. Students can search the Internet, using special browsers (such as *Lynx*, *Netscape Navigator*, or *Microsoft Internet Explorer*) and search engines (such as AltaVista, Lycos, and WebCrawler) that allow keyword searches, to locate information to use for reports or unit studies. This information may be in the form of text, sound clips, video clips, and/or graphics. Students will need instruction in use of browsers and search engines. They will probably also need practice in generating keywords to use with the search engines. An enjoyable way to practice searching for information on school topics is to participate in an Internet scavenger hunt for information specified by the teacher (Cotton, 1996). Another way is described in the following Model Activity.

**Model
Activities**

Internet Research for Book Making

Read several informational alphabet books to your class. (See Chapter 10 for suggestions of thematic alphabet books.) Discuss the characteristics of these alphabet books.

Next, choose a topic, such as "Mammals," that you are studying in a particular content area. Discuss what has already been discovered about this topic.

Then divide the class into small groups, assigning one or more letters to each group. Let group members search the Internet for mammals that would fit the assigned letters. Have each group choose from the mammals they locate the ones to use for their book pages. Then have them write and print book pages for their assigned letters, using desktop publishing software or word-processing software. Put the pages together to form a class book. Print multiple copies to use in the classroom, to share with other classes, and to send home to promote parent communication.

Finally, read the book to the class and let the group members responsible for each page tell about their search strategies.

The World Wide Web (WWW) is part of the Internet. The Web allows users to choose special words or symbols, with a mouse click or a keyboard stroke, and be automatically connected to related Web locations. Locating information on research topics in this way is much easier than having to know and enter each address for the locations of interest.

One problem with letting students use the Internet for research is that the accuracy of material that is posted to electronic bulletin boards or placed on Web pages is not monitored. Much inaccurate information is on the Internet, along with the useful material. Students should be encouraged to cross-check information found on the Internet in printed reference books, whenever possible. They need to see if the material is documented and to treat both undocumented and anonymous material as questionable.

Teachers may want to supply students with a list of reliable sites that contain information related to the current topic of study. McVey (1997) suggests that teachers may want to perform Internet searches, compile a set of links, and use this material as a tailor-made textbook. The material can be made to fit specific course needs and the particular group of students. Students may also use a teacher-supplied list as a basis for class research. Reliable sites include the Library of Congress site at **http://www.loc.gov**, NASA's Internet in the Classroom at **http://quest.arc.nasa.gov/interactive.html**, and the Smithsonian site at **http://www.si.edu**. The material in boldface gives the Internet addresses (called URLs, or Uniform Resource Locators) of the listed sites. The ones listed here are stable sites, but another hazard of providing students with a list of sites that you have found to have good information is that many sites are not stable. The World Wide Web is changing daily, and a site that you find today may not be there tomorrow. This situation can result in frustration on the part of the searchers. Example 11.5 shows a screen from an Internet site.

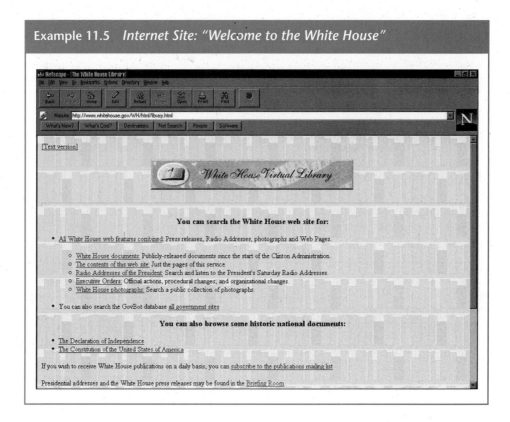

Example 11.5 *Internet Site: "Welcome to the White House"*

Some sites contain the full texts of some children's literature selections. This availability could make possible class activities that would ordinarily require multiple copies of the texts. The selections available are generally classics in the public domain. Check **gopher://lib.nmsu.edu/11/.subjects/Education/.childlit/.childbooks/** for some works of Louisa May Alcott, Mark Twain, and others. Folktales and fairy tales may be found at **http://itpubs.ucdavis.edu/richard/tales/**, printed in large letters (Kinnersley, 1997).

Teachers may want to guide their classes in developing their own Web home pages (Cotton, 1996). Many classes have done this, and the students have posted everything from creative writing to research reports to results of scientific experiments. Class newspapers or magazines may be published on the Web page. It is possible to include text, graphics, photographs, and animations. Since Web pages can be accessed from all over the world, the motivation for accuracy and clarity of information presented is great. Students may therefore be more inclined to revise and edit material.

The most common use of the Internet today is communication, which is discussed in the next section. Since communication is a language function, this use of the Internet is highly pertinent to literacy instruction.

Electronic Communications

There are a number of types of electronic communications that are useful for literacy instruction. Electronic mail (e-mail), electronic mailing lists (listservs), electronic bulletin boards (newsgroups), and electronic videoconferencing all have possible applications.

Electronic Mail. E-mail has many applications for literacy instruction. Students can e-mail other students in different classes, states, or countries. They can discuss the locales in which they live, customs of their countries, current events, topics being studied in school, and literature they are reading. Students in the Kentucky Telecommunications Writing Project read the same books as students at other Kentucky schools and communicate about their reading through e-mail (Bell et al., 1995; Holland, 1996). Students may also e-mail experts in different areas about their areas of specialization to obtain information needed for study topics. Students have the opportunity to interact with published authors in the Kentucky Authors Project, sharing both personal information and works-in-progress. "Authors provide feedback to each student's work, share their own ideas and approaches to writing, and, on occasion, offer direct instruction. . . . Students also have a chance to read and discuss each author's work directly with the author through on-line 'literature conferences'" (Paeth et al., 1995, p. 1). In a number of programs, college classes and public school students have had e-mail exchanges about books (Roe and Smith, 1997), instruction, or general conversation. Stivers (1996) paired college methods students with middle-school students with special needs, for e-mail conversation and skill instruction about writing. The public school students responded well, and the college students showed enhanced self-esteem as a result of the program. One e-mail project is described in the following Focus on Strategies (Roe and Smith, 1997).

Focus on Strategies

E-mail Conversations About Literature

During each of two semesters, students from Livingston Middle School, a rural public school, were paired with teacher education students enrolled in Betty Roe's reading and language arts methods classes at Tennessee Technological University to discuss literature selections that both groups were reading. In the fall semester both groups read *Bridge to Terabithia*, and in the spring semester both groups read *Tuck Everlasting*. The books were read on a predetermined schedule, and the partners communicated about their reading each week for seven weeks. During the fall semester, the university students also posted comments about literary features of the book to a newsgroup that was limited to the university students in the project. (Technical problems with the newsgroup caused its deletion from the second semester of the project.) Both groups also viewed a videotape of the book that had been

(continued)

read and communicated with partners by e-mail, comparing and contrasting the book and the video. (See the Focus on Strategies in the Videotapes section for more detail about this facet of the project.) The middle-school students also prepared an *mPower* presentation about each book at the conclusion of the reading. (See the Focus on Strategies in the Using Multimedia for Classroom Presentations and Projects section for more detail on this part of the program.)

Evaluations of the program by public school and university teachers and students were positive. The public school teachers felt that receiving e-mail motivated their students and enhanced the students' self-esteem. They felt that interacting with college students gave their students a sense of status and of doing high-level work. Some of the middle-school students had never read a novel before, but they read these books in order to communicate with their partners. Of course, they got additional reading practice when they read the e-mail correspondence from their partners in order to respond. These students had rarely done much writing, and the teachers saw the writing skills of many increase during the project. The university students had been encouraged to model good writing for their partners in their e-mail exchanges, and most did. Some partners continued to correspond, even after the semesters had ended. The e-mail communications reflected thinking on all levels of Bloom's Taxonomy, and the university students were sometimes surprised at the higher-order thinking displayed by their partners.

The university students gave the project high evaluations, also. One wrote, "This particular project not only introduced students to a good piece of literature; it introduced them to interactive technology, which is a skill that will be useful and probably necessary to their futures. It provided feedback that was fun and involving. I would definitely use this technique again" (Roe and Smith, 1997, p. 372).

Electronic Mailing Lists. Electronic mailing lists distribute messages to a group of readers who have "subscribed" to the list because of an interest in the topic. All "subscribers" receive all messages sent to the list until they "unsubscribe." The flow of mail to subscribers on these mailing lists is often exceedingly heavy, and the mail must be read and deleted frequently (usually daily). A class may want to subscribe to a mailing list that is related to a topic of study during the study and cancel the subscription after the topic is covered in class. Teachers may want to monitor the contents of the mailing list communications, because some outside participants may send inappropriate comments and use inappropriate language.

Jayne Everitt wanted her first graders to use the Internet to learn about effects of severe weather. She asked subscribers to the Kidsphere mailing list to send personal accounts of such effects. The children read the responses and charted the locations of the correspondents (Serim and Koch, 1996).

Electronic Bulletin Boards. Electronic bulletin boards, or newsgroups, differ from electronic mailing lists in that messages are posted to a network location, and readers who are interested in the topic can read the messages electronically by going to the newsgroup address. These messages may be posted and read by people from all over the world (Grabe and Grabe, 1998). Once again, teachers may want to monitor the content of newsgroups that students in class want to access, because inappropriate material may be posted. Some schools set up limited-access newsgroups to meet the needs of students who are studying a topic. These groups would be less risky to use with elementary school students.

Electronic Videoconferencing.   At present, most classrooms do not have the cameras and software needed for videoconferencing, but this may be an application on the horizon for literacy instruction. In videoconferences individuals hold conferences over the Internet with others who can be seen on their computer monitors and heard through their speakers. The advantages of this method for bringing such people as authors of children's books, scientists, and historians into contact with elementary school students are obvious. Students could be responsible for researching the person, literature, or topic of conversation ahead of time, writing interview questions, conducting a controlled interview, taking notes on the discussion, and writing reports on the results—all valid literacy activities. This type of interaction could also take place between two groups of elementary students from different parts of the world.

Computer-Assisted Instruction (CAI)

Computer-assisted instruction refers to use of computers to promote learning. The heart of a CAI system is the software, the programs that actually provide the instruction. These programs vary in quality, depending on the developers; the computer can only carry out the instructions its programmers have given it. To be instructionally sound, the program should present accurate information in a reasonable sequence with an appropriate amount of student interaction. It should not reward incorrect answers with clever messages or graphics, while not doing this for correct answers. It should be easy to use, providing clear instructions about what to do (1) to advance material on the screen, (2) to respond to questions (Should students use a letter or an entire typed-out answer to respond to a multiple-choice question? Should they touch the screen or click on beside the correct answer?), and (3) to receive help when needed. Erroneous keystrokes should not "dump" a student out of the program; the program should allow him or her to recover in a clear and easy way.

The four most common types of computer-assisted instruction are drill-and-practice programs, tutorial programs, simulation programs, and educational games programs. Computer-assisted instructional programs often have a component that takes care of such tasks as record keeping, diagnosis, and prescription of individualized assignments. Such a component is a computer-managed system, and many packages of instructional materials contain both an instructional and a management component.

Drill-and-Practice Programs.   These programs consist of practice lessons on skills students have previously been taught and are the simplest types of computer applications and the ones most commonly found in classrooms. They generally focus on learning factual information. With drill-and-practice programs, students receive information in a programmed sequence of small, sequential steps; enter responses to the material; and receive immediate feedback on the correctness of their answers. Some programs give students more than one opportunity to respond to an item before telling them the correct answer.

Practice is important for developing accuracy in, and automaticity of, reading skills. Computer drill-and-practice programs help students do this by providing repetition without the impatience teachers sometimes manifest. When the goal is developing accuracy, the computer can be used to present a few exercises accompanied by clear, immediate feedback, particularly for incorrect answers. After children have attained accuracy, the teacher can have them practice using computer programs with larger numbers of exercises, sometimes emphasizing speed, that are accompanied by less extensive feedback. Some drill-and-practice programs recirculate missed items for further practice, without requiring the teacher to plan or execute such repetition. These programs can take the place of worksheets that are designed for the same purpose, but lack the motivational advantage or interactive nature of computer use or the capability to give immediate reinforcement or planned repetition. Drill-and-practice programs can conserve a teacher's time while providing individualized instruction. Computer drills can also provide such things as graphics, animations, and sound that increase the appeal of the lessons and offer support for the textual material.

Tutorial Programs. With these programs, the computer actually presents instruction, then follows it with practice activities. Depending on the correct and incorrect responses a student gives as the program progresses, he or she may be branched to a remedial sequence of instruction, taken back through the initial instruction, directed through the typical sequence for the instruction, or skipped ahead in the program to avoid unnecessary practice. Some programs do not give students direct control over the sequence; others allow them to request review, remedial help, or additional practice.

Programs may be self-paced or computer-paced. Self-paced programs allow students to move at their own rates through the material, thereby providing more attention to individual differences than computer-paced programs, which progress through the material at a predetermined rate. Sometimes the programs are self-paced on a page-by-page basis; the student presses "Enter" to continue. Other programs are designed to allow the student to choose a pace for the entire program when the study session starts.

Programs can also be linear or branching. Linear programs take all students through the same sequence of material, although they generally allow the students to progress at their own rates. Branching programs, on the other hand, adjust the instructional sequence according to each student's performance. Branching programs are obviously more helpful for individualizing instruction.

Tutorial programs are available at a number of difficulty levels, and some provide a wide range of choices of difficulty level in one package, making them more versatile tools in a diverse classroom. They are particularly helpful for offering individual instruction to students who are far above or far below the instructional levels of the others in the class, allowing them to proceed through individually appropriate material. They also can offer make-up instruction for students who have missed that instruction in class, while the teacher is freed for other tasks.

Simulation Programs. These programs set up situations that simulate real-life activities, such as running a business or traveling west in a wagon train, that cannot be offered in other ways in the curriculum because of limited time, changed conditions (when the past is being simulated), or limited financial and physical resources. Geisert and Futrell (1995, p. 93) point out that such a computer model "is not a complete rendition of reality, but it can be made sufficient to enable users to examine events and study relationships, such as the behavior of objects when colliding." Simulations give students the opportunity to use critical reading skills as they examine the current situation and their options and make decisions about how to proceed. The computer responds to the students' decisions and presents different outcomes, depending upon these decisions. This practice in evaluating options and drawing conclusions often seems more like play than study to students.

Simulation programs are often time-consuming to use, but if the programs can be saved and re-entered from the same place in a later session, students will be likely to stay with them until a conclusion is reached. Motivation for using these programs is often high.

Students enjoy joint work with simulation programs (with discussion about each needed decision and collaborative decision-making). Even university students can feel the excitement as they work as a group to complete a simulation activity designed for elementary school children. Discussion becomes animated and thoughtful, and logic is applied in arguments that try to sway others toward a particular decision.

Interactive fiction programs present stories that offer readers options for actions, as if they were characters involved in the story. The story lines are affected by the decisions of the students, so that each time a story is read it may proceed differently. These are a type of simulation program that show the consequences of decisions based on critical reading. They closely resemble the printed Choose Your Own Adventure books. These programs are generally highly motivational, and, because they can be used multiple times by each student, they are cost-effective items. Pairs of students may work with these programs together, making decisions collaboratively.

Educational Game Programs. These programs offer a variety of formats, often resembling arcade games. They are distinguished from other computer games in that they give students experiences related to educational goals, as well as providing a degree of entertainment. Computer graphics and sound effects allow presentation of informational material in a gamelike format; for example, the user might be asked to "shoot down" balloons containing words with long vowel sounds. Educational games offer one type of drill and practice, allowing students to work repetitively on fast, accurate responses, gaining automaticity.

Electronic games should be used to reinforce skills that have been taught. They should not be used only as a reward to students who finish work early, or the students who need the practice are the ones least likely to get it. Rather, games that are found to be instructionally sound should be assigned as a regular part of the curriculum to students who will likely benefit from the practice, and perhaps used as an option for free time for those who are not in particular need of practice, but enjoy the games.

Adventure games can advance reading skills in some instances. Using them requires reading instructions and reading for clues (Downes and Fatouros, 1995).

Computer-Managed Instruction (CMI)

Computer-managed instruction (CMI) can help teachers keep track of students' performance and guide their learning activities. CMI systems vary greatly in complexity. CMI systems may provide computer-scored tests on specific objectives and then match the students' deficiencies to available instructional materials, suggest instructional sequences for the teacher to use, or assign material directly to the student. Some systems produce reports for parents on the objectives that their children have mastered. The computer may also perform tasks such as averaging grades on a series of tests, thereby removing quite a bit of burdensome record keeping from the teacher's shoulders. Many electronic gradebook programs are available, and they offer many options. Some even have parent and student access possibilities, through which parents and students can dial in to the school computer and, using an identification number, access an individual student's grades and teacher comments. Electronic portfolios allow teachers to "save students' work in a variety of formats, such as text, graphics, audio, and video. They also provide a framework for organizing these collections" (Willis, Stephens, and Matthew, 1996, p. 153). An example is the *Grady Profile*, an electronic portfolio for the Macintosh computer. Complete CMI systems are expensive programs, and they should be evaluated carefully (Willis, Stephens, and Matthew, 1996; Bitter, Camuse, and Durbin, 1993). Some publishers of educational materials offer adjunct computer materials that include computer-managed lessons and tests, but computer-managed instructional materials are not as widely used as computer-assisted instructional materials (Geisert and Futrell, 1995).

Management components are built into some individual CAI programs. They allow the teacher to see how well children perform, and sometimes they indicate which items were answered incorrectly. The management components in some programs tell students when to move on to more difficult levels of the program or when to drop back to easier ones. Some of these management components, however, do not save results from session to session.

Using Multimedia for Classroom Presentations and Projects

Multimedia publishing software allows students to "expand classroom publishing to include colorful graphics, moving images, sound effects . . . , music, and written and spoken words" (D'Ignazio, 1991, p. 250). Such possibilities make high-interest projects possible. For example, *The Bank Street Writer for the Macintosh* (Scholastic Software) offers multiple fonts and has a hypertext function with buttons that allows students to provide additional explanations about their text, create databases of information about their subjects, or create sounds for their products. A graphic gallery, spelling checker, and thesaurus come with the package, and other Macintosh graphics can be imported. With today's multimedia programs students can input text with the keyboard, draw onscreen (or on paper and scan the material into the computer), use predrawn pictures and backgrounds, record sounds to include in documents, or select sounds from prerecorded ones. This helps students with varied learning styles to approach compositions more easily (Rose and Meyer, 1994).

Students and teachers can develop multimedia presentations with a variety of special software, including *ClarisWorks* (Claris Corporation), Microsoft's *PowerPoint*, Multimedia Design's *mPower*, and *HyperStudio* (Roger Wagner). The following Focus on Strategies describes how two middle-school classes completed such a presentation.

Focus on Strategies

Multimedia Presentations

The two middle-school classes that were discussed in the two previous Focus on Strategies features in this chapter developed an *mPower* presentation on each of the books that they read along with their university partners, and the university partners viewed the presentations just before the end-of-semester meetings.

The middle-school classroom teachers organized their classes into cooperative groups to work on specific portions of the multimedia presentation and developed a schedule for the group assignments. Each group produced a rough draft to show what it planned to do. Then each group used the computer to create its portion of the presentation. To do this, the students had to make decisions about important incidents to include, sequence to follow, visual and sound features to incorporate, transitions to use, and other considerations. They used the *mPower* program to develop a series of carefully designed and sequenced slides that represented main events and characters in the books. They incorporated student-produced drawings, photography, and music to develop powerful presentations of content. The university students were impressed by the professional appearance and the thoroughness of the presentations. Such productions required a depth of understanding of the material that went far beyond the ability to describe the stories in words.

Teachers face a challenge in evaluating students' multimedia projects. They need to consider the prior planning (storyboarding); the variety, appropriateness, and documentation of sources; the organization and design; the clarity of navigation signals; and the choice and integration of media (Brunner, 1996). Slick presentation cannot be allowed to overshadow accuracy and organization.

Some educators believe that extensive use of computers in classroom instruction will cause children to develop into social isolates, as they sit and interact with a computer screen instead of people. Others say that computers can be used by two or more students in collaborative ways that result in even more positive social interactions than are ordinarily found in a traditional classroom. What do *you* think?

Adjusting Instruction Through Technology

Many computers are now capable of reading texts aloud, using synthetic speech. This enhances the utility of computer programs for young children and for readers with visual disabilities. Computers can also provide larger print for visually impaired readers, and the color and typeface of print shown on the monitor can be changed. With *Wiggleworks: Scholastic Beginning Literacy System* (Scholastic), a program that presents established children's books on CD-ROM, students can record sentences in their own voices, enter the sentences into the computer, have the computer read what has been entered in synthetic speech, and replay their recorded speech at any point for comparison. This capability allows self-monitoring of students' writing, a feature that is useful for younger and less adept students (Rose and Meyer, 1994; Mike, 1994).

There are special pads that serve as input devices for young children who have not yet developed the fine-motor control necessary for keyboarding, and the same devices can be helpful for students with physical disabilities that affect motor control. Zorfass, Corley, and Remz (1994) describe a computer keyboard with Braille "sticky" overlays on the keys used in conjunction with a word-processing program with speech feedback to allow a blind girl with cerebral palsy to type and monitor her writing. An application referred to as *word prediction* allows students who have fine-motor difficulties to begin typing a word, and, as they type, a list of words beginning that way appears, allowing the student to choose the desired word without having to type it all. Another application, called *abbreviation expansion*, allows whole messages to be encoded and retrieved with a given keystroke combination. Headsticks, mouthsticks, and customized hand-held pointers are also available for students with physical problems. If a student can make a consistent movement of some kind, the computer can be used. Braille translation programs are available to allow printouts on Braille printers (Zorfass, Corley, and Remz, 1994).

Some people think that the motivational effect of using technology—particularly computers—will decline because of regular opportunities for such use. Others think the varied possibilities for using technological tools—especially computers—provide a constant stream of fresh motivation for using technology. What do *you* think?

Summary

Teachers are faced with a bewildering array of possible technological applications for their literacy classrooms. They need to understand the range of technology available, how to evaluate the different applications, and how to make technology an integral part of core learning.

Among the many technological tools that can be applied to literacy instruction are instructional transparencies, television programs, audiotapes, videotapes, CD-ROMs and videodiscs, and computer applications. Various combinations of technological tools are also used for multimedia applications. These tools can be used to present information and to allow students to do research and create presentations and written products. Computers are used in literacy instruction for word processing; for desktop publishing; to access databases, electronic books, electronic reference works, and the Internet; for electronic communications such as electronic mail, electronic mailing lists, electronic bulletin boards, and electronic videoconferencing; for computer-assisted instruction, including drill-and-practice, tutorial, simulation, and educational game programs; for computer-managed instruction; and for multimedia applications for classroom presentations and projects.

There are computer applications and materials that make possible the participation of students with special needs. Synthetic speech and large print on computer screens and printouts, as well as special input devices and output systems, are available today.

Test Yourself

True or False

_____ 1. Overhead projectors are outdated technology that no longer have valid classroom uses.

_____ 2. All teachers now have computers with CD-ROM drives available in their classrooms.

_____ 3. Any computer software can be used on any computer that a teacher happens to have in the classroom.

_____ 4. The best practice is for teachers to try out software before purchasing it.

_____ 5. Only one student at a time can work at a single classroom computer.

_____ 6. There are no television programs that fit comfortably into literacy instruction.

_____ 7. Videotaping and/or audiotaping student presentations can facilitate assessment.

_____ 8. Comparing a print version of a children's literature selection with a video version of the same story can be a good literacy experience for students.

_____ 9. CD-ROMs and videodiscs allow users to access information from them in a nonlinear fashion.

_____ 10. Many electronic books are available on CD-ROM.

_____ 11. Hypertext and hypermedia allow text and media, respectively, to be accessed in a nonsequential manner.

_____ 12. Hypertext and hypermedia usage may lead to "navigational problems" for users.

_____ 13. Teachers have to be programmers to use computers effectively in their classrooms.

_____ 14. CMI can help teachers keep track of students' performances on learning activities.

_____ 15. Management functions are built into some individual CAI programs.

_____ 16. Word-processing software takes much of the labor out of editing and revising written products.

_____ 17. Database programs allow the categorization, storage, and orderly retrieval of data collected during research reading.

_____ 18. Students can search the Internet using special browsers and search engines that allow keyword searches to locate information for reports or unit studies.

_____ 19. The accuracy of material that is posted to electronic bulletin boards or placed on Web pages is carefully monitored and can be accepted as accurate without students' doing further checking.

_____ 20. World Wide Web home pages are too complicated for elementary teachers and students to develop and maintain.

_____ 21. Web pages can include only text; no sound or graphics are possible.

_____ 22. E-mail projects can allow students to discuss literature selections with authors and other students all over the world.

_____ 23. Most classrooms currently use electronic videoconferencing.

_____ 24. Computer-assisted instructional programs vary widely in quality.

_____ 25. Drill-and-practice programs offer initial instruction in skills.

_____ 26. CAI programs may be self-paced or computer-paced.

_____ 27. Simulation programs set up situations that simulate real-life adventures.

_____ 28. *Multimedia* refers to the mixing of different media.

_____ 29. Computers are now capable of reading texts aloud, enhancing their utility for young children and readers with visual disabilities.

_____ 30. If a student can make a consistent movement of some kind, the computer can be used.

For your journal...

Keep a section in your journal for reviews of pertinent videotapes, video-discs, audiotapes, and computer programs that you might wish to use in your literacy program. If you can, try each one with students, and write a reaction about its effectiveness in the journal. You may want to include your reviews in your portfolio.

...And your portfolio

1. Develop a multimedia presentation on a literacy topic of your choice for a grade level of your choice and include a copy of it on disk or videotape in your portfolio.

2. Make a series of transparencies, using a computer program such as *Power-Point* or *mPower*, to help explain a literacy topic, such as "Propaganda Devices in Advertising." Use the transparencies with a group of students to teach a lesson. Evaluate the results in your journal. Put photocopies of your transparencies in your portfolio, along with the lesson plan that you taught.

12

Assessment of Student Progress

SETTING OBJECTIVES

When you finish reading this chapter, you should be able to

▶ Describe some ways in which authentic assessment differs from traditional assessment.

▶ Explain the importance of observation and identify some ways to record observations.

▶ Implement portfolio assessment in an elementary classroom.

▶ Identify some ways for students to assess their own progress.

Construct and interpret informal tests.

▶ Recognize and analyze the significance of a reading miscue.

▶ Identify some features and limitations of standardized tests.

*A*ssessment is the collection of data, such as test scores and informal records, to measure student achievement, and *evaluation* is the interpretation and analysis of these data. Evaluating student progress is important because it enables the teacher to discover each student's strengths and weaknesses, to plan instruction accordingly, to communicate student progress to parents, and to evaluate the effectiveness of teaching strategies. Assessing student learning is essential for good teaching and should be an integral part of instructional procedures. Although assessment is often simply equated with testing, multiple measures—such as day-to-day observation, student conferences, and samples of students' work—provide a more valid evaluation of a student's capabilities.

The field of assessment is undergoing a great many changes as researchers strive to make procedures correspond more closely with current views about the reading process. This chapter first examines some views of assessment and then presents several types of alternative assessment, many of which reflect the current emphasis on using authentic reading and writing tasks to evaluate student progress. After a brief look at criterion-referenced tests, the chapter concludes with a discussion of formal assessment.

Current Views of Assessment

Assessment serves many purposes (Leslie and Jett-Simpson, 1997; Serafini, 1997; Walbergh et al., 1994). Its primary intent is to evaluate student performance in order to provide accountability, classify and place students, or—most importantly—guide instruction. Standardized tests yield scores that school districts use for comparing student achievement with that from previous years and for comparing district scores with national norms. These tests, though often mandated, frequently fail to reflect current views of teaching reading and are of little use to teachers for day-to-day instruction. Schools often use test scores to place students in groups, determine who should receive enrichment or extra help, and decide if children should pass or fail. Assessment that guides instruction consists of observation, samples of students' work, and informal measures that enable teachers to make classroom decisions. By reflecting on these sources of information, teachers can gain understanding of each student's performance in order to plan long- and short-term instruction, determine lesson content, drive instructional decisions, and decide who needs to be engaged in certain types of learning experiences (Parker et al., 1995).

To bring assessment into line with current views of the reading process, many educators are moving toward *authentic assessment* (DeLain, 1995; Eby, 1998). Because it takes place during the teaching-learning process, this type of assessment is an integral part of the curriculum. Authentic assessment does not measure language as a set of fragmented subskills; rather, it treats oral and written language as an integrated whole. Such assessment occurs in the context of functional, relevant learning. "The aim of authentic assessment is to assess many different kinds of literacy abilities in contexts that closely resemble the actual situations in which

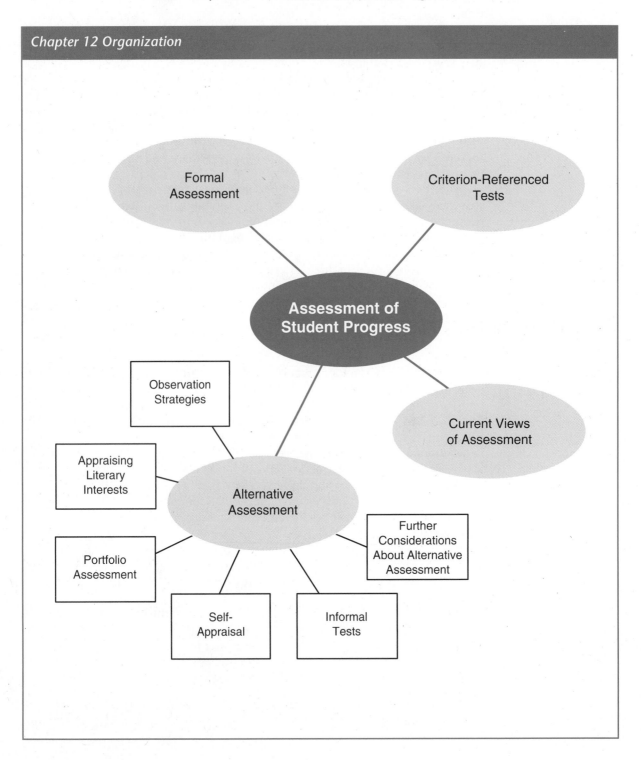

those abilities are used," according to Hiebert, Valencia, and Afflerbach (1994, p. 9). Teachers also use various types of *alternative assessment* to measure student performance in authentic situations, such as observation and analysis of work samples. Some types of alternative assessment, such as paper-and-pencil tests, however, are inappropriate for this purpose.

Ideally, instruction and assessment should merge (Brown and Lytle, 1988; Y. Goodman, 1989). "Evaluation is part of curriculum; it cannot be divorced from classroom organization, from the relationship between teachers and students, from continuous learning experiences and activities" (Y. Goodman, 1989, p. 4). Assessment should be a continuous process in which teachers observe and interact with students in various types of learning activities throughout the day. To provide a match between the strategies students use when they read and the skills that are being assessed, many educators are turning to kidwatching, portfolios, response journals, checklists, and retellings. They are also evaluating debates, collaborative activities, presentations, projects, journals, performances, exhibitions, process writing, and experiments (Sugarman, Allen, and Keller-Cogan, 1993; Wiggins, 1990). Assessment resembles good instruction when it occurs during typical learning activities, periods of social interaction, and times for reflection (Kapinus, 1994).

Assessment that corresponds with instruction should relate to students' prior knowledge, use complete text passages, accept different interpretations, and allow the reader to vary reading strategies. Many standardized tests do not exhibit these features, however (Kapinus, 1994; Shepard, 1989; Valencia and Pearson, 1987). Large-scale standardized tests must be objective, formal, time- and cost-efficient, widely applicable, centrally processed, and presented in a form useful to policy makers. They usually consist of multiple-choice items that primarily measure literal comprehension and isolated skills. Although efforts have been made to create standardized tests that more closely resemble authentic assessment, few changes in standardized-test format have actually been implemented.

Teachers who want their students to do well on tests therefore face a dilemma, because most tests still measure skill proficiency instead of the ability to read strategically. Many school systems exert pressure and provide incentives for high test scores; thus, teachers believe they must teach the subskills on the test instead of the more important concepts (Shepard, 1989). In the same vein, Winograd, Paris, and Bridge (1991, p. 109) say, "Misaligned tests force teachers to abandon their curricular goals to prepare students for skill-based tests."

Teachers today are gaining more control of assessment and are involving students in the process. Even though they want students to perform well on standardized tests, they realize that, in order to facilitate learning, they need the information that alternative assessments provide. Thus, as they reflect on ways to assess their students, they choose those that are most likely to be useful for making instructional decisions (Eby, 1998; Salinger, 1996).

Alternative assessment should be based on the following principles (Lipson and Wixson, 1997; Neill, 1997; *Standards for the Assessment of Reading and Writing*, 1994).

1. The major purpose of assessment is improvement of student learning.

2. Assessment is fair and equitable for all students.

3. Assessment involves all members of the educational community (i.e., parents, students, administrators, the public).

4. Communication about assessment is clear and regular.

5. Assessment includes a variety of perspectives and data.

6. Professional collaboration supports assessment.

7. Activities assessed are meaningful and contextualized (within daily instruction rather than on tests).

8. Assessment is continuous.

Alternative Assessment

Alternative assessment refers to all types of assessment other than formal, standardized tests. Concern about the inadequacies of standardized tests and about the need to look carefully at students' work in order to evaluate student performance have caused educators to take more interest in alternative assessment. This type of assessment involves students in creating and evaluating their own work, thus helping them develop a sense of responsibility and ownership. The following sections present some types of alternative assessment.

Observation Strategies

Since much student assessment occurs informally, teachers need to interpret their observations with insight and accuracy. Johnston (1987) suggests several characteristics of teachers who successfully evaluate students' literacy development. Expert evaluators recognize patterns of behavior and understand how reading and writing processes develop. They notice, for example, that one child is unable to make reasonable predictions or that another uses invented spellings effectively. Observant teachers listen attentively and perceptively, both at scheduled conferences and during the course of each day. Good observers evaluate as they teach, and they accept the responsibility for assessing children's needs and responding to them, instead of relying only on test data. On the basis of informal observations and even intuition, teachers can modify instructional strategies, clarify explanations, give individual help, use a variety of motivational techniques, adjust classroom management techniques, and provide reinforcement as needed.

Recordkeeping is an essential part of observation, and it may occur in different ways. Some teachers keep a notebook with a separate page to record observations for each child; others jot dated notes on sticky tags or on file cards that they later place in the students' files or portfolios. (See Example 12.1 for a sample observation card.) As they move about the room, teachers may carry clipboards for recording observations. Mickelson (1990) suggests that teachers use class sheets with a square for each name, similar in form to a calendar. As teachers write notes, they stick them on the children's names. At the end of the day or week, there may be many notes for some children and few for others. As children assume more responsibility for directing their own activities, teachers have more time to record observations (Rhodes and Nathenson-Mejia, 1992).

Example 12.1   *Observation Card*

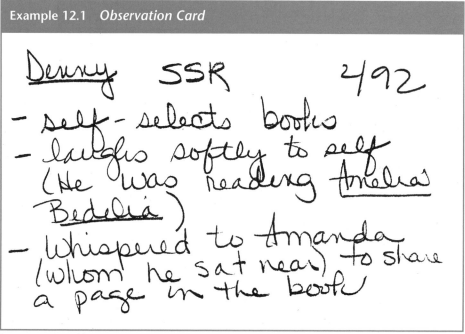

Source: Reprinted by permission from Beverly Mackie, Jere Whitson Elementary School, Cookeville, Tennessee, 1994.

Observation, Interaction, and Analysis

Three aspects of informal teacher evaluation are observation, interaction, and analysis (Goodman, Goodman, and Hood, 1989). During *observation*, the teacher carefully watches the activities of a single child, a group of children, or the whole class in order to evaluate language use and social behaviors. *Interaction* takes place when the teacher raises questions, responds to journal writing, and conferences with children in order to stimulate further language and cognitive growth. During *analysis*, the teacher gets information by listening to a child read or discuss and by examining a child's written work. The teacher then applies knowledge of learning principles to analyze the child's ability to use language.

Kidwatching

Kidwatching, a term introduced by Yetta Goodman (1978), is direct or informal observation of a child in various classroom situations. Based on the premise that language development is a natural process, kidwatching allows teachers to explore two questions: (1) What evidence exists that language development is occurring? and (2) What does a child's unexpected production say about the child's knowledge of language? It is based on three premises (Y. Goodman, 1985):

1. Observers should use a theoretically sound framework to make meaningful and unbiased interpretations of what they see.

2. Observers should watch children in a wide variety of literacy situations.

3. Observers should consider the interactions between children and adults in language learning.

<table>
<tr><td>Time for
Reflection</td><td>Although observation may be somewhat subjective and sporadic, many teachers are convinced that it is more useful for guiding instruction than test scores are. **What do *you* think?**</td></tr>
</table>

Anecdotal Records

Anecdotal records, written accounts of specific incidents in the classroom, are another option. The teacher records information about a significant language event: the time and place, the students involved, what caused the incident, what happened, and possibly the implications. Such records may be kept of individual students, groups, or the whole class. Their value lies mainly in evaluating progress, individualizing instruction, planning instruction, informing others (including the students), noting changes in language development, and understanding attitudes and behaviors (*A Kid-Watching Guide*, 1984; Rhodes and Nathenson-Mejia, 1992; Parker, 1995). Teachers who keep anecdotal records regularly become more sensitive to their students' special interests and needs than they were before they kept such records (Baskwill and Whitman, 1988). See Example 12.2 for a sample anecdotal record.

Example 12.2 *Anecdotal Record*

When Kim Ying was added to our class today, I asked Steve to be his buddy—to help him understand what we do in class, to eat lunch with him, to include him on the playground, etc. I was taking a big chance. Kim knew only a little English, and Steve has such a poor self-concept. Would putting them together work? I watched. Steve stuck to Kim like glue. When Kim was unsure what to do, Steve was there to show him. During free reading time, Steve showed Kim where to find books and recommended *The Very Quiet Cricket*, an easy favorite. Steve took Kim into a corner and helped him read, carefully pointing to the words and pictures. Steve was not only Kim's buddy, but also his tutor. I can see Kim beginning to feel comfortable in our class, and I am amazed at the way Steve's self-concept is blossoming with his new responsibility!

Checklists and Rating Scales

Some teachers also keep *checklists*, such as the literacy observation checklist in Example 12.3. Checklists are useful for recording information about student accomplishments and seeing at a glance what has been achieved and what needs further work. Rating scales provide additional information because teachers can assign numbers to each item, perhaps from 1 (lowest) to 5 (highest), according to each student's level of performance or achievement. Teachers can make several copies of the checklist or rating scale for each child and keep them in individual folders. By filling out the forms periodically and dating each one, teachers have a written record of each child's progress.

Example 12.3   *Literacy Observation Checklist*

Child's name _____ Teacher's name _____

Place a check beside each characteristic that the child exhibits.

Characteristics: **Dates:** _____ _____ _____

1. Uses variety of comprehension strategies.
2. Expresses interest in reading and writing.
3. Reads voluntarily.
4. Applies word recognition skills.
5. Writes coherently.
6. Reads aloud fluently.
7. Expresses ideas well orally.
8. Listens attentively.
9. Enjoys listening to stories.
10. Asks sensible questions.
11. Makes reasonable predictions.
12. Evaluates and monitors own work.
13. Works well independently.
14. Self-corrects errors.
15. Shows willingness to take risks.

An example of using a checklist for evaluation during literature circles, discussed in Chapters 7 and 8, comes from Natalie Knox's sixth-grade class (see the Classroom Scenario on evaluation in literature circles). This was Ms. Knox's and the children's first time to use multiple sets of books from quality literature instead of basal readers.

Classroom Scenario

Evaluation of Literature Circles

Natalie Knox reminds the students of their responsibilities for reading, discussing, writing in their literature logs, and planning for their next session while they are in their groups. She tries to meet with each group as both a participant and an evaluator. As she joins a group that is reading Lois Lowry's *Number the Stars*, she enters the discussion and also keeps a checklist of each student's status. One day's checklist is shown in Example 12.4.

Analysis of Scenario
As she visits different groups, Natalie is gaining a great deal of information over a period of time about students' interests and enthusiasm, ability to gain insights about characters and plot development, and skill in group interaction. From her observations, Natalie can make judgments about progress in student responses to literature and social interactions. The informal records of her observations can serve as a basis for parent conferences and entries on report cards.

Rubrics

A *rubric* provides specific criteria for describing student performance at different levels of proficiency in different content areas (O'Neil, 1994). Students receive a number of points that represent minimal to high-quality work, depending on the type of response. For example, during group reading, the criterion for a high-quality response that would earn the highest number of points might be "Carries on a meaningful conversation about reading," and the criterion for a minimal response with low or no points might be "Unable to express thoughts or feelings about reading material" (Winograd, 1994, p. 421). In some cases, educators establish criteria for district- or statewide standards and train scorers to be consistent in their grading (Garcia and Verville, 1994).

A well-constructed rubric lets students know in advance what is expected of them and helps teachers grade students' work fairly. When constructing rubrics, teachers may invite students to suggest criteria to include (Batzle, 1992). Then, when students receive their grades, they are more likely to understand them because they can refer to the criteria instead of just getting a letter grade without explanation. A rubric consists of *standards*, which refer to the levels at which students perform tasks, and *criteria*, or what is being evaluated. Some guidelines for writing rubrics include the following:

Base standards on samples of student work that represent each level of proficiency.

Example 12.4   Checklist for Literature Response Groups

Number the Stars — Meeting # 1

	Attended	Read to page	Shared # of items	Asked questions clarification	Made predictions &/or connections within the book (or other books)	Made connections to real situations	Responded to others in group	Read from response journal
Kristine Zeer	✓	60	✓	-Ellen's family?		-Far away relatives	✓ Missy Marie	hesitant
Marie Orby	✓	60	✓✓	-My star? -Buttons?	-Sisters death?		✓	excellent
Katie Smith	✓	125	✓✓✓✓	-Symbols? -Religion?		-Family friends religious difference		thorough
Missy Berg	✓	65	✓✓✓	-Peters involvement?			✓ Marie	detailed
Megan Clifton	✓	60	✓✓✓✓✓	-Symbols?	-Fishing? -Moms?s	-Aunts death		-skipped around -sequence?

Next meeting: 11/19
Read to: p. 94

Use precise wording that describes observable behaviors in terms that children can understand.

Avoid negative statements, such as "Cannot make predictions."

Construct rubrics with 3-, 4-, or 5-point scales, with the highest number representing the most desirable level.

Limit criteria to a reasonable number.

Example 12.5 is a sample rubric.

Example 12.5 *Rubric for Evaluating Research Reports*

Criteria	Standards		
	3	2	1
Content	This report covers all major aspects of the topic and is focused. It shows evidence of higher-order thinking and is based on three or more references.	This report covers several aspects of the topic, but omits some important information. It makes use of two or more references.	This paper is limited to one or two aspects of the topic. Only one source (or no source) of information is given.
Organization	This report is logically organized and easy to follow. The introduction presents the topic, the content follows in reasonable order, and the conclusion pulls information together.	This report shows some evidence of organization, but it lacks a clearly constructed beginning, middle, and end. Connections among subtopics are sometimes unclear.	This report is difficult to follow because it lacks a logical organizational plan. It shifts from one idea to another without making logical connections.
Use of Conventions	This paper shows consistent use of standard English and correct spelling, punctuation, capitalization, and paragraphing. It is neat and legible.	This paper indicates a general observance of conventions, but several errors exist in spelling, mechanics, and form.	This paper shows little awareness of writing conventions. Neatness and legibility are minimal.

Conferences and Interviews

Another type of informal assessment occurs when teachers have conferences with children (or interview them) about their attitudes, interests, and progress in reading. Conferences may be scheduled or may occur spontaneously when opportunities arise. Sample questions for teachers to ask include the following:

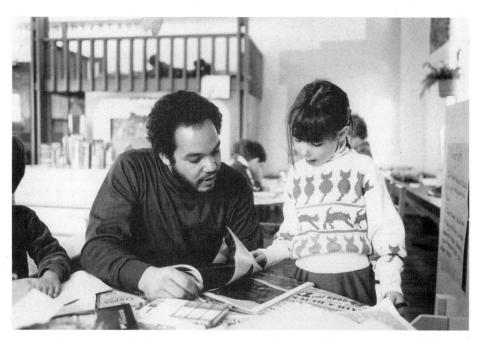

Teachers use informal assessment devices to observe and record individual strengths and weaknesses during the educational process, adjusting instruction to meet individual needs. (© *Susan Lapides*)

Do you like reading? Why or why not?

Do you think reading is important? Why or why not?

What books have you read recently? What did you like/dislike about them?

Are you a good reader? Why do you think that?

What do you do when you have a problem understanding what you are reading?

What do you do when you come to a word that you don't know?

Through interviews, teachers learn how students make interpretations and construct meaning. They also gain insights into the reasoning behind children's task performances as the children explain their answers (Seda and Pearson, 1991).

Retellings

Story retelling, another form of informal assessment, occurs when a student retells a story she or he has heard or read. Retellings can also be done with expository text and material from different genres, such as biographies, fables, and mysteries, so that the reader can explore different types of texts (Johnston, 1992). At first, the teacher encourages the student to retell without offering assistance, but when the student appears to have finished, the teacher may help by asking open-ended questions that will stimulate further retelling. By listening carefully and taking notes, the teacher can learn much about a student's understanding and appreciation of the story. Retellings also benefit students by improving their comprehension, sense of structure, and use of oral language (Fisette, 1993).

Appraising Literary Interests

An observant teacher who takes time to be a sensitive, yet critical, evaluator of children's progress is probably the best judge of the quality of their reactions to literature. The following questions will help the teacher in the evaluation process: Are the children

1. gaining an appreciation of good literature? How do I know?
2. making good use of time in the library and during free reading of books and periodicals?
3. enjoying storytelling, reading aloud, choral reading, and creative drama?
4. increasing their understanding of their own and other cultures through knowledge of the contributions of their own people and people of other lands?
5. maturing in awareness of the structure and forms of literature?
6. able to compare books by author's style, characterization, settings, plot development, and so forth?

Teachers can obtain answers to these questions through children's spontaneous remarks ("Do you know any other good books about space travel?"), through directed conversation with the class ("What books would you like to add to our classroom library?"), and during individual conferences, when children have opportunities to describe books they like and dislike.

One excellent device for showing changes in literary taste over a period of time is a *cumulative reading record*, in which children record each book they read, giving the author, title, kind of book, date of report, and a brief statement of how well they liked the book. Another device is a *personal reading record*, maintained separately by (or for) each child. This record classifies reading selections by topic such as poetry, fantasy, adventure, mystery, myths and folklore, animals (or more specifically, for example, horses and dogs), biography, other lands, and sports. By focusing on the types of literature the children read, teachers may encourage them to read about new topics and to expand their reading interests.

Portfolio Assessment

Many teachers—in some cases statewide—are adopting a portfolio approach to assessment. A *portfolio* is a collection of a student's work over a period of time, usually kept in an expandable file folder. The portfolio enables students and teachers to analyze and reflect on student work in order to evaluate progress. It should focus on what a student *can* do. There is no single way to implement portfolios unless a district mandates procedures and inclusions, so teachers and students must decide what works best for them. Three types of portfolios are listed below (Batzle, 1992; Leslie and Jett-Simpson, 1997; Salinger, 1996).

1. A *working portfolio*, a sampling of student work usually chosen by the student in collaboration with the teacher

2. A *showcase portfolio*, student-selected samples of best work only, likely to be shared with parents during conferences

3. A *record-keeping portfolio*, records of evaluation and test scores kept by the teacher, often for purposes of accountability

Contents of portfolios should be dated and will vary according to the purposes for using them and the criteria for selection. Possible inclusions are the following (Fiderer, 1995; Wiener and Cohen, 1997): writing samples (from first draft to published work, to show growth); literacy goals; accounts of authentic classroom experiences; a variety of tasks that demonstrate purposeful use of language; communications with others; audiotapes or videotapes; reasons for selecting certain pieces; and reflections and self-evaluations.

Valencia (1990) identifies four guiding principles based on research and classroom practice for implementing a working portfolio approach. Assessment must be authentic, continuous, multidimensional (including a wide range of cognitive processes and literacy activities), and collaborative (involving reflection by both teacher and student). It should be aligned with curriculum and instruction (Valencia and Place, 1994).

During the year students indicate their progress in a variety of ways; thus, selective samples of their work can provide an overview of the year's work. In deciding which samples to include in a portfolio, the teacher must first consider the goals of the instructional program (Valencia, 1990; Weaver, 1990). Samples should reflect broad, holistic curricular goals, not narrow tasks.

Implementing portfolio assessment is not easy (Stowell and Tierney, 1995). Teachers face many difficult decisions, such as what to include in order to reflect the range of activities students are pursuing and the extent of students' capabilities. They need to consider how to analyze the material, how to evaluate the contents for grading purposes, and how to guide students' selections of their best work. Teachers therefore must ask themselves: Who will see the portfolios? What should a portfolio look like? Who decides what to include? How should information be shared? Moving from traditional testing practices to assessing student progress with portfolios can be a difficult transition that may take several years.

In most cases, both students and teacher should decide what goes into the portfolio, and the portfolio should be accessible to both for review at all times. Farr (1989) suggests that students should be responsible for organizing and maintaining their portfolios so that they are ready to use as a basis for discussion with the teacher. For the portfolio to be passed along from year to year, it must be manageable in size, so some information must be summarized, some samples sent home at the end of the year, and only the most meaningful samples kept.

Although it is important for teachers and students to review portfolios together periodically, such reviews can consume considerable time. Teachers should develop rotating schedules in order to have conferences with students at least once a month. The Focus on Strategies illustrates one type of conferencing procedure.

Focus on Strategies

Using Portfolio Assessment

Although this was Mr. Fernandez's first year to use portfolios, he was quickly becoming aware of their usefulness. They were very helpful during parent conferences, because he could show the parents exactly what their children had done during a six-week period—the progress they had made or, in a few cases, the lack of progress. The parents seemed to understand better what their children were doing by looking at their work than by having him try to explain it.

Mr. Fernandez had also found the samples of students' work useful when it was time to give report card grades. He had always believed that grades should be more than averages of test scores, and now he could use their work samples to supplement the test score averages. Quite often, an examination of their work told him they were capable of better work than their tests indicated. If anyone questioned his judgment about his grades, he would be able to show these samples, along with the test scores, to support his evaluation.

Perhaps best of all, many children liked working on their portfolios. They really enjoyed looking back through their papers, recalling different pieces they had worked on and realizing they were getting better. They also liked being able to choose which pieces to include, although sometimes Mr. Fernandez suggested additional pieces.

He had told some of the students that he would meet with them today about their portfolios and asked them to pull their portfolios from the file in the back of the room and have them ready. Now, while they were reading independently, he would begin visiting these children at their seats. Taking along a stool, he seated himself beside Marcus and said quietly, "Marcus, let's see what you've included in your portfolio."

Marcus proudly showed his table of contents, which some of the children had decided to make. Then he turned to the section on his literature log. Marcus confided to Mr. Fernandez, "I really enjoyed reading *Hatchet*. I wanted to include what I wrote about it so I can remember why I liked the book so much." As Mr. Fernandez glanced through Marcus's responses, he could see that Marcus had some remarkable insights about Brian's problem-solving processes as Brian attempted to survive in the wilderness. Marcus had not simply summarized what happened, but had reflected on Brian's survival skills and identified them with his own. "I like the way you refer to Brian's problem-solving skills, Marcus," Mr. Fernandez said. "Can you think how you might learn more about survival skills?"

Leaving Marcus to ponder this question, Mr. Fernandez moved on to Tabitha and asked to see her portfolio. Reluctantly, Tabitha pulled it from her desk and opened it. Her papers were disorganized: math tests were mixed in with writing samples, and some work was undated. Mr. Fernandez asked her what she might do to get her papers ready to show him, and she said she would try to put all the reading and writing papers together. He agreed to return later. It was strange that some children seemed to care so much about their portfolios, whereas others took little interest in them.

Robin was next. She had been waiting for Mr. Fernandez and had her portfolio open. Eagerly, she produced a letter she had just completed about cleaning up the environment. "You know how we've been studying about the environment," Robin said. "I really got excited about doing something when you read us *A River Ran Wild*, so I decided to write a letter and send it to the editor of the *Tribune*. Do you think they'll print it?" As Mr. Fernandez read through the letter, he realized that Robin had picked up ideas from the book that she was applying to Simpson's Pond, the one that had become so polluted that fish couldn't live in it anymore. "This letter has many fine recommendations in it," Mr. Fernandez told Robin. "I think you should send it. Can you find the address?"

Moving on to Jeremy, Mr. Fernandez asked, "Jeremy, did you include your report on reptiles in your portfolio? You seemed really interested in writing about your findings, and I'd like to see what you've done." After shuffling through some papers, Jeremy found the report and showed it to Mr. Fernandez. "You have some good notes here and a rough draft," said Mr. Fernandez. "Where is your finished paper?" Jeremy admitted he hadn't done one, adding that he didn't like to have to write papers over. Reflecting on Jeremy's comment, Mr. Fernandez asked him how he would feel about using the computer to word process his paper. Glancing up, Jeremy said that idea might work. "Writing it on the computer is better because I can make the changes easier. Maybe I'll try that." "Be sure to show it to me when you finish," said Mr. Fernandez. "I'm interested in what you write."

Next, Mr. Fernandez came up to Kurt and asked to see his portfolio. "Show me whatever you like," he told Kurt. Kurt pulled out a review he had written of *Maniac Magee*. As Mr. Fernandez looked at the paper, he noticed that this review was little more than a summary and was carelessly written. He knew Kurt had done much better writing than this sample. "Why did you choose this, Kurt?" he asked. "I don't know," Kurt responded. "I guess I just put any old thing in. I don't see what difference it makes." "It's important that you have a reason to place pieces in your portfolio," said Mr. Fernandez. "Think how you can select your most significant work."

When Mr. Fernandez completed his visits for the morning, he realized how much he had learned about the students' work as they explained their portfolios to him. From Kurt he learned that he would need to help students make judgments about their work so that they could decide which selections merited inclusion in their portfolios. He would need to spend more time with Tabitha. She really needed some help with organizing her portfolio and completing her work. Perhaps Robin

(continued)

would help her; they seemed to get along well, and Robin's portfolio was well organized. He needed to find a way to encourage Jeremy to finish his work. The computer seemed to motivate him this time, but he would need to help Jeremy set goals for completing his work. Robin had surprised him with her enthusiasm about the environment. He needed to encourage her to find ways to extend her interest. Marcus was such an avid reader that his responses to *Hatchet* were no surprise. What Marcus needed was a good supply of books, time to read, and opportunities to respond. Mr. Fernandez realized that periodic portfolio reviews were a fine way to get to know his students better and understand their work.

Next year, Mr. Fernandez thought, he would do a few things differently. He had heard of placing an audiotape in each portfolio and recording the children's oral reading periodically. That would be another way to measure their progress. He also needed a better system of weeding out some of their work; their portfolios would be quite bulky by the end of the year. He would try to get some ideas from teachers who were already using portfolios so that he could make the procedure run more smoothly next time. "We're off to a good start this year, though," Mr. Fernandez thought, "and next year will be even better."

How can portfolios be used for evaluation? No grades should be given on the portfolios themselves (Farr and Tone, 1994), but portfolio assessment can (1) show what students have learned over a period of time, (2) enable students to develop criteria for judging their own work, (3) relate to real-life learning opportunities that reflect day-to-day thinking, (4) offer guidance for setting individual goals, and (5) enable teachers to evaluate teaching practices and curricula (DeFina, 1992).

Self-Appraisal

Assessment should help students develop the ability to judge their own accomplishments—to set their own goals, decide how to achieve those goals, and assess their progress in meeting the goals—in order to experience a sense of ownership in the assessment process (Au, 1990). Teachers can guide students toward self-assessment in a number of ways (Hansen, 1992; Winograd, Paris, and Bridge, 1991). By sharing audiotapes of oral reading, observation note cards, and checklists, teachers can help students become aware of their strengths and ways they might improve. Through interviews, they can help students focus on their own progress by asking such questions as "How has your reading improved in the last month?" and "What goals would you like to set for yourself in reading and writing?" By including student self-evaluations as part of report card grades, teachers show students that they value their judgments.

Students who display metacognition are aware of how they learn and of their personal strengths and weaknesses in relation to specific learning tasks.

They ask themselves questions in order to assess the difficulty of an assignment, the learning strategies they might use, any potential problems, and their likelihood of success. While reading or studying, their self-questioning might proceed as follows:

1. Do I understand exactly what I am supposed to do for this assignment?
2. What am I trying to learn?
3. What do I already know about this subject that will help me understand what I read?
4. What is the most efficient way for me to learn this material?
5. What parts of this chapter may give me problems?
6. What can I do so that I will understand the hard parts?
7. Now that I am finished reading, do I understand what I read?

The self-appraisal form in Example 12.6 is designed primarily for intermediate and middle-school children. It enables them to assess their competency in various reading skills and recognize areas of strength or weakness. Teachers can use the results to understand students' perceptions of their own needs and plan appropriate instruction. Another application for self-appraisal is found in Natalie Knox's literature circles (see the Classroom Scenario on literature circle self-evaluation).

Example 12.6 *Self-Check Exercise*

Directions: Read the following sentences and put a number beside each one.
Put 1 beside the sentence if it is nearly always true.
Put 2 beside the sentence if it is sometimes true.
Put 3 beside the sentence if it is hardly ever true.

_____ I understand what I read.

_____ I can find the main idea of a paragraph.

_____ I think about what I read and what it really means to me.

_____ I can "read between the lines" and understand what the author is trying to say.

_____ I think about what I already know about the subject as I read.

_____ I can figure out new words by reading the rest of the sentence.

_____ I can figure out new words by "sounding them out."

_____ I can use a dictionary to figure out how to pronounce new words.

_____ I can use a dictionary to find word meanings.

_____ I know how to find information in the library.

Example 12.6   *Self-Check Exercise (cont.)*

_____   I can find books I like to read in the library.
_____   I can read aloud easily and with expression.
_____   I know what is important to learn in my textbooks.
_____   I know how to use the indexes in my books.
_____   I know how to study for a test.
_____   I ask myself questions as I read to make sure I understand.

**Classroom
Scenario**

Literature Circle Self-Evaluation

The students have completed the book for their literature circle, and it is time to fill out the self-evaluations Natalie has given them. They rate themselves from 0 (not at all) to 3 (above average) on criteria related to their reading, their group responses, and their writing logs. After carefully rating themselves, they give themselves grades and justify their grades with reasons. Some of the children wrote as follows:

The grade I think I deserve for this literature group is ___*A*___ because

most of the answers above are number threes. And I love discussing questions and other things about my book.

The grade I think I deserve for this literature group is ___B___ because

I think I deserve a B because I sometimes took my vocabulary folder home and left it and then didn't have it.

The grade I think I deserve for this literature group is ___B___ because

I did ok but I didn't do perfect a C is rediculous but an A is way too much!

The grade I think I deserve for this literature group is ___B___ because

I guess I deserved this grade because sometimes I didn't keep up with litterature responce and reading.

The grade I think I deserve for this literature group is ___B___ because

Because I really made disturbances when it was supposed to be quiet reading time   But I do apoligize.

The grade I think I deserve for this literature group is ___C___ because

I think I can do better in keeping up with my journal. Mostly, I keep my voice level down and rarely get called down.

Analysis of Scenario
Such self-evaluation encourages children to reflect on their work and to become aware of their strengths and weaknesses. In so doing, they become independent learners.

Time for Reflection

Traditionally, teachers have felt that assessment was their job and that students should have little or nothing to say about their own work. Today, however, many teachers give students opportunities for appraising their own work. Should students be encouraged to do so? **What do *you* think?**

Informal Tests

In addition to such informal assessments as observations, checklists, rubrics, and portfolios, teachers may administer informal tests for specific purposes. Teachers may construct these tests or may find them commercially available in manuals or books.

Informal Tests of Specific Content or Skills

Sometimes the classroom teacher needs to administer an informal test to check students' knowledge and understanding of a specific skill or content area. For instance, the teacher might construct a vocabulary test from words students have studied during a thematic unit. Basal reader programs usually include tests to be used for determining how well students have learned the content of a specific unit of instruction. Workbooks also contain skill tests to be given periodically. Whenever such tests are given, they should be used for diagnosing students' strengths and weaknesses, deciding if reteaching is needed, and providing direction for future learning experiences.

Cloze Procedure

The cloze procedure, described in Chapter 10, helps the teacher know if a textbook is easy or difficult for a child to read. By filling in words that have been deleted from a textbook selection, the student reveals his or her familiarity with the subject and ability to read the text with understanding. Test results give information about the student's independent, instructional, or frustration levels for both narrative and expository material.

Multimedia and Computer Approaches

Multimedia and computers provide motivational alternatives to traditional testing. Photographs of completed projects, audiotapes of children retelling stories or reading orally, and videotapes of student performances and students at work are useful for recording and evaluating children's learning experiences throughout the year. Multimedia computer presentations, prepared by students, show evidence of facility with a number of literacy skills.

Teachers can use computers for assessment in several additional ways. Online testing allows students to work at terminals connected to a computer that analyzes their responses. Sometimes computers are used to scan mark-sensitive answer sheets that students have completed while working with test booklets. The computer scores the tests, thus freeing the teacher from this task. Software is also available to help teachers modify test items and entire tests, perform test and item analysis, collect and analyze test scores and student grades, record grades for various assignments, and compute final grades (Kubiszyn and Borich, 1987). With *Grady Profile Portfolio Assessment* software, teachers can gather and review all of a student's written work, as well as samples of oral presentations. *Gradebook Plus* enables teachers to record grades daily and compute a student's average grade at any time (McCarthy, 1994).

Informal Reading Inventory

Teachers administer *informal reading inventories (IRIs)* to get a general idea of a child's strengths and weaknesses in word recognition and comprehension. IRIs help teachers identify specific types of word recognition and comprehension difficulties so that they can use this information to plan appropriate instruction. An IRI can indicate a child's

1. independent reading level (level to be read "on his or her own").

2. instructional level (level of the material the child can read with teacher guidance).

3. frustration level (level that thwarts or baffles).

4. capacity level (potential reading level).

The oral reading sequence in an informal reading inventory should begin on the highest level at which the child achieves 100 percent on a sight word recognition test. After the oral reading, the teacher asks questions about the selection; then the child reads the silent reading part and is asked questions about that selection.

Material is written at a child's *independent* reading level when he or she correctly pronounces 99 words in 100 (99 percent correct) and correctly responds to at least 90 percent of the questions. The material for which the child correctly pronounces 95 percent of the words and correctly answers at least 75 percent of the questions is roughly at the child's *instructional* level, the level at which teaching may effectively take place.

If a student needs help on more than one word out of ten or responds correctly to fewer than 50 percent of the questions, the material is too advanced and is at the child's *frustration* level. After the frustration level has been reached, the teacher should read aloud higher levels of material until the child reaches the highest reading level for which he or she can correctly answer 75 percent of the comprehension questions. The highest level achieved indicates the child's probable *capacity* (potential reading) level.

Teachers may make their own informal reading inventories, or they may use commercially prepared inventories. Example 12.7 shows a sample reading selection with comprehension questions and scoring aid from the *Burns/Roe Informal Reading Inventory*.

It is important to remember that the result of an informal reading inventory is an *estimate* of a reader's abilities. The percentages the child achieves are a significant indication of levels of performance, but the teacher's observations of the child taking the test are equally important.

Miscue Analysis

Similar in form and procedures to the informal reading inventory, the *reading miscue inventory (RMI)* considers both the quantity and quality of *miscues*, or unexpected responses. Instead of simply considering the number of errors with equal weight for each, the teacher analyzes the RMI for the significance of each miscue. Knowing the type of miscue and what might have caused it provides more information about reading difficulties than knowing the number of miscues. (Some commercial IRIs, such as the one in Example 12.7, also include a qualitative analysis.)

Miscue analysis helps teachers gain insight into the reading process and helps them analyze students' oral reading (Y. Goodman, 1995). Analysis of the types of miscues each student makes helps the teacher interpret why students are having

Example 12.7 *Reading Selection and Questions from an Informal Reading Inventory*

TEACHER 5 ☆

INTRODUCTORY STATEMENT: Read this story to find out about a harbor seal pup that has a special problem.

In the sea, a harbor seal pup learns to catch and eat fish by watching its mother. By the time it is weaned, at the age of four or five weeks, it is able to feed on its own.

Without a mother, and living temporarily in captivity, Pearson had to be taught what a fish was and how to swallow it. Eventually, he would have to learn to catch one himself.

Holly started his training with a small herring—an oily fish which is a favorite with seals. Gently, she opened his mouth and slipped the fish in headfirst. Harbor seals have sharp teeth for catching fish but no teeth for grinding and chewing. They swallow their food whole.

But Pearson didn't seem to understand what he was supposed to do. He bit down on the fish and then spit it out. Holly tried again. This time, Pearson got the idea. He swallowed the herring in one gulp and looked eagerly for more.

Within a week, he was being hand-fed a pound of fish a day in addition to his formula. This new diet made him friskier than ever. He chased the other pups in the outside pen. He plunged into the small wading pool and rolled in the shallow water, splashing both seals and people.

Source: Pearson, A Harbor Seal Pup, by Susan Meyers, New York: E.P. Dutton, 1980, pp. 15–16.

[Note: Do not count as a miscue mispronunciation of the name Pearson. You may pronounce this name for the student if needed.]

FORM A

COMPREHENSION QUESTIONS

_____ main idea	1.	What is this story about? (teaching a harbor seal pup to catch and eat fish; teaching Pearson to catch and eat fish)
_____ detail	2.	How does a harbor seal pup learn to catch and eat fish in the sea? (by watching its mother)
_____ vocabulary	3.	What does the word "temporarily" mean? (for a short time; not permanently)
_____ vocabulary	4.	What does the word "captivity" mean? (the condition of being held as a prisoner or captive; confinement; a condition in which a person or animal is not free)
_____ cause and effect/ inference	5.	What caused Pearson to need to be taught what a fish was and how to swallow it? (He didn't have a mother to show him.)
_____ inference	6.	What is an oily fish that seals like? (herring)
_____ cause and effect/ inference	7.	What causes harbor seals to swallow their food whole? (They have no teeth for grinding and chewing.)
_____ sequence	8.	Name in order the two things that Pearson did the first time Holly put a fish in his mouth. (bit down on the fish and then spit it out)
_____ inference	9.	How fast did Pearson learn how to eat a fish? (He learned on the second try.)
_____ detail	10.	What made Pearson get friskier? (his new diet of fish and formula; his new diet)

5 PASSAGE ☆

SCORING AID

Word Recognition
%–Miscues
99–3
95–11
90–22
85–33

Comprehension
%–Errors
100–0
90–1
80–2
70–3
60–4
50–5
40–6
30–7
20–8
10–9
0–10

214 Words
(for Word Recognition)

217 Words
(for Rate)

WPM
13020

Source: Betty D. Roe, *Burns/Roe Informal Reading Inventory*, Fifth Edition. Copyright © 1999 by Houghton Mifflin Company. Used with permission.

difficulties. To some extent, miscues are the result of the thought and language the student brings to the reading situation. Therefore, analyzing miscues in terms of the student's background or schemata enables the teacher to understand why some miscues were given and to provide appropriate instructional strategies that build on strengths.

Teachers should consider whether miscalled words indicate lack of knowledge about phonics or structural analysis, show inability to use context, reveal limited sight word knowledge, result from dialect differences, or suggest some other type of difficulty. Therefore, while listening to a child read, a teacher must evaluate the significance of different miscues. For example, the child who reads "The boys are playing" as "The boys is playing" may be a speaker of a nonstandard dialect and may be using his or her decoding ability to translate the printed text to meaning. This miscue does not intefere with meaning, but many miscues do reflect problems.

In studying the miscues, the teacher should check for specific items such as the following:

1. Is the miscue a result of the reader's dialect? If he says *foe* for *four*, he may simply be using a familiar pronunciation that does not affect meaning.

2. Does the miscue change the meaning? If the reader says *dismal* for *dismiss*, the meaning is likely changed and the substitution would not make sense.

3. Does the reader self-correct? If he says a word that does not make sense but self-corrects, he is trying to make sense of reading.

4. Is he using syntactic cues? If he says *run* for *chase*, he still shows some use of syntactic cues, but if he says *boy* for *beautiful*, he is probably losing the syntactic pattern.

5. Is he using graphic cues? Comparing the sounds and spellings of miscues and expected words in substitutions will reveal how a reader is using graphic cues. Examples of graphic miscues include *house* for *horse*, *running* for *run*, *is* for *it*, and *dogs* for *dog*.

Time for Reflection	Some educators believe that counting the total number of miscues a reader makes is sufficient for purposes of evaluation, but others consider it important to analyze miscues to find the reasons for unexpected responses. **What do *you* think?**

Running Records

The *running record* is a strategy that tells how well a student is reading (Clay, 1979). The procedure for completing the running record is similar to that used with the IRI or RMI. While a child is reading, the teacher places a check above every word read correctly. When a child makes a miscue, the teacher uses a coding system to mark the type of miscue. After completing the running record for the three samples, the teacher considers why the child made each miscue by asking, "What made him/her say that?"

Running records are particularly useful for classroom teachers because they can handle them quickly and easily in any oral reading situation in which they can see the text that a student is reading (Lipson and Wixson, 1997). Students' miscues offer insights into how well they use various reading strategies, construct meaning from text, and monitor their own reading (e.g., self-correct if something doesn't make sense). As a result, teachers become aware of students' strengths and weaknesses and gain information to guide their instruction (Salinger, 1996).

Further Considerations About Alternative Assessment

Although alternative assessment gives a great deal of information about how well a child uses reading strategies, it has some limitations that teachers should consider. First, alternative assessment is subjective; that is, the teacher's personal biases may influence judgments about student performance. Therefore, it is possible for two teachers to assess the same work differently. Also, some teachers may not be knowledgeable about the use of informal strategies or may not have realistic expectations for students at a certain level, so their assessments may not be fair appraisals of student performance. Alternative assessment can also place a heavy burden on teacher time if teachers write frequent narrative reports on student progress instead of simply assigning numerical or letter grades based on objective test results. In addition, teachers must know how to interpret and apply information from informal records to help children improve their reading strategies.

Another limitation of alternative assessment becomes apparent when some parents and administrators insist on grade point records, which are not available through many types of informal assessment. School systems often stress accountability, which means that sets of scores must be available for each student. Thus, for a variety of reasons, most school systems require the use of formal tests along with informal assessment.

Criterion-Referenced Tests

A *criterion-referenced* (or objective-referenced) *test* is designed to yield scores that are interpretable in terms of specific performance standards, for example, to indicate that a student can identify the main idea of a paragraph 90 percent of the time. Such tests, which may be commercially prepared or teacher constructed, are intended to be used as guides for developing instructional prescriptions. For example, if a child cannot perform the task of identifying cause-and-effect relationships, the teacher should provide instruction in that area. Such specific applications make these tests useful in day-to-day decisions about instruction.

However, educators have important questions concerning criterion-referenced tests. How many correct answers are needed to show that the student has achieved an objective or performed up to standard? Should every child be expected to meet every objective? Most importantly, does knowing the skill mean that the child can apply it in authentic situations?

Criterion-referenced testing has both advantages and disadvantages. It is an effective way to diagnose a child's knowledge of reading skills, and it helps in prescribing appropriate instruction. Furthermore, students do not compete with other students, but only try to achieve mastery of each criterion or objective. On the other hand, reading can appear to be nothing more than a series of skills to be taught and tested, and skills may be taught in isolation rather than in combination. Knowledge gained in this way may be difficult for children to apply to actual reading situations.

Formal Assessment

Formal assessment refers to published standardized tests that have been constructed by experts in the field and are administered, scored, and interpreted according to specific criteria (Lipson and Wixson, 1997; Rubin, 1997). For seventy years or longer, standardized tests have remained essentially the same (VanLeirsburg, 1993). Comprehension sections consist of series of short passages followed by multiple-choice questions, and tests require students to identify a single correct answer for each test item. Estimates of a child's reading ability are based on the number of correct answers as found in an answer key. Many educators believe standardized tests fail to measure thinking and problem-solving skills, in-depth knowledge of subjects, and students' abilities to direct their own learning (Harp, 1994; Sugarman, Allen, and Keller-Cogan, 1993).

Norm-referenced tests are standardized. They measure a student's relative standing in relation to comparable groups of students across the nation or locally. Authors of these tests sample large populations of children to determine the appropriateness of test items. They seek to verify the *validity* and *reliability* of test results so that schools can be confident that the tests measure what they are intended to measure and that results will not vary significantly if students take the same test more than once.

Results of norm-referenced tests are most commonly expressed as grade equivalents (or grade scores), percentile ranks, or stanines. A *grade equivalent* indicates the grade level, in years and months, for which a given score was the average score in the standardization sample. *Percentile rank (PR)* expresses a score in terms of its position within a set of 100 scores. The PR indicates the percentage of scores in a reference group that is equal to or lower than the given score; therefore, a score ranked at the fortieth percentile is equal to or better than the scores of 40 percent of the people in the reference group. On a *stanine scale,* the scores are divided into nine equal parts, with a stanine of 5 as the mean.

Most schools administer standardized *achievement tests* in the spring or fall every year to assess the gains in achievement of groups of children. Most of these tests are actually batteries, or collections of tests on different subjects, and should be given under carefully controlled conditions and over the course of several days. They may be sent to the publisher for machine scoring. Many standardized achievement tests contain subtests in reading and language, which

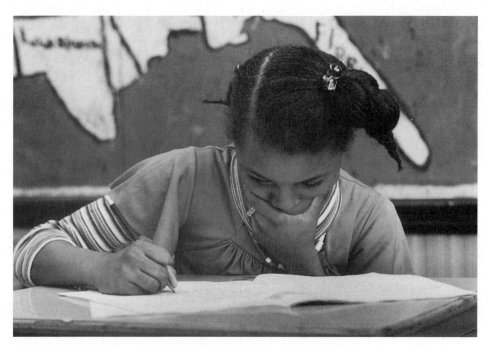

Norm-referenced tests can provide teachers with objective data about reading achievement, scholastic aptitude, and areas of strengths and weaknesses. (© *Jean Claude Lejeune*)

provide useful information for identifying students' general strengths and weaknesses in reading.

Standardized tests are often misused, however, and have serious limitations. In order to understand the limitations of standardized achievement tests, teachers should consider the following questions.

Do tests really measure what we know about the reading process today? Standardized tests often do not reflect current thinking about reading comprehension as a strategic process because

1. The test may check knowledge of vocabulary by asking students to find one of several words that most closely matches an isolated key word, instead of asking students to identify vocabulary in context, in the manner in which readers nearly always encounter words.

2. The test may assess reading comprehension on the basis of answers to series of short, unrelated paragraphs, instead of asking students to read longer passages as they would in real reading situations.

3. The test may present material without regard for students' prior knowledge, instead of considering the way students' existing schemata interact with the text as students construct meaning.

Is the test fair to all ethnic groups and inner-city children? Test publishers have been giving increasing attention to the question of the fairness of their tests. They do not want to state questions in a way that will give certain children an unfair advantage or discourage some children so that they will not do their best. Many writers and editors from different backgrounds are involved in testmaking, and members of several ethnic groups review questions to correct unintentional, built-in biases.

How are test scores being used? Too much emphasis is being placed on standardized test scores if they are the only source used to classify children as gifted or learning disabled, group children according to achievement levels, match materials designed for a particular reading level with children who scored at that level, or place children in remedial classes. Although standardized tests may be one consideration, placements in special groups should be the result of evaluating multiple assessments (Eby, 1998; Flippo, 1997).

Time for Reflection	Many teachers believe that children should not have to take standardized tests, yet most administrators and legislators require them. **What do** *you* **think?**

Recently, researchers have been seeking to establish more authentic ways to assess reading ability, by taking into consideration students' thought processes and reading strategies. Educators believe that because test scores often are used to direct instruction and predict performance, tests should measure the high-level thinking strategies students actually employ when reading (Powell, 1989). Therefore, developers of standardized tests have been seeking ways to measure a student's ability to apply reading strategies in a variety of authentic reading tasks.

Rather than focusing on single correct answers, researchers are considering the entire process of reading and the strategies used. Three ways that test developers are beginning to adapt new ideas about comprehension to their tests are (1) setting purposes for reading, (2) analyzing incorrect responses to multiple-choice questions to aid in diagnosing sources of difficulties, and (3) assessing vocabulary by asking readers to identify words embedded in text instead of words in isolation (Farr and Carey, 1986). New tests attempt to evaluate students' use of the reading process, application of prior knowledge, and depth of understanding (Harp, 1994).

Both Illinois and Michigan are at the forefront of developing new types of reading assessment that focus on larger concepts, such as problem solving and higher-order thinking skills, and on curriculum strands, such as language arts (VanLeirsburg, 1993). Other applications of performance-based assessment come from the 1992 National Assessment of Education Progress (NAEP) and the Arizona Student Assessment Program. In the NAEP revision, reading passages are longer and come from real texts. Tests consist of more open-ended responses, oral readings, interviews based on classwork, and discussions of reading selections (Flood and Lapp, 1993). In the Arizona program, one task calls for students to read high-quality fiction and nonfiction in order to solve problems. Because students must produce original thoughts about issues rather than repeat given information, they must use higher-order thinking skills (Peters, 1994).

Despite efforts to include more authentic tasks on standardized tests, however, "there is little evidence of their wide-scale feasibility, practicality, and utility" (Walberg et al., 1994, p. 37). Difficulties arise from lack of information about technical characteristics of the new assessments; from the inability to establish consistent ratings among judges; and from the variability in a student's scores, depending on which performance task is given.

Summary

Assessment procedures are changing as educators seek ways to measure student progress in reading that reflect current authentic views of the reading process. More than ever before, assessment is merging with instruction as teachers continuously observe students, interact with them, and analyze their strengths and weaknesses.

Alternative assessment can take many forms, and teachers can learn much about their students by using observation strategies. Daily observation, or kid-watching, is a key to effective assessment, and teachers can record their observations in a variety of ways, including anecdotal records and checklists and rating scales. Rubrics make students aware of expectations by giving specific criteria for scoring their work, and teachers gain insight into students' reading abilities through conferences, interviews, and retellings. Portfolios are useful for keeping samples of student work, and self-appraisal helps students evaluate their own accomplishments.

Informal tests over specific areas, including teacher-made tests on content or skills, provide information about student mastery of specific material. Cloze procedures enable teachers to determine whether a text is too easy or too difficult for students, and teachers can use multimedia and computers in various ways to assess students' knowledge. The informal reading inventory, reading miscue inventory, and running record are similar forms of informal measures that help the teacher identify students' strengths and weaknesses.

The teacher can use criterion-referenced tests to determine how well a student has mastered a specific skill. Skill mastery, however, does not always indicate whether or not the student can apply the skill to actual reading situations.

Formal assessment consists of standardized tests that are administered, scored, and interpreted according to designated procedures. Norm-referenced tests compare students with other students across the nation on the basis of test scores. Most schools require that achievement tests be given annually to measure the progress students have made in overall academic achievement. Most traditional standardized tests measure skill mastery by asking students to answer multiple-choice questions. Test developers are seeking ways to include more authentic tasks on standardized tests, but progress has been slow.

The following chart summarizes the purposes of alternative and formal assessment:

Alternative Assessment	Formal Assessment
Gives teacher useful day-to-day information about student progress	Compares students with other students across the nation
Informs teacher about planning instruction to meet students' needs	Provides accountability for school systems
Identifies individual strengths and weaknesses	Gives scores that can be interpreted statistically
Occurs continuously	Occurs once or twice a year
Uses classroom-based materials and procedures	Uses standardized materials and procedures

The teacher's most useful assessment tool is day-to-day observation. Informal tests may be used to reinforce or supplement such observation, whereas standardized tests are usually given only as mandated by the school system.

Test Yourself

True or False

_____ 1. Current practices in formal assessment correspond closely with what is known about the reading process.

_____ 2. Traditional standardized tests are more appropriate than alternative assessment for guiding instruction.

_____ 3. Instruction and assessment should be separate procedures.

_____ 4. Teachers must devise their own informal reading inventories, since none are commercially available.

_____ 5. Most standardized tests consist primarily of multiple-choice items.

_____ 6. Material written on a child's independent reading level is less difficult than material written on his or her instructional level.

_____ 7. Miscue analysis can help a teacher understand the nature of a child's unexpected responses in reading.

_____ 8. Self-questioning is an effective tool for reading and studying.

_____ 9. There is wide-scale feasibility, practicality, and utility for standardized tests that use authentic tasks.

_____ 10. A criterion-referenced assessment relates an individual's test performances to absolute standards rather than to the performances of others.

_____ 11. At present there are no computer programs for assessing reading skills.

_____ 12. Major changes have been occurring in standardized testing for much of the past seventy years.

_____ 13. Authentic assessment focuses on small, separate skills.

_____ 14. Three significant aspects of informal evaluation are observation, interaction, and analysis.

_____ 15. The term *kidwatching* refers to professional baby-sitting.

_____ 16. Record keeping is an essential part of observation.

_____ 17. Anecdotal records are written accounts of specific classroom incidents.

_____ 18. Story retelling enables teachers to learn about a child's comprehension of a story.

_____ 19. A rubric is used for scoring cloze tests.

_____ 20. It is considered desirable for students to assess their own progress.

_____ 21. In evaluating the results of a reading miscue inventory, the teacher focuses on the types of miscues rather than on the total number of miscalled words.

_____ 22. A running record is a narrative report of a child's overall progress.

_____ 23. Rubrics consist of standards (levels of proficiency) and criteria (skills or behaviors being evaluated).

_____ 24. The cloze procedure is an example of a norm-referenced test.

_____ 25. When using portfolios, samples of a student's work should be collected and reviewed by both the student and the teacher.

_____ 26. The best questions for a teacher to ask during a student conference or interview are those that can be answered with *yes* or *no*.

For your journal...

1. Reflect on the various types of alternative assessment discussed in this chapter. Which of them do you consider most useful? Why?

2. How can the misuse of standardized tests hurt both students and teachers? What can be done to avoid misusing them?

3. What do you think it means to merge instruction and assessment? How can one support the other?

...And your portfolio

1. Collect samples of student work that you could use as examples for each proficiency level, or standard, of a rubric. Be sure to focus on what you intend to measure.

2. Start an annotated list of recent journal articles that present current views of assessment. Consider how you can apply these views to your classroom.

3. Plan ways to use portfolio assessment in your classroom. Consider your purposes, a desirable format, ways to involve students in the selection and maintenance of portfolios, and ways to organize and store them.

Classroom Organization and Management

Key Vocabulary

Pay close attention to these terms when they appear in the chapter.

achievement grouping

community of learners

cooperative learning

friendship grouping

integrated language arts curriculum

interest grouping

learning center

paraprofessional

peer tutoring

project or research groups

pupil pairs or partners

special skills or needs groups

student contract

teacher-researcher

thematic unit

theme cycle

whole language classroom

SETTING OBJECTIVES

When you finish reading this chapter, you should be able to

▶ Explain some benefits of an integrated curriculum and how to implement it.

▶ Discuss some features of whole language classrooms and strategies for cooperative learning.

▶ Identify various ways teachers might group students for reading-related purposes.

▶ Name some ways to create a supportive physical and social-emotional environment in the classroom.

▶ Explain how the teacher can function as facilitator and manager of instruction, decision maker, researcher, and learner.

▶ Describe some ways teachers can communicate with parents.

▶ Explain the roles paraprofessionals and tutors play within the reading program.

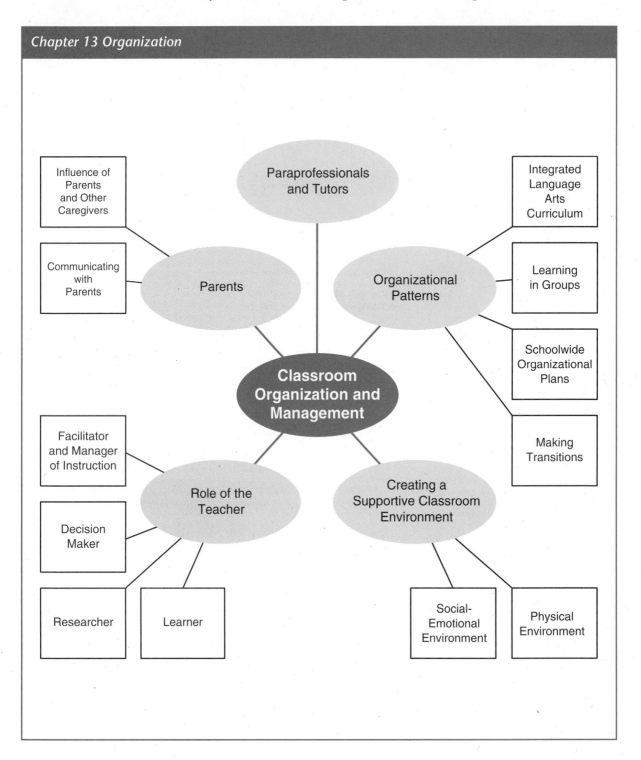

Paraprofessionals and Tutors

Influence of Parents and Other Caregivers

Communicating with Parents

Parents

Integrated Language Arts Curriculum

Learning in Groups

Organizational Patterns

Schoolwide Organizational Plans

Making Transitions

Classroom Organization and Management

Facilitator and Manager of Instruction

Decision Maker

Role of the Teacher

Researcher

Learner

Creating a Supportive Classroom Environment

Social-Emotional Environment

Physical Environment

Classroom organization does not directly involve the reading process or materials, methods, or approaches to teaching reading. Yet without good classroom organization and management, reading instruction may be totally ineffective. It is not enough for teachers to know what to teach; they must also know what organizational patterns and management techniques are conducive to learning.

This chapter presents various types of organizational plans and practical suggestions for forming and managing different kinds of groups. It considers an integrated language arts curriculum, a way to provide large blocks of time for students to learn and use language arts—reading, writing, listening, speaking, and viewing—meaningfully. It examines whole language classrooms and cooperative learning, as well as traditional classroom grouping arrangements. A variety of schoolwide organizational plans are presented, along with ideas for making transitions from one type of organization to another. The importance of creating supportive physical and social-emotional classroom environments is discussed.

Next, the chapter recognizes the teacher as the most important variable in the classroom and introduces four major roles of the teacher: the teacher as facilitator and manager of instruction, as decision maker, as researcher, and as learner. The chapter also considers the influence of parents and the home environment on children's reading attitudes and achievement. Finally, the chapter explains the value of paraprofessionals and tutors in the school program.

Organizational Patterns

It is no secret that students within a single class vary a great deal in chronological age, maturity, cognitive abilities, interests, and personal experiences. In view of the obvious need to provide the most appropriate instruction for each learner, teachers must give careful consideration to plans that provide for both individual differences and a sense of community. Students should participate in small-group, individualized, partner, and whole-class activities.

As educational practices become more holistic, changes are occurring in classroom organization. Instead of scheduling reading groups in half-hour segments, teachers are reserving larger blocks of time for reading and writing activities. Rather than grouping children by ability or achievement, teachers are allowing children to work together in more flexible patterns. Instead of assigning seats for all-day use, teachers are encouraging children to work at centers and other locations where they are comfortable.

Following are some general guidelines for classroom organization:

1. Remember that no single classroom organization is best for all situations.

2. Consider many criteria in deciding on a particular organizational plan, including children's needs and interests, your strengths and weaknesses, your educational philosophy, and specific goals of instruction.

3. Keep organizational plans and scheduling flexible; alter them as you discover improvements.

4. Organize your classroom so that it is structured and orderly, but provide a supportive emotional climate.

5. Offer opportunities for individualized learning, making sure to manage independent activities for the benefit of all students.

6. Whenever appropriate, provide whole-class instruction so that all students experience a sense of community.

Integrated Language Arts Curriculum

An *integrated language arts curriculum* emphasizes relationships among reading, writing, listening, speaking, and viewing in authentic situations. Growth in one area is likely to result in growth in the others, and the language arts become the building blocks for content area learning. As language learning extends into the various subject areas, teachers can create a holistic and connected curricular approach to learning (Tchudi, 1994). Routman (1994) cautions, however, that teachers will find it difficult to achieve a fully integrated curriculum in which language, content, and concepts are interrelated across the entire curriculum all of the time.

The National Association for the Education of Young Children supports the concept of an integrated curriculum by saying: "Children's learning does not occur in narrowly defined subject areas; their development and learning are integrated. Any activity that stimulates one dimension of development and learning affects other dimensions as well" (Ollila and Mayfield, 1992, p. 11). Integration of subjects is also supported by the associative theory of learning, which claims that students learn by associating material with other information, rather than by practicing isolated skills and memorizing facts (Cunningham and Allington, 1994). They learn by drawing on material from different but related sources to solve problems and reach goals.

Themes in an Integrated Curriculum

Thematic units integrate instruction meaningfully across the curriculum, thus enabling students to see connections among different subjects. During theme studies, students often extend their learning by pursuing ideas or concepts in-depth. They are using information for meaningful purposes instead of simply memorizing facts for test taking (Shanahan et al., 1995). A theme study is the core of the curriculum for an extended period of time. Most subjects can be integrated with the theme, although some subjects, such as math, must receive additional attention because they do not fit into it naturally. "A thematic approach provides an organizational framework for students to learn language as well as to learn through language" (Pike, Compain, and Mumper, 1994, p. 272).

Themes should be broadly based, to meet a variety of interests and individual differences and thereby ensure that students have choices within the theme structure (Lukasevich, 1996; Pike, Compain, and Mumper, 1994). The teacher should choose themes by considering curriculum guidelines, students' interests and areas of expertise, school-wide themes, parental concerns, and the teacher's own sense of what is worth knowing. At the beginning of the school year, students might brainstorm topics they want to study, and the teacher can try to match their ideas with topics suggested in the curriculum framework. Ideally, teacher and students *negotiate* curriculum: that is, students have a say in planning and directing their own learning while teachers provide guidance. Students generally find a negotiated curriculum to be motivational, relevant, and meaningful (Davenport, 1995).

Teachers sometimes mistake topics for themes. Topics, such as *koalas* or *apples*, are limited in the depth of thinking they afford, whereas themes present issues or perspectives, such as "Ways to make our community a better place" or "Oceans contain vast resources" (Shanahan et al., 1995). To be worthy of study, themes should have the potential for developing concepts that extend students' knowledge of their social and physical world. Examples are themes dealing with culture, energy, and social organization (Wilson et al., 1991). Selections from children's literature can also be the focus for developing worthy themes (see Chapter 8).

In *theme cycles*, teachers and students work together in negotiating the curriculum (Harste, Short, and Burke, 1988). Teachers bring their knowledge and experiences from encounters with experts and fields of study, and students bring their knowledge and experiences with life and learning. Together they plan what to study, make webs of "What We Know" and "What We Want to Know," and create lists of resources for obtaining information. As students explore a theme, they continue acquiring new information until they are ready to report their new knowledge to their classmates. The teacher's role is to help organize individual and group learning and to encourage students to consider new questions, search for resources, and discover different ways to present their ideas to their peers.

Scheduling

Scheduling for an integrated language arts curriculum calls for large blocks of time instead of small, fragmented, 15- or 20-minute chunks each for handwriting, spelling, grammar, and so forth. Ideally, this hour-and-a-half to two-hour block comes in the morning without interruption, providing time for a variety of language experiences. Many teachers are abandoning their segmented lesson plans in favor of larger, open-ended arrangements that allow more flexibility for language activities (Eisele, 1991; Lukasevich, 1996). Scheduling is unique for each classroom; it is a reflection of how the teacher believes children learn and a response to their needs and interests.

On the timetable shown in Example 13.1 is a large language arts block in the morning and a time for themes in the afternoon. Language arts time includes such activities as journal writing, process writing (including drafting, revising, and publishing), shared reading, author studies, reading and writing workshops, and literature circles. Whenever possible, the language arts should be related to the theme or topic; that is, spelling words may be theme-related words, and reading, research, and writing activities may center on the theme as well. During the afternoon theme study, students will continue using language arts to investigate the theme, while also learning about social studies, science, and other areas of the curriculum.

Example 13.1   *Schedule for an Integrated Language Arts Curriculum*

Time	Monday	Tuesday	Wednesday	Thursday	Friday
8:00– 8:30	Attendance, lunch money, announcements, sharing, story ----------------				
8:30–10:10	Language Arts	Language Arts	Language Arts	Language Arts	Language Arts
10:10–10:30	------------------------- Recess -------------------------------------				
10:30–11:30	Math	Math / P.E.	Math	Library / Math	Math
11:30–12:05	------------------------- Lunch -------------------------------------				
12:05–12:25	SSR	SSR	SSR	SSR	SSR
12:25– 2:25	Theme Study	Theme Study	Theme Study	Art / Theme Study	Theme Study / Music
2:25– 3:00	Free activity time (extension of theme, independent or group projects, free reading)				

Teachers may hold conferences with individual students any time during the day that children are working independently, to offer help and evaluate progress. Three ways to schedule conferences are daily; on a regular schedule, such as once or twice a week; or on an as-needed basis (Galda, Cullinan, and Strickland, 1993). Since students are not always aware that they need conferences and therefore do not request them, teachers should probably visit briefly with most or all students daily or schedule regular conferences as well as holding occasional unscheduled ones. Scheduled conferences enable both teacher and student to prepare in advance by gathering and reviewing pertinent materials. Although the length of time varies depending on the needs of the students, teachers usually average about five minutes per student. Thus, in a class of 30 students, a teacher could schedule conferences with six students each day within a half-hour's time. Teachers may go to students' desks or work areas, meet with students by calling them one by one to a designated area (not the teacher's desk), or assemble the group scheduled for that day at a conference table.

Some teachers believe that it is better to teach individual skills during discrete time periods, but other teachers prefer to teach skills in an integrated, holistic way during large blocks of time. **What do** *you* **think?**

Whole Language Classrooms

An integrated language arts curriculum is a basic tenet of whole language classrooms. The language arts, along with the content areas, are taught in purposeful ways during flexible blocks of time. Children read and write throughout the day as they work independently, with partners, or in small groups.

A whole language classroom might seem disorganized to the casual observer, but in reality it is carefully structured. For whole language to work, teachers, along with their students, must develop and implement a basic management and organizational plan. Such a plan considers room arrangement, availability and location of resources, and time allocations (Baumann, 1992; Garan, 1994). Effective whole language teachers are well organized, aware of each child's needs, and able to provide situations that promote student-directed learning.

Resources in a whole language classroom consist of authentic reading and writing materials arranged so that students can access them easily. Reading materials may include newspapers and magazines (both children's and adults'), a large quantity of trade books, reference materials (atlases, dictionaries, almanacs, and so forth), student-published books, tape-recorded stories with accompanying books, scrapbooks, and textbooks. Writing materials include lined and unlined paper, simply constructed booklets, computer paper, mailboxes to hold individual correspondence, a variety of writing tools (felt-tipped markers, pencils, pens), and a message board for students' messages. Because students often participate in organizing, storing, and maintaining these materials, they feel responsible for them and thus tend to take good care of them.

The following Classroom Scenario illustrates the organization of a whole language classroom.

Classroom Scenario

Whole Language Classroom

The children in Melanie Childress's third grade are busily involved in a variety of reading and writing activities. Most children are working independently or with one another, while Ms. Childress acts as a consultant to children who need help. On the board, Ms. Childress has written "mystery questions" for which the children must find answers by searching through newspapers. She has also given them the option of

(continued)

writing letters to Miss Beth and Ms. Ann or of completing the following assignment: You are a pioneer. You can have three animals. What three animals would you choose, and why?

Other children are getting ready to publish books they have been working on for several weeks. Ms. Childress is helping them with their final drafts, while classmates also offer editorial advice.

One girl attaches herself to a visitor and eagerly reads the book she has written. She points out that her book is patterned after another story but uses different names for the characters and a slightly different sequence of events. Another child enthusiastically shows the classroom library to a visitor and picks up a milk crate full of books by Robert Munsch, the children's favorite author. Meanwhile, three boys excitedly approach a visitor and offer to act out a play that a fourth member of their group has written.

Analysis of Scenario

In Ms. Childress's classroom, children are enthusiastic about a multitude of reading and writing experiences. The classroom is neither quiet nor obviously organized, but each child has found some type of purposeful language project to pursue. Ms. Childress has provided an environment in which children are free to choose, take risks, and explore their own interests in reading and writing.

Program Evaluation

In moving toward an integrated language arts classroom, teachers might ask themselves some of the following questions to determine their progress: Am I . . .

- using themes to integrate the language arts?
- valuing students' ideas in choosing and developing themes?
- involving students in language arts activities that extend into various subject areas?
- helping students find authentic purposes for using language arts throughout the day?
- teaching the language skills that enable students to pursue theme studies?
- providing the tools and resources students need for exploring ideas in depth?
- scheduling large blocks of time, for flexibility?
- evaluating progress in terms of students' ability to use language arts effectively in pursuit of goals?
- informing parents of the reasons for integrating the language arts?
- modeling good language usage for students?

Affirmative answers to these questions may take time to achieve, but are worth working toward in order to provide a meaningful, authentic learning environment.

Learning in Groups

Students learn from one another as well as from the teacher and on their own. In many classrooms, children have opportunities throughout the day to work in different kinds of groups that may vary in purpose, format, and materials (Flood et al., 1992). Purposes for groups may be skill development or shared interest; formats may be teacher or student led with varying numbers of participants; and materials may be the same for all groups or differ according to levels and themes. Grouping should be flexible, with students moving in and out of groups as needs and interests change (Salinger, 1996). This section begins with a discussion of cooperative learning groups, then moves into more traditional types of reading groups, and concludes with whole-class and individualized learning.

Cooperative Learning

In *cooperative learning*, students approach tasks cooperatively by working in mixed-ability groups to achieve certain goals. The organization of cooperative learning groups is generally highly structured, with students working in teams and assuming responsibility for their own learning, as well as for that of their teammates. Students must use social skills that enable them to interact productively, and they are accountable both individually and as a group.

Before initiating cooperative learning groups, the teacher should help children acquire the necessary social skills: speaking softly, showing respect for others, avoiding negative comments, appreciating other points of view, establishing trust, communicating accurately, and so forth (Johnson and Johnson, 1989/1990; Madden, 1988). The teacher is then ready to form mixed ability groups of three to six students and present the guidelines, such as equal participation by group members and attention to the task.

One language arts-related application of cooperative learning for upper elementary grades is Cooperative Integrated Reading and Composition (CIRC). This model features integrated language arts with basal or literature-based readers. It involves teacher presentation, partner and independent practice activities, and testing. While the teacher works with one group, pairs of students from two different reading groups may engage in activities such as the following:

1. Partner reading, in which students first read silently, then take turns reading aloud, with the listener correcting the reader when necessary

2. Story structure and story-related reading, with students answering questions about story elements and making predictions about how the problem will be resolved

3. Story retellings, in which students summarize stories for their partners

4. Peer conferencing during writers' workshops (Slavin, Madden, and Stevens, 1989/1990; Slavin, 1991)

As measured by standardized and informal tests, students engaged in CIRC showed significant growth in decoding and comprehension, as well as consistently positive growth in writing and language (Roehler and Duffy, 1991).

Another popular model for cooperative learning is Jigsaw, in which six-member heterogeneous teams investigate academic material that has been divided into sections. Each team member is assigned a different section to study. During preparation time, students work individually to find the information they need. Those who have the same assignment are then placed together into "expert groups" to discuss their sections. Then the students are regrouped into their original teams to teach their teammates about their sections. Learning is evaluated by testing or through a team project, and teams receive recognition for their achievement (Slavin, 1991).

There is evidence that many students benefit from opportunities to learn together in mixed-ability groups (Pearson and Fielding, 1994). Research supports the use of cooperative learning for improving thinking skills, retaining information, earning higher achievement test scores, making decisions, and accepting responsibility for learning. There are also claims that cooperative learning increases students' eagerness to learn and helps low-achieving and mainstreamed students develop positive attitudes toward learning (Augustine, Gruber, and Hanson, 1989/1990; Slavin, 1989/1990; Slavin, 1991; Smith, 1989; Uttero, 1988; Wood, 1990). The following Classroom Scenario demonstrates one form of cooperative learning for reading instruction.

Classroom Scenario

Cooperative Learning

Barbara Eldridge was using the CIRC model of cooperative learning with her fifth graders for the basal reader lesson, in which each child would work with a partner. During the teacher-presentation segment of the lesson, she led into the story by asking the children to share their experiences with animals and then to read the introductory paragraph and look at the pictures to predict what the story might be about. Ms. Eldridge went over the word mastery list of eleven words by pronouncing each word clearly and distinctly, having the students say the word, asking them to define it if they could, clarifying the definition, and once again pronouncing the word with the class.

Before the children moved into the partner activities, Ms. Eldridge reminded them that they would do silent reading to a predetermined page and then do oral partner reading in their "one-inch voices." The children found comfortable places in the room to read, some sitting on the floor, others in chairs with their feet up. As they finished reading, each child sat beside a partner, with the partners facing opposite directions, and read softly into the partner's ear. Partners discussed the answers to a short list of comprehension questions and then wrote their answers separately. Before resuming the same procedure for the second part of the story, the children made further predictions.

Analysis of Scenario
Ms. Eldridge had formed partnerships randomly except for her three poorest readers, whom she had paired with patient, better readers. The children thoroughly enjoyed reading with partners, and their teacher felt that they were doing very well in reading.

Time for Reflection

Many educators support the concept of cooperative learning, believing that children learn better when they interact socially and share ideas. Others, however, believe each child needs to work individually in order to make sure that each one is learning necessary skills. What do *you* think?

Grouping for Reading

To accommodate a wide range of reading levels, many teachers group children within their classrooms as a compromise between providing whole-class or totally individualized instruction. Literature circles, discussed in Chapters 7 and 8, are one type of group, but teachers may form many other types of groups for reading-related purposes. Table 13.1 summarizes grouping patterns by showing the composition of each group and the materials that are generally used by group members. A more complete discussion of various types of groups follows.

Table 13.1 *Grouping Patterns*

Type of Group	Basis for Membership	Material
Literature circles	Book preferences	Trade books, especially junior novels
Achievement	Similar reading levels	Basal readers, workbooks
Skills or needs	Common areas of skill deficiencies	Practice exercises
Interest	Shared interests	Books, materials on topic
Project and research	Participation in special project	Materials related to project
Friendship	Social preferences	Favorite stories
Pupil pairs or partners	Assigned or self-chosen partners	Trade books, journals, basal readers
Cooperative learning	Placement in mixed-ability teams	Trade books, basal readers, other materials

Achievement Groups. *Ability* or *achievement grouping*, a method of grouping children according to the level of material they can read for instructional purposes, has been a popular practice. The teacher·may divide the class into two, three, or four groups, usually using basal readers as the main fare because the manuals and workbooks provide a careful and detailed skill-building program. The teacher should continuously monitor students' progress within achievement groups and consider making changes in placement when a child's progress is either substantially slower or more rapid than that of the rest of the group. It is important to keep groupings flexible.

Grouping by achievement levels, however, has limitations. It only reduces individual differences; it in no way eliminates them. Even if a teacher tries to conceal the identities of the high and low groups, children are well aware of each group's level. Many students remain in the low group over the years and form poor self-concepts as a result. Placement in a low group can hinder reading development, and children in the low group rarely achieve grade-level reading and writing skills (Hall, Prevatte, and Cunningham, 1995). Teachers also generally use poorer-quality teaching strategies with low groups (Brown, Palincsar, and Armbruster, 1994; Wiggins, 1994).

Interest Groups. Based on shared interests, *interest grouping* is recommended for investigating topics through reading, writing, and literature. Children who are familiar with a topic and have a special interest in it can usually read material about it at higher levels than they normally read (Anderson et al., 1985).

Project or Research Groups. Another type of grouping is based on *projects* or *research*, usually related to a theme. Students of varying ability levels work together by investigating a topic, pooling their information, and planning a presentation.

Friendship Groups. A popular form of grouping among students is *friendship grouping*, in which good friends work together for a specific purpose and within a specified time frame. Because friends understand one another, enjoy being together, and usually cooperate well, this type of group can be particularly effective.

Special Skills or Needs Groups. As children show deficiencies in their use of reading strategies, the teacher may form *special skills* or *needs groups* for direct instruction. Each group includes children who need help with the same strategy, regardless of their placement within a high, middle, or low group. A teacher can assemble such groups on a temporary basis and present minilessons, followed by student applications of the strategy.

Pupil Pairs or Partners. Yet another type of grouping involves *pupil pairs* or *partners*, who may work cooperatively on such activities as

1. reading orally and listening to stories from trade books.
2. revising and editing stories.
3. corresponding through buddy journals.
4. providing assistance when one partner is a more proficient reader than the other.

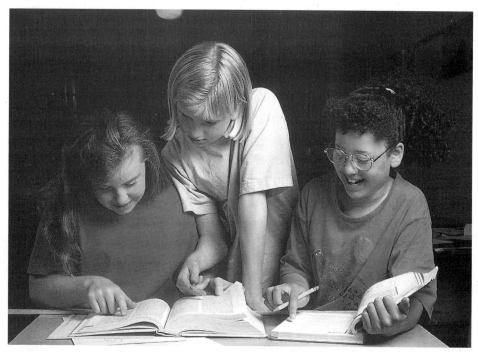

Students of varying achievement levels may work together in project or research groups.
(© *Jeffrey W. Myers/Stock Boston*)

Individualized and Whole-Class Activities

Although much learning takes place in groups and partnerships, students also need time to work both individually and as part of a whole-class community. Individualizing instruction allows children to make choices, pursue personal goals, explore special interests, move at their own paces, and work up to their capacity levels. Independent activities may take place as children work at computers, engage in Sustained Silent Reading, and publish their own books.

Many teachers begin and end each day with whole-class participation. Early morning is a good time for making announcements, letting students share, and reading aloud. When teachers become aware of specific skills that students need to learn, they teach minilessons to the whole class, often at the beginning of reading and writing workshops. Just before students go home, teachers may remind them of homework assignments and review what students have accomplished during the day. Among whole-class language activities are creative dramatics and choral reading, listening to stories read by the teacher or other students, learning about reading/study skills, going to the library, watching educational television, writing a class newspaper, creating a language experience chart, watching and discussing a video of a story, sharing multiple copies of a student magazine or newspaper, and participating in a poetry hour.

Schoolwide Organizational Plans

Over the years, education reformers have experimented with various organizational plans in order to find the best ways to help all children learn. Guided by research findings, school systems implement new programs and provide professional development for teachers. In many schools, teachers find opportunities to meet together by grade level during the week to discuss plans, develop themes, find ways to integrate various areas of the curriculum, and search for resource materials. Some meetings occur after school on a designated afternoon every week or two. Others, however, can be arranged during a free period, such as recess or library, if these periods are scheduled at the same time for all teachers at a particular grade level.

A wide range of organizational alternatives exists. In some schools, teachers participate in *team teaching*, which works particularly well for teachers who share similar educational philosophies. These teachers communicate with one another regularly and arrange for individualized, group, and whole-class instruction as needed. The team leader organizes and plans, but considers the ideas of team members. In *departmentalized* classrooms, each teacher assumes responsibility for teaching a different subject. This plan is more effective in middle schools, where there is more emphasis on teaching content, than in elementary schools, where children and teachers benefit from the sense of community that develops within self-contained classrooms.

A more recent trend is toward *multi-age classrooms*, which consist of children from contiguous grade levels, such as first grade through third, or grades four and five. Although most instruction occurs within these multi-age groupings, teachers may collaborate to provide specific skill instruction for children by grade levels at some time during the day. Theme studies allow students of such varying levels to work together in all areas of the curriculum. The wide range of abilities in multi-age classes leads to a cooperative spirit, with younger students learning from older ones and older students reinforcing their own knowledge as they teach younger ones (Wall, 1994).

Teachers find that by arranging partnerships between children at different grade levels, they allow both younger and older students to benefit from interacting in cooperative learning situations. *Cross-grade pairings* are often initiated and implemented by the teachers of the two classes involved, with meetings generally occurring during one or two class periods each week. This arrangement often results in personal growth and academic achievement for both older and younger learners. Partnerships across grades with low-achieving upper-grade students reading to kindergartners has proven to be worthwhile for both sets of partners (Labbo and Teale, 1990; Leland and Fitzpatrick, 1993/1994).

Time for Reflection	Some school systems try out different organizational plans in response to educational reform movements. Other systems believe it is better to stay with the tried-and-true, traditional organizational plans. What do *you* think?

Making Transitions

For a variety of reasons, a teacher may wish to move from one organizational pattern to another. Some teachers become dissatisfied with their present organizational patterns and seek better plans, or beginning teachers wish to try some of the ideas they have learned in college, even though they vary from traditional organizational plans. Changing from one pattern to another requires careful consideration and study. Professional meetings, journal articles, books, and the experiences of other teachers can provide helpful information about both the theoretical basis for another type of classroom organization and ways to implement it. The Focus on Strategies that follows shows a teacher making the transition from traditional instruction to whole language instruction.

**Focus on
Strategies**

From Traditional to Whole Language Instruction

As Linda walked into the Fourth Street Elementary School library, she noticed she was among the first to arrive at the TAWL (Teachers Applying Whole Language) meeting. "Good," Linda thought to herself, "I like this informal get-together before the meeting starts because it gives me a chance to find out what other teachers are doing."

Linda had taken a graduate-level whole language course last summer and was committed to becoming a whole language teacher. Enthusiasm was contagious throughout the course, with nearly all of the students thinking of ways to implement this exciting, student-centered philosophy in their classrooms when school started. The professor had warned them, however, not to try too many new ideas at once—that it takes time to become a whole language teacher. He had also advised them to find a support group, another teacher, or someone else with whom they could share their triumphs and disappointments.

Spotting Carole, a former whole language classmate, looking at the display of professional books on whole language, Linda quickly walked over to her and asked, "How is it going? Are you trying some whole language strategies?"

Carole answered cautiously, "I am, but it's not easy. No one else is using whole language in my school, although some teachers seem interested. I've started journal writing, and I've given the class more time for free-choice reading."

Linda agreed that journal writing and SSR were good ways to begin. "I'm not using the basal much anymore either," said Linda, "although we sometimes use it because it has some really good stories."

Carole admitted that she was still using the basal two days a week. "We aren't using workbooks and skill charts now, though, and we never did do round-robin reading. That always seemed like such a poor way to teach, and so boring for all of us. What a waste of time to take turns reading aloud what the children had already

(continued)

read to themselves! I enjoy reading aloud to them more often, though. I had always felt somewhat guilty doing that, but we learned that reading aloud is really legitimate!" laughed Carole. "How about you?"

Linda replied, "I guess I'm lucky. Another fourth-grade teacher, Angelo, has been doing whole language for a few years, and he's sort of taken me under his wing. It's so helpful to be able to observe him and talk to him about what I'm trying to do. My students are writing in journals, too, and we've just started literature circles. Angelo's class and mine share sets of books. He already had some sets, and I was able to get two more with PTO money."

"At least we have TAWL, even if I don't get much help at school," said Carole. "It's a great support group for me, and I get new ideas from each meeting."

As Linda and Carole wandered over to the refreshment table, they heard Rachel and Tom talking about theme studies. Rachel was saying, "We've started a theme on the solar system. The children came up with the topic after I showed them a film on outer space, and it fits into the curriculum framework. They are really excited about it, bringing in books and reference materials and volunteering to work on projects. I worry, though, that we're spending too much time on science and neglecting other areas of the curriculum."

Tom replied, "I'll bet you're covering more of the curriculum than you realize. There's a lot of math in calculating distances and speeds, and a lot of reading and writing with the reference materials they're investigating."

"There are even social studies applications if you consider possible cooperation among nations in exploring outer space," Linda added. "That's a great topic. I wonder if my fourth graders could do it."

Just then Sarah interrupted by placing a student-made big book in front of them. "You've just got to see what my fifth graders made for Dean's first graders! Look at these illustrations—and such a clever pattern for the story. They really did it all themselves after they looked at some big books in the library to get ideas." The book was indeed impressive; no wonder Sarah was proud of her students.

Linda noticed that Beverly, TAWL president, was trying to get everyone's attention to start the meeting, so she found a seat. The meeting usually began with some announcements about whole language events, and then someone read a new book—a shared pleasure for them all. Today's program was on portfolio assessment, something Linda knew a little about, and she was eager to learn more. She already had file folders and a few samples of student work, but she wasn't very clear about how to choose the samples and what to do with them. Now she had a chance to get some ideas for implementing portfolios in her classroom. That would be her next step in applying whole language philosophy.

Making changes is a difficult process for many reasons, and complete transitions are likely to take several years. The teacher must understand and be able to justify reasons for changing from one philosophical stance to another. Parents and administrators must be convinced that this move will benefit the students and that standardized test scores will not drop as a result (Pike, Compain, and Mumper, 1994).

Transitions allow teachers to move gradually from one theoretical position to another, implementing new ideas as they feel comfortable with them. Many basal reader teachers are moving toward literature-based instruction and then to whole language classrooms. In the process, they must make major changes in materials, planning, classroom organization, and assessment techniques (Harris, 1996).

In his book *Reading in the Middle School*, Duffy (1990) includes several case studies in which schools have moved from traditional organizational patterns to other plans. In one middle school, teachers designed a reading curriculum that focused on developing reading strategies in cooperative learning groups (Monahan, 1990), and teachers in another school concentrated on integrating language with content across the curriculum (Roehler et al., 1990). Key points in effecting change were administrative support, careful planning, willingness to take risks, energy, time, and a background of information and knowledge about how to bring about change.

Creating a Supportive Classroom Environment

The physical environment and social-emotional climate of a classroom can significantly affect children's literacy development. By understanding what children need, teachers are able to create supportive environments that facilitate learning and promote positive attitudes (Prosise, 1996).

Physical Environment

A classroom's furnishings and arrangement reflect a teacher's philosophy about how children learn (Wilson et al., 1991). Teachers who believe children learn from and with one another provide areas where the children can work in pairs and small groups. Teachers who understand that children have individual interests to pursue arrange quiet areas for independent work, and teachers who know that children need to work in groups of differing sizes and composition provide flexible room arrangements.

Teachers should consider many factors in creating a classroom's physical environment. Furniture should be arranged so that traffic flows easily, there are no safety hazards, and the teacher is able to see each child. Young children need well-defined areas, perhaps set off by a rug, marked with colored tape, or identified with bookcases and shelves set perpendicular to the walls (Mayfield, 1992). These classrooms may also need book racks for storing big books and easels for displaying them. The library area should be attractive, with comfortable chairs, large cushions, and displays of books and magazines. Many teachers are replacing individual student desks with tables, which permit more flexiblity but also necessitate setting up storage areas for students' books and supplies (Lukasevich, 1996; Pike, Compain, and Mumper, 1994).

Many classrooms have *learning centers*, which are areas of the classroom that contain sets of materials related to a theme. The materials may be attached to a piece of Masonite, hung on a pegboard, placed on shelves or in boxes, filed in kits, contained in folders or large envelopes, or displayed in some other way for children to use independently. Commercial kits are available for use at learning centers, but teachers often produce their own materials or collect those that are readily available from various sources. Learning centers should contain attractive, varied, and interesting materials that are inviting to children and are related to the theme. All centers should contain necessary supplies for carrying out activities and should include a comfortable place for children to work.

Learning centers require careful preparation and planning by the teacher. Students need to understand when they may go to the centers, how to use them, and where to place their completed work. They should be able to work independently or with classmates. Teachers need to provide protective coverings for frequently used materials, replenish supplies regularly, and replace center activities before children lose interest in them. Some types of learning centers that teachers may provide include computer centers; audiovisual stations; centers for puppet shows and creative drama; well-equipped writing centers; and classroom library centers. (More information on learning centers appears in Chapter 2.)

Many teachers have acquired large numbers of trade books to place in classroom libraries, but keeping track of the books can be a problem. Hollie Brooks (1995) suggests a useful procedure that includes separating books into categories, such as mystery, science, and reference; alphabetizing them by authors' last names within each category or section; using the computer to enter such database fields as title, author, subject, and section; placing book information in corresponding fields; letting students enter in a spiral notebook the books they check out; and choosing students to be class librarians. An organizational plan such as this provides students with real-life applications, lets them use the computer, and instills a sense of responsibility.

Many schools face the challenge of how to use a limited number of computers to best advantage. The number of computers in schools has increased rapidly in recent years, but even so, few students get sufficient exposure to computers. In some cases teachers allow more aggressive students to dominate the computers, thereby limiting their use by less assertive students. One solution to inequitable distribution of computer time is for the teacher to post a schedule chart with each student's name, class, and time for use so that students can take turns using the computer. Another possibility is to let two or more children work together on one computer.

Computer-managed instruction (CMI) simplifies teachers' work by providing gradebook and test-development software (Yellin and Blake, 1994). Gradebook programs enable teachers to develop class lists, enter grades, and average grades quickly, and testmaking programs let teachers create test banks from which they may select items to include on tests. More information on computers is in Chapter 11.

Social-Emotional Environment

Perhaps even more important than the physical environment is the social-emotional environment within the classroom. In this section, we consider three aspects of this environment: establishing a community of learners, creating a learning-centered classroom, and providing motivation.

Developing a sense of community begins with letting the students get to know one another well, perhaps exchanging points of view through class meetings or dialogue circles (Letts, 1994). Together, teacher and students establish the rules they perceive as necessary for reaching the goals for learning in their class (Roberts, 1993). When students feel part of a *community of learners*, they are likely to take reasonable risks, support one another, and control their behavior.

Membership in a community of learners varies, but it usually consists of the teacher and the students within the class and often extends to supplementary teachers and reading buddies from another class (Knight, 1994). The teacher is viewed as the "senior member" of the community of learners because he or she is more knowledgeable, experienced, and skilled in important learning processes. The teacher thus has an obligation to share and model ways to negotiate learning situations (Tierney and Pearson, 1994).

A community of learners flourishes in a learner-centered classroom where the environment supports children's interests and needs. Here students display their work, interact with one another, collaborate on projects, and explore issues that interest them. The teacher confers with students, works among them, shows warmth and respect, and manages several different activities simultaneously. Children find a learner-centered classroom nonthreatening, so they feel comfortable making decisions, expressing ideas, and asking questions that may ultimately drive much of the curriculum (Kohn, 1996).

Effective, mature readers must have both the *skill* and the *will* to read (Gambrell, 1996). Reading skills are discussed earlier in this book, so here we will focus on ways to promote the will, or desire, to read. Motivated readers choose to read for different purposes, such as acquiring knowledge or enjoying a good story. They spend more time reading and are better readers, whereas nonmotivated readers may be at risk of failure (Palmer et al., 1994).

The elementary school years are critical for developing motivated readers, so teachers must create environments that make children want to read, such as the following (Gambrell, 1996; Turner and Paris, 1995):

- Provide a book-rich class environment.
- Be a reading model; make your love of reading visible.
- Let children interact with others about their reading.
- Give them opportunities to become acquainted with a wide variety of books.
- Provide reading-related incentives (books or bookmarks).
- Allow children the freedom to choose the books they read.

- Challenge them with moderately difficult tasks.
- Let children share control over their learning.
- Encourage them to discover how literacy tasks can be meaningful and purposeful.

Role of the Teacher

Establishing a supportive classroom environment is only one of a teacher's many important responsibilities in the classroom. A competent, effective teacher makes a major difference in students' learning. For instance, researchers have found that "about 15 percent of the variation among children in reading achievement at the end of the school year is attributable to factors that relate to the skill and effectiveness of the teacher," but only "about 3 percent of the variation in reading achievement at the end of the first grade was attributable to the overall approach of the program" (Anderson et al., 1985, p. 85). Thus, the most essential ingredient of a good reading program is the teacher.

If teachers play such a key role in student learning, we need to know what makes them effective. Researchers have found that effective teachers balance authentic literacy experiences with direct teaching through minilessons, modeling, and explanations (Wharton-McDonald et al., 1997). They integrate skills instruction with authentic activities and avoid teaching skills in isolation. In addition to providing balanced instruction, highly effective primary literacy teachers use scaffolding extensively, integrate reading and writing, manage their classrooms competently, are aware of their purposes for instruction, encourage students to be self-regulated learners, and hold high expectations for all students.

The Teacher as Facilitator and Manager of Instruction

As a facilitator of instruction, the teacher must provide conditions that enable students to learn. The teacher should employ a variety of methods to meet the needs of a diverse student population. Through such procedures as modeling and direct instruction, the teacher can help students acquire the strategies and knowledge they need to succeed. By providing a learner-centered environment, the teacher can support students in their efforts to become responsible, independent learners.

No matter how good a lesson is, students will learn little if the teacher is unable to manage their behavior. Classroom management is a crucial factor in learning, especially when instruction is individualized or conducted in groups. Clear, sensible, consistent procedures can contribute to an orderly classroom.

Near the beginning of the year, teacher and students should agree on rules of behavior, which should be stated positively whenever possible. Generally, students should have reasonable freedom of movement and be able to talk quietly about task-related topics, but low voices and quiet movements should be stressed.

Children must know exactly what they are to do to be able work well independently and with their peers.

One way that teachers manage their classrooms effectively is by modeling appropriate behavior and learning strategies. Their actions and words set expectations for students, and these expectations become powerful motivators. Teachers model by *inference* as they read along with students during SSR, and they model with *talk-alouds* by asking themselves questions out loud while performing academic tasks. When they use *think-alouds*, they model their reasoning by describing aloud their thought processes (Roehler and Duffy, 1991).

One way to manage or keep track of individual activities is through *student contracts*. Students may "contract" to complete certain projects designed to help them with their individual needs. The agreement, formalized through the use of a written contract and signed by teacher and child, simply states what the student is to do and when the task is to be completed. A teacher can prepare and have available contracts that call for a variety of assignments and tasks, from which children can select those that best suit their needs, or a student can propose a contract and negotiate it with the teacher. Once the terms have been agreed on, the student should complete the contract as specified. Example 13.2 illustrates one such contract.

Example 13.2   *Sample Student Contract Form*

1. After listening to the librarian read aloud *The Cay* by Theodore Taylor, read one of the following to learn more about the idea of survival.
   a. *Island of the Blue Dolphins* by Scott O'Dell
   b. *Stranded* by Matt Christopher
   c. *Hatchet* by Gary Paulsen
   d. *Call It Courage* by Armstrong Sperry
   e. *The Summer I Was Lost* by Philip Viereck

2. Share your research in one of these ways:
   a. Illustrate one incident in the story.
   b. Write a play dramatizing one incident.
   c. Make a model of an object that may be useful for survival.
   d. Interview an authority on the subject of some sort of survival technique, and write a report.
   e. Compare the character(s) of your story with Robinson Crusoe in terms of self-reliance.

Choose one book from Number 1 and one method from Number 2 for your contract.

I plan to do (1) _____ and (2) _____ .

I will have this contract completed by _____ .

Student's signature _____

Teacher's signature _____

Teachers also need a record of the activities students complete at learning centers. Since students do this work independently and check their own answers, teachers may not know exactly what the children are doing unless they keep account of their activities in some way. Example 13.3 presents one way for a child to record learning center work.

Example 13.3 *Sample Learning Center Record*

Name _____

I worked at the _____ center or station.

Time in _____ Time out _____

The work was _____ . (good, fair, poor)

Activity:

I read _____

I worked on _____

I listened to _____

I read aloud with _____

I wrote _____

I also _____

The Teacher as Decision Maker

Some commercial reading programs prescribe what teachers should do and say and how they should do and say it. Many teachers believe that unless they use a manual with detailed instructions, their students will fail to learn. Although expert assistance may simplify teaching, it can also limit teachers' responsibilities as decision makers. The important point for teachers to consider is that they must use their own professional judgments in deciding how best to teach instead of implicitly following someone else's directions.

Classroom teachers make countless decisions daily as they manage their classrooms. Some decisions are made quickly and intuitively, but others require conscious reflection. Teachers may ask themselves:

How can I prevent potential behavior problems?

What is the best way to motivate these children?

What are the most appropriate materials to use?

What types of classroom organization will be most effective?

What teaching strategies are most appropriate to use?

What assessment techniques will tell me how well the children are learning?

What are the best ways to keep my students working productively?

How can I best meet individual needs?

How can I establish a supportive classroom environment?

What are the most effective ways to communicate with children, parents, and administrators?

Although the teacher has the final authority in the classroom, students should also assume some responsibility for making decisions about their learning (Garan, 1994; Sumara and Walker, 1991). There should be a balance between teacher and student control. When students internalize the behavior and reading strategies modeled by the teacher, they are able to direct their own learning within certain limits. For example, classroom teachers may retain control of the kinds of tasks and when they are to be completed, but give students choices about how, with whom, and where to do them.

The Teacher as Researcher

Teachers may participate in two kinds of research: *action research* and *naturalistic research*. *Action research* is designed to improve instruction through controlled methods and statistical procedures; *naturalistic research* occurs within the teacher-researcher's setting through systematic observations and detailed recordkeeping. Essentially, research directly involving teachers may take three forms: individual teacher research conducted by a single teacher; collaborative action research carried out by a group of teachers working with a university professor or with staff development personnel; and schoolwide action research, in which an entire faculty works with a school consortium (Calhoun, 1993).

Many teachers have become more involved in research in order to improve their own educational practices by gaining a better understanding of how their students learn. Education today is focusing on the process of how students learn—how they approach a learning task, how they self-correct misunderstandings, and what strategies they use as they read and write. As teachers carefully observe and record what their students are doing, they gain insights into effective educational procedures (Strickland, 1988).

On the basis of her own experiences in a first-grade classroom, Avery (1990) suggests steps to follow in becoming a teacher-researcher:

1. *Begin with a question.* Often the question blends with other questions and evolves as the investigation unfolds.

2. *Listen and observe.* Children reveal much about how they learn through their words and behaviors.

3. *Talk.* Conversing with the children offers glimpses into their thinking processes.

4. *Write.* Recording observations while they are still fresh helps retain details.

5. *Read.* Reading about the question under investigation supports classroom observations and helps clarify connections between theory and practice.

From the teacher's viewpoint, the role of teacher-researcher is a constant reminder to analyze the environment, gather evidence about how children learn, and reconstruct beliefs about children's growth and development. From the researcher's point of view, this role enables the teacher to connect scholarly work with classroom investigations that are based on extensive, in-depth, long-term contact with students (Milz, 1989).

The Teacher as Learner

One of the most refreshing, yet challenging, truths about being a teacher is that the role is constantly evolving. Changing situations and different groups of children each year call for modifications of teaching strategies to meet student needs. Recently published research may point in fresh directions, and the administration may introduce new programs. Teachers who view themselves as learners ask questions and *want* to learn more about new ideas that may be useful to them in the classroom.

Jaggar (1989) has identified sources of knowledge and ways of learning that appear to be common among teachers as learners. The first is *theory and research*, a knowledge base that is useful for observing and interpreting student behavior. To be meaningful, however, research must be viewed in terms of the teacher's personal knowledge and experience. Teachers also learn through *practice* by reflecting on their teaching experiences. Careful *observation* of students in various settings informs teachers about students' prior knowledge, use of language, interests, and learning styles. From insights into students' capabilities and preferences, teachers can plan appropriate instruction. Finally, teachers learn through *social dialogue* as they share ideas about theory, research, and practice.

Teachers also learn by interacting with other teachers. In addition to getting ideas from visiting other schools, teachers can arrange to meet at after-school meetings, during lunch periods set up to facilitate small-group meetings, while attending professional conferences, and at grade-level meetings during school hours while students are attending special classes such as music or art (Scharer and Detwiler, 1992).

Teachers can continue to learn and develop professionally in a variety of ways. They may take college courses for advanced degrees and recertification; they may participate in in-service activities; and they may join professional organizations. Through these associations, they can subscribe to publications and participate in conferences to learn about and apply new ideas. Some professional organizations related to the interests of elementary reading teachers are listed here, and along with their addresses and major publications.

Children's Book Council, 568 Broadway, New York, NY 10012. *CBC Features.*

International Reading Association, 800 Barksdale Road, P.O. Box 8139, Newark, DE 19714-8139, *The Reading Teacher, Journal of Adolescent & Adult Literacy, Reading Research Quarterly.*

National Association for the Education of Young Children, 1509 16th Street, N.W., Washington, DC 20036-1426. *Young Children.*

National Council of Teachers of English, 1111 W. Kenyon Road, Urbana, IL 61801-1096. *Language Arts, Primary Voices K–6*, and *Voices from the Middle.*

Parents

Parents and teachers should work together to create a positive learning environment for children. A child's first learning experiences occur in the home, and the home continues to provide educational opportunities that supplement learning activities in the classroom. Therefore, it is important that teachers understand a child's home environment and communicate with those responsible for the child's well-being.

Influence of Parents and Other Caregivers

Research generally shows positive correlations between children's success in reading and the availability of reading and writing materials in the home, the family's reading habits, parents' educational levels, and the language of the home. Literacy should be embedded early in children's social lives through meaningful interactions with family and community members (Sulzby and Teale, 1991). Recent emphasis on family literacy has resulted in numerous programs supported by schools, libraries, and community service groups to promote literacy among family members (Morrow et al., 1995).

Parents or caregivers who read to children, take them to the library, model positive reading behaviors, and encourage their children to read increase their children's likelihood of becoming good readers. If parents provide these services for their children and have positive attitudes toward reading, their children should look on reading as a pleasurable activity and, as a result, read more. The amount of time spent reading with parents is one of the clearest predictions of early reading achievement (Paris, Wasik, and Turner, 1991).

Communicating with Parents

Schools that value parent participation have more effective programs, more positive attitudes, and higher achievement than schools that do not encourage parents to participate (Jones, 1991). Some information parents usually want to know includes goals of the school and the teacher, what the child is learning and how it is taught, attendance and homework policies, and the child's progress.

It is therefore important that teachers and parents establish and maintain communication. Among the traditional methods of communication are newsletters (carefully written letters and bulletins to keep the parents informed about happenings at school), school booklets (including rules and regulations and information parents need to know before and after sending their children to school), parent-teacher association meetings, written reports in the form of personal letters or checklists, telephone calls, conferences, home visits (which give parent and teacher a chance to discuss particular problems and acquaint the teacher with the child's home environment), and Open House days (when the parents visit in the child's classroom to familiarize themselves with the materials, schedules, and routines of the school day). For years schools have utilized these methods, in various combinations, to foster communication between school and home.

The report card is the traditional way to inform parents and children about the child's performance in school, but report cards often give information that is incomplete and can be misunderstood. Simple A, B, or C grades for each subject tell very little about a student's interests, progress, attitudes, and effort. Example 13.4 shows a sample holistic report card for language arts with four grading periods.

Another option for communicating with parents is to use portfolios that contain samples of the children's work (Flood and Lapp, 1989). Parents often have difficulty understanding percentiles and standardized achievement test scores, but they can readily see the progress (or lack of progress) their children have made over time on informal measures such as writing samples. The portfolio should contain a broad array of children's work, including informal assessments, voluntary reading activities, self-evaluations, standardized test scores, and writing samples.

Many schools schedule conferences two or three times throughout the school year, but teachers can arrange conferences whenever they are necessary. During a conference, the teacher needs to listen to the parent's concerns, share samples of the child's schoolwork, show records of achievement (test scores, for example), and offer constructive suggestions for ways the parent and teacher can work together for the child's benefit. Conferences can include students; in fact, students sometimes lead them. They prepare by evaluating their own work, assembling selected pieces in portfolios, reflecting on their areas of strength and weakness, and role-playing conferences in order to be ready (Austin, 1994; Lenski et al., 1996).

The fall conference or Open House is a good time to introduce parents to the reading materials used in the school and to describe the reading experiences and skills being emphasized that year. A teacher may want to explain how the reading program is organized and the general approaches he or she uses. The teacher may also point out what (if anything) will be required of the child in terms of homework, as well as what the parents can do when the child requests help.

Teachers also communicate with parents through letters, progress reports, and notices they send home with children. The school may publish brochures informing parents of school policies and special events; libraries may provide lists

Example 13.4 *Holistic Report Card for Language Arts*

	1	2	3	4
Literature Appreciation				
Chooses appropriate literature				
Selects a variety of reading materials				
Reads willingly and with interest				
Responds creatively to literature				
Reading Strategies				
Reads for meaning				
Uses context clues				
Uses word structure clues				
Uses phonics clues				
Organizes ideas				
Recalls information				
Reads aloud fluently				
Draws conclusions				
Uses a variety of strategies				
Writing Strategies				
Expresses ideas clearly				
Organizes material				
Uses capitals and punctuation				
Revises and edits material				
Initiates and enjoys writing				
Listening and Speaking				
Communicates effectively				
Shows courtesy and respect				
Participates in class discussions				
Spelling				
Is learning dictionary skills				
Learns assigned words				
Uses correct spelling in revisions				
Handwriting				
Writes legibly and neatly				

Parents who read to their children, take them to the library, model positive reading behaviors, and encourage their children to read increase their children's likelihood of becoming good readers. (© *Elizabeth Crews*)

of recommended recreational reading suitable for various age levels; professional societies may have helpful bulletins or pamphlets for teachers to send home; and children may write letters to their parents about forthcoming events. The classroom teacher may write a personal note to a parent, especially to praise a child's performance; send home a summer calendar of reading-related activities for each day at the end of the school year; provide parents with activities to do with children that correspond to current reading objectives; or send a form letter, such as the one in Example 13.5, that applies to a group or whole class of children.

| Time for Reflection | Teachers differ in their views about parent involvement. Whereas some encourage it because they feel that parents in the classroom can strengthen the instructional program, others oppose it because they believe that parents may interfere and cause problems. What do *you* think? |

> **Example 13.5**   *Letter to Parents*
>
> Dear _____ ,
>
> During the past six weeks, your child has been working on a folklore unit in reading class. He or she has studied the characteristics of tall tales and has attempted to write an original tall tale of his or her own after reading several examples and hearing other examples read by the teacher. Your child's story is attached to this report. You may wish to read it and discuss it with him or her. All the children produced tall tales that indicated an understanding of this form of literature.
>
> Sincerely,

Paraprofessionals and Tutors

Many adults work as paid or volunteer assistants to the teacher by helping with individual or small-group instruction, constructing books for children to use for publishing their writing, grading student work, making displays, supervising computer-assisted instruction, and performing clerical tasks. Employment of *paraprofessionals* has increased steadily and duties have expanded in recent years so that paraprofessionals now work along with teachers to provide instruction and services (Pickett, Vasa, and Steckelberg, 1993). These paraprofessionals need some training in how to relate to children positively, how to teach simple skills, and how to judge student progress. Basically, the classroom teacher is responsible for the activities the assistant performs and for preparing the paraprofessional to carry out assigned activities. The teacher and paraprofessional need to communicate regularly, perhaps through structured conferences and shared planning times.

Peer tutoring occurs when one child tutors another child of the same age, whereas *cross-age tutoring* refers only to students of different ages (Foster-Harrison, 1997). Results of peer tutoring reveal improved academic achievement and better self-concepts for both tutor and tutee, improved social interactions between the partners, and more positive attitudes toward reading for both (Pearson and Fielding, 1991; Foster-Harrison, 1997).

When matching peer tutors with students, teachers must consider both the academic strengths and the emotional behavior of each student pair so that the two will work well together. Each tutor should receive training in planning appropriate lessons, selecting materials, following acceptable teaching procedures, and assessing the progress of the tutee. During peer conferencing, students learn how to interact by observing the teacher's modeling so that they can ask one another helpful questions (Forman and Cazden, 1994).

Summary

Orderly, efficient classroom organization is an important component of effective reading instruction. Many teachers are moving toward an integrated language arts curriculum, which allows children to understand the relationships among reading, writing, listening, speaking, and viewing, as they use these skills in meaningful situations. Teachers, with student input, select worthy themes as the focus of an integrated curriculum, and they use large blocks of time to schedule language arts and content-area activities. Whole language classrooms usually follow the integrated curriculum model.

Several other possibilities exist for organizing a classroom, including different ways of grouping children. Cooperative learning is an organizational plan that allows children to work with partners and in small groups to meet academic goals. Types of reading-related groups include literature circles, achievement groups, interest groups, project or research groups, friendship groups, special skills or needs groups, and pupil pairs or partners. Teachers create most of these arrangements for a limited time and a specific purpose. Students also benefit from individualized and whole-class instruction.

Some schools form larger organizational patterns, including departmentalization, team teaching, multi-age classrooms, and cross-grade arrangements. As teachers strive to find which organizational plans work best for them and their students, they may go through a transition period in which they gradually introduce new ideas.

The classroom's physical environment is an important factor in determining how well children learn. Some teachers use learning centers, classroom libraries, and computers in the instructional program. The classroom's social-emotional environment is also important. Teachers should establish a community of learners within a learner-centered classroom and develop motivated readers.

Four roles of the teacher are featured in this chapter: facilitator and manager of instruction, decision maker, researcher, and learner. The teacher is the key figure in the classroom and makes countless decisions daily that affect student learning. In some cases, the teacher assumes the role of researcher by making systematic observations and records of student behaviors. The teacher is also a learner, always alert to information supplied by research and theory, professional interactions, and the children themselves.

Parents strongly influence children's acquisition of reading skills and their attitudes toward achievement. Teachers should communicate with parents frequently in a variety of ways, including conferences, report cards, meetings, and publications. Teachers can offer suggestions to parents to help them create supportive reading environments in the home.

Teachers can benefit from the assistance of both paraprofessionals and tutors in the classroom. Paraprofessionals can provide a variety of reading-related services, including listening to children read, grading papers, preparing instructional materials, and assisting children in locating and using reference materials. Peer tutoring and cross-age tutoring are also effective for helping children learn to read.

True or False

_____ 1. Once organizational patterns have been established, they should be consistently maintained.

_____ 2. Most children placed in low reading groups quickly achieve grade-level reading and writing skills.

_____ 3. *Community of learners* refers to children who live in the same part of the school district.

_____ 4. Every classroom should contain three reading achievement groups.

_____ 5. In a negotiated curriculum, the teacher considers children's ideas for planning and directing learning.

_____ 6. Other than achievement groups, most groups are formed for limited times and specific purposes.

_____ 7. If the teacher tries to conceal the identities of high and low reading groups, children are unaware of any differences.

_____ 8. Organizational changes should be made slowly and gradually.

_____ 9. If reading skills are adequately covered during the reading instructional period, there is no need for any other type of reading during the day.

_____ 10. Classroom management is an important factor in how well students learn.

_____ 11. Even within groups based on reading achievement, diverse abilities exist.

_____ 12. Specific needs grouping puts together children who need to work on the same skill.

_____ 13. Learning centers allow children to carry out activities independently.

_____ 14. Computer-assisted instruction can be used only with one student for each computer.

_____ 15. According to current research and theory, children learn better when they can associate new material with prior knowledge.

_____ 16. When implementing an integrated language arts curriculum, teachers allocate brief periods of time for teaching each of the language arts.

_____ 17. Student contracts are one method teachers can use to manage individual activities.

_____ 18. The best time to hold teacher-student conferences is before or after school.

_____ 19. The organizational pattern of a classroom is more important than the teacher.

_____ 20. In cooperative learning, students learn in partnerships or as teams.

_____ 21. Effective teachers teach skills in isolation.

_____ 22. A child's first learning experiences occur in the home.

_____ 23. CIRC is a form of cooperative learning for upper elementary students in the area of language arts.

_____ 24. Whole language classrooms have no organization or structure.

_____ 25. Active student participation in language learning is an important aspect of whole language classrooms.

_____ 26. Teachers who observe students and record information about them are acting as researchers.

_____ 27. Just as students learn from teachers, teachers learn from students.

_____ 28. Peer tutoring benefits both the tutor and the tutee.

_____ 29. In reading to their children, parents provide a foundation for the school's reading program.

_____ 30. Sending bulletins or letters to parents is a valuable way for teachers to communicate about the school's reading program.

_____ 31. Paraprofessionals should do only clerical work in the classroom.

For your journal...

1. Reflect on your own home environment. How did it support, or fail to support, your progress in reading?

2. Think back about your involvement in elementary school reading groups. How were you grouped? How did your group placement make you feel?

3. How can you promote positive self-esteem in low-achieving students?

4. Think about effective teachers you know or have known. What characteristics did they possess?

...And your portfolio

1. Brainstorm a list of ideas for thematic units for which you have resource materials and special knowledge.

2. Conduct your own mini-research project by focusing on a child in your classroom or in one where you are observing. How does this child respond to different types of motivation? What works best, and what seems ineffective? Keep an ongoing record and then summarize your findings at the end of your study.

3. Sketch one or more floor plans for your classroom, or the one you hope to have. Take into consideration such factors as centers, desk or table arrangements, computers, classroom library, ease of traffic flow, flexible groupings, and so forth.

Readers with Special Needs

Key Vocabulary

Pay close attention to these terms when they appear in the chapter.

Americans with Disabilities Act (ADA)

attention-deficit hyperactivity disorder (ADHD)

bilingualism

dialect

English as a Second Language (ESL)

exceptional learner

gifted learner

hearing impairment

inclusion

Individuals with Disabilities Education Act (IDEA)

individualized education program (IEP)

learning disability

limited English proficiency (LEP)

mainstreaming

mild mental retardation

multidisciplinary team

multicultural students

PL 94-142

speech impairment

visual impairment

SETTING OBJECTIVES

When you finish reading this chapter, you should be able to

▶ Explain mainstreaming and inclusion and their effects in a regular classroom.

▶ Identify learners who are classified as exceptional and suggest several guidelines for instructing them.

▶ Name and briefly define several types of disabilities commonly encountered in classrooms.

▶ Describe some strategies that are generally effective in working with readers who have difficulties.

▶ Explain some ways to adjust teaching strategies for gifted students.

▶ Describe the effects of a child's culture on his or her reading achievement.

▶ Discuss several important features and promising approaches to consider in a reading program for children with cultural or dialectal differences.

▶ Describe some special needs of bilingual children and ways to meet these needs.

Chapter 14 Organization

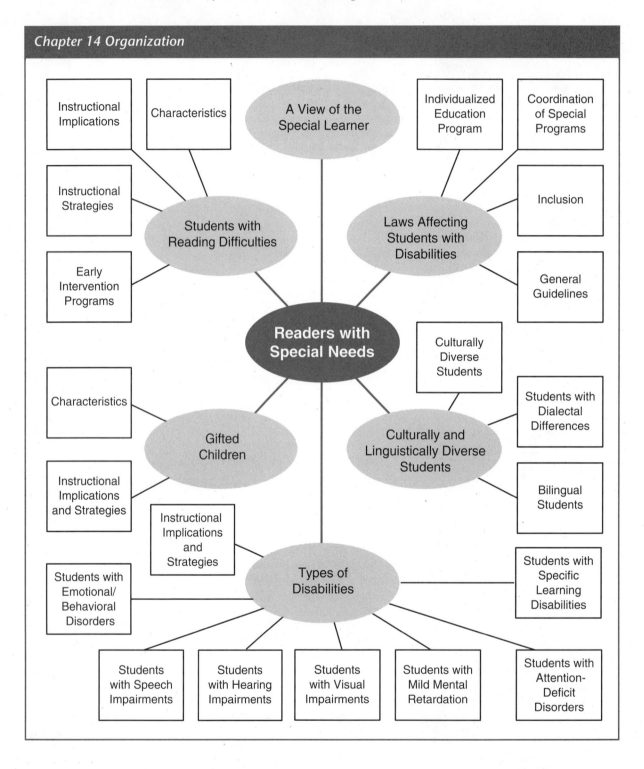

This chapter considers exceptional learners, those who differ in some way from the majority of learners. These children also need well-balanced holistic reading instruction, but they may need some instructional modifications or supplements to help them reach their full potential. The chapter discusses special types of learners who may be mainstreamed or *included* in regular classrooms, but makes no attempt to cover children with severe disabilities. This chapter focuses on what the classroom teacher, rather than the specialist, can do.

Since many children who were formerly enrolled in special education classes are now being integrated into regular classes, teachers are responsible for working with more exceptional children than they were in the past. Educators today realize that association with children in a regular classroom may be beneficial for exceptional children, and schools are making special provisions for these children by placing them in the educational mainstream.

This chapter begins with a presentation of laws affecting students with disabilities, in particular, the Individuals with Disabilities Education Act (IDEA), based on Public Law 94-142, and its effects on the education of children with disabilities. Then it discusses inclusion and presents a list of guidelines for working with students who have special needs. Next, the chapter focuses on different types of exceptional learners: students with learning disabilities, attention-deficit disorders, or mental retardation; children with visual, hearing, or speech impairments; youngsters who are emotionally disturbed; children who are gifted, as well as those who are not proficient readers; and students with cultural and linguistic variations. The chapter concludes with a list of multiethnic children's books to use with culturally different students.

A View of the Special Learner

Diversity is on the rise in today's classrooms. Children vary in terms of their racial, ethnic, cultural, and economic backgrounds, as well as their physical and mental abilities (Jasmine, 1995). Some students are said to be at risk; these students have normal intelligence but are unable to acquire the skills they need to achieve success. Circumstances that place them at risk include (1) low teacher expectations; (2) failure to achieve in a competitive school structure, particularly for children with academic, functional, or physical disabilities; and (3) family stress or instability, low socioeconomic background, and low self-perceptions regarding school (Bertrand, 1995).

Since family situations seem to play a major role in placing children at risk, many educators are promoting family literacy, thus encouraging adult learners to enhance their own literacy skills while promoting the literacy of their children (Morrow and Neuman, 1995). One school-based family literacy program, in which 95 percent of the families are members of minority groups with low socioeconomic backgrounds, offers support in language and literacy development as it increases parental awareness of the importance of reading books to further their children's education. Specifically, the program involves parents in planning, includes workshops, invites parent volunteers to read or tell stories to children, provides books for children to take home and share with parents, and encourages teachers to communicate with parents regularly and suggest ideas for them to try at home (Come and Fredericks, 1995).

Students are more alike than they are different in their needs and interests, so by accepting the premise that all children differ from one another, teachers can view differences among learners as variabilities, not necessarily disabilities. Given choices, children can select activities consistent with their abilities and interests (Roller, 1996).

Each child is an individual with a unique set of characteristics; there is no consensus on a definition of a typical child. It is the individual learner, not the label, that matters, and caring teachers do their best to facilitate each child's ability to learn.

Laws Affecting Students with Disabilities

In recent years, Congress has passed laws to protect the rights of individuals with disabilities. The *Americans with Disabilities Act of 1990 (ADA)* is intended to eliminate discrimination against all individuals with disabilities. Its implications for school children include enabling them to participate more fully in all school programs and to learn more effectively by using telecommunication systems.

In 1975 Congress passed PL 94-142, the Education for All Handicapped Children Act, which altered the placement of students with disabilities in the public schools. Instead of being assigned to special rooms, many of these children are now being mainstreamed into regular classrooms. In 1990, Congress amended PL 94-142 by modifying some of the provisions and changing the terminology to reflect greater sensitivity to the individual, rather than focusing on the disability (First and Curcio, 1993). The act, reauthorized in 1997 (HR5 to HR5-121), was renamed the *Individuals with Disabilities Education Act (IDEA)*.

Individualized Education Program (IEP)

A major provision of the IDEA is the development of an *individualized education program (IEP)* for each child with disabilities who receives support through federal funding. The IEP states the child's present levels of educational performance, the projected starting date of the program, and the duration of the special services. It sets annual goals for the child's level of educational performance as well as short-term instructional objectives, which must be defined in measurable terms. The IEP also specifies educational services and special instructional media for the child.

The IEP is developed by a *multidisciplinary team*, sometimes called a *core evaluation team*, consisting of a representative (other than the child's teacher) of the local education agency (usually the school), the teacher, and one or both parents. The child and other professional personnel may be included when appropriate.

The multidisciplinary team for children with specific learning disabilities must also include a person qualified to give individual diagnostic exams and, when available, an appropriate learning disabilities specialist.

Coordination of Special Programs

When working with students who have disabilities, the classroom teacher should cooperate with other teachers, such as the resource or Title I teacher, who may provide special reading instruction for some children during part of the day. In fact, Title I, a federally funded compensatory education program, now requires its teachers to coordinate compensatory instruction with classroom instruction (Allington, 1993).

To coordinate a special learner's reading instructional program, the classroom teacher and the support teacher must communicate on a regular basis so that the support teacher's instruction supplements the instruction provided in the regular classroom. Sometimes children are in "pull-out" programs in which they go to resource rooms, and sometimes they are tutored in the regular classrooms by reading specialists or aides in an "in-class" program. Bean and Eichelberger (1985) studied both types of programs and found that reading specialists concentrated more on reinforcing classroom skills and less on diagnosing needs in in-class programs than they did in pull-out programs, but there were problems with having two teachers in one room and with implementing the program in terms of time and space. Neither program guarantees greater coordination among teachers; the important issue is that teachers communicate with one another about students' strengths and needs to provide an integrated reading program for each special learner (Allington and Shake, 1986).

Inclusion

Inclusion means that students with disabilities are assigned to regular classrooms in a neighborhood school for the entire day and participate in all school activities. It differs from mainstreaming in that mainstreamed students move in and out of their regular classrooms during the day to receive special instruction. Inclusion requires adequate support services, such as physical accommodations, sufficient personnel, staff development and technical assistance, and collaboration among personnel involved. In some cases, a special education teacher joins the regular classroom teacher, not only to give support to students with disabilities, but to co-teach the entire class so that students are unaware that some of them need special assistance ("CEC Policy . . . ," 1993; Friend and Cook, 1992; Twiss, 1995). Inclusion is still a new idea, however, and its effectiveness and full impact on the regular teacher cannot yet be measured (Smelter, Rasch, Yudewitz, 1994). The following Focus on Strategies and Classroom Scenario, both based on actual situations, show the effects of inclusion in two classrooms.

Classmates can offer support by fully accepting the mainstreamed or included child, providing necessary services, and involving the child in activities. (© *Crews/The Image Works*)

Focus on Strategies

Inclusion

Long after the children had left, Faye sat at her desk reflecting on the year she had spent with this group of children. She remembered surveying her class of twenty-six second graders at the beginning of the year and thinking that this year would be quite a challenge. "It certainly has been," she thought, "and there was no way I could have predicted how it would turn out. I've had some very stressful experiences. It hasn't been easy."

Just before school started, Faye learned she would have two students in wheelchairs, Mickey with muscular dystrophy and Adam with spina bifida; Carlotta with attention-deficit hyperactivity disorder (ADHD); Yvonne, who was brain traumatized; and Leslie, who had been identified as seriously emotionally disturbed (SED). Ruby, a support teacher, would spend most of her time with Mickey but part of her time with Adam. Both children needed considerable help in completing their work.

One problem that demanded immediate attention was how to manage two wheelchairs and one or two additional adults in an already crowded classroom. Faye had tried several arrangements until she settled on one that seemed to work best. Maneuvering the wheelchairs to reading groups, learning centers, and special instructional areas had created some serious traffic jams! Faye had also found that she had to allow more time when preparing to leave the classroom for lunch and recess; it took time to position the wheelchairs and move them through the hallways.

It had been interesting to watch the children's relationships with Mickey and Adam develop. At first, they had eyed the two boys in wheelchairs somewhat suspiciously. Then they approached them cautiously, and finally warmed up to them. Mickey, with his bright, alert eyes, showed that he was eager to participate, and the children soon considered it a privilege to attend him. Adam was more reticent, being somewhat overprotected by his mother, who often sat with him in class, and the children found it more difficult to communicate with him.

Believing both boys were bright enough to do second-grade work, Faye held the same expectations for them that she did for the other children. Adam could speak well enough to answer her questions, but she found she had to modify his assignments because he was unable to track the work on the board to the paper on his tray. Mickey, on the other hand, could usually respond with only one or two words, so Ruby usually interpreted Mickey's answers for him. In small groups Mickey could speak more easily, perhaps as much as a sentence or two at a time.

Getting used to having another teacher in the room with her hadn't been easy either, Faye thought. Sometimes hearing another adult speaking at the same time she was talking had been quite disturbing; it was something she had had to get used to. Mickey needed Ruby's attention almost constantly in order to participate in the lessons. The only way he could take a spelling test was to spell the words to her so that she could write them down for him.

Recalling some of the better times, Faye thought of the way the class interacted with Mickey. "I really like the way the children took to Mickey," she thought. "They would bring him those toy trucks and stuffed animals to play with on his tray. Of course, he'd hit at them and knock them down when he'd try to pick them up because he couldn't control his arm movements, but the children didn't mind; they'd just pick them up for him. Mickey had a sparkle in his eye and was fun to be with."

One of the best ways the children worked with Mickey was as peer tutors during his therapy sessions. Pat, the physical therapist, would ask a couple of the children to accompany Mickey to therapy and teach them how to help Mickey with his body movements. On a few occasions, Mickey and his peer tutors went swimming at a nearby indoor pool during therapy sessions. That had been a real treat for the peer tutors as well as for Mickey.

Adam, however, hadn't benefited from the experience as much as Mickey had, Faye observed. Perhaps the children felt intimidated by his mother's presence, or maybe it was Adam's reluctance to participate in class activities. In any case, they seemed to prefer being with Mickey and spent little time with Adam voluntarily. Of course, they willingly pushed Adam's wheelchair when it was time for him to move to a different location.

Thinking back, Faye was well aware that Mickey and Adam certainly hadn't been the only children with special needs this year. Carlotta, Leslie, and Yvonne had been taking medication to help them control their behavior, but occasionally Carlotta's

(continued)

mother forgot to give her the medicine. On those days, Faye had to spend extra time helping Carlotta focus on her work.

Leslie's problems were more serious, sometimes causing her to be hospitalized for treatment for days or weeks at a time. After her first long-term hospitalization, Leslie had been reassigned to a special education self-contained room. Even though Leslie was being mainstreamed into Faye's room for periods of time each day, Faye recalled how much easier it had been to manage the class without Leslie's disruptive behaviors.

Getting the class to pay attention to her had been a constant struggle, too. The children were so easily distracted! Faye remembered the day she had used Mickey as an example of attentive behavior because of his eagerness and alertness. She recalled saying, "I really like the way Mickey is paying attention. Look at his eyes—they are always watching me when I'm talking." Looking over at Mickey, one of the children had said, "I know. Let's call him 'Eagle Eyes,'" and the nickname had stuck.

This year had been a learning experience for them all, Faye observed—probably more for herself than for the children. She had made it through somehow, but she hoped that accommodations would be made if she had so many children with special needs another year. A smaller class size would help, as would additional support teachers, even on a part-time basis. She would have also benefited from some training on how to work with these children. Although she had done her best, Faye believed that because of the special demands on her time and attention by a few children, the remaining children had been somewhat shortchanged.

**Classroom
Scenario**

Inclusion

Danny, who has cerebral palsy, has been admitted to Alan Stanton's third-grade class. Danny can move only his head and is unable to speak, but his IQ has been placed at 110. By moving his head and using his eyes, Danny indicates his wishes and answers questions. He also holds a pencil in his teeth to type written work, which is displayed along with the work of his peers, and he reads from an open book placed on a music stand.

Alan's positive attitude toward Danny and the children's eagerness to include him in *everything* they did created a positive learning environment. A larger child pushed his wheelchair so that Danny could go with them on field trips, take his turn as class leader, and participate in activities on the playground. When paired with a student of lower academic ability, Danny supplied the "brains" for a project while the other child carried out the plan. When the class learned folk dancing, Danny was the hub of the wheel and a child turned his chair. The children were protective, respectful, and accepting.

Analysis of Scenario
As a result of this experience, Danny benefited by being accepted as part of the class. Perhaps even more important, class members gained an appreciation of how much a student with disabilities can do.

Inclusion without adequate supplementary aids and services can create a situation such as the one Faye experienced in the first vignette. On the other hand, *responsible* inclusion, which occurs when regular and special educators are properly trained and supported (Lombardi and Ludlow, 1996), can positively affect achievement of educational objectives, communication skills, and social interactions. Schools, therefore, should offer the necessary support and services to students with disabilities within the regular classroom so that *all* the children can learn (Fisher, Sax, and Pumpian, 1996; Lombardi and Ludlow, 1996).

As the two vignettes on inclusion indicate, classmates play an important role in terms of offering acceptance and support to the mainstreamed or included child. The teacher therefore should prepare students to accept these class members by frankly explaining the nature of the disabilities and each student's special needs. It is important that the child who is mainstreamed or included be fully accepted as an integral part of the class and not just occupy space in the classroom. Students should become actively supportive by providing necessary services, tutoring when special help is needed, including the child in activities, and working with her or him in cooperative groups (Twiss, 1995).

Cooperative learning strategies allow groups of students with varied abilities, including those who are mainstreamed or included, to work together on projects relating to the content areas (Maring, Furman, and Blum-Anderson, 1985). Being included in these groups enables youngsters with disabilities to contribute to the activities, thereby improving their self-concepts, and to learn from their peers. Other effective strategies for including children with special needs are workshops, described in Chapter 8 (Caldwell, 1997; Roller, 1996), and integrated, theme-centered activities, described in Chapters 7, 8, 10, and 13 (Fisher, Sax, and Pumpian, 1996). Both allow children to work at developmentally appropriate levels.

Time for Reflection	Although some educators endorse inclusion, others oppose it. What do *you* think?

General Guidelines

Most of the procedures and materials already recommended in this book can be effectively used with exceptional children when teachers make reasonable adjustments for particular difficulties. The exceptional child's basic needs and goals are not so different from those of other children, but the means of achieving those goals and fulfilling those needs may differ. The following general practices, which apply to all learners, are crucial in teaching exceptional children:

1. *Maintain a positive attitude toward exceptional learners.* Children with special needs require a great deal of encouragement and understanding. Show that you are interested in them: talk with them about their interests; have high but reasonable expectations; note things they have done.

2. *Consider learning styles and modalities when planning instruction.* An exceptional child might be an auditory learner who readily associates sounds with symbols, a visual learner who remembers sight words easily, or a kinesthetic-tactile learner who needs to touch, manipulate, and move in order to learn to read. Such factors as lighting, space, time of day, and temperature may also affect children's ability to learn.

3. *Provide appropriate materials and direct instruction as needed.* Use high-interest materials that the children are capable of using successfully. Do not use the types of reading materials with which the children have previously failed. Arrange direct instruction to teach necessary skills that children lack.

4. *Communicate with others who work with special children.* Be sure to coordinate each special learner's program with all others involved in his or her instruction, particularly Title I and resource teachers. Where inclusion is used, make arrangements to co-teach so that children may benefit from the special skills and knowledge of each teacher.

5. *Provide a positive classroom environment.* Help the children in the regular classroom to accept and appreciate the unique qualities of children with disabilities by including the special learners in class activities and providing opportunities for them to make worthwhile contributions.

6. *Use varied instructional and assessment techniques.* Present concepts by means of concrete objects, manipulative devices, and multimedia presentations (films, television, videotapes, recordings) to make use of the child's five senses.

7. *Provide opportunities for success in tasks.* Assign tasks at or below ability levels of exceptional children who have problems to ensure reasonable success. Provide short-term goals and give immediate feedback to encourage good work. Use progress charts to make growth apparent, and have children compete against their own records, not those of their classmates.

Types of Disabilities

In any classroom, a teacher is likely to find one or more students with some type of disability. This section discusses various disabilities and impairments.

Students with Specific Learning Disabilities

Over the recent past, students with specific learning disabilities have comprised the largest group of students entitled to receive special education services (Wood, 1993). The most widely accepted definition of specific learning disabilities is from the *Federal Register*, 1977, p. 65083:

> The term "children with specific learning disabilities" means those children who have a disorder in one or more of the basic psychological processes involved in understanding or in using language, spoken or written, which disorder may manifest itself in imperfect ability to listen, think, speak, read, write, spell, or do mathematical calculations. Such disorders include such conditions as perceptual handicaps, brain injury, minimal brain dysfunction, dyslexia, and developmental aphasia. Such term does not include children who have learning problems which are primarily the result of visual, hearing, or motor disabilities, of mental retardation, of emotional disturbance, or of environmental, cultural or economic disadvantage.

Although some students with learning disabilities have excellent verbal skills, many exhibit severe communication deficits in their oral language and reading performance. They may have difficulty with articulation, following oral and written directions, and accurately expressing their thoughts orally and in writing. Reading improvement is the most widely recognized academic need of the child with learning disabilities (Beattie, 1994; Gaskins, 1982). The general guidelines presented earlier apply to students with learning disabilities.

Students with Attention-Deficit Disorders (ADD)

Many students with learning disabilities have difficulty focusing on tasks and maintaining attention. Some of these children are said to have *attention-deficit hyperactivity disorder (ADHD)* if the behavior occurs much more frequently in them than in others of the same mental age and if the onset is before age seven. Sample criteria include impulsiveness, fidgeting and squirming, high distractibility, difficulty in waiting for turn or playing quietly, excessive talking and interrupting, and inability to pay attention (Gearheart and Gearheart, 1989; Pfiffner, 1996; Richek, List, and Lerner, 1989). Another type of attention-deficit disorder, referred to as *undifferentiated attention-deficit disorder*, exists without hyperactivity and is characterized by marked inattention (Lerner, 1988).

Children who cannot concentrate are likely to have trouble learning to read and write. In some cases, doctors prescribe stimulant or antidepressant medication to help control behavior, but this has become a controversial practice. Children should realize that medication is used only for support and they are ultimately responsible for their own behavior (Fouse and Brians, 1993). These children will do best with short reading assignments and sessions.

Students with Mild Mental Retardation

Primary characteristics of children with *mild mental retardation* are subaverage intellectual functioning; that is, with I.Q.'s from about 50 to 75 (Lukasevich, 1996), and limitations in age-appropriate and situation-appropriate adaptive skills, including social, self-help, maturational, and communicative acts (Hunt and Marshall, 1994). In other words, children with mild mental retardation fail to meet certain expectations for their ages and situations. These children do not learn as readily as others of the same chronological age. They are usually unable to make complicated generalizations and learn material incidentally. According to Sedlak and Sedlak (1985), they are often deficient in oral and silent reading, locating details, recognizing main ideas, using context clues, and drawing conclusions.

Students with Visual Impairments

A child who is *visually impaired* has difficulty but is able to learn to read print, as opposed to the blind child who must learn to read braille. Teachers can make provisions for children with visual impairments by adjusting lighting, providing tape-recorded stories and books with large print, and reading orally to the whole class frequently. They should refer children to visual specialists if they observe such symptoms as squinting, closing or covering one eye, rubbing eyes frequently, or making frequent errors when copying board work.

Students with Hearing Impairments

The term *hearing impaired* applies to individuals whose sense of hearing is defective but adequate for ordinary purposes, with or without a hearing aid. When providing reading instruction for children with hearing impairments, teachers should speak slowly, clearly, and with adequate volume; seat the child as far as possible from distracting sounds; use a whole-word approach to word recognition rather than a phonics approach because the child cannot hear sounds well; use the language experience approach to connect meaningful experiences to words; and supplement reading lessons with visual aids. Teachers should refer students to hearing specialists if they observe such symptoms as inattentiveness in class, requests for repetition of verbal information, frowning when trying to listen, or turning the head so that one or the other ear always faces the teacher.

Students with Speech Impairments

Speech is considered abnormal "when it deviates so far from the speech of other people that it calls attention to itself, interferes with communication, or causes the speaker or his listener to be distressed" (Van Riper, 1978, p. 43). Two of the most common *speech impairments* the classroom teacher encounters are articulation problems and stuttering. Teachers of young children with articulation problems can make considerable use of rhymes, stories, and songs in groups, as well as planning more formal lessons organized around the speech sounds that are causing difficulties. In working with children who stutter, teachers should accept their speech and avoid prompting them.

Students with Emotional/Behavioral Disorders

Although all children sometimes misbehave, a few children have emotional/behavioral disorders characterized by long-term, extremely unacceptable behaviors across many situations. These behaviors interfere with personal and social development, as well as with learning. Emotional/behavioral disorders are usually exhibited through aggressiveness and destructiveness or through withdrawal and anxiety (Deiner, 1993).

Instructional Implications and Strategies

The guidelines already given are useful for working with special learners, but each student has specific needs. When teachers identify students who appear to be having difficulties, they should refer them for special services (for example, auditory testing, psychological counseling) and use good judgment when helping them. The following section presents some instructional strategies for helping students who are experiencing difficulties with reading.

Students with Reading Difficulties

In any classroom some children are more likely to have problems learning to read than others. Educators have recommended a number of strategies to help these students.

Characteristics

A student who has difficulty learning to read may be labeled dyslexic, remedial, underachieving, at risk, disabled, retarded, impaired, or language learning disabled, but these labels are often difficult to apply accurately and serve no real purpose (Kamhi and Catts, 1989). The terms *learning disabled* and *remedial reader* are often confused, although the degree of underachievement for students with learning disabilities is more severe than that for remedial readers (Rhodes and Dudley-Marling, 1988).

In addition to problems with decoding and comprehension, these students often have behavioral and emotional problems (Beck, 1988). They may have difficulty initiating and completing tasks, working accurately, maintaining attention, remaining in their seats, and following oral and written directions.

Emotional issues, such as low self-concept, poor frustration tolerance, and negative attitudes, may make these children unable to concentrate or unwilling to attempt learning tasks.

Instructional Implications

Strategies that are appropriate for teaching developmental readers, those who are making normal progress in reading, are generally the same as those for nonproficient readers. Instruction for readers with difficulties, however, may be more direct than it would be in regular reading classes. There may be highly specialized techniques for students with severe problems and instruction that is based on a thorough diagnosis of the problem (Richek, List, and Lerner, 1989). Often these readers need opportunities to develop positive attitudes toward reading and to build positive self-concepts. In the following Classroom Scenario, an undergraduate student enrolled in a reading practicum course helped low-achieving readers find success and build self-esteem.

Classroom Scenario

Providing Success for Nonproficient Readers

During her third-grade practicum, Molly Johnson had been assigned to work with three boys who hated to read and were reading at a first-grade level. After deciding to do a language experience chart with them, Molly began by reading Tomie de Paola's *The Quicksand Book* (Holiday House, 1977). After a discussion about quicksand, she involved the students in making quicksand in a large tub. The children made several charts related to the experience on such topics as what to do if trapped in quicksand, where quicksand is found, and the steps in conducting the experiment. When the three boys finished their work, Molly arranged for them to share their information with the rest of the class. They stood in the front of the classroom and read their charts to their peers, who were visibly impressed by what these boys had done.

Analysis of Scenario
By choosing an interesting topic and holding high expectations, Molly had found a way to motivate these students. They became excited about their special project and looked forward to the reading and writing activities related to their study of quicksand. By reading their charts in front of the room, they gained self-esteem and a measure of respect from their classmates.

Many researchers have found that direct, systematic instruction in skills and strategies benefits students who have difficulty grasping important reading-writing concepts on their own (Adams, 1990; French, Ellsworth, and Amoruso,

1995; Gaskins, 1988; Wong-Kam and Au, 1988; Sears, Carpenter, and Burstein, 1994). These children seem to learn best when direct instruction in basic skills is part of their instructional program. Direct instruction is defined as instruction with clearly stated goals that students understand, carefully sequenced and structured materials, detailed explanations and extensive modeling of reading processes, monitoring of student work with immediate feedback, and continued instruction until skill mastery is achieved.

Direct instruction is particularly helpful for students who have difficulty acquiring phonics and decoding skills that are essential for learning to read. After reviewing research on phonics skills, Lyon (1991) concluded that systematic, phonics-based instruction produces more positive outcomes than approaches that rely on contextual reading for students who cannot intuitively learn the alphabetic code. A potential danger with direct instruction of reading skills in isolation, however, is that children may learn to recognize and pronounce words but be unable to comprehend what they read.

Some educators favor holistic instruction for children with reading difficulties (Lukasevich, 1996; Moustafa, 1997; Scala, 1993; Truax and Kretschmer, 1993; Weaver, 1990; Zucker, 1993), but research is limited in this area. In one study Stice and Bertrand (1990) found that at-risk students in whole language classrooms scored slightly higher on achievement tests than at-risk students from traditional classrooms and also outperformed them on less formal measures.

A blend of direct and holistic instruction may be the solution to the controversy between the two (French, Ellsworth, and Amoruso, 1995). Direct instruction in phonics can occur in holistic classrooms within the context of story reading. For example, the teacher reads a big book with the class and on later readings calls attention to beginning sounds of words or to rhyming words. Minilessons (direct instruction) drawn from words in the story follow. (See "Focus on Strategies" in Chapter 3 for ways to teach phonics through literature.) According to Stahl (1994), direct instruction in phonics seems most effective when integrated into a meaningful reading-writing program, and Sears and her colleagues (1994) recommend teaching strategies explicitly or directly, but within the context of authentic reading activities.

Instructional Strategies

Direct instruction focuses on academics and is teacher-directed. Such instruction is not a matter of asking children to complete skill sheets; instead, it is a planned instructional sequence of explaining and modeling. By modeling, the teacher is helping readers understand the "invisible mental processes which are at the core of reading" (Duffy, Roehler, and Herrmann, 1988, p. 762). Direct instruction enables students to become independent readers by providing them with additional strategies for attacking unknown words and applying higher-level comprehension skills. (See Table 14.1 for examples of common reading difficulties and related direct instruction lessons.)

Table 14.1 *Common Reading Problems and Suggested Remedial Approaches*	
If a student . . .	**Let the student . . .**
1. Reads word by word or uses incorrect phrasing.	a. Read easy, familiar, and interesting material.
	b. Tape-record a paragraph, listen to the tape, record it again with attention to units of meaning, and listen for improvement. Repeat this process until fluency is reached.
	c. Read orally with a good reader and imitate the good reader's phrasing and expression.
	d. Participate in choral reading or choral speaking.
	e. Read a part in a play; do readers' theater.
2. Lacks knowledge of sight words.	a. Associate pictures with words that have concrete referents.
	b. Identify names of familiar products that appear in advertisements.
	c. Read words from language experience charts and student-written stories as they appear both in context and on word cards.
	d. Build word banks of sight words and use them to create sentences or organize them by naming or action words. (See Chapter 7 for ideas about word banks.)
3. Has difficulty using context clues.	a. Watch the teacher modeling ways of using semantic and syntactic context clues.
	b. Fill in blanks with appropriate words in cloze selections. (See Chapter 10 for construction of cloze passages.)
	c. Brainstorm words that would make sense for the unknown word in a sentence and then consider phonics clues (especially beginning sound) in deciding on the word.
	d. Underline specific types of context clues, such as definition or comparison. (See Chapters 3 and 4 for more types of context clues.)
4. Cannot make inferences or draw conclusions.	a. Observe the teacher modeling ways to draw inferences by thinking aloud about clues for meaning.
	b. Look at pictures or collections of objects, find reasonable connections among them, and create stories from them.
	c. Listen to a story and predict what will happen next.
	d. Underline word and phrase clues that lead to making an inference. (What season is it? The snow fell and the streets were icy. It was very cold outside.)
	e. Solve short mysteries. (See Donald Sobol's Encyclopedia Brown books, for example.)

Table 14.1 *Common Reading Problems and Suggested Remedial Approaches (cont.)*

If a student . . .	Let the student . . .
5. Has a limited vocabulary.	a. Expand experiences by watching films and listening to stories that contain new concepts and words. b. Keep a file or notebook of new words with their meanings and use some of these words in writing. c. Play games that use word knowledge, such as *Password*. d. Brainstorm with other children lists of synonyms and antonyms. e. Compare figurative and literal meanings of figurative expressions. f. Experience a rich environment with many varied, concrete experiences.

Two uses of literature are particularly effective with students who have reading difficulties. Sustained Silent Reading (SSR), discussed in Chapter 8, enables them to choose familiar, predictable, or high-interest books that are easy to read. The basic plan for SSR can be modified for these students so that they may read their books orally to partners and discuss them in pairs (Ford and Ohlhausen, 1988; Rhodes and Dudley-Marling, 1988). Another useful strategy is repeated shared readings of predictable and repetitive stories and poetry, a procedure that enables students to sense language patterns (Ford and Ohlhausen, 1989; Wicklund, 1988). Students may then compose their own pieces based on the now familiar patterns.

Semantic mapping (explained in Chapters 4 and 5) is a particularly useful strategy for nonproficient readers because it helps them visualize relationships (Flood and Lapp, 1988; Pehrsson and Denner, 1989; Rhodes and Dudley-Marling, 1988). Journal writing and process writing are also useful procedures for low-achieving students because they allow readers to choose their own topics, use invented spellings, and ignore writing conventions initially. By revising and editing selected pieces, even these students get to be published authors (Gaskins, 1988). Of special benefit during the writing process is peer conferencing, in which children help one another by offering suggestions and asking questions that lead to better composition (Wong-Kam and Au, 1988).

Involving children in authentic tasks promotes their understanding of reading and writing as meaning-making processes. The functional situations given in Example 14.1 and the list of authentic activities that follows are appropriate for any reader, but particularly for one who is having difficulties.

Example 14.1 *Imaginary Functional Situations*

Your dog is sick. What number do you call for help? Where could you take your dog?

Choose a magazine you would like to order. Fill out the order form.

Your mother is coming home on the bus, but you forget what time she is supposed to arrive. Look it up in the schedule.

You want to watch a television special, but you can't remember the time or channel. Find it in the newspaper.

Look through a catalogue and choose four items you would like to have for less than $100 in all. Fill out the order blank.

If a house is on fire, what number would you call? What are some other emergency phone numbers?

You want to write a lost-and-found ad for the bicycle you lost. Write the ad and find the address and phone number of the newspaper.

You want to order a game that is advertised on the back of a cereal box. Follow the directions for placing the order.

Look at a menu and order a meal for yourself. Find out how much it costs.

You want to go to a football game in a nearby town. Find the stadium on the map and be able to give directions.

Activities

1. Have the children set up a post office in which they write notes and address envelopes to their classmates.

2. Obtain multiple copies of last year's telephone directories, and let the students look up their own phone numbers; find emergency numbers; and look through the Yellow Pages to find restaurants, a skating rink, movie theaters, and other places that are familiar to them. Have each student make a telephone directory of these numbers.

3. Give children forms to fill out about themselves, including their names, addresses, telephone numbers, Social Security numbers, and so on.

4. Make cards of words and phrases found in public places, such as *Wet Paint, No Trespassing, Danger, Restroom*, and so on. Have the children see how many terms they can recognize.

5. Have students use newspapers to locate grocery store and other advertisements, find the classified section and look for items that are for sale and jobs that are

available, use the index to find the comics page, read headlines, and look at the sports pages to find out about local athletic events.

6. Keep a collection of simple recipes, arranged alphabetically within categories, in a recipe box. Obtain basic ingredients and allow the children to make something.

7. Collect coupons and distribute some to each child. Encourage children to figure out who will save the most money by using the coupons. Be sure they check expiration dates and any other specifications (such as two for the price of one).

Early Intervention Programs

As a result of a growing consensus that remedial reading instruction is often ineffective, particularly above second or third grade, a trend toward early intervention programs for students who are experiencing difficulty in learning to read is emerging (Johnston and Allington, 1991; Pikulski, 1994; Pinnell, 1991). Reading educators contend that the emphasis should be on prevention rather than correction. Intensive early intervention followed by long-term, effective instruction appears to bring about lasting and substantial gains in reading achievement.

Intervention should begin as soon as a student shows signs of difficulty, usually in first grade. Typically, an intensive program is provided by a trained instructor and lasts for a short period of time, although some students may need additional intensive support beyond first grade. Two early intervention programs are briefly described here: Reading Recovery and Success for All.

Reading Recovery, developed in New Zealand by Marie Clay, is a temporary intervention program intended for first graders who are at risk of early reading failure (Clay, 1979; Sensenbaugh, 1995). A specially trained tutor works daily with each child for thirty minutes, usually for a period of twelve to sixteen weeks, until the child has developed effective strategies for independent learning and can function adequately in the regular classroom. From a selection of approximately 500 "little books," the tutor selects those that meet a student's particular interests and needs. Each lesson consists of having the child read many little books and compose a brief story or message. Research evidence indicates that Reading Recovery has enabled children to retain initial gains in reading and continue to make progress.

Success for All focuses on low-achieving inner-city populations. This program involves school reorganization to provide excellent instruction from preschool through the primary grades (Slavin et al., 1994). Its three premises are innovative curriculum and instruction in reading, intensive one-on-one tutoring if reading problems emerge, and regrouping by reading level across the grades for ninety-minute reading instructional periods. The tutor reinforces the direct instruction provided by the regular classroom teacher, but also seeks to identify problems and find different strategies. In addition, a family support team attempts to involve parents, making them feel welcome in the school and providing special services. Research results are extremely positive and affirm the belief that reading failure in the primary grades is preventable.

Gifted Children

Characteristics

Identifying the gifted and talented student can be a perplexing problem, with different school systems using various criteria to select those students entitled to special services. Commonly used criteria are high IQ scores; high overall grade point averages; outstanding performance in such areas as art, music, math, or science; or superior creative abilities (Davis and Rimm, 1994). In his theory of multiple intelligences, Howard Gardner claims there are seven or more forms of intelligence (Armstrong, 1994; Lazear, 1992). An individual may be gifted in any one or more of these areas:

1. *Linguistic intelligence*, the ability to use written and spoken words effectively
2. *Logical-mathematical intelligence*, the ability to reason, think deductively, and use numbers effectively
3. *Spatial intelligence*, the capacity to perceive visual-spatial aspects of the world accurately and to create mental images
4. *Bodily-kinesthetic intelligence*, knowledge of one's body and its physical movements
5. *Musical intelligence*, recognition of tonal patterns and sensitivity to rhythm
6. *Interpersonal intelligence*, the capacity to understand and relate to other people
7. *Intrapersonal intelligence,* knowledge of self, including metacognition, spirituality, and self-reflection

Instructional Implications and Strategies

Gifted students need to be part of the community of learners within a classroom, participating in whole-class activities and working cooperatively with other students. Despite the widely recognized benefits of cooperative learning, however, gifted students also need opportunities to work alone and with their gifted peers on advanced projects related to their special abilities, as shown in the following Classroom Scenario. The current trend against grouping students by achievement or ability may actually have negative consequences for gifted students if they must always work in heterogeneous groups. In some school districts, special classes and programs for gifted children are being abolished (Davis and Rimm, 1994).

**Classroom
Scenario**

Gifted Education Class

Sandy Smith, a countywide gifted education coordinator, schedules one-hour meetings with her classes each week. A creative person herself, she encourages her students to be creative and use higher-order thinking skills. As her group of fifth graders assembles, she poses a question: "If we value creativity in here, how can we share it with others? Let's brainstorm some ideas." Marcia says, "We could put on a play." Stephen suggests, "Let's teach some kids to make origami." "How about helping them make collages of their lives?" asks Karla. Thor excitedly calls out, "I know—let's tell stories creatively!" Ms. Smith asks, "What do you mean, creatively?" "You know," says Thor. "With sound effects and expression so that it's almost like drama." Several children begin talking about the stories they'd like to tell. "Whoa!" laughs Ms. Smith. "We didn't get very far with our brainstorming. Are there any other ideas?" After pausing a moment, Craig says he really likes the storytelling idea and thinks it would be good to share stories with other classes. Several of the others nod agreement.

"If that's what you want to do, let's see how we can work it out," says Ms. Smith. "First, does everyone agree?" The children eagerly affirm the choice. "Then what plans should we make?" asks Ms. Smith. "We'll need to decide which stories to tell," suggests Stephen. "How should we do that?" asks Ms. Smith. "We could have a sign-up sheet and write down our stories as soon as we've decided which ones to tell," offers Gretchen. "Is it okay if Amy and I do a tandem story together?" asks Marcia. "Of course," replies Ms. Smith. "I'd like to do our stories for a kindergarten," says Thor. "Why not?" Ms. Smith responds. "I'll ask Ms. Masters; she always likes us to come visit her kindergartners."

Analysis of Scenario

Although Ms. Smith meets each group of gifted education students only once a week, she presents them with challenging, thought-provoking ideas that they greet with brainstorming and other problem-solving techniques. Because they support one another and value everyone's ideas, the children are a community of enthusiastic learners. Ms. Smith encourages her students to take ideas back to their classes and share them, and she arranges to have them spend extra time in the library. She coordinates activities with the classroom teachers, librarians, and parents so that support for special activities comes from all directions. When doing a special storytelling project such as the one described here, the students prepare and practice during gifted education class, then later present their material to other students, especially to those in lower grades.

Whether or not a school system offers special programs for gifted students, the classroom teacher should challenge gifted students to reach their potential. Even though they are capable of completing their work more rapidly than other students, the teacher should not require them to do more of the same kind of work if they finish their assignments early. Instruction for gifted students should focus on higher-level critical and creative reading (Collins and Aiex, 1995). Curriculum compacting enables students who demonstrate proficiency in the basic curriculum to skip instruction in basic skills. This procedure frees gifted students to participate in accelerated programs and enrichment activities, such as in-depth reading on topics of special interest, creative responses to books, and long-term research projects.

Computers offer intellectually gifted students opportunities to think, create, and explore (Perry, 1989). Students should view computers as tools for helping them with writing assignments, keeping track of information, and comparing sets of data. See Chapter 11 for information on using computers.

Time for Reflection	Some schools have special programs for the gifted and talented, but other schools support enrichment experiences within the regular classroom without any supplementary program. **What do** *you* **think?**

Culturally and Linguistically Diverse Students

America was long known as the "melting pot" because of its assimilation of people from all parts of the world. In recent years, this idea has been modified by people who believe in the "salad bowl" concept, or the rights of different minority groups to retain their cultural diversity within American society. The following discussions examine how children's backgrounds and specific language characteristics may affect the way they learn. They also consider the strategies teachers can use as they work with these children.

Culturally Diverse Students

Characteristics

Culturally diverse students come from many regional cultures, ethnic groups, and religions. Ethnic groups include

1. African Americans, whose origins are in Africa
2. Native Americans, whose origins are North American
3. Hispanic Americans, including those of Spanish descent or cultural heritage
4. Asian Americans, whose origins are in the Far East or Southeast Asia (Au, 1993; Norton, 1995; Wood, 1993)
5. White Americans, whose origins are in Europe

In recent years the enrollment of culturally diverse students in public schools has increased dramatically (Wood, 1993), and the ethnic and racial composition of students has changed. The trend is toward an increase in Hispanic American,

African American, and Asian American populations ("Why Multicultural Education?", 1994).

Children from some families may differ in their values, orientations toward school, and speech patterns from those in the American mainstream. Both their cultural and linguistic divergencies can influence how these children learn and consequently how they should be taught; thus, their presence and needs have affected educational policies in our schools.

Instructional Implications and Strategies

Multicultural education involves developing an understanding and appreciation of various cultural groups. Children should be taught with consideration for their cultural heritages, their language preferences, and their lifestyles. On the other hand, too much attention to the cultural characteristics of special groups may lead to stereotyping and perhaps to a differentiated, segregated curriculum (Guild, 1994). It can also weaken the educational program. Thus, teachers need to concentrate on teaching the strategies and content necessary for all students to achieve success in American society.

According to Banks (1994, p. 4), "[m]ulticultural education tries to create equal educational opportunities for all students by ensuring that the total school environment reflects the diversity of groups in classrooms, schools, and the society as a whole." Banks continues by saying that teachers implement multicultural education in different ways. The *contributions* approach deals with isolated facts about heroes from different cultures, and the *additive* approach adds units on special topics such as African Americans and the women's rights movement. Instead of these approaches, Banks recommends the *transformation approach*, which changes the curriculum so that students view content from the perspectives of a variety of groups. This approach involves fundamental changes in instructional materials and teaching techniques.

Following are some general guidelines for working with children of diverse cultural backgrounds (Au, 1993; Coelho, 1994; Wood, 1993).

1. *Learn about their cultures.* Find out about the children's language and learn cultural variations in word meanings. Learn about children's living conditions and what things are important to them. Try to discover cultural traits that affect how students learn. Show that you accept and value their cultures, even though they may differ from your own.

2. *Value their contributions.* Take an interest in what children bring to share, and listen to what they say. Create opportunities for their families to share their cultural heritages through learning experiences in the curriculum.

3. *Provide a supportive classroom environment.* Let the environment reflect the various cultures represented in the classroom by displaying multicultural materials and including instruction related to multicultural education.

4. *Provide opportunities for cooperative learning.* Let students work collaboratively to develop social and academic skills, understand and appreciate the

diversity among themselves, and learn strategies to use in their interactions outside of school.

5. *Use multicultural literature.* When possible, choose stories related to students' cultural backgrounds. Exposure to such stories benefits all children. They gain self-esteem by reading about their own heritage and broaden their concepts of the world and the people in it as they read about other cultures.

The use of multicultural literature merits special attention because it affirms and legitimizes various cultures (Diamond and Moore, 1995). It helps children connect with people of different cultures and provides them with information and insights about their own heritage. Because it implicitly acknowledges individuals' rights to be who they are, multicultural literature increases understanding of and respect for differences.

The teacher is the key to any literature program that embraces cultural themes (Aiex, 1989). The approach to cultural diversity is usually either positive, reflecting a willingness to accept differences, or negative, projecting an attitude of rejection. The teacher should use literature that values cultural pluralism and avoid books that portray negative stereotypes. Some questions for teachers to ask when evaluating books for stereotypes include the following:

1. Do the illustrations and text depict the character in the story as a distinct individual or as a stereotype of a particular ethnic group?

2. Is dialect used as a natural part of the story, or contrived to reinforce stereotypes?

3. Is the culture treated respectfully, or portrayed as inferior?

4. Are the people and the settings described authentically?

Hadaway and Florez (1990) point out several ways to use multicultural literature. Teachers, with the help of librarians, should select books that represent cultural groups realistically and integrate these books into literature and social studies programs. As they tell or read the stories to the class, teachers can promote vocabulary, comprehension, and writing skills, along with values education. Some teachers may wish to keep a continuing record on a world map of the settings for various multicultural books and encourage students to identify the sites of their family origins. The chapter appendix lists some multiethnic books that are classified by four of the ethnic groups mentioned earlier in this section.

Students with Dialectal Differences

Children who exhibit cultural differences are also likely to show linguistic variations, often manifested as dialectal differences. A *dialect* is a variation of a language that is sufficiently different from the original to be considered a separate entity but not different enough to be classified as a separate language. Dialectal variations are usually associated with socioeconomic level, geographical region, or national origin. In truth, we all speak a dialect of some sort, and differences exist even within a regional pattern.

Characteristics

Differences in dialects occur in phonology (pronunciation), vocabulary, and grammatical construction. Examples of phonological dialect differences are *de* for *the, nofin'* for *nothing*, and *brovah* for *brother*. Regional usage determines whether the speaker says *sack, tote, poke*, or *bag*. Dialectal variations in grammatical construction often result from the influence of another language.

Each dialect is a complete and functional language system, and no dialect is superior or inferior to another for purposes of communication. However, for individuals to be accepted in some social classes and attain certain career goals, use of standard English is desirable. Standard language is the form of language recognized in dictionaries and grammar books, the "culturally dominant language in a country or region; language of well-educated people" (Harris and Hodges, 1995, p. 242). Teachers should therefore accept and respect children's dialects as part of their cultures and environments, but should make them aware of standard English as an important alternative. Currently, perhaps the most widely accepted view among linguists and educators is support of *bidialectalism*, which affirms both the value of home dialect and its use within the community and the value of teaching students standard English (Ovando and Collier, 1985). This means students should be able to speak their home dialects in school some of the time without being criticized.

Reading teachers should be familiar with the principal differences in pronunciation and syntactic rules of a child's dialect in order to evaluate oral reading. Without this knowledge, teachers cannot distinguish between a child's oral misreading that results from a lack of decoding skills and oral misreading that results from dialectal differences.

Instructional Implications and Strategies

The language experience approach (see Chapter 7) offers many advantages as a method for teaching reading to students whose dialect differs considerably from standard English. However, critics argue that it simply reinforces the dialect without providing contact with standard English. Gillet and Gentry (1983) propose a variation of this approach that values children's language but also provides exposure to standard English. The teacher transcribes the children's story exactly as dictated. The process continues in the traditional way, but later the teacher writes another version of the dictated chart in standard English with conventional sentence structure, using the same format and much of the same vocabulary. The teacher presents it as another story, not a better one, and children compare the two versions. The students then revise the original chart, making their sentences longer, more elaborate, and more consistent with standard English. They then practice echo reading and choral reading with this version until they can read it fluently and have acquired additional sight words.

For those readers who plan to teach in regions where children have divergent dialects, these classroom practices may be useful:

1. Provide purposeful literacy activities so that students can readily see applications for using standard English to communicate.

2. Relate reading to personal experiences and oral language forms that are familiar to the child.

3. Accept the student's nonstandard usage, but model standard English. For example, if a child says, "I ain't got no pencil," you might respond with "You don't have a pencil? I'll help you find one."

4. Focus on the ideas the children are expressing rather than on their ways of expressing them.

5. Connect reading and writing whenever possible. Read stories to the children, let them write their own stories, and then have them read their stories to the class.

Bilingual Students

The term *bilingualism* refers to the ability to speak or understand a language in addition to one's native tongue. Many people in the United States are bilingual or have non-English language backgrounds, and an estimated 6 to 8 million school-age children (about one out of every six) speak a non-English language at home (Hieshima, 1994; McKeon, 1994; "Why Multicultural Education?", 1994).

English as a Second Language (ESL) programs are designed for teaching English to students whose primary language is not English. (© Elizabeth Crews/Stock Boston)

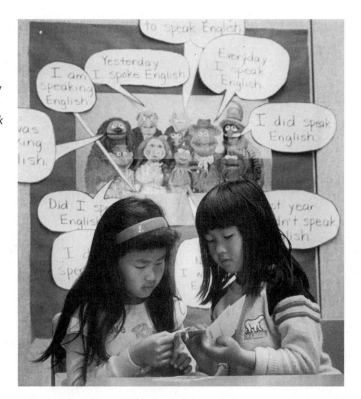

Characteristics

In the classroom, some bilingual students may speak very little English and others may speak English almost as well as they do their primary language. A number of students give the impression of English competence in informal social settings but have not yet attained the standard English of the classroom, and many are unable to use their fragmented knowledge of home and school languages effectively in the classroom (Thonis, 1990).

Bilingual children may be from families of indigenous groups, such as Native Americans; immigrants, who have left a country to settle permanently elsewhere; or refugees, who have fled a country to escape from an intolerable situation. Their home backgrounds and their families' attitudes toward language, school, and culture often affect how well they learn English as a second language.

Instructional Implications

English as a Second Language (ESL) instruction is designed for teaching English to students who live in an English-speaking environment but whose primary language is not English. It is common for students in ESL programs to receive content instruction in English and to spend part of the day in pull-out programs to learn English (Willis, 1994). Limited-English-proficient (LEP) students receive ESL instruction because they lack sufficient English language skills to achieve in a regular classroom and need special instruction to develop linguistic and academic skills.

Many schools follow a policy of immersion for LEP students, which means that students are exposed only to English, without special provisions to help them make the transition from their primary language to English. This practice is common because teachers are rarely available who speak the LEP student's first language. The belief is that children who are immersed in English during the school day will be able to learn it on their own, but this is not necessarily the case.

Research indicates that LEP students learn to read better if initial instruction is in their primary language than if they are simply immersed in an English-speaking environment (Allen, 1994; Baca and Cervantes, 1989; Flood et al., 1996/1997; Schifini, 1994). Students who can already read and write in their first language generally learn to read much faster in English than those who are non-literate in the first language. Once students perceive similarities in reading processes, they can transfer not only general reading strategies and attitudes, but also specific skills, such as awareness of text structure and knowledge of story grammar, from one language to the other.

Many teachers are monolingual and thus are unable to speak a bilingual child's primary language. In this case, there are several alternatives that still support language development (Freeman and Freeman, 1991). These include the following strategies:

1. Have bilingual aides or parent volunteers read and discuss literature in the child's primary language.

2. Ask older students who speak the child's first language to serve as peer tutors.

3. Encourage children to send pen-pal letters to students in another class who share the same primary language.

4. Pair students of the same primary language within a classroom so that the more proficient one can guide the other.

5. Place books in languages other than English in the classroom library.

6. Place signs or labels written in the children's first languages around the classroom, along with the English words.

7. Let children write in journals and ask a bilingual adult to respond to them.

Time for Reflection

Some people advocate immersion in English for speakers of another language, but others claim children make more progress if they first become literate in their primary language and then transfer skills to English. **What do *you* think?**

In addition to the guidelines presented for teaching culturally and linguistically diverse students, the following suggestions are useful for working with bilingual students (Allen, 1994; Altwerger and Ivener, 1994; Au, 1993; Cummins, 1994; Fitzgerald, 1993):

1. *Provide a literate environment.* Set up a library corner with many predictable, repetitive books that are easy for children to read. Use words and sentences in meaningful ways, such as labeling objects and exhibits, writing directions for taking care of a pet, making class books of shared experiences, putting captions on bulletin board displays, and encouraging children to share books they write.

2. *Involve parents.* Encourage parents to view themselves as partners in the education of their children in order to promote their academic and linguistic growth. If some parents are intimidated by the idea of coming to the school, ask them to listen to their children read books at home, help their children do research on their family backgrounds, and collaborate on writing projects.

3. *Encourage risk taking.* Let students experiment with using language without fear of embarrassment or ridicule. Emphasize the importance of communication, not the correctness of words and structure, during writing, conversation, and oral reading.

4. *Give feedback.* Reward students who are making efforts to communicate in English with praise and encouraging facial expressions and gestures. Be patient and realize that bilingual students may need more time to express themselves in English than many monolingual English students do.

5. *Use alternative forms of assessment.* Collect samples of students' writing, such as journal entries, reports, and published pieces, and keep records of their

reading. Tape-record oral reading and discussions, and keep observational records of students' progress in oral language development. Such informal assessment, assembled in portfolios, is more useful than standardized test scores.

6. *Encourage active participation.* Provide opportunities for students to become actively involved in class activities, take responsibility for their learning, work in cooperative groups, and make decisions about topics of study and classroom policies.

Instructional Strategies

A major focus in bilingual instruction is on language as a meaning-making process. Krashen (1991) uses the term *comprehensible input* to mean that it is important for the student to understand the meaning of the message instead of focusing on standard form and structure. According to Coelho (1994), the trend for second-language teaching is away from traditional instruction that focuses on information about language with many rules and examples. Cox and Batstone (1997) point out that instruction should emphasize language as communication, not as a set of rules to study. They contrast traditional grammar-based instruction (focus on language forms) with communicative-based instruction (focus on meaningful learning experiences), pointing out that communicative competence develops as children use language for functional purposes. The Classroom Scenario "Acquiring English Proficiency" shows how LEP children can learn language naturally.

**Classroom
Scenario**

Acquiring English Proficiency

Kelly Walker, a second grade teacher with a large number of ESL students, found that children develop proficiency in English by writing collaboratively. Sun-Hee from Korea began school with no knowledge of English, but by second grade she had made considerable progress. Kelly placed Sun-Hee with two strong writers, gave the three children materials for writing their own book, and provided time each day for them to discuss the book and write their story. Sun-Hee contributed ideas but sometimes used nonstandard expressions. Her two collaborators liked her ideas but altered the wording to correspond with standard English. Sun-Hee readily accepted their modifications and, as a result, fine-tuned her use of English.

Analysis of Scenario
Kelly realized that Sun-Hee would learn English more quickly by interacting informally with her peers than by memorizing rules of grammar. By composing a book collaboratively, Sun-Hee intuitively learned English syntax and increased her language proficiency.

Some teachers believe that speakers of another language must first learn the grammar, rules, and structure of English in order to become proficient users of English. Other teachers feel strongly that children will acquire proficiency in English naturally, through interactions with others. What do *you* think?

The following specific strategies, along with those already presented for dialectal speakers, may benefit students with limited English proficiency.

Drama. Through creative drama, bilingual students can interpret the stories they hear, thereby clarifying their understanding of story structure and vocabulary. Role playing enables them to experiment with vocabulary and sentence structure as they explore their feelings.

Authentic Experiences. Heidger (1991) suggests purposeful tasks for bilingual students: compiling bilingual dictionaries, reading children's books in primary languages, making books on the home or family, supplemented with illustrations or photographs and captioned in both English and the first language, listening to teacher-made or commercial audiotapes that accompany children's books written in English, and making arrangements for projects such as giving a party and inviting special people.

Purposeful Writing. Teachers should encourage bilingual students to write for authentic purposes even before they are proficient in English. The students may use a combination of symbols, drawings, and invented spellings to communicate their ideas. The writing workshop (discussed in Chapter 8) provides many opportunities for language development (Au, 1993; Roller, 1996; Ruiz, 1991). Good literature provides models for writing, minilessons help students acquire the skills they need for writing, and conferences develop communication skills.

Dialogue journals (described in Chapter 8) are actually written conversations that enable teachers to move LEP children toward competency in English by providing them with a nonthreatening, nonstructured medium for exchanging ideas. In addition to writing in journals, bilingual children can benefit from process writing instruction. Jonas Lindgren had completed one year of English in Sweden before coming to the United States, where he entered a sixth-grade ESL classroom. At the end of the year, Jonas wrote three drafts of a story about a subject that was very important to him. The first and last drafts, which show his progress in making revisions, appear in Example 14.2.

Language Experience Approach. The language experience approach (presented in Chapter 7) is particularly useful for helping LEP students learn to read (Heald-Taylor, 1989; Johns, 1988). Students who know very little English, however, need to acquire additional vocabulary and knowledge of oral language before they dictate sentences (Moustafa and Penrose, 1985). To increase students' vocabularies, teachers can ask them to touch, name, label, and talk about concrete objects.

Literature. When read aloud, literature offers bilingual students opportunities to hear the intonation and rhythm of the English language in meaningful contexts

Example 14.2   *Process Writing Drafts by an ESL Student*

The soccer final

It is year 2001 and Italy and Gurmeny is in the soccerfinal. Five minits in the game Gurmeny gets a very good clans, they kik the ball right outsid the gol. then Gurmeny gets a new clans 44 minits in the game. They cros it over to the mit spot of the penaly eria where ther mit for word is to hit it right in the kworner of the gol.

(then the first hafe finich) The sakend hafe was Italis hafe the started with a gol in the 23 mit and the finiched wit a goll in the 43 menit. I italy won the world campion agen.

①

Jonas Lindgren ③

The world champion soccer game

It is year 2009, and Italy and Germany are in the world champion soccer final.

Five minuts in the game Germany, gets a very good chance, they kick the ball right outside the gol.

Then Germany gets a new chance 44 minuts in the game, they crossed the ball over to the mit spot in the middle of the penalty area, where there striker was standing wating to hit it in the corner of the gool, and he did it. (Then the first half was finiced.

The second half was Italys half, they started with a gool in the 23rd minute and then, they finiched with a gool in the 43rd.

ITALY WON THE WORLD CUP AGAIN.

and to become familiar with the structure of the language. Of particular value to second-language learners are observing English print characteristics and directional patterns, making predictable stories into big books, and developing an awareness and appreciation of literature (Heald-Taylor, 1989). During shared big book reading (see Chapter 2), the teacher can help LEP students learn to read English by reinforcing reading strategies, modeling good reading, and inviting the children to read along (Lukasevich, 1996). Reader response (see Chapter 8) is also a particularly useful strategy for these students because it allows them to respond to literature uniquely in terms of their own cultural backgrounds and levels of English proficiency (Cox and Boyd-Batstone, 1997).

Summary

Every teacher should be especially aware of the needs of exceptional children, considering the passage of the Education for All Handicapped Children Act (PL 94-142). This law was amended by the Individuals with Disabilities Education Act (IDEA), which provides for the mainstreaming or inclusion of many exceptional students into regular classrooms. Teachers work with other professionals in designing individualized education programs (IEPs) for children with disabilities. General guidelines for working with these children include providing opportunities for success, having positive attitudes toward them, providing appropriate instruction, using suitable materials, and communicating with others who work with them.

Several types of special learners are being integrated into regular classrooms. Children with learning disabilities usually show a significant discrepancy between achievement level and potential in one or more areas. Many have communication problems, and reading improvement is their greatest academic need. One form of learning disability is attention-deficit disorder (ADD), characterized by inattentive behaviors. Students with mild mental retardation do not learn as readily as other children do. Some children have emotional/behavioral disorders or vision, hearing, or speech impairments.

Students who are having difficulty learning to read can benefit from well-balanced holistic instruction, including authentic reading and writing activities. Early intervention programs, such as Reading Recovery and Success for All, appear to be successful in helping young children overcome reading problems.

Gifted children can progress more rapidly than their peers and often show advanced development in one or more of the intelligences identified by Howard Gardner. Teachers should provide challenging tasks for these students and help them reach their full potential.

America's schools have children from a wide variety of ethnic, cultural, and racial origins who bring diverse backgrounds and experiences to the classroom. Carefully selected multicultural literature helps these students develop an appreciation of their heritage. Many of them speak nonstandard dialects or are bilingual. English as a Second Language (ESL) programs attempt to provide them with equal educational opportunities. Effective instructional strategies and activities include drama, authentic experiences, purposeful writing, the language experience approach, and the use of literature.

Test Yourself

True or False

_____ 1. The exceptional child's basic needs and goals are quite different from those of the average child.

_____ 2. The language experience approach is generally a good approach to use with the exceptional learner.

_____ 3. Many children who have been enrolled in special education classes are being integrated into regular classrooms.

_____ 4. The IDEA is a modification of the Americans with Disabilities Act.

_____ 5. Children who are being mainstreamed or included may have difficulty adjusting to a regular classroom.

_____ 6. IEP stands for Instant Environmental Plan.

_____ 7. A student with a learning disability has a low level of functioning in all areas.

_____ 8. Two of the most common speech disorders the classroom teacher encounters are faulty articulation and stuttering.

_____ 9. Children from different cultures are likely to exhibit linguistic differences.

_____ 10. Understanding the backgrounds of multicultural students is a good way to begin relating to them.

_____ 11. For purposes of general communication, some dialects are superior to others.

_____ 12. ESL students appear to read better if they learn to read in their native language first.

_____ 13. Many children with learning disabilities have severe communication deficits.

_____ 14. Enrollment of students from diverse cultures in public schools has decreased dramatically.

_____ 15. If a child is identified as ADHD, it means visual and auditory problems are present.

_____ 16. Reading Recovery is a program designed to help children with speech impairments pronounce words correctly during oral reading.

_____ 17. The use of multicultural literature helps children of diverse cultural backgrounds gain self-respect.

_____ 18. Teachers should choose multicultural literature that retains racial and ethnic stereotypes.

_____ 19. Cooperative learning strategies are generally effective for helping mainstreamed and included children adjust to the classroom.

_____ 20. When teaching students who are having difficulty with reading, teachers should focus on word attack skills without regard for meaning.

_____ 21. The typical at-risk child has low intelligence.

_____ 22. Predictable and repetitive stories are useful for helping low-achieving readers understand language patterns.

_____ 23. In bilingual programs, students receive some instruction in their primary languages.

_____ 24. A student with mild mental retardation is generally considered to have poor adaptive behavior and an IQ score between 50 and 75.

_____ 25. Teacher modeling is an effective strategy for helping students develop efficient mental processes for reading.

_____ 26. Because gifted children are capable of working more rapidly than their classmates, they should be assigned more of the same kind of work.

_____ 27. Title I teachers are required to coordinate instruction with classroom teachers.

_____ 28. Inclusion is an individualized educational plan designed especially for each child with a disability.

_____ 29. Standardized test scores are the most valid way to assess the achievement of bilingual students.

_____ 30. Holistic strategies seem to be effective for special learners.

_____ 31. The best way for ESL students to learn English is to memorize rules and practice skills.

For your journal...

1. Select an example of multicultural literature and reflect on its potential for building a child's self-esteem.

2. From your observations of a child who has one or more special needs, how do you think school could be made easier for the child, and how could he or she develop a more positive self-image?

3. Look at Howard Gardner's multiple intelligences in the section on gifted children. Which ones represent your strengths, and which do you need to strengthen?

...And your portfolio

1. Keep a list (annotated, if possible) of multicultural books that you believe have value for promoting self-esteem.

2. During a practicum, observe a child with a disability. Keep records of how this child copes and the intervention strategies that the teacher uses.

3. From your experiences and reading, add to the list of common reading problems and remedial approaches given in Table 14.1.

Chapter Appendix A

Multiethnic Literature

Books suitable for the primary level are marked *(P)*, those for the intermediate level are marked *(I)*, and those for all ages are marked *(A)*.

African American

Aardema, Verna. *Bringing the Rain to Kapiti Plain: A Nandi Tale*. New York: Dial, 1981. (P)

Aardema, Verna. *Who's in Rabbit's House?* New York: Dial, 1977. (P)

Aardema, Verna. *Why Mosquitoes Buzz in People's Ears*. New York: Dial, 1975. (P)

Adoff, Arnold. *Black Is Brown Is Tan*. New York: Harper & Row, 1972. (P)

Adoff, Arnold. *In for Winter, Out for Summer*. San Diego: Harcourt Brace Jovanovich, 1991. (A)

Bradby, Marie. *More Than Anything Else*. New York: Orchard, 1995. (A)

Cooper, Floyd. *Coming Home*. New York: Philomel, 1994. (A)

Feelings, Muriel. *Jambo Means Hello: Swahili Alphabet Book*. New York: Dial, 1974. (A)

Flournoy, Valerie. *The Patchwork Quilt*. New York: Dial, 1985. (P, I)

Greene, Bette. *Philip Hall Likes Me, I Reckon Maybe*. New York: Dial, 1974. (I)

Haley, Gail E. *A Story, a Story*. New York: Atheneum, 1970. (P)

Hamilton, Virginia. *M. C. Higgins, the Great*. New York: Macmillan, 1974. (I)

Hamilton, Virginia. *The People Could Fly: American Black Folktales*. New York: Knopf, 1985. (I)

Harris, Joel Chandler. *The Adventures of Brer Rabbit*. Skokie, Ill.: Rand McNally, 1980. (P, I)

Hoffman, Mary. *Amazing Grace*. New York: Dial, 1991. (P)

Keats, Ezra Jack. *John Henry: An American Legend*. New York: Pantheon, 1965. (P, I)

Mathis, Sharon B. *The Hundred Penny Box*. New York: Viking, 1975. (P)

McDermott, Gerald. *Anansi the Spider: A Tale from the Ashanti*. New York: Holt, Rinehart and Winston, 1972. (P)

McKissack, Patricia. *The Dark-Thirty: Southern Tales of the Supernatural*. New York: Knopf, 1992. (I)

McKissack, Patricia. *Flossie and the Fox*. New York: Scholastic, 1986. (P)

McKissack, Patricia. *Mirandy and Brother Wind*. New York: Knopf, 1988. (P)

Mendez, Phil. *The Black Snowman*. New York: Scholastic, 1989. (I)

Musgrove, Margaret. *Ashanti to Zulu, African Traditions*. New York: Dial, 1976. (P, I)

Myers, Walter Dean. *Glorious Angels*. New York: HarperCollins, 1995. (A)

Myers, Walter Dean. *Scorpions*. New York: Harper & Row, 1988. (I)

Polacco, Patricia. *Pink and Say*. New York: Philomel, 1994. (I)

Ringgold, Faith. *Aunt Harriet's Underground Railroad in the Sky*. New York: Crown, 1993. (P)

Ringgold, Faith. *Tar Beach*. New York: Crown, 1991. (P)

Steptoe, John. *Stevie*. New York: Harper & Row, 1969. (P)

Taylor, Mildred. *Roll of Thunder, Hear My Cry*. New York: Dial, 1976. (I)

Williams, Sherley Anne. *Working Cotton*. San Diego: Harcourt Brace Jovanovich, 1992. (P)

Asian American

Bang, Molly. *The Paper Crane*. New York: Mulberry, 1985. (P)
Coerr, Eleanor. *Sadako*. New York: Putnam's, 1993. (A)
Friedman, Ina R. *How My Parents Learned to Eat*. Boston: Houghton Mifflin, 1984. (P)
Garland, Sherry. *The Lotus Seed*. San Diego: Harcourt Brace Jovanovich, 1993. (P)
Hamanaka, Sheila. *Peace Crane*. New York: Morrow, 1995. (A)
Ishii, Momoko. *The Tongue-Cut Sparrow*. New York: Dutton, 1987. (I)
Paterson, Katherine. *The Tale of the Mandarin Ducks*. New York: Scholastic, 1990. (A)
Say, Allen. *Grandfather's Journey*. Boston; Houghton Mifflin, 1993. (A)
Yee, Paul. *Tales from Gold Mountain: Stories of the Chinese in the New World*. New York: Macmillan, 1990. (I)
Yep, Lawrence. *Child of the Owl*. New York: Harper & Row, 1977. (I)
Yep, Lawrence. *The Rainbow People*. New York: Harper & Row, 1989. (I)
Yep, Lawrence. *Star Fisher*. New York: Morrow, 1991. (I)

Hispanic American

Brown, Tricia. *Hello, Amigos!* New York: Henry Holt, 1986. (P)
de Paola, Tomie. *The Lady of Guadalupe*. New York: Holiday, 1980. (I)
Dorros, Arthur. *Abuela*. New York: Trumpet, 1991. (P)
Ehlert, Lois. *Moon Rope*. San Diego: Harcourt Brace Jovanovich, 1992. (A)
Garza, Carmen. *Family Pictures*. San Francisco: Children's Book Press, 1990. (A)
Grossman, Patricia. *Saturday Market*. New York: Lothrop, Lee & Shepherd, 1994. (P)
Jamarillo, Nelly. *Grandmother's Nursery Rhymes*. New York: Henry Holt, 1994. (P)
Meltzer, Milton. *The Hispanic Americans*. New York: Crowell, 1982. (I)
Mora, Pat. *Pablo's Tree*. New York: Macmillan, 1994. (P)
Soto, Gary. *Too Many Tamales*. New York: Putnam, 1993. (P)

Native American

Baker, Olaf. *Where the Buffaloes Begin*. New York: Murray, 1981. (P)
Baylor, Byrd. *When Clay Sings*. New York: Scribner's, 1972. (A)
Begay, Shonto. *Navajo*. New York: Scholastic, 1995. (I)
Carlstrom, Nancy. *Northern Lullaby*. New York: Putnam & Grosset, 1992. (P)
dePaola, Tomie. *The Legend of Bluebonnet*. New York: Putnam, 1983. (A)
Dixon, Ann. *How Raven Brought Light to People*. New York: Macmillan, 1993. (A)
George, Jean Craighead. *The Talking Earth*. New York: Harper & Row, 1983. (I)
Goble, Paul. *The Girl Who Loved Wild Horses*. New York: Bradbury, 1978. (A)
Joosse, Barbara. *Mama, Do You Love Me?* New York: Chronicle, 1991. (P)
Martin, Bill, Jr., and John Archambault. *Knots on a Counting Rope*. New York: Henry Holt, 1987. (A)
McDermott, Gerald. *Arrow to the Sun*. New York: Viking, 1974. (A)
McDermott, Gerald. *Raven: A Trickster Tale from the Pacific Northwest*. San Diego: Harcourt Brace Jovanovich, 1993. (A)

Miles, Miska. *Annie and the Old One*. Boston: Little, Brown, 1971. (P)

O'Dell, Scott. *Sing Down the Moon*. Boston: Houghton Mifflin, 1970. (I)

Paulsen, Gary. *Dogsong*. New York: Bradbury, 1988. (I)

Sneve, Virginia Driving Hawk. *Dancing Teepees: Poems of American Indian Youth*. New York: Holiday House, 1989. (A)

Speare, Elizabeth George. *The Sign of the Beaver*. Boston: Houghton Mifflin, 1983. (I)

Steptoe, John. *The Story of Jumping Mouse*. New York: Lothrop, Lee & Shepard, 1984. (A)

Wood, Douglas. *Northwoods Cradle Song*. New York: Simon & Schuster, 1996. (P)

Bibliography

Aaron, Ira E., Jeanne S. Chall, Dolores Durkin, Kenneth Goodman, and Dorothy S. Strickland. "The Past, Present, and Future of Literacy Education: Comments from a Panel of Distinguished Educators, Part I." *The Reading Teacher,* 43 (January 1990), 302–311.

Aaron, Ira E., Jeanne S. Chall, Dolores Durkin, Kenneth Goodman, and Dorothy Strickland. "The Past, Present, and Future of Literacy Education: Comments from a Panel of Distinguished Educators, Part II." *The Reading Teacher,* 43 (February 1990), 370–380.

Adams, Marilyn Jager. *Beginning to Read: Thinking and Learning about Print.* Cambridge, Mass.: MIT Press, 1990.

Adams, Marilyn Jager. "Modeling the Connections Between Word Recognition and Reading." In *Theoretical Models and Processes of Reading,* 4th ed., edited by Robert B. Ruddell, Martha Rapp Ruddell, and Harry Singer. Newark, Del.: International Reading Association, 1994, pp. 838–863.

Adams, Marilyn Jager, et al. "*Beginning to Read*: A Critique by Literacy Professionals and a Response by Marilyn Jager Adams." *The Reading Teacher,* 44 (February 1991), 370–395.

Adelman, Howard S., and Linda Taylor. *An Introduction to Learning Disabilities.* Glenview, Ill.: Scott, Foresman, 1986.

Aiex, Nola Kortner. "Literature as Lessons on the Diversity of Culture." *ERIC Digest.* Bloomington, Ind.: ERIC Clearing House on Reading and Communication Skills, 1989.

Aiex, Nola Kortner. "Literature-Based Reading Instruction." *The Reading Teacher,* 41 (January 1988), 458–461.

Aiex, Nola Kortner. "Storytelling: Its Wide-Ranging Impact in the Classroom." In *ERIC Digest Number 9.* Bloomington, Ind.: ERIC Clearinghouse on Reading and Communication Skills, 1988.

Airasian, Peter W., and Mary E. Walsh. "Constructivist Cautions." *Phi Delta Kappan,* 78 (February 1997), 444–449.

Aliki. *A Weed Is a Flower: The Life of George Washington Carver.* Englewood Cliffs, N.J.: Prentice-Hall, 1965.

Allen, R. V. "The Language-Experience Approach." In *Perspectives on Elementary Reading: Principles and Strategies of Teaching,* edited by Robert Karlin. New York: Harcourt Brace Jovanovich, 1973.

Allen, Virginia. "Selecting Materials for the Reading Instruction of ESL Children." In *Kids Come in All Languages: Reading Instruction for ESL Students,* edited by Karen Spangenberg-Urbschat and Robert Pritchard. Newark, Del.: International Reading Association, 1994, pp. 108–131.

Allington, Richard. "Literacy Lessons in the Elementary Schools: Yesterday, Today, and Tomorrow." In *No Quick Fix,* edited by Richard Allington and Sean Walmsley. Newark, Del.: International Reading Association, 1995.

Allington, Richard. "Michael Doesn't Go Down the Hall Anymore." *The Reading Teacher,* 46 (April 1993), 602–604.

Allington, Richard L. "Oral Reading." In *Handbook of Reading Research,* edited by P. David Pearson. New York: Longman, 1984.

Allington, Richard L., and Mary C. Shake. "Remedial Reading: Achieving Curricular Congruence in Classroom and Clinic." *The Reading Teacher,* 39 (March 1986), 648–654.

Altwerger, Bess, and Bonnie Lee Ivener. "Self-Esteem: Access to Literacy in Multicultural and Multilingual Classrooms." In *Kids Come in All Languages: Reading Instruction for ESL Students,* edited by Karen Spangenberg-Urbschat and Robert Pritchard. Newark, Del.: International Reading Association, 1994, pp. 65–81.

Alvermann, Donna E. "The Discussion Web: A Graphic Aid for Learning Across the Curriculum." *The Reading Teacher,* 45 (October 1991), 92–99.

Alvermann, Donna E., and Paula R. Boothby. "Text Differences: Children's Perceptions at the Transition Stage in Reading." *The Reading Teacher,* 36 (December 1982), 298–302.

Anders, Patricia L., and Candace S. Bos. "Semantic Feature Analysis: An Interactive Strategy for Vocabulary Development and Text Comprehension." *Journal of Reading,* 29 (April 1986), 610–616.

Anderson, Gary, Diana Higgins, and Stanley R. Wurster. "Differences in the Free-Reading Books Selected by High, Average, and Low Achievers." *The Reading Teacher,* 39 (December 1985), 326–330.

Anderson, Nancy A. "Teaching Reading as a Life Skill." *The Reading Teacher,* 42 (October 1988), 92.

Anderson, Richard C., Elfrieda H. Hiebert, Judith A. Scott, and Ian A. G. Wilkinson. *Becoming a Nation of Readers: The Report of the Commission on Reading.* Washington, D.C.: National Institute of Education, 1985.

Anderson, Richard C., J. Mason, and L. Shirey. *The Reading Group: An Experimental Investigation of a Labyrinth.* Technical Report No. 271. Urbana–Champaign, IL: Center for the Study of Reading, University of Illinois, 1983.

Anderson, Richard C., and William E. Nagy. "Word Meanings." In *Handbook of Reading Research, Volume II,* edited by Rebecca Barr, Michael L. Kamil, Peter Mosenthal, and P. David Pearson. New York: Longman, 1991, pp. 690–724.

Anderson, Richard C., and P. David Pearson. "A Schema-Theoretic View of Basic Processes in Reading." In *Handbook of Reading Research,* edited by P. David Pearson et al. New York: Longman, 1984.

Anderson, Thomas H., and Bonnie B. Armbruster. "Studying." In *Handbook of Reading Research,* edited by P. David Pearson et al. New York: Longman, 1984.

Anderson-Inman, Lynne. "The Reading-Writing Connection: Classroom Applications for the Computer, Part I." *The Computing Teacher,* 14 (November 1986), 23–26.

Anderson-Inman, Lynne, Mark A. Horney, Der-Thang Chen, and Larry Lewin. "Hypertext Literacy: Observations from the Electro Text Project." *Language Arts,* 71 (April 1994), 279–287.

Ankney, Paul, and Pat McClurg. "Testing Manzo's Guided Reading Procedure." *The Reading Teacher,* 34 (March 1981), 681–685.

Antal, James. "To Simile or Not to Simile." *The Reading Teacher,* 41 (April 1988), 858–859.

Aoki, Elaine, Evelyn Freeman, Barbara Elleman, Rosemary Bamford, and Myra Zarnoski. "Bookalogues: Outstanding Nonfiction Choices for 1995." *Language Arts,* 73 (October 1996), 436–444.

Armbruster, Bonnie B. "On Answering Questions." *The Reading Teacher,* 45 (May 1992), 724–725.

Armbruster, Bonnie B. "Readings about Reading to Learn." *The Reading Teacher,* 46 (April 1993), 598–600.

Armbruster, Bonnie B. "Science and Reading." *The Reading Teacher,* 46 (December 1992/January 1993), 346–347.

Armbruster, Bonnie B., T. H. Anderson, and J. Ostertag. "Does Text Structure/Summarization Instruction Facilitate Learning from Expository Text?" *Reading Research Quarterly,* 22 (1987), 331–346.

Armbruster, Bonnie B., Thomas H. Anderson, and Joyce Ostertag. "Teaching Text Structure to Improve Reading and Writing." *The Reading Teacher,* 43 (November 1989), 130–137.

Armbruster, Bonnie B., and William E. Nagy. "Vocabulary in Content Area Lessons." *The Reading Teacher,* 45 (March 1992), 550–551.

Armstrong, Thomas. *Multiple Intelligences in the Classroom.* Alexandria, Va.: Association for Supervision and Curriculum Development, 1994.

Arnold, Richard D. "Teaching Cohesive Ties to Children." *The Reading Teacher,* 42 (November 1988), 106–110.

Aron, Helen, and Ernest Balajthy. "Local Area Networks." *The Reading Teacher,* 42 (March 1989), 532–533.

Artley, A. Sterl. "Controversial Issues Relating to Word Perception." *The Reading Teacher,* 50 (September 1996), 10–13.

Ashby-Davis, Claire. "Improving Students' Comprehension of Character Development in Plays." *Reading Horizons,* 26, no. 4 (1986), 256–261.

Ashton-Warner, Sylvia. *Teacher.* New York: Simon & Schuster, 1963.

Atwell, Nancie. *In the Middle: Writing, Reading, and Learning with Adolescents.* Upper Montclair, N.J.: Boynton/Cook, 1987.

Atwell, Nancie. "Writing and Reading from the Inside Out." In *Breaking Ground: Teachers Relate Reading and Writing in the Elementary School,* edited by Jane Hansen, Thomas Newkirk, and Donald Graves. Portsmouth, N.H.: Heinemann, 1985.

Au, Kathryn. *Literacy Instruction in Multicultural Settings.* Fort Worth: Harcourt Brace, 1993.

Au, Kathryn H. "Constructing the Theme of a Story." *Language Arts,* 69 (February 1992), 106–111.

Au, Kathryn H. "An Overview of New Concepts of Assessment: Impact on Decision Making and Instruction." Paper presented at the International Reading Association Convention, Atlanta, May 6, 1990.

Au, Kathryn H., and Judith A. Scheu. "Guiding Students to Interpret a Novel." *The Reading Teacher,* 43 (November 1989), 104–110.

Augustine, Dianne, Kristin Gruber, and Lynda Hanson. "Cooperation Works!" *Educational Leadership,* 47 (December 1989/January 1990), 4–8.

Austin, Terri. *Changing the View: Student-Led Parent Conferences.* Portsmouth, N.H.: Heinemann, 1994.

Avery, Carol S. "Learning to Research/Researching to Learn." In *Opening the Door to Classroom Research,* edited by Mary W. Olson. Newark, Del.: International Reading Association, 1990.

Avery, Charles W., and Beth Faris Avery. "Merging Reading and Cooperative Strategies Through Graphic Organizers." *Journal of Reading,* 37 (May 1994), 689–690.

Babbs, Patricia J. "Monitoring Cards Help Improve Comprehension." *The Reading Teacher,* 38 (November 1984), 200–204.

Babbs, Patricia J., and Alden J. Moe. "Metacognition: A Key for Independent Learning from Text." *The Reading Teacher,* 36 (January 1983), 422–426.

Baca, Leonard, and Hermes T. Cervantes. *The Bilingual Special Education Interface,* 2d ed. Columbus, Ohio: Merrill, 1989.

Bader, Lois A. "Instructional Adjustments to Vision Problems." *The Reading Teacher,* 37 (March 1984), 566–569.

Bagford, Jack. "What Ever Happened to Individualized Reading?" *The Reading Teacher,* 39 (November 1985), 190–193.

Bailey, Mildred Hart. "The Utility of Phonic Generalizations in Grades One Through Six." *The Reading Teacher,* 20 (February 1967), 413–418.

Baker, Linda, and Ann L. Brown. "Metacognitive Skills and Reading." In *Handbook of Reading Research,* edited by P. David Pearson et al. New York: Longman, 1984.

Balajthy, Ernest. *Computers and Reading.* Englewood Cliffs, N.J.: Prentice-Hall, 1989.

Balajthy, Ernest. "Keyboarding and the Language Arts." *The Reading Teacher,* 41 (October 1987), 86–87.

Balajthy, Ernest. "Only One Computer in the Classroom?" *The Reading Teacher,* 41 (November 1987), 210–211.

Balajthy, Ernest. "What Are Basal Publishers Doing with Computer Based Instruction?" *The Reading Teacher,* 41 (December 1987), 344–345.

Balajthy, Ernest, and Gordon Link. "Desktop Publishing in the Classroom." *The Reading Teacher,* 41 (February 1988), 586–587.

Ball, E. W., and B. A. Blachman. "Does Phoneme Awareness Training in Kindergarten Make a Difference in Early Word Recognition and Developmental Spelling?" *Reading Research Quarterly,* 26, no. 1 (1991), 49–66.

Bank Street College of Education, F. E. Smith, and G. Brackett. *The Bank Street Writer for the Macintosh.* Jefferson City, Mo.: Scholastic Software, 1991.

Banks, James A. "Transforming the Mainstream Curriculum." *Educational Leadership,* 51 (May 1994), 4–8.

Barnard, Douglas P., and Robert W. Hetzel. *Selecting a Basal Reader Program: Making the Right Choice.* Lancaster, Pa.: Technomic Publishing, 1988.

Barnitz, John G. "Developing Sentence Comprehension in Reading." *Language Arts,* 56 (November/December 1979), 902–908, 958.

Barone, Tom, Maryann Eeds, and Kathleen Mason. "Literature, the Disciplines, and the Lives of Elementary School Children." *Language Arts,* 72 (January 1995), 30–38.

Baroni, Dick. "Have Primary Children Draw to Expand Vocabulary." *The Reading Teacher,* 40 (April 1987), 819–820.

Barr, Rebecca. "Beginning Reading Instruction." In *Handbook of Reading Research,* edited by P. David Pearson. New York: Longman, 1984.

Barr, Rebecca, and Robert Dreeben. "Grouping Students for Reading Instruction." In *Handbook of Reading Research, Vol. II,* edited by Rebecca Barr, Michael L. Kamil, Peter B. Mosenthal, and P. David Pearson. White Plains, N.Y.: Longman, 1991, pp. 885–910.

Barrentine, Shelby. "Engaging with Reading through Interactive Read-alouds." *The Reading Teacher,* 50 (September 1996), 36–43.

Barrow, Lloyd H., Janice V. Kristo, and Barbara Andrew. "Building Bridges Between Science and Reading." *The Reading Teacher,* 38 (November 1984), 188–192.

Barta, Jim, and Martha Crouthers Grindler. "Exploring Bias Using Multicultural Literature for Children." *The Reading Teacher,* 50 (November 1996), 269–270.

Barton, James. "Interpreting Character Emotions for Literature Comprehension." *Journal of Adolescent and Adult Literacy,* 40 (September 1996), 22–28.

Bash, Barbara. *Tree of Life: The World of the African Baobab.* Boston: Little, Brown, 1989.

Baskwill, Jane, and Paulette Whitman. *Evaluation: Whole Language, Whole Child.* Toronto: Scholastic, 1988.

Batzle, Janine. *Portfolio Assessment and Evaluation.* Cypress, Calif.: Creative Teaching Press, 1992.

Baumann, James. "Organizing and Managing a Whole Language Classroom." *Reading Research and Instruction,* 31 (Spring 1992), 3–14.

Baumann, James F., and P. Z. Ballard. "A Two Step Model for Promoting Independence in Comprehension." *Journal of Reading,* 30 (1987), 608–612.

Baumann, James F., Leah A. Jones, and Nancy Seifert-Kessell. "Using Think-Alouds to Enhance Children's Comprehension Monitoring Abilities." *The Reading Teacher,* 47 (November 1993), 184–193.

Baumann, James F., and Maribeth C. Schmitt. "The What, Why, How, and When of Comprehension Instruction." *The Reading Teacher,* 39 (March 1986), 640–646.

Baumann, James F., and Jennifer A. Stevenson. "Using Scores from Standardized Reading Achievement Tests." *The Reading Teacher,* 35 (February 1982), 528–533.

Beach, R., and S. Hynds. "Research on Response to Literature." In *Handbook of Reading Research, Vol. II,* edited by R. Barr, M.L. Kamil, P. Mosenthal, and P.D. Pearson. New York: Longman, 1991, pp. 453–489.

Bean, Rita, M., and R. Tony Eichelberger. "Changing the Role of Reading Specialists: From Pull-Out to In-Class Programs." *The Reading Teacher,* 38 (March 1985), 648–653.

Beattie, John. "Characteristics of Students with Disabilities and How Teachers Can Help." In *Teaching Reading to High-Risk Learners,* edited by Karen Wood and Bob Algozzine. Boston: Allyn & Bacon, 1994, pp. 99–121.

Beaty, Janice J. *Picture Book Storytelling.* Fort Worth: Harcourt Brace, 1994.

Beck, I., and C. Juel. "The Role of Decoding in Learning to Read." *American Educator,* 8 (Summer 1995), 8–23.

Beck, I. L., C. A. Perfetti, and M. G. McKeown. "Effects of Long-Term Vocabulary Instruction on Lexical Access and Reading Comprehension." *Journal of Educational Psychology,* 74 (1982), 506–521.

Beck, Isabel L. "Reading and Reasoning." *The Reading Teacher,* 42 (May 1989), 676–682.

Beck, Isabel L., and Margaret G. McKeown. "Learning Words Well—A Program to Enhance Vocabulary and Comprehension." *The Reading Teacher,* 36 (March 1983), 622–625.

Beck, Isabel L., and Margaret G. McKeown. "Research Directions: Social Studies Texts Are Hard to Understand:

Mediating Some of the Difficulties." *Language Arts,* 68 (October 1991), 482–490.

Beck, Isabel, and Margaret McKeown. "Conditions of Vocabulary Acquisition." In *Handbook of Reading Research, Volume II,* edited by Rebecca Barr, Michael L. Kamil, Peter Mosenthal, and P. David Pearson. New York: Longman, 1991, pp. 789–814.

Beck, Judith S. "A Problem Solving Framework for Managing Poor Readers in Classrooms." *The Reading Teacher,* 41 (April 1988), 774–779.

Bell, Barbara. "Literature Response Groups." Presentation at Richard C. Owen Workshop "Whole Language in the Classroom." Oak Ridge, Tennessee, June 12, 1990.

Bell, Kathy. "Books for Telling Time." *The Reading Teacher,* 42 (November 1988), 179.

Bell, Kathy. "Books to Supplement a Unit on Measurement." *The Reading Teacher,* 42 (December 1988), 256.

Bell, Kathy. "Using Literature to Teach Addition and Subtraction." *The Reading Teacher,* 42 (October 1988), 90.

Bell, Nancy, Debbie Cambron, Kathy Rey-Barreau, and Beverly Paeth. "Online Literature Groups." Handout at the National Council of Teachers of English Convention, San Diego, 1995.

Bellows, Barbara Plotkin. "Running Shoes Are to Jogging as Analogies Are to Creative/Critical Thinking." *Journal of Reading,* 23 (March 1980), 507–511.

Bennett, Rand Elliot. "Cautions for the Use of Informal Measures in the Educational Assessment of Exceptional Children." *Journal of Learning Disabilities,* 15 (June/July 1982), 337–339.

Berger, Linda R. "Reader Response Journals: You Make the Meaning . . . and How." *Journal of Adolescent & Adult Literacy,* 39 (February 1996), 380–385.

Bergeron, Bette S. "Seeking Authenticity: What Is 'Real' About Thematic Literacy Instruction." *The Reading Teacher,* 49 (April 1996), 544–551.

Berglund, Roberta L., and Jerry L. Johns. "A Primer on Uninterrupted Sustained Silent Reading." *The Reading Teacher,* 36 (February 1983), 534–539.

Berkowitz, S. J. "Effects of Instruction in Text Organization on Sixth-Grade Students' Memory for Expository Reading." *Reading Research Quarterly,* 18 (1986), 161–178.

Bernhardt, Bill. "Reading and Writing Between the Lines: An Interactive Approach Using Computers." *Journal of Reading,* 37 (March 1994), 458–463.

Bertrand, John. "Children at Risk of School Failure." In *Empowering Children at Risk of School Failure: A Better Way,* edited by John Bertrand and Carole Stice. Norwood, Mass.: Christopher-Gordon, 1995, pp. 1–15.

Beutler, Suzanne A. "Using Writing to Learn about Astronomy." *The Reading Teacher,* 41 (January 1988), 412–417.

Bidwell, Sandra M. "Ideas for Using Drama to Enhance Reading Instruction." *The Reading Teacher,* 45 (April 1992), 653–654.

Biehler, Robert F., and Jack Snowman. *Psychology Applied to Teaching,* 5th ed. Boston: Houghton Mifflin, 1986.

Bierne-Smith, Mary, James Patton, and Richard Ittenbach. *Mental Retardation,* 4th ed. New York: Merrill, 1994.

Bird, Lois. "Joyful Literacy at Fair Oaks School." In *The Whole Language Catalog,* edited by Kenneth Goodman, Lois Bird, and Yetta Goodman. Santa Rosa, Calif.: American School Publishers, 1991.

Bird, Lois. "Resource: Periodical." In *The Whole Language Catalog,* edited by Kenneth Goodman, Lois Bird, and Yetta Goodman. Santa Rosa, Calif.: American School Publishers, 1991.

Bitter, Gary G., Ruth A. Camuse, and Vicki L. Durbin. *Using a Microcomputer in the Classroom.* Boston: Allyn and Bacon, 1993.

Blachowicz, Camille L. Z. "C(2)QU: Modeling Context Use in the Classroom." *The Reading Teacher,* 47 (November 1993), 268–269.

Blachowicz, Camille L. Z. "Making Connections: Alternatives to the Vocabulary Notebook." *Journal of Reading,* 29 (April 1986), 643–649.

Blachowicz, Camille L. Z. "Showing Teachers How to Develop Students' Predictive Reading." *The Reading Teacher,* 36 (March 1983), 680–683.

Blachowicz, Camille L. Z. "Vocabulary Development and Reading: From Research to Instruction." *The Reading Teacher,* 38 (May 1985), 876–881.

Blachowicz, Camille L. Z., and John J. Lee. "Vocabulary Development in the Whole Literacy Classroom." *The Reading Teacher,* 45 (November 1991), 188–195.

Blachowicz, Camille L. Z., and Barbara Zabroske. "Context Instruction: A Metacognitive Approach for At-Risk Readers." *Journal of Reading,* 33 (April 1990), 504–508.

Blanchard, Jay S., and Claire J. Rottenberg. "Hypertext and Hypermedia: Discovering and Creating Meaningful Learning Environments." *The Reading Teacher,* 43 (May 1990), 656–661.

Blanton, William E., Gary B. Moorman, and Karen D. Wood. "A Model of Direct Instruction Applied to the Basal Skills Lesson." *The Reading Teacher,* 40 (December 1986), 299–304.

Blanton, William E., Karen D. Wood, and Gary B. Moorman. "The Role of Purpose in Reading Instruction." *The Reading Teacher,* 43 (March 1990), 486–493.

Blass, Rosanne J., Nancy Allan Jurenka, and Eleanor G. Zirzow. "Showing Children the Communicative Nature of Reading." *The Reading Teacher,* 34 (May 1981), 926–931.

Bloomfield, Leonard, and Clarence Barnhart. *Let's Read: A Linguistic Approach.* Detroit: Wayne State University Press, 1961.

Bode, Barbara A. "Dialogue Journal Writing." *The Reading Teacher,* 42 (April 1989), 568–571.

Bonds, Charles W., Lella Gant Bonds, and Walter Peach. "Metacognition: Developing Independence in Learning." *The Clearing House,* 66 (September/October 1992), 56–59.

Boodt, Gloria M. "Critical Listeners Become Critical Readers in Remedial Reading Class." *The Reading Teacher,* 37 (January 1984), 390–394.

Booth, David. *Classroom Voices.* Toronto: Harcourt Brace, 1994.

Borkowski, J.G., and B.E. Kurtz. "Metacognition and Executive Control." *Cognition in Special Children: Comparative Approaches to Retardation, Learning Disabilities, and Giftedness,* edited by J.G. Borkowski and J.D. Day. Norwood, N. J.: Ablex, 1987, 123–152.

Bormuth, J. R. "The Cloze Readability Procedure." In *Readability in 1968,* edited by J. R. Bormuth. Champaign, Ill.: National Council of Teachers of English, 1968.

Bouffler, Chrystine, and Bruce Knight. "Assessment and Evaluation in Reading." *PEN 81.* New South Wales, Australia: Primary English Teaching Association, 1991.

Boyd, Reta. "The Message Board." In *Whole Language: Theory in Use,* edited by Judith Newman. Portsmouth, N.H.: Heineman, 1985.

Boyle, Owen F., and Suzanne F. Peregoy. "Literacy Scaffolds: Strategies for First- and Second-Language Readers and Writers." *The Reading Teacher,* 44 (November 1990), 194–200.

Bradley, L., and P. Bryant. "Categorizing Sounds and Learning to Read—A Causal Connection." *Nature,* 301 (1983), 419–421.

Bransford, John D., and Barry S. Stein. *The IDEAL Problem Solver.* New York: W. H. Freeman, 1984.

Braselton, Stephania, and Barbara C. Decker. "Using Graphic Organizers to Improve the Reading of Mathematics." *The Reading Teacher,* 48 (November 1994), 276–281.

Breen, Leonard. "Connotations." *Journal of Reading,* 32 (February 1989), 461.

Brennan, A. D., and W. P. Dunlap. "What Are Prime Factors of Reading Mathematics?" *Reading Improvement,* 22 (1985), 152–159.

Bridge, Connie A. "Focusing on Meaning in Beginning Reading Instruction." In *Counterpoint and Beyond: A Response to Becoming a Nation of Readers,* edited by Jane L. Davidson. Urbana, Ill.: National Council of Teachers of English, 1988.

Bristow, Page Simpson. "Are Poor Readers Passive Readers? Some Evidence, Possible Explanations, and Potential Solutions." *The Reading Teacher,* 39 (December 1985), 318–325.

Bromley, Karen D. "Buddy Journals Make the Reading-Writing Connection." *The Reading Teacher,* 43 (November 1989), 122–129.

Bromley, Karen D. *Webbing with Literature.* Boston: Allyn & Bacon, 1991.

Bromley, Karen D'Angelo. "Teaching Idioms." *The Reading Teacher,* 38 (December 1984), 272–276.

Brooks, Ellen. *Just-Right Books for Beginning Readers.* New York: Scholastic, 1996.

Brooks, Hollie. "'I Know That Book's Here Somewhere!': How to Organize Your Classroom Library." *The Reading Teacher,* 48 (April 1995), 638–639.

Brown, A. L., and J. D. Day. "Macrorules for Summarizing Texts: The Development of Expertise." *Journal of Verbal Learning and Verbal Behavior,* 22, no. 1 (1983), 1–14.

Brown, A. L., J. D. Day, and R. Jones. "The Development of Plans for Summarizing Texts." *Child Development,* 54 (1983), 968–979.

Brown, Ann L., Annemarie Palincsar, and Bonnie Armbruster. "Instructing Comprehension." In *Theoretical Models and Processes,* 4th ed., edited by Robert Ruddell, Martha Rapp Ruddell, and Harry Singer. Newark, Del.: International Reading Association, 1994, pp. 757–787.

Brown, Carol S., and Susan L. Lytle. "Merging Assessment and Instruction: Protocols in the Classroom." In *Reexamining Reading Diagnosis: New Trends and Procedures,* edited by Susan Mandel Glazer, Lyndon W. Searfoss, and Lance M. Gentile. Newark, Del.: International Reading Association, 1988.

Brozo, William G., and Carl M. Tomlinson. "Literature: The Key to Lively Content Courses." *The Reading Teacher,* 40 (December 1986), 288–293.

Bruck, Maggie, and Rebecca Treiman. "Learning to Pronounce Words: The Limitations of Analogies." *Reading Research Quarterly,* 27, no. 4 (1992), 374–388.

Brunner, Cornelia. "Judging Student Multimedia." *Electronic Learning,* 15 (May/June 1996), 14–15.

Bufe, Bruce N. "Word Sort to Improve Comprehension." *The Reading Teacher,* 37 (November 1983), 209–210.

Bulletin Board Maker—Happy Habitats: The Pond. Fairfield, Conn.: Pelican, 1991.

Burchby, Marcia. "Literature and Whole Language." *The New Advocate,* 1 (Spring 1988), 114–123.

Burmeister, Lou E. *Foundations and Strategies for Teaching Children to Read.* Reading, Mass.: Addison-Wesley, 1983.

Burmeister, Lou E. "Usefulness of Phonic Generalizations." *The Reading Teacher,* 21 (January 1968): 349–356, 360.

Busching, Beverly A., and Betty Ann Slesinger. "Authentic Questions: What Do They Look Like? Where Do They Lead?" *Language Arts,* 72 (September 1995), 341–351.

Butler, Andrea, and Jan Turbill. *Towards a Reading-Writing Classroom.* Portsmouth, N.H.: Heinemann, 1987.

Butler, Dorothy, and Marie Clay. *Reading Begins at Home.* Auckland, New Zealand: Heinemann Educational Books, 1979.

Butler, Syd, and Barbara Cox. "DISKovery: Writing with a Computer in Grade One: A Study in Collaboration." *Language Arts,* 69 (December 1992), 633–640.

Cairney, T. *Teaching Reading Comprehension.* Milton Keynes, U.K.: Open University Press, 1990.

Caldwell, JoAnne. "Critical Questions." *The Reading Teacher,* 50 (February 1997), 436–437.

Calhoun, Emily. "Action Research: Three Approaches." *Educational Leadership,* 51 (October 1993), 62–65.

Calkins, Lucy M. *Lessons from a Child.* Portsmouth, N.H.: Heinemann, 1983.

Carlsen, Joanne M. "Between the Deaf Child and Reading: The Language Connection." *The Reading Teacher,* 38 (January 1985), 424–426.

Carney, J. J., D. Anderson, C. Blackburn, and D. Blessing. "Preteaching Vocabulary and the Comprehension of Social Studies Materials by Elementary School Children." *Social Education,* 48 (1984), 71–75.

Carnine, D., and D. Kinder. "Teaching Low-Performing Students to Apply Generative and Schema Strategies to Narrative and Expository Material." *Remedial and Special Education,* 6 (1985), 20–30.

Carnine, Douglas W. "Phonics Versus Look-Say: Transfer to New Words." *The Reading Teacher,* 30 (March 1977), 636–640.

Carr, Eileen. "The Vocabulary Overview Guide: A Metacognitive Strategy to Improve Vocabulary Comprehension and Retention." *Journal of Reading,* 21 (May 1985), 684–689.

Carr, Eileen, and Karen K. Wixson. "Guidelines for Evaluating Vocabulary Instruction." *Journal of Reading,* 29 (April 1986), 588–595.

Carr, Joan A. "Verbalizing Character Roles in Novels." *Journal of Reading,* 35 (October 1991), 145–146.

Carr, Kathryn S. "The Importance of Inference Skills in the Primary Grades." *The Reading Teacher,* 36 (February 1983), 518–522.

Carroll, John B., Peter Davies, and Barry Richman. *The American Heritage Word Frequency Book.* Boston: Houghton Mifflin, 1971.

Casson, Lucinda, Joel Bauman, Elaine Rideout Fisher, Mark Lindblad, Jennifer R. Sumpter, Louis G. Tornatzky, and Ben S. Vickery. *Making Technology Happen.* Research Triangle Park, N.C.: Southern Technology Council, 1997.

Casteel, Carolyn P., and Bess A. Isom. "Reciprocal Processes in Science and Literacy Learning." *The Reading Teacher,* 47 (April 1994), 538–545.

Catterson, Jane. "Discourse Forms in Content Texts." *Journal of Reading,* 33 (April 1990), 556–558.

"CEC Policy on Inclusive Schools and Community Settings." Reston, Va.: The Council for Exceptional Children, 1993.

Ceprano, Maria A. "A Review of Selected Research on Methods of Teaching Sight Words." *The Reading Teacher,* 35 (December 1981), 314–322.

Chaney, Jeanne H. "Alphabet Books: Resources for Learning." *The Reading Teacher,* 47 (October 1993), 96–104.

"Chapter I Gains Questioned." *AAP Reading Initiative,* 4 (Winter 1994), 1–2.

Cheng, Pui-wan. "Metacognition and Giftedness: The State of the Relationship." *Gifted Child Quarterly,* 37 (Summer 1993), 105–112.

Chew, Charles. "Instruction Can Link Reading and Writing." In *Breaking Ground: Teachers Relate Reading and Writing in the Elementary School,* edited by Jane Hansen, Thomas Newkirk, and Donald Graves. Portsmouth, N.H.: Heinemann, 1985.

Chittenden, Edward, and Rosalea Courtney. "Assessment of Young Children's Reading: Documentation as an Alternative to Testing." In *Emerging Literacy: Young Children Learn to Read and Write,* edited by Dorothy Strickland and Lesley Morrow. Newark, Del.: International Reading Association, 1989.

Church, Susan M. "Is Whole Language Warm and Fuzzy?" *The Reading Teacher,* 47 (February 1994), 362–370.

Clark, L. K. "Invented Versus Traditional Spelling in First Graders' Writings: Effects on Learning to Spell and Read." *Research in the Teaching of English,* 22 (1988), 281–309.

Clay, M. M. *The Early Detection of Reading Difficulties,* 3d ed. Auckland, New Zealand: Heinemann, 1993.

Clay, Marie. "Concepts about Print in English and Other Languages." *The Reading Teacher,* 42 (January 1989), 268–276.

Clay, Marie. *The Early Detection of Reading Difficulties.* Auckland, New Zealand: Heinemann, 1979.

Clay, Marie. "Involving Teachers in Classroom Research." In *Teachers and Research,* edited by Gay Su Pinnell and Myna L. Matlin. Newark, Del.: International Reading Association, 1989.

Clay, Marie. *Reading: The Patterning of Complex Behavior,* 2d ed. Auckland, New Zealand: Heinemann, 1979.

Clemmons, Joan, and Lois Laase. *Language Arts Mini-Lessons.* New York: Scholastic, 1995.

Clymer, Theodore. "The Utility of Phonic Generalizations in the Primary Grades." *The Reading Teacher,* 50 (November 1996), 182–187.

Coate, Sheri, and Marrietta Castle. "Integrating LEA and Invented Spelling in Kindergarten." *The Reading Teacher,* 42 (March 1989), 516–519.

Cochran-Smith, M., J. Kahn, and C. L. Paris. "When Word Processors Come into the Classroom." In *Writing with Computers in the Early Grades,* edited by J. L. Hoot and S. B. Silvern. New York: Teachers College Press, 1988.

Coelho, Elizabeth. *Learning Together in the Multicultural Classroom.* Markham, Ontario: Pippin, 1994.

Cohen, Ruth. "Self-Generated Questions as an Aid to Reading Comprehension." *The Reading Teacher,* 36 (April 1983), 770–775.

Collier, Calhoun C., and Lois A. Redmond. "Are You Teaching Kids to Read Mathematics?" *The Reading Teacher,* 27 (May 1974), 804–808.

Collins, Norma, and Nola Aiex. "Gifted Readers and Reading Instruction." *ERIC Digest.* Bloomington, Ind.: Indiana University, April, 1995.

Colt, Jacalyn M. "Support for New Teachers in Literature-Based Reading Programs." *Journal of Reading,* 34 (September 1990), 64–65.

Combs, Martha, and John D. Beach. "Stories and Story-telling: Personalizing the Social Studies." *The Reading Teacher,* 47 (March 1994), 464–471.

Come, Barbara, and Anthony Fredericks. "Family Literacy in Urban Schools: Meeting the Needs of At-Risk Children." *The Reading Teacher,* 48 (April 1995), 566–570.

Commeyras, M. "Were Janell and Neesie in the Same Classroom? Children's Questions as the First Order of Reality in Storybook Discussion." *Language Arts,* 71 (1994), 517–523.

Commeyras, Michelle. "Promoting Critical Thinking through Dialogical-Thinking Reading Lessons." *The Reading Teacher,* 46 (March 1993), 486–493.

Commeyras, Michelle. "Using Literature to Teach Critical Thinking." *Journal of Reading,* 32 (May 1989), 703–707.

Commeyras, Michelle, and Georgiana Sumner. "Literature Discussions Based on Student-Posed Questions." *The Reading Teacher,* 50 (November 1996), 262–265.

Committee on Geographic Education. *Guidelines for Geographic Education: Elementary and Secondary Schools.* Washington, D.C.: National Council for Geographic Education and the Association of American Geographers, 1983.

Conrad, Lori L. "Charting Effect and Cause in Informational Books." *The Reading Teacher,* 42 (February 1989), 451–452.

Cooper, Charles R., and Anthony R. Petrosky. "A Psycholinguistic View of the Fluent Reading Process." *Journal of Reading,* 20 (December 1976), 184–207.

Cooper, J. David. *Improving Reading Comprehension.* Boston: Houghton Mifflin, 1986.

Cooter, Robert B., Jr. *The Teacher's Guide to Reading Tests.* Scottsdale, Ariz.: Gorsuch Scarisbrick, 1990.

Cooter, Robert B., Jr., and Robert Griffith. "Thematic Units for Middle School: An Honorable Seduction." *Journal of Reading,* 32 (May 1989), 676–681.

Cordts, Anna D. *Phonics for the Reading Teacher.* New York: Holt, Rinehart and Winston, 1965.

Cornett, Claudia E. "Beyond Retelling the Plot: Student-led Discussions." *The Reading Teacher,* 50 (March 1997), 527–528.

Cotton, Eileen Giuffre. *The Online Classroom: Teaching with the Internet.* Bloomington, Ind.: ERIC Clearinghouse on Reading, English, and Communication, 1996.

Cowan, Hilary. "Software At-A-Glance: New and Hot!: *Classroom Publisher.*" *Electronic Learning,* 15 (May/June 1996), 61–62.

Cowin, Gina. "Implementing the Writing Process with Sixth Graders, *Jumanji*: Literature Unit." *The Reading Teacher,* 40 (November 1986), 156–161.

Cox, Carole. "Literature-Based Teaching: A Student Response–Centered Curriculum." In *Reader Response in Elementary Classrooms,* edited by Nicholas Karolides. Mahwah, N.J.: Lawrence Erlbaum, 1997.

Cox, Carole, and Joyce Many. "Toward an Understanding of the Aesthetic Response to Literature." *Language Arts,* 69 (January 1992), 28–33.

Cox, Carole, and Paul Boyd-Batstone. *Crossroads.* Upper Saddle River, New Jersey: Merrill, 1997.

Cox, Susan, and Lee Galda. "Multicultural Literature: Mirrors and Windows on a Global Community." *The Reading Teacher,* 43 (April 1990), 582–589.

Crafton, Linda K. "Comprehension Before, During, and After Reading." *The Reading Teacher,* 36 (December 1982), 293–297.

Criscuolo, Nicholas P. "Creative Vocabulary Building." *Journal of Reading,* 24 (December 1980), 260–261.

Crook, Patricia R., and Barbara A. Lehman. "Themes for Two Voices: Children's Fiction and Nonfiction as Whole Literature." *Language Arts,* 68 (January 1991), 34–41.

Cudd, Evelyn T., and Leslie L. Roberts. "A Scaffolding Technique to Develop Sentence Sense and Vocabulary." *The Reading Teacher,* 47 (December 1993/January 1994), 346–349.

Cudd, Evelyn T., and Leslie Roberts. "Using Writing to Enhance Content Area Learning in the Primary Grades." *The Reading Teacher,* 42 (February 1989), 392–404.

Cullinan, Bernice E. *Children's Literature in the Reading Program.* Newark, Del.: International Reading Association, 1987.

Cullinan, Bernice E. "Whole Language and Children's Literature." *Language Arts,* 69 (October 1992), 426–430.

Cullinan, Bernice E., and Lee Galda. *Literature and the Child,* 3d ed. Fort Worth: Harcourt Brace, 1994.

Cummins, Jim. "The Acquisition of English as a Second Language." In *Kids Come in All Languages: Reading Instruction for ESL Students.* Newark, Del.: International Reading Association, 1994, pp. 36–62.

Cunningham, James W., and Hunter Ballew. "Solving Word Problem Solving." *The Reading Teacher,* 36 (April 1983), 836–839.

Cunningham, James W., and Lisa K. Wall. "Teaching Good Readers to Comprehend Better." *Journal of Reading,* 37 (March 1994), 480–486.

Cunningham, Pat. "Knowledge for More Comprehension." *The Reading Teacher,* 36 (October 1982b), 98–101.

Cunningham, Patricia M. "A Compare/Contrast Theory of Mediated Word Identification." *The Reading Teacher,* 32 (April 1979), 774–778.

Cunningham, Patricia M. "Decoding Polysyllabic Words: An Alternative Strategy." *The Reading Teacher,* 21 (April 1978), 608–614.

Cunningham, Patricia M. *Phonics They Use: Words for Reading and Writing.* New York: HarperCollins, 1991.

Cunningham, Patricia M., and James W. Cunningham. "Content Area Reading-Writing Lessons." *The Reading Teacher,* 40 (February 1987), 506–512.

Cunningham, Patricia M., and James W. Cunningham. "Making Words: Enhancing the Invented Spelling-Decoding Connection." *The Reading Teacher,* 46 (October 1992), 106–115.

Cunningham, Patricia, and Richard Allington. *Classrooms that Work: They Can All Read and Write.* New York: HarperCollins, 1994.

Curtis, Mary E., and Linn McCart. "Fun Ways to Promote Poor Readers' Word Recognition." *Journal of Reading,* 35 (February 1992), 398–399.

Dailey, Kathleen, and Kimberly Owen. "Dramatic Play and Literacy Development." Presentation at International Reading Association Convention, Toronto, Canada, May, 1994.

Daisey, Peggy. "Three Ways to Promote the Values and Uses of Literacy at Any Age." *Journal of Reading,* 36 (March 1993), 436–440.

Dale, Edgar, and Jeanne S. Chall. "A Formula for Predicting Readability." *Educational Research Bulletin,* 27 (January 21, 1948), 11–20, 28; (February 18, 1948), 37–54.

Daneman, Meredyth. "Individual Differences in Reading Skills." In *Handbook of Reading Research, Vol. II,* edited by R. Barr, M. L. Kamil, P. Mosenthal, and P. D. Pearson. New York: Longman, 1991, pp. 512–538.

Daniel, Twyla. "Extending Literacy with School Libraries." *Language Arts,* 67 (November 1990), 746–749.

Danielson, Kathy E. *Dialogue Journals: Writing as Conversation.* Bloomington, Ind.: Phi Delta Kappa, 1988.

Danielson, Kathy Everts. "Picture Books to Use with Older Students." *Journal of Reading,* 35 (May 1992), 652–654.

Davenport, Ruth, Michael Jaeger, and Carol Lauritzen, eds. "Negotiating Curriculum." *The Reading Teacher,* 49 (September 1995), 60–62.

Davis, Gary, and Sylvia Rimm. *Education of the Gifted and Talented,* 2d ed. Englewood Cliffs, N.J.: Prentice-Hall, 1994.

Davis, Susan J. "Synonym Rally: A Vocabulary Concept Game." *Journal of Reading,* 33 (February 1990), 380.

Davis, Zephaniah T., and Michael D. McPherson. "Story Map Instruction: A Road Map for Reading Comprehension." *The Reading Teacher,* 43 (December 1989), 232–240.

Deaton, Cheryl D. "Idioms As a Means of Communication: Writing in the Middle Grades." *The Reading Teacher,* 45 (February 1992), 473.

DeFina, Allan A. *Portfolio Assessment.* New York: Scholastic, 1992.

DeGroff, Linda. "Informational Books: Topics and Structures." *The Reading Teacher,* 43 (March 1990), 496–501.

DeGroff, Linda. "Is There a Place for Computers in Whole Language Classrooms?" *The Reading Teacher,* 43 (April 1990), 568–572.

Deiner, Penny. *Resources for Teaching Children with Diverse Abilities.* Fort Worth: Harcourt Brace, 1993.

DeLain, Marsha. "Equity and Performance-Based Assessment: An Insider's View." *The Reading Teacher,* 48 (February 1995), 440–442.

DeSerres, Barbara. "Putting Vocabulary in Context." *The Reading Teacher,* 43 (April 1990), 612–613.

Dever, Christine T. "Press Conference: A Strategy for Integrating Reading with Writing." *The Reading Teacher,* 46 (September 1992), 72–73.

Diamond, Barbara, and Margaret Moore. *Multicultural Literacy.* White Plains, New York: Longman, 1995.

Dickerson, Dolores Pawley. "A Study of Use of Games to Reinforce Sight Vocabulary." *The Reading Teacher,* 36 (October 1982), 46–49.

Dickinson, David K. "Oral Language, Literacy Skills, and Response to Literature." In *The Dynamics of Language Learning,* edited by James R. Squire. Urbana, Ill.: ERIC Clearinghouse on Reading and Communication Skills, 1987.

D'Ignazio, Fred. "DISKovery: The Starship Enterprise: New Opportunities for Learning in the 1990's." *Language Arts,* 68 (March 1991), 248–252.

Dillner, Martha. "Using Hypermedia to Enhance Content Area Instruction." *Journal of Reading,* 37 (December 1993/January 1994), 260–270.

Dionisio, Marie. "Responding to Literary Elements through Mini-lessons and Dialogue Journals." *English Journal,* 80 (January 1991), 40–44.

Dionisio, Marie. "Write? Isn't This Reading Class?" *The Reading Teacher,* 36 (April 1983), 746–750.

Dixon-Krauss, Lisbeth. *Vygotsky in the Classroom.* White Plains, N.Y.: Longman, 1996.

Doiron, Ray. "Using Nonfiction in a Read-Aloud Program: Letting the Facts Speak for Themselves." *The Reading Teacher,* 47 (May 1994), 616–624.

Dougherty, Wilma Holden, and Rosalind E. Engel. "An 80s Look for Sex Equality in Caldecott Winners and Honor Books." *The Reading Teacher,* 40 (January 1987), 394–398.

Dowd, Cornelia A., and Richard Sinatra. "Computer Programs and the Learning of Text Structure." *Journal of Reading,* 34 (October 1990), 104–112.

Downes, Toni, and Cherryl Fatouros. *Learning in an Electronic World.* Portsmouth, N.H.: Heinemann, 1995.

Downing, John. "How Children Think about Reading." In *Psychological Factors in the Teaching of Reading,* compiled by Eldon E. Ekwall. Columbus, Ohio: Charles E. Merrill, 1973.

Downing, John. "Reading—Skill or Skills?" *The Reading Teacher,* 35 (February 1982), 534–537.

Doyle, Denis P. "The 'Unsacred' Texts: Market Forces that Work Too Well." *American Educator,* 8 (Summer 1984), 8–13.

Dreher, Joyce. "Character Contrast." *The Reading Teacher,* 42 (March 1989), 551–552.

Dreher, Mariam Jean, and Harry Singer. "Story Grammar Instruction Unnecessary for Intermediate Grade Students." *The Reading Teacher,* 34 (December 1980), 261–268.

Dreher, Miriam J., and Harry Singer. "The Teacher's Role in Students' Success." *The Reading Teacher,* 42 (April 1989), 612–617.

Duchein, M. A., and D. L. Mealey. "Remembrance of Books Past . . . Long Past: Glimpses into Aliteracy." *Reading Research and Instruction,* 33, no. 1 (1993), 12–28.

Duffelmeyer, Frederick A. "Effective Anticipation Guide Statements for Learning from Expository Prose." *Journal of Reading,* 37 (March 1994), 452–457.

Duffelmeyer, Frederick A. "The Influence of Experience-Based Vocabulary Instruction on Learning Word Meanings." *Journal of Reading,* 24 (October 1980), 35–40.

Duffelmeyer, Frederick A. "Introducing Words in Context." *The Reading Teacher,* 35 (March 1982), 724–725.

Duffelmeyer, Frederick A. "Teaching Word Meaning from an Experience Base." *The Reading Teacher,* 39 (October 1985), 6–9.

Duffelmeyer, Frederick A. "Word Maps and Student Involvement." *The Reading Teacher,* 41 (May 1988), 968–969.

Duffelmeyer, Frederick A., and Dale D. Baum. "The Extended Anticipation Guide Revisited." *Journal of Reading,* 35 (May 1992), 654–656.

Duffelmeyer, Frederick A., and Barbara Blakely Duffelmeyer. "Developing Vocabulary Through Dramatization." *Journal of Reading,* 23 (November 1979), 141–143.

Duffelmeyer, Frederick A., and Barbara Blakely Duffelmeyer. "Topic and Main Idea: Clearing Up the Confusion." *The Reading Teacher,* 45 (November 1991), 252–254.

Duffy, Gerald G. *Reading in the Middle School,* 2d ed. Newark, Del.: International Reading Association, 1990.

Duffy, Gerald G., and Laura R. Roehler. *Improving Classroom Reading Instruction.* New York: Random House, 1986.

Duffy, Gerald G., and Laura R. Roehler. "Improving Reading Instruction Through the Use of Responsive Elaboration." *The Reading Teacher,* 40 (February 1987), 514–520.

Duffy, Gerald G., Laura R. Roehler, and Beth Ann Herrmann. "Modeling Mental Processes Helps Poor Readers Become Strategic Readers." *The Reading Teacher,* 41 (April 1988), 762–767.

Duncan, Patricia H. "I Liked the Book Better: Comparing Film and Text to Build Critical Comprehension." *The Reading Teacher,* 46 (May 1993), 720–725.

Durkin, Dolores. "What Classroom Observations Reveal about Reading Comprehension Instruction." *Reading Research Quarterly,* 14 (1978/1979), 481–533.

Durkin, Dolores. "What Is the Value of the New Interest in Reading Comprehension?" *Language Arts,* 58 (January 1981b), 23–43.

Dwyer, David. "Apple Classrooms of Tomorrow: What We've Learned." *Educational Leadership,* 51 (April 1994), 4–10.

Dwyer, Edward J. "Comprehending Figurative Language." *The Reading Teacher,* 45 (December 1991), 328–329.

Dwyer, Edward J. "Solving Verbal Analogies." *Journal of Reading,* 32 (October 1988), 73–75.

Dymock, Susan. "Reading But Not Understanding." *Journal of Reading,* 37 (October 1993), 86–91.

Eads, Maryann. "What to Do When They Don't Understand What They Read—Research-Based Strategies for Teaching Reading Comprehension." *The Reading Teacher,* 34 (February 1981), 565–571.

Ebel, Carolyn Williams. "An Update: Teaching Reading to Students of English as a Second Language." *The Reading Teacher,* 33 (January 1980), 403–407.

Eby, Judy. *Reflective Planning, Teaching, and Evaluation K–12,* 2d ed. Upper Saddle River, N.J.: Merrill, 1998.

Edinger, Monica. "Empowering Young Writers with Technology." *Educational Leadership,* 51 (April 1994), 58–60.

Edwards, Anthony T., and R. Allan Dermott. "A New Way with Vocabulary." *Journal of Reading,* 32 (March 1989), 559–561.

Egan, Margaret. "Capitalizing on the Reader's Strengths: An Activity Using Schema." *Journal of Reading,* 37 (May 1994), 636–640.

Egawa, Kathy. "Harnessing the Power of Language: First Graders' Literature Engagement with *Owl Moon.*" *Language Arts,* 67 (October 1990), 582–588.

Ehri, L. C. "Development of the Ability to Read Words." In *Handbook of Reading Research, Vol. II,* edited by R. Barr, M. L. Kamil, P. Mosenthal, and P. D. Pearson. New York: Longman, 1991, pp. 383–417.

Ehri, L. C., and C. Robbins. "Beginners Need Some Decoding Skill to Read Words by Analogy." *Reading Research Quarterly,* 27, no. 1 (1992), 13–26.

Ehri, L. C., and L. S. Wilce. "Does Learning to Spell Help Beginners Learn to Read Words?" *Reading Research Quarterly,* 22 (1987), 47–65.

Eisele, Beverly. *Lesson Plan Book for the Whole Language and Literature-Based Curriculum.* Cypress, Calif.: Creative Teaching Press, 1991.

Eisele, Beverly. *Managing the Whole Language Classroom.* Cypress, Calif.: Creative Teaching Press, 1991.

Elkind, David. "Developmentally Appropriate Practice: Philosophical and Practical Implications." *Phi Delta Kappan,* 71 (October 1989), 113–117.

Emans, Robert. "The Usefulness of Phonic Generalizations Above the Primary Grades." *The Reading Teacher,* 20 (February 1967), 419–425.

Emery, Donna W. "Helping Readers Comprehend Stories from the Characters' Perspectives." *The Reading Teacher,* 49 (April 1996), 534–541.

Englot-Mash, Christine. "Tying Together Reading Strategies." *Journal of Reading,* 35 (October 1991), 150–151.

Enz, Billie, ed. "Strategies for Promoting Parental Support for Emergent Literacy Programs." *The Reading Teacher,* 49 (October 1995), 168–170.

Evans, Carol. "*Monstruos, Pesadillas,* and Other Frights: A Thematic Unit." *The Reading Teacher,* 47 (February 1994), 428–430.

Faber, D. *Eleanor Roosevelt: First Lady of the World.* New York: Viking Kestrel, 1985.

Fallon, Irmie, and JoBeth Allen. "Where the Deer and the Cantaloupe Play." *The Reading Teacher,* 47 (April 1994), 546–551.

Farr, Roger. "Portfolio Assessment." *The Reading Teacher,* 43 (December 1989), 264.

Farr, Roger. "Portfolios: Assessment in Language Arts." *ERIC Digest* (1991), 3 pp. [ED334603].

Farr, Roger, and Robert F. Carey. *Reading: What Can Be Measured?,* 2d ed. Newark, Del.: International Reading Association, 1986.

Farr, Roger, and Nancy Roser. *Teaching a Child to Read.* New York: Harcourt Brace Jovanovich, 1979.

Farr, Roger, and Bruce Tone. *Portfolio and Performance Assessment.* Fort Worth: Harcourt Brace, 1994.

Farrar, Mary Thomas. "Asking Better Questions." *The Reading Teacher,* 38 (October 1984a), 10–15.

Farrar, Mary Thomas. "Why Do We Ask Comprehension Questions? A New Conception of Comprehension Instruction." *The Reading Teacher,* 37 (February 1984b), 452–456.

Farris, Pamela J., and Carol J. Fuhler. "Developing Social Studies Concepts through Picture Books." *The Reading Teacher,* 47 (February 1994), 380–387.

Fay, Leo. "Reading Study Skills: Math and Science." In *Reading and Inquiry,* edited by J. Allen Figurel. Newark, Del.: International Reading Association, 1965.

Feitelson, D., B. Kita, and Z. Goldstein. "Effects of Listening to Series Stories on First Graders' Comprehension and Use of Language." *Research in the Teaching of English,* 20 (1986), 339–356.

Felber, Sheila. "Story Mapping for Primary Students." *The Reading Teacher,* 43 (October 1989), 90–91.

Fennessey, Sharon. "Living History through Drama and Literature." *The Reading Teacher,* 49 (September 1995), 16–19.

Ferguson, Anne M., and Jo Fairburn. "Language Experience for Problem Solving in Mathematics." *The Reading Teacher,* 38 (February 1985), 504–507.

Fiderer, Adele. *Practical Assessments.* New York: Scholastic, 1995.

Field, James C., and David W. Jardine. "'Bad Examples' as Interpretive Opportunities: On the Need for Whole Language to Own Its Shadow." *Language Arts,* 71 (April 1994), 258–263.

Fielding, L. G., R. C. Anderson, and P. D. Pearson. *How Discussion Questions Influence Story Understanding* (Technical Report No. 490). Urbana–Champaign, Ill.:

University of Illinois, Center for the Study of Reading, January 1990.

Fields, Marjorie, and Deborah Hillstead. "Whole Language in the Play Store." *Childhood Education,* 67 (Winter 1990), 73–76.

Fields, Marjorie, and Katherine Spangler. *Reading Right,* 3d ed. Englewood Cliffs, N.J.: Merrill, 1995.

Finn, Patrick. *Helping Children Learn to Read.* New York: Random House, 1985.

First, Patricia, and Joan Curcio. *Implementing the Disabilities Acts: Implications for Educators.* Bloomington, Ind.: Phi Delta Kappa, 1993.

Fisette, Dolores. "Practical Authentic Assessment: Good Kid Watchers Know What to Teach Next." *The California Reader,* 26 (Summer 1993), 4–7.

Fish, John. *Special Education: The Way Ahead.* Philadelphia: Open University Press, 1985.

Fisher, Bobbi. "The Environment Reflects the Program." *Teaching K–8,* 20 (August/September 1989), 82, 84, 86.

Fisher, Bobbi. *Joyful Learning.* Portsmouth, N.H.: Heinemann, 1991.

Fisher, Bobbi. *Thinking and Learning Together.* Portsmouth, N.H.: Heinemann, 1995.

Fisher, Douglas, Caren Sax, and Ian Pumpian. "From Intrusion to Inclusion: Myths and Realities in Our Schools." *The Reading Teacher,* 49 (April 1996), 580–584.

Fitzgerald, Jill. "Enhancing Two Related Thought Processes: Revision in Writing and Critical Reading." *The Reading Teacher,* 43 (October 1989), 42–48.

Fitzgerald, Jill. "Helping Readers Gain Self-Control over Reading Comprehension." *The Reading Teacher,* 37 (December 1983), 249–253.

Fitzgerald, Jill. "Helping Young Writers to Revise: A Brief Review for Teachers." *The Reading Teacher,* 42 (November 1988), 124–129.

Fitzgerald, Jill. "Literacy and Students Who Are Learning English as a Second Language." *The Reading Teacher,* 46 (May 1993), 638–647.

Fitzgerald, Jill. "Research on Stories: Implications for Teachers." In *Children's Comprehension of Text: Research into Practice,* edited by K. Denise Muth. Newark, Del.: International Reading Association, 1989.

Flippo, Rona. *Reading Assessment and Instruction: A Qualitative Approach to Diagnosis.* Fort Worth: Harcourt Brace, 1997.

Flitterman-King, Sharon. "The Role of the Response Journal in Active Reading." *The Quarterly of the National Writing Project and the Center for the Study of Writing,* 10, no. 3 (1988), 4–11.

Flood, James. "The Text, the Student, and the Teacher: Learning from Exposition in the Middle Schools." *The Reading Teacher,* 39 (April 1986), 784–791.

Flood, James, and Diane Lapp. "Clearing the Confusion: A Closer Look at National Goals and Standards." *The Reading Teacher,* 47 (September 1993), 58–61.

Flood, James, and Diane Lapp. "Conceptual Mapping Strategies for Understanding Information Texts." *The Reading Teacher,* 41 (April 1988), 780–783.

Flood, James, and Diane Lapp. "Reading and Writing Relations: Assumptions and Directions." In *The Dynamics of Language Learning,* edited by James R. Squire. Urbana, Ill.: ERIC Clearinghouse on Reading and Communication Skills, 1987.

Flood, James, and Diane Lapp. "Reading Comprehension Instruction for At-Risk Students: Research-Based Practices That Can Make a Difference." *Journal of Reading,* 33 (April 1990), 490–496.

Flood, James, and Diane Lapp. "Reporting Reading Progress: A Comparison Portfolio for Parents." *The Reading Teacher,* 42 (March 1989), 508–514.

Flood, James, Diane Lapp, and Nancy Farnan. "A Reading-Writing Procedure that Teaches Expository Paragraph Structure." *The Reading Teacher,* 39 (February 1986), 556–562.

Flood, James, Diane Lapp, Sharon Flood, and Greta Nagel. "Am I Allowed to Group? Using Flexible Patterns for Effective Instruction." *The Reading Teacher,* 45 (April 1992), 608–616.

Flood, James, Diane Lapp, Josefina Tinajero, and Sandra Hurley. "Literacy Instruction for Students Acquiring English: Moving beyond the Immersion Debate." *The Reading Teacher,* 50 (December 1996/January 1997), 356–359.

Flynn, Linda L. "Developing Critical Reading Skills Through Cooperative Problem Solving." *The Reading Teacher,* 42 (May 1989), 664–668.

Flynn, Rosalind M., and Gail A. Carr. "Exploring Classroom Literature Through Drama: A Specialist and a Teacher Collaborate." *Language Arts,* 71 (January 1994), 38–43.

Ford, Michael, and Marilyn Ohlhausen. "Tips from Reading Clinicians for Coping with Disabled Readers in Regular Classrooms." *The Reading Teacher,* 42 (October 1988), 18–23.

Forell, Elizabeth. "The Case for Conservative Reader Placement." *The Reading Teacher,* 38 (May 1985), 857–862.

Forman, Ellice A., and Courtney B. Cazden. "Exploring Vygotskian Perspectives in Education: The Cognitive View of Peer Interaction." In *Theoretical Models and Processes of Reading,* 4th ed., edited by Robert Ruddell, Martha Rapp Ruddell, and Harry Singer. Newark, Del.: International Reading Association, 1994.

Fortescue, Chelsea M. "Using Oral and Written Language to Increase Understanding of Math Concepts." *Language Arts,* 71 (December 1994), 576–580.

Fortson, Laura, and Judith Reiff. *Early Childhood Curriculum.* Boston: Allyn and Bacon, 1995.

Foster-Harrison, Elizabeth. *Peer Tutoring for K–12 Success.* Bloomington, Ind.: Phi Delta Kappa, 1997.

Fouse, Beth, and Suzanne Brians. *A Primer on Attention Deficit Disorder.* Bloomington, Ind.: Phi Delta Kappa, 1993.

Fowler, Gerald. "Developing Comprehension Skills in Primary Students Through the Use of Story Frames." *The Reading Teacher,* 36 (November 1982), 176–179.

Fox, Lynn H., and William G. Durden. *Educating Verbally Gifted Youth.* Bloomington, Ind.: Phi Delta Kappa, 1982.

Frager, Alan M. "Affective Dimensions of Content Area Reading." *Journal of Reading,* 36 (May 1993), 616–622.

Fredericks, Anthony D. "Mental Imagery Activities to Improve Comprehension." *The Reading Teacher,* 40 (October 1986), 78–81.

Freedman, Glenn, and Elizabeth G. Reynolds. "Enriching Basal Reader Lessons with Semantic Webbing." *The Reading Teacher,* 33 (March 1980), 667–684.

Freedman, R. *Lincoln: A Photobiography.* New York: Clarion, 1987.

Freeman, David E., and Yvonne S. Freeman. "Bilingual Learners: How Our Assumptions Limit Their World." Occasional paper. Tucson: Arizona Center for Research and Development, May 1988.

Freeman, Yvonne S. "The California Reading Initiative: Revolution or Merely Revision?" *The New Advocate,* 1 (Fall 1988), 241–249.

Freeman, Yvonne S., and David E. Freeman. "Ten Tips for Monolingual Teachers of Bilingual Students." In *The Whole Language Catalog,* edited by Kenneth Goodman, Lois Bird, and Yetta Goodman. Santa Rosa, Calif.: American School Publishers, 1991.

Freeman, Yvonne S., and David E. Freeman. *Whole Language for Second Language Learners.* Portsmouth, N.H.: Heinemann, 1992.

French, Joyce, Nancy Ellsworth, and Marie Amoruso. *Reading and Learning Disabilities: Research and Practice.* New York: Garland, 1995.

Fresch, Mary Jo. "Self-Selection of Early Literacy Learners." *The Reading Teacher,* 49 (November 1995), 220–227.

Frew, Andrew W. "Four Steps Toward Literature-Based Reading." *Journal of Reading,* 34 (October 1990), 98–102.

Fried, J., K. Grey, and S. Swanson. *Monsters & Make-Believe.* Fairfield, Conn.: Pelican, 1991.

Friend, Marilyn, and Lynne Cook. "The New Mainstreaming." *Instructor,* 101 (March 1992), 30–34.

Fritz, J. *What's the Big Idea, Ben Franklin?* New York: Coward, McCann & Geoghegan, 1976.

Fry, Edward. *Elementary Reading Instruction.* New York: McGraw-Hill, 1977.

Fry, Edward. "Fry's Readability Graph: Clarifications, Validity, and Extension to Level 17." *Journal of Reading,* 21 (December 1977), 249.

Fry, Edward. "A Readability Formula for Short Passages." *Journal of Reading,* 33 (May 1990), 594–597.

Fuhler, Carol J. "Let's Move Toward Literature-Based Reading Instruction." *The Reading Teacher,* 43 (January 1990), 312–315.

Fuhler, Carol J. "Response Journals: Just One More Time with Feeling." *Journal of Reading,* 37 (February 1994), 400–405.

Furleigh, Mary A. "Teaching Comprehension with Editorials." *The Reading Teacher,* 44 (March 1991), 523.

Galda, Lee. "Children and Poetry." *The Reading Teacher,* 43 (October 1989), 66–71.

Galda, Lee. "History as Story: Books for the Social Studies." *The Reading Teacher,* 45 (November 1991), 224–233.

Galda, Lee. "Our Natural World." *The Reading Teacher,* 43 (January 1990), 322–326.

Galda, Lee. "Readers, Texts and Contexts: A Response-Based View of Literature in the Classroom." *The New Advocate,* 1 (Spring 1988), 92–102.

Galda, Lee. "Saving Our Planet, Saving Ourselves." *The Reading Teacher,* 45 (December 1991), 310–317.

Galda, Lee. "What a Character!" *The Reading Teacher,* 43 (December 1989), 244–249.

Galda, Lee, Emily Carr, and Susan Cox. "The Plot Thickens." *The Reading Teacher,* 43 (November 1989), 160–166.

Galda, Lee, Bernice Cullinan, and Dorothy Strickland. *Language, Literacy and the Child.* Orlando: Harcourt Brace, 1993.

Galda, Lee, with Donna Diehl and Lane Ware. "One World, One Family." *The Reading Teacher,* 46 (February 1993), 410–419.

Galda, Lee, and Pat MacGregor. "Nature's Wonders: Books for a Science Curriculum." *The Reading Teacher,* 46 (November 1992), 236–245.

Galda, Lee, and Kathy G. Short. "Visual Literacy: Exploring Art and Illustration in Children's Books." *The Reading Teacher,* 46 (March 1993), 506–516.

Galda, Lee, and Jane West. "Exploring Literature through Drama." In *Book Talk and Beyond,* edited by Nancy Roser and Miriam Martinez. Newark, Del.: International Reading Association, 1995.

Gale, David. "Why Word Play?" *The Reading Teacher,* 36 (November 1982), 220–222.

Gallagher, Janice Mori. "Pairing Adolescent Fiction with Books from the Canon." *Journal of Adolescent and Adult Literacy,* 39 (September 1995), 8–14.

Gambrell, L., W. Pfeiffer, and R. Wilson. "The Effects of Retelling upon Reading Comprehension and Recall of Text Information." *Journal of Educational Research,* 78 (1985), 216–220.

Gambrell, Linda. "Creating Classroom Cultures That Foster Reading Motivation." *The Reading Teacher,* 50 (September 1996), 14–25.

Garan, Elaine. "Who's in Control? Is There Enough 'Empowerment' to Go Around?" *Language Arts,* 71 (March 1994), 192–199.

Garcia, Eugene. *Student Cultural Diversity.* Boston: Houghton Mifflin, 1994.

Garcia, Mary, and Kathy Verville. "Redesigning Teaching and Learning: The Arizona Student Assessment Program." In *Authentic Reading Assessment: Practices and Possibilities,* edited by Sheila Valencia, Elfrieda Hiebert, and Peter Afflerbach. Newark, Del.: International Reading Association, 1994.

Gardner, Howard. *Frames of Mind: The Theory of Multiple Intelligences.* New York: Basic Books, 1983.

Gardner, Howard. "Relfections on Multiple Intelligences." *Phi Delta Kappan,* 77 (November 1995), 200–209.

Gardner, Michael K., and Martha M. Smith. "Does Perspective Taking Ability Contribute to Reading Comprehension?" *Journal of Reading,* 30 (January 1987), 333–336.

Garrison, James W., and Kenneth Hoskisson. "Confirmation Bias in Predictive Reading." *The Reading Teacher,* 42 (March 1989), 482–486.

Gaskins, I. W., L. C. Ehri, C. Cress, C. O'Hara, and K. Donnelly. "Analyzing Words and Making Discoveries about the Alphabetic System: Activities for Beginning Readers." *Language Arts,* 74 (March 1997), 172–184.

Gaskins, I. W., M. A. Downer, R. C. Anderson, P. M. Cunningham, R. W. Gaskins, M. Schommer, and The Teachers of Benchmark School. "A Metacognitive Approach to Phonics: Using What You Know to Decode What You Don't Know." *Remedial and Special Education* 9 (1988), 36–41.

Gaskins, Irene W. "Let's End the Reading Disabilities/Learning Disabilities Debate." *Journal of Learning Disabilities,* 15 (February 1982), 81–83.

Gaskins, Irene West. "Reading for Learning: Going Beyond the Basals in the Elementary Grades." *The Reading Teacher,* 35 (December 1981), 323–328.

Gaskins, Irene West, et al. "Classroom Talk about Text: Learning in Science Class." *Journal of Reading,* 37 (April 1994), 558–565.

Gaskins, Irene West, et al. "Procedures for Word Learning: Making Discoveries about Words." *The Reading Teacher,* 50 (December 1996/January 1997), 312–327.

Gaskins, Robert W. "The Missing Ingredients: Time on Task, Direct Instruction, and Writing." *The Reading Teacher,* 41 (April 1988), 750–755.

Gaskins, Robert W., Jennifer C. Gaskins, and Irene W. Gaskins. "A Decoding Program for Poor Readers—And the Rest of the Class, Too!" *Language Arts,* 68 (March 1991), 213–225.

Gauthier, Lane Roy. "A Strategy to Increase Punctuation Awareness." *Journal of Reading,* 36 (February 1993), 401–402.

Gauthier, Lane Roy. "Understanding Content Material." *The Reading Teacher,* 43 (December 1989), 266–267.

Gauthier, Lane Roy. "Using Capsulization Guides." *The Reading Teacher,* 42 (March 1989), 553–554.

Gauthier, Lane Roy. "Using Journals for Content Area Comprehension." *Journal of Reading,* 34 (March 1991), 491–492.

Gearheart, Bill R., and Carol J. Gearheart. *Learning Disabilities.* Columbus, Ohio: Merrill, 1989.

GEONews Handbook, November 11–17, 1990, 7.

Geisert, Paul G., and Mynga K. Futrell. *Teachers, Computers, and Curriculum: Microcomputers in the Curriculum.* 2d ed. Boston: Allyn and Bacon, 1995.

Gestwicki, Carol. *Developmentally Appropriate Practice.* Albany, N.Y.: Delmar, 1995.

Gill, J. Thomas, Jr. "Development of Word Knowledge as It Relates to Reading, Spelling, and Instruction." *Language Arts,* 69 (October 1992), 444–453.

Gilles, Carol. "Reading, Writing, and Talking: Using Literature Study Groups." *English Journal* (January 1989), 38–41.

Gillet, Jean Wallace, and J. Richard Gentry. "Bridges Between Nonstandard and Standard English with Extensions of Dictated Stories." *The Reading Teacher,* 36 (January 1983), 360–365.

Gipe, Joan P. "Use of a Relevant Context Helps Kids Learn New Word Meanings." *The Reading Teacher,* 33 (January 1980), 398–402.

Gitelman, Honore F., and Gayle Burgess Rasberry. "Bring on the Books: A Schoolwide Contest." *The Reading Teacher,* 39 (May 1986), 905–907.

Glass, Gerald G. "The Strange World of Syllabication." *The Elementary School Journal,* 67 (May 1967), 403–405.

Glynn, Shawn. "Teaching with Analogies: Building on the Science Textbook." *The Reading Teacher,* 49 (March 1996), 490–492.

Glynn, Shawn M. "The Teaching with Analogies Model." In *Children's Comprehension of Text: Research into Practice,* edited by K. Denise Muth. Newark, Del.: International Reading Association, 1989.

Gold, Lillian. *The Elementary School Publishing Center.* Bloomington, Ill.: Phi Delta Kappa. 1989.

Golden, Joanne M. "Children's Concept of Story in Reading and Writing." *The Reading Teacher,* 37 (March 1984), 578–584.

Golden, Joanne M., Annyce Meiners, and Stanley Lewis. "The Growth of Story Meaning." *Language Arts,* 69 (January 1992), 22–27.

Goldenberg, Claude. "Instructional Conversations: Promoting Comprehension through Discussion." *The Reading Teacher,* 46 (December 1992/January 1993), 316–326.

Goldstein, Bobbye S. "Looking at Cartoons and Comics in a New Way." *Journal of Reading,* 29 (April 1986), 647–661.

Gonzales, Phillip. "Beginning English Reading for ESL Students." *The Reading Teacher,* 35 (November 1981), 154–162.

Gonzales, Phillip. "Second Language Literacy." *Illinois Reading Council Journal,* 22 (Winter 1994), 13–16.

Goodall, Marilyn. "Can Four Year Olds 'Read' Words in the Environment?" *The Reading Teacher,* 37 (February 1984), 478–482.

Gooden, Andrea A. *Computers in the Classroom.* San Francisco: Apple Press and Jossey-Bass Publishers, 1996.

Goodman, Kenneth S. "As I See It: Evaluation in Whole Language." In *The Whole Language Catalog,* edited by Kenneth S. Goodman, Lois B. Bird, and Yetta M. Goodman. Santa Rosa, Calif.: American School Publishers, 1991.

Goodman, Kenneth S. "Reading: A Psycholinguistic Guessing Game." In *Perspectives on Elementary Reading,* edited by Robert Karlin. New York: Harcourt Brace Jovanovich, 1973.

Goodman, Kenneth S. "Reading, Writing, and Written Texts: a Transactional Sociopsycholinguistic View." In *Theoretical Models and Processes of Reading,* 4th ed., edited by Robert B. Ruddell, Martha Rapp Ruddell, and Harry Singer. Newark, Del.: International Reading Association, 1994, pp. 1093–1130.

Goodman, Kenneth S. "Unity in Reading." In *Theoretical Models and Processes of Reading,* 3d ed., edited by Harry Singer and Robert B. Ruddell. Newark, Del.: International Reading Association, 1985.

Goodman, Kenneth S. *What's Whole in Whole Language?* Portsmouth, N.H.: Heinemann Educational Books, 1986.

Goodman, Kenneth S. "Why Whole Language Is Today's Agenda in Education." *Language Arts,* 69 (September 1992), 354–363.

Goodman, Kenneth S., and Catherine Buck. "Dialect Barriers to Reading Comprehension Revisited." *The Reading Teacher,* 50 (March 1997), 454–459.

Goodman, Kenneth S., Yetta M. Goodman, and Wendy J. Hood, eds. *The Whole Language Evaluation Book.* Portsmouth, N.H.: Heinemann, 1989.

Goodman, Yetta. "Children Coming to Know Literacy." In *Emergent Literacy,* edited by William H. Teale and Elizabeth Sulzby. Norwood, N.J.: Ablex, 1986.

Goodman, Yetta. "Kid Watching: An Alternative to Testing." *National Elementary Principal,* 57 (June 1978), 41–45.

Goodman, Yetta. "Kidwatching: Observing Children in the Classroom." In *Observing the Language Learner,* edited by Angela Jagger and M. T. Smith-Burke. Newark, Del.: International Reading Association, 1985.

Goodman, Yetta. "Miscue Analysis for Classroom Teachers: Some History and Some Procedures." *Primary Voices K–6,* 3 (November 1995), 2–9.

Goodman, Yetta. "Test Review: Concepts about Print Test." *The Reading Teacher,* 34 (January 1981), 445–448.

Goodman, Yetta. "Using Children's Reading Miscues for New Teaching Strategies." *The Reading Teacher,* 23 (February 1970), 455–459.

Goodman, Yetta M. "Evaluation of Students: Srehcaet fo Noitaulave." In *The Whole Language Evaluation Book,* edited by Kenneth S. Goodman, Yetta M. Goodman, and Wendy J. Hood. Portsmouth, N.H.: Heinemann, 1989.

Goodman, Yetta M., and Myna M. Haussler. "Literacy Environment in the Home and Community." In *Roles in Literacy Learning: A New Perspective,* edited by Duane R. Tovey and James E. Kerber. Newark, Del.: International Reading Association, 1986.

Gordon, Christine J. "Teaching Narrative Text Structure: A Process Approach to Reading and Writing." In *Children's*

Comprehension of Text: Research into Practice, edited by K. Denise Muth. Newark, Del.: International Reading Association, 1989.

Gordon, Christine, and P. David Pearson. *Effects of Instruction in Metacomprehension and Inferencing on Students' Comprehension Abilities* (Technical Report No. 269). Urbana–Champaign, Ill.: University of Illinois, Center for the Study of Reading, 1983.

Gordon, Naomi, ed. *Classroom Experiences: The Writing Process in Action.* Exeter, N.H.: Heinemann, 1984.

Gough, Philip B. "Word Recognition." In *Handbook of Reading Research,* edited by P. David Pearson et al. New York: Longman, 1984.

Gove, Mary. "Clarifying Teachers' Beliefs about Reading." *The Reading Teacher,* 37 (December 1983), 261–268.

Grabe, Mark, and Cindy Grabe. *Integrating Technology for Meaningful Learning.* Boston: Houghton Mifflin, 1998.

Grabe, Mark, and Cindy Grabe. "The Microcomputer and the Language Experience Approach." *The Reading Teacher,* 38 (February 1985), 508–511.

Grabe, Nancy White. "Language Experience and Basals." *The Reading Teacher,* 34 (March 1981), 710–711.

Grace, Marsha. "Implementing a Portfolio System in Your Classroom." *Reading Today,* 10 (June/July 1993), 27.

Grady, Emily. *The Portfolio Approach to Assessment.* Bloomington, Ind.: Phi Delta Kappa, 1992.

Graves, D. H. *Investigate Nonfiction.* Portsmouth, N.H.: Heinemann, 1989.

Graves, Donald, and Jane Hansen. "The Author's Chair." *Language Arts,* 60 (February 1983), 176–183.

Graves, Michael F., and Maureen C. Prenn. "Costs and Benefits of Various Methods of Teaching Vocabulary." *Journal of Reading,* 29 (April 1986), 596–602.

Gray, Mary Ann. "Creatively Developing Research Writing Skills." *The Reading Teacher,* 42 (January 1989), 347.

Greaney, Vincent. "Parental Influences on Reading." *The Reading Teacher,* 39 (April 1986), 813–818.

Greenewald, M. Jane, and Rosalind L. Rossing. "Short-Term and Long-Term Effects of Story Grammar and Self-Monitoring Training on Children's Story Comprehension." In *Solving Problems in Literacy: Learners, Teachers, and Researchers,* edited by Jerome A. Niles and Rosary V. Lalik. Rochester, N.Y.: National Reading Conference, 1986.

Griffith, Priscilla, and Mary Olson. "Phonemic Awareness Helps Beginning Readers Break the Code." *The Reading Teacher,* 45 (March 1992), 516–523.

Groff, Patrick. "The Maturing of Phonics Instruction." *The Reading Teacher,* 39 (May 1986), 919–923.

Groff, Patrick J. "Resolving the Letter Name Controversy." *The Reading Teacher,* 37 (January 1984), 384–388.

Gronlund, Gaye. "Bringing the DAP Message to Kindergarten and Primary Teachers." In *Early Childhood Education 96/97,* edited by Karen Paciorek and Joyce Munro. Guilford, Conn.: Dushkin, 1996–1997, pp. 78–86.

Guild, Pat. "The Culture/Learning Style Connection." *Educational Leadership,* 51 (May 1994), 16–21.

Gunderson, Lee. "L2 Reading Instruction in ESL and Mainstream Classrooms." In *Issues in Literacy: A Research Perspective,* Thirty-Fourth Yearbook of the National Reading Conference, edited by Jerome A. Niles and Rosary V. Lalik. Rochester, N.Y.: National Reading Conference, 1985.

Gunning, Thomas G. "Word Building: A Strategic Approach to the Teaching of Phonics." *The Reading Teacher,* 48 (March 1995), 484–488.

Guri-Rozenblit, Sarah. "Impact of Diagrams on Recalling Sequential Elements in Expository Text." *Reading Psychology,* 9, no. 2 (1988), 121–139.

Guthrie, John T. "Children's Reasons for Success and Failure." *The Reading Teacher,* 36 (January 1983), 478–480.

Guthrie, John T. "Models of Reading and Reading Disability." *Journal of Educational Psychology,* 65 (1973), 9–18.

Guthrie, John T. "Preschool Literacy Learning." *The Reading Teacher,* 37 (December 1983), 318–320.

Guthrie, John T., Solomon Alao, and Jennifer M. Rinehart. "Engagement in Reading for Young Adolescents." *Journal of Adolescent and Adult Literacy,* 40 (March 1997), 438–446.

Guzzetti, Barbara J., Barbara J. Kowalinski, and Tom McGowan. "Using a Literature-Based Approach to Teaching Social Studies." *Journal of Reading,* 36 (October 1992), 114–122.

Hacker, Charles J. "From Schema Theory to Classroom Practice." *Language Arts,* 57 (November/December 1980), 866–871.

Hadaway, Nancy L., and Terrell A. Young. "Content Literacy and Language Learning: Instructional Decisions." *The Reading Teacher,* 47 (April 1994), 522–527.

Hadaway, Nancy, and Viola Florez. "Teaching Multiethnic Literature, Promoting Cultural Pluralism." *The Dragon Lode,* 8 (Winter 1990), 7–13.

Hafner, Lawrence E., and Hayden B. Jolly. *Teaching Reading to Children,* 2d ed. New York: Macmillan, 1982.

Haggard, Martha Rapp. "Developing Critical Thinking with the Directed Reading-Thinking Activity." *The Reading Teacher,* 41 (February 1988), 526–533.

Haggard, Martha Rapp. "The Vocabulary Self-Collection Strategy: Using Student Interest and World Knowledge to Enhance Vocabulary Growth." *Journal of Reading,* 29 (April 1986), 634–642.

Hahn, Amos L. "Teaching Remedial Students to Be Strategic Readers and Better Comprehenders." *The Reading Teacher,* 39 (October 1985), 72–77.

Hall, Dorothy, Connie Prevatte, and Patricia Cunningham. "Eliminating Ability Grouping and Reducing Failure in the Primary Grades." In *No Quick Fix*, edited by Richard Allington and Sean Walmsley. Newark, Del.: International Reading Association, 1995.

Hall, MaryAnne. "Teaching and Language Centered Programs." In *Roles in Literacy Learning*, edited by Duane Tovey and James Kerber. Newark, Del.: International Reading Association, 1986.

Hall, Nigel. *The Emergence of Literacy*. Portsmouth, N.H.: Heinemann Educational Books, 1987.

Haller, E. P., D. A. Child, and H. J. Walberg. "Can Comprehension Be Taught? A Quantitative Synthesis of 'Metacognitive' Studies." *Educational Researcher,* 17 (1988), 5–8.

Hamann, Lori S., Loree Schultz, Michael W. Smith, and Brian White. "Making Connections: The Power of Autobiographical Writing Before Reading." *Journal of Reading,* 35 (September 1991), 24–28.

Hancock, Marjorie R. "Character Journals: Initiating Involvement and Identification through Literature." *Journal of Reading,* 37 (September 1993), 42–50.

Hancock, Marjorie R. "Literature Response Journals: Insights Beyond the Printed Page." *Language Arts,* 69 (January 1992), 36–42.

Handloff, Elaine, and Joanne Golden. "Writing as a Way of 'Getting to' What You Think and Feel about a Story." In *Book Talk and Beyond,* edited by Nancy Roser and Miriam Martinez. Newark, Del.: International Reading Association, 1995.

Hansell, Stevenson F. "Stepping Up to Outlining." *Journal of Reading,* 22 (December 1978), 248–252.

Hansen, Jane. "The Effects of Inference Training and Practice on Young Children's Reading Comprehension." *Reading Research Quarterly,* 16, no. 3 (1981a), 391–417.

Hansen, Jane. "An Inferential Comprehension Strategy for Use with Primary Grade Children." *The Reading Teacher,* 34 (March 1981b), 665–669.

Hansen, Jane. "Literacy Portfolios Emerge." *The Reading Teacher,* 45 (April 1992), 604–607.

Hansen, Jane. "Organizing Student Learning: Teachers Teach What and How." In *The Dynamics of Language Learning,* edited by James R. Squire. Urbana, Ill.: National Council of Teachers of English, 1987.

Hansen, Jane. "Skills." In *Breaking Ground,* edited by Jane Hansen, Thomas Newkirk, and Donald Graves. Portsmouth, N.H.: Heinemann Educational Books, 1984.

Hansen, Jane. "Students' Evaluations Bring Reading and Writing Together." *The Reading Teacher,* 46 (October 1992), 100–105.

Hansen, Jane. "Synergism of Classroom and School Libraries." *The New Advocate,* 6 (Summer 1993), 201–211.

Hansen, Jane, and Ruth Hubbard. "Poor Readers Can Draw Inferences." *The Reading Teacher,* 37 (March 1984), 586–589.

Hansen, Jane, Thomas Newkirk, and Donald Graves, eds. *Breaking Ground: Teachers Relate Reading and Writing in the Elementary School.* Portsmouth, N.H.: Heinemann, 1985.

Hansen, Jane, and P. David Pearson. "An Instructional Study: Improving the Inferential Comprehension of Fourth Grade Good and Poor Readers." *Journal of Educational Psychology,* 75, no. 6 (1983), 821–829.

Hare, Victoria Chou. "What's in a Word? A Review of Young Children's Difficulties with the Construct 'Word.'" *The Reading Teacher,* 37 (January 1984), 360–364.

Hargis, Charles H., et al. "Repetition Requirements for Word Recognition." *Journal of Reading,* 31 (January 1988), 320–327.

Harlin, Rebecca, Sally Lipa, and Stephen Phelps. "Portfolio Assessment: Interpretations and Implications for Classroom Teachers and Reading Teachers." In *Literacy Research and Practice: Foundations for the Year 2000,* edited by Nancy Padak, Timothy Rasinsky, and John Logan. Pittsburg, Kan.: College Reading Association, 1992.

Harp, Bill. "Principles of Assessment and Evaluation in Whole Language Classrooms." In *Assessment and Evaluation for Student Centered Learning,* 2d ed., edited by Bill Harp. Norwood, Mass.: Christopher-Gordon, 1994, 47–66.

Harp, Bill. "When the Principal Asks, 'How Are We Using What We Know about Literacy Processes in the Content Areas?'" *The Reading Teacher,* 42 (May 1989), 726–727.

Harp, Bill. "When the Principal Asks, 'Why Are You Doing Guided Imagery During Reading Time?'" *The Reading Teacher,* 41 (February 1988), 588–590.

Harp, Bill. "When the Principal Asks: 'Why Are You Doing Piagetian Task Testing When You Have Given Basal Placement Tests?'" *The Reading Teacher,* 41 (November 1987), 212–214.

Harp, Bill. "When the Principal Asks: 'Why Aren't You Using the Phonics Workbooks?'" *The Reading Teacher,* 42 (January 1989), 326–327.

Harp, Bill. "When the Principal Asks, 'Why Don't You Ask Comprehension Questions?'" *The Reading Teacher,* 42 (April 1989), 638–639.

Harris, Albert J., and Edward R. Sipay. *How to Increase Reading Ability,* 8th ed. New York: Longman, 1985.

Harris, Larry A., and Carl B. Smith. *Reading Instruction.* New York: Macmillan, 1986.

Harris, Sandra. "Bringing About Change in Reading Instruction." *The Reading Teacher,* 49 (May 1996), 612–618.

Harris, Theodore, and Richard Hodges. *A Dictionary of Reading and Related Terms.* Newark, Del.: International Reading Association, 1981.

Harris, Theodore L., and Richard E. Hodges, eds. *The Literacy Dictionary: The Vocabulary of Reading and Writing.* Newark, Del.: International Reading Association, 1995.

Harris-Sharples, Susan D., Gail Kearns, and Margery Miller. "A Young Authors Program: One Model for Teacher and Student Empowerment." *The Reading Teacher,* 42 (April 1989), 580–583.

Harste, J. C., K. G. Short, and C. Burke. *Creating Classrooms for Authors: The Reading-Writing Connection.* Portsmouth, N.H.: Heinemann, 1988.

Harste, Jerome C. *New Policy Guidelines for Reading: Connecting Research and Practice.* Urbana, Ill.: National Council of Teachers of English and ERIC Clearinghouse on Reading and Communication Skills, 1989.

Hayden, Carla, ed. *Venture into Cultures.* Chicago: American Library Association, 1992.

Hayes, David A. "Initiate Cartographic Literacy with the MAP Activity." *Journal of Reading,* 35 (May 1992), 659–661.

Heald-Taylor, B. Gail. "Three Paradigms for Literature Instruction in Grades 3 to 6." *The Reading Teacher,* 49 (March 1996), 456–466.

Heald-Taylor, Gail. *Whole Language Strategies for ESL Students.* San Diego: Dormac, 1989.

Heide, Ann, and Dale Henderson. *The Technological Classroom: A Blueprint for Success.* Toronto: Trifolium Books, 1994.

Heide, F. "Rocks." In *By Myself,* compiled by L. B. Hopkins. New York: Crowell, 1980.

Heidger, Barbara. "No Need to Panic." In *The Whole Language Catalog,* edited by Kenneth Goodman, Lois Bridges, and Yetta Goodman. Santa Rosa, Calif.: American School Publishers, 1991.

Heimlich, Joan E., and Susan D. Pittelman. *Semantic Mapping: Classroom Applications.* Newark, Del.: International Reading Association, 1986.

Heine, Patricia. "The Power of Related Books." *The Reading Teacher,* 45 (September 1991), 75–77.

Helfeldt, John P., and William A. Henk. "Reciprocal Question-Answer Relationships: An Instructional Technique for At-Risk Readers." *Journal of Reading,* 33 (April 1990), 509–514.

Heller, Mary F. "Comprehending and Composing through Language Experience." *The Reading Teacher,* 42 (November 1988), 130–135.

Henderson, Alayna. "Kindergarteners 'Choose' to Read." *The Reading Teacher,* 49 (April 1996), 590–591.

Henke, Linda. "Beyond Basal Reading: A District's Commitment to Change." *The New Advocate,* 1, no. 1 (1988), 42–51.

Herman, Patricia A., Richard C. Anderson, P. David Pearson, and William E. Nagy. "Incidental Acquisition of Word Meaning from Expositions with Varied Text Features." *Reading Research Quarterly,* 22, no. 3 (1987), 263–284.

Hermes, Joan. "Read Me a Story: 101 Good Books Kids Will Love." In *Early Childhood Education 96/97,* edited by Karen Paciorek and Joyce Munro. Guilford, Conn.: Dushkin, 1996.

Herrell, Adrienne L., and Joel P. Fowler, Jr. *Camcorder in the Classroom: Using the Videocamera to Enliven Curriculum.* Columbus, Ohio: Prentice Hall, 1998.

Herriott, John. "CAI: A Philosophy of Education and a System to Match." *Creative Computing,* 8 (April 1982), 80–86.

Herrmann, Beth Ann. "Two Approaches for Helping Poor Readers Become More Strategic." *The Reading Teacher,* 42 (October 1988), 24–28.

Hess, Mary Lou. "Understanding Nonfiction: Purpose, Classification, Response." *Language Arts,* 68 (March 1991), 228–232.

Hewett, Frank M., with Steven R. Forness. *Education of Exceptional Learners,* 3d ed. Boston: Allyn & Bacon, 1984.

Hickman, Janet. "Children's Response to Literature: What Happens in the Classroom." In *Readings on Reading Instruction,* edited by Albert J. Harris and Edward R. Sipay, 3d ed. New York: Longman, 1984.

Hickman, Janet. "Not by Chance: Creating Classrooms that Invite Responses to Literature." In *Book Talk and Beyond,* edited by Nancy Roser and Miriam Martinez. Newark, Del.: International Reading Association, 1995.

Hiebert, Elfrieda, and Terry Hutchison. "Research Directions: The Current State of Alternative Assessments for Policy and Instructional Uses." *Language Arts,* 68 (December 1991), 662–668.

Hiebert, Elfrieda, Sheila Valencia, and Peter P. Afflerbach. "Definitions and Perspectives." In *Authentic Reading Assessment: Practices and Possibilities,* edited by Sheila W. Valencia, Elfrieda H. Hiebert, and Peter P. Afflerbach. Newark, Del.: International Reading Association, 1994, pp. 6–21.

Hiebert, Elfrieda H., and Jacalyn Colt. "Patterns of Literature-Based Reading Instruction." *The Reading Teacher,* 43 (October 1989), 14–20.

Hiebert, Elfrieda H., and Barbara M. Taylor. "Interventions and the Restructuring of American Literacy Instruction." In *Getting Reading Right from the Start,* edited by Elfrieda H. Hiebert and Barbara M. Taylor. Boston: Allyn & Bacon, 1994.

Hieshima, Joyce. "Literacy Instruction and ESL Learners: A Need for Re-examination." *Illinois Reading Council Journal,* 22 (Winter 1994), 17–20.

Hilbert, Sharon B. "Sustained Silent Reading Revisited." *The Reading Teacher,* 46 (December 1992/January 1993), 354–356.

Hills, Tynette. "Assessment in Context—Teachers and Children at Work." In *Early Childhood Education 94/95,* 15th ed., edited by Karen Paciorek and Joyce Munro. Guilford, Conn.: Dushkin, 1994, pp. 150–157.

Hoffman, James V. "Critical Reading/Thinking Across the Curriculum: Using I-Charts to Support Learning." *Language Arts,* 69 (February 1992), 121–127.

Hoffman, James V., and Sarah J. McCarthey. "Ongoing Research: Teachers' Practices and the New Basals." *NRRC News* (May 1995), 6–7.

Holbrook, Hilary Taylor. "The Quality of Textbooks." *The Reading Teacher,* 38 (March 1985), 680–683.

Holdaway, Don. *The Foundations of Literacy.* Portsmouth, N.H.: Heinemann Educational Books, 1979.

Holdaway, Don. "Guiding a Natural Process." In *Roles in Literacy Learning,* edited by Duane R. Tovey and James E. Kerber. Newark, Del.: International Reading Association, 1986.

Holland, Holly. "Way Past Word Processing." *Electronic Learning,* 15 (May/June 1996), 22–26.

Holmes, Betty C. "A Confirmation Strategy for Improving Poor Readers' Ability to Answer Inferential Questions." *The Reading Teacher,* 37 (November 1983), 144–147.

Holzberg, Carol S. "Software Reviews: *Jack and the Beanstalk: An Animated Storybook.*" *The Apple IIGS Buyer's Guide,* Fall 1989, 57–58.

Hood, Joyce. "Why We Burned Our Basic Sight Vocabulary Cards." *The Reading Teacher,* 27 (March 1972), 579–582.

Hoppes, Ginny. "Spinning a Prereading Lesson." *The Reading Teacher,* 42 (February 1989), 450.

Hornsby, David, Deborah Sukarna, and Jo-Ann Parry. *Read On: A Conference Approach to Reading.* Portsmouth, N.H.: Heinemann, 1986.

Howell, Helen. "Language, Literature, and Vocabulary Development for Gifted Students." *The Reading Teacher,* 40 (February 1987), 500–504.

Hoyt, Linda. "Many Ways of Knowing: Using Drama, Oral Interactions, and the Visual Arts to Enhance Reading Comprehension." *The Reading Teacher,* 45 (April 1992), 580–584.

HR5 to HR5–121. 1997. Publication of the 105th Congress of the United States of America, unpaged.

Huck, Charlotte S., Susan Hepler, and Janet Hickman. *Children's Literature in the Elementary School,* 6th ed. Fort Worth: Harcourt Brace, 1997.

HuffBenkoski, Kelly Ann, and Scott C. Greenwood. "The Use of Word Analogy Instruction with Developing Readers." *The Reading Teacher,* 48 (February 1995), 446–447.

Hughes, Sandra M. "Impact of Whole Language on Four Elementary School Libraries." *Language Arts,* 70 (September 1993), 393–399.

Humanities Software. *Great Scary Imaginings.* Hood River, Ore.: Humanities Software, 1991.

Humanities Software. *Terrible Days I.* Hood River, Ore.: Humanities Software, 1991.

Hunt, Nancy, and Kathleen Marshall. *Exceptional Children and Youth.* Boston: Houghton Mifflin, 1994.

Hunter-Grundin, Elizabeth. "Spoken Language in Emergent Literacy Learning." *Reading Today,* 7 (February/March 1990), 22.

Hutchins, Pat. *The Doorbell Rang.* New York: Mulberry Books, 1986.

"The Inclusive School." *Educational Leadership* (Special issue), 52 (December 1994/January 1995).

Ingham, Rosemary Oliphant. "Poetry Preferences with Great References." *Kentucky Reading Journal,* 5 (Spring 1984), 11–15.

International Business Machines. *Stories and More.* Atlanta: International Business Machines, 1991.

Irwin, Judith Westphal. "Implicit Connectives and Comprehension." *The Reading Teacher,* 33 (February 1980), 527–529.

Irwin, Judith Westphal. *Teaching Reading Comprehension Processes,* 2d ed. Englewood Cliffs, N.J.: Prentice-Hall, 1991.

Isaacson, Richard, et al., eds. *The Children's Catalog,* 16th ed. New York: H. W. Wilson, 1988.

Isaak, Troy, and John Joseph. "Authoring Software and Teaching." *The Reading Teacher,* 43 (December 1989), 254–255.

Iwicki, Ann L. "Vocabulary Connections." *The Reading Teacher,* 45 (May 1992), 736.

Jachym, Nora, Richard Allington, and Kathleen A. Broikou. "Estimating the Cost of Seatwork." *The Reading Teacher,* 43 (October 1989), 30–35.

Jaggar, Angela M. "Teacher as Learner: Implications for Staff Development." In *Teachers and Research,* edited by Gay Su Pinnell and Myna L. Matlin. Newark, Del.: International Reading Association, 1989.

Jasmine, Julia. *Addressing Diversity in the Classroom.* Westminster, Calif.: Teacher Created Materials, 1995.

Jasmine, Julia. *Portfolios and Other Assessments.* Huntington Beach, Calif.: Teacher Created Materials, 1993.

Jenkins, Barbara L., et al. "Children's Use of Hypothesis Testing When Decoding Words." *The Reading Teacher,* 33 (March 1980), 664–667.

Jenks, Carolyn, and Janice Roberts. "Reading, Writing, and Reviewing: Teacher, Librarian, and Young Readers Collaborate." *Language Arts,* 67 (November 1990), 742–745.

Jensen, Julie M., and Nancy L. Roser. "Are There Really 3 R's?" *Educational Leadership,* 47 (March 1990), 7–12.

Jett-Simpson, Mary. "Writing Stories Using Model Structures: The Circle Story." *Language Arts,* 58 (March 1981), 293–300.

Johns, Kenneth M. *How Children Learn a Second Language.* Bloomington, Ind.: Phi Delta Kappa, 1988.

Johns, Kenneth M., and Connie Espinoza. *Mainstreaming Language Minority Children in Reading and Writing.* Bloomington, Ind.: Phi Delta Kappa, 1992.

Johnson, Dale D., and James F. Baumann. "Word Identification." In *Handbook of Reading Research,* edited by P. David Pearson et al. New York: Longman, 1984.

Johnson, Dale D., and P. David Pearson. *Teaching Reading Vocabulary,* 2d ed. New York: Holt, Rinehart and Winston, 1984.

Johnson, Dale D., Susan D. Pittelman, and Joan E. Heimlich. "Semantic Mapping." *The Reading Teacher,* 39 (April 1986), 778–783.

Johnson, Dale D., and Bonnie von Hoff Johnson. "Highlighting Vocabulary in Inferential Comprehension Instruction." *Journal of Reading,* 29 (April 1986), 622–625.

Johnson, David, and Roger Johnson. "Social Skills for Successful Group Work." *Educational Leadership,* 47 (December 1989/January 1990), 29–33.

Johnson, Lori Beckmann. "Windows Computing: Finding the Right Words: Dictionaries, Thesauruses, and Quotations." *PC Novice,* 5 (September 1994), 21–23.

Johnson, Nancy M., and M. Jane Ebert. "Time Travel Is Possible: Historical Fiction and Biography—Passport to the Past." *The Reading Teacher,* 45 (March 1992), 488–495.

Johnson, Terry D., and Daphne R. Louis. *Literacy Through Literature.* Portsmouth, N.H.: Heinemann, 1987.

Johnston, Francine R. "Improving Student Response in DR-TAs and DL-TAs." *The Reading Teacher,* 46 (February 1993), 448–449.

Johnston, Peter H. "Assessment in Reading." In *Handbook of Reading Research,* edited by P. David Pearson et al. New York: Longman, 1984.

Johnston, Peter, and Richard Allington. "Remediation." In *Handbook of Reading Research, Vol. II.,* edited by Rebecca Barr, Michael L. Kamil, Peter B. Mosenthal, and P. David Pearson. White Plains, N.Y.: Longman, 1991, pp. 984–1012.

Johnston, Peter H. *Constructive Evaluation of Literate Activity.* New York: Longman, 1992.

Johnston, Peter H. "Teachers as Evaluation Experts." *The Reading Teacher,* 40 (April 1987), 744–748.

Jolly, Hayden B., Jr. "Teaching Basic Function Words." *The Reading Teacher,* 35 (November 1981), 136–140.

Jones, Linda L. "An Interactive View of Reading: Implications for the Classroom." *The Reading Teacher,* 35 (April 1982), 772–777.

Jones, Linda T. *Strategies for Involving Parents in Their Children's Education.* Bloomington, Ind.: Phi Delta Kappa, 1991.

Jones, Margaret B., and Denise D. Nessel. "Enhancing the Curriculum with Experience Stories." *The Reading Teacher,* 39 (October 1985), 18–22.

Jongsma, Kathleen S., and Eugene A. Jongsma. "Test Review: Commercial Informal Reading Inventories." *The Reading Teacher,* 34 (March 1981), 697–705.

Jongsma, Kathleen Stumpf. "Mathematics and Reading." *The Reading Teacher,* 44 (February 1991), 442–443.

Joranko, Joyce. "Reading and Writing Informational Texts." *The Reading Teacher,* 44 (November 1990), 276–277.

Josel, Carol Anne. "In a Different Context." *Journal of Reading,* 31 (January 1988), 375–377.

Jossart, Sarah A. "Character Journals Aid Comprehension." *The Reading Teacher,* 42 (November 1988), 180.

Juel, Connie. "Beginning Reading." In *Handbook of Reading Research, Vol. II,* edited by R. Barr, M. L. Kamil, P. Mosenthal, and P. D. Pearson. New York: Longman, 1991, pp. 759–787.

Juel, Connie. "Learning to Read and Write: A Longitudinal Study of Fifty-four Children from First through Fourth Grade." *Journal of Educational Psychology,* 80 (1988), 437–447.

Kachuck, Beatrice. "Relative Clauses May Cause Confusion for Young Readers." *The Reading Teacher,* 34 (January 1981), 372–377.

Kaiden, Ellen, and Linda Rice. "Paragraph Patterns and Comprehension: A Tactical Approach." *Journal of Reading,* 30 (November 1986), 164–166.

Kaisen, Jim. "SSR/Booktime: Kindergarten and 1st Grade Sustained Silent Reading." *The Reading Teacher,* 40 (February 1987), 532–536.

Kamhi, Alan, and Hugh Catts. *Reading Disabilities: A Developmental Language Perspective.* Boston: Little, Brown, 1989.

Kapinus, Barbara. "Looking at the Ideal and the Real in Large-Scale Reading Assessment: The View from Two Sides of the River." *The Reading Teacher,* 47 (April 1994), 578–580.

Kaplan, Elaine M., and Anita Tuchman. "Vocabulary Strategies Belong in the Hands of Learners." *Journal of Reading,* 24 (October 1980), 32–34. ·

Karnowski, Lee. "Using LEA with Process Writing." *The Reading Teacher,* 42 (March 1989), 462–465.

Keegan, Suzi, and Karen Shrake. "Literature Study Groups: An Alternative to Ability Grouping." *The Reading Teacher,* 44 (April 1991), 542–547.

Keller, Paul F. G. "Maryland Micro: A Prototype Readability Formula for Small Computers." *The Reading Teacher,* 35 (April 1982), 778–782.

A Kid-Watching Guide: Evaluation for Whole Language Classrooms. Tucson, Ariz.: TAWL (Tucsonans Applying Whole Language), 1984.

Kimmel, Susan, and Walter H. MacGinitie. "Helping Students Revise Hypotheses While Reading." *The Reading Teacher,* 38 (April 1985), 768–771.

Kinman, Judith R., and Darwin L. Henderson. "An Analysis of Sexism in Newbery Medal Award Books from 1977 to 1984." *The Reading Teacher,* 38 (May 1985), 885–889.

Kinnersley, Ruth T. "Children and Young Adult Literature on the Internet: An Introduction." In *Rethinking Teaching and Learning through Technology.* Proceedings of the Mid-South Instructional Technology Conference. Murfreesboro, Tenn.: Mid-South Technology Conference, 1997.

Kinney, Martha A. "A Language Experience Approach to Teaching Expository Text Structure." *The Reading Teacher,* 38 (May 1985), 854–856.

Kitagawa, Mary M. "Improving Discussions or How to Get the Students to Ask the Questions." *The Reading Teacher,* 36 (October 1982), 42–45.

Klare, George R. "Readability." In *Handbook of Reading Research,* edited by P. David Pearson et al. New York: Longman, 1984.

Kleiman, Glenn, and Mary Humphrey. "Learning with Computers: Word Processing in the Classroom." *Compute,* 4 (March 1982), 96, 98–99.

Knight, Jenny. "Learning in a Community." *The Reading Teacher,* 47 (March 1994), 498–499.

Koeller, Shirley, and Samina Khan. "Going Beyond the Dictionary with the English Vocabulary Explosion." *Journal of Reading,* 24 (April 1981), 628–629.

Koeze, Scott. "The Dictionary Game." *The Reading Teacher,* 43 (April 1990), 613.

Kohn, Alfie. "What to Look for in a Classroom." *Educational Leadership,* 54 (September 1996), 54–55.

Kolb, Gayla. "Read with a Beat: Developing Literacy through Music and Song." *The Reading Teacher,* 50 (September 1996), 76–77.

Koskinen, Patricia S., and Irene H. Blum. "Repeated Oral Reading and the Acquisition of Fluency." In *Changing Perspectives on Research in Reading/Language Processing and Instruction,* Thirty-Third Yearbook of the National Reading Conference, edited by Jerome A. Niles and Larry A. Harris. Rochester, N.Y.: National Reading Conference, 1984.

Koskinen, Patricia S., Linda B. Gambrell, Barbara A. Kapinus, and Betty S. Heathington. "Retelling: A Strategy for Enhancing Students' Reading Comprehension." *The Reading Teacher,* 41 (May 1988), 892–896.

Koskinen, Patricia S., Robert M. Wilson, Linda B. Gambrell, and Susan B. Neuman. "Captioned Video and Vocabulary Learning: An Innovative Practice in Literacy Instruction." *The Reading Teacher,* 47 (September 1993), 36–43.

Kotrla, Melissa. "What's Literacy?" *The Reading Teacher,* 50, (May 1997), 702–703.

Kranz, Bella. *Identifying Talents among Multicultural Children.* Bloomington, Ind.: Phi Delta Kappa, 1994.

Krashen, Stephen D. "The Input Hypothesis and Language Education." In *The Whole Language Catalog,* edited by Kenneth Goodman, Lois Bridges, and Yetta Goodman. Santa Rosa, Calif.: American School Publishers, 1991.

Krieger, Evelyn. "Developing Comprehension Through Author Awareness." *Journal of Reading,* 33 (May 1990), 618–619.

Krushenisky, Cindy. "Lightening Your Load with Multimedia Encyclopedias." *PC Novice,* 4 (October 1993), 62–65.

Kubiszyn, Tom, and Gary Borich. *Educational Testing and Measurement,* 2d ed. Glenview, Ill.: Scott, Foresman, 1987.

Kupiter, Karen, and Patricia Wilson. "Updating Poetry Preferences: A Look at the Poetry Children Really Like." *The Reading Teacher,* 47 (September 1993), 28–35.

Kuta, Katherine Wiesolek. "Teaching Text Patterns to Remedial Readers." *Journal of Reading,* 35 (May 1992), 657–658.

Laase, Lois. "Study Skills: Note-taking Strategies That Work." *Instructor,* 106 (May/June 1997), 58.

Labbo, Linda, and William Teale. "Cross-age Reading: A Strategy for Helping Poor Readers." *The Reading Teacher,* 43 (February 1990), 362–369.

LaBerge, David, and S. Jay Samuels. "Toward a Theory of Automatic Information Processing in Reading." In *Theoretical Models and Processes of Reading,* 3d ed., edited by Harry Singer and Robert B. Ruddell. Newark, Del.: International Reading Association, 1985.

Lamme, Linda L. "Children's Literature: The Natural Way to Learn to Read." In *Children's Literature in the Reading Program,* edited by Bernice Cullinan. Newark, Del.: International Reading Association, 1987.

Lamme, Linda Leonard, and Linda Ledbetter. "Libraries: The Heart of Whole Language." *Language Arts,* 67 (November 1990), 735–741.

Lancia, Peter. "Literary Borrowing: The Effects of Literature on Children's Writing." *The Reading Teacher,* 50 (March 1997), 470–475.

Landis, Ken. "Software Review: *Where in the World Is Carmen Sandiego?*" *The Apple IIGS Buyer's Guide,* Fall 1989, 59.

Lange, Bob. "Making Sense with Schemata." *Journal of Reading,* 24 (February 1981), 442–445.

Lapp, Diane, and James Flood. "Are There 'Real' Writers Living in Your Classroom? Implementing a Writer-Centered Classroom." *The Reading Teacher,* 48 (November 1993), 254–258.

Lapp, Diane, and James Flood. "Integrating the Curriculum: First Steps." *The Reading Teacher,* 47 (February 1994), 416–419.

Lapp, Diane, and James Flood. "Where's the Phonics? Making the Case (Again) for Integrated Code Instruction." *The Reading Teacher,* 50 (May 1997), 696–700.

Lapp, Diane, James Flood, and Linda Lungren. "Issues and Trends: Strategies for Gaining Access to the Information Superhighway: Off the Side Street and on to the Main Road." *The Reading Teacher,* 48 (February 1996), 432–436.

Larson, Jennifer. "Make New Friends: Introducing Children to Computers." *PC Novice,* September 1994, 34–36.

Larson, Jennifer. "Pick Up a Good Program: Reading Software for Children of All Ages." *PC Novice,* September 1994, 44–47.

Lathlaen, Peggy. "A Meeting of Minds: Teaching Using Biographies." *The Reading Teacher,* 46 (March 1991), 529–531.

Laughlin, Catherine E., and Mavis D. Martin. *Supporting Literacy.* New York: Teachers College Press, 1987.

Lauritzen, Carol, Michael Jaeger, and M. Ruth Davenport. "Integrating Curriculum: Contexts for Integrating Curriculum." *The Reading Teacher,* 49 (February 1996), 404–406.

Layton, Kent, and Martha E. Irwin. "Enriching Your Reading Program with Databases." *The Reading Teacher,* 42 (May 1989), 724.

Lazear, David. *Teaching for Multiple Intelligences.* Bloomington, Ind.: Phi Delta Kappa, 1992.

Leal, Dorothy L. "The Power of Literary Peer-Group Discussions: How Children Collaboratively Negotiate Meaning." *The Reading Teacher,* 47 (October 1993), 114–120.

Lee, Tosca Moon. "From Stories to Essays: Writing Software for School Children." *PC Novice,* September 1994, 44–47.

Leland, Christine, and Ruth Fitzpatrick. "Cross-Age Interaction Builds Enthusiasm for Reading and Writing." *The Reading Teacher,* 47 (December 1993/January 1994), 292–301.

Lenski, Susan, Marsha Riss, and Gayle Flickinger. "Honoring Student Self-Evaluation in the Classroom Community." *Primary Voices K–6,* 4 (April 1996), 24–32.

Lerner, Janet. *Learning Disabilities,* 5th ed. Boston: Houghton Mifflin, 1988.

Letts, Nancy. "Building Classroom Unity." *Teaching K–8,* 25 (August/September 1994), 106–107.

Leslie, Lauren, and Mary Jett-Simpson. *Authentic Literacy Assessment.* New York: Longman, 1997.

Leu, Donald J., Jr. "Exploring Literacy Within Multimedia Environments." *The Reading Teacher,* 50 (October 1996), 162–165.

Levine, Daniel U. "Successful Approaches to Improving Academic Achievement in Inner-City Elementary Schools." *Phi Delta Kappan,* 63 (April 1982), 523–526.

Levstick, Linda S. "Research Directions: Mediating Content Through Literary Texts." *Language Arts,* 67 (December 1990), 848–853.

Lewis, Maureen, David Wray, and Patricia Rospigliosi. ". . . And I Want It in Your Own Words." *The Reading Teacher,* 47 (April 1994), 528–536.

Lewkowicz, Nancy K. "The Bag Game: An Activity to Heighten Phonemic Awareness." *The Reading Teacher,* 47 (March 1994), 508–509.

Lipson, Marjorie Y., Sheila W. Valencia, Karen K. Wixon, and Charles W. Peters. "Integration and Thematic Teaching: Integration to Improve Teaching and Learning." *Language Arts,* 70 (April 1993), 252–263.

Lipson, Marjorie, and Karen Wixson. *Assessment and Instruction of Reading Disability.* New York: HarperCollins, 1991.

Lipson, Marjorie, and Karen Wixson. *Assessment & Instruction of Reading and Writing Disability,* 2d ed. New York: Longman, 1997.

Lombardi, Thomas, and Barbara Ludlow. *Trends Shaping the Future of Special Education.* Bloomington, Ind.: Phi Delta Kappa, 1996.

Long, Emily S. "Using Acrostic Poems for Research Reporting." *The Reading Teacher,* 46 (February 1993), 447–448.

Loughlin, Catherine E., and Mavis D. Martin. *Supporting Literacy.* New York: Teachers College Press, 1987.

Lukasevich, Ann. "Meeting Special Needs in the Whole-Language Classroom." In *Whole Language,* 2d ed., edited by Victor Froese. Boston: Allyn and Bacon, 1996, pp. 306–337.

Lukasevich, Ann. "Organizing Whole-Language Classrooms." In *Whole Language Practice and Theory,* 2d ed., edited by Victor Froese. Boston: Allyn and Bacon, 1996, pp. 362–388.

Lundberg, I., J. Frost, and O. Peterson. "Effects of an Extensive Program for Stimulating Phonological Awareness in Preschool Children." *Reading Research Quarterly,* 23 (1988), 263–284.

Lunsford, Susan H. "'And They Wrote Happily Ever After': Literature-Based Mini-Lessons in Writing." *Language Arts,* 74 (January 1997), 42–48.

Lynch-Brown, Carol. "Translated Children's Books: Voyaging to Other Countries." *The Reading Teacher,* 44 (March 1991), 486–492.

Lyon, G. Reid. *Research in Learning Disabilities: Research Directions (Technical Report).* Bethesda, Md.: National Institutes of Child Health and Human Development, 1991.

Macey, Joan Mary. "Word Lines: An Approach to Vocabulary Development." *The Reading Teacher,* 35 (November 1981), 216–217.

Maclean, Rod. "Two Paradoxes of Phonics." *The Reading Teacher,* 41 (February 1988), 514–517.

Macon, James M., Diane Bewell, and MaryEllen Vogt. *Responses to Literature: Grades K–8.* Newark, Del.: International Reading Association, 1991.

Madden, Lowell. "Improve Reading Attitudes of Poor Readers through Cooperative Reading Teams." *The Reading Teacher,* 42 (December 1988), 194–199.

Mallow, Jeffry V. "Reading Science." *Journal of Reading,* 34 (February 1991), 324–338.

Mandler, J. M. *Stories, Scripts, and Scenes: Aspects of Schema Theory.* Hillsdale, N.J.: Erlbaum, 1984.

Mandler, Jean M., and Nancy S. Johnson. "Remembrance of Things Parsed: Story Structure and Recall." *Cognitive Psychology,* 9 (January 1977), 111–151.

Mangieri, John N., and Michael S. Kahn. "Is the Dolch List of 220 Basic Sight Words Irrelevant?" *The Reading Teacher,* 30 (March 1977), 649–651.

Manna, Anthony. "Making Language Come Alive Through Reading Plays." *The Reading Teacher,* 37 (April 1984), 712–717.

Manning, Gary L., and Maryann Manning. "What Models of Recreational Reading Make a Difference?" *Reading World*, 23 (May 1984), 375–380.

Manning, Maryann, Gary Manning, and Jackie Hughes. "Journals in 1st Grade: What Children Write." *The Reading Teacher*, 41 (December 1987), 311–315.

Manolakes, George. "Comprehension: A Personal Experience in Content Area Reading." *The Reading Teacher*, 42 (December 1988), 200–202.

Maria, Katherine. "Developing Disadvantaged Children's Background Knowledge Interactively." *The Reading Teacher*, 42 (January 1989), 296–300.

Maric, K., and J. M. Johnson. "Correcting Misconceptions: Effect of Type on Text." In *Literacy Theory and Research: Analyses from Multiple Paradigms*, edited by S. McCormick and J. Zutell. Chicago: National Reading Conference, 1990.

Maring, Gerald H., Gail Chase Furman, and Judy Blum-Anderson. "Five Cooperative Learning Strategies for Mainstreamed Youngsters in Content Area Classrooms." *The Reading Teacher*, 39 (December 1985), 310–313.

Marshall, Nancy. "Using Story Grammar to Assess Reading Comprehension." *The Reading Teacher*, 36 (March 1983), 616–620.

Marston, Marilyn. "Bag the Magic E." *The Reading Teacher*, 42 (January 1989), 339.

Martinez, Miriam. "Motivating Dramatic Story Reenactments." *The Reading Teacher*, 46 (May 1993), 682–688.

Martinez, Miriam, and Marcia F. Nash. "Bookalogues: Talking about Children's Books." *Language Arts*, 68 (February 1991), 140–147.

Martinez, Miriam, and Marcia F. Nash. "Bookalogues: Talking about Children's Literature." *Language Arts*, 67 (October 1990), 599–606.

Martinez, Miriam, and Marcia F. Nash. "Bookalogues: Talking about Children's Literature." *Language Arts*, 67 (December 1990), 854–861.

Martinez, Miriam, and William H. Teale. "The Ins and Outs of a Kindergarten Writing Program." *The Reading Teacher*, 40 (January 1987), 444–451.

Marzano, Lorraine. "Connecting Literature with Cooperative Writing." *The Reading Teacher*, 43 (February 1990), 429–430.

Marzano, Robert J. "A Cluster Approach to Vocabulary Instruction: A New Direction from the Research Literature." *The Reading Teacher*, 38 (November 1984), 168–173.

Marzano, Robert J. "Lessons from the Field about Outcome-Based Performance Assessments." *Educational Leadership*, 51 (March 1994), 44–50.

Mason, George. "The Word Processor and Teaching Reading." *The Reading Teacher*, 37 (February 1984), 552–553.

Mason, George E. *Language Experience Recorder Plus.* Gainesville, Fla.: Teacher Support Software, 1987.

Mason, Jana M. "Early Reading from a Developmental Perspective." In *Handbook of Reading Research,* edited by P. David Pearson et al. New York: Longman, 1984.

Mateja, John. "Musical Cloze: Background, Purpose, and Sample." *The Reading Teacher*, 35 (January 1982), 444–448.

Mathewson, Grover C. "Teaching Forms of Negation in Reading and Reasoning." *The Reading Teacher*, 37 (January 1984), 354–358.

Mathison, Carla. "Activating Student Interest in Content Area Reading." *Journal of Reading*, 33 (December 1989), 170–176.

Maudeville, Thomas F. "KWLA: Linking the Affective and Cognitive Domains." *The Reading Teacher*, 47 (May 1994), 679–680.

Mavrogenes, Nancy A. "What Every Reading Teacher Should Know about Emergent Literacy." *The Reading Teacher*, 40 (November 1986), 174–178.

Mayfield, Margie. "The Classroom Environment: A Living-in and Learning-in Space." In *Emerging Literacy*, edited by Lloyd O. Ollila and Margie I. Mayfield. Boston: Allyn & Bacon, 1992, pp. 166–195.

Mayfield, Margie. "Organizing for Teaching and Learning." In *Emerging Literacy*, edited by Lloyd O. Ollila and Margie I. Mayfield. Boston: Allyn & Bacon, 1992, pp. 196–228.

McAloon, Noreen. "Prereading and Background Knowledge." *Journal of Reading*, 38 (October 1994), 142–144.

McAloon, Noreen. "Time for Nonfiction?" *Journal of Reading*, 36 (March 1993), 502–503.

McCarthy, Robert. "Assessing the Whole Student." *Instructor Special Supplement* (May/June 1994), 18.

McClure, Amy A., and Connie S. Zitlow. "Not Just the Facts: Aesthetic Response in Elementary Content Area Studies." *Language Arts*, 68 (January 1991), 27–33.

McConaughy, Stephanie H. "Word Recognition and Word Meaning in the Total Reading Process." *Language Arts*, 55 (November/December 1978), 946–956, 1003.

McCord, D. "This Is My Rock." In *Anthology of Children's Literature*, 4th rev. ed., edited by E. Johnson, E. R. Sickels, and C. R. Sayers. Boston: Houghton Mifflin, 1970.

McCormick, S., and D. S. Hill. "An Analysis of the Effects of Two Procedures for Increasing Disabled Readers' Inferencing Skills." *Journal of Educational Research*, 77 (1984), 219–226.

McCracken, Robert, and Marlene McCracken. *Stories, Songs & Poetry to Teach Reading & Writing.* Winnipeg, Canada: Peguis, 1987.

McDonell, Gloria M., and E. Bess Osburn. "New Thoughts about Reading Readiness." In *Readings on Reading Instruction*, edited by Albert J. Harris and Edward R. Sipay. New York: Longman, 1984.

McGee, Lea. "Talking about Books with Young Children." In *Books and Beyond*, edited by Nancy Roser and Miriam

Martinez. Newark, Del.: International Reading Association, 1995.

McGee, Lea M. "Exploring the Literature-Based Reading Revolution." *Language Arts,* 69 (November 1992), 529–537.

McGee, Lea M., and Donald J. Richgels. *Literacy's Beginnings.* Boston: Allyn & Bacon, 1990.

McGee, Lea M., and Donald J. Richgels. "Teaching Expository Text Structure to Elementary Students." *The Reading Teacher,* 38 (April 1985), 739–748.

McGee, Lea M., and Gail E. Tompkins. "Literature-Based Reading Instruction: Who's Guiding the Instruction?" *Language Arts,* 72 (October 1995), 405–414.

McGee, Lea M., and Gail E. Tompkins. "The Videotape Answer to Independent Reading Comprehension Activities." *The Reading Teacher,* 34 (January 1981), 427–433.

McGill-Franzen, Anne. "'I Could Read the Words!': Selecting Good Books for Inexperienced Readers." *The Reading Teacher,* 46 (February 1993), 424–426.

McGinley, William, and Daniel Madigan. "The Research 'Story': A Forum for Integrating Reading, Writing, and Learning." *Language Arts,* 67 (September 1990), 474–483.

McGuinness, Diane. *When Children Don't Learn.* New York: Basic Books, 1985.

McInnes, John. "Children's Quest for Literacy." In *Roles in Literacy Learning,* edited by Duane Tovey and James Kerber. Newark, Del.: International Reading Association, 1986.

McIntosh, Margaret E. "What Do Practitioners Need to Know about Current Inference Research?" *The Reading Teacher,* 38 (April 1985), 755–761.

McKenzie, Gary R. "Personalize Your Group Teaching." In *Readings on Reading Instruction,* 3d ed., edited by Albert J. Harris and Edward R. Sipay. New York: Longman, 1984.

McKeon, Denise. "When Meeting 'Common' Standards is Uncommonly Difficult." *Educational Leadership,* 51 (May 1994), 45–49.

McKeown, M. G., I. L. Beck, R. C. Omanson, and C. A. Perfetti. "The Effects of Long-Term Vocabulary Instruction on Reading Comprehension: A Replication." *Journal of Reading Behavior,* 15 (1983), 3–18.

McKeown, Margaret G., Isabel L. Beck, and M. Jo Worthy. "Grappling with Text Ideas: Questioning the Author." *The Reading Teacher,* 46 (April 1993), 560–566.

McKeown, Margaret G., Isabel L. Beck, Richard C. Omanson, and Martha T. Pople. "Some Effects of the Nature and Frequency of Vocabulary Instruction on the Knowledge and Use of Words." *Reading Research Quarterly,* 20, no. 5 (1985), 522–535.

McLane, Joan, and Gillian McNamee. *Early Literacy.* Cambridge, Mass.: Harvard University Press, 1990.

McMahon, Susan I., and Taffy E. Raphael. "Teacher Assessment Plan (TAP)." Paper presented at the International Reading Association Convention, Atlanta, May 6, 1990.

McMillan, Merna M., and Lance M. Gentile. "Children's Literature: Teaching Critical Thinking and Ethics." *The Reading Teacher,* 41 (May 1988), 876–878.

McNutt, Gaye, and Nancy Bukofzer. "Teaching Early Reading at McDonald's." *The Reading Teacher,* 35 (April 1982), 841–842.

McVey, Michael. "The Death of the Textbook: Shaping a New Learning Environment." *Talking Points,* 8 (May/June 1997), 5–7.

McWhirter, Anna M. "Whole Language in the Middle School." *The Reading Teacher,* 43 (April 1990), 562–565.

Means, Barbara, and Kerry Olson. "The Link Between Technology and Authentic Learning." *Educational Leadership,* 51 (April 1994), 15–18.

Meir, Margaret. "Comprehension Monitoring in the Elementary Classroom." *The Reading Teacher,* 37 (April 1984), 770–774.

Melnick, Steven A. "Electronic Encyclopedias on Compact Disk." *The Reading Teacher,* 44 (February 1991), 432–434.

Meltzer, Nancy S., and Robert Herse. "The Boundaries of Written Words as Seen by First Graders." *Journal of Reading Behavior,* 1 (Summer 1969), 3–14.

Memory, David M., and Carol Y. Yoder. "Improving Concentration in Content Classrooms." *Journal of Reading,* 31 (February 1988), 426–435.

Mendoza, Alicia. "Reading to Children: Their Preferences." *The Reading Teacher,* 38 (February 1985), 522–527.

Menke, Deborah J., and Michael Pressley. "Elaborative Interrogation: Using 'Why' Questions to Enhance the Learning from Text." *Journal of Reading,* 37 (May 1994), 642–645.

Merkley, Donna J. "Modified Anticipation Guide." *The Reading Teacher,* 50 (December 1996/January 1997), 365–368.

Meyer, Carol. "What's the Difference between *Authentic* and *Performance* Assessment?" *Educational Leadership,* 49 (May 1992), 39–40.

Miccinati, Jeannette L. "Using Prosodic Cues to Teach Oral Reading Fluency." *The Reading Teacher,* 39 (November 1985), 206–212.

Michener, Darlene M. "Test Your Reading Aloud IQ." *The Reading Teacher,* 42 (November 1988), 118–122.

Mickelson, Norma. "Adventures in Evaluation." Paper presented at the Whole Language Umbrella Conference, St. Louis, August 4, 1990.

Miholic, Vincent. "An Inventory to Pique Students' Metacognitive Awareness of Reading Strategies." *Journal of Reading,* 38 (October 1994), 84–86.

Mike, Dennis G. "Interactive Literacy." *Electronic Learning,* 13 (May/June 1994), 50–52, 54.

Mikel, Vesta L. "Using Cooperative Learning in Teaching Content Reading." *Journal of Reading,* 36 (May 1993), 659–660.

Miller, Etta. "The Seeing Sticks." *Journal of Adolescent and Adult Literacy,* 39 (April 1996), 584–585.

Miller, Etta, Luther B. Clegg, and Bill Vanderhoff. "Creating Postcards from the Famous for Social Studies Class." *Journal of Reading,* 36 (October 1992), 134–135.

Miller, G. Michael, and George E. Mason. "Dramatic Improvisation: Risk-Free Role Playing for Improving Reading Performance." *The Reading Teacher,* 37 (November 1983), 128–131.

Milz, Vera E. "Comments from a Teacher Researcher." In *Teachers and Research,* edited by Gay Su Pinnell and Myna L. Matlin. Newark, Del.: International Reading Association, 1989.

Minnesota Educational Computing Consortium. *Story Book Weaver.* North Minneapolis, Minn.: MECC.

Moldofsky, Penny Baum. "Teaching Students to Determine the Central Story Problem: A Practical Application of Schema Theory." *The Reading Teacher,* 36 (April 1983), 740–745.

Monahan, Joy N. "Developing a Strategic Reading Program." In *Reading in the Middle Schools,* 2d ed., edited by Gerald G. Duffy. Newark, Del.: International Reading Association, 1990.

Moore, David W., and James W. Cunningham. "Task Clarity and Sixth-Grade Students' Main Idea Statements." In *Changing Perspectives on Research in Reading/Language Processing and Instruction,* edited by Jerome A. Niles and Larry A. Harris. Rochester, N.Y.: National Reading Conference, 1984.

Moore, David W., and John E. Readence. "Processing Main Ideas Through Parallel Lesson Transfer." *Journal of Reading,* 23 (April 1980), 589–593.

Moore, David W., and Greg P. Stefanich. "Middle School Reading: A Historical Perspective." In *Reading in the Middle School,* 2d ed., edited by Gerald G. Duffy. Newark, Del.: International Reading Association, 1990.

Moore, Margaret. "Computers Can Enhance Transactions Between Readers and Writers." *The Reading Teacher,* 42 (April 1989), 608–611.

Moore, Margaret. "Electronic Dialoguing: An Avenue to Literacy." *The Reading Teacher,* 45 (December 1991), 280–286.

Moore, Sharon Arthur, and David W. Moore. "Literacy through Content/Content through Literacy." *The Reading Teacher,* 43 (November 1989), 170–171.

Moore, Sharon Arthur, David W. Moore, and Jeanne Swafford. "Reading and Mathematics Comprehension." *The Reading Teacher,* 44 (May 1991), 684–686.

"More Disabled Students Now in Regular Classes." *Reading Today,* 11 (April/May 1994), 28.

Morden, Dawn L. "Crossroads to the World." *Educational Leadership,* 51 (April 1994), 36–38.

Morrow, Lesley, Diane Tracey, and Caterina Maxwell, eds. *A Survey of Family Literacy in the United States.* Newark, Del.: International Reading Association, 1995.

Morrow, Lesley Mandel. "Manipulative Learning Materials: Merging Reading Skills with Content Area Objectives." *Journal of Reading,* 25 (February 1982), 448–453.

Morrow, Lesley Mandel. "Reading and Retelling Stories: Strategies for Emergent Readers." *The Reading Teacher,* 38 (May 1985), 870–875.

Morrow, Lesley Mandel. "Using Story Retelling to Develop Comprehension." In *Children's Comprehension of Text: Research into Practice,* edited by K. Denise Muth. Newark, Del.: International Reading Association, 1989.

Morrow, Lesley Mandel, and Susan B. Neuman. "Introduction: Family Literacy." *The Reading Teacher,* 48 (April 1995), 550–551.

Morrow, Lesley Mandel, and Diane H. Tracey. "Strategies Used for Phonics Instruction in Early Childhood Classes." *The Reading Teacher,* 50 (May 1997), 644–651.

Mosenthal, P. "Children's Strategy Preference for Resolving Contradictory Story Information under Two Social Conditions." *Journal of Experimental Child Psychology,* 28 (1979), 323–443.

Mosenthal, P. "Reading Comprehension Research from a Classroom Perspective." In *Promoting Reading Comprehension,* edited by J. Flood. Newark, Del.: International Reading Association, 1984.

Mosenthal, P., and T. J. Na. "Quality of Children's Recall under Two Classroom Testing Tasks: Toward a Socio-Psycholinguistic Model of Reading Comprehension." *Reading Research Quarterly,* 15 (1980a), 501–528.

Mosenthal P., and T. J. Na. "Quality of Text Recall as a Function of Children's Classroom Competence." *Journal of Experimental Child Psychology,* 30 (1980b), 1–21.

Mosenthal, Peter B. "Defining Reading: Freedom of Choice but Not Freedom from Choice." *The Reading Teacher,* 39 (October 1985), 110–112.

Mosenthal, Peter B. "Defining Reading: Operational Definitions and Other Oracles." *The Reading Teacher,* 39 (December 1985), 362–364.

Mosenthal, Peter B. "Defining Reading: Taxonomies and Stray Definitions." *The Reading Teacher,* 39 (November 1985), 238–240.

Mosenthal, Peter B. "Defining Reading: Translating Definitions of Reading in Research into Practice." *The Reading Teacher,* 39 (January 1986), 476–479.

Mosenthal, Peter B. "From Pyramid Taxonomy to Reading Theories: The Complexity of Simplification." *The Reading Teacher,* 39 (March 1986), 732–734.

Mosenthal, Peter B. "Improving Reading Practice with Reading Theory: The Procrustean Approach." *The Reading Teacher,* 40 (October 1986), 108–111.

Mosenthal, Peter B. "The Whole Language Approach: Teachers Between a Rock and a Hard Place." *The Reading Teacher,* 42 (April 1989), 628–629.

Mosenthal, Peter B., and Irwin S. Kirsch. "Understanding Documents: Understanding Graphs and Charts, Part I." *Journal of Reading,* 33 (February 1990), 371–373.

Mosenthal, Peter B., and Irwin S. Kirsch. "Understanding Documents: Understanding Graphs and Charts, Part II." *Journal of Reading,* 33 (March 1990), 454–457.

Mosenthal, Peter B., and Irwin S. Kirsch. "Understanding Documents: Understanding Thematic Maps." *Journal of Reading,* 34 (October 1990), 136–140.

Moss, Barbara. "Children's Nonfiction Trade Books: A Complement to Content Area Texts." *The Reading Teacher,* 45 (September 1991), 26–32.

Moss, Barbara, and Harry Noden. "Pointers for Putting Whole Language into Practice." *The Reading Teacher,* 47 (December 1993/January 1994), 342–344.

Moss, Joy F., and Sherri Oden. "Children's Story Comprehension and Story Learning." *The Reading Teacher,* 36 (April 1983), 784–789.

Mountain, Lee. "Math Synonyms." *The Reading Teacher,* 46 (February 1993), 451–452.

Moustafa, Margaret. *Beyond Traditional Phonics: Research Discoveries and Reading Instruction.* Portsmouth, N.H.: Heinemann, 1997.

Moustafa, Margaret. "Comprehensible Input PLUS the Language Experience Approach: A Longterm Perspective." *The Reading Teacher,* 41 (December 1987), 276–286.

Moustafa, Margaret. "Recoding in Whole Language Reading Instruction." *Language Arts,* 70 (October 1993), 483–487.

Moustafa, Margaret, and Joyce Penrose. "Comprehensible Input PLUS the Language Experience Approach: Reading Instruction for Limited English Speaking Students." *The Reading Teacher,* 38 (March 1985), 640–647.

Muller, Dorothy H., and Liz Savage. "Mapping the Library." *The Reading Teacher,* 35 (April 1982), 840–841.

Munson, Jennie Livingston. "Story and Poetry Maps." *The Reading Teacher,* 42 (May 1989), 736–737.

Nagy, William E. *Teaching Vocabulary to Improve Reading Comprehension.* Urbana, Ill.: National Council of Teachers of English, 1988.

Nagy, William E., and Richard C. Anderson. "How Many Words Are There in Printed School English?" *Reading Research Quarterly,* 19, no. 3 (1984), 304–330.

Nagy, William E., Patricia A. Herman, and Richard C. Anderson. "Learning Words from Context." *Reading Research Quarterly,* 20, no. 2 (1985), 233–253.

Naughton, Victoria M. "Creative Mapping for Content Reading." *Journal of Reading,* 37 (December 1993/January 1994), 324–326.

Neill, Monty. "Principles for 'Assessment.'" *Talking Points,* 8 (February-March 1997), 26–27.

Nelson, Carol. "Language Diversity and Language Arts." *ERIC Digest.* Bloomington, Ind.: Indiana University, June 1995.

Nelson-Herber, Joan. "Expanding and Defining Vocabulary in Content Areas." *Journal of Reading,* 29 (April 1986), 626–633.

Nessel, Denise D. "Storytelling in the Reading Program." *The Reading Teacher,* 38 (January 1985), 378–381.

Neuman, Susan B., and Patricia S. Koskinen. "Captioned Television as Comprehensible Input: Effects of Incidental Word Learning in Context for Language Minority Students." *Reading Research Quarterly,* 27 (1992), 95–106.

Neuman, Susan, and Kathleen Roskos. *Language and Literacy Learning in the Early Years.* Orlando: Harcourt Brace Jovanovich, 1993.

Neville, Rita. "Critical Thinkers Become Critical Readers." *The Reading Teacher,* 35 (May 1982), 947–948.

Newman, Judith. "Insights from Recent Reading and Writing Research and Their Implications for Developing Whole Language Curriculum." In *Whole Language: Theory in Use,* edited by Judith M. Newman. Portsmouth, N.H.: Heinemann, 1985.

Newman, Judith M. "Online: From Far Away." *Language Arts,* 66 (1989), 791–797.

Newman, Judith M. "The Computer Is Only Incidental." *Language Arts,* 67 (April 1990), 439–444.

Newman, Judith M., and Susan M. Church. "Myths of Whole Language." *The Reading Teacher,* 44 (September 1990), 20–26.

Nolan, Thomas E. "Self-Questioning and Prediction: Combining Metacognitive Strategies." *Journal of Reading,* 35 (October 1991), 132–138.

Nolte, Ruth Yopp, and Harry Singer. "Active Comprehension: Teaching a Process of Reading Comprehension and Its Effects on Reading Achievement." *The Reading Teacher,* 39 (October 1985), 24–31.

Noonan, Norma. "Parents as Partners in Reading Development." In *Readings on Reading Instruction,* 3d ed., edited by Albert J. Harris and Edward R. Sipay. New York: Longman, 1984.

Norton, Donna E. "Circa 1942 and the Integration of Literature, Reading, and Geography." *The Reading Teacher,* 46 (April 1993), 610–614.

Norton, Donna E. *The Impact of Literature-Based Reading.* New York: Merrill, 1992.

Norton, Donna E. "Modeling Inferencing of Characterization." *The Reading Teacher,* 46 (September 1992), 64–67.

Norton, Donna E. *Through the Eyes of a Child,* 4th ed. Columbus, Ohio: Merrill, 1995.

Norton, Donna E. "Understanding Plot Structures." *The Reading Teacher,* 46 (November 1992), 254–258.

Norton, Donna E. "Webbing and Historical Fiction." *The Reading Teacher,* 46 (February 1993), 432–436.

Noyce, Ruth M. "Team Up and Teach with Trade Books." *The Reading Teacher,* 32 (January 1979), 442–448.

Nurss, Joanne. "Evaluation of Language and Literacy." In *Emerging Literacy,* edited by Lloyd Ollila and Margie Mayfield. Boston: Allyn & Bacon, 1992, pp. 229–252.

O'Brien, Kathy, and Darleen K. Stoner. "Increasing Environmental Awareness through Children's Literature." *The Reading Teacher,* 41 (October 1987), 14–19.

Ogle, Donna M. "K-W-L: A Teaching Model that Develops Active Reading of Expository Text." *The Reading Teacher,* 39 (February 1986), 564–570.

Ogle, Donna M. "The Know, Want to Know, Learn Strategy." In *Children's Comprehension of Text: Research into Practice,* edited by K. Denise Muth. Newark, Del.: International Reading Association, 1989.

Oja, Leslie Anne. "Using Story Frames to Develop Reading Comprehension." *Journal of Adolescent and Adult Literacy,* 40 (October 1996), 129–130.

Oldfather, Penny. "Commentary: What's Needed to Maintain and Extend Motivation for Literacy in the Middle Grades." *Journal of Reading,* 36 (March 1995), 420–422.

Oldfather, Penny. "What Students Say about Motivating Experiences in a Whole Language Classroom." *The Reading Teacher,* 46 (May 1993), 672–681.

Oleneski, Sue. "Using Jump Rope Rhymes to Teach Reading Skills." *The Reading Teacher,* 46 (October 1992), 173–175.

Ollila, Lloyd O., and Margie I. Mayfield. *Emerging Literacy: Preschool, Kindergarten, and Primary Grades.* Boston: Allyn & Bacon, 1992, pp. 166–195.

Ollmann, Hilda E. "Creating Higher Level Thinking with Reading Response." *Journal of Adolescent & Adult Literacy,* 39 (April 1996), 576–581.

Ollmann, Hilda E. "Integrating Content Area Skills with Fiction Favorites." *Journal of Reading,* 34 (February 1991), 398–399.

Olson, Mary W., and Thomas C. Gee. "Content Reading Instruction in the Primary Grades: Perceptions and Strategies." *The Reading Teacher,* 45 (December 1991), 298–307.

O'Neil, John. "'Inclusive' Education Gains Adherents." *ASCD Update,* 35 (November 1993), 1, 3–4.

O'Neil, John. "Making Assessment Meaningful." *ASCD Update,* 36 (August 1994), 1, 4–5.

O'Neil, John. "Portfolio Assessment Bears the Burden of Popularity." *ASCD Update,* 35 (October 1993), 3, 8.

O'Neil, John. "The Promise of Portfolios." *ASCD Update,* 35 (September 1993), 1, 5.

"Open to Suggestion: Electronic Access to the Library of Congress in Washington, D.C." *Journal of Reading,* 37 (May 1994), 691.

Otto, Wayne, Anne Wolf, and Roger G. Eldridge. "Managing Instruction." In *Handbook of Reading Research,* edited by P. David Pearson et al. New York: Longman, 1984.

Ovando, Carlos J., and Virginia P. Collier. *Bilingual and ESL Classrooms.* New York: McGraw-Hill, 1985.

Owston, R. D., S. Murphy, and H. H. Wideman. "The Effects of Word Processing on Students' Writing Quality and Revision Strategies." *Research in the Teaching of English,* 26 (1992), 249–276.

Pace, Glennellen. "When Teachers Use Literature for Literacy Instruction: Ways That Constrain, Ways That Free." *Language Arts,* 68 (January 1991), 12–25.

Padek, Nancy D. "The Language and Educational Needs of Children Who Speak Black English." *The Reading Teacher,* 35 (November 1981), 144–151.

Paeth, Beverly, and others. "Kentucky Telecommunication Writing Program." Handout presented at the National Council of Teachers of English Convention, San Diego, 1995.

Pahl, Michele M., and Robert J. Monson. "In Search of Whole Language: Transforming Curriculum and Instruction." *Journal of Reading,* 35 (April 1992), 518–524.

Palincsar, Annemarie Sullivan, and Ann L. Brown. "Interactive Teaching to Promote Independent Learning from Text." *The Reading Teacher,* 39 (April 1986), 771–777.

Palmer, Barbara. "Dolch List Still Useful." *The Reading Teacher,* 38 (March 1985), 708–709.

Palmer, Barbara, Rose Marie Codling, and Linda Gambrell. "In Their Own Words: What Elementary Students Have to Say About Motivation to Read." *The Reading Teacher,* 48 (October 1994), 176–178.

Palmer, Gerry. "Process Writing Is Alive and Well." *Teaching K–8,* 20 (May 1990), 86–87.

Palmer, Rosemary G., and Roger A. Stewart. "Nonfiction Trade Books in Content Area Instruction: Realities and Potential." *Journal of Adolescent & Adult Literacy,* 40 (May 1997), 630–641.

Pardo, Laura S., and Taffy E. Raphael. "Classroom Organization for Instruction in Content Areas." *The Reading Teacher,* 44 (April 1991), 556–565.

Paris, Scott G., Barbara A. Wasik, and Julianne C. Turner. "The Development of Strategic Readers." In *Handbook of Reading Research, Vol. II,* edited by Rebecca Barr, Michael L. Kamil, Peter B. Mosenthal, and P. David Pearson. White Plains, N.Y.: Longman, 1991, pp. 609–640.

Parker, Emelie, Regla Armengol, Leigh Brooke, Kelly Carper, Sharon Cronin, Anne Denman, Patricia Irwin, Jennifer McGunnigle, Tess Pardini, and Nancy Kurtz. "Teachers' Choices in Classroom Assessment." *The Reading Teacher,* 48 (April 1995), 622–624.

Pearson, P. David. "Changing the Face of Comprehension Instruction." *The Reading Teacher,* 38 (April 1985), 724–738.

Pearson, P. David. "Focus on Research: Teaching and Learning Reading: A Research Perspective." *Language Arts,* 70 (October 1993), 502–511.

Pearson, P. David, et al. *The Effect of Background Knowledge on Young Children's Comprehension of Explicit and Implicit Information.* Urbana–Champaign, Ill.: University of Illinois, Center for the Study of Reading, 1979.

Pearson, P. David, and Kaybeth Camperell. "Comprehension of Text Structures." In *Comprehension and Teaching:*

Research Reviews, edited by John T. Guthrie. Newark, Del.: International Reading Association, 1981, 815–860.

Pearson, P. David, and Kaybeth Camperell. "Comprehension of Text Structures." In *Theoretical Models and Processes of Reading,* 4th ed., edited by Robert Ruddell, Martha Rapp Ruddell, and Harry Singer. Newark, Del.: International Reading Association, 1994, pp. 448–468.

Pearson, P. David, and Linda Fielding. "Comprehension Instruction." In *Handbook of Reading Research, Volume II,* edited by Rebecca Barr, Michael L. Kamil, Peter Mosenthal, and P. David Pearson. New York: Longman, 1991, 815–860.

Pearson, P. David, and Linda Fielding. "Comprehension Instruction." In *Theoretical Models and Processes of Reading,* 4th ed, edited by Robert Ruddell, Martha Rapp Ruddell, and Harry Singer. Newark, Del.: International Reading Association, 1994, 815–860.

Pearson, P. David, and Dale D. Johnson. *Teaching Reading Comprehension.* New York: Holt, Rinehart and Winston, 1978.

Peck, Jackie. "Using Storytelling to Promote Language and Literacy Development." *The Reading Teacher,* 43 (November 1989), 138–141.

Pehrsson, Robert, and Peter Denner. *Semantic Organizers: A Study Strategy for Special Needs Learners.* Rockville, Md.: Aspen, 1989.

Pelican Press. Fairfield, Conn.: Toucan, 1992.

Perry, Margaret. *Using Microcomputers with Gifted Students.* Bloomington, Ind.: Phi Delta Kappa, 1989.

Perry, Merry. *The New Talking Stickybear Alphabet. The Apple IIGS Buyer's Guide,* Fall 1989, 58–59.

Peters, Charles. "Commentary on Redesigning Teaching and Learning: The Arizona Student Assessment Program." In *Authentic Reading Assessment: Practices and Possibilities,* edited by Sheila Valencia, Elfrieda Hiebert, and Peter Afflerbach. Newark, Del.: International Reading Association, 1994, pp. 247–254.

Peters, L. *The Sun, the Wind, and the Rain.* New York: Holt, Rinehart and Winston, 1988.

Peterson, B. "Selecting Books for Beginning Readers." In *Bridges to Literacy: Learning from Reading Recovery,* edited by D. DeFord, C. Lyons, and G. S. Pinnell. Portsmouth, N.H.: Heinemann, 1991, pp. 119–147.

Peterson, Susan, and Patricia H. Phelps. "Visual-Auditory Links: A Structural Analysis Approach to Increase Word Power." *The Reading Teacher,* 44 (March 1991), 524–525.

Petrick, Pamela Bondi. "Creative Vocabulary Instruction in the Content Area." *Journal of Reading,* 35 (March 1992), 481–482.

Pettersen, Nancy-Laurel. "Grate/Great Homonym Hunt." *Journal of Reading,* 31 (January 1988), 374–375.

Pfiffner, Linda. *All About ADHD.* New York: Scholastic, 1996.

Pickert, Sarah M., and Martha L. Chase. "Story Retelling: An Informal Technique for Evaluating Children's Language." *The Reading Teacher,* 31 (February 1978), 528–531.

Pickett, Anna Lou, Stanley Vasa, and Allen Steckelberg. *Using Paraeducators Effectively in the Classroom.* Bloomington, Ind.: Phi Delta Kappa, 1993.

Piech, Pat. "Science Learning Centers: Seatwork Alternatives." *The Reading Teacher,* 44 (February 1991), 446–447.

Pierce, Kathryn Mitchell, and Kathy G. Short, eds. "Children's Books: Contemporary Social and Political Issues." *The Reading Teacher,* 47 (October 1993), 148–157.

Pierce, Kathryn Mitchell, and Kathy G. Short, eds. "Children's Books: Environmental Issues and Actions." *The Reading Teacher,* 47 (December 1993/January 1994), 328–335.

Pigg, John R. "The Effects of a Storytelling/Storyreading Program on the Language Skills of Rural Primary Students." Unpublished paper. Cookeville, Tenn.: Tennessee Technological University, 1986.

Pike, Kathy, Rita Compain, and Jean Mumper. *Connections: An Integrated Approach to Literacy.* New York: HarperCollins, 1994.

Pikulski, John. "The Assessment of Reading: A Time for Change?" *The Reading Teacher,* 43 (October 1989), 80–81.

Pikulski, John. "Preventing Reading Failure: A Review of Five Effective Programs." *The Reading Teacher,* 48 (September 1994), 30–39.

Pikulski, John. "The Role of Tests in a Literacy Assessment Program." *The Reading Teacher,* 43 (May 1990), 686–688.

Pikulski, John J. "Questions and Answers." *The Reading Teacher,* 42 (April 1989), 637.

Pinnell, Gay Su. *Restructuring Beginning Reading with the Reading Recovery Approach.* Bloomington, Ind.: Phi Delta Kappa, 1991.

Pittelman, Susan D., Joan E. Heimlich, Roberta L. Bergund, and Michael T. French. *Semantic Feature Analysis: Classroom Applications.* Newark, Del.: International Reading Association, 1990.

Phillips, Melissa. "Beyond the 'Best CDs' List." *Electronic Learning,* 15 (May/June 1996), 16.

Plisko, Valena White, and Joyce D. Stern, eds. "Educating Handicapped Students." *The Condition of Education.* Washington, D.C.: Statistical Report, National Center for Education Statistics, U.S. Department of Education, 1985.

Poe, Virginia L. "Mind Reading Made Easy: A Game for Practicing Word Recognition Skills." *The Reading Teacher,* 38 (April 1985), 822–824.

Poindexter, Candace. "Guessed Meanings." *Journal of Reading,* 37 (February 1994), 420–422.

Poole, Bernard J. *Education for an Information Age.* Boston: WCB/McGraw-Hill, 1997.

Popp, Marcia. *Learning Journals in the K–8 Classroom.* Mahwah, N.J.: Lawrence Erlbaum, 1997.

Powell, Janet L. "How Well Do Tests Measure Real Reading?" *ERIC Clearinghouse on Reading and Communication Skills* (June 1989), 1.

Powell, William R. "Teaching Vocabulary Through Opposition." *Journal of Reading,* 29 (April 1986), 617–621.

Preece, Alison. "Oral Language Competence and the Young Child." In *Emerging Literacy: Preschool, Kindergarten, and Primary Grades,* edited by Lloyd Ollila and Margie Mayfield. Needham Heights, Mass.: Allyn and Bacon, 1992, pp. 42–70.

Prill, Pat. "Helping Students Use the Classroom Library." *The Reading Teacher,* 48 (December 1994/January 1995), 365.

Prince, A. T., and D. S. Mancus. "Enriching Comprehension: A Schema-Altered Basal Reading Lesson." *Reading Research and Instruction,* 27, no. 1 (1987), 45–54.

Probst, Robert E. "Transactional Theory in the Teaching of Literature." *Journal of Reading,* 31 (January 1988), 378–381.

Prosise, Roger. *Beyond Rules and Consequences for Classroom Management.* Bloomington, Ind.: Phi Delta Kappa, 1996.

Pugh, Sharon L., and Jesus Garcia. "Portraits in Black: Establishing African American Identity Through Nonfiction Books." *Journal of Reading,* 34 (September 1990), 20–25.

Quiocho, Alice. "The Quest to Comprehend Expository Text: Applied Classroom Research." *Journal of Adolescent & Adult Literacy,* 40 (March 1997), 450–455.

Radebaugh, Muriel Rogie. "Using Children's Literature to Teach Mathematics." *The Reading Teacher,* 34 (May 1981), 902–906.

Radencich, Marguerite C. "Books That Promote Positive Attitudes Toward Second Language Learning." *The Reading Teacher,* 38 (February 1985), 528–530.

Ramsey, Patricia. *Teaching and Learning in a Diverse World.* New York: Teachers College Press, 1987.

Rand, Muriel K. "Story Schema: Theory, Research and Practice." *The Reading Teacher,* 37 (January 1984), 377–382.

Raphael, Taffy E. "Question-Answering Strategies for Children." *The Reading Teacher,* 36 (November 1982), 186–190.

Raphael, Taffy E. "Teaching Learners about Sources of Information for Answering Comprehension Questions." *Journal of Reading,* 27 (January 1984), 303–311.

Raphael, Taffy E. "Teaching Question-Answer Relationships, Revisited." *The Reading Teacher,* 39 (February 1986), 516–522.

Raphael, Taffy E., and P. David Pearson. *The Effect of Metacognitive Awareness Training on Children's Question Answering Behavior* (Technical Report No. 238). Urbana–Champaign, Ill.: University of Illinois, Center for the Study of Reading, 1982.

Raphael, Taffy, et al. "Research Directions: Literature and Discussion in the Reading Program." *Language Arts,* 69 (January 1992), 54–61.

Rasinski, Timothy V. "Mental Imagery Improves Comprehension." *The Reading Teacher,* 41 (April 1988), 867–868.

Rasinski, Timothy V. "The Role of Interest, Purpose, and Choice in Early Literacy." *The Reading Teacher,* 41 (January 1988), 396–400.

Rasinski, Timothy V., and Nancy D. Padak. "Multicultural Learning Through Children's Literature." *Language Arts,* 67 (October 1990), 576–580.

Readence, John E., R. Scott Baldwin, and Martha H. Head. "Direct Instruction in Processing Metaphors." *Journal of Reading Behavior,* 18, no. 4 (1986), 325–339.

Readence, John E., R. Scott Baldwin, and Martha H. Head. "Teaching Young Readers to Interpret Metaphors." *The Reading Teacher,* 40 (January 1987), 439–443.

Readence, John E., R. Scott Baldwin, Robert J. Rickelman, and G. Michael Miller. "The Effect of Vocabulary Instruction on Interpreting Metaphor." In *Solving Problems in Literacy: Learners, Teachers, and Researchers,* edited by Jerome A. Niles and Rosary V. Lalik. Rochester, N.Y.: National Reading Conference, 1986.

"Reading Recovery 1984–1988." Columbus, Ohio: The Ohio State University, 1988.

Reading/Language in Secondary Schools Subcommittee of IRA. "A Reading-Writing Connection in the Content Areas." *Journal of Reading,* 33 (February 1990), 376–378.

Reardon, S. Jeanne. "The Development of Critical Readers: A Look Into the Classroom." *The New Advocate,* 1, no. 1 (1988), 52–61.

Recht, Donna. "Teaching Summarizing Skills." *The Reading Teacher,* 37 (March 1984), 675–677.

Reed, Arthea J. S. *Comics to Classics: A Parent's Guide to Books for Teens and Preteens.* Newark, Del.: International Reading Association, 1988.

Reese, Colleen. "Story Development Using Wordless Picture Books." *The Reading Teacher,* 50 (October 1996), 172–173.

Reimer, Beck L. "Recipes for Language Experience Stories." *The Reading Teacher,* 36 (January 1983), 396–401.

Reinking, David. "Me and My Hypertext :) A Multiple Digression Analysis of Technology and Literacy (Sic)." *The Reading Teacher,* 50 (May 1997), 626–643.

Resnick, Lauren B. *Education and Learning to Think* (report). Washington, D.C.: National Academy Press, 1987.

Reutzel, D. Ray. "C[6]: A Reading Model for Teaching Arithmetic Story Problem Solving." *The Reading Teacher,* 37 (October 1983), 28–34.

Reutzel, D. Ray. "Reconciling Schema Theory and the Basal Reading Lesson." *The Reading Teacher,* 39 (November 1985), 194–197.

Reutzel, D. Ray. "Story Maps Improve Comprehension." *The Reading Teacher,* 38 (January 1985), 400–404.

Reutzel, D. Ray, and Robert Cooter. "Organizing for Effective Instruction: The Reading Workshop." *The Reading Teacher,* 44 (April 1991), 548–554.

Reutzel, D. Ray, and Parker C. Fawson. "Using a Literature Webbing Strategy Lesson with Predictable Books." *The Reading Teacher,* 43 (December 1989), 208–215.

Rhodes, Lynn K. "I Can Read! Predictable Books as Resources for Reading and Writing Instruction." *The Reading Teacher,* 34 (February 1981), 511–518.

Rhodes, Lynn K., and Curt Dudley-Marling. *Readers and Writers with a Difference.* Portsmouth, N.H.: Heinemann, 1988.

Rhodes, Lynn, and Sally Nathenson-Mejia. "Anecdotal Records: A Powerful Tool for Ongoing Literacy Assessment." *The Reading Teacher,* 45 (March 1992), 502–509.

Richards, Janet Clarke, and Joan P. Gipe. "Activating Background Knowledge: Strategies for Beginning and Poor Readers." *The Reading Teacher,* 45 (February 1992), 474–478.

Richek, Margaret Ann. "Relating Vocabulary Learning to World Knowledge." *Journal of Reading,* 32 (December 1988), 262–267.

Richek, Margaret, Lynne List, and Janet Lerner. *Reading Problems.* Englewood Cliffs, N.J.: Prentice-Hall, 1989.

Richgels, Donald. "Experimental Reading with Invented Spelling (ERIS): A Preschool and Kindergarten Method." *The Reading Teacher,* 40 (February 1987), 522–529.

Richgels, Donald, Karla Poremba, and Lea M. McGee. "Kindergartners Talk about Print: Phonemic Awareness in Meaningful Contexts." *The Reading Teacher,* 49 (May 1996), 632–642.

Richgels, Donald J., Lea M. McGee, and Edith A. Slaton. "Teaching Expository Text Structure in Reading and Writing." In *Children's Comprehension of Text: Research into Practice,* edited by K. Denise Muth. Newark, Del.: International Reading Association, 1989.

Richler, Howard. "Word Play: You're Likely to Be Clipped." *Notes Plus* (March 1996), 11–12.

Rickelman, Robert J., William A. Henk, and Stephen A. Melnick. "Electronic Encyclopedias on Compact Disk." *The Reading Teacher,* 44 (February 1991), 432–434.

Ridout, Susan Ramp. "Sing Your Way to Better Reading." *The Reading Teacher,* 42 (October 1988), 95.

Riel, M. "The Impact of Computers in Classrooms." *Journal of Research on Computing in Education* (1989), 180–189.

Roberts, Patricia. *Counting Books Are More Than Numbers: An Annotated Action Bibliography.* Hamden, CT.: Shoe String Press, 1990.

Roberts, Patricia. *A Green Dinosaur Day: A Guide for Developing Thematic Units in Literature-Based Instruction, K–6.* Boston: Allyn & Bacon, 1993.

Robertson, Julie Fisher, and Donna Rane-Szostak. "Using Dialogues to Develop Critical Thinking Skills." *Journal of Adolescent & Adult Literacy,* 39 (April 1996), 552–556.

Robinette, Michelle. *Mac Multimedia for Teachers.* Foster City, Calif.: IDG Books Wordwide, 1995.

Robinson, Francis P. *Effective Study,* rev. ed. New York: Harper & Row, 1961.

Robinson, H. Alan, Vincent Faraone, Daniel R. Hittleman, and Elizabeth Unruh. *Reading Comprehension Instruction: 1783–1987.* Newark, Del.: International Reading Association, 1990.

Rock, Heidi Marie, and Alysa Cummings. "Can Videodiscs Improve Student Outcomes?" *Educational Leadership,* 51 (April 1994), 46–50.

Roe, Betty D. *Report on Non-Instructional Assignment.* Cookeville, Tenn.: Tennessee Technological University, 1990.

Roe, Betty D. *Use of the Computer to Improve Writing Instruction in the Second Grade.* Cookeville, Tenn.: Rural Education Research and Service Consortium, 1987.

Roe, Betty D. *Use of Storytelling/Storyreading in Conjunction with Follow-up Language Activities to Improve Oral Communication of Rural First Grade Students: Phase I.* Cookeville, Tenn.: Rural Education Consortium, 1985.

Roe, Betty D. *Use of Storytelling/Storyreading in Conjunction with Follow-up Language Activities to Improve Oral Communication of Rural Primary Grade Students: Phase II.* Cookeville, Tenn.: Rural Education Consortium, 1986.

Roe, Betty D., and Sandy H. Smith. "University/Public Schools Keypals Project: A Collaborative Effort for Electronic Literature Conversations." In *Rethinking Teaching and Learning through Technology.* Proceedings of the Mid-South Instructional Technology Conference. Murfreesboro, Tenn.: Mid-South Technology Conference, 1997.

Roe, Betty D., Suellen Alfred, and Sandy Smith. *Teaching Through Stories: Yours, Mine, and Theirs.* Norwood, Mass.: Christopher-Gordon, 1998.

Roe, Mary F. "Reading Strategy Instruction: Complexities and Possibilities in Middle School." *Journal of Reading,* 36 (November 1992), 190–196.

Roehler, Laura, and Gerald Duffy. "Teachers' Instructional Actions." In *Handbook of Reading Research, Vol. II,* edited by Rebecca Barr, Michael L. Kamil, Peter B. Mosenthal, and P. David Pearson. White Plains, N.Y.: Longman, 1991, pp. 861–884.

Roehler, Laura R., Kathryn U. Foley, Mara T. Lud, and Carol A. Power. "Developing Integrated Programs." In *Reading in the Middle Schools,* 2d ed., edited by Gerald G. Duffy. Newark, Del.: International Reading Association, 1990.

Rogers, Wanda C. "Teaching for Poetic Thought." *The Reading Teacher,* 39 (December 1985), 296–300.

Roller, Cathy. *Variability Not Disability.* Newark, Del.: International Reading Association, 1996.

Romney, David M. *Dealing with Abnormal Behavior in the Classroom.* Bloomington, Ind.: Phi Delta Kappa, 1986.

Roney, R. Craig. "Background Experience Is the Foundation of Success in Learning to Read." *The Reading Teacher,* 38 (November 1984), 196–199.

Rose, David H., and Anne Meyer. "Focus on Research: The Role of Technology in Language Arts Instruction." *Language Arts,* 71 (April 1994), 290–294.

Rosenblatt, Louise M. *Literature as Exploration.* New York: Noble & Noble, 1938/1983.

Rosenblatt, Louise M. "Literature—S.O.S.!" *Language Arts,* 68 (1991), 444–448.

Rosenblatt, Louise M. *The Reader, the Text, and the Poem: The Transactional Theory of the Literary Work.* Carbondale, Ill.: Southern Illinois University Press, 1978.

Rosenblatt, Louise M. "The Transactional Theory of Reading and Writing." In *Theoretical Models and Processes of Reading,* 4th ed., edited by Robert B. Ruddell, Martha Rapp Ruddell, and Harry Singer. Newark, Del.: International Reading Association, 1994, pp. 1057–1092.

Rosenblatt, Louise M. "Viewpoints: Transaction Versus Interaction—A Terminological Rescue Operation." *Research in the Teaching of English,* 19 (February 1985), 96–107.

Rosenbloom, Cindy Shultz. "From *Ox-Cart Man* to *Little House in the Big Woods*: Response to Literature Shapes Curriculum." *Language Arts,* 68 (January 1991), 52–57.

Rosenholtz, Susan J., and Carl Simpson. "Classroom Organization and Student Stratification." *Elementary School Journal,* 85 (September 1984), 21–37.

Rosenshine, Barak, and Carla Meister. "Reciprocal Teaching: A Review of the Research." *Review of Educational Research,* 64 (Winter 1994), 479–530.

Rosenshine, Barak, and Robert Stevens. "Classroom Instruction in Reading." In *Handbook of Reading Research,* edited by P. David Pearson et al. New York: Longman, 1984.

Roser, N., and C. Juel. "Effects of Vocabulary Instruction on Reading Comprehension." In *New Inquiries in Reading Research and Instruction,* Thirty-First Yearbook of the National Reading Conference, edited by J. A. Niles and L. A. Harris. Rochester, N.Y.: National Reading Conference, 1982.

Roser, Nancy L., James Hoffman, Linda D. Labbo, and Cindy Forest. "Language Charts: A Record of Story Time Talk." *Language Arts,* 69 (January 1992), 44–52.

Roser, Nancy L., James V. Hoffman, and Cynthia Farest. "Language, Literature, and At-Risk Children." *The Reading Teacher,* 43 (April 1990), 554–559.

Roskos, Kathy, and Carol Vukelich. "Promoting Literacy in Play." *Day Care and Early Education,* 19 (Fall 1991), 30–34.

Ross, Elinor. *Using Children's Literature Across the Curriculum.* Bloomington, Ind.: Phi Delta Kappa, 1994.

Ross, Elinor. *The Workshop Approach: A Framework for Literacy.* Norwood, Mass.: Christopher-Gordon, 1996.

Ross, Elinor P. "Classroom Experiments with Oral Reading." *The Reading Teacher,* 40 (December 1986), 270–275.

Ross, Elinor Parry. "Checking the Source: An Essential Component of Critical Reading." *Journal of Reading,* 24 (January 1981), 311–315.

Rosso, Barbara Rak, and Robert Emans. "Children's Use of Phonic Generalizations." *The Reading Teacher,* 34 (March 1981), 653–657.

Rouse, Michael W., and Julie B. Ryan. "Teacher's Guide to Vision Problems." *The Reading Teacher,* 38 (December 1984), 306–307.

Routman, Regie. *Invitations.* Portsmouth, N.H.: Heinemann, 1994.

Rowe, Deborah, and Jerome C. Harste. "Metalinguistic Awareness in Writing and Reading: The Young Child as Curricular Informant." In *Metalinguistic Awareness and Beginning Literacy,* edited by David B. Yaden, Jr., and Shane Templeton. Portsmouth, N.H.: Heinemann Educational Books, 1986.

Rubin, Dorothy. *Diagnosis and Correction in Reading Instruction,* 3d ed. Boston: Allyn and Bacon, 1997.

Rubino, Ann. "The Science/Language Connection: Why to Make It . . . How to Do It." *The Reading Teacher,* 45 (November 1991), 248–249.

Ruddell, Robert B. "A Whole Language and Literature Perspective: Creating a Meaning-Making Instructional Environment." *Language Arts,* 69 (December 1992), 612–620.

Ruddell, Robert B., and Norman J. Unrau. "Reading as a Meaning-Construction Process: The Reader, the Text, and the Teacher." In *Theoretical Models and Processes of Reading,* 4th ed., edited by Robert B. Ruddell, Martha Rapp Ruddell, and Harry Singer. Newark, Del.: International Reading Association, 1994, 996–1056.

Ruddiman, Joan. "The Vocab Game: Empowering Students Through Word Awareness." *Journal of Reading,* 36 (February 1993), 400–401.

Ruiz, Nadine. "Effective Instruction for Language Minority Children with Mild Disabilities." *ERIC Digest* #E499, 3 pp., 1991.

Rule, Audrey, and Joan Atkinson. "Choosing Picture Books about Ecology." *The Reading Teacher,* 47 (April 1994), 586–591.

Rumelhart, David. *Toward an Interactive Model of Reading* (Technical Report 56). San Diego, Calif.: Center for Human Information Processing, March 1976.

Rumelhart, David E. "Schemata: The Building Blocks of Cognition." In *Comprehension and Teaching: Research Reviews,* edited by John T. Guthrie. Newark, Del.: International Reading Association, 1981.

Rush, R. Timothy. "Assessing Readability: Formulas and Alternatives." *The Reading Teacher,* 39 (December 1985), 274–283.

Russell, David L. *Literature for Children,* 2d ed. New York: Longman, 1994.

Sabey, Brenda, and Linda Squier. "Environmental Print: Trash or Treasure." *Contemporary Issues in Reading,* 9 (Fall 1993), 45–51.

Saccardi, Marianne. "Predictable Books: Gateways to a Lifetime of Reading." *The Reading Teacher,* 49 (April 1996), 588–590.

Saccardi, Marianne C. "Predictable Books: Gateways to a Lifetime of Reading." *The Reading Teacher,* 49 (May 1996), 632–642.

Sadow, Marilyn W. "The Use of Story Grammar in the Design of Questions." *The Reading Teacher,* 35 (February 1982), 518–522.

Salinger, Terry S. *Literacy for Young Children,* 2d ed. Englewood Cliffs, N.J.: Merrill, 1996.

Sameroff, Arnold, and Susan McDonough. "Educational Implications of Developmental Transitions: The 5- to 7-Year Shift." In *Early Childhood Education 96/97,* edited by Karen Paciorek and Joyce Munro. Guilford, Conn.: Dushkin, 1996–1997, pp. 40–44.

Sammons, Rebecca Bell, and Beth Davey. "Assessing Students' Skills in Using Textbooks: The Textbook Awareness and Performance Profile." *Journal of Reading,* 37 (December 1993/January 1994), 280–286.

Sampson, Mary Beth, Michael R. Sampson, and Wayne Linek. "Circle of Questions." *The Reading Teacher,* 48 (December 1994/January 1995), 364–365.

Samuels, S. Jay. "Decoding and Automaticity: Helping Poor Readers Become Automatic at Word Recognition." *The Reading Teacher,* 41 (April 1988), 756–760.

Samuels, S. Jay. "Toward a Theory of Automatic Information Processing in Reading, Revisited." In *Theoretical Models and Processes of Reading,* 4th ed., edited by Robert B. Ruddell, Martha Rapp Ruddell, and Harry Singer. Newark, Del.: International Reading Association, 1994, pp. 816–837.

Samuels, S. Jay, and Sumner W. Schachter. "Controversial Issues in Beginning Reading Instruction: Meaning Versus Subskill Emphasis." In *Readings on Reading Instruction,* edited by Albert J. Harris and Edward R. Sipay. New York: Longman, 1984.

Samway, Katherine Davies, et al. "Reading the Skeleton, the Heart, and the Brain of a Book: Students' Perspectives on Literature Study Circles." *The Reading Teacher,* 45 (November 1991), 196–205.

Sanacore, Joseph. "Creating the Lifetime Reading Habit in Social Studies." *Journal of Reading,* 33 (March 1990), 414–418.

Sandholtz, Judith Haymore, Cathy Ringstaff, and David C. Dwyer. *Teaching with Technology.* New York: Teachers College Press, 1997.

Santino, Betsy H. "Improving Multicultural Awareness and Story Comprehension with Folktales." *The Reading Teacher,* 45 (September 1991), 77–79.

Savage, John F. *Teaching Reading Using Literature.* Madison, Wis.: WCB Brown & Benchmark, 1994.

Sawyer, John Michael. "Using Media Knowledge to Enhance the Literary Schema of Literarily Impoverished Students." *Journal of Reading,* 37 (May 1994), 683–684.

Scala, Marilyn. "What Whole Language in the Mainstream Means for Children with Learning Disabilities." *The Reading Teacher,* 47 (November 1993), 222–229.

Schachter, Sumner W. "Using Workbook Pages More Effectively." *The Reading Teacher,* 35 (October 1981), 34–37.

Scharer, Patricia L., and Deana B. Detwiler. "Changing as Teachers: Perils and Possibilities of Literature-Based Language Arts Instruction." *Language Arts,* 69 (March 1992), 186–192.

Schatz, Elinore K., and R. Scott Baldwin. "Context Clues Are Unreliable Predictors of Word Meanings." *Reading Research Quarterly,* 21, no. 4 (1986), 439–453.

Schaudt, Barbara A. "Another Look at Sustained Silent Reading." *The Reading Teacher,* 36 (May 1983), 934–936.

Schell, Leo M. "Teaching Decoding to Remedial Readers." *Journal of Reading,* 31 (May 1978), 877–882.

Schell, Vicki J. "Learning Partners: Reading and Mathematics." *The Reading Teacher,* 35 (February 1982), 544–548.

Schifini, Alfredo. "Language, Literacy, and Content Instruction: Strategies for Teachers." In *Kids Come in All Languages: Reading Instruction for ESL Students,* edited by Karen Spangenberg-Urbschat and Robert Pritchard. Newark, Del.: International Reading Association, 1994, pp. 158–179.

Schipper, D., and K. Vincent. *Alexander and the Terrible, Horrible, No Good, Very Bad Day.* Pleasantville, N.Y.: Sunburst Communications, 1991.

Schmitt, M. C., and D. O'Brien. "Story Grammars: Some Cautions about the Translation of Research into Practice." *Reading Research Quarterly,* 26, no. 1 (1986), 1–8.

Schmitt, Maribeth Cassidy, and James F. Baumann. "How to Incorporate Comprehension Monitoring Strategies into Basal Reader Instruction." *The Reading Teacher,* 40 (October 1986), 28–31.

Schoenfeld, Florence G. "Instructional Uses of the Cloze Procedure." *The Reading Teacher,* 34 (November 1980), 147–151.

Schuder, Ted, Suzanne F. Clewell, and Nan Jackson. "Getting the Gist of Expository Text." In *Children's Comprehension of Text: Research into Practice,* edited by K. Denise Muth. Newark, Del.: International Reading Association, 1989.

Schumm, Jeanne Shay. "Overcoming Students' Misconceptions about Science." *Journal of Reading,* 35 (October 1991), 161.

Schumm, Jeanne Shay, and Linda Saumell. "Aliteracy: We Know It Is a Problem, But Where Does It Start?" *Journal of Reading,* 37 (May 1994), 701.

Schumm, Jeanne Shay, and Linda Saumell. "Word Processors: Their Impact on Process and Product." *Journal of Reading,* 37 (November 1993), 190.

Schwartz, David M. *How Much Is a Million?* New York: Scholastic, 1985.

Schwartz, Robert M. "Learning to Learn Vocabulary in Content Area Textbooks." *Journal of Reading,* 32 (November 1988), 108–118.

Schwartz, Robert M., and Taffy E. Raphael. "Concept of Definition: A Key to Improving Students' Vocabulary." *The Reading Teacher,* 39 (November 1985), 198–205.

Sears, Sue, Cathy Carpenter, and Nancy Burstein. "Meaningful Reading Instruction for Learners with Special Needs." *The Reading Teacher,* 47 (May 1994), 632–638.

Sebesta, Sam Leaton, James William Calder, and Lynne Nelson Cleland. "A Story Grammar for the Classroom." *The Reading Teacher,* 36 (November 1982), 180–184.

Seda, Ileana, and P. David Pearson. "Interviews to Assess Learners' Outcomes." *Reading Research and Instruction,* 31 (Fall 1991), 22–32.

Sedlak, Robert A., and Denise M. Sedlak. *Teaching the Educable Mentally Retarded.* Albany, N.Y.: State University of New York Press, 1985.

Seitz, Ernest R., Jr. "Using Media Presentations to Teach Notetaking, Main Idea, and Summarization Skills." *Journal of Adolescent and Adult Literacy,* 40 (April 1997), 562–563.

Seminoff, Nancy Wiseman. "Children's Periodicals Throughout the World: An Overlooked Educational Resource." *The Reading Teacher,* 39 (May 1986), 889–895.

Sensenbaugh, Roger. "Reading Recovery." *ERIC Digest.* Bloomington, Ind.: Indiana University, September, 1995.

Serafini, Frank. "Stances to Assessment." *Talking Points,* 8 (February–March 1997), 2–4.

Serebrin, Wayne. "A Writer and an Author Collaborate." *Language Arts,* 63 (March 1986), 281–283.

Serim, Ferdi, and Melissa Koch. *Netlearning: Why Teachers Use the Internet.* Sebastopol, Calif.: Songline Studios, Inc., and O'Reilly & Associates, 1996.

Shanahan, Timothy. "Predictions and the Limiting Effects of Prequestions." In *Solving Problems in Literacy: Learners, Teachers, and Researchers,* edited by Jerome A. Niles and Rosary V. Lalik. Rochester, N.Y.: National Reading Conference, 1986.

Shanahan, Timothy, Bonita Robinson, and Mary Schneider. "Avoiding Some of the Pitfalls of Thematic Units." *The Reading Teacher,* 48 (May 1995), 718–719.

Shanahan, Timothy, Bonita Robinson, and Mary Schneider. "Integrating Curriculum." *The Reading Teacher,* 48 (May 1995), 718–719.

Shanklin, Nancy L., and Lynn K. Rhodes. "Comprehension Instruction as Sharing and Extending." *The Reading Teacher,* 42 (March 1989), 496–500.

Shannon, Patrick. "Commentary: Teachers Are Researchers." In *Opening the Door to Classroom Research,* edited by Mary W. Olson. Newark, Del.: International Reading Association, 1990.

Sharp, Peggy Agostino. "Teaching with Picture Books Throughout the Curriculum." *The Reading Teacher,* 38 (November 1984), 132–137.

Shaw, Evelyn. "A Novel Journal." *The Reading Teacher,* 41 (January 1988), 489.

Shepard, Lorrie. "Why We Need Better Assessments." *Educational Leadership,* 46 (April 1989), 4–9.

Shoop, Mary. "InQuest: A Listening and Reading Comprehension Strategy." *The Reading Teacher,* 39 (March 1986), 670–674.

Short, Kathy, and Gloria Kauffman. "'So What Do *I* Do?': The Role of the Teacher in Literature Circles." In *Book Talk and Beyond,* edited by Nancy Roser and Miriam Martinez. Newark, Del.: International Reading Association, 1995.

Silvers, Penny. "Process Writing and the Reading Connection." *The Reading Teacher,* 39 (March 1986), 684–688.

Silverstein, Alvin, and Virginia Silverstein. *Life in a Tidal Pool.* Boston: Little, Brown, 1990.

Simpson, Anne. "Critical Questions: Whose Questions?" *The Reading Teacher,* 50 (October 1996), 118–127.

Sinatra, Richard, and Cornelia Dowd. "Using Syntactic and Semantic Clues to Learn Vocabulary." *Journal of Reading,* 35 (November 1991), 224–229.

Singer, Harry. "The Substrata-Factor Theory of Reading." In *Theoretical Models and Processes of Reading,* 4th ed., edited by Robert B. Ruddell, Martha Rapp Ruddell, and Harry Singer. Newark, Del.: International Reading Association, 1994, pp. 895–927.

Singer, Harry, John D. McNeil, and Lory L. Furse. "Relationship Between Curriculum Scope and Reading Achievement in Elementary Schools." *The Reading Teacher,* 37 (March 1984), 608–612.

Sippola, Arne E. "K-W-L-S." *The Reading Teacher,* 48 (March 1995), 542–543.

Sippola, Arne E. "What to Teach for Reading Readiness—A Research Review and Materials Inventory." *The Reading Teacher,* 39 (November 1985), 162–167.

Slater, Wayne H., and Michael F. Graves. "Research on Expository Text: Implications for Teachers." In *Children's Comprehension of Text: Research into Practice,* edited by K. Denise Muth. Newark, Del.: International Reading Association, 1989.

Slaughter, Helen B. "Indirect and Direct Teaching in a Whole Language Program." *The Reading Teacher,* 42 (October 1988), 30–34.

Slavin, Robert. "Research on Cooperative Learning: Consensus and Controversy." *Educational Leadership,* 47 (December 1989/January 1990), 52–54.

Slavin, Robert. "Synthesis of Research on Cooperative Learning." *Educational Leadership,* 48 (February 1991), 71–82.

Slavin, Robert. "Synthesis of Research on Grouping in Elementary and Secondary Schools." *Educational Leadership,* 47 (September 1988), 67–77.

Slavin, Robert, Nancy Madden, and Robert Stevens. "Cooperative Learning Models for the 3R's." *Educational Leadership,* 47 (December 1989/January 1990), 22–28.

Slavin, Robert E. "IBM's Writing to Read: Is It Right for Reading?" *Phi Delta Kappan,* 72 (November 1990), 214–216.

Slavin, Robert E., Nancy L. Karweit, and Barbara A. Wasik. "Preventing Early School Failure: What Works?" *Educational Leadership,* 50 (December 1992/January 1993), 10–18.

Slavin, Robert E., Nancy A. Madden, Nancy L. Karweit, Lawrence J. Dolan, and Barbara A. Wasik. "Success for All: Getting Reading Right the First Time." In *Getting Reading Right from the Start,* edited by Elfrieda H. Hiebert and Barbara M. Taylor. Boston: Allyn & Bacon, 1994, pp. 125–147.

Smardo, Frances A. "Using Children's Literature to Clarify Science Concepts in Early Childhood Programs." *The Reading Teacher,* 36 (December 1982), 267–273.

Smelter, Richard, Bradley Rasch, and Gary Yudewitz. "Thinking of Inclusion for All Special Needs Students? Better Think Again." *Phi Delta Kappan,* 76 (September 1994), 35–38.

Smit, Edna K. "Teaching Theme to Elementary Students." *The Reading Teacher,* 43 (May 1990), 699–701.

Smith, Carl. "Shared Learning Promotes Critical Reading." *The Reading Teacher,* 43 (October 1989), 76–77.

Smith, Carl. "Teachers as Decision Makers." *The Reading Teacher,* 42 (April 1989), 632.

Smith, Carl, and Roger Sensenbaugh. "Helping Children Overcome Reading Difficulties." *ERIC Digest.* Bloomington, Ind.: ERIC Clearinghouse on Reading and Communication Skills, 1992. [ED344190]

Smith, Carl B. "Building a Better Vocabulary." *The Reading Teacher,* 42 (December 1988), 238.

Smith, Carl B. "Learning Through Writing." *The Reading Teacher,* 43 (November 1989), 172–173.

Smith, Carl B. "Prompting Critical Thinking." *The Reading Teacher,* 42 (February 1989), 424.

Smith, Carl B. "The Role of Different Literary Genres." *The Reading Teacher,* 44 (February 1991), 440–441.

Smith, Carl B. "Vocabulary Development in Content Area Reading." *The Reading Teacher,* 43 (March 1990), 508–509.

Smith, Frank. *Essays into Literacy.* Exeter, N.H.: Heinemann, 1983.

Smith, Frank. *Understanding Reading.* 4th ed. Hillsdale, N.J.: Lawrence Erlbaum, 1988.

Smith, J. Lea, and Holly Johnson. "Models for Implementing Literature in Content Studies." *The Reading Teacher,* 48 (November 1994), 198–209.

Smith, Jamie. "DISKovery: Goin' Wild in HyperCard." *Language Arts,* 68 (December 1991), 674–680.

Smith, Marilyn, and Thomas W. Bean. "Four Strategies That Develop Children's Story Comprehension and Writing." *The Reading Teacher,* 37 (December 1983), 295–301.

Smith, Nancy J., M. Jean Greenlaw, and Carolyn J. Scott. "Making the Literate Environment Equitable." *The Reading Teacher,* 40 (January 1987), 400–407.

Smith, Richard J., et al. *The School Reading Program.* Boston: Houghton Mifflin, 1978.

Smith, William Earl, and Michael D. Beck. "Determining Instructional Reading Level with the 1978 Metropolitan Achievement Tests." *The Reading Teacher,* 34 (December 1980), 313–319.

Smolkin, Laura, and David Yaden, Jr. "*O* Is for Mouse: First Encounters with the Alphabet Book." *Language Arts,* 69 (October 1992), 432–441.

Smyers, Teresa. "Add SQ to the DRTA—Write." *The Reading Teacher,* 41 (December 1987), 372–374.

Solem, Maizie. "Junior First Grade: A Year to Get Ready." In *Prototypes,* edited by Stanley Elam. Bloomington, Ind.: Phi Delta Kappa, 1989.

Sorenson, Nancy L. "Basal Reading Vocabulary Instruction: A Critique and Suggestions." *The Reading Teacher,* 39 (October 1985), 80–85.

Spache, George D. *Good Reading for Poor Readers,* 6th ed. Champaign, Ill.: Garrard Press, 1966.

Spiegel, Dixie Lee. "Adaptability and Flexibility of Literature Resource Materials." *The Reading Teacher,* 43 (April 1990), 590–592.

Spiegel, Dixie Lee. "Blending Whole Language and Systematic Direct Instruction." *The Reading Teacher,* 46 (September 1992), 38–44.

Spiegel, Dixie Lee. "Comprehension Materials: Quality of Directions and Instructional Language." *The Reading Teacher,* 43 (March 1990), 502–504.

Spiegel, Dixie Lee. "Content Bias in Reference and Study Skills." *The Reading Teacher,* 44 (September 1990), 64–66.

Spiegel, Dixie Lee. "Critical Reading Materials: A Review of Three Criteria." *The Reading Teacher,* 43 (February 1990), 410–412.

Spiegel, Dixie Lee. "Decoding and Comprehension Games." *The Reading Teacher,* 44 (November 1990), 258–261.

Spiegel, Dixie Lee. "Materials for Integrating Science and Social Studies with the Language Arts." *The Reading Teacher,* 44 (October 1990), 162–165.

Spiegel, Dixie Lee. "Materials to Introduce Children to Poetry." *The Reading Teacher,* 44 (February 1991), 428–430.

Spiegel, Dixie Lee. "Materials to Promote Vocabulary Development." *The Reading Teacher,* 44 (March 1991), 504–507.

Spiegel, Dixie Lee. "Reinforcement in Phonics Materials." *The Reading Teacher,* 43 (January 1990), 328–329.

Spiegel, Dixie Lee. "The Role of Trust in Reader-Response Groups." *Language Arts,* 73 (September 1996), 332–339.

Spiegel, Dixie Lee. "Six Alternatives to the Directed Reading Activity." *The Reading Teacher,* 34 (May 1981), 914–920.

Spiegel, Dixie Lee, and Jill Fitzgerald. "Improving Reading Comprehension Through Instruction about Story Parts." *The Reading Teacher,* 39 (March 1986), 676–682.

Spiro, Rand J. *Etiology of Comprehension Style.* Urbana–Champaign, Ill.: University of Illinois, Center for the Study of Reading, 1979.

Squire, James. "Composing and Comprehending: Two Sides of the Same Basic Process." *Language Arts,* 60 (May 1983), 581–589.

Stahl, Steven A. "Saying the 'P' Word: Nine Guidelines for Exemplary Phonics Instruction." *The Reading Teacher,* 45 (April 1992), 618–625.

Stahl, Steven A. "Separating the Rhetoric from the Effects: Whole Langauage in Kindergarten and First Grade." In *Reading, Language, and Literacy: Instruction for the Twenty-first Century,* edited by F. Lehr and J. Osborn. Hillsdale, N.J.: Lawrence Erlbaum, 1994, pp. 101–114.

Stahl, Steven A. "Three Principles of Effective Vocabulary Instruction." *Journal of Reading,* 29 (April 1986), 662–668.

Stahl, Steven A., and Barbara A. Kapinus. "Possible Sentences: Predicting Word Meanings to Teach Content Area Vocabulary." *The Reading Teacher,* 45 (September 1991), 36–43.

Stahl, Steven A., Jean Osborn, and Fran Lehr. *Beginning to Read: Thinking and Learning about Print—A Summary.* Champaign, Ill.: University of Illinois, Center for the Study of Reading, 1990.

Stahl, Steven A., and Sandra J. Vancil. "Discussion Is What Makes Semantic Maps Work in Vocabulary Instruction." *The Reading Teacher,* 40 (October 1986), 62–67.

Stahl-Gemake, Josephine, and Francine Guastello. "Using Story Grammar with Students of English as a Foreign Language to Compose Original Fairy and Folktales." *The Reading Teacher.* 38 (November 1984), 213–216.

Standards for the Assessment of Reading and Writing. Prepared by the IRA/NCTE Joint Task Force on Assessment. Newark, Del.: International Reading Association, 1994.

Standards for the English Language Arts. Newark, Del.: International Reading Association and Urbana, Ill.: National Council of Teachers of English, 1996.

Stanger, D., P. Elseth, and S. Clough. *Magic Slate II.* Pleasantville, N.Y.: Sunburst Communications, 1988.

Stanovich, Keith. "Romance and Reality." *The Reading Teacher,* 47 (December 1993/January 1994), 280–291.

Staton, Jana. "ERIC/RCS Report: Dialogue Journals." *Language Arts,* 65 (February 1988), 198–201.

Stauffer, Russell G. "Reading as a Cognitive Process." *Elementary English,* 44 (April 1968), 348.

Stauffer, Russell G. *Teaching Reading as a Thinking Process.* New York: Harper & Row, 1969.

Stetson, Elton G., and Richard P. Williams. "Learning from Social Studies Textbooks: Why Some Students Succeed and Others Fail." *Journal of Reading,* 36 (September 1992), 22–30.

Stevens, Kathleen C. "Can We Improve Reading by Teaching Background Information?" *Journal of Reading,* 25 (January 1982), 326–329.

Stewart, Oran, and Dan S. Green. "Test-Taking Skills for Standardized Tests of Reading." *The Reading Teacher,* 36 (March 1983), 634–638.

Stewart, Roger A., Edward E. Paradis, Bonita D. Ross, and Mary Jane Lewis. "Student Voices: What Works in Literature-Based Developmental Reading." *Journal of Adolescent and Adult Literacy,* 39 (March 1996), 468–478.

Stewig, John Warren. *Children and Literature.* Chicago: Rand McNally, 1980.

Stice, Carole, and Nancy Bertrand. *Whole Language and the Emergent Literacy of At-Risk Children: A Two Year Comparative Study.* Nashville, Tenn.: Center of Excellence: Basic Skills, June, 1990.

Stivers, Jan. "The Writing Partners Project." *Phi Delta Kappan,* 77 (June 1996), 694–695.

Stoll, Donald R., ed. *Magazines for Kids and Teens,* rev. ed., Glassboro, N.J.: Educational Press Association of America and Newark, Del.: International Reading Association, 1997.

Storey, Dee C. "Reading in the Content Areas: Fictionalized Biographies and Diaries for Social Studies." *The Reading Teacher,* 35 (April 1982), 796–798.

Stotsky, Sandra. "Research on Reading/Writing Relationships: A Synthesis and Suggested Directions." *Language Arts,* 60 (May 1983), 627–642.

Stowell, Laura, and Robert Tierney. "Portfolios in the Classroom: What Happens When Teachers and Students Negotiate Assessment?" In *No Quick Fix,* edited by Richard Allington and Sean Walmsley. Newark, Del.: International Reading Association, 1995, 78–94.

Strange, Michael. "Instructional Implications of a Conceptual Theory of Reading Comprehension." *The Reading Teacher,* 33 (January 1980), 391–397.

Strickland, Dorothy. "Emergent Literacy: How Young Children Learn to Read and Write." *Educational Leadership,* 47 (March 1990), 18–23.

Strickland, Dorothy. "Some Tips for Using Big Books." *The Reading Teacher,* 41 (May 1988), 966–968.

Strickland, Dorothy, and Lesley Morrow. "Creating a Print Rich Environment." *The Reading Teacher,* 42 (November 1988), 156–157.

Strickland, Dorothy, and Lesley Morrow. "The Daily Journal: Using Language Experience Strategies in an Emergent Literacy Curriculum." *The Reading Teacher,* 43 (February 1990), 422–423.

Strickland, Dorothy, and Lesley Morrow. "Family Literacy: Sharing Good Books." *The Reading Teacher,* 43 (March 1990), 518–519.

Strickland, Dorothy, and Lesley Morrow. "New Perspectives on Young Children Learning to Read and Write." *The Reading Teacher,* 43 (October 1988), 70–71.

Strickland, Dorothy S. "Reinventing Our Literacy Programs: Books, Basics, Balance." *The Reading Teacher,* 48 (December 1994/January 1995), 294–302.

Strickland, Dorothy S. "The Teacher as Researcher: Toward the Extended Professional." *Language Arts,* 65 (December 1988), 754–764.

Strickland, Dorothy S., and Bernice E. Cullinan. "Literature and Language." *Language Arts,* 63 (March 1986), 221–225.

Strickland, Dorothy S., Rose M. Dillon, Leslie Funkhouser, Mary Glick, and Corrine Rogers. "Research Currents: Classroom Dialogue during Literature Response Groups." *Language Arts,* 66 (February 1989), 192–205.

Strickland, Dorothy S., and Lesley Mandel Morrow. "Integrating the Emergent Literacy Curriculum with Themes." *The Reading Teacher,* 43 (April 1990), 604–605.

Strube, Penny. *Getting the Most from Literature Groups.* New York: Scholastic, 1996.

Sudol, Peg, and Caryn King. "A Checklist for Choosing Nonfiction Trade Books." *The Reading Teacher,* 49 (February 1996), 422–424.

Sugarman, Jay, James Allen, and Meg Keller-Cogan. "Make Authentic Assessment Work for You." *Instructor,* 103 (July/August 1993), 66–68.

Sullivan, Joanne. "The Global Method: Language Experience in the Content Areas." *The Reading Teacher,* 39 (March 1986), 664–668.

Sulzby, Elizabeth. "I Can Write! Encouraging Emergent Writers." In *Early Childhood Education 94/95,* 15th ed., edited by Karen M. Paciorek and Joyce H. Munro. Guilford, Conn.: Dushkin, 1994, 204–207.

Sulzby, Elizabeth. "Using Children's Dictated Stories to Aid Comprehension." *The Reading Teacher,* 33 (April 1980), 772–778.

Sulzby, Elizabeth, and William Teale. "Emergent Literacy." In *Handbook of Reading Research, Vol. II,* edited by Rebecca Barr, Michael L. Kamil, Peter B. Mosenthal, and P. David Pearson. White Plains, N.Y.: Longman, 1991, pp. 727–758.

Sulzby, Elizabeth, William H. Teale, and George Kamberelis. "Emergent Writing in the Classroom: Home and School Connections." In *Emerging Literacy,* edited by Dorothy Strickland and Lesley Morrow. Newark, Del.: International Reading Association, 1989.

Sumara, Dennis, and Laurie Walker. "The Teacher's Role in Whole Language." *Language Arts,* 68 (April 1991), 276–285.

Sweet, M. *The Scholastic Process Writer.* New York: Scholastic, 1990.

"A Talk with Marilyn Adams." *Language Arts,* 68 (March 1991), 206–212.

Taylor, Barbara M. "A Summarizing Strategy to Improve Middle Grade Students' Reading and Writing Skills." *The Reading Teacher,* 36 (November 1982), 202–205.

Taylor, Barbara, and Elfrieda Hiebert. "Early Literacy Interventions: Aims and Issues." In *Getting Ready Right from the Start,* edited by Elfrieda Hiebert and Barbara Taylor. Boston: Allyn & Bacon, 1994, pp. 3–11.

Taylor, Barbara M., and Linda Nosbush. "Oral Reading for Meaning: A Technique for Word Identification." *The Reading Teacher,* 37 (December 1983), 234–237.

Taylor, Denny, and Dorothy S. Strickland. *Family Storybook Reading.* Portsmouth, N.H.: Heinemann, 1986.

Tchudi, Susan. *Integrated Language Arts in the Elementary School.* Belmont, Calif.: Wadsworth, 1994.

Teale, William, and Elizabeth Sulzby. "Emergent Literacy: New Perspectives." In *Emerging Literacy: Young Children Learn to Read and Write,* edited by Dorothy Strickland and Lesley Morrow. Newark, Del.: International Reading Association, 1989.

Teale, William H., and Elizabeth Sulzby. *Emergent Literacy: Writing and Reading.* Norwood, N.J.: Ablex, 1986.

Temple, Charles, Ruth Nathan, Nancy Burris, and Frances Temple. *The Beginnings of Writing,* 2d ed. Boston: Allyn and Bacon, 1988.

Templeton, Shane. "Literacy, Readiness, and Basals." *The Reading Teacher,* 39 (January 1986), 403–409.

Thames, D. G., and J. E. Readence. "Effects of Differential Vocabulary Instruction and Lesson Frameworks on the Reading Comprehension of Primary Children." *Reading Research and Instruction,* 27, no. 2 (1988), 1–12.

Thelen, Judith N. "Vocabulary Instruction and Meaningful Learning." *Journal of Reading,* 29 (April 1986), 603–609.

Thompson, Deborah L. "The Alphabet Book as a Content Area Resource." *The Reading Teacher,* 46 (November 1992), 266–267.

Thompson, Stephen J. "Teaching Metaphoric Language: An Instructional Strategy." *Journal of Reading,* 30 (November 1986), 105–109.

Thonis, Eleanor Wall. "Teaching English as a Second Language." *Reading Today,* 7 (February/March 1990), 8.

Tierney, R. J., and T. Shanahan. "Research on the Reading-Writing Relationship: Interactions, Transactions, and Outcomes." In *Handbook of Reading Research, Vol. II,* edited by R. Barr, J. L. Kamil, P. Mosenthal, and P. D. Pearson et al. New York: Longman, 1991, pp. 246–280.

Tierney, Robert J., and James W. Cunningham. "Research on Teaching Reading Comprehension." In *Handbook of Reading Research,* edited by P. David Pearson et al. New York: Longman, 1984.

Tierney, Robert J., and P. David Pearson. "A Revisionist Perspective on 'Learning to Learn from Text: A Framework for Improving Classroom Practice.'" In *Theoretical Models and Processes of Reading,* 4th ed., edited by Robert Ruddell, Martha Rapp Ruddell, and Harry Singer. Newark, Del.: International Reading Association, 1994, pp. 514–519.

Tinajero, Josefina. "Are We Communicating? Effective Instruction for Students Who Are Acquiring English as a Second Language." *The Reading Teacher,* 48 (November 1994), 260–264.

Tipton, Juanita. "Extending Context Clues to Composition and Cooperative Learning." *Journal of Reading,* 35 (September 1991), 50.

Tompkins, Gail E., and Lea M. McGee. *Teaching Reading with Literature.* New York: Merrill, 1993.

Tompkins, Gail E., and Lea M. McGee. "Teaching Repetition as a Story Structure." In *Children's Comprehension of Text: Research into Practice,* edited by K. Denise Muth. Newark, Del.: International Reading Association, 1989.

Topping, Keith. "Peer Tutoring and Paired Reading: Combining Two Powerful Techniques." *The Reading Teacher,* 42 (March 1989), 488–494.

Tovey, Duane R. "Children's Grasp of Phonics Terms vs. Sound-Symbol Relationships." *The Reading Teacher,* 33 (January 1980), 431–437.

Trachtenburg, Phyllis. "Using Children's Literature to Enhance Phonics Instruction." *The Reading Teacher,* 43 (May 1990), 648–654.

Trachtenburg, Phyllis, and Ann Ferruggia. "Big Books from Little Voices: Reaching High Risk Beginning Readers." *The Reading Teacher,* 42 (January 1989), 284–289.

Trelease, Jim. *The New Read-Aloud Handbook.* 4th ed. New York: Viking Penguin, 1995.

Truax, Roberta, and Richard Kretschmer, Jr. "Focus on Research: Finding New Voices in the Process of Meeting the Needs of All Children." *Language Arts,* 70 (November 1993), 592–601.

Tunnell, Michael O., and James S. Jacobs. "Using 'Real' Books: Research Findings on Literature-Based Reading Instruction." *The Reading Teacher,* 42 (March 1989), 470–477.

Turner, Julianne, and Scott Paris. "How Literacy Tasks Influence Children's Motivation for Literacy." *The Reading Teacher,* 48 (May 1995), 662–673.

Tway, Eileen. *Writing Is Reading: 26 Ways to Connect.* Urbana, Ill.: National Council of Teachers of English, 1985.

Twiss, Lindy. "Inclusion of Children with Disabilities in Elementary School Classrooms." *The Reading Teacher,* 49 (September 1995), 66–68.

Twiss, Lindy. "Innovative Literacy Practices for ESL Learners." *The Reading Teacher,* 49 (February 1996), 412–414.

Tyson, Eleanore S., and Lee Mountain. "A Riddle or Pun Makes Learning Words Fun." *The Reading Teacher,* 36 (November 1982), 170–173.

Unia, Sumitra. "From Sunny Days to Green Onions: On Journal Writing." In *Whole Language: Theory in Use,* edited by Judith M. Newman. Portsmouth, N.H.: Heinemann, 1985.

Unsworth, Len. "Meeting Individual Needs Through Flexible Within-Class Grouping of Pupils." *The Reading Teacher,* 38 (December 1984), 298–304.

Uttero, Debbra. "Activating Comprehension Through Cooperative Learning." *The Reading Teacher,* 41 (January 1988), 390–395.

Vacca, Jo Anne L., Richard T. Vacca, and Mary K. Gove. *Reading and Learning to Read.* Boston: Little, Brown, 1987.

Valencia, Sheila. "A Portfolio Approach to Classroom Reading Assessment: The Whys, Whats, and Hows." *The Reading Teacher,* 43 (January 1990), 338–340.

Valencia, Sheila, and Nancy Place. "Portfolios: A Process for Enhancing Teaching and Learning." *The Reading Teacher,* 47 (May 1994), 666–669.

Valentine, Sonia L. "Beginning Poets Dig for Poems." *Language Arts,* 63 (March 1986), 246–252.

Valenza, Joyce Kasman. "Library as Multimedia Studio." *Electronic Learning,* 16 (November/December 1996), 56–57.

Valmont, William J. "Cloze Deletion Patterns: How Deletions Are Made Makes a Big Difference." *The Reading Teacher,* 37 (November 1983), 172–175.

Van Horn, Leigh. "The Character Within Us: Readers Connect with Characters to Create Meaning and Understanding." *Journal of Adolescent & Adult Literacy,* 40 (February 1997), 342–347.

VanLeirsburg, Peggy. "Standardized Reading Tests: Then and Now." In *Literacy: Celebration and Challenge,* edited by Jerry Johns. Bloomington, Ill.: Illinois Reading Council, 1993, pp. 31–54.

Van Riper, C. *Speech Correction: Principles and Methods,* 6th ed. Englewood Cliffs, N.J.: Prentice-Hall, 1978.

Veatch, Jeanette. "From the Vantage of Retirement." *The Reading Teacher,* 49 (1996), 510–516.

Vukelich, Carol. "Parents' Role in the Reading Process: A Review of Practical Suggestions and Ways to Communicate with Parents." *The Reading Teacher,* 37 (February 1984), 472–477.

Vygotsky, Lev. *Thought and Language* (rev. ed.), edited by Alex Kozulin. Cambridge, Mass.: MIT Press, 1986.

Wade, Suzanne E., and Ralph E. Reynolds. "Developing Metacognitive Awareness." *Journal of Reading,* 33 (October 1989), 6–14.

Walberg, Herbert, Geneva Haertel, and Suzanne Gerlach-Downie. *Assessment Reform: Challenges and Opportunities.* Bloomington, Ind.: Phi Delta Kappa, 1994.

Walberg, Herbert J., Victoria Chou Hare, and Cynthia A. Pulliam. "Social-Psychological Perceptions and Reading Comprehension." In *Comprehension and Teaching: Research Reviews,* edited by John T. Guthrie. Newark, Del.: International Reading Association, 1981, pp. 140–159.

Walker-Dalhouse, Doris. "Using African-American Literature to Increase Ethnic Understanding." *The Reading Teacher,* 45 (February 1992), 416–422.

Walker-Dalhouse, Doris, A. Derick Dalhouse, and Dennis Mitchell. "Development of a Literature-Based Middle School Reading Program: Insights Gained." *Journal of Adolescent & Adult Literacy,* 40 (February 1997), 362–370.

Wall, Bonnie. "Managing Your Multi-Age Classroom." *Teaching K–8,* 25 (August/September 1994), 68–73.

Waller, T. Gary. *Think First, Read Later! Piagetian Prerequisites for Reading.* Newark, Del.: International Reading Association, 1977.

Walmsley, Sean A. "Reflections on the State of Elementary Literature Instruction." *Language Arts,* 69 (November 1992), 508–514.

Walmsley, Sean A., and Ellen L. Adams. "Realities of 'Whole Language.'" *Language Arts,* 70 (April 1993), 272–280.

Walshe, R. D. "Donald Graves in Australia." In *Donald Graves in Australia—"Children Want to Write . . . ,"* edited by R. D. Walshe. Rozelle, NSW, Australia: Primary English Teaching Association, 1986.

Watson, Dorothy J. "Whole Language: Why Bother?" *The Reading Teacher,* 47 (May 1994), 600–607.

Watson, Jerry J. "An Integral Setting Tells More Than When and Where." *The Reading Teacher,* 44 (May 1991), 638–646.

Waugh, Joyce Clark. "Using LEA in Diagnosis." *Journal of Reading,* 37 (September 1993), 56–57.

Waugh, R. P., and K. W. Howell. "Teaching Modern Syllabication." *The Reading Teacher,* 29 (October 1975), 20–25.

Weaver, Constance. *Psycholinguistics and Reading: From Process to Practice.* Cambridge, Mass.: Winthrop, 1980.

Weaver, Constance. *Understanding Whole Language.* Portsmouth, N.H.: Heinemann, 1990.

Weaver, Phyllis, and Fredi Shonhoff. "Subskill and Holistic Approaches to Reading Instruction." In *Readings on Reading Instruction,* edited by Albert J. Harris and Edward R. Sipay. New York: Longman, 1984.

Weber, Rose Marie. "Linguistic Diversity and Reading in American Society." In *Handbook of Reading Research, Vol. II,* edited by Rebecca Barr, Michael L. Kamil, Peter B. Mosenthal, and P. David Pearson. White Plains, N.Y.: Longman, 1991, pp. 97–119.

Webre, Elizabeth Cancienne. "Using Children's Choices Books to Enhance Math and Health Instruction." *The Reading Teacher,* 44 (February 1991), 445–446.

Weiss, Maria J. "Who Needs a Teacher's Guide?" *The Reading Teacher,* 41 (October 1987), 119–120.

Weissman, Kathleen E. "Using Paragraph Frames to Complete a K-W-L." *The Reading Teacher,* 50 (November 1996), 271–272.

Wepner, Shelley B. "Holistic Computer Applications in Literature-Based Classrooms." *The Reading Teacher,* 44 (September 1990), 12–19.

Wepner, Shelley B. "Linking Logos with Print for Beginning Reading Success." *The Reading Teacher,* 38 (March 1985), 633–639.

Wepner, Shelley B. "Technology and Author Studies." *The Reading Teacher,* 46 (April 1993a), 616–619.

Wepner, Shelley B. "Technology and Textsets." *The Reading Teacher,* 46 (September 1992a), 68–71.

Wepner, Shelley B. "Technology and Thematic Units: An Elementary Example on Japan." *The Reading Teacher,* 46 (February 1993b), 442–445.

Wepner, Shelley B. "Technology and Thematic Units: A Primary Example." *The Reading Teacher,* 46 (November 1992b), 260–263.

Wepner, Shelley B. "Technology Based Literature Plans for Elementary Students." *The Reading Teacher,* 45 (November 1991), 236–238.

Wepner, Shelley B. "Using Technology with Content Area Units." *The Reading Teacher,* 45 (April 1992c), 644–646.

Wepner, Shelley B., Nancy E. Seminoff, and Jay Blanchard. "Navigating Learning with Electronic Encyclopedias." *Reading Today,* 12 (June/July 1995), 28.

Werner, Patrice Holden, and JoAnna Strother. "Early Readers: Important Emotional Considerations." *The Reading Teacher,* 40 (February 1987), 538–543.

Wertheim, Judy. "Teaching Guides for Novels." *The Reading Teacher,* 42 (December 1988), 262.

Wharton-McDonald, Ruth, Michael Pressley, Joan Rankin, Jennifer Mistretta, Linda Yokoi, and Shari Ettenberger. "Effective Primary-Grades Literacy Instruction = Balanced Literacy Instruction." *The Reading Teacher,* 50 (March 1997), 518–521.

Whaley, Jill Fitzgerald. "Story Grammars and Reading Instruction." *The Reading Teacher,* 34 (April 1981), 762–771.

"What's in Store Software Guide." *Family Computing,* March 1986, 82–91.

White, Maureen C., and Susan Mary Lawrence. "Integrating Reading and Writing Through Literature Study." *The Reading Teacher,* 45 (May 1992), 740–743.

White, Thomas G., Joanne Sowell, and Alice Yanagihara. "Teaching Elementary Students to Use Word-Part Clues." *The Reading Teacher,* 42 (January 1989), 302–308.

Whitin, David J., and Sandra Wilde. *Read Any Good Math Lately? Children's Books for Mathematical Learning, K–6.* Portsmouth, N.H.: Heinemann, 1992.

Whitin, Phyllis E., and David J. Whitin. "The Numbers and Beyond: Language Lessons for the Mathematics Classroom." *Language Arts* 74 (February 1997), 108–115.

Whitmer, Jean E. "Pickles Will Kill You: Use Humorous Literature to Teach Critical Reading." *The Reading Teacher,* 39 (February 1986), 530–534.

"Why Multicultural Education?" *Program News.* Alexandria, Va.: Association for Supervision and Curriculum Development (May 1994), 4–5.

Wicklund, LaDonna. "Shared Poetry: A Whole Language Experience Adapted for Remedial Readers." *The Reading Teacher,* 42 (March 1989), 478–481.

Wiener, Roberta, and Judith Cohen. *Literacy Portfolios.* Upper Saddle River, N.J.: Merrill, 1997.

Wiesendanger, Katherine D. "Comprehension: Using Anticipation Guides." *The Reading Teacher,* 39 (November 1985), 241–242.

Wiewandt, Thomas. *The Hidden Life of the Desert.* New York: Crown, 1990.

Wiggins, Grant. *The Case for Authentic Assessment.* Washington, D.C.: ERIC Clearinghouse, 1990 [ED328611].

Wiggins, Robert A. "Large Group Lesson/Small Group Follow-Up: Flexible Grouping in a Basal Reading Program." *The Reading Teacher,* 47 (March 1994), 450–460.

Wilkinson, Phyllis A., and Del Patty. "The Effects of Sentence Combining on the Reading Comprehension of

Fourth Grade Students." *Research in the Teaching of English,* 27 (February 1993), 104–125.

Williams, Mary Ann. "Teaching Vocabulary Through Rephrasing." *The Reading Teacher,* 41 (April 1988), 858–859.

Willis, Jerry W., Elizabeth C. Stephens, and Kathryn I. Matthew. *Technology, Reading, and Language Arts.* Boston: Allyn and Bacon, 1996.

Willis, Scott. "Teaching Language–Minority Students." *ASCD Update,* 36 (June 1994), 1, 4–5.

Willis, Scott. "Teaching Young Children." In *Early Childhood Education 96/97,* edited by Karen Paciorek and Joyce Munro. Guilford, Conn.: Dushkin, 1996–1997, pp. 87–94.

Wilson, Cathy Roller. "Teaching Reading Comprehension by Connecting the Known to the New." *The Reading Teacher,* 36 (January 1983), 382–390.

Wilson, Lorraine, David Malmgren, Shirl Ramage, and Leanne Schulz. *An Integrated Approach to Learning.* South Melbourne, Australia: Nelson, 1991.

Wilson, Patricia J., and Richard F. Abrahamson. "What Children's Literature Classics Do Children Really Enjoy?" *The Reading Teacher,* 41 (January 1988), 406–411.

Winograd, Peter. "Developing Alternative Assessments: Six Problems Worth Solving." *The Reading Teacher,* 47 (February 1994), 420–423.

Winograd, Peter, and Karen W. Higgins. "Writing, Reading, and Talking Mathematics: One Interdisciplinary Possibility." *The Reading Teacher,* 48 (December 1994/January 1995), 310–318.

Winograd, Peter, Scott Paris, and Connie Bridge. "Improving the Assessment of Literacy." *The Reading Teacher,* 45 (October 1991), 108–116.

Winograd, Peter N., Karen K. Wixson, and Marjorie Y. Lipson, eds. *Improving Basal Reading Instruction.* New York: Teachers College Press, 1989.

Wiseman, Donna L. "Helping Children Take Early Steps Toward Reading and Writing." *The Reading Teacher,* 37 (January 1984), 340–344.

Wittrock, Merlin C. "Process Oriented Measures of Comprehension." *The Reading Teacher,* 40 (April 1987), 734–737.

Wixson, Karen K. "Questions about a Text: What You Ask about Is What Children Learn." *The Reading Teacher,* 37 (December 1983), 287–293.

Wolchock, Carol. "Interpreting Idioms." *The Reading Teacher,* 43 (April 1990), 614–615.

Wolfe, Ronald, and Alice Lopez. "Structured Overviews for Teaching Science and Terms." *Journal of Reading,* 36 (December 1992/January 1993), 315–317.

Wollman-Bonilla, Julie E. "Reading Journals: Invitations to Participate in Literature." *The Reading Teacher,* 43 (November 1989), 112–120.

Wong, B. Y. L. "Self-Questioning Instructional Research: A Review." *Review of Educational Research,* 55(1985), 227–268.

Wong, Jo Ann, and Kathryn Hu-pei Au. "The Concept-Text-Application Approach: Helping Elementary Students Comprehend Expository Text." *The Reading Teacher,* 38 (March 1985), 612–618.

Wong Fillmore, Lily. "Research Currents: Equity or Excellence?" *Language Arts,* 63 (September 1986), 474–481.

Wong-Kam, Jo Ann, and Kathryn Au. "Improving a 4th Grader's Reading and Writing: Three Principles." *The Reading Teacher,* 41 (April 1988), 768–772.

Wood, Delores, and Joanne Nurss. "Print Rich Classrooms Support the Development of Print Awareness." *Georgia Journal of Reading,* 14 (Fall/Winter 1988), 21–23.

Wood, Judy. *Mainstreaming,* 2d ed. Columbus, Ohio: Merrill, 1993.

Wood, Julie M., and Nell K. Duke. "Inside 'Reading Rainbow': A Spectrum of Strategies for Promoting Literacy." *Language Arts,* 74 (February 1997), 95–106.

Wood, Karen D. "Fostering Collaborative Reading and Writing Experiences in Mathematics." *Journal of Reading,* 36 (October 1992), 96–103.

Wood, Karen. "Collaborative Learning." *The Reading Teacher,* 43 (January 1990), 346–347.

Wood, Karen. "Using Cooperative Learning Strategies." *Middle School Journal,* 20 (May 1989), 23–26.

Wood, Karen, and Bob Algozzine, eds. *Teaching Reading to High-Risk Learners.* Boston: Allyn & Bacon, 1994.

Wood, Karen D. "Probable Passages: A Writing Strategy." *The Reading Teacher,* 37 (February 1984), 496–499.

Wood, Karen D., and John A. Mateja. "Adapting Secondary Level Strategies for Use in Elementary Classrooms." *The Reading Teacher,* 36 (February 1983), 492–496.

Wortham, Sue. *The Integrated Classroom.* Englewood Cliffs, N.J.: Merrill, 1996.

Worthy, Jo. "A Matter of Interest: Literature that Hooks Reluctant Readers and Keeps Them Reading." *The Reading Teacher,* 50 (November 1996), 204–212.

Wysocki, Katherine, and Joseph R. Jenkins. "Deriving Word Meanings Through Morphological Generalization." *Reading Research Quarterly,* 22, no. 1 (1987), 66–81.

Yatvin, J. *Developing a Whole Language Program.* Richmond, Va.: Virginia State Reading Association, 1991.

Yellin, David, and Mary Blake. *Integrating Language Arts: A Holistic Approach.* New York: HarperCollins, 1994.

Yopp, Hallie. "Read-Aloud Books for Developing Phonemic Awareness: An Annotated Bibliography." *The Reading Teacher,* 48 (March 1995), 538–542.

Yopp, Hallie Kay. "Developing Phonemic Awareness in Young Children." *The Reading Teacher,* 45 (May 1992), 696–703.

Yopp, Hallie Kay. "A Test for Assessing Phonemic Awareness in Young Children." *The Reading Teacher,* 49 (September 1995), 20–29.

Yopp, R. E. "Questioning and Active Comprehension." *Questioning Exchange,* 2 (1988), 231–238.

Young, Terrell A., and Sylvia Vardell. "Weaving Readers Theatre and Nonfiction Into the Curriculum." *The Reading Teacher,* 46 (February 1993), 396–406.

Ysseldyke, James, and Bob Algozzine. *Introduction to Special Education,* 2d ed. Boston: Houghton Mifflin, 1990.

Zabrucky, Karen, and Hilary Horn Ratner. "Children's Comprehension Monitoring: Implications of Research Findings for the Classroom." *Reading Improvement,* 27 (Spring 1990), 46–53.

Zack, Vicki. "'It Was the Worst of Times': Learning about the Holocaust through Literature." *Language Arts,* 68 (January 1991), 42–48.

Zarillo, James. "Teachers' Interpretations of Literature-Based Reading." *The Reading Teacher,* 43 (October 1989), 22–28.

Zarillo, James, and Carole Cox. "Efferent and Aesthetic Teaching." In *Stance and Literary Understanding: Exploring the Theories, Research, and Practice,* edited by Joyce Many and Carole Cox. Norwood, N.J.: Ablex, 1992.

Zarnowski, Myra. "Learning about Fictionalized Biographies: A Reading and Writing Approach." *The Reading Teacher,* 42 (November 1988), 136–142.

Zastrow, Holly. "Word Play for 3rd to 7th Grade Readers." *The Reading Teacher,* 41 (January 1988), 495.

Zimet, Sara Goodman. "Teaching Children to Detect Social Bias in Books." *The Reading Teacher,* 36 (January 1983), 418–421.

Zirkelbach, Thelma. "A Personal View of Early Reading." *The Reading Teacher,* 37 (February 1984), 468–471.

Zogby, Grace. "Literature Groups: Empowering the Reader." Presentation at Whole Language Umbrella Conference, St. Louis, Missouri, August 4, 1990.

Zorfass, Judith, Patricia Corley, and Arlene Remz. "Helping Students with Disabilities Become Writers." *Educational Leadership,* 51 (April 1994), 62–66.

Zucker, Carol. "Using Whole Language with Students Who Have Language and Learning Disabilities." *The Reading Teacher,* 46 (May 1993), 660–670.

Glossary

achievement grouping Placing students into various groups on the basis of achievement.

achievement test A measure of the extent to which a person has assimilated a body of information.

affective Relating to attitudes, interests, values, appreciations, and opinions.

alphabetic principle Concept that letters represent speech sounds.

alternative assessment All types of assessment other than standardized tests.

Americans with Disabilities Act (ADA) A law designed to eliminate discrimination against all individuals with disabilities.

analogies Comparisons of two similar relationships, stated in the form of the following example: *Author* is to *book* as *artist* is to *painting*.

analytic approach to phonics instruction Teaching the sounds of letters in already known words. Sight words are taught first; letter sounds second, in context.

anaphora Use of a word as a substitute for another word or group of words.

anecdotal record Written account of specific incidents or behaviors in the classroom.

anticipation guides Sets of declarative statements related to materials about to be read that are designed to stimulate thinking and discussion.

antonyms A pair of words that have opposite meanings.

appositive A word or a phrase placed beside another word or phrase as a restatement.

articulation Production of speech sounds.

assessment The collection of data, such as test scores and informal records, to measure student achievement.

attention-deficit disorder (ADD) Syndrome characterized by inability to focus attention on tasks and maintain attention.

auditory acuity Sharpness of hearing.

auditory discrimination The ability to differentiate among sounds.

auditory memory The ability to recall information or stimuli that one has heard.

auditory perception The way the brain comprehends information it receives by sound.

auditory sense Sense of hearing.

authentic assessment Measurement of a student's performance on activities that reflect real-world learning experiences.

author's chair A chair in which children sit when they read their own books or trade books to an audience.

bandwagon technique An approach that utilizes the urge to do what others are doing. The impression is given that everyone else is participating in a particular activity.

bar graphs Graphs that use vertical or horizontal bars to compare quantities.

basal reader series Coordinated, graded set of textbooks, teacher's guides, and supplementary materials.

bidialectalism Ability to communicate in more than one dialect of a language.

big books Large books that the entire class can share together, often characterized by predictability, repetition, and rhyme.

bilingualism Ability to speak or understand another language in addition to one's native tongue.

bottom-up models Models that depict reading as being initiated by examination of the printed symbols, with little input being required from the reader.

Caldecott Award An annual award for excellence in illustration.

capacity level Potential reading level.

card stacking Telling only one side of a story by ignoring information favorable to the opposing point of view.

categorization Classification into related groups.

cause-and-effect pattern A writing pattern organized around causes and their effects.

CD-ROM Compact Disc–Read Only Memory. A digital data storage device from which information can be accessed in nonlinear fashion.

characterization The way people come to life through words of the author.

checklist A convenient form on which the teacher can record observations about specific student behaviors or attitudes.

choral reading Dramatic reading of poetry in a group.

chronological order pattern A writing pattern based on time order.

cinquain A simple five line poem that follows a prescribed pattern.

circle or pie graphs Graphs that show relationships of individual parts to a whole circle.

classification pattern A writing pattern in which information is ordered under common headings and subheadings.

cloze procedure Method of estimating reading difficulty by omitting every nth (usually fifth) word in a reading passage and observing the number of correct words a reader can supply; an instructional technique in which words or other structures are deleted from a passage by the teacher, with blanks left in their places for students to fill in by using the surrounding context.

cognitive development The acquisition of knowledge.

community of authors A supportive and cooperative relationship among students and teacher during writing activities.

community of learners A cohesive group of class members who develop and pursue similar goals.

comparison/contrast pattern A writing pattern organized around likenesses and differences.

computer-assisted instruction Instruction that makes use of a computer to administer a programmed instructional sequence or other educational experience.

computer-managed instruction Use of the computer for such tasks as record-keeping, diagnosis, and prescription of individualized assignments.

concept-text-application approach A way to organize lessons to help elementary school students understand expository text.

concept/vocabulary development The acquisition of words and their meanings.

concrete experiences Direct experiences, involving all senses.

concrete-operational period Piaget's third stage of cognitive development (approximately ages seven to eleven).

connotations The feelings and shades of meaning that a word tends to evoke.

content area textbooks Textbooks in areas of information, such as literature, social studies, science, and mathematics.

context clues Clues to word meanings or pronunciations found in the surrounding words or sentences.

cooperative learning Learning through an instructional and grouping procedure utilizing mixed ability groups of students who work cooperatively to achieve certain goals.

creative dramatics Acting out stories spontaneously, without a script.

creative reading Reading beyond the lines.

criterion-referenced test Test designed to yield measurements interpretable in terms of specific performance standards.

critical reading Reading for evaluation.

cross-age tutoring Tutoring between those of different ages.

culturally diverse Pertaining to those who come from homes that differ economically, socially, and culturally.

database An organized body of information which can be sorted and searched electronically.

database programs Programs that facilitate the development of databases.

denotations Dictionary definitions.

departmentalization Instructional systems in which there is a different teacher for each major subject area.

derivatives Words formed by adding prefixes and suffixes to root words.

desktop publishing Application of computers combining text and graphics for classroom publishing.

developmentally appropriate practice A framework or an approach for working with young children in which the teacher considers each child's competencies and adjusts instruction accordingly.

dialect Regional or social modifications of a language; distinguishing features may include pronunciation, vocabulary, and syntax.

dialectal miscue Miscalling of a word due to dialect.

diorama A three-dimensional miniature scene.

direct instruction Teacher control of learning environment through structured lessons, goal setting, choice of activities, and feedback.

directed inquiry activity A technique based upon the directed reading-thinking activity, in which predictions related to who, what, when, where, how, and why questions are made after previewing, but before reading, the content material, in order to set reading purposes.

directed reading activity A strategy in which detailed lesson plans are followed to teach the reading of stories.

directed reading-thinking activity A general plan for directing the reading of content area reading selections or basal reader stories and for encouraging children to think as they read, to predict, and to check their predictions.

directionality Reading from left to right and top to bottom.

drafting The second stage of the writing process, in which the author sets ideas on paper without regard for neatness or mechanics.

dramatic play Simulating real experiences, such as playing the mother or father in a housekeeping center.

eclectic approaches Approaches that combine desirable aspects of a number of different major approaches.

editing The fourth stage of the writing process, in which the author corrects spelling and mechanics.

electronic bulletin boards Network locations to which messages are posted so that readers interested in the topic can read the messages electronically. Sometimes referred to as newsgroups.

electronic mail Messages sent electronically from one computer user to another.

electronic mailing list Electronic distributor of messages on a particular topic to a group of readers who have "subscribed" to the list.

ellipsis The omission of a word or group of words that are to be "understood" by the reader.

emergent literacy A developing awareness of the interrelatedness of oral and written language.

environmental print Words that children frequently see around them.

ESL (English as a second language) program A program for teaching English language skills to those whose native language is not English.

etymology The origin and history of words.

euphemism The substitution of a less offensive word or phrase for an unpleasant term or expression.

exceptional child One who deviates from the majority of learners to such an extent that he or she cannot derive maximum benefit from regular classroom instruction; additional or different curriculum, instruction or setting may be required.

experience charts Written accounts about common experiences, dictated by the student(s) and recorded by the teacher.

experiential background Fund of total experiences that aid a reader in finding meaning in printed symbols.

explanation of a process pattern A writing pattern in which processes are described, frequently involving illustrations, such as pictures, charts, or diagrams, which are designed to clarify the textual material.

expository passage organizers (EPOs) Reading and writing process study guides designed to help students see the structure of expository text and use that knowledge in writing it.

expository style A precise, factual writing style.

expository text A text written in a precise, factual writing style.

fable A brief moral tale in which animals or inanimate objects speak.

figurative language Nonliteral language.

fixations Stops made by the eyes during reading in order to take in words and phrases and to react to them.

flexibility of reading habits Ability to adjust reading habits to fit the materials and purposes for reading.

formal (standardized) test Testing instrument based on extensive normative data and for which reliability and validity can be verified.

format The size, shape, design of pages, illustrations, typography, paper, and binding of a publication.

friendship grouping Allowing friends to work together for a specific purpose and within a specified time frame.

frustration level A level of reading difficulty with which a reader is unable to cope; when reading material is on this level, the reader usually recognizes 90 percent or less of the words he or she reads or comprehends 50 percent or less of what he or she reads.

genre A type of classification of literature, such as historical fiction, biography, or folktales.

gifted (intellectually) Possessing high intellectual development with a mental age that is substantially above the norm.

glittering generalities Using vague phrases to influence a point of view without providing necessary specifics.

grade equivalent scores Test scores expressed in terms of grade level, comparing a student's score with average achievement of the population used to standardize the test. (A score of 6.4 represents achievement equal to that of an average child in the fourth month of the sixth school year.)

grapheme A written symbol that represents a phoneme.

graphic cue Clue provided by the written form of the word.

guide words Words used in dictionaries, encyclopedias, and other reference books to aid users in finding entries.

The first guide word names the first entry on the page; the second guide word names the final entry on the page.

guided reading procedure A method designed to help readers improve organizational skills, comprehension, and recall.

hearing impaired One whose sense of hearing is defective but functional for ordinary purposes.

heterogeneous Different or unlike.

holistic assessment A process-oriented approach for evaluating a student's abilities to integrate separate skills in order to comprehend an entire selection.

homogeneous Similar or like.

homographs Words that have identical spellings but sound different and have different meanings.

homonyms Pairs or groups of words that are spelled differently but are pronounced alike; homophones.

hyperbole An extreme exaggeration.

hypermedia Text, sound, or pictures (still or animated) linked in a nonsequential manner, allowing access to the material in an order chosen by the user.

hypertext Information that is linked in a nonsequential manner, allowing students to choose the paths they will take through the information.

idiom A group of words that, taken as a whole, has a meaning different from that of the sum of the meanings of the individual words.

IEP (Individual Education Program) A written account of objectives, strategies, curriculum modifications, and classroom accommodations for a student with learning problems.

improvisation Acting without a script.

inclusion The assignment of students with disabilities to regular classrooms in neighborhood schools for the entire school day. These children participate in all school activities.

independent level A level of reading difficulty low enough that the reader can progress without noticeable hindrance; the reader can ordinarily recognize at least 99 percent of the words and comprehend at least 90 percent of what he or she reads.

individualized reading approach An approach to reading instruction that is characterized by pupils' self-selection of reading materials and self-pacing and by pupil-teacher conferences.

Individuals with Disabilities Education Act (IDEA) An amended version of PL 94-142 that modifies some of the provisions and changes some terminology to show greater sensitivity for the individual.

inference Conclusion drawn from stated facts.

inflectional endings Endings that when added to nouns change the number, case, or gender; when added to verbs change the tense or person; and when added to adjectives change the degree.

informal assessment Nonstandardized measurement.

Informal drama Spontaneous and unrehearsed acting.

informal reading inventory An informal instrument designed to help the teacher determine a child's independent, instructional, frustration, and capacity levels.

InQuest Investigative Questioning, a comprehension strategy that combines student questioning with creative drama.

insertions Words that do not appear in the printed passage but are inserted by the reader.

instructional level A level of difficulty at which the reader can read with understanding with teacher assistance; the reader can ordinarily recognize at least 95 percent of the words in a selection and comprehend at least 75 percent of what he or she reads.

instructions for experiment pattern A writing pattern containing step-by-step procedures to be followed.

integrated curriculum A curriculum in which content and concepts are interrelated across subject areas.

integrated language arts curriculum The integration of purposeful reading, writing, listening, and speaking activities.

interactive processing Processing in which one uses both information supplied by the text and information from one's own prior world knowledge and background of experiences to interpret the text.

interactive theories Theories that depict reading as a combination of reader-based and text-based processing.

interclass grouping Forming groups from a number of classrooms.

interest grouping Placing pupils into various groups on the basis of common interests.

interest inventory Device used to assess a person's preferences in various areas.

Internet International "network of networks" that links a multitude of computers.

interpretive reading Reading between the lines.

invented spellings Unconventional spellings resulting from children's attempts to associate sounds with letters.

irregularly spelled words Words not spelled the way phonics rules indicate that they would be, based on the way they sound.

journals Written records of reflections, events, and ideas.

juncture Pauses in the flow of speech (marking the ends of phrases, clauses, or sentences).

kidwatching Observing children to gain insights into their learning.

knowledge-based processing Bringing one's prior world knowledge and background of experiences to the interpretation of the text.

K-W-L Teaching Model A teaching model for expository text; stands for What I *Know,* What I *Want* to Learn, What I *Learned.*

language arts Listening, speaking, reading, and writing skills.

language experience approach An approach in which reading and the other language arts are interrelated in the instructional program and the experiences of children are used as the basis for reading materials.

language experience story A story composed by a child or a group of children and recorded by them or the teacher.

language facility Listening comprehension, speaking ability, reading skill, and writing ability.

learning center An area containing several independent learning activities based on a theme.

learning disabled Having a developmental disorder that interferes with the ability to learn certain skills.

least restrictive environment A setting in which a child can master skills and content; it resembles the regular classroom as closely as possible.

legend (of a map) The map's key to symbols used.

limited English proficiency (LEP) Describing those who lack sufficient English language skills to achieve in a regular classroom and who thus require special instruction for developing linguistic and academic skills.

line graphs Graphs that show changes in amounts by connecting with line segments points representing the amounts.

linguistics The scientific study of human speech.

linguists Scientists who study human speech.

literacy club A group with membership consisting of children who have quite naturally acquired knowledge of purposes and activities related to reading and writing.

literal comprehension Understanding ideas that are directly stated.

literature-based approaches Approaches that use quality literature as a basis for reading instruction.

literature circles Groups established to allow students to exchange ideas about books they are reading.

mainstreaming Integrating children who are disabled into the general reading program of the classroom.

mental retardation General intellectual ability that is significantly below average, coupled with deficits in adaptive behavior during the developmental period.

metacognition A person's knowledge of the functioning of his or her own mind and his or her conscious efforts to monitor or control this functioning.

metacognitive strategies Techniques for thinking about and monitoring one's own thought processes.

metalinguistic awareness The ability to think about language and manipulate it objectively.

metaphor A direct comparison not using the word *like* or *as.*

metaphoric language Nonliteral language.

minimally contrasting spelling patterns Words that vary in spellings by only a single letter.

miscue An unexpected oral reading response (error).

modality A sensory system for receiving and processing information (visual, auditory, kinesthetic, tactile).

morphemes The smallest units of meaning in a language.

motivation Incentive to act.

multicultural students Students who represent a variety of regional cultures, ethnic groups, and religious groups.

multidisciplinary team A group of people who construct an IEP for a student with disabilities.

multiethnic Pertaining to various racial and ethnic groups.

multimedia The use of a number of different media (graphics, text, moving images, sound effects, etc.) in the same application.

name calling Using derogatory labels to create a negative reaction without providing evidence to support such an impression.

Newbery Award An annual award for the most distinguished contribution to American literature for children.

newsgroups Network locations to which messages are posted so that readers who are interested in the topic can read the messages electronically. Sometimes referred to as electronic bulletin boards.

nonrestrictive clauses Appositive clauses; clauses that do not restrict the information in the main clause but add information.

norm-referenced test Test designed to yield results interpretable in terms of a norm, the average or mean results of a sample population.

onsets and rimes Word parts, with onsets being the consonants or consonant clusters at the beginning of a syllable and rimes being the vowel(s) and any consonants that follow.

oral reading strategy A technique in which the teacher reads material to the students and has them restate it in their own words.

ownership A sense of complete responsibility for something, such as a piece of writing.

paired-associate learning Learning in which a stimulus is presented along with a desired response.

pantomime Dramatizing through movement without using words.

paraprofessional A teacher's assistant or other adult with some professional training who works in the classroom to assist the teacher.

peer tutoring One student helping another student learn.

percentile rank Test score expressed in terms of its position within a set of 100 scores.

perception The interpretation of sensory impressions.

performance-based assessment Measurement of a student's ability to create an assigned response or product to demonstrate her or his level of competence.

performance sampling Examples of children's work collected periodically for later analysis.

personification Giving the attributes of a person to an inanimate object or abstract idea.

phoneme The smallest unit of sound in a language.

phonemic awareness An understanding that speech consists of a series of small sound units.

phonemic segmentation The process of separating the sounds within words.

phonics The association of speech sounds with printed symbols.

picture graphs Graphs that express quantities with pictures.

pitch Highness or lowness of sound.

PL 94-142 The Education for All Handicapped Children Act, which provides federal assistance for the education of students who are disabled.

plain folks talk Relating a person or proposed program to the common people in order to gain their support.

plot The plan of a story.

poor reader One who has difficulty learning to read; also sometimes identified as dyslexic, remedial, underachieving, at-risk, disabled, retarded, impaired, or language learning disabled.

portfolio A collection of a child's work over a period of time.

potential reading level An estimate of a person's possible reading achievement level based upon intelligence or listening comprehension.

predictable books Books that use repetition, rhythmic language patterns, and familiar concepts.

preoperational period Piaget's second stage of cognitive development, extending from age two to age seven.

prewriting The first stage of the writing process in which the author prepares for writing by talking, reading, and thinking about the piece; organizing ideas; and developing a plan.

print conventions Generally accepted concepts about writing.

process-oriented assessment Measures a student's use of thought processes and reading strategies.

programmed instruction A method of presenting instructional material in which small, sequential steps; active involvement of the learner; immediate reinforcement; and self-pacing are emphasized.

project or research grouping Placing students of varying ability levels together so that they may investigate a topic.

propaganda techniques Techniques of writing used to influence people's thinking and actions, including bandwagon technique, card stacking, glittering generalities, name calling, plain folks talk, testimonials, and transfer techniques.

publishing The last stage of the writing process in which the writer puts the piece into finished form.

pupil pairs Partners who work cooperatively on activities.

rating scale A device for recording estimates of the levels of student functioning.

readability An objective measure of the difficulty of written material.

readers' theater Reading aloud from scripts in a dramatic style.

reading and writing workshop Instructional procedure consisting of a minilesson, a status-of-the-class report, reading or writing, and sharing.

reading checklist Listing of significant reading behaviors and a convenient form for recording results of teacher observation.

reading miscue inventory An informal instrument that considers both the quality and quantity of miscues made by the reader.

reading rate Speed of reading, often reported in words per minute.

reading readiness The level of preparedness for formal reading instruction.

reading readiness test A test for predicting a child's readiness to begin formal reading instruction.

reading/study techniques Techniques designed to enhance comprehension and retention of written material.

realistic story A story that could have happened to real people.

reciprocal teaching A technique to develop comprehension and metacognition in which the teacher and students take turns being "teacher." They predict, generate questions, summarize, and clarify ideas.

regressions Eye movements back to a previously read word or phrase for the purpose of rereading.

reinforcement Something done to strengthen a response.

relative clauses Clauses that refer to an antecedent (may be restrictive or nonrestrictive).

reliability The degree to which a test gives consistent results.

ReQuest A technique in which the teacher and the students alternate asking questions about a passage.

resource room A classroom where children with disabilities spend a period of time on a regular basis, with instruction provided by the resource-room teacher.

restrictive clauses Clauses that restrict the information in the main clause by adding information.

reversals Changing the position or orientation of letters, parts of a word, or words.

reversibility The ability to reverse an operation to produce what was there initially.

revising The third stage of the writing process, in which the author makes changes in the initial draft.

rubric A set of criteria used to describe and evaluate a student's level of proficiency in a particular subject area.

running record A strategy for recording miscues during a student's oral reading.

scaffolding Offering support through modeling or feedback, and then withdrawing support gradually as the learner gains competence.

scale (of a map) The part of a map showing the relationship of a given distance on a map to the same distance on the area represented.

schema A pre-existing knowledge structure developed about a thing, place, or idea.

selection aids References that identify and evaluate publications.

self-concept An individual's perception of himself or herself as a person, his or her abilities, appearance, performance, and so on.

semantic cues (or clues) Meaning clues.

semantic feature analysis A technique in which the presence or absence of particular features in the meaning of a word is indicated through symbols on a chart, allowing comparisons of word meanings.

semantic maps Graphic representations of relationships among words and phrases in written material.

semantic webbing Making a graphic representation of relationships in written material through the use of a core question, strands (answers), strand supports (facts and inferences from the story), and strand ties (relationships of the strands to each other).

sensory handicap Hearing and/or visual impairment.

sequence The order in which the events in a story occur.

setting The time and place of a story.

shared book experiences Reading and rereading books in a group activity for understanding and enjoyment.

sight words Words that are recognized immediately, without having to resort to analysis.

simile A comparison using *like* or *as*.

special skills (needs) grouping Placing pupils into various groups on the basis of skills deficiencies.

specific learning disability A developmental disorder exhibited by imperfect ability to learn certain skills.

speech impaired Those whose speech deviates sufficiently from normal speech to interfere with satisfactory oral communication.

spreadsheets Computer programs that allow the manipulation of numerical data that is entered into cells arranged in columns and rows.

SQRQCQ A study method consisting of six steps: Survey, Question, Read, Question, Compute, Question.

SQ3R A study method consisting of five steps: Survey, Question, Read, Recite, Review.

standardized test A published test that has been constructed by experts in the field and is administered, scored, and interpreted according to specific criteria.

stanine scale A ranking of test scores on a scale of one through nine.

story grammar A set of rules that define story structures.

story mapping Making graphic representations of stories that make clear the specific relationships of story elements.

stress Degree of emphasis placed on a syllable or sound.

structural analysis Analysis of words by identifying prefixes, suffixes, root words, inflectional endings, contractions, word combinations forming compound words, and syllabication.

student contract Negotiated agreement about what the pupil is to do and when the task is to be completed.

study guides Duplicated sheets prepared by the teacher and distributed to the children to help guide reading in content fields and alleviate some difficulties that interfere with understanding.

stuttering A type of speech impairment characterized by hesitation, sound prolongations, and/or repetition.

style An author's mode of expressing thoughts in words.

subskill theories Theories that depict reading as a set of subskills that children must master and integrate.

survey test A test that measures general achievement in a given area.

Sustained Silent Reading (SSR) A program for setting aside a certain period of time daily for silent reading.

synonyms Groups of words that have the same, or very similar, meanings.

syntactic cues (or clues) Clues derived from the word order in sentences.

syntax The rules for combining words to form grammatical sentences.

synthetic approach to phonics instruction Teaching pupils to blend together individual known letter sounds in order to decode written words. Letter sounds are taught first; then they are blended into words.

teacher research Teacher participation in classroom action or naturalistic research.

team arrangement Two or more classes combined with a staff of several teachers.

testimonial technique Using a highly popular or respected person to endorse a product or proposal.

text-based processing Trying to extract the information that resides in the text.

thematic unit An integrated learning experience with a topic or concept that is the core of the curriculum for an extended period of time.

theme The main idea that the writer wishes to convey to the reader.

theme cycle A theme study negotiated by the teacher and the students.

theory A set of assumptions or principles designed to explain phenomena.

top-down models Models that depict reading as beginning with the generation of hypotheses or predictions about the material by the reader.

topic sentence A sentence that sets forth the central thought of the paragraph in which it occurs.

topical order pattern A writing pattern organized around central themes or topics.

trade book A book for sale to the general public.

transactive theories Theories based on Rosenblatt's idea that every reading act is a transaction that involves a reader and a text and occurs at a particular time in a specific context, with meaning coming into being during the transaction between the reader and the text.

transfer technique Associating a respected organization or symbol with a particular person, project, or idea.

validity The extent to which a test represents a balanced and adequate sampling of the instructional outcomes it is intended to cover.

variants Words formed by adding inflectional endings to root words.

vicarious experiences Indirect experiences.

videoconferencing The holding of conferences over the Internet with others who can be seen on their computer monitors and heard through the speakers.

videodisc An analog data storage device from which information can be accessed in nonlinear fashion.

visual acuity Sharpness of vision.

visual discrimination Ability to differentiate between different shapes.

visual memory The ability to recall an image one has seen.

visual perception The result of the brain's processing and understanding of visual stimuli.

visualization Picturing events, places, and people described by the author.

visually impaired Those who are partially sighted but able to read print.

webbing A technique that graphically connects a central topic or theme to related ideas.

whole language A philosophy that supports an integrated curriculum, authentic learning tasks, social interactions, learner-centered classrooms, and the use of literature across the curriculum.

whole language classroom A child-centered environment where language is integrated with content through authentic experiences.

word bank A collection of sight words that have been mastered by an individual pupil, usually recorded on index cards.

word configuration Word shape.

word-processing software Computer software designed to allow entry, manipulation, and storage of text (and sometimes images).

word webs Graphic representations of the relationships among words that are constructed by connecting the related terms with lines.

wordless picture books Picture books without words.

World Wide Web (WWW) A part of the Internet that allows users to choose special words or symbols with a mouse click or keyboard stroke and be automatically connected to related Web locations.

writing process A child-centered procedure for writing consisting of prewriting, drafting, revising, editing, and publishing.

zone of proximal development The span between a child's actual level and potential level when assistance is given.

Appendix

Answers to "Test Yourself"

Chapter 1   *True-False*

1. F	11. F	21. T
2. T	12. T	22. T
3. F	13. T	23. T
4. F	14. F	24. F
5. T	15. F	25. T
6. T	16. T	26. F
7. T	17. T	27. T
8. F	18. F	28. F
9. F	19. F	
10. T	20. T	

Chapter 2   *True-False*

1. T	11. F	21. F
2. F	12. T	22. F
3. T	13. T	23. T
4. T	14. F	24. F
5. F	15. F	25. T
6. F	16. F	26. T
7. F	17. F	27. T
8. T	18. F	28. F
9. F	19. T	
10. F	20. F	

Chapter 3   *True-False*

1. F	13. T	25. T
2. F	14. T	26. F
3. T	15. T	27. F
4. F	16. T	28. T
5. T	17. T	29. T
6. T	18. F	30. F
7. F	19. T	31. T
8. T	20. F	32. T
9. F	21. F	33. T
10. T	22. T	34. T
11. T	23. T	35. F
12. F	24. T	

Chapter 3   *Multiple-Choice*

1. a	5. c	9. b
2. c	6. a	10. b
3. a	7. c	11. a
4. b	8. b	

Chapter 4   *True-False*

1. F	11. T	21. T
2. T	12. F	22. F
3. F	13. T	23. T
4. F	14. T	24. T
5. T	15. T	25. T
6. T	16. T	26. F
7. T	17. T	27. T
8. T	18. T	28. F
9. T	19. T	
10. F	20. F	

Chapter 5   *True-False*

1. T	7. F	13. T
2. T	8. T	14. F
3. T	9. T	15. F
4. T	10. T	16. F
5. F	11. F	17. T
6. T	12. T	18. F

Chapter 6   *True-False*

1. T	8. F	15. F
2. T	9. T	16. F
3. T	10. F	17. F
4. F	11. T	18. T
5. T	12. T	19. T
6. F	13. F	20. F
7. T	14. T	21. T

Chapter 7 *True-False*

1. F	9. T	17. F
2. T	10. F	18. F
3. F	11. T	19. T
4. F	12. T	20. T
5. T	13. T	21. F
6. T	14. F	22. F
7. F	15. T	
8. T	16. T	

Chapter 8 *True-False*

1. T	9. F	17. T
2. T	10. T	18. F
3. F	11. T	19. T
4. F	12. F	20. F
5. F	13. T	21. F
6. F	14. F	22. T
7. T	15. F	23. T
8. F	16. T	24. T

Chapter 9 *True-False*

1. F	10. T	19. T
2. T	11. T	20. T
3. T	12. F	21. F
4. T	13. T	22. F
5. F	14. F	23. T
6. T	15. T	24. T
7. F	16. T	25. F
8. F	17. F	26. T
9. T	18. T	

Chapter 10 *True-False*

1. F	11. F	21. T
2. T	12. T	22. T
3. T	13. T	23. T
4. F	14. T	24. T
5. F	15. F	25. F
6. T	16. T	
7. F	17. T	
8. F	18. F	
9. T	19. T	
10. T	20. T	

Chapter 11 *True-False*

1. F	11. T	21. F
2. F	12. T	22. T
3. F	13. F	23. F
4. T	14. T	24. T
5. F	15. T	25. F
6. F	16. T	26. T
7. T	17. T	27. T
8. T	18. T	28. T
9. T	19. F	29. T
10. T	20. F	30. T

Chapter 12 *True-False*

1. F	11. F	21. T
2. F	12. F	22. F
3. F	13. F	23. T
4. F	14. T	24. F
5. T	15. F	25. T
6. T	16. T	26. F
7. T	17. T	
8. T	18. T	
9. F	19. F	
10. T	20. T	

Chapter 13 *True-False*

1. F	12. T	23. T
2. F	13. T	24. F
3. F	14. F	25. T
4. F	15. T	26. T
5. T	16. F	27. T
6. T	17. T	28. T
7. F	18. F	29. T
8. T	19. F	30. T
9. F	20. T	31. F
10. T	21. F	
11. T	22. T	

Chapter 14 *True-False*

1. F	12. T	23. T
2. T	13. T	24. T
3. T	14. F	25. T
4. F	15. F	26. F
5. T	16. F	27. T
6. F	17. T	28. F
7. F	18. F	29. F
8. T	19. T	30. T
9. T	20. F	31. F
10. T	21. F	
11. F	22. T	

Index

Chapter 11 Organization

- Evaluating Technological Applications
- The Role of the Teacher
- Understanding the Range of Technology Available
- **Use of Technology for Literacy Learning**
- Adjusting Instruction Through Technology
- Using Multimedia for Classroom Presentations and Projects
- Computer Applications
- Techno_____ as a To_____ Literacy I_____

Technology as a Tool for Literacy Instruction **461**

period of time, as is true in unit studies. Means and Olson (1994) have described one such example of integration. A summary is found in the following Classroom Scenario.

Classroom Scenario

Integrating Technology into Classroom Activities

Students in a fifth-grade class in California needed funds to go to a science camp, and they also needed appropriate materials, on easy reading levels, about Hispanic leaders. They decided on a multimedia project to develop their own materials, not only about local Hispanic heroes, but also about African-American and Vietnamese-American community leaders as well. They planned to sell the materials to others to raise funds for science camp.

The fifth-graders identified people that they wished to interview; planned, conducted, and videotaped the interviews; and wrote up the main points from each one. The students carried out their plans by first studying existing interviews of famous people to help them construct their questions, they formed groups and practiced interviewing skills on each other. The actual interviews were conducted by collaborative groups, with one student videotaping, one asking questions, and one taking notes. The interviews were critiqued and transcribed, and the key points were summarized. This task involved much proofreading and editing. The teacher, Cliff Gilkey, moved from group to group, monitoring progress and offering assistance.

Analysis of Scenario

The students were working on an authentic task to meet two real-life needs. The technology was used as a tool to help meet these needs. The process involved a number of important literacy skills as the students read interviews, composed questions, took notes, summarized material, and proofread and edited material. Cliff Gilkey was a coach and a facilitator of learning.

Time for Reflection

Some people think that only "cutting edge" technology should be used in today's classrooms. They would discard applications that have been around a long time, referring to them as "antiquated." Others consider it possible to embrace newer technologies without casting aside older ones that accomplish curricular goals effectively. *What do *you* think?*

Technology as a Tool for Literacy Instruction

This chapter, of course, _____ _____ imarily with the application of technol-_____ _____ her than for instruction in general. Fol-_____ _____ nology can be used for this purpose.

Model Activities

Internet Research for Book Making

Read several informational alphabet books to your class. (See Chapter 10 for suggestions of thematic alphabet books.) Discuss the characteristics of these alphabet books.

Next, choose a topic, such as "Mammals," that you are studying in a particular content area. Discuss what has already been discovered about this topic.

Then divide the class into small groups, assigning one or more letters to each group. Let group members search the Internet for mammals that would fit the assigned letters. Have each group choose from the mammals they locate the ones to use for their book pages. Then have them write and print book pages for their assigned letters, using desktop publishing software or word-processing software. Put the pages together to form a class book. Print multiple copies to use in the classroom, to share with other classes, and to send home to promote parent communication.

Finally, read the book to the class and let the group members responsible for each page tell about their search strategies.